D0268888

When Saturday Comes
The Half Decent Football Book

When Saturday Comes

The Half Decent Football Book

Penguin Books

PENGUIN BOOKS

Published by the Penguin Group
Penguin Books Ltd, 80 Strand, London WC2R 0RL, England
Penguin Group (USA) Inc., 375 Hudson Street, New York, New York 10014, USA
Penguin Group (Canada), 90 Eglinton Avenue East, Suite 700, Toronto, Ontario, Canada M4P 2Y3
(a division of Pearson Penguin Canada Inc.)
Penguin Ireland, 25 St Stephen's Green, Dublin 2, Ireland (a division of Penguin Books Ltd)
Penguin Group (Australia), 250 Camberwell Road, Camberwell, Victoria 3124, Australia
(a division of Pearson Australia Group Pty Ltd)
Penguin Books India Pvt Ltd, 11 Community Centre, Panchsheel Park, New Delhi – 110 017, India
Penguin Group (NZ), cnr Airborne and Rosedale Roads, Albany, Auckland 1310, New Zealand
(a division of Pearson New Zealand Ltd)
Penguin Books (South Africa) (Pty) Ltd, 24 Sturdee Avenue, Rosebank, Johannesburg 2196, South Africa

Penguin Books Ltd, Registered Offices: 80 Strand, London WC2R 0RL, England

www.penguin.com

First published 2005
Published in paperback 2006
1

Copyright © *When Saturday Comes*, 2005
Illustrated letters copyright © Tim Bradford
All rights reserved

The moral right of the author has been asserted

Set in 9/12 pt Monotype Amasis
Typeset by Rowland Phototypesetting Ltd, Bury St Edmunds, Suffolk
Printed in England by Clays Ltd, St Ives plc

Contents

Preface

In compiling this book, we have tried to avoid a straightforwardly factual account of the game's history, which has been covered in numerous other reference works. The book is not intended to be a source of up-to-date information about trophies won during the 2005–06 season; nor will you find any mention of, for example, the Greene King IPA Essex Intermediate League or the fact that the *Rothmans Yearbook* habitually gave Tottenham full back Chris Hughton's height as 5' 7³/₄". Instead, the *WSC Half Decent Football Book* offers a personalized perspective on the game's development as an important part of popular culture in the UK, in a way that we hope will be accessible to the general reader as well as the informed football fan. Hopefully the book will entertain as much as it provides a source of information, which is after all what it's supposed to be all about.

We would like to thank our principal collaborators – Matthew Brown, Cameron Carter, Ian Plenderleith and Mike Ticher – and the following contributors: Richard Guy, Neil Forsyth, Roger Titford, Harry Pearson, Philip Cornwall, Huw Richards, Taylor Parkes, Ben Lyttleton, Joyce Woolridge, Adam Powley, Neil White, Gavin Willacy, Matt Barker, John Carter, Paul Hutton, Neil Hurden, Ian Farrell, Chris Bainbridge, Phil Ball, Al Needham, Nick House, Tom Davies, Phil Kyte, Chris Upton, Steve Westby, Dave Jennings, Steve Wilson, David Wangerin, Simon Tyers, James Medhurst, Andrew Turton, Jonathan Paxton, Csaba Abrahall, Steve Morgan, Tim Springett, Steve Menary, Glen Wilson, Piers Pennington, John Earls, David Harrison, Graham Lightfoot, Dave Espley, Paul Giess, Darren Fletcher, Paul Lewis, Martin Atherton, Jim Gwinnell, Joe Boyle, Craig Gurney, Steven Heath, Andrew Bennett, Helen Duff, Mark Herron, John Secker, Andrew Frazier, Tom Rance, Colin Dobell, Nigel Wheatley, Jon Matthias, Tony Morris, Ken Fox, Andrew Firmin, Robert Jeffery, Mark Griffiths, John Bourn, Rob Rushton, Maison Urwin, Chris Forth, Kevin Bartholemew, Steven Agnew and Duncan Young.

Andy Lyons and Barney Ronay
May 2006

abandoned matches

The large majority of football matches are ended neatly with one of three possible results. Despite this there are scattered about the game's history – like forgotten, rusting hulks – a select group of matches that were abandoned before a result could be reached.

The most common reason for abandoning a match is extremely bad weather. During his first brief spell with Manchester City in 1961, Denis **Law** scored six goals against Luton in heavy rain on a quagmire of a pitch, only for the match to be abandoned with half an hour to go. City lost the rearranged cup tie 3–1. At the other end of the scale, a match between Dundee United and Dunfermline in 1998 lasted precisely 90 seconds before it was called off because of high winds. Current procedure dictates that if a match is abandoned before kick-off, fans get free admission to the rearranged fixture. If it is called off after the game has started, this generosity wanes to half-price admission to the rearranged game. An expensive minute and a half of football, then, for the Dundee United and Dunfermline faithful.

In October 1996, Scotland won their World Cup qualifying match in Estonia with one small kick. The ball having been nudged off the centre spot at the first whistle, the referee blew again immediately for the end of the match, with no Estonian player in sight. FIFA had ordered the game to be rearranged from evening to afternoon because of the poor state of floodlighting at the Kadriorg Stadium and, as a protest against interference with international television coverage (and consequent loss of revenue), Estonia stayed at home. Unusually for a match not played out for its allotted time, the result stood.

West Brom had slightly more opposition from Sheffield United in March 2002. Their match was abandoned with only eight minutes remaining when United's Robert Ullathorne left the field injured, leaving United with only six players on the pitch, fewer than the minimum seven that constitutes a team. With West Brom leading 3–0, referee Eddie Wolstenholme had no choice but to call the whole thing off (though the final result stood). The official Sheffield roll of honour read: three sent off, two injured. West Brom's manager, Gary Megson, was available for comment for a long, long time after the game.

Aberdeen

Aberdeen is a city built on oil and a history of the city's football club displays the 'boom–bust' characteristic of that industry, with the success of Alex **Ferguson**'s 1980s reign being unmatched before or after. Its status as the sole provider of top-class football in Scotland's third city has spared the club the worst ravages of the recent depressed financial status of Scottish football, yet Aberdeen are presently a pale memory of former glories.

A football club named Aberdeen was formed in 1881 but 1904 is seen as the year of the club's true birth, when an amalgamation of local clubs entered the Scottish League under the one name and based at Pittodrie, formerly a dunghill for police horses. Aberdeen football club were soon displaying a willingness to provide historical footnotes, firstly in 1923 when Peterhead were sent packing 13–0 at Pittodrie. Then, eight years later, a less celebrated incident named the 'Great Mystery' rocked the club and city to the core when an alleged betting scandal saw five players dropped.

The Second World War was to prove a time for muted celebration for the club as they swept up six wartime titles, finally finding a use for the Pittodrie trophy room, and this form was maintained after the ending of hostilities with 1947 seeing League Cup Final defeat and the capture of the Scottish Cup. Two further Scottish Cup finals were lost before the Scottish League title was won in 1955, with 'fortress Pittodrie' witnessing only one defeat all season.

Trips to Hampden were commonplace for the club's followers throughout this extended period, and one of the most memorable was for the crowning of 'cup tie Mackay', in 1970, after Derek Mackay had been plucked from the reserves to star in the quarter- and semi-finals of the Scottish Cup, then score another two goals in the 3–1 defeat of Celtic. Up to now, the club had not mustered any significant European achievement to go with their domestic success but the two would be spectacularly married after Ferguson's 1978 appointment.

Twenty-one years later Ferguson was handed the keys to the city, and this is why; 1980, Scottish League title; 1982, Scottish Cup win; 1983, European Cup Winners' Cup win; 1983, Scottish Cup win; 1983, European Super Cup win; 1984, Scottish League title; 1984, Scottish Cup win; 1985, Scottish League Cup win; 1986, Scottish Cup win.

It's a staggering roll call and left Aberdeen as a team renowned throughout Europe. The capture of the European Cup Winners' Cup in 1983 had been a stirring 2–1 victory over Real Madrid in Gothenburg and the Super Cup defeat of European Cup holders Hamburg had been beamed to more than 80 countries worldwide as players such as Jim Leighton, Willie Miller, Alex McLeish and Gordon Strachan temporarily became the nation's ambassadors.

Every Aberdeen manager since Ferguson's departure for Old Trafford has struggled with the 'Ferguson effect', with Alex Smith coming closest to regaining the League title with a heart-breaking last-day defeat to Rangers in 1991. The club's failure to be taken entirely seriously since is perhaps best summarized by the Scottish Cup Final defeat of 2000, when striker Robbie Winters was forced to play in goal after an injury to Leighton, eccentric Danish manager Ebbe Skovdahl having neglected to pick a reserve goalkeeper.

Tony Adams

The consequences of Gareth Southgate's penalty shoot-out miss in the Euro 96 semi-final defeat to Germany did not just extend to the pizza advertising industry. That miss was the catalyst for Tony Adams to start a seven-week drinking binge, which ended with a pint of stout at 5pm on Friday, 16 August. A week later, Adams started the rest of his life and attended his first Alcoholics Anonymous meeting.

Tony Adams, born in Romford in 1966, signed schoolboy forms for Arsenal aged 14 and at 17 was the second-youngest player to make his debut, memorable only because he wore his shorts back-to-front. On the pitch he was imposing, decisive and aggressive, the perfect leader to get the best out of an ageing team when George **Graham** appointed him captain in 1987. The 21-year-old spent most of that season yelling at seasoned internationals like Viv Anderson and Charlie Nicholas, leaving no-one in any doubt about who was the boss.

Adams was successful on the pitch, winning the 1987 League Cup, playing for England in their ill-fated Euro 88

campaign and captaining the side to their 2–0 last-gasp win at Anfield to clinch the 1989 title (despite Arsenal having been 19 points ahead in February). But he was haunted by fear and insecurity off it, and developed an alcohol addiction in between matches. Occasionally the angry Adams would reveal himself – he called miked-up referee David Elleray 'a fucking cheat' – though more often than not he was the inarticulate Essex boy loved by the Clock End. But he was stung by a sense of rejection when he missed out on the 1990 World Cup squad, and the drinking was getting worse: he needed 29 stitches in a head wound when he fell down the stairs, he regularly wet himself in the night, and he spent two months in Chelmsford jail for drink-driving in December 1990.

More trophies followed, but still Adams was five years away from admitting his problem. In 1991, Arsenal won the League and two years later the FA Cup and League Cup, celebrating which Adams dropped goalscorer Steve Morrow and broke his arm. In 1994, Arsenal beat Parma to win the European Cup Winners' Cup.

Tony Adams reached a personal water-shed in August 1996, when he declared himself an alcoholic to his Arsenal team-mates after new signings Remi Garde and Patrick Vieira's first training session with the club. 'It was pretty surreal,' said Garde. 'We'd just turned up and the mythical emblem of the club had told us all he was an alcoholic. We wondered what the hell we were doing.' Graham has since admitted that he smelt alcohol on Adams's breath every morning but never did anything about it.

Adams became the antithesis of his former self: he learnt the piano, read Shakespeare and went to the opera. He wore scarves tied in a bow at the neck, and spoke in a quiet voice. The only time he came close to blowing his 'new man' act was when he went out with Caprice. Meanwhile Arsenal's new manager, Arsène **Wenger**, was teaching Adams about the science of football, persuading him to stay at the club and elongating his career thanks to a new diet and training regime.

Adams captained Arsenal to the League and Cup **Double** in 1998 and his international career flourished: he played in the 1998 World Cup and then captained his country under Kevin **Keegan**. His final international appearance was as captain in the defeat to Germany in the last-ever game at Wembley: it was fitting as it was his 60th Wembley appearance, a record that is unlikely to be beaten. By now an MBE, Adams finally quit after winning another Double with Arsenal in 2002. The club retired his number 6 shirt, and Adams did a university course in sports science and got his UEFA coaching licence. He had already set up the Sporting Chance Clinic, a charity whose patrons include Paul Merson and Elton John, to help sportsmen with addictions.

He took his scientific ideas and psycho-speak to Wycombe Wanderers in November 2003, but they were unsurprisingly relegated and he quit 12 months later. He married whisky heiress and Arsenal fan Poppy Teacher and now devotes most of his time to his clinic. The sober Adams is much happier but, echoing the thoughts of many Tottenham fans, he admits that 'the old Tony Adams would have looked at me now and thought, "What an arsehole."'

agents

'The majority of players are still paid slaves,' protested football agent Rachel Anderson in an interview with *When Saturday Comes* in November 1999 – in the process striking a blow for workers everywhere who receive several thousand pounds a week for working half-days and having the whole summer off.

Had Anderson been speaking in 1905 she may have had more of a point. Alf **Common**, the first-ever £1,000 player, pocketed a signing-on fee of just £10 after his move from Sunderland to Middlesbrough. Common's transfer was completed without an intermediary, although agents had been a feature of professional football since the legalization of professionalism in 1885. The modern agent will act for a portfolio of players, arranging transfers and new contracts and helping maximize a player's off-field earnings.

Early football agents such as J. P. Campbell of Liverpool were typical Victorian entrepreneurs. They filled a vacuum in the professional game, which at that time lacked any kind of coaching or scouting network. An advert placed by Campbell in *Athletic News* in 1891 proclaimed: 'Secretaries, now is the time to introduce new blood, drop out the weeds and strike in your teams for next year. My agent in Scotland is hard at work and I expect some tip-top men from him next week.'

It wasn't until the 1970s that agents began to feature significantly, as football developed the tentacles that would link it increasingly with the world of product endorsement and entertainment. In 1977 Kevin **Keegan** made himself the wealthiest footballer in Europe by signing the first-ever 'face' contract, giving his agent and his club, Hamburg, the right to use his image to promote whatever products they deemed fit. Through the power of aftershave, petrol and argyle-patterned golfing tank-tops, Keegan quickly became the most recognizable footballer in the world. Following the increase in player mobility after the **Bosman** ruling, British football has seen an overwhelming increase in agent activity. FIFA lists 220 licensed agents operating in England, almost as many as the combined number in Italy, Germany and Spain.

Agents have traditionally come into football from a variety of backgrounds. One of the first agents in the UK, Reg Hayter, was a sports journalist; Dennis Roach, once the most powerful agent in Europe, got into the business after meeting Johan Cruyff on a seaside holiday; the unctuous, cigar-chomping Eric Hall has his roots in the entertainment industry; and Barry Silkman, one of the busiest of a more recent generation, was a player with Crystal Palace and Manchester City. The UK's largest agency, the SFX Sports Group, has built up a huge portfolio of footballing representation, including among its clients Michael **Owen**, Alan **Shearer** and, until recently, David **Beckham**.

Another agency, Pro-Active Sports, was the first such organization to face suggestions of a conflict of interest, with several Premiership managers selling shares in the company in order to avoid suspicion of improper conduct when signing players Pro-Active represented. In 2004, Manchester United stopped dealing with the Elite Sports agency, run by Sir Alex **Ferguson**'s son, Jason, after a television documentary criticized his role in the transfer of several players to United. There has also been comment about the fact that Darren Dein, the son of the Arsenal vice-chairman, works for Jerome Anderson, an agent who represents several members of Arsenal's first-team squad.

Agents have been blamed for many of the modern game's ills. The unscrupulous agent will agitate for a transfer, or approach a club speculatively claiming to represent a player they have no contact with. In some transfers, incredibly,

agents are able to represent the buying and the selling club as well as the player. Often criticized for knowing nothing about the game they trade in (Harry Redknapp: 'It's a well-known fact that few football agents know one end of a football from the other'), and for providing little more than financial distractions, agents will claim in their defence that they serve to redress the balance of power between footballing plc's and their employees. Either way, agents will remain in football as long as there is money to be made, their numbers always proportionate to the amount of cash circulating through the game.

Airdrie United

Airdrie United were founded in 2002, as the successor to Airdrieonians, who became the first Scottish League club to go out of business since Third Lanark in 1967. They had been in administration for two years before slipping under in 2002. A primary factor in the club's demise was the decision to sell their stadium, Broomfield, before a new one, aimed at meeting the criteria of the newly reorganized Scottish Premier League, was completed. Airdrieonians groundshared for four financially ruinous years at Cumbernauld before moving to the 'new Broomfield' (officially called the Shyberry Excelsior Stadium) in 1998.

When Airdrieonians went bust (their League place being taken by Gretna), a consortium of local businessmen set about buying up another struggling League side, Clydebank. On 7 July 2002, Clydebank's shares were transferred to Airdrie United, who assumed that club's position in Division 2. The new club, which adopted its predecessor's distinctive white shirts with a red 'V', has had quick success: their second season ended in the Division 2 championship under the stewardship of Sandy Stewart, a long-serving Airdrieonians player.

There had been a football club in the Lanarkshire industrial town since 1878, though they didn't join the Scottish League for a further 16 years: it was as a regional league club in 1886 that they inflicted Glasgow Rangers' worst-ever home defeat, 10–2. Promoted to Division 1 in 1903, Airdrieonians stayed up for 33 years and were League runners-up for four consecutive seasons from 1923.

Their greatest moment was a 2–0 victory over Hibernian in the 1924 Scottish Cup Final, with a team featuring the great Hughie Gallacher, later a prolific goalscorer with Newcastle and Chelsea, and their most-capped Scottish international, full-back Jim Crapnell. On the back of their Cup success, Airdrieonians were invited to tour Scandinavia and made a big impression. A match watched by the king and queen of Norway drew lavish praise from a local newspaper, which marvelled at the visitors' 'phenomenal dribbling' and how 'everything seemed so easy yet, for us, so unbelievable'.

Airdrieonians reached the Scottish Cup Final on three more occasions, losing each time – the 1992 defeat to the League champions Rangers led to their only European appearance, a defeat to Sparta Prague in the UEFA Cup – and appeared in several League Cup semi-finals. In 1972 they were runners-up to Derby in the Texaco Cup. In their death throes Airdrieonians won the Challenge Cup for lower-division clubs in 2000 and 2001, the first of the victories with an almost entirely Spanish team managed by former Barcelona and Scotland striker Steve Archibald.

Albion Rovers

Albion Rovers' hour of near-glory came when they reached the 1920 Scottish Cup Final after beating Glasgow Rangers in the semi-final over three games. A crowd of more than 95,000 saw them go down to Kilmarnock at Hampden by the odd goal in five, despite twice holding the lead.

The loss gave 'The Wee Rovers' from Coatbridge the distinction of being the only team besides Dumbarton (in 1897 when they were at the foot of Division 2) to reach the final in the same year as finishing bottom of the League. They made the semi-final again the following season, but this time Rangers took their revenge, and that was the last time that Albion threatened the record books aside from a brace of Division 2 championships, thriftily spaced apart in 1934 and 1989.

Albion are honoured by a sole Scottish cap – Jock White played for Scotland against Wales in 1922 – and they also played a footnote role in the 1949 title race, when their 1–4 home loss to Rangers on the season's final day allowed the Glasgow side to overtake Dundee, who were busy falling to Falkirk. Rovers finished bottom with just eight points from 30 games, but at least they could say the title had been decided at Cliftonhill.

Formed in 1882, when two local clubs called Rovers and Albion merged, the side joined Division 2 in 1903 and the expanded Division 1 in 1919, the same year they moved into their Cliftonhill stadium. It held over 27,000 for a Scottish Cup tie with Rangers in 1936, but its capacity now is a much-reduced 2,500. Cliftonhill seems to be under the perpetual shadow of demolition as the club stands on the brink of selling the ground and building a new 3,000-seater stadium with a training academy. In 2004 they were made an offer by property developers, but decided to defer moving for at least another year.

alcohol

British football has enjoyed a long, intimate and at times destructive relationship with alcohol. From its medieval folk beginnings, playing football has been intimately tied up with drinking. Early football games were often played at rural festivals. The rowdiness of the fabled Shrovetide football matches of the Middle Ages was fuelled, in part, by the availability of local grog, with football spontaneously taken up as a more robust adjunct to all the other village festivities. In the Victorian era many professional football clubs were formed either in or around a favoured pub.

The first football pitches tended to be on pub land and the pub, or club bar, remains the traditional social headquarters of most football teams. Publicans played an important part in the financing and administration of the earliest football clubs, with clubs often seeking financial support from local breweries. Manchester United was created out of the ashes of the defunct Newton Heath by a brewer called John Davies, who distributed shares in the new club among directors of his brewery.

Football has long been a favourite advertising medium for the drinks industry. Grounds, programmes and billboards have been visible testimony to the link between the two. In the first half of the century it was common for names of local breweries to be painted on the roof of a covered stand. During the 1960s players began to advertise brands of beer and stout.

'My name is Jimmy Greaves. I am a professional footballer. And I am an alcoholic.' So begins Jimmy **Greaves**'s autobiography, *This One's on Me*, published in 1979, providing both a fairly comprehensive summary of the book's contents, and also the first public admission of a serious drinking problem from any high-profile footballer. Players have always drunk together. Evenings spent drinking at favoured pubs or in a club bar have long been a part of the machinery of creating the British notion of team spirit. Even now, with the various modernizing and cosmopolitan influences at the top end of the British game, it is rare for any of the larger clubs to actively discourage players from drinking.

In fact excessive drinking and alcoholism have been recurrent malevolent forces throughout the game's history. It was only in the 1960s, with changes in the method and content of newspaper reporting, that the private lives of footballers came under increasing scrutiny and the drinking exploits of professional footballers became a staple of the tabloid newspapers. George **Best** was the first footballing celebrity to make headlines because of his off-field carousing, and his escalating alcoholism was periodically chronicled in newspaper scoops.

Footballers have always drunk: Derby and England striker Steve **Bloomer** was frequently called to account by the club's directors over his late nights and tendency to arrive for training reeking of alcohol; and Dixie **Dean** combined record-breaking scoring feats with the lifestyle of a late-night local celebrity. Best set the template for a new kind of public footballing figure: the talented wastrel. Greaves, Paul **Gascoigne** and Paul Merson have all since played at the highest level despite widely reported addiction problems.

'I don't want angels in the team. In fact they can get out of their brains every night as long as they are man of the match on Saturday,' Aston Villa manager John Gregory said in 1999. Unfortunately, evidence suggests that players are far less likely to be man of the match on Saturday if they have been out of their brains every night of the preceding week. Part of the revolutionary training and dietary influence of foreign players and managers has been to restrict the amount of alcohol consumed.

Even now, foreign players coming to English football for the first time frequently register their surprise and often horror at the sheer quantity of alcohol consumed by fellow players. The book *The Keeper of Dreams* describes German goalkeeper Lars Leese's experiences during his time playing in the Premiership for Barnsley: 'On the continent it was well known that many English professionals thought it was all part of a good night out to down nine or ten pints of beer.' What amazed Lars was that they never had to go to the toilet. He had drunk four beers and been to the gents several times. 'How do they do that?' he wondered. He worked it out when he heard a splashing noise under the table; midfielder Darren Sheridan had rolled up one leg of his shorts and was watering the pub garden grass under the table. 'Above the table he went on talking as though nothing was happening.'

all-rounders

While most footballers are happy to spend their summers either lounging on a fashionable beach or sweating in some Middle Eastern golfing inferno, there have been those who have used the off-season to pursue a career in another sporting discipline.

Denis Compton of Middlesex County Cricket Club and Arsenal has a fair claim to be the greatest all-round British sportsman ever. Compton was a cricketing phenomenon, the finest stroke-player of his generation, scorer of 18 first-class centuries in the summer of 1947 and the man who made the winning hit to claim the Ashes back from Australia in the Coronation summer of 1953. Compton also played for England at football, winning 12 unofficial wartime and Victory match caps, appearing on the left wing while Stanley **Matthews** patrolled the right. Compton also picked up an FA Cup winner's medal as part of the Arsenal team that beat Liverpool 2–0 at Wembley in 1950, the high point of a football career spanning 54 League games over 16 war-interrupted years. In the process Compton became the sporting face of his generation, the original Brylcreem poster boy, a flamboyantly cravated icon of raffish male grooming and all-round sporting excellence.

At the other end of the scale Chesterfield goalkeeper Chris Marples spent several summers keeping wicket for Derbyshire during the 1980s, while Leicestershire batsman Chris Balderstone played cricket for England and first-division football for Carlisle during the 1970s. The last man to play at the top level in both sports, Balderstone once played in an evening League match after a whole day of Championship cricket. More famously, cricketing legend Ian Botham played 11 games at centre-half for Scunthorpe between 1979 and 1984, while Geoff **Hurst** – described as an 'outstanding fielder' – played one first class game for Essex against Lancashire in June 1962, scoring 0 and 0 not out. As yet the closest thing to a Caledonian Denis Compton, Rangers and Scotland goalkeeper Andy Goram also played cricket for his country, keeping wicket in several one-day internationals during his time at Hibernian.

More recently, Phil Neville – over 50 England caps and six Premiership medals

– broke England batsman John Crawley's Lancashire schoolboy run-scoring records before opting for a career in football instead of cricket. Similarly, Gary **Lineker** was a successful schoolboy cricketer, as was Italy centre-forward Christian Vieri, who during his youth in Australia forged a reputation as a useful seam bowler before moving to Italy to concentrate on scoring goals, being constantly linked with a move to the Premiership and having almost his entire body covered in tattoos.

Probably the greatest all-rounder of them all, C. B. Fry, had only the briefest of brushes with football, playing at full-back with Southampton, for whom he appeared in an FA Cup Final and for England against Ireland in 1901. Otherwise he spent most of his time playing cricket for England, standing as a member of parliament, breaking the long-jump world record and being offered the throne of Albania. Further down the scale of modern-day Renaissance men, West Ham and Liverpool left-back Julian 'The Terminator' Dicks pursued a brief career in semi-professional golf after retiring from top-level football, ultimately finding a life of painstaking frustration on the greens no substitute for the adrenaline rush of the studs-up tackle.

Phil Neale played at right-back for Lincoln City between 1974 and 1985, spending his summers playing as a batsman for Worcestershire County Cricket Club. He is currently part of the England cricket coaching staff. Arnie Side-bottom had a long football career with Manchester United and Huddersfield Town and also played cricket for Yorkshire for 18 years and made a single Test Match appearance for England.

As the start of the football season edges closer to July every year, and after a hundred years of retreat from a sporting landscape in which a gifted amateur could take up the cudgels alongside the professional, it seems increasingly unlikely that a place remains for the dual sportsman. Part of the reason for this is financial: before the boom in players' wages, the likes of Compton and Balderstone were well paid for their summers out of football. On the other hand, had he opted for a career in cricket Philip Neville would have earned less in a year as a county player than in two weeks as a professional footballer.

Ivor Allchurch

Ivor Allchurch was the quintessential local hero in a time when such heroes could also be of national and international significance. Among the extraordinarily gifted generation who emerged from Swansea in the decade after the Second World War, he was the player most closely associated with the town and its club.

He was an unhurriedly elegant inside-forward of whom Jimmy Murphy, Wales manager in the 1950s, wrote: 'Ivor had the lot. He was two-footed: a superb runner on the ball with a glorious body swerve. He could shoot hard and accurately with both feet, and he was very good in the air.' Swansea fans and newspapers called him the 'Golden Boy', a title his biographers were frustrated to have pre-empted by Wilf **Mannion**'s chroniclers.

His League debut delayed until he was 20 by National Service, he arrived in Swansea Town's Division 2 squad at Christmas 1949 as a mature talent. A spectacular FA Cup performance against Arsenal brought him to wider notice within weeks and initiated transfer speculation that would last for most of the 1950s. A move in the early 1950s would have smashed the British transfer record, but, already on the maximum wage and an automatic choice for Wales from his debut in 1950, there were few pressures to move. The closest he came to leaving, for Wolves in 1952, was a response to the club's financial problems, not pressure from the player.

It was also reasonable to hope that he might play Division 1 football with Swansea. He might have made it had the club's board been prepared to buy defenders to supplement locally generated attacking talents such as Allchurch, Terry Medwin, Mel Charles and Cliff Jones. As other, younger players began to leave, Allchurch finally joined them, saying 'It is now or never' when he joined Newcastle United in 1958. In the same year he had been a star of Wales's run to the quarter-finals of the World Cup, scoring with an extraordinary dipping volley in a play-off against Hungary. While watching a tournament illuminated by such talents as Johnny Haynes, Nils Liedholm and Didi, Santiago Bernabéu, president of Real Madrid, called him 'the greatest inside-forward in the world'.

His 68 caps and 24 goals for Wales in an international career spread over 16 years were both records at the time. As recently as 2004 former Wales manager Terry Yorath argued that Wales's cardinal weakness over the last four decades has been an absence of the creative qualities Allchurch epitomized.

His League career was similarly long and productive, with totals of 694 games and 245 goals, also a record for a Welshman at the time of his retirement in 1968. After four seasons at Newcastle United and three with Cardiff City, he had returned to Swansea for the final three years. Allchurch played on at non-League level with Worcester City, Haverfordwest and Pontardawe until his wife demanded he burn his boots at the age of 50. Awarded an MBE in 1966, he died in 1997.

Malcolm Allison

Malcolm Allison was one of the most innovative coaches of his era, but like some of the maverick players with whom he was associated, he might have achieved a lot more. All his successes in English football were crammed into four years at Manchester City. In Allison's first full season as assistant to manager Joe **Mercer**, City won the 1966 Division 2 championship, then took the League title, with rivals United second, in 1968.

Renowned for a free-flowing style developed by Allison (who introduced a red-and-black away kit because he wanted them to look like AC Milan), City also won the FA Cup, League Cup and European Cup Winners' Cup over the next two seasons, They flopped badly in the European Cup of 1968–69, however, losing to Fenerbahçe of Turkey in the first round after Allison, prone to making extravagant boasts, had said, 'We will take football to the moon.'

Allison's modest playing career as a centre-half with West Ham in Division 2 was ended by tuberculosis when he was 30 (a teenage Bobby **Moore** was his replacement). Like many of his contemporaries at Upton Park he took an interest in coaching and soon went into management with non-League Bath City in 1962, moving on to Plymouth Argyle two years later, then to Manchester City in 1965.

Joe Mercer, seen as a calming influence on his mercurial assistant, stepped down in 1971 leaving Allison in sole charge – he later claimed to have turned down an offer to coach Juventus shortly before Mercer's departure. City nearly won the League in Allison's first full season but lost key matches after the balance of the side was disrupted by the signing of the flamboyant Rodney Marsh from QPR. Allison tinkered with the team to little effect over the next year before resigning to take over at Crystal Palace, who were already doomed to relegation from Division 1.

Despite taking Palace down again the following year, Allison's public stock remained high, helped by starring performances as 'Big Mal' on ITV's World Cup panels and press interest in a convoluted private life (first divorced in 1975, he was to become a father for the sixth time at the age of 63). His standing was bolstered by Palace's FA Cup run of 1975–76, when they reached the semifinals before losing to Southampton, with the manager resembling a Chicago gangster in the lucky fedora worn for each match. But Palace, still stuck in the third, sacked him later that year and his career fell away.

After a spell abroad Allison returned, unsuccessfully, to three previous clubs: Plymouth, Man City and Palace. At City, where he spent £1.43m on the unexceptional Wolves midfielder Steve Daley, one player later wearily recalled that they would run laps of the training pitch while the manager periodically shouted 'How do you feel?', to which they were meant to respond, 'Sharp!'

After one final triumph, winning the Portuguese League with Sporting Lisbon in 1982, Allison took on the more prosaic task of keeping impoverished Middlesbrough in Division 2. This he achieved, though the club didn't take up his suggestion, inspired by a coaching spell in America, that they should play on an astroturf pitch dyed orange. After a final spell in management at Bristol Rovers, where he introduced a tactical concept called the 'Whirl', which involved players regularly swapping positions, Allison settled into semi-retirement as a radio pundit on Teesside, which survived his exclaiming 'Oh fuck!' on air when Middlesbrough let in a goal.

With his enthusiam for expansive football, Malcolm Allison would have made a fine director of coaching at the FA in the 1970s in place of the long-ball advocate Charles Hughes, but his extravagant lifestyle seemed to colour his approach to club management – he couldn't be left alone with a chequebook. He remains the only English football manager to have published an autobiography that sounds like a psychedelic LP, *Colours of My Life*.

Alloa Athletic

Alloa stormed on to the Scottish League scene in their 1921 debut season when they won Division 2 by 13 points. However, despite the 49 goals netted that year by 'Wee' Willie Crilly, it was a false dawn. The next season they went straight back down and have not played in Scotland's top flight since. Gold and black have always been the chosen colours of 'The Wasps', formed in 1883 and residents of Recreation Park since 1895. The team's solitary Scottish cap was won by Jock Hepburn in 1891.

Alloa's long sojourn in Division 2 would have been broken when they pipped East Fife for second place in the 1938–39 season. Having played little wartime football, in 1946 they were one of a handful of teams who lost their rightful place in Division A, and were placed in Division B when play resumed and the league was reorganized. They finally reached Division 1 in 1977, but by that time the league had been reformed again to incorporate the Scottish Premier League, and over the subsequent years they bobbed around the lower divisions, picking up a Division 3 title in 1998 to add to their seven runners-up spots in Division 2.

There were few Cup shocks to brighten up the half-century of stasis, unless you count losing 1–0 to Tarff Athletic (an alliance of villages between Dumfries and Stranraer) in the Scottish Cup second preliminary round at the end of 1969. Although Alloa have never progressed further than the quarter-finals of either League or FA Cup, their most successful year in 1999–2000 included not just a promotion from Division 2, but lifting the Challenge Cup as well – a dramatic win on penalties against Inverness Caledonian Thistle after the game had finished 4–4 at the end of extra time.

Alloa fans are rewarded with better views of the Ochil Hills from the Recreation ground than their counterparts at Stenhousemuir's Ochilview Park. Visitors complain, however, that in spite of Alloa's brewing tradition, the 3,100 capacity stadium lies a good 15-minute yomp from the nearest pub.

Anglo-Italian Cup

This unlikely tournament was conceived in 1969 partly as a way of rewarding League Cup winners Swindon Town with European football, a path denied them by UEFA because of their lower division status. To add to the confusion, there were two separate tournaments – one involved six sides from each nation, the other was a direct face-off over two legs between the Coppa Italia and the English League Cup winners (although from 1975 it became the FA Cup winners). This was known as the Anglo-Italian League Cup.

Still, the whole mess duly granted Swindon their hour of European glory. In 1969 they beat Roma 5–2 on aggregate to take the Anglo-Italian League Cup, and later that season they also qualified for the final of the Anglo-Italian Cup as the best-placed English side from the complicated group system, having beaten Juventus home and away. They were leading Napoli 3–0 in the single-tie final in

Naples in front of 55,000 when the game was abandoned after 79 minutes because of rioting by the home crowd. So at least somebody was taking it seriously.

Blackpool twice made the final of the Anglo-Italian Cup, winning 2–1 in Bologna after extra time in 1971. They lost to Roma the following year, while Newcastle won the last trophy contested by professional clubs, in Florence. A curious statistic: two years later Newcastle also won the last-ever Texaco Cup and maintain a reputation as the grim reaper of doomed trans-national club competitions. The Anglo-Italian did continue until 1986 as a competition for, theoretically, semi-professional sides (English non-League clubs played opponents from Italy's Serie C, many of whom were in fact full-time), giving Sutton United their lone European honour in 1979.

The Anglo-Italian League Cup, meanwhile, limped on until 1976, although it was not held from 1972 to 1974. Manchester City, Spurs and Southampton all count the cup among their honours, while West Ham were the only English side to lose, falling to Fiorentina in 1975.

Unbelievably, the idea was revived in 1992 for a tortuously complex tournament between English and Italian second-tier sides. In the face of chronic indifference, especially in Italy, where fans could not be lured out to watch the likes of Stoke City and Tranmere, the contest once more breathed its last after just four years. Notts County were the sole English victors, beating Ascoli 2–1 at Wembley in 1995 in front of fewer than 12,000 spectators, and it was perhaps scant consolation for finishing bottom of Division 2.

Arbroath

Since 12 September 1885, Arbroath have been living in the past, basking in the glory of their greatest achievement. To this day, their defeat of Aberdeen Bon Accord in the first round of the Scottish Cup, by 36 goals to nil, stands as a British record. Unfortunately, the Red Lichties (named after the red light used to guide fishing boats to the harbour) have had precious little to cheer in the 120 years since that remarkable win. Despite six promotions Arbroath are still waiting for their first major trophy. They dropped to Division 3 in 2005, suffering more than most from the cash flow problem blighting the game in Scotland.

Life started brightly for Arbroath. They won their first competitive match in 1878, against Our Boys of Dundee, and in 1880 they laid their roots at Gayfield, a former refuse dump that they still call home. The ground provided controversy in 1884, when they beat Rangers 4–3 in the 1884 Scottish Cup only for the Glasgow side to complain that the pitch was too narrow. A replay was ordered, which Arbroath duly lost 8–1.

One year later Arbroath etched their name in football history. John 'Jocky' Petrie scored 13 of the 36 goals that day, also a record. Shortly afterwards, the club signed their only international player to date, 'Ned' Doig, a goalkeeper who would later play for Sunderland and Liverpool. In 1888 Doig won the 300 yard sprint, the skipping race and the hop, step and jump at the town's annual games. Doig was still in his early 20s when he left and Arbroath would continue to sell their best players, often out of necessity. In 1934 George Mutch was sold to Manchester United at the age of 21. He would score the goal that won the FA Cup for Preston North End in

1938. George Cumming, another goalkeeper, followed him south in 1936, joining Middlesbrough for £3,000, then a Scottish record fee. He would be capped for Scotland only after he left Gayfield.

But there'll always be Bon Accord. A rematch finally took place between Arbroath and the Aberdeen junior club in 1996. The Red Lichties came out on top again, falling a mere 32 goals short of equalling their proud record.

Arsenal

Arsenal are by a distance the most successful London football club, and the standard-bearers for the south in a sport historically dominated by northern teams. The Gunners have played in the top division since 1919, a record run during which they have won the League or Premiership title 13 times and the League and FA Cup Double three times. Despite beginning their north London life as ambitious upstarts, a modern club in an art-deco stadium, Arsenal have come to be seen as one of English football's old guard: a middle-class club in a north London suburb, with a board of directors that resemble public school headmasters and a support that includes more teachers, graduates and shaggy-haired media types than any other.

Much is made of Arsenal's 'marble halls' – in reality a single stairwell with a bust of Herbert **Chapman**, the club's first great manager. In fact the dynamism of the current coaching and playing staff are consistent with Arsenal's history as a brash and innovative English football club. There may have been resistance to the idea of leaving Highbury for the monstrously corporate new stadium at Ashburton Grove, but the move itself is within the Arsenal tradition of speculative self-improvement.

The club was founded in 1886 by workers at the Royal Arsenal in Woolwich under the name Dial Square, one of the workshops at the south London shipyard. The word 'Arsenal' is derived from the Arabic for a military port, and like Woolwich itself the club was built around the munitions factory workers. Known as the Woolwich Reds for a while and then Woolwich Arsenal, the team's early games were played on Plumstead Common, followed by the Manor Ground and later the Invicta Stadium.

Arsenal were the first southern team to turn professional and the first to join the Football League, entering Division 2 in 1893. Promotion nine years later was followed by the club's only ever relegation in 1913, a campaign during which they didn't win a game from September to March and won only once at home all season. Within two seasons Arsenal were back in the top flight, having been controversially readmitted to the expanded Division 1 ahead of Tottenham thanks to the machinations of chairman Henry Norris. By this time the club had also relocated to its new ground at Highbury, having made the move north from Plumstead to Islington.

At the time it seemed like an act of great folly. Clapton and Tottenham, two established clubs, were hostile to another professional football club moving into the area. Tottenham in particular seem to have never quite got over the shock of having an upstart – and ultimately more successful – neighbour. The move was generally considered a bizarre and desperate act by a team that had lost a great proportion of its core support through the impoverishment of the Woolwich area and the hiatus in the club's existence brought about by the Boer War, when its activities were briefly suspended so that workers could concentrate on the war effort.

However, rather than extinction in exile, with the move to Highbury the club was heading for the first of its successful eras. This is a common theme in the club's history: a spectacular burst of success under a particular manager, interspersed by periods of retrenchment. During Herbert Chapman's nine years in charge it became the finest football team Britain had seen. After his appointment in 1925, Arsenal won the League four times in five years from 1931, the last two of these after Chapman had died suddenly, catching pneumonia while watching a reserve team game. The first great Arsenal team – in common with the most recent – was famed for its advanced diet, fitness and tactical precision, and for the fast, direct attacking interplay of players such as Ted Drake, Cliff **Bastin** and Joe Hulme. The club also began to spend unprecedented amounts of money on new players.

After further League titles in 1948 and 1953, it would be 18 years before Arsenal experienced another spectacular success, the League and Cup Double of 1971. In 1966 Arsenal had finished just four points ahead of relegated Northampton Town. Five years later, under Bertie Mee and with a team built around captain Frank McLintock, midfielder George **Graham** and the goalkeeping of Bob Wilson, they took the title with a 1–0 victory at White Hart Lane in the final match of the season, beating Liverpool 2–1 after extra time in the FA Cup Final a few days later.

A period of decline during the 1970s was leavened by successive FA Cup Final appearances in 1978, 1979 (victorious) and 1980, but it took the arrival of George Graham in 1986 to begin the club's next great era. Graham built an utterly defensive team. A relentlessly drilled offside trap, masterminded by Tony **Adams**, alongside Steve Bould and the full-backs Nigel Winterburn and Lee Dixon, was supported by mobile, skilful young midfielders – including the youth team products David Rocastle and Paul Davis – and the kind of forward designed either to head (Niall Quinn, Alan Smith) or chase (Ian **Wright**) the long ball over the top. Graham's Arsenal won League titles in 1989 (dramatically, with Michael Thomas's goal in injury time at Anfield) and 1991, and earned a reputation as a team that was both boring and lucky. In fact they were simply highly effective, although unable to develop beyond a couple of attritionally hard-earned League titles (plus two domestic cups in 1993 and a European Cup Winners' Cup).

Arsenal have had relatively few managers. There have been only 11 since Chapman, including both Don **Howe** and Bruce Rioch for just a single season. The most recent manager, Arsène **Wenger**, arrived in 1996 and is on his way to becoming the most successful in the club's history. Wenger took over a club with a reputation for bad habits – an enthusiastically embraced drinking culture and various tabloid-friendly romps and mishaps – and with an ageing core in David Seaman, the famous George Graham defence and Ian Wright, born in Woolwich and holder of the club's goalscoring record until it was beaten by Thierry Henry. Wenger intro-duced changes in training and lifestyle that have since been adopted across the Premiership. Controls on diet and alcohol intake were enthusiastically taken up, as were innovative physical-conditioning techniques.

During Wenger's tenure English players such as Ray Parlour and Martin Keown revived or prolonged their careers, while devoted skipper Tony Adams was transformed from an injury-prone alcoholic to a reformed alcoholic Double-winning skipper with a passing interest in Shakespeare, motivational techniques and painting.

Arsenal's £400m new stadium at Ashburton Grove represents a gamble as the club has taken on an enormous debt in order to complete it. In return they should be able to generate enough in revenue to compete with their stellar rivals. Wenger's team took the FA Cup again in 2005 with a penalty shoot-out victory over Manchester United and they were defeated by Barcelona in the 2006 Champions League Final. Much depends on continued success on the field.

art

'What the fuck is art? A picture of a bottle of sour milk lying next to a smelly old jumper? To me it's a load of shit. I'd say football is art' – the thoughts of then Aston Villa manager John Gregory, as recorded in *Loaded* magazine in 1999. In fact Gregory is wrong. Football is not art; it's an 11-a-side team sport. However, the game has been depicted in pictorial form by various British artists over the last 200 years. Thomas Webster's *The Football*, painted in 1839, shows a group of boys engaged in a boisterous game of rural village football, a full 25 years before the Football Association would codify the game with its first set of official laws and regulations. Previously, sketchy cartoons of village football had been fairly common, a style that found an echo in the anecdotal pen-and-ink drawings which sometimes accompanied match reports around the turn of the century.

Football was largely ignored by the art establishment during the first half of the 20th century. Bloomsbury aesthete Duncan Grant produced *Football* in 1911, a panel painting currently hanging in the Tate Gallery in London, which shows a group of lithe young men in athletic suits engaged in a kind of bucolic gambol, seeming to pay more attention to one another's muscular physiques than the ball one of them holds casually beneath an arm. John Singer Sargent's First World War painting *Gassed* features a train of walking wounded approaching a trench field hospital, while in the background a football match is taking place with players in full kit and boots. Some critics have claimed that the artist is making an analogy between the horrors of modern warfare and organized sport, in which case *Gassed* could be the first ever *anti*-football painting.

Later the modernist Paul Nash summoned up a – perhaps perversely – Cubist vision of what remains a very spherical game in *Footballers Prefer Shell* (1933), part of a popular poster campaign for Shell Oil. In 1954 football was the subject of perhaps its first dedicated exhibition when the Arts Council organized a collection called Football and the Fine Arts. The curators may have intended the title as a pithy paradox given the tone of most of the paintings, which tended to portray football as a means of collective existential release from the kitchen-sink misery of working-class life.

One of the works exhibited was L. S. Lowry's *Going to the Match* (1953), perhaps the most famous football painting. It shows supporters walking towards Bolton Wanderers' Burnden Park, while in the background factory chimneys belch smoke. The painting was bought as an investment by the PFA in 1999, and the £2m purchase was much trumpeted in sections of the press as a means of discrediting the union when it threatened to bring its members out on strike in a dispute over television payments in 2001.

During the 1960s football was a recurrent motif in the work of influential Pop artist Peter Blake. Blake included a foot-baller – Albert Stubbins, a Liverpool player of the 1950s – in his artwork for the cover of the Beatles' *Sgt Pepper's Lonely Hearts Club Band*, and in 1991 his *F is for Football* featured cigarette card portraits of footballers and images of Spurs players from the 1961 Double-winning team. However, the decades following the 1954 exhibition saw a general dwindling of public footballing art, which has only recently been reversed with the market-led softening of the game's image during the 1990s and an increasingly close relationship between football and various areas of entertainment and the media. During Euro 96 exhibitions of football paintings were held at the City Gallery in Manchester and at London's Gallery 27. Subsequently the opening of the National Football Museum in Preston in 2001 has created a site for footballing art to be gathered under one roof.

Despite this, 'good' footballing art remains a tiny adjunct of the cultural landscape. Bad footballing art, on the other hand, is a huge and thriving industry. The market for hastily knocked-up ('lovingly hand-crafted'), mass-produced memorabilia ('highly collectible artworks') is as vibrant as any other footballing spin-off. For example, for just £150 fans of Manchester United can buy *The Dream. The Hope. The Reality*, a tribute to the club's 1999 treble-winning season, a series of hastily executed mug shots, which bills itself as 'a sports illustration without equal . . . breathtakingly detailed'. There is a huge amount of this kind of footballing art for sale, infinitely more than there is of the 'serious' or 'good' or simply non-money-making variety. And while relatively few artists may have deemed the game worthy of their attentions, there is clearly a hunger for footballing art among those who follow the game.

ashes

The boom in football's popularity during the 1990s had many unexpected side-effects. One of these was the increasing fashion for newly deceased football fans to have their ashes sprinkled on the pitch of their chosen team. In 1993 the FA issued guidelines to groundsmen to help deal with the rise in the number of such requests from families of the recently cremated. At the time Manchester United were receiving up to 25 a year and Manchester City at least a dozen. Goal-mouths and centre circles proved to be favoured spots among the deceased, with crucial areas of match day turf suffering as a result. In response to this the Football Association magazine *FC* published a series of handy hints under the headline 'Scattering tips for groundsmen'. These included 'on a windy day it is best to scatter ashes upwind'; 'brush the ashes about to ensure an even spread'; and 'a large pile could kill the grass'. Not to mention alarm the players.

Aston Villa

Often referred to as English football's original aristocrats, Aston Villa were formed in 1874 and boast a varied history that includes a notable period of success before the First World War, as well as one of the more unlikely triumphs in European Cup history. The club's rapid rise to early football prominence was largely the product of three famous figures. William McGregor, the most familiar amongst them, was a Perthshire-born shopkeeper whose pursuit of the breathtakingly simple idea of a group of teams playing regular fixtures against each other helped to establish the Football League in 1888.

By this time Villa had already won the first of its seven FA Cups, defeating West Bromwich 2–0 at the Oval (after a semi-final victory over Glasgow Rangers). Equally significant was the arrival of George Ramsey, a slight Glaswegian whose dazzling dribbling skills – frequently undertaken in a natty polo cap – earned him a place on the team and then the captaincy. From 1888 to 1926 Ramsey served as club secretary; during his tenure Villa won the League six times and the Cup five.

The other critical presence was chairman Fred Rinder, the dynamic surveyor who in 1897, a week after his club had claimed English football's second-ever Double, orchestrated Villa's return to Aston Lower Grounds, known today as Villa Park. Such was the scale of Rinder's architectural ambition that by 1914 he was drafting plans to expand the ground's capacity to 104,000. His legacy was the Trinity Road Stand, christened in 1924 by the future King George VI and probably the finest the country had then seen. It was demolished in 2001 as the ground was redeveloped.

By the late 1930s, all three men had died, and Villa had dropped into Division 2, though they scrambled out again after only two seasons. Few could have expected the drought which lay ahead: only an FA Cup triumph in 1957, soon followed by relegation in the dying minutes of the season at West Brom in 1959. The arrival of the League Cup in 1960 would offer a welcome tonic. In beating Rotherham over two legs with a goal in extra time Villa became the new cup's first champions; two more successes followed in the seventies, by which time the club had tasted life in Division 3 and flirted with bankruptcy amidst boardroom power struggles and dwindling gates.

With the arrival of Ron Saunders in 1974, Villa's fortunes changed. Within three seasons the famously dour disciplinarian had steered the club to fourth place in Division 1 and its first-ever crack at Europe. Four years later, Villa claimed the championship for the first time in 71 years, using only 14 players all season.

History may have underrepresented their unlikely conquest of Europe the following season – particularly the final, which saw evergreen goalkeeper Jimmy Rimmer going off after eight minutes complaining of a sore neck. Young replacement Nigel Spink, with just one first-team match to his name, proceeded to keep Karl-Heinz Rummenigge and Bayern Munich at bay largely through a combination of deft goalkeeping and a four-leaf clover he must have tucked into a sock. Peter Withe scored the game's only goal, using his shin, midway through the second half and Villa hung on for dear life to lift the trophy.

By the time of Villa's greatest triumph Saunders had resigned in acrimony, having fallen out with directors. Long-time chairman Doug Ellis, who had first joined the board in 1968, wasn't at Villa for their title win and European success but returned in 1983 and his grip on the club would grow ever more tenacious as the club fell from grace. By 1987 Villa were in Division 2 again, playing before gates as low as 9,000. Graham **Taylor** guided them out – and to a League runners-up spot – before promptly leaving to become England manager; another second place followed under Ron Atkinson in 1993.

The 1990s produced two further League Cup Final triumphs: the first, under Atkinson, over a treble-chasing Manchester United; the second, with 1970s terrace idol Brian Little now in charge, against Leeds United. By then Ellis's 'deadly' disposition and hands-on style of chairmanship had produced a parade of ten different managers since Saunders's former assistant Tony Barton guided the club to European glory.

Despite this, Taylor's ill-judged return in 2002 marked the first time Villa had finished out of positions four to eight since 1994. A penalty shoot-out with Bolton in 2000 put Villa in the FA Cup Final for the first time in 43 years, but they lost to Chelsea.

attendances

Counting and publicizing the number of people who attend a football match may seem a mundane activity, but the bald figures that have been collected since the game became a business in the 1880s can be read in any number of ways. To administrators they are a barometer of the health of the game in general and each club in particular; to players they have given a sense of their own financial worth (and, until the 1960s, a cause for grievance); for fans they can be an indicator of the passion or loyalty attached to their own club, especially in hard times.

In England, club attendances have gone through five broad phases: rapid increase from the start of the League until it began to taper in the mid-1920s; a plateau during the Depression of the 1930s; the huge post-Second World War boom; a long decline from the early 1950s until 1986, only briefly halted after England's 1966 World Cup win; then a strong and totally unexpected recovery. The reasons for each – except perhaps the recent boom – are not much in doubt.

The development of the league system, with more clubs added at regular intervals, went in tandem with the building of stadiums that could hold more people. By the 1920s, most grounds had the basic shape (and in many cases the exact stands and terraces) that would last until the 1990s, and the League had expanded to include

88 clubs by 1923. More uncertain economic times helped keep a lid on crowds until after the Second World War, when the first few seasons saw records set that mostly still stand. That frenzy could not last, but the decline accelerated in the 1950s and '60s as the variety of leisure activities increased and the old inner-city working-class communities began to fracture. The blight of hooliganism – perhaps exacerbated by a particularly negative period on the field – then drove more fans away in the 1970s and early '80s, as football seemed locked in a permanent downward spiral of violent fans ruling over outdated and dangerous stadiums.

In the season after the **Heysel disaster** and the **Bradford fire**, 1985–86, League crowds amounted to only 16.5 million – at their peak in 1949 they topped 41 million and were still hovering around 30 million in the late 1960s. Clubs that had pulled huge crowds throughout their history, such as Tottenham, played League matches in front of fewer than 10,000 people that season. Yet from that nadir, things have improved beyond all expectation, with crowds climbing back to more than 29 million by 2004.

While some of that improvement can be attributed to the marketing of the Premiership (although the rise started six years before the new league began), it is heartening to note that crowds have risen just as steadily in the lower divisions. More people watched second-flight football in 2003–04 (albeit with a 24-team division) than in any season since 1955–56. And even further down, the arrival of the Conference as an effective fifth division has lifted non-League crowds to remarkable levels – the second season of automatic promotion to the League, 1987–88, ended with what is still a Conference record crowd of 9,432 for Lincoln v Wycombe.

The teams that have drawn the most fans have remained remarkably similar since the beginning of the League. For the first ten years Everton were clearly dominant – their average crowd rose from 7,260 in 1889 to 17,420 by 1898. Aston Villa and Newcastle also had spells at the top of the crowd charts before and after the First World War, largely matching their success on the field, but the appeal of the northern clubs (with the two Manchester giants already to the fore) was more than matched by perennially underachieving Chelsea, who were the biggest draw in the country in 1907–08 (averaging nearly 32,000), only their third season in existence.

Even they could not resist the glamour of all-conquering Arsenal in the 1930s, and after the war Tottenham also proved their appeal, along with Newcastle and Everton again, before Manchester United finally established themselves beyond doubt as the most popular team in the country in 1967. Since then, despite many years of relative failure, they have only been headed on a few occasions, the last in 1989 by Liverpool.

Away from the elite, more than one club has been strongly identified with its drawing power, or lack of it. Manchester City fans in recent years have revelled in their loyalty as the club slid to the third level, perhaps more self-consciously in these media-dominated times than with other struggling big clubs in the past, such as Aston Villa, Sheffield Wednesday or Wolves. Wimbledon, by contrast, almost made a virtue of their lack of support during their spell in the top flight – the 3,039 who saw them play Everton in 1993 is a record low for that division – but sadly their much more pitiful crowds ten years later had a more contentious cause and a more demoralizing effect.

Ayr United

Ayr United are nicknamed 'The Honest Men' after a line in native son Robert Burns's poem 'Tam O'Shanter' that declares Ayr to be a town of 'honest men and bonnie lassies'. Founded in 1910 after a merger of Ayr FC, who'd joined the League in 1898, and Ayr Parkhouse, who arrived in 1903 but finished bottom of Division 2 on three occasions, the team is the only example of two Scottish League sides from the same town successfully forming an alliance. From the start they've played at Somerset Park.

The team began promisingly, lifting the Division 2 title in 1912 in only its second season, but they were denied a place in the top flight after the League deferred automatic relegation that season. The following season Ayr took the title again, and this time there were no such shenanigans. Protective Scottish League policies weren't the only problems visited on the club. In 1920, Ayr was the venue for some heavy stone-throwing at a game against Rangers, a disturbance caused by the notorious Brake Clubs. These were travelling fan clubs, founded pre-First World War, who went to games by horse wagonette. After the war they upgraded to charabancs and acquired a reputation for trouble.

An Ayr player was at the centre of an early bribe scandal too. In 1935, Falkirk manager Robert Orr told United's Robert Russell not to appear in a vital relegation clash between the two if he valued his job at a coach-building company in Falkirk. Russell accepted three pounds not to play and declared himself unfit, but when Falkirk won the game he confessed all and the match was replayed. This time Ayr won. Russell was fined £10 and banned until the season's end, while Orr was banned for life.

From 1969 onwards Ayr enjoyed their longest continuous period in the top flight, surviving as part-timers for almost a decade. Led by future Scotland boss Ally McLeod, they could never quite finish high enough to qualify for Europe, and have kicked around the lower divisions since relegation in 1997. The Honest Men have won eight Division 2 titles, and have been three times runners-up, but Cup success has eluded them. In 1950 they shipped late goals to Motherwell after being seven minutes away from the League Cup Final. In 1973 they were pipped 2–0 by Rangers in the Scottish Cup semis, while in the 1990s they twice reached the final of the new League Challenge Cup (for lower-division sides only), but lost to Dundee and Hamilton.

In 2002, in the same season they were knocked out of the Scottish Cup by Celtic at the semi-final stage, Ayr finally reached a major final, the League Cup, but lost 4–0 to Rangers. In the weeks preceding the game the town's statue of Robert Burns was adorned with an Ayr United scarf. He didn't look happy about it.

bad behaviour

Throughout its recorded history in this country football has, in one form or another, been associated with rowdiness, poor sportsmanship, violence and general bad behaviour. Something about the game has always attracted censure, usually from the governing classes. In Shakespeare's *King Lear* the King's courtier Kent calls the rascally Oswald 'you base football player', while there is a case of a man being sent to the Tower for playing football in a churchyard on a Sunday during the reign of Henry VIII. The deviant worsened the situation by calling the King an adulterer and added that if he had the opportunity he would like to play football with the monarch's head – in defence he claimed drunkenness.

As long ago as 1846 the traditional Shrovetide match between the parishes of All Saints and St Peter's in Derby was broken up by a cavalry charge on the orders of the local governor, after years of attempted suppression by the town mayor. The professional game has its roots in the mass village free-for-alls of the Middle Ages, usually violent, often drunken affairs where societies dissolved and the local populace were allowed to disport themselves in as disorderly a manner as they pleased. Football was a liberation from polite society and, by this time, a disreputable activity that threatened to subvert a carefully marshalled social order. Something of this exists to the modern day, undoubtedly grounded in the lingering attitudes of the British class system.

Something of the game's disreputable air, its association with the lower orders, springs from the introduction of the professional player in 1885 and the steady departure from amateurism at the turn of the 20th century, anathema to the public school men who had founded the

Football Association and many of the League's most prominent clubs.

As the game's popularity increased and the enormous crowds of the inter-war years confirmed its place as the primary public entertainment of the masses, so the notion of the football fan entered the national lexicon, yet another focus for the opprobrium that surrounds the game. Although football has always been a very physical pursuit, with fouling, injuries and violent disputes a regular part of competition, mass sendings off, bans and suspensions are a relatively recent phenomenon. The proliferation of yellow cards in the years since their introduction in 1976 and the frequency with which players are now sent off are more a function of strict refereeing guidelines than a sign that the game has become dirtier or players more badly behaved. Arsenal and Manchester United are the only teams ever to have points deducted, two and one respectively, after a particularly spectacular brawl during the 1990–91 season.

Despite football's reputation for rowdiness, gamesmanship and acts of physical violence, the game has a fairly strict unwritten law of good conduct. Players from the same team don't argue with one another. Derek Hales and Mike Flanagan became the first players from the same English League team ever to be sent off for fighting one another, the two Charlton Athletic front men coming to blows during an FA Cup tie against Maidstone in 1979. Apparently Hales had wanted the ball played through to him *before* he'd strayed offside. Flanagan offered a curt reply to the effect that even when Hales received a pass in an onside position, he had always missed it. In 2004–05 Newcastle's Lee Bowyer and Kieron Dyer were the second pair of sparring team-mates to be dismissed.

In 1995, while playing Spartak Moscow in the Champions' League, Blackburn's Graeme Le Saux baulked at David Batty's motivational abuse and threw a punch at his team-mate. Le Saux had to be substituted in the second half with a hand injury. Bradford's Stuart McCall and Andy Myers and Liverpool's Steve McManaman and Bruce Grobbelaar have also put on a show for their public in the heat of the moment.

The best-known football fight of modern times occurred at a Derby v Leeds match in 1975, between Francis Lee and Norman Hunter. Hunter, lurching viciously forward, threw a couple of haymakers at Lee, one of which split his lip, and Lee responded with a whirring of fists in the general direction of Hunter's head. Brilliantly, having been dismissed, they continued throwing punches on their way to the dressing room and squared up again in the players' lounge (20 years later, when both were attending a player's memorial service, Lee mimed throwing a punch at Hunter as he walked past him).

Brought about by referees' increased willingness to halt play if a player is lying injured, teams will now routinely return the ball to the opposition if they had possession before a stoppage. Failure to do this is seen as the ultimate in bad sportsmanship. In 1997 Blackburn striker Chris Sutton enraged Arsenal players and supporters by refusing to surrender easy possession from a throw-in awarded after Patrick Vieira had put the ball out of play so that his team-mate Stephen Hughes could receive attention for an injury. Arsenal were forced to concede a corner, from which Rovers' Garry Flitcroft scored an equalizing goal that effectively ended Arsenal's championship challenge. In February 2000, Wolves substituted their striker Michael Branch after he scored from a ball that, unknown to him, was supposed to have been given back to opponents Nottingham Forest; beaten goalkeeper Dave Beasant then chased the bewildered Branch up to the halfway line.

In 1999 an FA Cup fifth-round tie between Arsenal and Sheffield United was replayed after Arsenal had won the first game 2–1. The winning goal had provoked an exchange of blows among players and an attempt by United manager Steve Bruce to bring his players off the field. Marc Overmars had scored for Arsenal from a pass by Kanu, who had intercepted Ray Parlour's attempt to return possession to the opposition after goalkeeper Alan Kelly had put the ball out of play so that an injured player could be treated. Amid the post-match furore Arsène **Wenger** offered to replay the entire game. Kanu had been making his debut for Arsenal, who won the return 2–1.

bad signings

Bad signings are nothing new. In 1938 Arsenal caused public outrage by spending a record £14,000 on Welsh inside-forward Bryn Jones, a fee so inflated that questions were asked in the House of Commons. A year of anonymous performances followed ('his limitations are marked,' commented one newspaper), and disappointment was mixed with relief when Jones was spared another season by Hitler's invasion of Poland.

Despite a long history of failed transfers, the mid-1990s were a particular low point for the British game, a side-effect largely of the force-fed TV rights income stream in the top two divisions. Notably poor Premiership signings include Ade Akinbiyi (nickname: 'Puff' – as in 'Puff Ade'), for whom Peter Taylor paid Wolves £5m while he was manager of Leicester City. During seven months without a goal, in which time he acquired the new alias 'panic-buyi', the whole-hearted Akinbiyi became a catch-all byword for overpriced purchases.

Joey Beauchamp moved to West Ham from his hometown club Oxford United for £1m in 1994, but found the 50 mile trip up the M40 such a wrench that he never actually played a game for the Hammers, moving back west after two months' suffering from homesickness. Hammers manager Harry Redknapp's most notorious signing remains 'Mad' Marco Boogers, a Dutch striker signed on the basis of a highlights video sent by his agent. Boogers' brief spell at the club is already a part of Upton Park folklore. Coming on as sub against Manchester United in only his second appearance, Boogers was immediately red-carded for a violent tackle on Gary Neville. The striker promptly disappeared and was discovered several weeks later hiding in a mobile home in a Dutch caravan park.

Before the start of the Premiership bad signings tended to stand out. Manchester United paid Nottingham Forest £1.25m for England centre-forward Garry Birtles, only for Birtles to take almost a year to score his first United goal before being sold back to Forest for a £1m discount. A year earlier Wolves midfielder Steve Daley was signed for £1.43m by Manchester City (see Malcolm **Allison**). After a single season he was offloaded to the Seattle Sounders in the USA, a high-water mark of pre-Premiership bad business.

Recently, expensive foreign signings have tended to stand out. Winston Bogarde's career at Chelsea remains one of the absurdities of the modern game. Bogarde made only two League starts for the Blues over four years, during which time he earned an estimated £7m in wages, handsome reward for training with the youth team all week and going to the cinema on Saturday afternoons. Spanish international Marcelino joined

Newcastle from Mallorca for £5m with a reputation as a no-nonsense defensive hardman. He started just 15 League games in three and a half years and missed almost a whole season with a damaged finger before leaving the club on a free transfer. Italian forward Michele Padovano signed for Crystal Palace from Juventus for £1.7m in November 1997. In a year at the club Padovano scored once in 12 appearances, never played more than two games in a row and eventually left on a free transfer as Palace were relegated. Padovano then returned to Selhurst Park after his departure to claim £1m in unpaid wages from the club's administrators during a financial crisis that almost saw Palace go out of existence.

With English football seemingly in thrall to the expensive expats of Serie A, Frank Clark brought Andrea Silenzi to the City Ground in August 1995. Nicknamed 'The Paintbrush', the beanpole Silenzi spent most of his 15 appearances strolling sulkily around a small area of the pitch. His time at the club ended in acrimony as he refused to return to England after a loan spell at Venezia. By the time his contract was cancelled the languid target man had cost bankruptcy-bound Forest £2.75m. He scored two goals.

Often bad signings are just a consequence of bad chemistry. In an ITV poll Chris Sutton's move to Chelsea from Blackburn Rovers was voted the worst signing in the history of British football. Gianluca Vialli paid £10m for the former Norwich striker, who scored just one League goal during a solitary season at Stamford Bridge. Sold for £6m to Celtic, under Martin O'Neill, Sutton has become one of the finest players of that club's modern era.

the ball

Doggedly ever-present, the founding father of a game that really wouldn't be the same without it, the ball has remained the one constant in all of football's many forms. Early manifestations of the ball ranged from Roman soldiers reputedly enjoying a kickabout with the severed heads of enemy soldiers to the pig's heads and inflated sheep's bladders used in village free-for-alls in the Middle Ages.

Currently the definition of what is and isn't a football is governed by FIFA's Laws of the Game. *Law 2 – The Ball* states that the ball shall be 'spherical', made of 'leather or other suitable material', and between 68 and 70 cm in circumference and 410 and 450 grams in weight. In his 1810 opus *Sports and Pastimes of the People of England*, Joseph Strutt describes an 18th-century football as 'made of a blown bladder and cased in leather', which would remain the model for the first manufactured balls produced in early Victorian England. The ball remained largely in this form – stitched leather with an opening bound by laces around a central core made of animal skin – until the 1950s, when plastic balls with valves were first produced, thereby avoiding the tendency of old-style leather balls to become bloated with water and mud during the course of a game, or for the pig or sheepskin bladder to burst: the FA Cup finals of both 1946 and 1947 were delayed by a burst ball.

After the introduction of floodlights in the 1950s white balls began to replace the standard orangey brown, although the ball over which 1966 World Cup hat-trick hero Geoff **Hurst** fought a tabloid-fuelled custody battle in 1999 was a robust terracotta. Gradually black or coloured panels were incorporated into a predominantly white design, notably in the case of the classic Mexico 1970 Telstar ball, with its black and white hexagons, developed with colour television pictures in mind.

Although FIFA regulations prohibit any kind of advertising on the ball beyond the maker's name and the competition the ball is being used in, manufacturers have used successive World Cups to promote the most significant developments in ball design. The Azteca Ball used at Mexico 86 was the first FIFA-sanctioned ball made entirely of synthetic materials, while the World Cup 2002 Fevernova ball – hailed as the 'roundest' ball ever – contained 'millions of gas-filled micro balloons'. Innovations in the design and manufacture of the ball continue apace, not all of them merely in the cause of merchandising or brand-promotion: in football for the partially sighted, balls containing 150 ball-bearings are used, creating a ball that players can actually hear coming.

The ball has often been used for purposes beyond the merely footballing: it has been kicked away as an expression of disgust – Spurs' Christian Ziege was sent off against Manchester City in December 2002 after twice being yellow-carded for kicking the ball away; used as a weapon – mild-mannered Ray Wilkins became the first England player dismissed in a World Cup match after inexplicably hurling the ball at the referee during England's 0–0 draw with Morocco in Monterey in 1986; sat on as a form of protest or mockery – Alan Ball, Jim **Baxter** and Spurs' Alfie Conn are all rumoured to have done so at some point during a match; or more commonly kept as a souvenir, usually after scoring a hat-trick.

The relationship between player and ball remains an infinitely varied one. South Americans 'love' the ball; English players on the other hand are frequently described as going to great lengths to distance themselves from it (they are often implored to 'get rid of it' by spectators). 'Another feature of England training is "mime practice",' wrote Liverpool full-back Phil Neal in his 1981 book *Attack from the Back*. 'As you jog round you go through all the motions without the ball . . . You trap, pass, volley, head for goal, and weight imaginary passes. All that is missing is the ball.' Football without the ball remains, and always will be, nothing more than men jumping up and down.

Gordon Banks

Many young football fans growing up in the 1960s and early '70s would have picked first Leicester City and later Stoke City as their second-favourite clubs simply because they were Gordon Banks's teams. A towering figure capable of tremendous agility, Banks was the England goalkeeper for over a decade, during which time he was one of the best in the world.

Banks kept 35 clean sheets in 73 matches of which England lost only nine, playing in 23 consecutive matches without defeat from May 1964, including the 1966 World Cup Final. His most famous moment came in the next World Cup, in Mexico four years later, when he stretched low at his post to get fingertips to Pelé's downward header, pushing it over the bar. It was a fantastic piece of athleticism, often cited as one of the best saves ever seen. According to an England team-mate, Pelé was shouting 'Gol!' as Banks reached the ball.

Like Peter **Shilton**, his successor at both Leicester and Stoke, Gordon Banks didn't get a chance to play for one of the bigger League clubs. Unlike Shilton, an English and European champion with Nottingham Forest, Banks won only one medal in his club career, a League Cup with Stoke in 1972. Born in Sheffield into an Anglo-Chinese family, he was working as a bricklayer and playing non-League football when he was spotted by Division 3 Chesterfield, for whom he signed as part-timer, starring in the club's run to the final of the 1956 FA Youth Cup, where they lost 4–3 to Manchester United. After two years away on National Service in Germany, he turned professional then quickly moved on to Leicester, with whom he was twice an FA Cup runner-up in the early 1960s.

The year after the World Cup win, with the 17-year-old Shilton judged to be ready for the first team, Leicester placed a surprised Banks on the transfer list ('I felt', he said later 'that I had given them fantastic service for the poor wages they paid me'). Liverpool and West Ham both showed an interest but Stoke, whose manager Tony Waddington had gained a reputation for reviving careers, bid the highest. They just avoided relegation in Banks's first two seasons, and never finished higher than ninth while he was there, but his form didn't suffer and he was voted Footballer of the Year shortly after the League Cup win.

Banks had played a crucial role in Stoke reaching the final, saving Geoff **Hurst**'s last-minute penalty in a marathon semi-final against West Ham that went to two replays. Two months into the following season, however, his League career ended when he lost the sight in his right eye after a car accident. After six months of playing only in non-competitive matches he retired, making a brief comeback in the glitzy North American Soccer League with Fort Lauderdale ('I felt like a circus act . . . Roll up, roll up, to see the greatest one-eyed goalkeeper in the world') before stopping for good, aged 38, in 1978.

banners

In the 1970s and '80s homemade banners were as much a feature of FA Cup Final Saturday as a special edition of *It's a Knockout* and interviews with celebrity fans who clearly hadn't watched 'their team' since the abolition of National Service. Painted on to a bedsheet using some gloss black paint Dad had left over from doing the coal shed door and held aloft on a couple of broom handles by a pair of lads in tank-tops, they fell broadly into three categories: humorous ('Currie Gives Hoddle The Runs', QPR fans, 1982), celebratory ('Pearson Strikes More Than British Leyland', Man Utd, 1977) and rude about the UK's favourite football pundit ('Up Your Arse 'N' All, Jimmy Hill', Ipswich Town, 1978).

Supporters had carried homemade standards – usually featuring a cardboard cut-out of the club symbol, mounted on a single pole and generally resembling a vernacular version of the sort of thing the Roman legions used to march behind – as far back as the 1920s. There were also isolated cases of banners being used to protest against unpopular boardroom decisions (the signing of Bert Trautmann by Manchester City just after the Second World War saw irate City fans brandishing one that read 'Off With The German'), but it was not until the 1960s that inventive homemade banners became such a feature of the English game.

Arguably the most famous was one held aloft by Leeds supporters at Wembley in 1973: 'Norman Bites Yer Legs'. This sentiment proved so popular that it not only became Norman Hunter's nickname but was also echoed on other banners down the years, notably by Newcastle fans with their 'Broon Ale Bites Yer Legs' effort in 1974.

By the mid-1980s the opportunity for banner displays was receding largely because the police, worried about hooliganism, were reluctant to allow people to take long sticks with them into the ground. The banner still made occasional and telling appearances (the destructive reign of chairman Peter Johnson at Everton gave rise to one at Anfield that read 'Congratulations Agent Johnson – Mission Accomplished'), often, as in the past, to protest, but its heyday had passed. Since health and safety regulations now require that all flags and banners waved at football must have been treated to make them inflammable, it seems unlikely they will return. Unless, of course, Dad has some spare fire retardant spray in the shed.

Barnet

By the start of the 20th century, there were several clubs battling it out in the hilly suburb on London's northernmost tip, and the latter-day Barnet are the product of various mergers in the early part of the century. The original Barnet FC was dissolved in 1901, passing on its Queens Road ground to rivals Barnet Avenue, who promptly renamed themselves Barnet FC and spent the next decade lifting various amateur trophies. They merged in 1912 with nearby Alston Works AFC, alias 'The Dentals', a team from a false-teeth factory who'd already caused a minor stir in the FA Cup, and whose distinctive amber-and-black strip replaced the more traditional (but disconcertingly Rothko-esque) violet and black as the colours of the new team Barnet and Alston – inevitably renamed Barnet FC at the end of the First World War.

After many years in the Athenian League (including their appearance in the first-ever live televised football match, a hotly anticipated scrap with Tooting and Mitcham), Barnet went semi-pro in 1965. Their history since is largely a catalogue of struggle against financial ruin, lightened by the regular signings of great and good players in their dotage (Jimmy **Greaves**, Bob McNab, Mark Lawrenson and Terry Mancini all pulled on the amber and black in later life, though star managers like Ray Clemence and Tony Cottee have enjoyed considerably less success). In the 1990s, during the controversial reign of ticket-tout turned chairman Stan Flashman and the never-popular Barry Fry, the club ascended to the Football League (at the end of the 1990–91 season), while simultaneously plumbing the financial depths, avoiding liquidation and enforced relegation on more than one occasion. More recently, the problem has been the inadequacy of their Underhill ground, a dilapidated structure with a sloping pitch, which charms visitors with its scurvy rootsiness but which, post-**Taylor Report**, threatened to mire Barnet perpetually in the Conference, to which they returned in 2001.

Since Fry and Flashman's departure, the appeal of the ground, the club's perennial minnow status and its ongoing survival battles have made Barnet a second-favourite club for many fans of larger London sides (there are strong links with Arsenal and West Ham in particular). The 'Keep Barnet Alive' campaign, set up during the most recent period of crisis, has attracted goodwill, and more importantly money, from supporters at every level of the game. Under manager Paul Fairclough the club returned to the Football League at the end of 2004–05, winning the Conference title by 22 points.

Barnsley

Until 1997, Barnsley were the only FA Cup-winning team of the professional era never to have played in the top division. Their promotion that year, decided by a 2–0 win over Bradford in the penultimate match – accompanied by the regular supporters' chant of 'It's just like watching Brazil!' – sealed a period of stability for the south Yorkshire club which had been playing at the second level for 16 seasons.

Danny Wilson's team made a poor start to the following season, losing eight of their first ten matches, including a 6–0 home defeat to Chelsea. They rallied, winning away at Liverpool and Aston Villa and beating Manchester United in the FA Cup, but were finally relegated by five points. Barnsley, in common with several other clubs, then began to suffer the financial effects of trying and failing to stay in the Premiership. They were to reach the Division 1 playoff final in 2000 under Dave Bassett, but a large wage bill prompted a slide that took the club to the lower reaches of Division 2 and administration within three years.

Barnsley should have been up before, however. At the end of 1914–15, three seasons after the club's FA Cup victory in a replay against West Bromwich, they had finished third in Division 2. On the resumption of League football four years later, it was decided to expand the top level by bringing in three teams but Barnsley were scandalously overlooked for the final spot, awarded instead to fourth-placed Arsenal. Another third-place finish in 1921–22 led to their missing promotion by one goal.

Formed in 1887 as Barnsley St Peter, and always based at the Oakwell stadium, the club were elected to Division 2 of the Football League 11 years later. A quiet first decade for the Tykes (a nickname taken from a general term for Yorkshiremen) was followed by an eventful flurry: they reached the FA Cup Final for the first time in 1910, losing to Newcastle, were forced to seek re-election the next year after finishing one off the bottom of Division 2, then in the following season took their only major trophy. It was a monumental slog – their six goalless draws on the way to the Final is a record and the replay was still goalless until two minutes from the end, when winger Harry Tufnell scored after a 45-yard run.

Until 1959, Barnsley had spent just five seasons below Division 2 but relegation that year precipitated the worst period in their history: seven years later, they finished in their lowest-ever league position, 16th in Division 4. However, the club has not been back to the bottom division since 1979, when they achieved two promotions in three seasons under former Leeds players Allan Clarke and Norman Hunter.

Asked to name a footballer associated with Barnsley, some might suggest Danny **Blanchflower**, who began his English League career at Oakwell in the early 1950s. More would think of one of his teammates, Sid 'Skinner' Normanton, a formidable wing-half frequently lionized by the club's best-known fan, Michael Parkinson. The first name that would occur to many Barnsley supporters, however, would be Ronnie Glavin. A burly, deceptively skilful midfielder signed by Allan Clarke from Celtic in 1980, Glavin was to average almost a goal in every two games for the club, finishing their top scorer in three of his four seasons. It was appropriate that he should score the goal that got the Tykes back into Division 2 at the end of 1980–81. Despite several changes of manager, and a distinct dip in home crowds as a result of the miners' strike, Barnsley spent the eighties consolidating as a solid second-level club prior to Danny Wilson's arrival in 1993.

Ten years on and strapped for cash, the club experienced two changes of ownership, the first involving former Leeds chairman Peter Ridsdale, who stepped down in 2004. Meanwhile, some disaffected fans formed a breakaway club, AFC Barnsley, now in the Central Midlands League. In 2006 Barnsley beat Swansea in the League One play-off final.

Cliff Bastin

Cliff 'Boy' Bastin was a prodigious young footballer. He scored for Exeter City when he was 16, became at 17 a crucial part of the Arsenal team that would dominate the 1930s, and won every honour in domestic football by the age of 21. Renowned for his cool head as much as his turn of pace and finishing skills, Bastin was Arsenal's regular penalty-taker at the age of 18. His goalscoring record with Arsenal is remarkable – 178 goals in 396 games, including 33 League goals in one season – particularly given that almost all of them were scored from a position on the left wing.

Having lured a reluctant Bastin away from his West Country roots, Arsenal manager Herbert **Chapman** devised a successful innovation whereby his wingers were encouraged to stray from the accepted practice of running pell mell up and down a short stretch of the touchline in the hope of being able to deliver a cross from the corner flag. Chapman urged Bastin and his right-wing counterpart, Joe Hulme, to cut inside and head for goal. In this way Bastin used his eye for space, his acceleration and powerful left foot to set an Arsenal goalscoring record that was only bettered by Ian **Wright** in 1997 and by Thierry **Henry** in 2004–05.

Cliff Bastin's understanding with Hulme and Alex **James** was the cornerstone on which Arsenal's success in the 1930s was based. As if to emphasize this, it was Bastin who scored to complete a 2–2 comeback against Hull City in the semi-final of the 1930 FA Cup, forcing a replay which Arsenal won. Had the semi-final result gone the other way it's conceivable that Chapman's team would have foundered at this crucial stage in its development.

Throughout his career Bastin was troubled by the cartilage in his left knee 'slipping' during a game, leading to physio Tom Whittaker regularly manipulating it back into place at half-time. When it was finally removed, the gristle was so misshapen that it was snapped up by the Royal College of Surgeons as an exhibit with which to frighten young medical students. Bastin's increasing deafness – he confessed he could never fully understand what Glaswegian Alex James was saying – meant that he saw out the Second World War on ARP duty at Highbury. However, his career was effectively ended by the war. He played his last game for the Gunners in 1946.

Jim Baxter

Having never come close to a World Cup final themselves, Scots like to cite a match which, in their eyes, qualified as the next best thing: the 3–2 victory at Wembley in 1967 over an England side that had been crowned world champions nine months before.

The chief orchestrator of that victory was the cultured, left-sided midfielder 'Slim Jim' Baxter, who could not only control games, but also loved to taunt his opponents in a number of ways. On this occasion he stood on the wing of the enemy's sacred turf juggling the ball on his left foot, and reportedly spent much of the game mimicking Alan Ball's high-pitched whiney voice into the diminutive Englishman's ear. It wasn't the first time that Baxter, who played for Scotland 34 times, had helped see off the English in their own stadium. In 1963 he scored both of Scotland's goals in a 2–1 victory there. And he thrived on the big occasion when playing for his main club, Rangers, finishing on the losing side only twice in the 18 games he played against Celtic during two spells at Ibrox.

Rangers signed the elegant 20-year-old ex-miner Baxter from Raith Rovers in 1960 for £17,500, and he won three League titles and a bevy of Cup medals in Scot Symon's formidable side before moving to Sunderland five years later for £72,500. His price tag increased to a round a hundred grand by the time he arrived at Nottingham Forest in 1967, but by this time there was baggage attached to the tag – like many a footballing genius down the years, Baxter liked to drink, but he didn't much like to train, and his play suffered accordingly. 'It'd be just my luck to get George Best's liver,' he quipped in 1994 when entering hospital for one of two transplant operations he underwent that year. Like **Best**, Baxter was a supreme natural talent who squandered his gifts with too much booze, causing him to prematurely end his career at the age of 31 after a second and far less successful spell at Rangers. He then bought himself a pub.

Baxter's second liver operation allowed him to live another seven years before he succumbed to pancreatic cancer in 2001. In between times he was spotted drinking in a Glasgow bar wearing his pyjamas. Once an exhibitionist, always an exhibitionist.

David Beckham

After a decade of relentless tabloid exposure, the words 'David Beckham' tend to conjure up an unwanted mental flip chart. This usually goes something like: goal from the halfway line, floppy hair, Posh Spice, sarong, petulant kick, hanged in effigy, *Hello!* magazine, gay icon, England captain, kids with silly names, free kick, runs around a lot, Mohican, sunglasses, Japan, metatarsal, flying boot, Real Madrid, hanging out in LA, tattoos, steamy text messages, wife very skinny.

During this period there have been at least 50 major books published in Beckham's honour, as well as shoe-horned name-checks across every conceivable cultural outlet. In her book *Burchill on Beckham*, Julie Burchill writes that in 'his incredible dignity and grace . . . his breathtaking boldness and beauty . . . his feet of fire, his incredible journey . . . his relentless beauty . . . we seem to see all that men could be'. More honestly, perhaps, *Attitude* magazine described him as having the 'face of an angel and the bum of a Greek god'. Ludicrously, Beckham was once the subject of 12-week media studies course at the University of Staffordshire. Publicity-seeking Buddhist monks built a shrine to him before the 2002 World Cup. His image has been used to boost sales of soft drinks, sportswear, mobile phones, chocolate bars, children's clothing and almost every newspaper and magazine in Europe. He is the most famous current football player in the world and probably the most famous of all time.

Despite this, Beckham has never been voted European or World Player of the Year, or Player of the Year in England. Off the pitch he may appear a hybrid of gold-chain-draped Essex dandy, tabloid show-off and spendthrift international playboy, but Beckham has never been a flashy footballer. A direct player rather than a crowd-pleaser, he remains a brave, hard-working midfielder with obvious deficiencies – a lack of pace or trickery on the ball – and obvious strengths: mainly an ability to play long passes and crosses very accurately. Wiry and slightly bandy-legged, he has stamina but no great athleticism. The level of his fame (vast) in relation to his abilities (respectable) is a precise barometer of football's progress towards becoming a branch of the entertainment industry. The only really exceptional things about David Beckham are that he is very good-looking and very determined. The world would have been a very different place, and Beckham's career a very different thing, if his name was Nigel Onions and he'd grown up looking like Peter Beardsley.

Beckham was born in Leytonstone in 1975 and grew up in Chingford in Essex. His father was a Manchester United fan, part of a generation of supporters attracted by the success of Matt **Busby**'s team of the 1960s. Beckham's inherited passion for the club would make his career there a visible symbol of United's nationwide appeal, a totem for Essex Reds and migratory southern fans. At the age of 11 Beckham came first in his class in Bobby **Charlton**'s three-day soccer skills school after hearing about the competition on *Blue Peter*. He joined United as a 14-year-old and made his Premiership debut in 1995 after a loan spell at Preston North End.

Over nine seasons he made 397 appearances, scoring 86 goals and winning six Premiership titles, two FA Cups and the Champions' League in 1999. His goal against Wimbledon in August 1996 – a driven shot from the halfway line that caught keeper Neil Sullivan off his line – is usually seen as the point at which Beckham announced his arrival as a Premiership star. Significantly, news footage of his photogenic, floppy-haired celebrations probably made as much impression as the goal itself. No other long-range punt has been so widely celebrated. Nayim, for example, has yet to be invited to Los Angeles to present an MTV Movie Award.

In July 1999 Beckham married Victoria Adams after two years of high-profile courtship. Their wedding, complete with matching lavatorial gold thrones, a flock of white doves and a cake featuring naked effigies of the newlyweds, was a riveting collision of newly naff Premiership millionaire and enduring pop star tackiness. The Beckhams have been observed in minute public detail ever since. Occasionally, while Beckham is cosying up to P Diddy, touring Japan or signing autographs in Woolworth's to aid his wife's musical ambitions, it has been tempting to ask: why exactly is he doing this? The answer being: for the cash and the fame of course. Constantly mindful of his pocket money-swallowing behemoth of a brand, Beckham was the 34th best-paid person in the country in 2003.

His international career has been varied but always hysterically high profile. A goal from a free kick against Colombia in England's final World Cup group game at France '98 seemed to promise much. However, Beckham was sent off in the team's next game after kicking out at Argentina's Diego Simeone, having just been fouled by the same player. The score remained at 2–2, England lost on penalties and Beckham received a disproportionate level of personal abuse in the English tabloid press. He improved dramatically as a player over the next three years, showcased by his excellent performance in a below-par Manchester United team in their victorious Champions' League Final of 1999.

Made captain of the national team by Peter Taylor during his one-match spell in charge for the friendly against Italy in November 2000, Beckham was retained by Sven-Göran **Eriksson** and entered the most influential phase of his international career. After the stunning 5–1 victory over Germany in Munich, Eriksson's team needed a point against Greece at Old Trafford to qualify for the finals. Twice behind in a scrappy game, England were dragged back into the game by Beckham's manic promptings from the right wing. A free kick created the first equalizer, and in injury time a spectacular goal direct from a free kick provided the decisive moment.

For a while this hyperactivity became something of a signature. In recent times, however, a different kind of David Beckham has emerged. Clearly unfit at both the 2002 World Cup and the 2004 European Championships, Beckham was a disappointment at both tournaments, at times flapping about the pitch in a self-important elbows-out parody of his perpetual motion against Greece in 2001. He seemed physically diminished and, at 29, prematurely aged as an athlete. Beckham moved to Real Madrid from Manchester United in the summer of 2003. To his credit, during the first six months of his time at the Bernabéu he performed to a level that suggested his move had been motivated by something other than a desire to sell shirts in the Far East.

Subsequently, however, he experienced the first genuine crisis of his career. Madrid finished fourth in the Primera Liga, and three seasons later Beckham has yet to win a trophy there. Worse, his adulterous affair with a personal assistant has been exposed in full and unflattering detail in the tabloid press. Always struggling to meet his considerable reputation, Beckham has become a slightly tarnished figure both on and off the field. Whether through overkill, unrealistic expectations or, simply, the built-in obsolescence of any pop celebrity, even now he has much to prove, if only as a footballer.

Berwick Rangers

The identity of Berwick Rangers revolves around a single fact – that they are the only English club to play in the Scottish League – and a single result: their 1–0 victory over Glasgow Rangers in the first round of the 1966–67 Scottish Cup. 'We have no complaints, we beat ourselves,' said Rangers' captain, John Greig, after the shock result, the game won by a single goal from Sammy Reid. Reid left 'The Borderers' for Dumbarton and quit football the following year, but Berwick's manager, Jock Wallace, who had put his team through a stringent three-week fitness regime, later went on to successfully manage the Glasgow giants. In the next round Berwick lost 1–0 to Hibs.

Once Scotland's richest port, Berwick changed hands between Scotland and England 13 times before the English took it for good in 1482. The football team, however, has mostly stayed true to Division 2 since gaining League membership in 1951. After a few years in the old Division C, its League career proper took off in 1955. Twenty-four years later in 1979, winning the Division 2 title under the fondly remembered player-manager Davie Smith lifted them to the giddy heights of Division 1 for just two seasons. A two-year visit to Division 3 ended with promotion in 2000, they dropped back to the bottom division five years later and were promoted again in 2006.

Prior to turning senior the club was more peripatetic, and after its 1881 founding switched between various English and Scottish leagues while playing at a number of different home venues, including the threateningly named Bull Stob Close. A healthy Scottish Cup run in 1954, culminating in a 4–0 quarter-final defeat in front of 60,000 at Ibrox, helped finance the move to their present home at Shielfield Park. This was topped off with the purchase of a stand from Bradford City's Valley Parade that was dismantled, transported north, and then rebuilt.

In the cash-strapped 1980s it was a familiar story as the struggling club was forced to sell the ground to the local council and lease it back. At one point the directors sold the lease to a grey-hound promoter, who then threw the club out and forced them into various groundshares. They returned when fans, sponsors and the club's bank bought the lease back, and in 2003 the side was bought by a local consortium.

This was not the first threat to the club's existence. In the mid-1960s Glasgow Rangers had proposed reducing the Scottish league to 32 clubs, and Berwick was one of five teams on its hit list. The teams took legal action and the idea was eventually dropped, so that famous 1967 Cup win was made all the sweeter for its sense of revenge. In 2002 the sides met again in the Cup at Shielfield Park, but this time the score was 0–0 and Rangers took the replay.

George Best

An early photograph shows that at 13 months old George Best could dribble a ball in a way that many adult footballers would envy. Matt **Busby** described him in his prime as gifted with more indi-vidual ability than any other player he had seen, unique for the range of his talents. His strength and courage belied his deceptively skinny frame, every aspect of ball control came naturally to him. He used both feet, was an accom-plished header of the ball and could beat other players by a variety of means.

Above all, he was supremely confident in his own powers. An elegant and graceful winger, with a limber dribbling style, he was also a prolific marksman who, in 1970, memorably scored six of United's eight goals in an FA Cup tie against Northampton Town. Many consider him the best British player ever. However, despite playing 466 games for Manchester United during one of the club's most successful periods, he is generally thought to have underachieved and squandered his prodigious talent, his later years blighted by alcoholism.

Born in May 1946, Best grew up on Belfast's Cregagh estate, playing football for the local boys' club. Scout Bob Bishop recommended him to Manchester United when he was 15, five feet tall and eight stone in weight. Homesick, he took the boat home next day. Two weeks later he was back at Old Trafford. He made his first team debut aged 17 in September 1963 and began his inter-national career with Northern Ireland in 1964. In Best's first full season, United became League champions.

Overcoming his painful shyness, Best began to enjoy the pleasures of Manchester's nightlife, usually partnered by City player Mike Summerbee. He was formally disciplined for the first time at the start of the 1965–66 season by Matt Busby, who claimed late nights had adversely affected the 19-year-old's performance, but his transgressions were minor. In March 1966, when Best impul-sively donned an unfeasibly large som-brero as he disembarked from a flight back from a scintillating performance against Benfica in the European Cup, he entered a new phase of celebrity. The Portuguese press christened him 'El

Beatle', and Best and his *outré* headgear made the front pages. His dark good looks and fashionable clothes led to many offers of promotional work: his first big TV advert was for Cookstown sausages.

Best helped United to another League title in 1967, and in 1967–68 he dethroned Denis **Law** as the club's leading scorer. When United won the European Cup in 1968, he rounded the Benfica goalkeeper in extra time to score United's bravura second goal. Best added European Footballer of the Year to his trophies. But his once modest alcohol consumption had escalated. He began to buckle under the pressures of intrusive, constant media and public attention and the strain of playing in a team which was in decline. He missed training, disappeared before games, on one such occasion besieged by the press for four days in actress Sinéad Cusack's London flat. After tormenting various Busby replacements who needed his genius but could not solve his problems, he eventually left United in 1974, turning out for clubs as diverse as Dunstable Town and Cork Celtic. Following a brief purple patch at Fulham in 1976 and spells in the USA, he became an after-dinner speaker and pundit. His unsuccessful battles with addiction provided regular tabloid fare, while dismaying his admirers, who preferred to remember him as the 'dark ghost' drifting effortlessly past defenders. Best died in hospital in November 2005.

Birmingham City

Birmingham City Football Club was formed in 1875 as Small Heath Alliance, a winter occupation for the members of the Holy Trinity Cricket Club. The club's first fixture was against Holte Wanderers from Aston, the district that was to produce the club's city rivals, Aston Villa.

Small Heath moved to current ground St Andrews in 1906 and rechristened themselves as Birmingham City FC, entering the Football League two years later. Without ever threatening to challenge for the title, the club has remained in the top two divisions for all but four seasons of its League existence. The majority of these have been spent in a regular exchange of promotions and relegations, with the odd false dawn of a mid-table finish in the top division.

Apart from a League Cup success against Villa in 1963, Birmingham have never won a major trophy. They have twice been runners-up in the FA Cup: in 1931 (when they lost to local rivals West Brom); and in 1956, the club's best-ever season, during which they also finished sixth in Division 1. Rivalry with Aston Villa has been intensified by their neighbours' relative success, lending the Blues fans a reputation for being characteristically long-suffering in their loyalty. In fact, the club has generally ploughed a furrow of even-keeled mediocrity. Birmingham have probably the least successful record of any big city club in English football.

The late 1950s and early '60s proved the most notable period for the club to date, starting with promotion to the top flight under Arthur Turner in 1955. The League Cup win in 1963 was preceded by successive appearances in the Fairs Cup in 1960 and 1961. Birmingham were the first professional English club to take part in the competition, losing in the final on both occasions, the first a 4–1 aggregate defeat by Barcelona, the second to AS Roma.

In keeping with a history of mediocre achievement, Birmingham have produced few great players. Those that have emerged remain deeply revered by the club's supporters. During the 1920s and '30s Joe Bradford scored a record 267 goals in 445 appearances for the club. In 1970 Trevor Francis made his debut as a 15-year-old and went on to become Birmingham's best-ever player during nine years at St Andrews. Francis was sold to Nottingham Forest in 1979 for £999,999, scored the winning goal in the European Cup Final that year and went on to play for England 52 times. He also had the honour of being name-checked in the 1981 theme tune to *Only Fools and Horses*, with the line 'at a push some Trevor Francis track suits from a mush in Shepherd's Bush'.

After a difficult period in the late 1980s and early '90s, which saw the club sink deep into debt and spend three seasons in the old Division 3, Birmingham were bought by adult-publishing magnate David Sullivan and the Gold brothers, David and Ralph. Despite immediate . relegation, the club was on the rise, with money made available to buy new players and redevelop the ground. In 1995 Barry Fry took Birmingham back into Division 1 as champions and captured the Auto Windscreens Shield (see **LDV Vans Trophy**). At the same time St Andrews was being massively redeveloped to make it an all-seater ground for the first time.

The club was promoted to the Premier League under Steve Bruce and had enjoyed three seasons of relative stability before being relegated in 2006. Never quite a sleeping giant, more of a dozing middleweight, the club's greatest attribute is the strength of its support relative to achievements on the pitch. This has long been the case. It was the 80,000 turnout to a midweek Cup replay against Derby at Maine Road that prompted the government to ban week-night matches in order to aid the rebuilding of the country after the Second World War.

black footballers

In February 1972 *The Football League Review* contained a report on the efforts being made at Bradford City to encourage young players from the local Pakistani and West Indian communities to join the club at youth level. 'One particular player has made a deep impression so far. He is Joe Cooke, the 16-year-old West Indian centre-half who is one of three West Indians on the playing staff. Says manager Bryan Edwards: "Like the other coloured lads he looks deceptively casual. He has the same sort of style as the Brazilians, easy moving and so lithe and supple. He looks casual but he's so tremendously quick. He's going to do really well."'

Cooke did do well, playing 307 League and Cup matches for City and scoring 79 goals, and later going on to captain Oxford United. And, despite the old-fashioned language and stereotyped description, the *Review*'s article tells one of the happier stories from a time when there was a great deal of prejudice against non-white players.

Currently English football boasts one of the most racially integrated professional leagues in the world. In fact football, so often chastised for the behaviour of its players and supporters, is ahead of many other British institutions in this respect. In 2002 the Premiership champions Arsenal regularly fielded up to eight black or mixed-race first-team players, while the England team eliminated from the 2002 World Cup by Brazil in Shizuoka featured seven non-white outfield players: Ashley Cole, Sol Campbell, Rio Ferdinand, Trevor Sinclair, Emile Heskey, Darius Vassell and Kieron Dyer. Administrative positions within the game's ruling bodies do not yet follow a similar pattern of integration, although there is reason to suspect that in time they will. However, the current integration of black players has not been achieved without their first suffering a great deal of segregation, ignorance and abuse, particularly during the 1970s and '80s, when the first generation of players with West Indian immigrant parents to make a significant impact on the English League began to emerge.

The first black amateur in British football was Andrew Watson, about whom very little is known other than that he was an outfield player who also played for Scotland in the 1870s. A few years later Arthur Wharton became the first black professional footballer in Britain. Wharton was a Ghanaian who moved to Durham to complete his education in the 1880s, during which time he also played in goal for Darlington, Sheffield United and then Rotherham. Wharton was notable for his unusual athleticism and habit of exchanging banter with the crowd during a game. He was also briefly the fastest man on the planet after winning an AAA 100-yard dash, and was at one point talked about as a possible England international. Well known as a carouser, Wharton retired in 1902 and died in 1930, a penniless syphilitic.

In 1909 Spurs' Walter Tull became the first black outfield player in Division 1, and was also later the first black combat officer in the First World War. During the inter-war years Eddie Parris became the first black international for Wales, while Jack Leslie, a London-born Anglo-African, played for Plymouth Argyle in the 1920s and '30s, and was the first black footballer to enjoy genuine longevity in the British game, scoring more than 400 goals for Plymouth between 1921 and 1935.

Jamaican-born Lloyd 'Lindy' Delapenha played for Middlesbrough between 1950 and 1957. A great crowd favourite at Ayresome Park, he scored 90 goals in 260 appearances, having previously played for Portsmouth during their winning 1948–49 League championship campaign. Another black player, Charlie Williams, made 158 appearances for Doncaster Rovers between 1948 and 1958. Barnsley-born Williams achieved greater fame during the early 1970s as a television entertainer, starring in *The Comedians* and *The Golden Shot.*

Giles Heron – father of jazz poet Gil Scott-Heron – played briefly for Celtic in the 1950–51 season, making just a handful of first-team appearances despite his popularity with the club's support. Heron was criticized by some for being unable to transfer his fighting qualities (he had previously been a boxer) to the football field, being described in the local press as 'lacking resource when challenged'.

Perhaps the most famous black player in England during the 1960s was Albert Johanneson, a South African signed by Leeds United in 1961 who, four years later, became the first black player to play in an FA Cup Final. Johanneson was often subjected to racial abuse, both from spectators and from opposing players, and he retired early from the game in 1970. In the late 1980s, shortly before his death, Johanneson was unearthed by the tabloid press living in poverty in Leeds, his years as a great local player forgotten or ignored. Clyde Best, a powerful Bermuda-born centre-forward, made his debut for West Ham in 1969. At a time of increasing television coverage, Best's appearances in a West Ham side that included Geoff **Hurst** and Bobby **Moore**, and his ability to withstand the abuse he received, proved an inspiration to a generation of aspiring young black footballers. In 1970 the racially diverse Brazil national team won a thrilling World Cup in Mexico, the first to receive blanket TV coverage. Players such as Pelé and Jairzinho, who scored in every game, would also become role models for a generation of young black men in the UK.

During the 1977–78 season, Ron Atkinson's West Bromwich Albion became the first club to field three black players. Cyrille Regis, Laurie Cunningham and Brendan Batson, a centre-forward, a winger and a full-back, paved the way for a slow but steady stream of local black players to emerge in the Midlands. More than 25 years later Atkinson was forced to resign from his position as a pundit for ITV and as a columnist for the *Guardian* after making a racist comment about Chelsea defender Marcel Desailly while commentating on a Champions' League game on live television. Batson, as chairman of the PFA, was among those to condemn Atkinson outright for revealing, through his comments, a residue of old-fashioned prejudice that still hinders the game at some levels. His stupidity aside, the players Atkinson helped to bring through contributed far more to the game than a roundly condemned moment of ignorance could ever undo. As Wimbledon player Robbie Earle said: 'without the inspiration provided by the likes of these players, I might never have considered football as a career'.

Around this time Viv Anderson emerged at Nottingham Forest, a skilful attacking full-back who, aged 22, became officially the first black player to represent England, making his debut in November 1978 against Czechoslovakia. (Leeds full-back Paul Reaney, who played internationally in the early 1970s, preferred not to publicly acknowledge his mixed-race background.)

Despite this, emerging black players endured horrific racial abuse during a period when National Front literature was regularly being distributed outside football grounds. When Regis was first selected for the full England squad he was sent a bullet through the post, accompanied by the words, 'You'll get one of these through your knees if you step on our Wembley turf.' Regis played for England five times in five years.

In 1987 John Barnes became Liverpool's first black signing (locally born Howard Gayle had been their first black player in the early 1980s). In his book *Fever Pitch* Nick Hornby describes witnessing Barnes being racially abused by a group of his own supporters on his first appearance for his new club at Highbury. 'We could see quite clearly, as the teams warmed up before kick-off, that banana after banana was being hurled from the away supporters' enclosure.' Barnes went on to become one of the finest players in the club's history and perhaps the most successful black player in the history of the English game, capped 79 times by his country and the 'double' footballer of the year (as voted for by fellow professionals and football writers) in 1988.

By the 1990s most of the traditional barriers to black players in domestic football had been overcome, and black fans were beginning to become less of a rarity, although still hugely underrepresented at grounds. In Scotland players such as Mark Walters at Rangers and Paul Elliott at Celtic were still being racially abused on the field by both fans and players, in part a reflection of the relatively unintegrated and racially monochrome society in Scotland at the time. Scotland and Northern Ireland have fielded a small selection of non-white players in recent years, including Jeff Whitley and Nigel Quashie, the first Scottish international with Afro-Caribbean roots in the modern era, while a generation of black Welshmen have represented their country in recent years, among them Nathan Blake, Robert Earnshaw and Daniel Gabbidon.

In stark contrast, the sizable Asian communities that have become established in many English cities are still massively underrepresented within professional football. Basic racial prejudice has undoubtedly played a part in this but, to a certain extent, social stereotypes are also to blame – notably the ideas that Asians aren't strong enough to play football, that they prefer cricket and hockey to football, and that they are more likely to seek careers as doctors and lawyers. There have been a small number of Asian players in British football over the years – notably Ricky Heppolette at Preston and Leyton Orient in the 1960s and '70s – but their lack of prominence means there are few role models for Asian youngsters who are otherwise just as likely to be fans of the sport as their black or white schoolmates.

In recent years, a few Asian players have broken through – Newcastle United's Michael Chopra has played in the Premiership and represented England at youth level, and Fulham's centre-half Zesh Rehman has made regular appearances in the first team. However, until an Asian player becomes a real star at the top level, it seems likely that promising teenage players from the various Asian communities will continue to be overlooked by the deeply conservative traditionalists who run many English football clubs.

Perhaps it is in the England squad that the ethnically diverse nature of domestic football finds its best representation. Players such as Rio Ferdinand, Ashley Cole and even Essex man David **Beckham** reflect the dominantly urban black cultural influence on the younger footballing generation, which expresses itself in dress, speech, musical tastes and enmities that tend to define themselves along club, rather than racial, lines.

Blackburn Rovers

Founded in 1875 as Blackburn Grammar School Old Boys, Blackburn Rovers have enjoyed two distinct periods of success: the pre-First World War era, when the club won the League title twice; and the 1990s, when, infused with the financial impetus of chairman Jack Walker's steel industry fortune, they won promotion from Division 1 and the Premiership title in the space of three years.

A wealthy manufacturing and mining town during the late Victorian period, Blackburn's football club was formed and initially run by members of the town's newly cotton-rich middle classes. The club's first ground was located at Oozehead, on a pitch that featured a watering hole for cows near the centre circle, a difficulty the club overcame by placing timber boards and turf over the hole while a match was being played. Rovers teams were based around a strong Scottish influence, notably after signing influential Rangers captain Hughie McIntyre. The Scottish influence would surface again almost a hundred years later as a Blackburn team managed by Kenny **Dalglish** and captained by Colin Hendry brought the League title back to Ewood Park; and a decade later still manager Graeme Souness would reinforce the Glasgow connection by signing another Rangers and Scotland captain in Barry Ferguson.

Blackburn won the FA Cup three times in a row between 1884 and 1886, and won again in 1890 (the year they moved to current ground Ewood Park) and 1891, the season that the club were involved in one of the strangest games in Football League history. Facing Burnley on a freezing December afternoon, all of

Rovers' outfield players left the pitch in protest after a series of fights between the two teams, leaving only goalkeeper Herby Arthur to face the 11 men of Burnley. Arthur managed to keep Burnley at bay by appealing successfully for offside, and then simply holding on to the ball for so long that the referee abandoned the game. The club later apologized for the boycott, claiming in its defence that its players were simply too cold to carry on, and rewarded Arthur with a benefit game.

After their early successes, including winning the Division 1 championship in 1912 and 1914 with a team captained by the legendary full-back Bob Crompton, Rovers' fortunes gradually declined, mirroring the town's economic erosion as the factories and collieries closed down before the Second World War. Still one of the best-supported teams in the country, Rovers were famed for their band of travelling fans, who followed the team to the accompaniment of brass bands, fireworks and a festive atmosphere on the terraces. However, a first-ever relegation to Division 2 in 1936 set the pattern for 35 years of a steadily yo-yoing existence between the top two divisions, leavened only by the emergence of the impressive team of the 1950s that featured long-serving England international Ronnie Clayton in central midfield and fellow internationals in winger Bryan Douglas and full-back Bill Eckersley.

The bleakest period in the club's history came with four consecutive seasons in Division 3 in the early 1970s. Finally, after 26 years away and the agony of three successive play-off defeats, the club returned to the top flight under Kenny Dalglish in 1992. Director and majority shareholder Jack Walker had by this stage begun to channel huge amounts of his private fortune into buying players – including breaking the British transfer record twice by spending £3.6m on Alan **Shearer** in 1992 and £5m on Chris Sutton in 1994 – and also into the club infrastructure, ground refurbishment and training facilities. One of only four teams ever to have won the Premiership, Blackburn are part of a small band of clubs to have emerged stronger and more stable from the galloping inflation of the 1990s.

Blackpool

Everybody knows one thing about Blackpool Football Club: they won the '**Matthews** Cup Final' in 1953 coming back from 3–1 down to beat Bolton 4–3 with a winner in the final moments. (Although the match belonged as much to striker Stan Mortensen, who became the first player ever to score a hat-trick in a final at Wembley.) That was part of Blackpool's most successful period: the club were Cup runners-up in 1948 and 1951 and in 1956 had their highest-ever League finish, second in the old Division 1 behind Manchester Utd. Life for Blackpool fans since then has been a story of slow but steady decline rather like the town itself. The Atomic Boys – Blackpool's fan club in the 1950s – have gone the same way as Kiss-Me-Quick hats and donkey rides on the sands.

If people know a second thing about Blackpool it is that they play in 'tangerine', the only League club to choose this colour. It is said the idea came from a director seeing Holland play in the 1920s. Until then Blackpool had played in a variety of mostly blue outfits since their founding in 1887. The club originally joined Division 2 in 1896, dropped out in 1899 but were re-elected in 1900 having amalgamated with South Shore and moved to their ground at Bloomfield Road. They have been a

League club ever since, and still play at the same ground.

The only League title was in 1930, when they were champions of Division 2, gaining promotion to the top flight for the first time. Since 1953 they have had to be content with success in minor cup competitions, winning the Anglo-Italian Cup in 1971 and the LDV Vans Trophy twice in the last four years.

Blackpool had two players in the England World Cup squad of 1966, Alan Ball and Jimmy Armfield, but the following year they dropped out of Division 1. In that season, 1966–67, the club set a record which still stands for the worst home season in the top flight, one win and five draws. That was the end of Division 1 life, apart from one disastrous season in 1970–71. Three years later they nearly made it back, and the next year Mickey Walsh won the Goal of the Season for his strike against Sunderland, but in 1978 the club slipped down another division, to the third, and have never risen above that level since.

Alan Ball returned as player-manager in the early 1980s, only to take Blackpool down to the bottom division, and a couple of years later came the final indignity of having to apply for re-election for the first time since 1899. Since then things have improved slightly. The club have bounced up and down between the two lower divisions, with three promotions and two more relegations. The closest Blackpool have come to higher things was defeat in the Division 2 play-off semi-finals in 1996 (losing 3–0 at home to Bradford having won 2–0 in the away leg), though recent managers have done well: three of the last four, Sam Allardyce, Gary Megson and Nigel Worthington, subsequently worked in the Premiership.

In 2002, after 20 years of promises, the old ground was finally demolished, and a new stadium began to rise in its place. Only two sides have been built so far (which leaves visiting supporters exposed to the elements in their temporary stand) but hopefully it is a mark of better things to come. Blackpool's sense of history is demonstrated by the fact that the main stand is named after their most famous player, and their current poverty by the fact that its full name is the Pricebusters Stanley Matthews Stand.

Danny Blanchflower

Arguably the key figure in Bill **Nicholson**'s Double-winning Spurs side, and captain of the Northern Ireland side of the 1950s, Danny Blanchflower was a sublimely elegant midfielder whose playing achievements ensured his legacy as one of the great footballers of the era. It was also his maverick attitude and his reputation as a visionary willing to challenge officialdom and authority that made Blanchflower stand out from his peers

His career as a player straddled the abolition of the maximum wage, yet real success came late. Born in Belfast in 1926, he began at Glentoran before switching to Barnsley and then Aston Villa. He signed for Spurs in 1954, but had to wait for the appointment of Nicholson as manager four years later before his talents found their reward, culminating in the Double year of 1961. He was an ever-present, marshalling the talents of a gifted side with an unerring ability to read and influence the game.

The relationship between Nicholson and Blanchflower was not an easy one – the manager was often exasperated by his skipper's contrariness – but they complemented each other perfectly. Prior to winning the European Cup Winners' Cup in 1963, Nicholson concentrated on the strengths of the opposition. Blanchflower countered by highlighting the qualities of his team-mates: Spurs promptly won 5–1.

Crucially, manager and captain shared an almost identical philosophy as to how football should be played. Blanchflower's belief that 'the game is about glory' cemented his image as a romantic, but he was also a pragmatist. In vain he expressed an interest in becoming Nicholson's successor as manager at White Hart Lane, remarking on the need to 'play the game within the game'.

Blanchflower also skippered Tottenham to another FA Cup victory in 1962, after leading Northern Ireland against the odds to the World Cup finals in 1958. Age and injury caught up with him by 1964 and he retired after over 600 appearances for clubs and country. Confounding predictions that he would immediately go into management, he became an eloquent sports journalist, working full-time in a profession he had dabbled in for years.

Typically forward-looking and provocative as a writer (he was a firm advocate of a United Kingdom team), Blanchflower famously became the first 'victim' to refuse to appear on the TV programme *This is Your Life*. The lure of management proved too strong, however, and after Tottenham's directors ignored his candidacy, Blanchflower took charge first with the Northern Ireland national side and then concurrently at Chelsea.

Out of step with the cynicism of the time, he was to prove successful in neither post, and returned to journalism until ill-health forced his retirement. Financial hardship was alleviated by a testimonial at Spurs in 1990, but he succumbed three years later to Alzheimer's – a cruel irony for a man much loved for his perceptive nature and keen wit. As Hunter Davies wrote, Danny

Blanchflower was 'an original piece of artwork'.

Steve Bloomer

Steve Bloomer was the first real star of professional football. A prolific striker with Derby and Middlesbrough for over 20 years up to 1914, he set records that still stand; long before the end of his remarkable career he was often referred to in headlines simply as 'Steve'.

Born in the West Midlands in 1874, Bloomer moved to Derby as a child and played for local junior clubs before singing for County at the age of 18. A gaunt figure, slightly built with cropped hair and a deceptively lazy style, Bloomer made an immediate impact, scoring two goals on his League debut at Stoke, ending up with 11 from 28 games. There are numerous photographs of Bloomer, in most of which he is staring intently from the middle of a team group – he was known variously as 'Stoneface' and 'Paleface' – but no film of him in action exists and he only recorded one radio interview, now lost, a year before his death in 1938. However, the impact he made on the early years of League football can be seen in a string of amazing statistics.

Bloomer is the earliest player for any League club whose club goalscoring record (292 for Derby) still stands, and one of only two from the 19th century. He was to be Derby's top scorer in 15 consecutive seasons, getting 18 hat-tricks and is still the only Derby player to have scored six in a League match, which he did against Sheffield Wednesday in 1899. His League career total of 352 goals – he was also top scorer at Middlesbrough in two of his four seasons there – has since been bettered by only three players. His 28 goals in 23 matches in the Home International Championships was a record for

50 years. He scored in his first ten matches for England, getting 19 in total and was on the losing side only twice.

Bloomer's achievements are made more remarkable by the fact that he didn't play for successful teams. The only winner's medal in his entire career was a Division 2 championship with Derby in 1911–12. He missed the club's 1903 FA Cup Final appearance through injury and had been on the beaten side in two earlier finals in 1898 and 1899.

After retiring, Bloomer took up a coaching job in Germany just before the First World War and was subsequently interned for four years. Later a coach in Spain he returned to Derby as a member of the backroom staff. Known for his sudden shooting from distance, a story told in Peter Seddon's biography of Bloomer shows that was still able to demonstrate his technique when in his 50s. Derby player Harry Storer recounted how he was talking to Bloomer by the side of the pitch when a stray ball from a player's shooting practice hurtled towards them. Rather than ducking, 'Bloomer turned quickly, sighted the dropping ball and, perfectly balanced, volleyed it into the net. We were left speechless. He was about forty yards from goal.'

Bloomer is commemorated in Derby by a memorial erected in the city centre in 1996 dedicated to 'The First King of English Football Goalscorers'.

Bolton Wanderers

Bolton Wanderers owe their life to Henry VIII – or at least to the strand of Christianity the fat king founded. An offshoot of local Anglicanism, the club emerged in 1874 as a recreational sideline of Christ Church Sunday School. Three years later, following a tiff with the parish vicar, they split from their godly roots, occupying various temporary bases around Bolton and – by this 'wandering' – inspiring their current name. Founder members of the Football League in 1888, the Trotters drew support from the industrial workers of Bolton and nearby towns like Leigh and Atherton.

Though never glamorous, Wanderers can claim to have been consistently, if gently, pioneering. From scouting trips to sign Welsh and Scottish players as early as the 1880s, to a latter-day embracing of holistic coaching techniques, steady pragmatism has governed their dealings – infrequently interrupted by crises and glory.

After a spell yo-yoing between divisions 1 and 2 (and the startling achievement of missing all 11 penalties awarded to them in the 1899–1900 season), the team's most sustained burst of high-flying came after the First World War. Under the indefatigable Charles Foweraker, whose tenure as manager eventually lasted 25 years, Wanderers enjoyed three FA Cup victories during the 1920s, driven by the formidable left-sided partnership of Joe Smith and Ted Vizard.

They also became the first club to receive £10,000 for a player, with the 1928 sale of David Jack to Arsenal: the fee would have been higher if Gunners manager Herbert **Chapman** hadn't succeeded in getting Bolton's negotiating officials drunk whilst himself remaining cunningly sober. Come the Second World War, Wanderers' squad enlisted en masse. Schoolboy Nat **Lofthouse** broke into the team and began the greatest virtuoso career in the club's history. Over 21 years, Lofthouse scored 285 goals for the Whites and featured in two FA Cup finals. Neither trip to Wembley proved entirely satisfying, though: in 1953, Stanley **Matthews**'s Blackpool staged a famous comeback to humble Bolton; five years later Wanderers triumphed but, in beating a Manchester United freshly devastated by the Munich crash, garnered little glory from their win.

Bolton's own disaster had occurred in 1946 when overcrowding during a Cup game against Stoke City killed 33 fans and injured hundreds more (see **Burnden Park disaster**). Ignominiously, the site of the tragedy was later sold. Although the late 1970s had seen a vigorous Wanderers squad – solidly managed by Ian Greaves and boasting the iconic Frank Worthington in its ranks – briefly flourish in the top flight, the subsequent decade found them slumping to Division 4. Close to ruin, Bolton allowed one side of Burnden Park to be redeveloped as a supermarket. Neither away fans nor the grocery shoppers loading their cars beneath the floodlights could subsequently take the club seriously.

Dignity was restored in 1997 with relocation to the impressive (if not impressively named) Reebok Stadium – a move that both signified and aided the club's resurrection. Promoted to the Premiership in 1995, Wanderers squeezed two further promotions, two relegations and two play-off near-misses into a six-season spell, before achieving relative stability under the charismatic management of Sam Allardyce. The club's contemporary reputation – encompassing wily budgeting and the wholehearted embrace of sports science – has diluted if not entirely displaced its former image of Lancastrian dourness. Today Wanderers are poised somewhere between mill town and Milan.

booking

A booking is the popular name for the action of the referee in cautioning a player who has committed one of seven offences and is so called because the referee writes the player's name and number down in his notebook.

The most common bookable offence is being 'guilty of unsporting behaviour', the category long known as 'ungentlemanly conduct' but renamed as the game became more noticeably one for both sexes to play. This covers any act of foul play deemed worthy of a caution in itself, as well as taking a free kick too quickly or anything else not covered elsewhere.

The other categories are: 'dissent by word or action'; persistently infringing the laws of the game – often signalled by a referee pointing to the sites of various offences; delaying the restart of play; failing to respect the required distance when play is restarted; entering or re-entering the field of play without the referee's permission; deliberately leaving the field of play without the referee's permission.

'A booking' has become synonymous with 'a yellow card', after the item whose use was proposed by the English former referee Ken Aston, after the confusion that surrounded the awarding of cautions in England's World Cup quarter-final against Argentina in 1966. Neither Bobby nor Jack **Charlton** was aware that they had been booked until they read the papers the next day. They rang the FIFA office – where Aston was working – to check. Aston had the idea while driving – yellow is effectively the amber traffic light. The cards were initially used in the 1968 Olympics, before being gradually introduced into other levels of the game.

The consequences of being booked can vary greatly. A booking is called a caution because you are being warned as to your future conduct: pick up two in the same game and you are supposed to be sent off. In August 2004, though, referee Andy D'Urso booked Blackburn's Barry Ferguson for the second time in a match at Southampton, but failed to send him off. Ferguson was later suspended for one game; D'Urso for a month.

In amateur football, where the rules are less rigorously enforced, bookings are rarer but can often result in the levying of a fine by the league or local association. In the professional game, suspensions are imposed for picking up a set number of bookings that varies according to the competition. In domestic football, the rate at which the number was reached can also determine the length or imposition of a suspension.

Famous bookings include the one that Holland captain Johan Cruyff talked himself into with his constant complaints to referee Jack Taylor in the 1974 World Cup Final; Paul **Gascoigne**'s in the 1990 World Cup semi-final, which prompted his tears as he realized he would be suspended if England reached the final; David **Beckham**'s, deliberately incurred against Wales in a 2004 World Cup qualifier; that imposed on Vinnie Jones after three seconds of a match; Bobby **Charlton**'s against Argentina, which was the only one he received; and all the ones Gary **Lineker** never received in his unblemished career.

Once players have retired and are looking for new careers, bookings, usually as after-dinner speakers or TV pundits but occasionally as minicab drivers, become highly sought-after.

boots

Until very recently the 150-year evolution of the football boot followed a surprisingly steady course. The original 1863 FA guidelines on appropriate playing attire stated that 'no one wearing projecting nails, iron plates or gutta percha [a tough type of rubber from

Malaysia] on the soles of his boots is allowed to play', and in the early years of organized football players would turn out in any kind of leather boots they could lay their hands on. By contrast, David **Beckham** is currently sporting his sixth custom-made pair in five years. Beckham's Predator Mania TRX kangaroo-skin boots feature 'modular outsole construction, external heel counter, asymmetric loop lacing system and X-Traxion outsole with magnesium studs'; they are available in gun metal grey, silver or Predator Red (not black); and they feature the embroidered names of his children. A fresh pair is selected for every third game Beckham plays and discarded – or, more likely, auctioned – afterwards.

Specialist football boots were first manufactured in the 1880s, to a design incorporating raised ankle support and toe-poke friendly reinforced uppers, all stitched together out of the most unforgiving leather available. So rigorous was the process of breaking in new boots that some players resorted to the army practice of urinating into a new pair and leaving the leather to soften. Legend has it that Newcastle United forward Jackie **Milburn** broke in a new pair of boots by wearing them down a damp coal mine. Milburn wore the same pair in three FA Cup finals over a five-year span during the 1950s, and persisted with the boots until his retirement.

As designs evolved, so boots became lighter and lower cut. During the early 1960s the reinforced upper gradually gave way to a soft toecap. This reflected both the evolution away from heavy, mud-bloated footballs and the accompanying change in kicking technique, with players favouring the instep and the top of the foot.

Moulded rubber studs were the norm until the 1970s, when the removable stud became widespread, allowing players to alter stud lengths depending on the condition of the playing surface. Before the current era of disposable footwear players tended to wear the same pair of boots for as long as possible. At the 1986 World Cup in Mexico Gary **Lineker** endured a goal-less opening couple of games before having a pair of ancient but 'lucky' boots flown out from home, with which he scored a hat-trick in England's final group game against Poland.

The evolution towards a lighter, more supple boot gained a commercial impetus in the mid-1990s with the introduction of the Adidas Predator boot, invented by former Liverpool player Craig Johnston. The Predator featured a series of plastic ridges and pimples in crucial areas such as instep and toe, intended to enhance ball control and increase the power and degree of curl in a shot. The boot inspired a sweeping redesign, with most of the major manufacturers incorporating similar soft-leather innovations. Moulded wedge-shaped studs returned, with professional players tending to carry several pairs of boots each with a different length of 'blade'. Benefiting from the recent explosion in football merchandising, professional players at all levels now have their boots supplied free of charge by manufacturers, with Premiership players able to command a large fee for favouring a particular brand. In 1993 the teenage Ryan **Giggs**'s £100,000 boot deal was widely marvelled over. Currently Michael **Owen**'s deal with Umbro is worth £2 million annually.

Boots remain a central feature of the language of the game. 'Booting it' has survived the evolution of the feather-light moulded slipper to refer still to a long and violent punt. In the 1970s 'have-boots-will-travel' strikers periodically posed for newspaper pictures at train

stations. And out of the inner domestic recesses of the professional game emerged two currently dead or dying institutions: the boot room culture; and the boot-cleaning apprentice, a part of football's feudal past that may soon die out as a consequence both of the current generation of disposable footwear and the income-fuelled mobilization of player power at even the most junior levels.

Bosman

Many great players have stamped their names into the history of European football but none has left such an indelible mark as a certain Belgian pro of mediocre talent called Bosman. The high point of Jean-Marc Bosman's career came when captaining the Belgium youth side, but his actions in a European court in the mid-1990s so rocked the football world that some commentators seriously predicted the end of the game as we know it. Football survived, of course, but so too did Jean-Marc's surname as the phrase 'on a Bosman' entered footballing parlance, understood by football people everywhere as referring to a footballer's ability to move on a free transfer at the end of his contract.

The story involves the tangled technicalities of European employment law and the peculiarities of the football transfer system. It started in 1990 when Bosman's contract with the Belgian club RFC Liège came to an end. He was offered a new contract on a quarter of his current salary and the club set his transfer fee four times higher than the one they'd paid for him. Not surprisingly, Bosman wanted to leave, and tried to join the French club Dunkerque, but they couldn't afford the fee.

He took his case to the European Court of Justice in Luxembourg, arguing that the club had no right to treat him differently from any other worker in the European Union – in other words that he, and by extension all players, should be free agents at the end of their contracts.

That prospect sent the football world into a fever. Bosman was challenging two fundamental canons of the modern game – the transfer system and the 'foreigners rule', which restricted the number of overseas players each club was allowed to use. Until then football had regarded itself as a 'special case', different in kind from other areas of economic activity, and free from the kind of European employment laws which applied to other industries. Yet, in failing to treat one of its employees fairly, the masters of the game had risked losing the right to make their own rules.

The predictions were dire. The transfer system, it was argued, was the lifeblood of the professional game, a means of circulating finances from the bigger clubs to smaller ones. The ruling would mean large clubs' best assets – the players – would be worthless outside their contracts. As a result they would simply pay less for players and the loss of income would threaten the very survival of small clubs who rely on their ability to cultivate and sell-on potential young stars. According to some (slightly hysterical) estimates as many as 50 professional clubs in England would go part-time and 35 go bust, while thousands of professional players would be unemployed.

Meanwhile, star players would demand higher wages as clubs tried to force them to sign new contracts. Youth development would suffer as it wouldn't be in clubs' interests to invest in young players. On the international stage, players would migrate from poorer European countries to richer ones, depriving their national games of funds and reducing the number of leagues and clubs. This too would be a threat to youth development in the richer states as clubs would buy foreign and neglect home-grown talent.

The case went to court in June 1995 with Liège, the Belgian FA and UEFA as defendants, and, as predicted, the court ruled in Bosman's favour later that year. On the transfer argument it was clear – a football player out of contract can freely move to play in any other member state. On the foreigner rule things were a bit more complicated, involving various articles of EU law. Essentially, it said all players who are EU citizens should be regarded as domestic players; therefore the foreigner rule could only apply to non-EU players.

On 19 February 1996, UEFA adopted 'the Bosman Ruling' for all its 49 countries (far more than the EU members, then 15). It abolished all restrictions on the number of players from EU member states who could play for European clubs and removed all conditions on the transfer of players at the end of their contracts between clubs in EU states. Individual FAs can still impose a fee for transfers between clubs within the same country, so the ruling encouraged transfers between European nations – hence unrestricted numbers of French, German, Italian, Dutch and Scandinavian players now play at Premier and Football League clubs.

Although many of the direst predictions did not (quite) come true, Bosman certainly changed the nature of the transfer system, and tipped the balance of power between clubs and players further in favour of the latter and their increasingly powerful agents. However 'special' it thought it was, the case also kicked football into begrudging acknowledgement of its responsibilities under law.

Boston United

Boston United's greatest moment nearly turned to disaster. The club won promotion to the Football League at the end of 2001–02 but celebrations were cut short when the FA checked the club's books and found that manager Steve Evans had broken the rules when registering player contracts. Evans was banned for 20 months while the club was fined £100,000 and docked four points from their total in their first League season. Conference runners-up Dagenham & Redbridge, who'd finished second on goal difference, protested that Boston should have the points deducted from that season's total but the decision stood. In February 2004, Steve Evans was reappointed, the day after his FA ban ended.

Boston United began in 1934 when supporters in the Lincolnshire market town reacted to the winding up of Boston FC by forming a new club which took over its predecessor's place in the Midland League. In United's second full season, striker Frank Bungay set a record of 61 goals which included scoring in nine consecutive FA Cup games. Among the many subsequent Cup runs, the most notable came in 1954 when Boston won 6–1 at Derby (a majority of the team were ex-Derby players), which remains a record away win in the Cup by a non-League club against League opposition.

With average crowds regularly reaching 6,000, Boston began to apply for election to the Football League on a regular basis, and attempted to boost their case by playing challenge matches against top opponents (Aston Villa, Sheffield United and Leeds United were all defeated at York Street, the club's ground since the 1870s). A switch to the Southern League in 1958 failed to pay off, however, and after finishing bottom

in 1961 they moved to the smaller Central Alliance rather than accept relegation. Three years later United effectively folded but their name was kept alive by turning out an amateur team in the Boston & District League for one season, though chairman Ernest Malkinson (whose family ran the club for nearly 70 years) refused to withdraw from the FA Cup, which resulted in a record 14–0 defeat to Spalding United.

Under the leadership of former Grimsby defender Don Donovan the club then began a spectacular rise through non-League football, winning league titles in three successive seasons before joining the inaugural Northern Premier League in 1968. A year later, former wing-half Jim Smith took over and put together a side that would go 51 League games unbeaten, a professional football record at the time. Under Smith, the club also gained its current nickname, 'The Pilgrims', reflecting the town's historical connections with the Pilgrim Fathers prior to their departure for America.

After winning four Northern Premier League titles, the majority under Smith's successor, Howard Wilkinson, Boston were founder members of the Alliance Premier Football League in 1979. Two years earlier, they might have been elected directly into the League but York Street failed to meet the ground inspectors' criteria and NPL runners-up Wigan were admitted instead.

The next 20 years included one Wembley appearance, a 2–1 defeat to Wealdstone in the FA Trophy final in their club's 50th anniversary season in 1985, and a spectacular cock-up by the club secretary in 1996 when application forms for Conference membership weren't posted on time (Boston had gone down to the NPL three years earlier). A sideways move to the Dr Martens League in 1998 was accompanied by the arrival of Steve

Evans as manager. He took the club up to the Conference in 2000 and then on to the League, where Boston struggled for several months under the effects of the points deduction but finally stayed up with six points to spare.

AFC Bournemouth

A statistic says if every bar in Bournemouth is full, 40,000 people are drinking – a huge number for a town with a population of 163,000. However, if AFC Bournemouth's stadium is full, there are just 9,000 fans watching; Bournemouth is a resort not a football town. That doesn't mean the fans don't care: three years ago, unpopular chairman Tony Swaisland tried to sell the recently revamped stadium, Dean Court, to a mystery property firm. With no links to the town, Swaisland faced so much opposition he stood down, though he remains on the board.

Bournemouth date back to 1899 and the formation of a team in the suburb of Boscombe, where Dean Court was built. That club became Bournemouth & Boscombe Athletic, who spent a record 43 seasons in Division 3 (South) after entering the Football League in 1923. After relegation to Division 4 in 1970–71 the club changed the name to AFC Bournemouth ('Boscombe, back of the net!' is still a supporters' chant) and recruited John Bond as manager. His exciting side included Ted MacDougall, who knocked a record nine goals out of the 11 put past Margate in the FA Cup in 1971, and came close to promotion to Division 2, regularly attracting 20,000 home fans.

Yet by the end of the decade, the club were relegated while nearby Southampton had won the FA Cup, had been promoted, were in Europe and had signed Kevin **Keegan** (together with

MacDougall and his old Bournemouth strike partner Phil Boyer). To this day the matchday train to Southampton is full of fans from Bournemouth and western neighbours Poole, which has a 135,000 population and not even a semi-professional team to support.

The following decade was the best era yet for the Cherries – the origins of the name come either from the cherry-red shirt or an old orchard once found near the ground. In 1984 Harry Redknapp's side knocked holders Manchester United out of the FA Cup, then won the first ever LDV Vans Trophy (then known as the Associate Members' Cup) and took the Division 3 title to lift the club up to the second level for the first time.

Redknapp could not keep them there, however. On the last day of 1989–90, Bournemouth needed a win to stay up while opponents Leeds also needed a victory for the title. Around 8,000 Leeds fans turned up for a game staged – against club advice – on a bank holiday. With thousands locked out of the 11,000 capacity stadium, the riots that ensued were to dispel any goodwill for the club among local businesses reliant on tourism.

In 1997, with Redknapp gone, the club sank into receivership. Fans rallied round and the council provided a £250,000 loan and a year later 34,000 fans watched the Cherries lose to Grimsby in another LDV final appearance in 1998. Today, Bournemouth teeter on the brink of solvency with £5m debts. Yet, after another relegation, things are looking up: after winning the play-offs, a young side playing good football under manager Sean O'Driscoll is challenging for promotion to the Championship.

Bradford City

In 1903, Manningham rugby club decided that playing football would be more profitable, and reinvented themselves as Bradford City AFC. Since then, the Bradford Bulls rugby league team have repeatedly become world club champions. This is not something that has ever seemed likely to happen to their football-playing neighbours; but Bradford City's history contains some successes along with some lengthy lean spells.

Before playing a match, City were welcomed into a Football League keen to make inroads into rugby territory, and they finished their first season halfway up the Division 2 table. In 1908 they were promoted as champions. The 1910–11 campaign saw City finish fifth in the top flight, still the club's best League performance. It also brought the FA Cup to Bradford, when a goal from City captain Jimmy Spiers proved sufficient to beat Newcastle in a Cup Final replay at Old Trafford.

But relegation came in 1922 and 1927. City dropped into Division 3 (North) and rattled around in the lower divisions for the next 58 years, handicapped by several serious local difficulties. Rugby remained a strong rival attraction, and many local football fans favoured Bradford Park Avenue, a League club between 1908 and 1970 (when they were voted out after having applied for re-election in four successive years). More importantly, Bradford suffered a steady economic decline during much of the century, largely owing to the waning of the wool trade that had been the city's main industry.

The 1984–85 City team rose above the area's adversity to win the Division 3 championship, but their success was overshadowed by one of Britain's worst sporting tragedies (see **Bradford fire**).

City were relegated in 1990, but six years later the Bantams' first-ever trip to Wembley brought promotion via the play-offs. In 1998 local icon Stuart McCall, a hero of the 1985 team, returned and starred in another successful promotion campaign. A nerve-shattering 3–2 win at Wolves in the season's final match took City into the Premiership.

Few expected them to stay there for more than a year, but David Wetherall's goal in the final game of the 1999–2000 season beat Liverpool and fended off relegation. The club enjoyed a European adventure, visiting Lithuania, the Netherlands and Russia in reaching the semi-finals of the Intertoto Cup, the preliminary competion for the UEFA Cup. City's line-up included foreign stars Benito Carbone and Dan Petrescu. In their first home League game of the new season, Bradford City beat Chelsea 2–0. And then it all fell apart.

It became clear that the financial foundations supporting the rise of the team and the construction of the big new stands at Valley Parade (their ground since 1903) had been decidedly shaky. The money ran out, and the famous names departed. Two relegations and two spells in administration followed, and in 2004 the club came desperately close to closure. Soon after leaving the Premiership, Bradford City fans seriously discussed the possible long-term benefits of bankruptcy and a relaunch in the Northern Premier League.

Thankfully, it didn't quite come to that. New chairman Julian Rhodes took the club out of administration in December 2004, when manager Colin Todd's team was already pushing for promotion despite the cash crisis. In recent years, supporters have seen Bradford City slide from beating Arsenal and Chelsea in the Premiership to losing to Accrington in the LDV Vans Trophy; but now, with the club's survival seemingly secured, City fans have grounds for cautious optimism.

Bradford fire

It is a short step between ill-fated and tragic. In 1968 Nottingham Forest's main stand caught fire during their game with Leeds. The game was abandoned and all 34,000 spectators were evacuated. On 11 May 1985, with a big crowd gathered to celebrate Bradford City's already-secured promotion to Division 2, a fire broke out in the wooden main stand of Valley Parade. The match was abandoned as, all other escape routes blocked, fans spilled out onto the pitch. On this occasion more than 50 were killed and many others seriously injured.

The Bradford tragedy happened because of a mixture of carelessness and cruel luck. The fire began when a dropped cigarette fell under the old wooden stand and ignited piles of rubbish that had been allowed to accumulate beneath the seating. Afterwards, the true scale of the horror took a few hours to emerge. At first, news reports suggested that relatively few had died. The gruesome truth emerged when wreckage at the rear of the burned-out stand was explored. Locked exit gates had brought a terrible death to dozens of people trying desperately to escape from the back of the stand. The death toll eventually reached 56.

Lord Justice Popplewell's report into the Bradford disaster brought some minor improvements to football safety standards. Readily accessible fire exits now had to be provided by clubs with wooden stands. In any case, no major club was now likely to build a new wooden stand. But the biggest changes to the culture of British football grounds would not come until after the tragedy of the **Hillsborough disaster** in 1989.

Brechin City

Formed in 1906 through the merger of two junior clubs, Hearts and Harp, Brechin City chiselled out a long tradition of stasis – remaining in or below the lowest professional division in Scotland for nearly 80 years – before earning their first ever promotion from Division 2 in 1982–83. The City moved to current ground Glebe Park in 1919 and entered the newly formed Scottish Division 3 in 1923. Early players included local favourite Frank Gray, a revered long throw-in specialist in the days when players were allowed to leap in the air to gain extra yardage. Brechin's early years as a League club were notable only for a string of record defeats in the 1937–38 season, losing 10–0 to Cowdenbeath in November, and by the same score to Albion Rovers in January and Airdrieonians in February.

After the Second World War it took the club nine years to regain its status in the professional leagues. They then remained in the bottom division until they achieved the notable feat of being relegated before winning their first promotion – as one of the clubs to 'go down' to the reduced Division 2 in 1975 when the League was reorganized to accommodate the Scottish Premier Division. Capturing the Division 2 title in 1983 ushered in a jaunty sequence of promotions and relegations – 11 in 20 years – that have seen Brechin see-saw between the divisions, without ever quite making it to the top flight; most recently Dick Campbell's buoyant team have been promoted three times in five seasons, with two relegations in between, and begin season 2006–07 in Division 2.

The club has yet to have a member of

its playing staff capped at international level; the record for League appearances is held by David Watt, who played in 459 matches between 1975 and 1989; and the all-time scoring record belongs to Ian Campbell, with 131. Despite the recent swelling of its population to just under 10,000, Brechin remains the smallest city in Britain to host a professional football club.

The Scottish Tourist Board describes Brechin's ancient cathedral as 'a classic example of an 11th-century round tower', despite which Brechin City are still perhaps best known for their home ground (record attendance 8,122 v Aberdeen in the third round of the Scottish Cup, February 1973), which is described on Brechin's official website as 'the only football ground in Europe with a hedge surrounding its perimeter' – a well-maintained box privet that runs halfway along the touchline opposite the Main Stand.

Billy Bremner

Billy Bremner's image is indelibly printed on football history as the ultra-competitive and incendiary captain of Leeds United during the club's greatest years from the mid-1960s to the mid-1970s under manager Don **Revie**. Born in Stirling in 1942 the widely coveted Bremner was persuaded to join Leeds in preference to his boyhood club Hibernian. He made his debut on 23 January 1960 in a 3–1 away win at Chelsea and scored his first goal at home to Birmingham six weeks later where, in front of Leeds's lowest gate of the season, he was joined on the scoresheet by Revie, who became manager a year later.

Some called Bremner Revie's 'second son' such was the apparent bond between them, but each was very much his own man, as Revie discovered when

he tried unsuccessfully to browbeat the still teenaged central midfielder into playing wide on the right. Bremner insisted on being in the thick of things, tackling ferociously, passing sublimely, winning headers despite his five foot five stature and contributing half a dozen often spectacular and vital goals per season.

In 1965 Bremner's late equalizer forced FA Cup Final extra time against Liverpool, but the latter ran out 2–1 winners. Disappointment also followed the 1967 Fairs Cup Final against Dinamo Zagreb, but Bremner finally collected silverware as the recently installed Leeds captain in 1968, when Leeds beat Arsenal 1–0 in the League Cup Final and then Ferencváros over two legs in the Fairs Cup.

The next seven years saw Bremner's indefatigable leadership spur Leeds to two championships (1969 and 1974), another Fairs Cup (1971) and an FA Cup triumph (1–0 over Arsenal again in 1972), though as many trophies slipped just out of his reach, including memorable FA Cup defeats to Chelsea and Sunderland as well as a heartbreaking 2–0 loss to Bayern Munich in the 1975 European Cup Final, where Bremner's own marginal offside denied Peter Lorimer an opening goal for Leeds. Along the way he picked up the 1970 Footballer of the Year award and 54 caps, many as captain, for Scotland, crowned by playing at the 1974 World Cup finals, where he came within inches of scoring in a goalless draw against Brazil.

After 771 games, one short of Jack **Charlton**'s club record, Bremner moved on in September 1976 to complete his playing career firstly at Hull City and then Doncaster Rovers, where he became player-manager in November 1978. In 1985 he was given the chance to take over from former team-mate Eddie

Gray as Leeds manager. Bremner steered the now Division 2 club to an FA Cup semi-final in 1987 and a desperate promotion play-off final replay reverse in extra time to Charlton six weeks later. He was replaced by Howard Wilkinson a year later and rejoined Doncaster from 1989 until 1991. He died of pneumonia on 7 December 1997 after a short illness, and a statue to the man voted their greatest-ever player by Leeds fans now stands as a landmark outside the Elland Road ground.

Brentford

Griffin Park, Brentford's home since 1904, is a popular ground among visiting fans not least because, uniquely, it has a pub on each of its four corners. The days of it hosting big crowds are long in the past, however, Brentford having spent more seasons in the bottom two divisions than any other London League club. The Bees draw most of their support from west and south-west London, the same approximate catchment area as three other clubs, Chelsea, Fulham and Queens Park Rangers. With the others having all had lengthy periods in the top division since Brentford's heyday – a few years either side of the Second World War – the Bees' hardcore support numbers no more than a few thousand.

Formed in 1889, Brentford joined the Southern League nine years later and became a founder member of Football League Division 3 in 1920. They were to remain at that level for 13 seasons, even when setting a League record by winning all their 21 home games during 1929–30, finishing second to Plymouth at a time when only one team went up from their section. Promoted four years later, they reached Division 1 in 1935 and were the highest-placed London club in their first

season, finishing fifth. Welsh winger Idris Hopkins became their most-capped British international player during this period with 12 appearances for Wales, though the record-holder is defender John Buttigieg, a regular for Malta during his two seasons at Griffin Park in the late 1980s.

After relegation in 1947, Brentford hung on in Division 2 for seven years, during which Tommy **Lawton** played 50 games for the club and Griffin Park featured in a film, *The Great Game*, starring the contrasting talents of Thora Hird and Diana Dors (who in one scene is passed over the heads of the crowd after fainting). Since slipping down to the third level in 1954, the Bees have only spent one season outside the lower divisions, in 1992–93. In 1962, facing relegation to Division 4 for the first time, the club attempted to sign striker Jim Towers from QPR. Towers was to meet Bees officials at Brentford Market but went to nearby Acton Market by mistake and never completed the transfer.

Five years later, with the club in an impoverished state, chairman Jack Dunnett invited QPR to groundshare at Griffin Park with a view to the clubs merging but the plan was scuppered by supporter opposition.

Brentford reached their lowest point in the next decade, narrowly avoiding applications for re-election in 1973–74 and 1975–76. With Terry Hurlock and Chris Kamara a fearsome combination in midfield, a solid Bees team established itself in Division 3 during the 1980s, reaching the Freight Rover Trophy final in 1985, where they lost to Wigan. Two years earlier, former player Stan Bowles saved Griffin Park from burning down when he saw it alight on returning to his nearby house from a nightclub at 3am.

Promoted in 1992, the club had several

other near misses in the play-offs, notably in 1995 when they finished second in Division 2 in a year when that wasn't enough to go up automatically because of League reorganization. 'It's a hell of a cup competition when you play 46 games to get to the semis,' said manager David Webb in angry despair after his side had been knocked out on penalties by Huddersfield. Webb's team led the division for most of the 1996–97 season but the surprising sale of striker Nicky Forster to Birmingham triggered a slump that saw them finish eight points adrift of the top two, and beaten in the play-offs again. With several other regulars sold amid fans' allegations of financial chicanery, Brentford went down the following year.

Former Crystal Palace chairman Ron Noades then took over, appointed himself manager for a year and got the club back up again straight away. Noades has since left after protracted arguments with the local council and supporters' groups about proposals to relocate Brentford in various parts of Surrey and west London. It now seems that the Bees will be staying put at Griffin Park, which is to be redeveloped.

Brighton

Brighton & Hove Albion midfielder Gordon Smith is responsible for a famous piece of football commentary. Brighton were drawing 2–2 with Manchester United in the final seconds of the 1983 FA Cup Final. The ball came to Smith, unmarked inside the United penalty area. 'And Smith must score!' shouted BBC radio's Peter Jones as he took a moment to place his shot, allowing Man Utd goalkeeper Gary Bailey time to make a block. The game went to a replay, which Brighton lost 4–0. Relegated from Division 1 that season,

they have since come close to going out of business.

Formed in 1901, Brighton joined the Football League Division 3 in 1920 having previously been in the Southern League, whose championship they had won in 1909–10. The club were to remain at the third level for 39 years, gaining a reputation for FA Cup exploits in the inter-war period, when they knocked out seven Division 1 opponents. Brighton reached Division 2 for the first time in 1958, surviving for four years. They returned in 1971 having often drawn 30,000-plus crowds to the increasingly ramshackle Goldstone Ground (their home since 1902) but were promptly relegated.

Brian **Clough**, lately sacked by Derby, took over a team struggling to avoid a further relegation in 1973 and oversaw two traumatic home defeats, 8–2 in a televised match against Bristol Rovers and 4–0 to non-League Walton & Hersham in an FA Cup replay. After Clough departed for Leeds in 1974, his assistant, Peter Taylor, stayed on as manager and led Brighton to a series of promotion campaigns, continued under Alan Mullery, who finally took the club up to Division 1 in 1979 with a team featuring young striker Peter Ward, central defender Mark Lawrenson and captain Brian Horton in midfield. During this period, matches with promotion rivals Crystal Palace generated an intense rivalry that has continued ever since and spawned a new nickname, Brighton fans chanting 'Seagulls!' as a response to their rivals' cries of 'Eagles!' The club stayed at the top level for four seasons but were hampered by problems with the Goldstone Ground, the North Stand having to be demolished because it was deemed to be unsafe.

Fourteen years after the Cup Final defeat, Brighton were 90 minutes away from a place in the Conference. Requiring a draw at Hereford on the final day of the 1996–97 season, Albion went in at half-time a goal down. Robbie Reinelt, Brighton's only cash signing that season, had only been on the pitch eight minutes when he scored the goal that saved his team and sent Hereford down because of fewer goals scored. Brighton had slipped into the old Division 3 in 1987 but the team's decline carried no hint of the dire financial problems to come – indeed, four years later they reached the Division 2 play-off final, losing 3–1 to Notts County. By 1993, however, gross mismanagement of the club's finances – with players' wages often unpaid and the Inland Revenue owed a large sum of PAYE arrears – left them having to urgently sell goalkeeper Mark Beeney to Leeds to avoid going out of business.

Two years later, it was revealed that the club's board had done a deal to sell the Goldstone Ground, without having found an alternative home first. Brighton fans soon became known for elaborate forms of protest, with chairman Bill Archer and chief executive David Bellotti being their chief targets. The demonstrations ranged from marches through London and Brighton to petitions to the FA, and most famously the birth of 'Fans United', when supporters from across the country attended a Brighton home match to show solidarity. In 1997, with the Goldstone Ground sold to developers, a groundshare was arranged at Gillingham, a 150-mile round trip for the club's fans (with many boycotting matches, just 1,025 saw a 3–0 defeat to Barnet on 5 November 1997).

After protracted negotiations, a consortium led by Dick Knight took over the club and arranged a temporary home back in Brighton at the Withdean athletic stadium. The club celebrated their cen-

tenary year by winning Division 3 under Micky Adams in 2001 – their first title in 36 years. Another championship followed just a year later but the struggle for a new stadium took precedence, with the club losing millions of pounds a year at their rented accommodation. The board have a site in mind, at Falmer in northeast Brighton, but still require planning permission. The search for a new home wasn't helped by relegation back to League One in 2005–06.

Bristol City

Bristol City are the more popular of the two professional clubs in arguably England's most underachieving football city, one that is still waiting for its first major trophy after over a century. Periodic suggestions that the clubs should merge have been resisted and increasingly heated derby matches over the last decade have only served to reinforce distinct identities: City are seen as the more 'aristocratic' of the two, yet draw on support from the rougher south of the city and Somerset; Rovers, from the north and Gloucestershire. The City club song, 'Drink Up Thy Zider', contains a briskly disparaging reference to the Rovers.

Formed as Bristol South End in 1894, the club adopted their current name three years later after joining the Southern League. They were elected to the Football League seven years later. Their first foray into the top division in 1906 was achieved on the back of the no-nonsense approach of Bill 'Fatty' Wedlock. The substantial centre-half – still City's most capped player with 26 appearances for England – led the club to their only Cup Final appearance, a 1–0 defeat against Manchester United in 1909, before retiring to a life of being mistaken for silent-film actors.

City went down two years later. In 1920 they reached the FA Cup semi-finals but two years after slipped down to Division 3 South. Three decades and much bumbling around in the middle two divisions later came the debut of John Atyeo, probably the finest, and most frequently mispronounced, player ever to pull on a red City shirt. His 395 goals in 700 appearances guaranteed Atyeo – one of the few England internationals of modern times never to have played in the top flight – his place in the hall of fame, and his legacy as the only British player ever to have had a surname that rhymes with 'patio' lives on to this day. The John Atyeo Stand replaced the old away terrace at Ashton Gate in 1994.

Atyeo's retirement to become a maths teacher in 1966 was followed almost immediately by the 13-year reign of manager Alan Dicks, who took City to the League Cup semi-finals in 1971 and promotion to Division 1 in 1976. Dicks's glorious epoch incorporated several players with distinctly odd names, beginning with winger Mike Brolly in the early 1970s. The promotion team contained Scottish midfielders Gerry Sweeney (subject of a menacing terrace chant) and the swashbuckling Donnie Gillies (scorer in the 1–0 win at mighty Leeds in the FA Cup fifth round in 1973–74). Striker Paul Cheesley made a telling contribution too, often in partnership with another local boy, Keith Fear, until forced into early retirement by a knee injury.

The steadying influence of several ex-internationals – Norman Hunter and Terry Cooper in defence, ex-Liverpool midfielder Peter Cormack and veteran striker Joe Royle – helped keep City in the top division for four seasons. Then, dogged by financial crises, they slid from the first to the fourth in successive years; Sweeney disappeared as one of the 'Ashton Gate Eight', who, in January 1982, ripped up their contracts to help the club stave off bankruptcy. City took two attempts to get out of Division 4. At one point in late 1982 they were bottom of the entire League on crowds of under 4,000. Promotion in 1984 and a Freight Rover Trophy victory in 1986 (see **LDV Vans Trophy**) remain the most unsung achievements in the club's history.

Since then, they have reached the League Cup semi-final for a second time – losing 2–1 to Nottingham Forest in 1989 – and been promoted back up to the second level twice, in 1990 and 1998, as well as suffering three Division 2 play-off defeats, the most recent in the 2004 final, which led to the immediate sacking of manager Danny Wilson. That 40,000 fans, the vast majority from Bristol, saw City win the LDV Vans Trophy for the second time in 2003 is testament to the club's potential.

Bristol Rovers

Bristol Rovers' current lowly status, struggling in the lowest reaches of the Football League, belies the club's history of thriving in perilous circumstances. Having gone through financial crisis, fires, floods and exile, it is a cruel irony that a club again established in its home city with no threat of financial collapse should lately have been in real danger of dropping out of the League.

Rovers' history can be traced through the various grounds that have been the club's home. After their foundation in 1883 as the Black Arabs, Rovers made use of an assortment of pitches mostly in the Eastville and Purdown areas of Bristol. Even in these early days financial worries were never far away and the club was once reprimanded for charging both the opposing players and match officials for entrance to a game (they had to refund it). Despite this, Rovers were able to purchase the former home of a rugby club at Eastville in 1896 for £150 and here they would stay for the next 90 years. The ground was next to a gasworks, hence Rovers fans are known as 'Gasheads'.

From here they would join the Football League in 1920 and build several successful teams all on a pitch that was regularly flooded by the nearby River Frome. Their best years were in the 1950s under manager Bert Tann, when they twice reached the quarter-finals of the FA Cup and finished in the top half of Division 2 for seven successive seasons following promotion in 1952–53. Outstanding players from this era included full-back Harry Bamford, wing-half Jackie Pitt and striker Geoff Bradford, who was capped by England.

The end for Rovers at Eastville came in 1986, the culmination of over 40 years of off-field problems: the club had to sell the ground to a greyhound company in 1940 and then lease or rent it back; in 1980 a fire destroyed the South Stand; finally a huge hike in rents left Rovers no option but to leave. A groundshare with local rivals City was never a realistic option, so Bath City's 'compact' Twerton Park became Rovers' temporary home. Here the club would gain promotion, reach Wembley twice, hold the then mighty Liverpool to an FA Cup draw – and lose only once in ten years to Bristol City. Visiting teams generally found Twerton an intimidating venue: 'maybe not a cauldron,' said one fan 'but at least a small saucepan'.

In 1996 the club returned to Bristol, first as tenants then as owners of Bristol RFC's Memorial Ground. Here Ian Holloway's team twice narrowly missed out on promotion, before the inexplicable slump that would see Rovers relegated to the bottom division for the first time in 2001. Expected to make a quick return to the third tier, things just got worse as they ended up in 91st place in 2002 and only slightly improved in 2003 before five different managers helped secure a mid-table finish the next season. Rovers fans will feel that a return to their historical level of mid-League respectability is long overdue.

British managers abroad

It is hard to imagine now but there was a time when British managers were in great demand overseas for their tactical know-how and revolutionary coaching methods. Very often such men were underappreciated at home; strong-willed, independent thinkers who rarely fitted into the authoritarian structure of many football clubs where the board of directors expected a say in running the team.

It's a sign of the English influence on Spanish football in the first half of the century that *el mister* is still a common term for a football coach. Legendary centre-forward Steve **Bloomer** won a Spanish championship with small Basque club Real Unión de Irún in 1924 (beating Real Madrid in the play-off final). He later took up a staff position at Derby County but was never a manager in England in his own right. The eccentric Fred Pentland, known as 'bombin' (bowler hat), was one of several English managers to work at Athletic Bilbao and also coached Spain when they became the first continental team to defeat England, in 1929.

Among the many others who worked overseas in the inter-war period, probably the outstanding figure was Jimmy Hogan. Formerly a winger with Fulham and Burnley among others, he became Austrian national coach just before the outbreak of the First World War and later worked in Hungary and Germany before returning to take charge of the Austrians, whom he led to the Olympic Games Final in 1936. Known for demonstrating his own ball skills when teaching players, Hogan's influence helped to establish a quick-passing Central European style which came to be seen as superior to the British approach, with its stress on fitness and power. He was to win a Division 2 title with Aston Villa in 1938, though the club's directors complained about his training methods, and later worked at Celtic. In 1953 he was a guest of the Hungarian FA for their team's 6–3 win at Wembley.

Jesse Carver, once a centre-half with Blackburn and Newcastle, held several jobs in Italy for a decade from the late 1940s, winning a league title with Juventus in 1950. Carver returned to England briefly for unsuccessful stints at West Brom and Coventry where, like Hogan, his routines based on ball work were popular with players but not with the board. He was also offered, and declined, the England manager's job by the far-sighted Stanley **Rous**, then secretary of the FA.

Carver's assistant, later replacement, at Coventry was George Raynor, who also coached Juventus and Lazio but was known chiefly for his work with the Swedish national team, with whom he was an Olympic winner in 1948 and World Cup runner-up ten years later. Sweden had drawn 2–2 in Hungary immediately prior to the latter's momentous 6–3 win at Wembley in 1953, but the England manager Walter **Winterbottom** ignored the defensive tactical plan suggested by Raynor. Forced out of Coventry by arguments with the board, Raynor was a store manager at a holiday camp before a brief spell at Doncaster.

After Raynor the next most successful among the stream of British coaches to work in Scandinavia was Bobby Houghton, who was the first Briton to manage an overseas team to a European Cup Final when his Malmö side lost to Nottingham Forest in 1979. Houghton won four league titles in Sweden, often in competition with another Englishman, Roy Hodgson, twice a champion with Halmstad. The two worked together for a brief and disastrous spell at Bristol City in the early 1980s; Hodgson also had a stint at Blackburn but has mostly worked abroad, including in Italy, the only coach from the UK employed there since the heyday of Carver and co, barring Graeme Souness and David Platt's brief spells at Torino and Sampdoria respectively.

Souness is one of several British coaches to have worked with Portugal's biggest club, Benfica, the most successful of whom was Jimmy Hagan (not Hogan), with three league titles in the 1970s. Malcolm **Allison** also won a championship with Benfica's Lisbon rivals, Sporting, in 1982. Bobby **Robson** worked at Sporting and Porto as well as Barcelona. Terry **Venables** took the latter to their first league title in 11 years in 1985 but fell out of favour quickly. Others to have brief spells in La Liga include Ron Atkinson, Colin Addison (both Atlético Madrid) and Jock Wallace (Sevilla).

Far and away the most successful British coach in southern Europe in modern times is John Toshack, who spent nearly 20 years in Spain – including two spells at Real Madrid – Portugal and France before becoming Wales manager in 2004. Many British managers continue to be employed by clubs and national teams around the world but technically and tactically the domestic game is seen to lag behind the continent; it may be a while before we see another Toshack cement a coaching reputation in a major European league.

British players abroad

The USA and France were the first countries to which British footballers moved in large numbers, dozens heading to both destinations in the 1920s. No transfer fees were required as the UK football associations were not then members of FIFA. The American Soccer League, which existed for a decade from 1921, was professional; French clubs were officially amateur but still able to offer inducements to sign. Many more players joined the professional league created in France in 1932, mostly from lower-division or amateur clubs – former Chelsea centre-half Peter O'Dowd was the only full international – but few stayed for long.

There was a second wave of migration to the US after the creation of the North American Soccer League in 1969; at its peak in the late 1970s several teams consisted almost entirely of British players. Most were on summer vacation from their League clubs, but some settled permanently (striker Jim Fryatt, once of Oldham and Southport among others, became a croupier in Las Vegas; ex-Blackpool and England goalie Tony Waiters was to coach Canada at the 1986 World Cup finals).

In 1950, England centre-half Neil Franklin was one of four Football League players to join the 'rebel' league in Colombia which existed outside FIFA jurisdiction (Stanley **Matthews** was one of several who turned down an invitation). Attracted by huge salaries at a time when the maximum wage inhibited their earnings at home, none of the players lasted longer than a year, Franklin returning home after just two months and six games. The next wave of migrations was to Italy from the mid-1950s, though only two players had sustained success – Welsh international

legend John **Charles**, three times a title-winner with Juventus after joining them from Leeds in 1957, and centre-forward Gerry Hitchens, who left Aston Villa for Internazionale in 1961 and spent eight seasons in Serie A, though all of his paltry seven England caps were won while with Villa. The lure of the Italian league is said to have influenced the football authorities' decision to abolish the maximum wage in 1962, after which Fulham, who had struggled to fend off AC Milan's interest in Johnny Haynes, immediately put their star player on £100 a week.

Numerous footballers from the UK were active in Europe (notably Scandinavia, Holland and Belgium) by the end of the 1960s but no famous names ventured abroad again until Kevin **Keegan** left new European champions Liverpool for Hamburg in 1977. After a shaky start, Keegan went on to win two league titles in Germany and was twice elected European Footballer of the Year during his time there (where he acquired the nickname Mighty Mouse). England striker Tony Woodcock also played in the Bundesliga in two spells with Cologne during the 1980s and has since worked in Germany as a coach and players' agent. Centre-half Dave Watson, however, returned to Manchester City after barely two months with Werder Bremen in 1979 having been sent off in only his second game with the club.

The same year, West Brom winger Laurie Cunningham became only the second British player of modern times to sign for Real Madrid (preceded by veteran Scottish midfielder Jock Wilson 30 years earlier) but his subsequent career was hampered by injury. He was playing for Real's modest neighbours Rayo Vallecano by the time of his car crash death in 1989. More recently, an English colony has been created at Real, beginning with Steve McManaman who joined on a free transfer from Liverpool in 1999 and became the first English player to score for a foreign team in a European final, getting the third goal in a 3–0 Champions' League victory over Valencia in 2000. After the 2002 World Cup David **Beckham** arrived in Madrid and was joined in summer 2004 by Michael **Owen** and, surprisingly, centre-half Jonathan Woodgate, who was unable to play in the first season owing to injury.

Fifty years on from the first wave, British players returned to French football during its short-lived financial boom from the mid-1980s, Mark Hateley (who had also played for AC Milan) and Glenn **Hoddle** winning a title with Arsène **Wenger**'s Monaco in 1987–88, while Chris Waddle ('Ouadull!') became a huge favourite at Olympique Marseille. Again, however, most of the migrants didn't settle. Scottish international striker Ian Wallace left Brest after half a season complaining that the coach had made no attempt to communicate with him in English.

Several Football League stars, including Graeme Souness, Trevor Francis and Ray Wilkins, moved to Italy shortly after a 14-year ban on foreign players was lifted in 1980. Irish midfielder Liam Brady, initially with Juventus, was the most successful, Ian **Rush**, who spent a year with the same club, probably the biggest flop. During the 1990s David Platt did well with Juventus and Sampdoria but Paul Ince and a rarely fit Paul **Gascoigne** made less impact with Inter and Lazio respectively. In the last eight years, only two English players have appeared in Serie A – Lee Sharpe played three games for Sampdoria in 1998–99 and Jay Bothroyd spent 2003–04 with Perugia before joining Blackburn. The enormous salaries

on offer in the Premiership has helped to keep its stars at home, but a history of not travelling well has surely affected British players' appeal to potential foreign buyers.

Sir Trevor Brooking

Trevor Brooking was a tall, languid creative midfielder, who spent his entire playing career at West Ham and was also capped 47 times by England over eight years. His reputation as an England international has mushroomed beyond his achievements as a player – he scored four goals for England and played very briefly at one World Cup. Despite this, his partnership with Kevin **Keegan**, his statesmanlike bearing and his subsequent career as an FA administrator have given his international career a lustre that other, more obviously successful England players might lack.

Brooking's huge popularity at West Ham is based on his loyalty to the club, his longevity in playing over 600 games, and his likable and courtly public demeanour. The perception that he is an all-round good egg seems to have sustained him through his subsequent career as a bland and equivocal television pundit, a successful and innovative administrator with Sport England, and as chief coaching guru at the FA, during which time he has also been awarded an OBE, an MBE and a knighthood.

As a player Brooking's finest moment will remain his winning goal for West Ham in the 1980 FA Cup Final against Arsenal. Much is made of the fact that Brooking scored the goal – rarely for him – with his head (and was apparently still concussed during his subsequent *Match of the Day* punditry appearances), but even more unusual was the fact that West Ham were in Division 2 at the time

Burnden Park disaster

The Burnden Park disaster was the result of serious overcrowding at a Cup tie between Bolton and Stoke in 1946. Thirty-three supporters died after 85,000 people were allowed to enter a ground with a capacity of 65,000. Before kick-off the turnstiles had become blocked by a sudden rush of people. Eventually large numbers of supporters were allowed to enter the ground over walls and fences. Amid the carnage, which included the fatal collapse of safety barriers at the Railway End, and with bodies laid out at the edge of the pitch, the game was allowed to go ahead. A subsequent inquiry into the disaster, the Moelwyn Hughes Report, recommended limitations on crowd sizes and licensing inside grounds.

Burnley

Burnley FC have reached dizzying heights and plumbed great depths, and continue to put a small Lancashire town on the map. The club was formed in the Bull Hotel in 1882, by a group of men who showed good sense in agreeing to stop playing rugby and adopt the association code. The next year, Burnley moved to Turf Moor, a patch of land where the club has stayed ever since. Burnley were one of the pioneers of professionalism, importing Scotsmen and, in 1884, convening a meeting of major clubs that threatened to form a breakaway British Football Association unless they could pay players.

Although one of the founders of the Football League, the club had little early

and Brooking, a current England international, had stayed with the club through relegation and subsequent promotion.

success, being relegated to Division 2 in 1897 and again three years later, an early nadir coming with a close call over re-election in 1902. Enter John Haworth, who arrived as manager in 1910 and had moulded the character of the club by the time of his death in 1924. Burnley were soon back in Division 1, and in 1914 the town emptied to see the team beat Liverpool to win the FA Cup, Bert Freeman writing himself into legend by scoring the only goal. By this stage Burnley were the Clarets, having abandoned their green colours. In 1921, they became League champions, having gone 30 games unbeaten during the season, a record that only Arsenal would beat eight decades on.

Following Haworth's death, things slipped. With the town's local industries hit hard by the Depression in the 1930s the club slid back into Division 2 anonymity. It was only after the Second World War that things picked up. In 1947 Burnley reached the FA Cup Final and won promotion. They would stay up for 24 years. During this time, Burnley won the League again, in 1960, climbing above Wolves after winning the final game at Maine Road, while in 1962 a Double came agonizingly close, the club finishing runners-up in both League and Cup.

Chairman Bob Lord ruled Turf Moor with a totalitarian grip, but oversaw innovations aided by manager Harry Potts, a quiet over-achiever. Burnley was a club that innovated. It used the latest training methods, had a model training ground (which, alas, remains in the 1960s), and pioneered a youth policy. The icon of Burnley's most successful years was Jimmy McIlroy, an outrageously skilled Northern Irish inside-forward, but his popularity didn't stop (perhaps contributed to?) Lord selling him to Stoke at the height of his powers. Some outraged souls never set foot inside Turf Moor again – those who stayed knew not to get too attached to players. Economics dictated that almost every season a high-priced player was sold. Internationals – players like John Connelly, Ray Pointer and Ralph Coates – would depart, and be replaced seamlessly by another teenager, usually from the north-east, on an apparently endless conveyer belt of talent identified by legendary scout Jack Hixon.

In the 1970s the miracle ended. The clock had been ticking since the abolition of the maximum wage, and other clubs caught up. The decision to use money from player sales to rebuild half the ground – some still call the Bob Lord Stand the Martin Dobson Stand, as it was said to have cost that player's transfer fee from Everton – was, in hindsight, mistaken. In 1971, Burnley were relegated, and although they came back and briefly flourished, in 1976 they went down again and are yet to return. There were occasional highs, but in 1985 they dropped into Division 4 for the first time. On 9 May 1987, automatic relegation into the non-League having been introduced, Burnley – managed by Brian Miller, a member of the 1960 championship team – went into the last game bottom, facing oblivion. With 15,000 in attendance, fives times the club's regular gate, Orient were beaten 2–1, and Burnley survived.

The lowest point had passed. In 1992, Burnley became the last winner, and therefore current holder, of the Division 4 championship, completing a clean sweep of titles. In 2000, they returned to the second level under Stan Ternent, since replaced by the talented Steve Cotterill. Burnley remain deeply impoverished, somehow staying up with no squad, and having just, to clear crushing debts, sold Turf Moor to a company headed by chairman Barry Kilby. The future is uncertain, but Burnley will continue to draw on its tradition of endurance.

Bury

Bury are one of those football clubs often described as 'unfashionable' – not many people support them and the mainstream media, even in the north-west, give them scant coverage. The club was founded in 1885 but until 2003, when the Supporters' Trust and Bury Council put up a number of signs around the area, it was said that some locals didn't even know the location of their ground, Gigg Lane.

Nicknamed 'The Shakers' after victory in the Lancashire Senior Cup of 1892, when their chairman said they had 'shaken' supposedly stronger opponents, Bury eke out an existence in the lowest division of the Football League, on a support of between 2,000 and 3,500. With the Manchester clubs, Bolton, Blackburn and Burnley only half an hour away, their realistic ambitions stretch to a Cup run or an occasional tilt at promotion.

It was not always thus. Bury has a rich footballing heritage, including several seasons playing at the highest level, and two amazing FA Cup Final victories. For their first 70 years, they were hardly out of the top two divisions, drawing crowds of up to 30,000. The club has had several international players (the most capped being Irish full-back Bill Morgan in the late 1930s) and in recent decades has discovered or nurtured players such as Colin Bell, Terry McDermott, Alec Lindsay, Lee Dixon, Neville Southall and David Johnson.

In 1894 Bury were Division 2 champions in their first season as Football League members. Six years later, they won the FA Cup for the first time, beating Southampton 4–0; in 1903 they surpassed this achievement, thumping

Derby County 6–0, the highest winning margin in an FA Cup Final. The club's best League season was fourth place in 1925–26, which included a 6–5 win over Manchester City on Christmas Day.

Bury swapped between the top two divisions a couple of times until being relegated to Division 3 North in 1957. They spent seven of the next eight seasons in Division 2, but from 1969 onwards their fairly frequent oscillations have been between the bottom two sections, apart from a glorious surge from Division 3 to Division 1 between 1995 and 1997. Manager Stan Ternent's team conceded just seven goals in 23 home games during their Division 2 championship season, and the club went on to draw some sell-out crowds to Gigg Lane the following year (Ternent lamented what he saw as a poor turn-out for the bus parade through their town with the Division 2 trophy, but it took place in a torrential downpour and was the club's third civic reception in as many years). Bury survived their first season, which included a win at Man City, but the major financial backer then pulled out after losing a fortune in the derivatives market, and the club tumbled back down the divisions.

Bury were threatened with extinction after going into administration in 2002, but the sterling efforts of the Supporters' Trust ('Forever Bury') has helped keep them afloat. The fans helped save the club once before, in 1971, when rejecting the directors' idiotic plan to rename the club Manchester North End.

Sir Matt Busby

'Never dare to say anything like that to me when other people can hear you!' A Manchester United director had just suggested to his rookie manager, Matt Busby, that a certain player should be dropped. Busby followed his adversary into the gents and made it clear that he wouldn't tolerate such 'advice'. In 1945, freshly demobbed company sergeant-major Matt Busby, a dapper, soft-spoken 35-year-old Scot, stepped off the bus at Cornbrook Cold Storage, temporary offices of Manchester United, confident that he could make his mark at the bombed-out, debt-laden club. By the time of his death in 1994, Busby was chiefly responsible for imbuing Manchester United with an aura of glamour and worldwide fame, as well as becoming an icon of modern football management. Massive crowds lined the streets for his funeral, at that time still an unusual outpouring of public respect for a sportsman.

Matt Busby grew up in the Lanarkshire mining village of Belshill, and later boasted proudly that as a boy he once lent his boots to Alex **James**. He became an elegant wing-half, compensating for a distinct lack of pace with his quick brain and accurate passing. He captained Liverpool, but the war gave him a taste for management; from February 1940 he ran a star-studded British Army XI, which toured Europe to raise morale. As the self-styled 'young dictator' of the ailing United, he was one of the new breed of tracksuit managers, playing in practice games with some style, while advocating football management as a profession for ex-players rather than 'civilians'.

Busby presided over three great teams. The first was built around the fine squad of players which had been brought together at Old Trafford on the eve of the war. It won the FA Cup in 1948, but the League Championship eluded this side, runners-up four times until their eventual triumph in 1952. The second was the youthful 'Busby Babes' (an appellation which did not please Busby, who thought it too 'soft'), products of his 'football nursery', which won successive titles in 1956 and 1957. Busby defied the FA to take United into European competition, and it was on the return from a European tie in Belgrade on 6 February 1958 that eight players were among the 23 killed when their plane crashed at Munich airport (see **Munich aircrash**).

His response to this tragedy won him legendary status. So gravely injured that his son Sandy did not recognize the 'old grey man' lying in an oxygen tent, he later admitted starkly, 'I wanted to die', and his wish was nearly granted. But he found the courage to resurrect United, ably supported by assistant-manager Jimmy Murphy, and constructed his glamorous third team, which swaggered to the FA Cup in 1963, added League titles in 1965 and 1967 and became the first English side to win the European Cup, in 1968. Pre-Busby, United had only won Division 1 twice, Division 2 once and bagged a solitary FA Cup. Furthermore, all his teams played in an attractive, attacking style.

As a manager Busby behaved with dignity and intelligence, inspiring genuine love. Though rarely raising his voice, he was no soft touch. In private he was a genial companion, always ready with a (tuneless) song. Critics have accused Busby of hamstringing his immediate successors by his failure to relinquish control after his retirement, condemning United to years of under-achievement. But his was an impossible act to follow. Knighted in 1968, he deserves his reputation as one of the great football managers. Appropriately, for the club which he stamped indelibly with his imprint, the main approach to Old Trafford is named the 'Sir Matt Busby Way'.

Cambridge United

A steady but progressive non-League club for nearly 60 years, Cambridge United spent the last three and a half turbulent decades as members of the the Football League before relegation to the Conference in 2005. Abbey United spent the 1920s and 1930s trundling up the Cambridgeshire League, with players such as 'Pimp' Stearn and 'Fanny' Freeman gracing the rutted pitch of the 'Celery Trenches' until a move to their present home in 1932, where the grass was kept in check by a flock of sheep and the club committee dutifully cleared up after them on matchdays.

After the war an ambitious and renamed Cambridge United progressed through the regional leagues, and when Bill Leivers was appointed manager in 1967, he promised League status within three years; after two championships the U's were duly elected in 1970 at the expense of Bradford Park Avenue. Leivers took them into Division 3 three years later, but the club's first-ever relegation in 1974, including 'attracting' a post-war record low League crowd of 450 at Rochdale, eventually cost him his job.

Enter Ron Atkinson. His rebuilding brought promotion in 1977 and another record, the fastest-ever own goal, by an obliging Pat Kruse of Torquay in six seconds. When Atkinson was poached by West Brom in 1978, his assistant John Docherty took United straight up to Division 2. Now punching way above their weight, the U's survived six seasons, their next record coming in 1983 with 12 consecutive home clean sheets; keeper Malcolm Webster was presented with an award before the 13th game, and duly let in four.

A Football League rule change enabling home clubs to keep all gate receipts sounded the death knell for little

Cambridge, and Docherty left as they attained the least desired record yet, 34 games without a win and relegation by 23 points. It got no better next season, player-boss John Ryan sent off twice in three games on his way to the sack and United finishing with a record 33 defeats, 25 points adrift at the foot of Division 3.

Chris Turner turned the club around in his five years in charge from 1985, but John Beck took over for the most extraordinary episode yet as his collection of free-transfer misfits achieved two consecutive promotions from 1990 and two runs to the FA Cup quarter-finals with increasingly extreme route one tactics: Swindon's Glenn **Hoddle** all but held a perfumed handkerchief to his nose when his team was defeated. For a time, the Premier League looked attainable. But Beck's rigid adherence to a system now sussed by the opposition kept his one-time leaders down to fifth, and play-off defeat by Leicester signalled the end of an unforgettable era. Shorn of star strikers Dublin, Claridge and Taylor, the fall was almost as rapid as the rise. Beck was gone by October 1992; last-day relegation followed and a plethora of managers could never recapture the halcyon days. Owing to League reorganization, the club became the only one ever to be relegated after finishing fifth from bottom, in 1995.

A promotion was achieved in 1999 under Roy McFarland, but he was released after a couple of seasons' struggle. A brief Beck comeback kept the team up before he was given the boot again in 2001. Now, back in non-League football, Cambridge United's dreams are restricted to keeping a penniless ship afloat. Those Celery Trenches look a lot closer now than at any time since the 1930s.

Eric Cantona

In the short preface to his 1994 autobiography, *Cantona: My Story*, Eric Cantona mentions rock singer Jim Morrison, poet Arthur Rimbaud, actors Marlon Brando and Mickey Rourke, and French anarchist musician Leo Ferré: not for Cantona the standard influences of parents, manager and – increasingly – God. 'Always be yourself,' he concludes and, during his relatively short time in English football, Cantona was a uniquely meteoric presence.

Signed for Leeds United from Nîmes by Howard Wilkinson in February 1992, having being released after a trial by Sheffield Wednesday, Cantona made an immediate impression on the second half of Leeds's title-winning season. He scored vital goals during the run-in but was surprisingly dropped from the first team the following season, despite scoring a hat-trick in a 4–3 Charity Shield win over Liverpool. Cantona's sale to Manchester United in November 1992 is said to have been discussed as an afterthought while Alex **Ferguson** and Wilkinson were negotiating the transfer of another player on the phone. Ferguson made a speculative £1m bid for Cantona, Wilkinson immediately accepted, and Cantona was set on a course that would see him become United's main inspiration in four Premiership titles in the next five years.

'Collar turned up, back straight, chest stuck out, he glided into the arena as if he owned the fucking place,' Roy **Keane** recalls in his autobiography, *Keane*. With five League titles from his time at Leeds and Manchester United, Cantona remains the most successful foreign player in the history of British football. He was also the catalyst, not just for a first League title in 25 years for Alex Ferguson's team, but for their subsequent decade of almost total domination.

Cantona scored 63 League goals in 144 appearances over five seasons at Old Trafford and was voted PFA Player of the Year in 1994 and Football Writers' Player of the Year in 1996. Despite this Cantona played with an occasionally brutal physical edge. He was banned for four European games in 1994 for becoming involved in a scuffle with Turkish policemen while leaving the field after being sent off against Galatasaray. The same year he was sent off twice in four days, against Swindon Town and Arsenal, and was ejected from a World Cup 94 press box after attempting to punch an official.

Increasingly violent on the field, Cantona reached a career-defining epiphany at Selhurst Park in January 1995 when, after being sent off against Crystal Palace, he attacked a member of the home support while leaving the pitch. Television cameras captured the Frenchman launching a spectacular flying kick at a man in the crowd who had been abusing him as he left the pitch. Cantona was duly arrested and held overnight at South Norwood police station. IS THIS THE END FOR THE MADMAN? screamed the front page of the *Sun* the next day. The answer to which was no. Suspended immediately by his club, Cantona was banned from all competitive matches for nine months, first by the FA and then by FIFA. In March he was sentenced to two weeks in jail for common assault, reduced to 120 hours of community service on appeal; the same month he was offered a new three-year contract by United.

Cantona returned to action in October, scoring in a 2–2 draw with Liverpool, and proved a pivotal figure in the regaining of the League title, scoring the winning goal in six separate 1–0

victories, captaining the team towards the end of the season and scoring the winner in the FA Cup Final against Liverpool. Rarely can a sporting redemption have been so rapid and so complete. In 1997 Cantona retired from football, preferring instead to concentrate on an acting career that has, as yet, failed to take off.

Cardiff City

Any schoolboy will tell you that when they won the FA Cup, back in 1927, Cardiff City became the only club to take the trophy out of England – an event yet to be repeated. Then again, there are only three non-English clubs in the League, all based in Wales. There were more, years ago, but one by one they've dropped into non-League football – a fate that nearly befell Cardiff City more than once.

The fans of Swansea and Wrexham may not agree, but Cardiff are Wales's biggest club in terms of levels of support and relative success. Formed as Riverside FC in 1899, in an effort to keep a cricket team together during the winter months, they were the brain-child of one man – Bartley Wilson, founder, secretary and, briefly, manager. Under Wilson, the club were renamed Cardiff City, gained their nickname, the Bluebirds (after changing to a blue strip from 'chocolate and amber'), and bought the land that would become their home – Ninian Park.

By 1910, Cardiff had turned professional; Wilson's efforts (and the team's success) saw City elected to the Southern League. By 1922, they were promoted into the Football League, and in 1924 lost the championship by the smallest-ever margin – 0.024 of a goal after centre-forward Len Davies missed a penalty in a goalless draw at Birmingham in the last match of the season.

In 1925, they reached Wembley, only to lose to Sheffield United in the FA Cup Final, but returned two years later when Arsenal were defeated by the strangest of goals – their goalkeeper, Dan Lewis, allowing a tame shot to slip under his arm and over the line. That season saw Fred Keenor captain Cardiff to victory in the FA Cup, the Welsh Cup, and the Charity Shield – still a unique treble. But that achievement was the pinnacle of many players' careers, and soon afterwards Cardiff went into decline. Just seven years later, they were rock-bottom, and forced to apply for re-election.

Cardiff emerged from the Second World War with an outstanding team, which was back in the top flight within five seasons on the back of average crowds of 35,000. Their last spell in Division 1 ended in 1961–62 but the next decade and a half was a good time for the club; Cardiff were a strong side in Division 2, hardened by regular European exposure, via the Welsh Cup – until the recent introduction of the Champions' League, and its dominance by a handful of sides, Cardiff had played more European ties than any other League club. They reached the semi-finals of the European Cup Winners' Cup in 1968, losing 4–3 on aggregate to Hamburg, who scored the decisive goal in the 88th minute of the second leg, and won the home leg of their quarter-final tie against Real Madrid three years later.

But after seasons of being desperately close to promotion, Cardiff gradually slipped backwards, a process that some say began in 1970 with the sale of talismanic striker John Toshack to Liverpool and that ended 25 years later with the Bluebirds finishing last but one in Division 4. A string of enthusiastic but cash-poor owners had kept the club afloat financially during that time, but the team had suffered; Cardiff City were at their lowest ebb.

The last few years have seen a dramatic revival. Since taking over in the summer of 2000, Sam Hammam, former owner of Wimbledon, has borrowed heavily to drag the team back up the tables, to their present place in the Championship. Cardiff are at their highest League position since the 1970s, but to go that bit further, Hammam has staked everything on building an expensive new stadium. In the meantime, the somewhat neglected side struggles, and the supporters hold their breath.

Carlisle United

For a couple of weeks in the late summer of 1974 Carlisle United were, to the astonishment of everyone except possibly their lavishly side-burned and self-confident striker Joe Laidlaw, top of the Football League. It was a heady and rare taste of success for the Cumbrian club. Founded in 1903 after the merger of Shaddongate United and Carlisle Red Rose, the club had begun life in the Lancashire Combination, been elected to Division 3 (North) in 1928 and – though briefly boasting Bill **Shankly** as manager and numbering Stan Bowles amongst former players – had won only one national honour, the Division 3 championship in 1962–63. Apart from that and a League Cup semi-final appearance in 1970 the Cumbrians' main claim to football fame was that they were the first club outside London to install floodlights.

Despite a team boasting an excellent goalkeeper, Alan Ross, the busy forwards Laidlaw and Bobby Owen, and the cultured Chris Balderstone (who also played cricket for England and went on to serve as a test match umpire), Carlisle couldn't sustain their bright start to the 1974–75 season, which began with a 2–0 win at Chelsea. They ended it in the relegation zone. It remains their only spell in the top flight. By 1984 they were in Division 4.

The arrival of new owner Michael Knighton in the summer of 1992 threatened to change the fortunes of the Foxes (so named in honour of local huntsman John Peel). Knighton had once come close to taking control of Manchester United, and now, possibly on the advice of aliens from outer space he claimed to have encountered on the M6, he was in charge of Carlisle United.

Knighton was soon telling everyone that European football – for which he claimed, bizarrely, the club was ideally placed – was on its way to Brunton Park, Carlisle's home since 1909. Initially the signs were positive. United were beaten in the Division 3 play-offs in 1993–94 and won the title the following year. They went to Wembley twice for the Auto Windscreens finals of 1995 and 1997, winning on the latter occasion. Financially, though, things had begun to unravel. The litigious Knighton's business dealings were Byzantine to say the least and his attempts to sell the club often ended in farce, as when one prospective buyer, 'millionaire' Stephen Brown, turned out to be a waiter in a local curry house.

Despite sales of players such as Matt Jansen and Rory Delap the fiscal problems at Brunton Park mounted. On the pitch things were little better. In 1998–99 Carlisle avoided relegation into the Conference only thanks to an injury time goal by on-loan keeper Jimmy Glass. In 2002 the club went into voluntary administration and the mysterious Knighton finally sold out to businessman John Courtenay. The trials of Carlisle were not over, however. The club dropped out of the League at the end of the 2003–04 season, but returned a year later after beating Stevenage in the Conference play-off final. A second

successive promotion followed in 2005–06, continuing a remarkable revival in the club's fortunes.

Raich Carter

Horatio 'Raich' Carter is widely regarded as the greatest inside-forward England has ever produced. While his England teammate Middlesbrough's Wilf **Mannion** was the better ball-player, Carter was the more complete footballer. Cool in possession, he was an incisive passer who brilliantly orchestrated midfield and attack and yet still averaged a goal every other game throughout his career.

Born in the Hendon district of Sunderland in December 1913, the eldest of three children, Carter had a tough upbringing. His father died when he was young and he was forced to become the family's main breadwinner at the age of 14. He won England caps as a schoolboy and played for Esh Winning in the Northern League while working as an apprentice engineer.

Appointed captain of Sunderland when he was just 21, Carter led his side to the League Championship in 1935–36, finishing joint top-scorer with 31 goals, including a hat-trick in a 5–4 win over reigning title-holders Arsenal. The following year Sunderland won the FA Cup, Carter scoring the winning goal in the final. In all, the man even his teammates called 'The Maestro' scored 127 goals in 276 appearances for the Rokermen.

In 1946 Carter signed for Derby County, hitting 34 goals in 63 appearances and masterminding Derby's victory in the 1946 FA Cup Final. He left Derby for Boothferry Park, Hull, where he soon became player-manager. By now age had tinted Carter's once black hair a steely grey; along with his scheming style of play this led to him being nicknamed 'The

Silver Fox'. (Another Carter sobriquet, 'The Great White Hunter', referred to his alleged fondness for women.)

Carter led the Tigers to the Division 3 (North) title and signed Don **Revie** from Leicester City before an argument with the club directors led to his resignation. After briefly running a cake shop in Hull he signed as player-coach with Cork Athletic. Though now turned 40, he was still good enough to play a vital part in his side's winning the Irish FA Cup.

He returned to England to manage Leeds United. He was at Elland Road for nine years. During that time the club won promotion to the top division but doubts still remain about the Silver Fox's ability as a manager. Certainly neither John **Charles** nor Jack **Charlton** was impressed by him, the latter remarking that 'He didn't coach and he didn't employ coaches.' He left Leeds United in 1959, and managed Mansfield Town and then Middlesbrough before retiring from the game. He died in 1994.

The consensus of those who played under Carter was that he held himself in high regard. 'You felt that he thought none of us was as good as he had been,' Charles observed. This is a common belief amongst great players, though in Carter's case it may also have been an accurate one.

Casuals

Like every teenage cult from Teds onwards, Casual was about going to extraordinary lengths to look different from everyone else, whilst having the security of a dozen or so mates who looked the same. Football grounds – hardly a bastion of sartorial elegance in previous or subsequent eras – were its catwalk.

Although argument still rages over the true origins of Casual – who first wore *that* jumper, which city first adopted

mauve, etc. – it's generally agreed upon that Liverpool fans kickstarted the movement in the late 1970s. While the team swept all before them in Europe, some of their travelling support plundered continental menswear retail outlets, setting themselves apart from their Doc Marten and star jumper-clad contemporaries.

By the turn of the decade, the fashion strongholds of Manchester and London had caught on, and introduced the defining factor of Casual: sportswear. Prior to this, the only time anyone wore a tracksuit top was during a games lesson when it was a bit nippy. On the continent, however, vast quantities of exotically coloured Adidas trainers and Tacchini trackie tops could be purchased, or stolen.

After going through a range of styles, from 'Italian Exchange Student' to 'PE Teacher at Posh Grammar School', the definitive Casual look emerged: 'Middle Management on Golfing Weekend'. Like the Teds and Mods, Casual was essentially a working-class movement that sought to subvert the fashions of their supposed betters. Unlike any other youth culture movement, however, Casual was aimed squarely at the football terraces – it would be hard to get into a 1980s nightclub with trainers on, even if they were Adidas Trimm-Trab imported from Munich and they cost two weeks' dole money.

The Casual look was perfect for hooligans; anyone that way inclined could instantly tell who was up for it (non-Casual fans, or 'scarfers', were generally left alone) and – for a short time – it greatly confused the police. This was Label Queendom taken to masculine extremes; the more expensive and exclusive, the better, even though much of the gear could never be worn in any decade other than the 1980s.

Casual wasn't tied to the musical trends of the day, so instead of copying whoever was in *Smash Hits* that month, it drew inspiration from the unlikeliest of sources – Bjorn Borg's Fila tracksuit top, an obscure golfer's Farah trousers and even Ronnie Corbett's Lyle and Scott jumpers. This enabled Casual to have a longevity far beyond its natural shelf-life. Indeed, the sartorial fortunes of a 'crew' revolved around the performance of their football club. If the team drew Italian opponents in the UEFA Cup, their stock rose dramatically. If they supported Middlesbrough, they had to make do with a coach trip down to London for the sole purpose of visiting the one shop that sold *that* particular polo shirt.

The golden age of Casual was ended by the **Heysel disaster** of May 1985. A ban on English clubs in Europe curtailed shopping/shoplifting expeditions, the media had finally cottoned on, and sportswear manufacturers had moved on to chunkier and even more ostentatious hip-hop fashions.

Casual still lives on a quarter-century later, for better or worse. Sadly, the 'Chav' phenomenon (Burberry cap, tracksuit bottoms tucked into socks, Hackett polo shirt) is a direct result of Casual, along with 'sports' shops that sell nothing one would need to actually play a sport with. On the upside, it excuses certain men in their forties and upward from forsaking the comfort and style of a nice pair of trainers.

celebrity fans

Celebrity football fans have tended to fall into two categories: the discreet biographical oddity (horse-racing commentator Julian Wilson is a Swindon Town fan; former Labour leader Michael Foot supports Plymouth); or, a more recent phenomenon, the publicity-chasing Premiership hanger-on. This category reached a definitive point during the

1990s with the high-profile attachment of TV presenter Zoë Ball to Manchester United, having already switched from a previous allegiance to Liverpool and no doubt fulfilled a lifetime ambition by publishing the book *Zoë Ball's Soccer Studs*. Also in the fairweather fan VIP lounge: the Prime Minister, Tony Blair, grinning in the stands at St James' Park, not far from his constituency; various members of S Club 7 talking about being 'Gooners'; and assorted television presenters, among them Angus Deayton and Eamonn Holmes, making wry remarks about Manchester United.

The celebrity fan who becomes involved with the financial management of their club is a rare breed. The most obvious example remains Elton John, who, during his time as chairman of Watford during the 1970s and 1980s, spent a huge amount of his own money in utterly transforming the club's fortunes, taking them from Division 4 to a second-place finish in the first and an FA Cup Final in 1984. This attachment to a little-known suburban fourth-division football club was hardly a publicity stunt. Elton, whose uncle had broken a leg while playing for Nottingham Forest in the 1959 FA Cup Final, had been a childhood fan.

Port Vale fans might have expected a similar *deus ex machina* intervention from celebrity fan Robbie Williams during the club's recent financial travails. Williams had frequently name-checked his local team during interviews and even appeared on stage wearing a Vale shirt, but turned down an appeal for financial help after the club had gone into administration in December 2002, despite having recently signed a record deal worth £80m. In 2006, however, the singer finally invested in the team.

Lists of celebrity fans have become a feature of club websites. Nigel Havers, Keith Deller and Trevor Nunn support

Ipswich Town. Kriss Akabusi is a West Ham fan. Def Leppard support Sheffield United, as do Sean Bean and The Human League. The official Liverpool website produced a list of Anfield celebrity fans that included Miss World, the Pope, Nelson Mandela, Ole Gunnar Solskjaer, Courtney Love, Halle Berry and Dr Dre, who is quoted as saying, 'Back in 1988 I was in London and one night we were watching TV and these cool cats in red came on the box. They whupped some poor dudes four or five zip.'

Traditionally, both Arsenal and, more successfully, Chelsea have had a reputation as the celebrity club of a particular era. Chelsea were popular with theatrical types, film stars and musicians during the 1960s. The club's central London location, its genesis as a branch of the entertainment industry rather than an inner-city sports club, and the proximity of the allegedly 'swinging' King's Road all seem to have promoted its status as a celebrity magnet. During the 1970s regular faces in the stands included Sir Richard Attenborough and a whole cast of actors, TV producers and musicians.

Celtic

Celtic and their Old Firm rivals Rangers have dominated Scottsh football for a century. The club have amassed so many domestic trophies – 40 League titles, 33 Scottish Cups, and 13 League Cups – that seasons in which they picked up one or two more often barely register in the memory of their supporters. It's the periods of sustained dominance that are celebrated, plus the time that they became the best team in Europe.

When Brother Walfrid proposed the establishment of a football club amongst the city's Irish immigrant community in 1888, he was not acting on a flight of fancy. The Catholic teacher had observed

the way in which Edinburgh's Hibernian club had become a positive force for that city's Irish community and he named his creation 'Celtic' to reflect those combined roots.

In the 1920s, by which time Celtic had gained considerable support and success, the simmering sectarian issues caused by the club's origins, which continue to this day, began against the background of the Irish Civil War. Even less welcome was the tragic death of goalkeeper and club stalwart John Thomson through a skull fracture sustained after diving at the feet of a Rangers forward in 1931.

The post-war years saw Celtic's worst-ever period, with a flirtation with relegation and low League finishes, though the one-off Coronation Cup was won in 1953 under the captaincy of Jock **Stein**. Retrospectively, some blame interfering chairman Robert Kelly for these barren years whilst others point to training involving only daily laps of the pitchside track. What is under no debate is that the tide turned with the installation of Stein as manager in 1965.

A tactically astute pioneer, Stein led Celtic to nine League titles in a row and a haul of cups. In Europe, they became the first British club to win the European Cup with a 2–1 victory over Inter Milan in Lisbon that was so impressive even Inter coach Helenio Herrera described it as 'a victory for sport'. Until his 1978 departure, Stein nurtured some of the finest talent the club has ever had in Jimmy Johnstone, Kenny **Dalglish** and Billy McNeill, amongst others.

It was McNeill who followed Stein as manager and, although he brought success, Rangers had gained ground and there was also the 'New Firm' challenge of Aberdeen and Dundee United. Whispers emerged of financial problems, especially over Charlie Nicholas's departure for Arsenal, and McNeill left after a ·

dispute over finances. A succession of managers (including McNeill again) ultimately failed to convince the board, and the pressure was also on the latter as fans' disillusionment grew.

In 1994, with the club close to bankruptcy, Fergus McCann took control. The Scots-born Canadian tycoon oversaw a hugely successful share flotation whilst rebuilding Parkhead into one of the finest stadiums in Britain. On the pitch, there was improvement under former player Tommy Burns before Wim Jansen stopped by for a season to win the title and stop Rangers gaining a record-breaking ten consecutive League wins.

It was the arrival of Martin O'Neill in 2000 that saw Celtic finally match their new ground in achievement. The treble in 2001 – with Swedish striker Henrik Larsson, widely rated the club's best-ever import, contributing 35 League goals – was followed by a march to the UEFA Cup Final two seasons later, defeating Liverpool on the way, though they lost the domestic battle to Rangers. Champions again in 2004, they lost the title the following year after a last-minute defeat in the final match of the season, signalling the end of the O'Neill era. The team were Scottish champions again in 2005–06, Gordon Strachan's first season in charge.

central defenders

Central defenders are usually strong rather than fast, and dogged rather than skilful. Despite this defending is clearly very difficult. The dourest of managers have hailed it as an art form and at any level the standard of football being played can usually be judged by how few goals are scored: the less interesting the scoreline, the higher the quality.

It has been said that central defenders win you championships, and during the early 1990s some of George **Graham**'s

Arsenal teams attempted to put this into practice by fielding a surplus of big blokes with cauliflower ears in both defence and midfield. This is no longer the case. The ability of the central defender to spoil, dominate and physically impose himself on a game has been steadily diminished by changes to the laws. Yellow cards for tackles from behind, a crackdown on shirt-pulling and a general speeding up of open play have weakened the central defender's armoury. Football has always adapted. The modern central defender evolved out of a change to the offside law in 1925. Perhaps a new kind of position will come about to replace the traditional stopper, at least in European competition where the ability to tackle, hoof the ball out of play, and point and shout a lot seems increasingly beside the point.

The change in the laws to require two rather than three players between an onside attacker and the opposition goal led to the emergence of the new 'stopper' centre-half, as pioneered by the all-conquering Arsenal team of the late 1920s and early 1930s (see Herbert **Chapman**). Under Chapman's newly fashionable tactics the withdrawn half-back had no responsibilities beyond defence. In practice this amounted to heading away an aerial bombardment aimed towards the new breed of bustling forward as 'direct play' became widespread. Arsenal's Herbie Roberts was perhaps the first great centre-half of the new breed.

Tactical evolution towards a defensive 4–4–2 system increased both the responsibilities and the individual prominence of the centre-half. Great post-war central defenders included Wolves's Billy **Wright**, who was also a notable captain of England. Wright could be said to have crystallized the notion of the centre-half as leader or strong-arm captain, an ideal taken to violent extremes by generations of relegation-haunted British sides and in the England team by Terry Butcher's much-photographed fist-pumping blood-stained schlock during the 0–0 qualifying draw with Sweden in 1988.

Bobby **Moore** was a crucial member of the England's World Cup-winning team and became the epitome of a different kind of defender, the 'ball-playing' centre-half. It was his cross that created Geoff **Hurst**'s first goal for England in the 1966 World Cup Final. Combining intelligence, tackling ability and easy passing skills, Moore is perhaps the greatest-ever British central defender. A very tough act to follow, he also spawned generations of imitators as the combination of a tough-tackling and a 'cultured' centre-half, in the style of Moore and Jack **Charlton**, emerged as an ideal within the flat 4–4–2 defence. Rio Ferdinand, who excelled as a ball-carrying defender at the 2002 World Cup, is perhaps the closest English football has come since Moore. Alan Hansen was comfortable in possession in a dominant Liverpool, but vulnerable under pressure as a stopper with Scotland.

The best centre-halves have been fearsome defenders with the ability to score goals from set-piece play. Terry Butcher and Tony **Adams** (once called 'a professor of defending' by Arsène **Wenger**) managed this for club and country. Larry Lloyd and Phil Thompson provided a simpler template for the physically dominant fulcrum of a backline that, above all, must refuse to be out-muscled. In British football the primary aim has always been to match the opposition for physical strength. Centre-halves are lost at the first hurdle if they don't possess the primary attributes of height, power and a loud shouting voice.

For this reason, among others, British teams have very rarely been able to keep possession long enough to compete consistently at international and European level. Whether this really matters is another argument altogether. Few things in football are as exciting to watch as an old-fashioned anvil-headed, no-frills centre-half making his presence felt at either end of the field.

Champions' League

The UEFA Champions' League is the first European football competition created entirely for the benefit of television. Now the most lucrative tournament in the world, the Champions' League was created out of the foundations of the old European Cup. The competition has been a success: currently the financial rewards and blanket television coverage have made it UEFA's club football flagship, a global rival to FIFA's World Cup. With the success of the Champions' League, however, has come a sense of anti-climax.

The old European Cup was a knock-out competition of rare intensity, competed for by the champions of the strongest leagues in Europe. The Champions' League is in effect a cartel of wealthy second- and third-raters. There is no great exclusivity to this club. A fourth place finish will do in the major leagues, throwing up midweek features of exceptional banality in the early stages, particularly during those seasons when UEFA insisted on a drawn-out sequence of two successive group stages in a single competition.

The first-ever Champions' League competition, in 1992–93, ended in sinister farce, with Basile Boli's header winning the Final for Marseille against Milan, only for the French team to be stripped of their medals after evidence was uncovered of a bribery conspiracy involving disgraced former owner

Bernard Tapie. Always a competition founded out of a weakness for large cash sums, the Champions' League has grown from these murky waters into a burgeoning money train, in the process making a cartel of leading clubs infinitely richer than their local competitors, and dividing up the pot between an ever-decreasing few. The semi-finals of the 1990–91 European Cup featured Red Star Belgrade and Spartak Moscow. The last 16 featured nine clubs who have no recent Champions' League presence at all, having been squeezed out by the many Spanish, English and Italian representatives.

Arsenal played in the first competition after the lifting of the post-**Heysel disaster** European ban but failed to reach the group stage. The following year, Leeds lost to Rangers in a knock-out round. The latter then got to within a point of making the final, but no Scottish team has had any serious impact since.

The early seasons of the Champions' League saw other clumsy and occasionally woeful showings from Blackburn and Manchester United, before Alex **Ferguson**'s team settled into a steady rhythm of reaching the quarter-final stage. Their victory in the Final against Bayern Munich in 1999 has occasionally been seen as fortunate because of the timing of their winning goals (both from corners in injury time) and the scrappy performance by both teams in the Final. However, the run to the trophy included fine victories over Juventus and Internazionale, and was the culmination of steady European improvement by a young team. Leeds United's unexpected run to the semi-finals in 2001 provided a cautionary tale. Failure to qualify for the following season's competition precipitated the club's dizzying descent into financial chaos and relegation. In 2005, Liverpool took the trophy in dramatic

fashion, coming back from three down to draw 3–3 with AC Milan, then winning on penalties. Arsenal reached the final in 2006, losing 2–1 to Barcelona.

The Champions' League may be a synthetic and over-long concoction devised to take advantage of a TV-fuelled revenue boom. And it may produce meaningless mid-November group-fillers between two uninterested teams in an empty stadium. But it is still extremely difficult to win.

Herbert Chapman

Herbert Chapman is the most influential club manager in the history of English football. The architect of the legendary Arsenal team of the late 1920s and early 1930s, during his time at Highbury Chapman implemented a thorough modernization of tactics, training and the all-round development of a game still only 40 years into its lifetime as a professional sport. Chapman had an unspectacular amateur playing career while still working as a mining engineer and later played as a professional with Northampton Town and Tottenham Hotspur.

He began his management career at Northampton, having been offered the post by a Spurs team-mate who had changed his mind about taking it – the two men sealing the arrangement with a handshake in the dressing room after Chapman's final game as a player. It was at Huddersfield Town that he enjoyed his first real success. Despite poor attendances and a lack of finance Chapman's team won the FA Cup and two League titles during a meteoric four-year reign.

Chapman became Arsenal manager in 1925. During his nine years in charge the club won two League titles and two FA Cups. In the process Chapman revolutionized the role of the manager and devised a tactical blueprint that still forms the basis of the traditional English style of play. At the beginning of the 1920s football managers had little say in the running of a club and often didn't even merit a mention in newspaper match reports. Chapman established himself as the first 'personality' manager, defining the manager's role as central to his club's success on and off the field. He constructed a young Arsenal team around players such as Alex **James**, Cliff **Bastin**, and Joe Hulme (also an England cricketer), often persuading players to switch from their accustomed positions to new and innovative roles.

Dapper and famously polite, Chapman was also a formidable authoritarian. He publicly sacked chief trainer George Hardy, an old friend from Yorkshire, in the middle of a Cup replay for shouting at a player to move upfield, unwittingly interfering with a tactical plan. He was also considered a master of man-management ('Chapman knew when to blow you up and when to blow you down,' revealed Gunners player Alec Jackson) and his team became renowned for its intimidating aura of invincibility, and its good fortune – the 'lucky Arsenal' tag dates back to the Chapman era. Besides coming up with the idea of renaming the nearby Gillespie Road tube station 'Arsenal', Chapman was also a driving force behind such innovations as using a white football, having numbers on players' shirts, using rubber studs and playing under floodlights. His greatest tactical coup was the creation of the 'stopper' centre-half, a direct response to the change to the offside law requiring two rather than three players between attacker and goal. Chapman instructed his central defender to stay in his own half at all times and concentrate solely on winning the ball in the air – common-

place now, but at the time this was considered a tactical masterstoke.

Chapman then trained his defence and midfield players to move the ball forward as quickly as possible. English football had its first experience of the 4–4–2 formation, and its first taste of concerted 'direct' play. In his 1957 book *Soccer Tactics* Bernard Joy (himself a former Arsenal player) introduces a chapter with the heading 'Imitation of Arsenal's Tactics Brings In Kick and Rush Football', and Chapman has occasionally been blamed for the subsequent and enduring fashion among English teams for the long-ball game. However, Chapman's tactics were enacted by players of unrivalled skill, for whom fast accurate forward passing bore no resemblance to the 'putting it in the mixer' game plan favoured by less skilful exponents.

Chapman died suddenly in January 1934 after contracting pneumonia while watching a reserve-team game on a freezing night at Guildford. His legacy remains: Arsenal won the League that year and the next; and at every level English teams, with various degrees of fidelity, still play to the Chapman blueprint.

Charity Shield

First staged in 1908, the annual FA Charity Shield, officially renamed the Community Shield in 2002, is British football's oldest fundraising occasion, with all receipts from the game donated to various favoured charities. The game has been the traditional curtain-raiser for the new season since 1960, and an occasion deemed fit for the national stadium since 1974. Initially the Charity Shield was competed for by the winners of the League championship and the holders of the Southern League title, and later by a team of amateurs against a team of professionals.

The current format of League champions versus FA Cup winners was established in 1928, although in 1950 a World Cup Team beat an eleven billed as 'Canadian Touring Team' 4–2. The League champions have tended to dominate, with Liverpool winning the Shield a record 13 times since 1964. Ipswich's two appearances have both ended in thumping defeats, 5–1 to Tottenham in 1962 and 5–0 v Nottingham Forest 16 years later. Until the 1997 penalty shoot-out between Chelsea and Manchester United, drawn matches had been permitted with both clubs keeping the Shield for six months. Goalkeeper Pat Jennings scored for Spurs in 1967 with a clearance from the edge of his own penalty area, the first goal in a 3–3 draw with Manchester United. The same game was also famous for one of the great televised goals, scored from 30 yards by Bobby **Charlton** after a flowing move begun near United's own corner flag, which prompted the commentating Kenneth Wolstenholme to proclaim it a goal 'good enough to win the Grand National'.

During the first-ever Shield game at Wembley, Kevin **Keegan** and Billy **Bremner** had a fist-fight after Keegan had been roughed up by Bremner's midfield partner Johnny **Giles** at a corner. Both players were sent off and later banned from playing for five weeks. The incident was made famous by live television pictures of both Keegan and Bremner removing their shirts in disgust and hurling them to the ground (perhaps having just remembered: Oh yes – it's only the Charity Shield) as they headed for the tunnel.

John Charles

If the game itself has been British football's most succesful export, John Charles is a good second. When Juventus fans voted in 1997 on the greatest player in their club's first century, Charles headed the poll ahead of Zidane and Platini.

Wales's youngest player (since superseded by Ryan **Giggs**) as an 18-year-old centre-half capped in 1949, he was still playing Southern League football in the early 1970s. His greatness, though, is defined by the five years after moving from Leeds to Juventus for a world record £65,000 in 1957. He scored 93 goals, won two championships and three cups, was both leading scorer and Player of the Year in 1958 and was the dominant individual in one of the world's strongest football cultures. Italy too conferred his enduring nickname of *Il Buon Gigante* – 'the Gentle Giant' – in recognition of the pacific temperament that was the despair of boxing promoters who had seen him as a British answer to Rocky Marciano.

Charles once said: 'If I have to knock them down to play well, I don't want to play this game.' Massive by the standards of his time at 6 ft 2 in and 14 stone he subverted the underlying assumption of footballing physics, that size will be in inverse proportion to ball skills. Danny **Blanchflower**, one of his greatest contemporaries, lamented that while he had to think every action and movement, Charles knew instinctively what to do and where to go. Those skills underpinned an ability to switch between positions with such facility that Nat **Lofthouse** considered him the best centre-half he had played against, while Billy **Wright** reckoned him the best centre-forward.

A member of Swansea's astonishing

immediate post-war generation, his move from Swansea Town's groundstaff to a contract with Leeds in 1948 led to a change in League regulations affecting players who were with clubs, but not on full professional contracts. Initially a centre-half, he was switched in 1952 to centre-forward with spectacular effect – his 42 goals in 1953–54 remain a club record, while his Leeds career total of 154, including the leading first-division scorer in 1956–57 with 38, has been beaten only by Peter Lorimer.

His Wales career was limited at his peak by difficulties in securing release from Juventus, making him a late arrival at the 1958 World Cup, where he was outshone by younger brother Mel, who played for Swansea and Arsenal with similar versatility, during Wales's run to the quarter-final. He won 38 caps, scoring 15 goals.

After a brief return to Leeds in 1962, he also played for AS Roma and Cardiff City before becoming player-manager of Hereford United and Merthyr Tydfil. The genial guilelessness that made him so adaptable and popular a team-mate served him less well off the field, making him an unsuccessful manager and businessman. While his later years were clouded by poverty and illness, he remained remarkably unembittered – a genial raconteur as appreciative of modern players as of those of his own era. He died aged 71 in February 2004.

Charlton Athletic

Charlton Athletic FC were established in 1903 by an alliance of local youth clubs, among them the pious late-Victorians of the East Street and Blundell Missions. Based in deepest south-east London, even the club's nickname reflects its geographical location: 'The Addicks' is the local pronunciation of the word

'haddock' – part London, part Kent, part Thames Estuary.

The club's first games were played on Siemens Meadow, now the site of a housing estate in the Charlton heartlands, before graduating to the big league of nearby Woolwich Common in 1907. Charlton played their first game at The Valley in 1913, the same year that local rivals Woolwich Arsenal moved north in search of a wealthier suburb and a catchier name, and the club was soon enjoying its most successful period to date during the 23-year managerial reign of Jimmy Seed, finishing second in Division 1 in 1937 and winning its only major honour so far, the 1947 FA Cup Final.

The following decade saw the club go into decline. Crowds dwindled, The Valley fell into disrepair, and Seed was sacked in 1956. The same year legendary goalkeeper Sam Bartram retired at the age of 42, having played in four Wembley finals during the 1940s, including the victorious one of 1947.

Bartram was burdened throughout his career with the tag of 'the finest goal-keeper never to play for England', although he is also remembered for one of the strangest stories in the club's history. In his autobiography he described how heavy fog had descended at one end of The Valley soon after kick-off during a game against Chelsea. 'The fog began to thicken rapidly at the far end, rolling steadily towards me,' he wrote. 'The referee stopped the game, and then, as visibility became clearer, restarted it. We were on top at this time, and I saw fewer and fewer figures as we attacked steadily.' The game had gone unusually silent but Bartram remained at his post, peering into the thickening fog from the edge of the penalty area. 'After a long time, a figure loomed out of the curtain of fog in front of me. It was a policeman. "What on earth are you doing here?" he gasped. "The game was stopped a quarter of an hour ago." '

Employing a similar single-mindedness throughout his career, Bartram made a record 579 first team appearances for the Addicks, and his memory was honoured in 1997 when a road next to The Valley was renamed Sam Bartram Close. Charlton were relegated to Division 2 the same year that Bartram retired, and the team from the pre-war suburbs entered a slough of slow decay that would only come to a head 30 years later.

Heroes came and went, even during the leaner times. Derek Hales, terrifyingly bearded, scored a record 168 goals in 368 games during the 1970s and early 1980s. Hales enjoyed a successful period in tandem with Mike Flanagan, slightly further down the list with 120 goals, with whom he famously traded punches during a match at The Valley in January 1979.

In 1982 Charlton surprised even themselves by signing former European Footballer of the Year Allan Simonsen from Barcelona. At the time the club was in Division 2, deep in debt and inhabiting a stadium not renovated since the good times before the war. It would prove a catalyst for the most troubled period in the Addicks' history.

Twelve months later Charlton were famously five minutes away from going into receivership. In 1985 chairman John Fryer led the exodus from the crumbling Valley, relocating the club across London to Selhurst Park.

Seven years of a vagrant existence followed, culminating in the extraordinary success of the 'Back to The Valley' campaign, a supporter-led movement to raise funds to buy and renovate the club's home ground. In 1992, after years of concerted action by volunteers and local people – and continual updates in the press on the height of the weeds growing on the Valley pitch – Charlton Athletic moved back to its historical home.

Neatly rounding off 70 years of boom and bust since the dawn of its last new era, the club is currently enjoying its most successful period since the reign of Jimmy Seed, finishing ninth in the Premiership in 2001 under the guidance of Alan Curbishley, who was in sole managerial charge from 1995 until 2006.

Sir Bobby Charlton

Before the emergence of David **Beckham** and his squadron of dedicated brand managers, Bobby Charlton was probably the most famous British footballer of all time. His playing career was incomparably successful: League championship winner with Manchester United three times, a World Cup winner in 1966, European Footballer of the Year the same season, a key member of the first English side to lift the Champions' Cup and record goalscorer for England with 49 in 106 games.

Charlton was a different type of player from Beckham in other ways. Equally feted for his gentlemanly demeanour (he was rarely booked and never sent off in his career) and reputation for diffident Englishness, during the 1960s Charlton's name was said to have become a byword for courteous good sportsmanship, its mere mention drawing back-slapping hospitality in obscure Mexican haciendas and remote Inuit fishing communities.

Whatever the truth of this, Charlton was certainly a great player and a very modest man. Raised in Ashington, he and his brother Jack were, according to folklore at least, coached by their mother, Cissie – a relative of Jackie **Milburn** – before Bobby, always the more talented of the two, was spotted by Manchester United scouts. He signed for United in

1954 and stayed at the club for his entire playing career of 754 appearances and 247 goals. Part of the Championship-winning team of 1957, Charlton was injured in the **Munich aircrash** in 1958, surviving after being thrown 40 yards clear of the wreckage. Charlton was traumatized by the crash and later revealed that it took him several years to recover his confidence away from the football pitch. Decades later the memory of that tragedy still moves this always emotional man to tears and may have explained a reserve that led some fellow pros to accuse him of being lugubrious.

He began his career at United playing on the wing, but matured into a peerless forward playmaker. His most obvious attributes were his balance and his shooting power with both feet, something he had worked on for hours as a boy. Charlton wore the number 9 but didn't play as a centre-forward, dropping deep instead to 'scheme' from a position behind a more physical front player. It was a style copied from one of his idols, Alfredo Di Stefano. A dignified, prematurely aged figure with a legendary scrape-over hairstyle the strands of which trailed behind him when he was in full flight like the tail of a kite, Charlton was nevertheless a graceful and dynamic presence on the field.

Charlton retired from playing in 1973. A lifelong smoker he would later say that the thing he missed most was lying in bed on Saturday morning, lighting up a cigarette and thinking about that after-noon's game.

He managed Preston North End for a while with no great distinction and was caretaker-manager at Wigan briefly before returning to Old Trafford as a board member and developing an ambassadorial presence promoting foot-ball and Manchester United around the world.

Jack Charlton

Jack Charlton was born in Ashington, Northumberland, on 8 May 1935. At that time his hometown was usually described as 'the world's biggest coal mine'. Jack's father Robert spent his working life down the pit and this was the future mapped out for his eldest son. After just a day at the coalface, however, Jack turned his back on mining. He applied for a job with the police, but before he could report for duty Leeds United signed him. The news came as a surprise to many people in Ashington, not least the Charltons' football-mad mother, Cissie. She regarded Jack's abili-ties as so limited that when the scout from Elland Road knocked on the door and asked to speak to him she assumed he had got the wrong house.

Initially Jack's experiences at Leeds seemed to bear out his mother's judge-ment. He signed professional forms in 1952 and for the next eight years was in and out of the first team, all the while upsetting management and colleagues with his forthright manner ('Jack wasn't always right but he was never wrong,' team-mate Johnny **Giles** would later observe).

It was not until Don **Revie** became manager at Elland Road in 1961 that Charlton's career really began. Encour-aged by the new boss, the raw and ill-disciplined centre-half began to apply his natural intelligence and resourcefulness to the game. By identifying his strengths and acknowledging his limitations he transformed himself into a defender of the highest calibre. In all 'The Giraffe' played 773 times for Leeds, scoring an impressive 96 goals, most of them headed in from corners while standing on or near the goal-line.

In 1965, at the age of 30, Jack won the first of his 35 England caps. He quickly established himself as first-choice partner for the elegant Bobby **Moore** and was a member of England's 1966 World Cup winning team. Typically his celebrations after that victory ended with him sleeping on the sofa of a total stranger he had met in a pub.

As a player Jack had a reputation for toughness. On a north-east television programme in 1970 he told an interviewer, 'I have a little book with players' names in it. If I get a chance to do them I will.' It was said in good humour, but many, including the FA, took it seriously. Charlton was banned from playing for England, a meaningless punishment as it happened since he had announced his international retirement after that year's World Cup.

After Charlton quit playing in 1973 he applied his uncompromising attitude to the management of Middlesbrough, who promptly won the Division 2 championship and established themselves in the top division. He went on to manage Sheffield Wednesday, briefly returned to Ayresome Park as caretaker boss and then had a short unhappy spell in charge of the club he had supported since boyhood, Newcastle United. In February 1986 he was surprisingly appointed manager of the Republic of Ireland. He took the Irish to their first major tournament, the 1988 European Championships, where they defeated England and narrowly missed out on qualification to the knock-out stages. In the 1990 World Cup the Irish did even better, reaching the quarter-finals. Four years later in the USA they beat Italy in the group stage. On returning to Ireland Charlton was awarded the freedom of Dublin and a year later retired.

Some Irish fans and reporters felt Charlton didn't get the best out of a talented bunch of players (he seemed particularly reluctant to utilize the talents of the nation's world-class midfielder, Liam Brady) and rebelled against the ball-over-the-top football – based on his own hatred as a defender of having to play facing his own goal – his side employed. But many more were charmed by Big Jack's easy manner, openness and self-deprecating humour – not a sentence anybody would have anticipated writing in the 1960s or 1970s.

Jack and Bobby were England's greatest-ever football brothers, but when their playing days were over the two men fell out over the latter's treatment of their mother. 'Our kid was the better footballer, but I am the better bloke' was how Jack Charlton summed up the situation. It is testimony to how public perceptions of the two men have changed since their playing days that you would find few people in the British Isles who would disagree with Big Jack's assessment.

Chelsea

Chelsea Football Club was formed as a means of filling the vacant Stamford Bridge athletics stadium, left empty in 1904 after Fulham refused to take up an offer to play their home games there. With stadium owner H. A. 'Gus' Mears attracted by the financial rewards of a sporting venue, Stamford Bridge – host to track and field events and later greyhound racing, speedway and American Football – became the home of Chelsea FC. Long before the current Chelsea Village complex took shape (concept: a high-end global branded leisure experience; reality: various empty restaurants a hundred yards off the wrong end of the King's Road), Chelsea was already an entrepreneurial concern. The club originally mooted as London FC has always been a glitzy affair, one whose achievements have not always matched the ambitions of its owners, the celebrity of its fans or the cachet of its post code.

Chelsea entered the Football League in 1905 and immediately won promotion from Division 2. The 'Pensioners' wasted no time in acquiring established players from other clubs, including legendary 23-stone England goalkeeper William 'Fatty' Foulke, who – among a great many other things – once famously polished off all 11 of his team-mates' breakfasts after arriving early in the team hotel dining room. Chelsea veered between divisions 1 and 2 for the next 50 years without ever winning anything, despite sparking a post-war transfer boom in 1945 by signing Tommy **Lawton** for a record £11,500.

It took the appointment of Ted Drake as manager in 1952 for the club to produce its first successful team. Dubbed 'Drake's Ducklings', a young Chelsea side surprised everybody by winning the title just two years after finishing 19th in Division 1. However, the Ducklings couldn't repeat their success; they finished 16th the following season and seven years later Chelsea were back in Division 2.

Moderate success followed under the guidance of Tommy Docherty (a League Cup triumph in 1965) and then Dave Sexton, whose genre-defining 1970s King's Road Swingers won the FA Cup in 1970 and the European Cup Winners' Cup a year later. In many ways the 1970 FA Cup Final crystallized the image of Chelsea as southern stylists pitted against their northern antithesis in Don **Revie**'s grimly pragmatic Leeds United. Chelsea didn't shrink from the confrontation and the Final is duly remembered as one of the most violent in the history of the competition.

For the next 20 years Chelsea went into decline both on and off the pitch.

Between 1976 and 1989 the club spent eight seasons outside the top flight, winning Division 2 in 1984 and 1989. Blues teams of this era tended to feature a series of hardmen and hotheads, bearing the chalice passed down by the archetypal Ron 'Chopper' Harris. The mountainous Micky Droy – who once dragged a posse of invading Chelsea fans off the pitch during a League game at Luton – was succeeded by the likes of Vinnie Jones, David Speedie and Dennis Wise, while off the field Chelsea fans – most notoriously in the case of the Chelsea Headhunters 'firm' – acquired a dismal reputation for thuggery.

In 1992 Chelsea were founder members of the Premier League. The 14 years since the creation of a TV-cash-fuelled elite have seen an upsurge in the club's fortunes. Crucially Ken Bates – an irritating, outspoken presence and the definitive 'personality' chairman – finally acquired the freehold to Stamford Bridge after a long-running battle with a now-defunct property company. And Chelsea went back to their roots: signing ready-made stars, notably in the shape of record £15 million signing Jimmy Floyd Hasselbaink and the man recently voted Chelsea's greatest-ever player in a club poll, the Sardinian Gianfranco Zola. The club mutated into the broad-based Chelsea Village plc, which pursued a leisure-based domination of west London and, perhaps, Western Europe through a hotchpotch of hotels, restaurants, finan-cial services and levels of debt as high as £100 million. At the same time Chelsea enjoyed a highly successful period on the field, with FA Cup wins in 1997 and 2000, a Cup-Winners' Cup in 1998 and various forays into the Champions' League.

In 2003 Chelsea Village plc was bought outright by the Russian billionaire oil magnate Roman Abramovich. A period of scarcely credible spending on players followed: £210m in two years, under Italian manager Claudio Ranieri, then his Portuguese successor, José **Mourinho**. Abramovich's vast wealth has almost single-handedly sustained a European transfer market feeling the chill after the fall in TV rights revenues. Mourinho's expensive team won the Premiership in 2005 and 2006, but the longevity of its Russian owner's interest is a matter that remains to be seen.

In a decade during which the club has transformed itself into a corporate leisure entity listing football as 'one of its activities', fielded a first XI without a single English player, acted as a magnet for celebrity hangers-on and the casual consumer, and now become a billionaire's plaything, Chelsea have only been doing what comes naturally. Gus Mears's Pensioners are a London enterprise, a speculative operation in a city grown out of commerce. In a sense the game is only just catching up with them.

Cheltenham Town

After the discovery of the local springs, Cheltenham developed from an obscure Cotswolds village to a fashionable 18th-century spa town, visited by George III, Samuel Johnson and Handel, possibly all at the same time. Like its football team over 200 years later, the town – home most famously of late to the government's GCHQ spying headquarters – recovered from its brief period of excitement to become a solid if unspectacular local middleweight. Formed in 1892, it took Cheltenham Town four decades to gather the confidence to venture out of local amateur football. Having done so, progress came swiftly. The Robins moved into their current Whaddon Road ground and breezed through the Birmingham Combination, before begin-

ning their long association with the Southern League in 1935.

Such progress was reflected in the 1933–34 FA Cup second round when Cheltenham claimed a League scalp, Carlisle United, for the first and only time. A record attendance of 10,389 witnessed the subsequent third round 3–1 defeat to Blackpool, whose players enjoyed the advantage of being able to stay in bed until 11am on the day of the game, while several of the home team were putting in half a shift at the day job.

For much of the next 40 years the Robins displayed an uncanny ability to compete at the top level of non-League football and yet achieve relatively little. There were neither championships nor FA Cup glory, although Arch Anderson's Scottish-influenced side of the 1950s flirted with the Southern League title. Manager Tommy Cavanagh set new standards, albeit low ones, in 1961 when he was dismissed during a game for using offensive language. Fortunes ebbed and flowed through the 1970s and 1980s, and the club's luck reached a new low when non-League restructuring meant the Robins were effectively relegated twice in four seasons.

After more than 100 years of waiting, Cheltenham's own golden age finally arrived with the managerial appointment of 32-year-old Steve Cotterill in January 1997. The Cheltenham-born boss successfully rescued a faltering Southern League promotion campaign by getting his players to perform above their natural level with organized and determined displays – a constant feature of the next five years.

Tipped to struggle on their return to the Conference, Cheltenham ended 1997–98 as runners-up to Halifax Town. But the club's greatest day thus far was reserved for a 1–0 win over Southport in the FA Trophy final, with 18,000 Cheltonians making the journey to Wembley. Although regarded as a hotbed of horse racing rather than football, Cheltenham was one of the largest towns outside the Football League and relatively free of competition from the professional game. So with the club finally making waves, the locals were quick to respond.

Backed by an upsurge in attendances, Cheltenham went one better in 1998–99, claiming the Conference championship and promotion to the Football League. Significantly, the Robins held their nerve against fellow title contenders, not least when a 90th-minute equalizer and injury-time winner secured all three points at league leaders Rushden & Diamonds during the run-in. The upward curve continued into Division 3 with a 3–1 victory over Rushden in the 2001–02 play-off final. But Cotterill's departure in May 2002, for Stoke City, left a gap that the club struggled to fill and Cheltenham were relegated from Division 2 12 months later. They were promoted to League One via the play-offs in 2006.

Chester City

Chester City are one of a handful of current League clubs to have never played at Wembley. The closest they got was an extraordinary run to the semi-finals of the League Cup in 1974–75, which ended with a 5–4 aggregate semi-final defeat to Aston Villa and included a 3–0 win over Leeds, who were to be European Cup finalists later that season. The team – featuring veteran Welsh striker Derek Draper, Michael **Owen**'s father, Terry, in midfield and a fine young goalkeeper, the splendidly named Grenville Millington – were promoted from Division 4 the same year.

The Leeds match was not, however, voted Chester's greatest moment in a fans' poll a few years ago, which also overlooked games from the 1964–65 season when the club scored 119 goals (a total not matched by any League team since). Instead, the popular vote went to a 2–2 draw at Wrexham in 1995, a match Chester finished with nine men. The Chester–Wrexham rivalry is the only international derby in the Football League – and one of the most keenly felt. Nevertheless, numerous footballers from Wales have turned out for the club, the most capped being Bill Lewis in the 1890s. Chester have also won the Welsh Cup three times, the last in 1946, 15 years after they entered the Football League.

Another Welshman, Ian **Rush**, is the club's most famous player, though he left for Liverpool aged only 18 in 1980, having scored 14 goals in 33 games. The construction of an ugly new main stand the year before Rush's departure plunged Chester into heavy debt. Long-serving chairman Reg Rowlands, who had been involved with the club since 1945, departed shortly afterwards and Chester passed through the hands of several property developer owners, one of whom added 'City' to the club name, in 1983. Each appeared to think that the club's financial woes could be solved by either selling the 20,000 capacity Sealand Road, Chester's home since 1906, or arranging to become a feeder club for a bigger neighbour. (In the 1960s, the club had rejected an approach from one of Britain's wealthiest landowners, the Duke of Westminster, whose family seat is just outside the city. The Duke's main condition was that the team switched from their blue and white strip to his family colours of gold and green.)

Sealand Road was finally knocked down in 1990; after two years of groundsharing at Macclesfield, the club returned home to the Deva Stadium. Promoted and relegated twice in just over a decade, Chester reached crisis point under the chairmanship of Mark Guterman in 1998. They owed a six-figure sum to creditors including the Inland Revenue and the city council, and manager Kevin Ratcliffe had to use his own bank account to pay the water rates after the water authority threatened to disconnect the supply. The club went into administration two months later.

Supporters had high hopes of American Terry Smith when he took over in the summer of 1999. But Ratcliffe resigned after three games of the following season, unable to work with the eccentric chairman. Smith, also owner of the Manchester Spartans gridiron team, made himself manager and introduced captains for defence, midfield and forwards. He also insisted that the team says the Lord's Prayer before home games. With the team stuck at the bottom of Division 3, having won just four of their 24 League games, Smith conceded that he needed help from someone who knew about football. Ian Atkins, brought in as 'coaching director' in January 1999, spurred a revival but Chester were still relegated to the Conference on goal difference.

Mark Wright took Chester back into the Football League in 2003–04 but resigned in the summer after a series of disagreements with the chairman Steve Vaughan. Wright returned in 2006 after Ian Rush and Keith Curle had both had unsuccessful spells in charge.

Chesterfield

The fourth-oldest football club in Britain, Chesterfield FC traces its roots back to 19 October 1867, when a motion was agreed to found a football team at a meeting of the Chesterfield Cricket Club at the County Hotel in Saltergate. A year later, wearing blue shirts and white shorts (as worn ever since except for during the 1890–91, season when the players turned out in Union Jack shirts), the team from the self-styled Capital of North Derbyshire played and lost its first-ever game against the Garrick Club of Sheffield.

By 1872 the Sheffield FA had outlawed catching the ball, but early games were still rough 14-a-side affairs, with Chesterfield's star performer Tommy Bishop – a tobacconist by trade – earning a reputation as the finest local player of his era. The club quickly became known as 'The Blues' or 'The Spireites', after the town's distinctive wonky parish church spire, which in 1994 earned the town membership of the Association of Twisted Spires of Europe.

In 1881 Chesterfield saw the first of its many battles with extinction, as the club was dissolved and then reformed a year later as Chesterfield Town, under which name it played its first game in the Football League in 1899. Local legend-in-the-making Herbert Munday scored the winner against Woolwich Arsenal. By 1915 they were back in liquidation again, only to rise from the ashes as Chesterfield Town FC under the guidance of a local restaurateur called O. W. Everest. Unfortunately Everest's club was disbanded two years later after an illegal-payments scandal, only for yet another alias – Chesterfield Municipal Football Club – to spring up in 1919 under the aegis of the local council, in which guise the club joined the newly formed Division 3 (North) in 1921.

Nine years later the team completed a run of scoring in 46 consecutive League matches – a record broken by Arsenal in 2003 – and in 1931 Chesterfield won the Division 3 (North) title, setting in motion a steady oscillation between divisions 2, 3 and 4.

During the 1940s Chesterfield went

international, loaning a set of shirts to the hard-pressed Ajax of Amsterdam in 1946 and seeing its plans to tour Brazil thwarted by FA regulations in 1948. Gordon **Banks** subsequently emerged as Chesterfield's first and only real star player, the future World Cup winner ending local favourite Ron Powell's run of 284 consecutive League games when he made his debut in 1958. In 1981 the club won its most significant trophy to date, the Anglo-Scottish Cup – this despite a looming financial crisis that would see Chesterfield rescued from closure in 1983 by two local business-men. Two years later they completed yet another remarkable rise from the treatment table by becoming champions of Division 4.

Since then a series of notable Cup successes have made headlines, including the 4–4 League Cup draw at Anfield against Liverpool in 1992 – which inspired Chesterfield player Dave Lancaster to comment, 'We thought there'd be eight goals in it, but we didn't think we'd get four of them' – a 2–0 Wembley play-off victory against Bury in 1995, and the gravity-defying Cup run of 1997, when the Spireites drew 3–3 with Premiership Middlesbrough in the semi-finals of the FA Cup before losing narrowly in the replay.

However, promotion to Division 2 in 2001 was overshadowed by off-field trauma as hundreds of thousands of pounds vanished from the club's coffers. True to Chesterfield's municipal roots, a fans' consortium calling itself the Chester-field Football Supporters' Society assumed control of the club, helping to stabilize off-field matters as the team renewed its long-standing struggle with fellow inhabitants of the lower half of League One.

Brian Clough

During his garrulous heyday in the 1970s Brian Clough was commonly compared to Muhammad Ali. The manager who led Derby County to a League championship and then, even more improbably, Nottingham Forest to the title and back-to-back European Cup triumphs had a similarly high opinion of himself and was not afraid to voice it.

Clough signed for Middlesbrough – his hometown club – in 1955. As centre-forward his scoring record for Boro was extraordinary. During his five full seasons in the first team his lowest tally was 36; he scored a total of 197 goals in 213 games. Yet he was never popular with his team-mates (many of whom seemed to him more interested in gambling than in winning matches), who accused him of being arrogant, scathing and confron-tational – charges that would follow him for most of his life.

When Clough was appointed team captain the rest of the team sent a letter to the board of directors asking for the decision to be reversed.

It was the final straw. He demanded a transfer and was sold to Sunderland for £55,000. At Roker Park he hit 63 goals in 74 appearances, before a collision with Bury goalkeeper Chris Harker smashed the cruciate ligaments in his knee. He struggled gamely to recover. But though 20,000 turned out at Roker Park to watch his comeback for the reserves he made only three more appearances for the first team before being forced to quit in 1964, aged 29.

The pain and the bitter disappointment led Clough into a prolonged bout of drinking. He pulled out of it when Sunder-land offered him the job of youth team coach, but alcohol would continue to play a large and ultimately destructive part in his life.

At Middlesbrough, Clough had become good friends with the goalkeeper Peter Taylor, a shrewd tactician. The two men joined up when Clough was offered the job of managing fourth-division Hartlepool United. The next stop for Clough and Taylor was the Baseball Ground, Derby. The Rams had once been a dominant force in English football and under Clough they became so again. They won promotion to the top flight in 1969 and took the League title three years later.

By now Clough had developed into a TV personality. He appeared on chat shows, boasting shamelessly and hectoring anybody who had the temerity to disagree with him. He became one of the most imitated men in the country. Clough left the Baseball Ground after a row with chairman Sam Longston. He resurfaced briefly at Brighton & Hove Albion before accepting the job of taking over from Don **Revie** at Leeds United.

Clough's spell at Elland Road was a disaster. As manager of Derby he had frequently criticized Leeds, then England's top club side, for their gamesmanship. Clough believed in good sportsmanship and good football. His teams always had excellent disciplinary records, never argued with referees and never sought illegal advantage.

On his first day at the Yorkshire club he told a dressing room full of established international stars, 'You lot have won everything going, but as far as I'm concerned you can chuck all your medals in the bin because you only got them by cheating.' As an opening address it made a good resignation speech. Forty-four days later he was sacked.

Taylor had not accompanied Clough to Leeds but he joined him at the City Ground, Nottingham, where the pair masterminded one of the most extraordinary achievements in the history of British football turning an unfashionable provincial team with average attendances of 25,000 into the champions of Europe.

In the mid-1980s Clough and Taylor fell out irreparably and bitterly. The former goalkeeper returned, unsuccessfully, to Derby County. Clough carried on at Forest but alcoholism was starting to skew his judgement. In 1989 he was fined for punching two fans who had invaded the pitch and shortly afterwards unproven allegations started to surface about him taking kick-backs on transfer deals. Forest went in to steady decline and at the end of Clough's final season in charge they were relegated.

Eccentric, funny, cruel, clever, a bully and a braggart, Clough – who died in 2004 – was at once brilliant and flawed. In later life he was asked what he would want people to say about him after he died. 'That I contributed' was his unexpectedly modest reply.

club colours

In the early days of professional football, clubs didn't wear specific colours, players instead turning out in whatever strip happened to be available. Hooped jerseys were popular initially but, with a few exceptions, came to be associated mainly with rugby; stripes have been tried by a majority of current English League clubs at some point, nearly always in white and one other colour, though Blackpool briefly turned out in a dazzling combination of red, blue and yellow.

When teams were required to adopt standard colours in 1891 many chose those of the county or municipality (blue and yellow in the case of Leeds, claret and amber for Bradford City). A year earlier it had been decreed that the home team should change in the event of a colour clash with their opponents – 30 years later this was altered to the away team. Goalkeepers were not required to wear a different colour shirt from their team-mates until 1909 and green didn't become standard for several years after that. Most teams tried a variety of combinations before setting on the colours which they are now known by. Everton had worn black shirts with a red sash before joining the inaugural Football League in 1888 and then spent a few seasons in red shirts with blue shorts. Liverpool wore blue and white halves in their first league season, switching to red only in the early 1900s after Everton had adopted their familiar blue. In 1903–04, and occasionally after that, the Scotland national team ditched their navy blue shirts for primrose and white hoops, the racing colours of Scottish FA honorary president Lord Roseberry.

Few teams wore mauve, which was to be a relatively popular colour in European football, as the dye was expensive. Black was not allowed from the end of the 19th century until 1992, when Premiership referees were given green shirts, nor brown (unless on a halved shirt with another colour) because it would be hard to distinguish opponents on muddy pitches. Claret and light blue was a combination largely unique to England, at least six other League clubs at some point adopting the kit first worn by Aston Villa (the equivalent shirt in Italy is the red and blue halves worn by Genoa, the most successful club before the First World War). Norwich City are a rare case of a club choosing colours to match a nickname: already known as the Canaries owing to the city's fame as a centre for bird-breeding, they switched to the appropriate strip of yellow and green in 1907.

Football shirts are now marketed as leisurewear and clubs change their kit designs regularly, but in modern times only a few have altered their basic colours. Leeds switched from blue and yellow to all-white in the early 1960s in imitation of Real Madrid; Watford adopted yellow and black in 1959 having played in a variety of strips before then, including turquoise; Oldham chairman Ken Bates changed their blue shirts with white shorts to orange and blue in 1965 – the club switched back a decade later. Others have made a significant small alteration: Liverpool began to wear red shorts rather than white only in 1965 but have kept them ever since; Coventry went from blue and white stripes to all sky blue under Jimmy **Hill**'s management in 1962 (though they had briefly returned to stripes when winning the FA Cup in 1987); Millwall and Brighton dallied briefly with striped shorts.

Clubs have often used distinctive terms to describe their shirt colour, thus Blackpool play in 'tangerine', Wolves in 'old gold', non-League Sutton United's yellow and brown combination is officially 'amber and chocolate', Chelsea insisted that their pale green away strip of the late 1980s was 'jade'. International team colours have been a popular second choice strip since the 1970s: Newcastle were the first to wear Brazil's yellow shirts with sky blue shorts; Derby likewise borrowed Argentina's sky-blue and white stripes, later worn as a first-choice kit by Stockport. In recent years some clubs have used their original colours as change strips, Portsmouth appearing in the pink shirts they'd worn before the First World War, while Manchester United reverted briefly to the yellow and green halves of their first incarnation, Newton Heath.

club nicknames

British club nicknames fall into five broad categories: colours (for those whose imagination has stretched no further than The Blues); animals (especially birds); the town's traditional industry (The Hatters, The Silkmen, The Railwaymen); local landmarks (The Spireites, The Cottagers); and the endlessly debated but ultimately obscure (The Baggies, Pompey). Thankfully football has been largely immune to the American-inspired rebranding efforts that have infected rugby league and minor sports in Britain (giving us the Halifax Blue Sox and the Basingstoke Bison). A glance through the League's nicknames is still a pretty reliable guide to 19th-century industrial England, when you could safely assume chairs came from Wycombe, saddles from Walsall and shoes from Northampton.

From the 1960s some clubs began to discard nicknames that didn't convey the right kind of image, notably Chelsea (formerly The Pensioners, now The Blues), Crystal Palace (The Glaziers now the Eagles) and Reading (The Biscuitmen now the Royals). Bristol Rovers are officially known as The Pirates, but more commonly as The Gas, after the gasworks next to their former ground at Eastville. Everton and Manchester City fans are these days only reluctant users of their given names, Toffees and Citizens respectively. Swansea City, officially The Swans, have also adopted the town's nickname of The Jacks, allegedly after the 1930s lifesaving exploits in Swansea docks of a black retriever called Jack. Charlton have been the least decisive nickname club in the league, flirting with The Robins, The Valiants and The Addicks (or even Haddicks).

More recently a few clubs have adopted more snazzy, go-getting names, such as QPR's Superhoops, Wimbledon's Crazy Gang and Livingston's lamentable 'Livi Lions'. Sunderland, formerly (though not very popularly) the Rokerites, decided they needed to be known as the Black Cats after leaving Roker Park in 1997. Scotland has its own tradition of colourful nicknames, most attached to modest clubs such as Arbroath (The Red Lichties), Forfar (The Loons) or Montrose (The Gable Endies). In fact it's a handy rule of thumb that the bigger the club, the less likely it is to have an intriguing or unusual name. Notable exceptions outside Britain include Real Madrid (The Meringues) and Juventus (The Old Lady).

club origins

The great wave of football enthusiasm that swept through Britain in the last 30 years of the 19th century latched on to all kinds of existing institutions for the administrative means and psychological bonds required to sustain a successful (or at least enduring) club. Churches saw benefits for themselves and for potentially delinquent youths in running organized sport, and religious institutions of one kind or another were responsible for setting up clubs such as Fulham, Everton, QPR, Southampton, Aston Villa, Bolton and Burnley. Others grew out of local industries, notably Coventry (the Singer bicycle factory), West Ham (a paternal initiative of the Thames Ironworks) and Arsenal, where migrant workers from the north and Midlands at the Woolwich Arsenal took the lead, a fact which may have influenced the club in its early adoption of professionalism compared with its southern neighbours.

Cricket clubs looking for winter recreation were another common starting point (Sheffield Wednesday, Derby, Preston and West Brom began this way), as were old boys' associations and looser collections of former schoolmates. Blackburn and Tottenham both owed something to such school ties, as did Leicester City, whose Wyggeston Boys Grammar founders are regrettably referred to today as Old Wyggestonians, whereas older reference books insist on Old Wigglestonians. Perhaps surprisingly, two of the most successful foundations in English football – Liverpool and Chelsea – came about simply because circumstances left a large ground with no club to fill it (Everton having decamped from Anfield, Fulham declining to make Stamford Bridge their home).

One kind of professional club not found in England is those either explicitly founded to represent a political, national or ethnic outlook, or those which quickly came to do so. In Scotland Celtic and Hibernian could be said to have emerged and grown in this way, as have Athletic Bilbao in Spain's Basque country, AEK Athens (the 'Athletic Union of Constantinople', founded by Greek refugees from Turkey in the 1920s) and perhaps even Internazionale, whose split from Milan came about because of different attitudes to using foreigners in the team. Football in the US has a long tradition of 'ethnic' clubs (from Scots via Italians to central Americans), as does Australia (notably Greek, Italian, Hungarian, Serb/Croatian and Jewish).

Clyde

The supporters of Clyde became known as the Gypsy Army in recent years as the club they follow travelled the West of Scotland in search of a home. Their first flit came back in 1897, 20 years after they started playing at Barrowfield Park, and took them to Shawfield Stadium, in Glasgow. There they stayed for 87 years, during which time they won the Scottish Cup three times, in 1955 and 1958 (with

teams featuring their most-capped player, Tommy Ring) and 1939, when the onset of the Second World War ensured a six-year grip on the trophy that remains a record.

The club by the River Clyde were relegated from Division 1 five times after the war but bounced straight back on each occasion. When Scottish football was reorganized with the creation of the Premier League in 1974–75, however, they fell into the second tier and have not returned to the top level. With attendances taking a dive the directors looked into relocating in East Kilbride and Hamilton. A takeover bid for that town's existing club, Hamilton Academical, was also proposed, but none of these schemes bore fruit and in 1986 they were forced out of Shawfield, a stadium they did not own and that was used principally for greyhound racing.

Thus began their nomadic wanderings, first to Firhill, shared with Partick Thistle for five years. Next stop was Douglas Park, Hamilton, where their landlords were the club they had tried to acquire in the 1980s. In 1994 the long-term aim of relocation was met. Cumbernauld, a new town, seemed the perfect new home. It boasted a large and growing population with no senior club to follow and in Broadwood Stadium had a modern ground with 8,000 seats.

Cumbernauld has never fully adopted its club, however, and Clyde were perilously close to relegation to Division 3 in 1998, a fate that could have brought dire consequences for the club. They rallied, however, and were promoted in 2000, finishing second in 2003 and 2004.

One area in which they are all but invincible is the matchday programme. Their publication dominates the annual awards with Old Firm-like predictability. They also possess one of the most impenetrable official nicknames in British football. Nobody is quite sure why they are known as the Bully Wee. Not even the Gypsy Army.

Colchester United

The sacking of Mike Walker on 1 November 1987, just days before he received the Division 4 Manager of the Month award for October, was the beginning of the end of the first phase of Colchester United's existence. Walker left to take Norwich City into Europe, United plummeted into the Conference within two and a half years.

Colchester is Britain's oldest recorded town but its professional football club is relatively young, founded only in 1937. The U's had been in the League for 40 years by the time of their sudden collapse, which can be largely credited to its takeover in May 1985 by millionaire businessman Jonathan Crisp at a time when the club were £140,000 in debt. He brought in comedian Frank Carson as a director in 1986 and Roger Brown, a former Fulham centre-half, was installed as Walker's replacement. When Brown left after an 8–0 defeat to Orient in 1988, the damage had been done. Third from bottom that year, Colchester dropped out of the League the following season. After six managers in six years, Crisp left, having sold the ground to the local council and increased the debt to well over £1 million.

Crisp's reign was a far cry from the giant-killing days for which Colchester are most commonly renowned. In 1947–48, just ten years after the establishment of the club, Colchester became the first non-League side in the modern history of the FA Cup to beat a Division 1 team – Huddersfield the victims of a shock 1–0 defeat at Layer Road in the third round. A still unbeaten attendance of 19,072 saw the visit of Reading in round one the next year, followed in 1950 by election to Football League Division 3 (South).

Colchester's most famous moment occurred in February 1971. In the fifth round of the FA Cup 16,000-plus squeezed in to Layer Road to see former England striker Ray Crawford score twice as Don **Revie**'s Leeds were beaten 3–2, making the U's only the second team from the fourth level ever to reach the last eight of the competition. They spent the next decade and a half as a steady lower-division club with two promotions and relegations, though crowds fell away as some locals were lured by the success of nearby Ipswich (others still travel to London, particularly West Ham, for their live football).

The club were to be rejuvenated after dropping out of the League in 1990. In the first of two successful seasons in the Conference, Ian Atkins took the U's to within a couple of points of the title. His successor, player-manager Roy McDonough, led a full-time professional but financially deprived club to the top of a league in which the considerably richer Wycombe Wanderers had become a force under Martin O'Neill. A last-minute drop-kick winner from 90 yards by U's goalkeeper, Scott Barratt, at Wycombe's Adams Park was a key moment in a season in which Colchester won the title on goal difference. The double was sealed by their first-ever visit to Wembley in the FA Trophy final. They would return to Wembley twice more within the decade.

The second phase of United's existence finds them established as a League One club. It took six seasons back in the bottom division to gain promotion through the play-offs. After eight seasons in the third level, with attendances more than doubled from their 1980s nadir, they were promoted to the Championship in

2006. His name is still mud, but perhaps Crisp did Colchester a favour after all.

commemorative games

The childish delight of picking teams to represent supranational regions, combined with the self-importance of many governing bodies, made the commemorative international match a regular and often popular occurrence in the days before football's global TV exposure. One of the first such occasions was the celebration of the FA's 50th anniversary in 1938, when England beat a Europe XI (managed by Italy's World Cup-winning coach Vittorio Pozzo) 3–0 at Highbury. After the war the reasons to celebrate mushroomed, beginning with unofficial 'victory internationals' between the home nations and their wartime allies (and, less logically, Switzerland).

In 1947, 137,000 turned up at Hampden to rejoice in the return of the British countries to FIFA (Great Britain beat Europe 6–1), while similar events followed for the 90th anniversary of the FA (4–4 v the Rest of Europe in 1953) and most famously for its 100th birthday in 1963, when England beat a genuinely star-laden World XI 2–1 at Wembley. For a while internationals were constantly in demand for even apparently minor occasions. Portuguese star Eusébio, for example, spent much of the 1960s and early 1970s gamely trekking from the 75th anniversary celebrations for the Danish FA (Scandinavia 2, Rest of Europe 4), to Ricardo Zamora's 65th birthday (Spain 0, World XI 3) to Uwe Seeler's farewell match (Hamburg 3, Europe XI 7).

Even in the 1970s there was room for oddities such as The Six v The Three to mark the entry of Britain, Ireland and Denmark to the EEC in 1973 and the tournament involving England, Brazil and Italy for the US bicentenary in 1976. Sometimes such matches threw up tantalizing line-ups – Johan Cruyff and Gunter Netzer both scored for a World XI against Red Star Belgrade in 1972. More often they produced incongruous combinations, such as the World XI that faced Real Madrid in 1967 featuring AC Milan's Gianni Rivera, Kurt Hamrin and the ubiquitious Eusébio, alongside Arsenal centre-half Ian Ure. By the 1980s, the days when you could get someone of the calibre of Real Madrid and France striker Raymond Kopa to show up for the 75th anniversary of the Irish FA were disappearing, even though 61,000 saw a Football League XI beat the Rest of the World 2–0 during the League's ineptly planned centenary celebrations in 1988.

These days FIFA tends to sanction world teams for charitable purposes (although they loyally raised teams to mark FA anniversaries in Russia, Turkey and Italy in the 1990s) and the participants are more likely to be veterans than the preciously guarded leading lights of Europe's top clubs. When the EU expanded again in 2004, no one suggested squeezing a match between The Ten and The Fifteen into the calendar – and they would have got a pretty dusty reaction if they had.

commentators

Today's match commentators are called John Motson or Alan Green. The first ever commentator on a live football match had a proper name: Captain Henry Blythe Thornhill Wakelam. Captain Wakelam took the helm on BBC radio on the afternoon of 22 January 1927 for the game between Arsenal and Sheffield United. Punctuating his distinct military description of events on the pitch was a colleague in the same room piping 'Square 1 . . . Square 3 . . .' and so on, every few seconds. Although the Captain sounds ever so slightly huffy at these interruptions, they were felt necessary at the time so that listeners could refer to their grid – printed in the *Radio Times* – to discover which area of the pitch the ball had arrived in.

While Thornhill Wakelam's delivery sounds like a parody to our sophisticated modern ears, he was the first of a long line of commentators who adopted a classic, measured style, running through Kenneth 'They Think It's All Over' Wolstenholme, Barry Davies, David Coleman, Brian Moore, Martin Tyler and Jon Champion. Restraint and objectivity is the key here. Others have trodden a more enthusiastic, excitable and populist path – trivia hound John Motson and, to a greater extent, Alan 'Roy Keane is a thug' Green and Jonathan 'Jürgen the German' Pearce being high-profile examples. Stranded somewhere between the two camps is Gerald Sinstadt, a difficult man to categorize or, indeed, recall. Tony Gubba's place in the pantheon, on the other hand, is clear; he is the BBC's supply teacher figure – versatile, available and not particularly heeded.

They may have all used thousands of words over football, but the individual styles of commentators are summed up in how they respond to a goal. Wolstenholme's 'A goal! – it's a beauty' method suggested an approving uncle witnessing a spectacle he could never understand. ITV's Hugh Johns ('wun *nuth*-ing, City') combined in his delivery a nasal, staccato quality with a surgical finality. David Coleman's momentous '*ONE* NIL' was given in the style of a man meeting his dead brother on the stairs.

With the popularity of the young *Match of the Day* in the late 1960s and 1970s, World Cup winner Wolstenholme was considered too old-fashioned to lead

the verbal charge on BBC1. Instead chirpy commoner Motson and philosophizing (later to become pontificating) grammar-school boy Davies gained the ascendancy. The regional accent was followed, in the evolution of football commentary, by the introduction of the sidekick for live games. ITV invariably saddled Brian Moore, Peter Drury or Clive Tyldesley with someone 'colourful' such as Ron Atkinson, while the BBC have tended to hitch John Motson and co with an honest, becalmed fellow like Trevor **Brooking** or Mark Lawrenson.

Sky have successfully twinned the thoughtful and economical Martin Tyler with the clamorous Andy Gray, rather as, years ago, Dean Martin worked with Jerry Lewis. On radio, BBC's Five Live's coverage has benefited from Steve Claridge's humour and honesty.

Unsurprisingly, because of the similarity of much of the action they describe, all commentators have their clichés and verbal tics. John Motson's exhaustive homework unfortunately includes heavily prepared soundbites dropped into his monologue and the man can nuzzle contentedly at a theme for hours, like a dog with a wrapped ham. During the 2002 World Cup he became obsessed with sizzling sausages and chinking teacups. Brian Moore was habitually convinced of something 'unless I am very much mistaken'. Kenneth Wolstenholme invented pronunciations of certain names, including famously, Everton's double-scorer in the 1966 FA Cup Final, Mike Trebilcock. His Cornish surname, pronounced as it is spelled, was changed on the day to 'Tre-beel-coh', presumably because Wolstenholme didn't want to say 'cock' on the BBC.

At its best, though, and most often spontaneously, commentary actually adds to the occasion. John Motson's 'Oh, for the youngster!' as 20-year-old Joe Waters scored both Leicester City goals in their FA Cup quarter-final win over QPR in 1974, Barry Davies with his 'Look at his face! Just look at his face!' as Francis Lee celebrated a screamer for Derby against his former club Manchester City, and Brian Moore's description of a goalkeeper 'flailing around like a man in a nightmare' in a 1970s goalmouth scramble are classics of the genre.

Alf Common

In 1905 Alf Common became the first player to command a four-figure transfer fee. A ruddy-cheeked, stocky forward (5 foot 8 inches tall, weighing 13 stone), Common was 25 years old when he moved from Sunderland to Middlesbrough for £1,000. During this period Boro created a minor scandal – and sparked heated debate in the House of Commons – by attempting to spend their way out of trouble at the bottom of the First Division table. Common scored on his debut to give Middlesbrough their first away win for two years and was promptly made captain. His goals helped the club escape relegation by two points.

Revered in the north-east, where he began his career with Jarrow before graduating to Sunderland, Common returned the compliment when he moved on to Sheffield United, asking his Yorkshire employers for a transfer back to Sunderland because he was homesick. Common still managed to win a Cupwinner's medal with United in 1902 and gained his first England cap while at the club.

At a time when transfers were few and the highest ever had been £400, Common's ambition took him to six clubs in twelve years. The transfer market was never quite the same again. Common's skill, strength and knack for scoring goals didn't desert him until he left Middlesbrough for Arsenal in 1910. Common moved on to Preston two years later but his powers were waning and he retired the next year. He became a publican in Darlington, an early adopter of a trend among retired footballers that continues to this day, and died in the same town in 1946.

community schemes

Football in the Community schemes started as a pilot project in 1985, the year of the **Heysel disaster**, when football clubs were wondering how to halt a decline in attendances and re-engage local people disenchanted with rising admission prices and hooliganism. The pilot, run by the PFA, involved six northwest clubs and had five objectives: to provide employment and training for unemployed people; to promote closer links between professional football clubs and the community; to involve ethnic minority groups in social and recreational activities; to attempt to prevent acts of hooliganism and vandalism; and to maximize the use of facilities at the football club.

A further ten clubs – also from the north-west – joined in 1987, and by 1990 there were 50 community schemes attached to professional clubs throughout the country. The scheme was run under the auspices of the Footballers' Further Education and Vocational Training Society, a wing of the PFA.

Community schemes only really took off, however, following the **Taylor Report**, which called for clubs to develop better relations with their local communities. So, in the early 1990s, while chairmen talked to their new architect friends about new stands and the layout of their executive boxes, community schemes expanded and by 1995 almost all professional and some semi-pro teams had programmes of their own, providing coaching to nearly a million schoolchildren across the country.

Inevitably, some schemes – chiefly those at bigger clubs – did little more than provide jobs for old pros, generate revenue by charging fees for coaching courses, and boost a club's supporter base. Others concentrated on developing football skills among young people who no longer played the game at school – amazing as it may seem now, some people genuinely feared for the game's popularity, and were keen to prevent losing future fans and players (and income) to other sports.

The best schemes used football's popularity and their club's central role in the area as a hook to attract youngsters to educational programmes and a lever for grass roots community development works, often in some of the country's most deprived areas. Schemes at clubs such as Leyton Orient, Millwall and Charlton became community projects that happened to be attached to football clubs. While football was still the main focus of their activities, they developed partnerships with charities and voluntary groups, schools, employment schemes and anti-drugs initiatives. The scheme at Leyton Orient, for example, grew from a one-man band in 1989 to a programme employing 40 people and working across three east London boroughs.

Getting chairmen to fund community work of this kind was more difficult, however, and by 2000 only 26 per cent of clubs provided funding for their own programmes. Many directors and managers still saw them as a way to get players to 'do their bit', or another

vehicle for tapping the talents of local kids in the hope that one of them would turn out to be the next David **Beckham**.

In 1999, the Leyton Orient Community Sports Programme became the first community scheme to gain charitable status and financial independence from the whims of its club chairman. This meant it could raise funds from sources which wouldn't normally give to sections of a football club, such as local authorities, charitable trusts and central government – others soon copied this model.

Community schemes have been at the forefront of developing education initiatives, such as Learning Through Football and Playing for Success, since promoted by government and football authorities. They've also been one of the main vehicles for government-backed sport and social inclusion projects and have played a major role in fighting racism. Now, even schemes at the biggest clubs – such as Arsenal and Chelsea – are community projects first and foremost.

corner flags

The corner flag came into existence shortly after the introduction of the corner kick in 1873. Rather like the human appendix, no-one is very sure why we have them. The flag stands as a clear demarcation between the award of a throw-in and a corner, the presence of a pole also preventing any dispute should the ball happen to run out of play precisely in the corner of the pitch. Beyond lending the suggestion of a carnival atmosphere to Stockport versus Rotherham on a Tuesday night in February, the corner flag is an extremely low-profile feature of the football pitch.

Clubs that have won the FA Cup are allowed to have triangular flags on their poles – the rest must make do with square – while the maverick Len **Shackleton** used corner flags to play one-twos to himself in order to humiliate post-war full-backs. Flags are also a useful prop for celebrating a goal through the medium of dance, as displayed by the likes of Lee Sharpe (Elvis impersonation) and Cameroon's Roger Milla (sexual virility display).

In 2004 Northern Ireland's David Healy was booked for kicking a corner flag in celebration after scoring a goal against Wales. He was then immediately booked again for making a celebratory gesture towards the stands, and was back in the dressing room before the game had even restarted.

corner kick

A corner kick is awarded when a defending team puts the ball out of play over the goal line. The attacking team will then take the corner kick from inside the quarter circle marked from the corner flag. As with a direct free kick, they can either pass or shoot for goal. Opponents are not allowed to stand within ten yards of the ball before the kick is taken.

In practice there are three types of corner: 1. the 'short' corner, where the ball is played quickly to a nearby team-mate in the hope of catching defenders off their guard (usual result: player with the ball is shepherded back towards the halfway line before passing back to his own goalkeeper); 2. the near post flick-on, as perfected by George **Graham**'s Arsenal team, where the ball is drilled in towards Steve Bould or some other pylon-like figure at the front of the six-yard box, who then flicks it on for a team-mate behind him (requires both guesswork and balletic choreography – usual result: goal kick); 3. the far post 'lump it in there' default option (usual

result: goalkeeper tumbles under light breeze and wins free kick).

The corner kick was first introduced in 1872, and then revised in 1924 after Everton's Sam Chedgzoy took advantage of a previously unnoticed loophole in the laws during a game against Tottenham Hotspur by passing a corner kick to himself, dribbling towards goal and scoring. The rules were hastily amended to prevent a player from touching the ball more than once before it has reached anybody else. Scoring directly from a corner remains an extremely rare occurrence, although in 2002 Artim Sakiri managed to embarrass England goalkeeper David Seaman by curling the ball in to put Macedonia 1–0 ahead in a Euro 2004 qualifying game at the St Mary's Stadium.

Corners are a regular attacking feature of any football match – the first game in which no corner kicks were awarded did not take place until 1931. But goals created from corners are still surprisingly rare: Manchester United managed to win the Premiership title in 2003 without scoring a single goal with a direct 'assist' from a corner.

corruption

A characteristic of organized football has long been the desire to push to the limit the regulations, financial and organizational, in order to seek an advantage. As long ago as 1884 Preston North End were expelled from the FA Cup for making payments to players in the days when it was an amateur competition. In 1919 Leeds City were expelled from the League for making illegal payments to players. Manager Herbert **Chapman** is reputed to have burnt the club's financial records before resigning his post. Chapman would win League titles with Huddersfield and Arsenal; City would go out of business shortly afterwards.

These kinds of scandals were largely eradicated by the transition to a fully professional league. Subsequently, money would change hands for other reasons: to influence the outcome of a transfer bid, or merely as part of a top-up or sweetener on the deal. Under-the-counter payments to players were widespread before abolition of the maximum wage and are alleged to have continued since, while some managers have received financial 'gifts' from agents when buying players. George **Graham** was sacked by Arsenal in 1995 after it was revealed that some of the £500,000 fee paid by the club for Norwegian defender Pal Lydersen had ended up with Graham via Lydersen's agent. Revelations about 'bung culture' made during Terry **Venables**'s court case against Tottenham in 1996 led to an FA enquiry which resulted in the banning of former Nottingham Forest assistant-manager Ronnie Fenton, who admitted using illicit cash from transfer dealings to pay for his daughter's wedding. Other, bigger names escaped censure. The FA then established a Compliance Unit, made up of one man, Detective Constable Graham Bean. With limited legal and financial power, he had some success in rooting out financial skulduggery at Chesterfield, Hull City and Boston United, but no action had been taken against managers or clubs at the top level by the time of Bean's departure from the job in 2002.

Gambling has always been a part of professional football. Whether through gambling on results through the football pools, players spending their afternoons in the bookie's or killing hotel time by forming a card school, or the more recent innovations of spread and online betting, having a flutter remains a large

part of watching and playing the game. The unavoidable corollary of this is the temptation among those involved to fix or engineer a result. Despite the tradition of gambling on British football – spectators at the ground were said to have staked a whole month's wages on the result of the 1887 FA Cup Final between Aston Villa and West Bromwich Albion – and despite the huge number of games played every season, there is very little hard evidence of match fixing.

Fixing the result of a football match is a very difficult thing to do. A single player would find it almost impossible to influence a result with any great certainty, while a conspiracy would be prone to discovery. Despite this, anecdotal evidence and the odd criminal conviction suggest that players and their associates have on occasion succeeded. In 1905 Manchester City player Billy **Meredith** was suspended for trying to bribe Aston Villa captain Alex Leake to throw a match between the two teams. The minor scandal that followed led to the framing of the Prevention of Corruption Act 1906, which made it a criminal offence to attempt to bribe a footballer. In 1915, in perhaps the most infamous recorded incident of this type, Enoch West of Manchester United was given a life ban and nine other players were suspended for engineering United's 2–0 Good Friday win over Liverpool. All of the accused were eventually pardoned except for West, who was banned from the game for 30 years.

Three Sheffield Wednesday players served prison sentences in the 1960s after a newspaper story over match fixing led to a police investigation. Tony Kay, David 'Bronco' Layne and England centre-half Peter Swan were all convicted of throwing a game against Ipswich Town in December 1962. Wednesday lost the game 2–0 although, oddly, Kay was adjudged man of the match. Swan, who had been a member of England's World Cup squad earlier that year, would make a brief comeback with the Owls in the early 1970s.

There were further murky accusations after Nottingham Forest had been eliminated from the semi-finals of the UEFA Cup by Anderlecht in 1984. Despite trailing 2–0 from the first leg, the Belgians managed to win the return 3–0 with the help of some unusual decisions by Spanish referee Emilio Guruceta, who awarded the home side a questionable penalty and disallowed a late Paul Hart header. In 1997 Anderlecht president Constant Vanden Stock admitted having given Guruceta a £15,000 'loan' before the second leg. The payment only came to light because of a blackmail attempt by unknown parties in Belgium.

There were unproven allegations in the mid-1990s that Premiership players had taken payments from a Far East betting syndicate in return for influencing the results of Premiership matches. The *Sun* newspaper alleged that Liverpool goalkeeper Bruce Grobbelaar had accepted £40,000 to throw a match. Former England striker John Fashanu, along with Grobbelaar, Wimbledon goalkeeper Hans Segers and businessman Richard Lim, were accused of conspiring to corruptly influence the outcome of matches. After a retrial all parties were acquitted but Grobbelaar and Fashanu were ordered to pay their own costs of up to £650,000 after the judge concluded their conduct 'had brought suspicion' on themselves.

In July 2003 Fashanu was again forced to deny renewed allegations of match fixing after apparently falling victim to a tabloid newspaper sting for the second time. The *News of the World* reported that Fashanu had agreed to set up and fix the result of a charity match on behalf of two reporters posing as Arab businessmen. The paper produced tapes that appeared to show Fashanu agreeing to organize a charity match between a World XI and an unspecified Arab national side, and then fix the result by paying three players up to £70,000 each. Fashanu's payment would be £40,000 and a new Mercedes 4 × 4 car.

The transcripts also showed Fashanu claiming to have to fixed a Premiership match in 1994, having some of the leading players in the game on his payroll, working on behalf of Chinese betting syndicates, collecting £5m in insurance when a knee injury ended his career, and using his charitable foundation to avoid paying income tax. Fashanu, however, had an explanation. He had gone along with the sting because he knew he was being set up, accepting the £5,000 only in order to provide the police with evidence. No litigation has yet to emerge, despite the protestations of both sides.

Usually bookmakers will become suspicious if 'unusual betting patterns' emerge before a particular game. Dundee's return UEFA Cup fixture with Vllaznia Shkodra in 2003 was removed from the coupon by many high-street bookies after suspicions were aroused before the Scots' 2–0 win in the first leg in Albania. However, with stakes of up to £10,000 on the result of a single game a common occurrence among punters, the English Premiership has become a far softer and a far more likely target for match-fixing syndicates.

A Malaysian, Ong Chee Kew, was caught trying to short-circuit the floodlights during a Premiership match between Charlton and Liverpool on 10 February 1999. Earlier, the same attempt to cause abandonments had been successfully applied during matches between West Ham and Crystal Palace, and Wimbledon and Arsenal. In both cases the floodlights were extinguished just after one team had scored early in the second half. Under Malaysian gambling rules a result will stand if a game is abandoned at this point.

With the emergence of more diverse forms of football gambling, fuelled by statistical data and the popularity of spread and internet betting, certain kinds of fixing have become more likely. The opportunity to bet on the time of the first throw-in led to rumours in the late 1990s that players had taken advantage of the chance to lay a heavy bet on a throw-in in the first ten seconds and then simply hoof the ball out of play from the kick-off. The success of the scam would, of course, be reliant on the right team winning the toss, and on the player concerned being able to accurately locate the touchline, the last of which should not be taken for granted at certain Premiership clubs.

Coventry City

Coventry City have been members of the Football League since joining Division 2 in 1919. During this time the club's most remarkable achievement was its uninterrupted stay in the top division between 1967 and 2001. Coventry won promotion to Division 1 for the first time in the 1966–67 season, and remained in the top flight for 33 seasons, during which they qualified for European competition just once and only finished higher then tenth on three occasions. By the time they were relegated, Coventry had enjoyed the longest spell of unremarkable success in the history of English League football.

The club was formed in 1883 as Singer's FC by workers at Singer's bicycle factory. Singer's joined the Birmingham and District League in 1894

changing their name to Coventry City four years later. Coventry were elected to the Southern League in 1908 and narrowly escaped relegation at the end of their second season of League football by beating Bury 1–0. It was later discovered that the win had been secured with the help of a hefty bribe and City chairman David Cooke was one of several people connected with the clubs to receive a life ban from football.

Subsequently Coventry floated around the lower divisions, winning the Division 3 (South) in 1936, the club's only honour during the first 65 years of its existence. A long period in Division 2 coincided with the career of Clarrie Bourton, still the club's leading goalscorer with 171 between 1931 and 1937. The arrival of Jimmy **Hill** as manager in 1961 revolutionized Coventry's fortunes.

Appointed by chairman Derrick Robins, Hill began by changing the club's colours to sky blue, and then introducing a succession of innovations: Sky Blue Special trains for travelling fans, Sky Blue Radio commentaries and pre-match entertainment and free soft drinks and crisps to lure more children to Highfield Road. Hill's aggressive promotion of the club was innovative and brash. Fortunately the team were successful on the field too. Promotion to Division 2 in 1964 was followed by another promotion three years later, with the final game of the season watched by a record 51,455 crowd.

Hill resigned to begin his television career that same year, but the club continued to flourish. Noel Cantwell took the Sky Blues to sixth place in 1970 and their only venture into European competition, beating Bulgarians Trakia Plodiv in the first round of the Fairs Cup but going out in the next to Bayern Munich. Hill returned to the club in 1974 as managing director, although his attempt to make

Highfield Road the country's first all-seater stadium ended in disaster in 1981 as rioting fans ripped out the seats and used them as missiles.

In 1987 Coventry won their first and only major trophy. Former players John Sillett and George Curtis led the team to a 3–2 extra-time FA Cup victory over Tottenham Hotspur, the winning goal coming via a deflection off Spurs' defender Gary Mabbutt's knee. Having avoided relegation on the last day of the season ten times, Coventry were finally relegated in 2001 after defeat to their bogey team, Aston Villa (who didn't lose any of the first 28 League matches between the clubs). Of the current Premier League clubs, only Arsenal, Liverpool and Everton had enjoyed longer unbroken stays in the top flight. The team's finest single performance in Division 1 is probably the 4–0 win over Liverpool in December 1983, a game in which Terry Gibson scored a hat-trick. It was Liverpool's biggest defeat for seven years during their most dominant period. That same season Coventry finished 19th. They also lost the return fixture at Anfield in May 5–0.

Cowdenbeath

Scottish football legend Jim **Baxter** was born in Cowdenbeath, as was the scientist who invented beta blockers. Both moved away, one to find better football, while the other presumably lacked a market among the excitement-starved local football fans, whose gallows humour is reflected in the club's latterly adopted nickname of 'The Blue Brazil'.

Elton John reportedly once told a Scottish radio station that Cowdenbeath was his favourite Scottish side because he liked the name, but the singer has never showed up with the kind of money that

helped Watford rise to the heights of the English game. Founded in 1881 and admitted to the League in 1905, the Fifeshire club's best years came early, when they were Division 2 champions in 1914 and 1915, but a time when there was no automatic promotion. In the 1920s the team consisted almost wholly of local miners and they were twice Division 2 runners-up, then finished a respectable fifth, seventh and seventh in the top flight over three successive years in the latter part of the decade.

They were finally relegated in 1934, then a third Division 2 championship came just in time for the Second World War. One of the club's finest hours came soon after in 1949, when they played Rangers in a two-legged League Cup quarter-final. Cowdenbeath sensationally won the first leg at Ibrox, 3–2. The return at Central Park spawned the club's record gate of 25,586, but the home side went out of the competition when they lost 3–1 on the night, after extra time. In 1970 they made it one stage further in the same competition, but once again the side from Ibrox stood between Cowdenbeath and silverware. They lost 2–0.

A promotion to Division 1 earlier that same year was followed by an immediate return back down, while the club responded to going up a flight in 1992 by sacking manager John Brownlie. Bar two seasons in Division 2 at the start of the 21st century, the team has played in the bottom division until being promoted in 2006. In the early 1990s chairman Gordon McDougall, a former world stock car champion, introduced stock car racing on the oval track surrounding the pitch. Race nights drew crowds roughly ten times larger than those for the football team.

Crewe Alexandra

The last ten years have been the most successful in Crewe Alexandra's history, although 'success' is probably going a bit too far for a club whose only major honours remain the Welsh Cup successes of 1936 and 1937. Crewe were formed in 1877 by railway workers who had previously met as the Crewe Alexandra Cricket Club. The Alexandra is believed to come either from Princess Alexandra, wife of the future king Edward VII, or from a pub of that name where early members met.

Crewe are based at the Alexandra Stadium on Gresty Road, the club's home since 1898. The ground backs on to a set of railway tracks, reason in part for the club nickname 'The Railwaymen'. During the first half of the last century games were often played against a background of steam from trains on the tracks behind the ground. The home team are reported to have scored a goal against a bemused Hull City under cover of almost total invisibility, after clouds of steam from a shunting locomotive had engulfed the pitch.

Prior to the appointment of current manager Dario Gradi, Crewe had one of the least remarkable track records of any Football League club. After reaching the semi-finals of the FA Cup in 1888 and spending four seasons in Division 2 at the end of the 19th century, the Railwaymen dropped out of the League in 1896 after a campaign in which they lost 22 of 30 games played. It would be 25 years before the club returned, joining the nascent Division 3 in 1921 and remaining there until relegation to the newly formed Division 4 in 1957. Apart from a couple of promotions – both followed by instant relegation – during the 1960s, Crewe's greatest achievement over 70 years of almost exclusive occupation of the lowest division was successfully staving off falling out of the League altogether. Fittingly for a team enjoying a period of such modest achievements, the club's record defeat – 13–2 to Spurs in an FA Cup fourth-round replay in 1960 – came after the drawn first game had attracted a record attendance of 20,000 to Gresty Road.

The appointment of Dario Gradi as manager in 1983 ushered in the club's most successful period. Promoted from Division 4 in 1992, Crewe have risen steadily, with only a couple of hiccups along the way, spending the best part of ten years in the First Division and Championship, before suffering relegation to League One in 2005–06. The team's success has been built around the production of good-quality homegrown players, who have either then been sold to finance the first team squad or stayed at the club to take part in its successful rise. A first XI drawn from players given their break in League football at Crewe could include Bruce Grobbelaar, Rob Jones, Seth Johnson, Neil Lennon, Danny Murphy, David Platt, Robbie Savage, Geoff Thomas, Ashley Ward, Dele Adebola and Dean Ashton.

crime

Professional footballers have a long and detailed history of breaking the law. Whether because of an obsessive press interest in the private lives of celebrities, the disorientating effects of extreme and immediate wealth, or just because they're more badly behaved then ever before, instances of footballers falling foul of the police seem to be more common now than in any previous era. During the first half of the 20th century there were plenty of examples of corruption relating to the game itself. From the 1960s onwards the actions of individual players outside football began to be reported, with the exploits of footballers under the influence of alcohol becoming a staple of tabloid newspaper reporting.

Bobby **Moore**'s arrest before the 1970 World Cup was the first high-profile brush with the law involving a British player. The team were staying at a hotel in Bogotá during a training camp before the tournament when a cashier in the hotel's jewellery shop accused Moore of stealing an emerald and diamond bracelet worth £600, a charge the England captain denied. When the team landed in Bogotá again on the way to Mexico, Moore was arrested and detained by police. The incident was given worldwide press coverage, during which it emerged that several other high-profile guests had also been accused of theft while staying at the hotel, many of them paying off the jewellery shop to keep the whole affair hushed up. Moore was released without charge, although the suspicion later emerged – after off-the-record and unreported comments made towards the end of his life – that he may, in fact, have been covering up for one of the younger players in the squad.

Former Arsenal player Peter Storey was convicted of running a brothel in 1979 and has been sent to prison on various occasions since then for his part in a counterfeiting ring and for stealing cars. Storey once described his experiences of professional football in a tabloid exposé: 'it's about the drunken parties that go on for days. The orgies, the birds and the fabulous money.' Unfortunately, for Storey life after football also turned out to be about the importing of pornographic videos into the country hidden inside the spare tyre of his car, for which he was again sent to prison.

From the criminal-as-lovable-rogue tradition, football has produced Mickey Thomas, who was jailed for passing forged bank notes to trainees while a player at Wrexham, and Robin Friday, whose short life included a prison sentence for burglary. Tony **Adams** served 56 days of a three-month sentence for drink-driving in 1990 after crashing his car into a brick wall in Essex. Adams, now a recovering alcoholic, later captained England and Arsenal and has since started his own charity for sports stars with similar problems. Drink-driving remains the most common form of criminal activity among footballers. Jan Mølby served three months of his sentence for a drunken two-mile high-speed car chase with police in 1988. More recently, one-time England full-back Gary Charles was sentenced to four months in prison after he was convicted of driving his sports car into a garden wall and being found drunk in charge of the vehicle. Three years previously Charles had also been convicted of drink-driving, reportedly reassuring passers-by with the words, 'don't tell the police – I'm a bank robber and I'm on the run', after crashing his car.

In 1987 offences committed on the field of play were tried for the first time in a court of law. Chris Woods, Terry Butcher, Graham Roberts and Frank McAvennie appeared before the judge after violent incidents during a Celtic–Rangers game, although all escaped without a prison sentence. Duncan Ferguson remains the only player to go to prison for an offence committed on the field of play. Ferguson served three months in 1995 after head-butting Raith defender John McStay while he was already on probation over previous assault charges. The same year Eric **Cantona** was sentenced to community service and banned from playing for almost a year after fighting with a spectator at Crystal Palace. Cantona had been sent off and interrupted his walk back to the away dugout to launch a flying kick at a member of the public who had been abusing him.

Over the last decade the behaviour of players has either worsened considerably or simply found a more willing audience with the success of the Premiership. In 2001 Jonathan Woodgate was convicted of affray after a case involving other Leeds footballers accused of assaulting a student in the city centre during a boozy night out. The case was the first of many criminal investigations and unpleasant tabloid revelations involving footballers during the recent years of the Premiership, prompting suspicions that the behaviour of English football's unprecedentedly wealthy young players may be reaching a nadir.

Crystal Palace

Crystal Palace are named after a reconstructed Victorian glass building that burnt down in 1936. The first Crystal Palace football team was formed in 1861 by workers at Joseph Paxton's famous structure. Originally erected in Hyde Park, the Crystal Palace had previously housed part of Prince Albert's Great Exhibition. The Palace had then been rebuilt on a vacant site on Sydenham Hill and finally reopened in 1854. Technically, there is no such place as Crystal Palace; and after the fire that completely destroyed it – a blaze which could be seen right across London – there is no such thing as the Crystal Palace. Only the name, an athletics stadium and the football team remain. (The club removed one further link to the old palace in the 1970s, changing their nickname from 'The Glaziers' to 'The Eagles'.)

The current club was formed in 1905 and was originally based at the Sydenham Hill site, a venue also for several early FA Cup finals. Following

eviction from the palace by army requisitioning in 1915, the club moved to nearby Herne Hill and briefly shared Millwall's Den, before settling at its current home, Selhurst Park, a few miles from the final resting place of the Palace itself. Crystal Palace have no great history of winning trophies. A collection of lower-divisional titles plus a Zenith Data Systems Cup win in 1991 are the sum total of the club's successes, despite a fairly lengthy Football League lifespan. Entering the League in 1920 Palace immediately won the Division 3 championship, finishing top of a division that also included now-traditional rivals Brighton and Millwall. This would be a misleading start to League life: Palace were relegated four years later and spent the next 26 seasons in the bottom division, during the first part of which forward Peter Simpson scored a club record 153 League goals between 1930 and 1936.

A steady series of promotions during the 1960s saw the club reach Division 1 for the first time in 1969. Within five years, however, they were back in the third, resuming a pattern of occasional promotions that culminated in Terry **Venables** leading the club back up to the top flight as champions in 1979. Having been dubbed the Team of the Eighties, Palace were relegated after just two seasons and spent the rest of the decade in Division 2.

Another run of success followed in the early 1990s. Under the guidance of controversial chairman Ron Noades – a publicity-seeking 'personality' chairman who, despite his subsequent departure, still owns the freehold on Selhurst Park – Steve Coppell created a highly effective and highly physical team that won promotion to Division 1 in 1989. Coppell's men would achieve the club's highest ever League position, third in

1990–91, a year after losing to Manchester United in an FA Cup final replay. Coppell's team, including future England internationals Geoff Thomas, John Salako and Ian **Wright**, scorer of 89 League goals for the Eagles, remains the most celebrated in the club's history. Despite this, Palace were relegated again in 1993, and went down from the top level twice more in the next five years during a period of financial meltdown off the field.

Palace suffered more than most from the boom and bust of the 1990s. Under the disastrous stewardship of local businessman Mark Goldberg, the club became a magnet for under-performing foreign players at the back-end of their careers. After promotion in 1997, Palace spent £14.2m in one season and were rewarded with 20th place and an instant return to the Nationwide League. Michele Padovano signed for £1.7m from Juventus, made eight League starts in a year and then took legal action to claim his unpaid wages during the club's most financially perilous period.

Palace are no strangers to upheaval off the field, having had 17 changes of manager since the start of the 1980s. Managers at Selhurst Park during recent times have included Venables, Malcolm **Allison**, Alan Mullery, Dario Gradi, Attilio Lombardo and Coppell himself a total of four times. Resuscitated financially by Simon Jordan the club found an equilibrium in Division 1 and began, once again, to rebuild its fortunes on the field under new manager Iain Dowie. A stunning late-season charge up the Division 1 table in 2003–04 was rewarded with a surprise promotion to the Premiership via the play-offs, but the team went straight back down.

Crystal Palace Stadium

Crystal Palace, the second regular venue for the FA Cup Final after the Oval, was a forerunner to Wembley in more ways than one. It had a grandeur that helped to cement the peculiarly English notion that there should be a neutral venue for the final, and that it should be in London.

But its reputation hid a host of practical problems. Having tried both Manchester's Fallowfield and Goodison Park after crowds became too big for the Oval, with unsatisfactory results, the FA returned to London for the 1895 final. The ground was laid out in the park that surrounded the original Crystal Palace, the huge iron and glass building that was constructed for the Great Exhibition of 1851.

The final venue was barely a stadium at all, even by the standards of the time, with just three small stands down one side and grassy banks forming a huge bowl around the rest. Photographs of big matches there make it plain that many in the crowd could barely see the pitch, and the banks with no terraces or barriers were treacherous at the best of times, let alone in the rain – fortunately almost all the Cup Finals at the Palace were on sunny days. Nevertheless, the setting gave the final an irresistible sense of occasion and crowds were consistently huge, with many watching from the trees that surrounded the ground. In 1901, when Tottenham became the first London team to reach the final in the professional era (and the only one to play in a final at Crystal Palace) their 2–2 draw with Sheffield United was attended, if not necessarily watched, by more than 110,000 (reported figures vary), smashing the previous record by almost 40,000.

When the League runners-up Aston Villa beat the champions Sunderland 1–0 in the 1913 final, a world record crowd of 120,081 was on hand. The following year's final, between Burnley and Liverpool, was the first attended by royalty, but the last at Crystal Palace. After the outbreak of the war the ground was taken over for storage, which also sent the Crystal Palace club on the search for a new home.

By the time the war was over, they had moved on and so had the Cup Final, first to Stamford Bridge and then to Wembley. 'There is a spectacular suitability about the Crystal Palace ground that cannot be beaten, however many disadvantages [it] possesses in other respects,' wrote one northern observer at the 1914 final. In establishing the tradition of the Cup Final as a special event in the football calendar, with fans travelling to London for a carnival as well as a match, Crystal Palace deserves at least part of the aura that later settled on Wembley. The site was rebuilt as a multi-sport venue in 1964, now part of the National Sports Centre, and has since been one of the top athletics stadiums in the country.

Stan Cullis

The very name Stan Cullis conjures up a bygone era. Like his club captain at Wolverhampton Wanderers, Billy **Wright**, he seems to belong to an age of liniment, austerity and unfeasibly knobbly kneecaps. The truth is, though, that had it not been for a series of heart attacks in early middle age, Cullis might well have carried on in football management until the 1980s.

In some respects the tense, almost tortured figure who led Wolves to three League titles and two FA Cup wins is the forgotten man of British football, rarely drawing the sort of attention routinely paid to his contemporaries Bill

Nicholson and Matt **Busby**. Yet Cullis's legacy lives on. For more than anyone it was he, inspired by the statistical work of Wing Commander Charles Reep and his 'Position of maximum opportunity', who invented the kind of all-action, no-frills style of football that would come to be identified as quintessentially British by the rest of the world. Cullis always denied that his team played a long-ball game, preferring to identify it as a game of long passes. What isn't in doubt is that the tactics he adapted were based on playing the percentages. If he was an unromantic and pragmatic coach there was plenty of mitigation, however.

Cullis grew up in Ellesmere Port, part of an immigrant Black Country community who had moved to Cheshire along with the Wolverhampton Corrugated Iron Company. His father Sydney – too old to work in the foundry – was dour and violent, the ten children desperate to escape. Denied a place at grammar school because his dad wouldn't let him go, young Stan instead threw himself into self-improvement. While working as a grocer's boy he attended night school and perhaps surprisingly for someone often identified as the prototypical Little Englander, became fluent in both French and Esperanto.

When his football career took off, as a tough, intelligent centre-half at Wolves Cullis might have been forgiven for thinking he had finally clawed his way free and could look forward to a more comfortable future. Not a bit of it. He had no sooner been named captain of England than the Nazis invaded Poland. By the time the war ended he was past his best. All in all, it was enough to give anybody a few sharp corners.

Right from the start of his managerial life at Molineux in 1948 Cullis was uncompromising to the point of brutality. He demanded total effort and commitment and detested anyone who wasn't as driven as he was. As one former Wolves player remarked, 'The whole team was united by one thing. We all hated Stan.'

The highpoint of his career came on a wet night in the west Midlands in 1954 when Wolves took on Hungarian champions Honved in a floodlit friendly match and beat them 3–2. Afterwards the press identified Cullis's team as 'The Champions of the World'. A claim which set such a debate raging across the continent that it would eventually lead to the establishment of the European Cup.

If Cullis upset his players he rubbed his employers up the wrong way too. After a 5–1 defeat at Luton he infamously ordered the coach driver to set off back to the Midlands even though the Wolves director John Ireland was still in the lounge at Kenilworth Road. It was an action Ireland did not forget when he became chairman a few years later. In the early 1960s Wolves' form began to slide. They finished the 1963–64 season in 16th place. The following term began badly and Ireland seized the opportunity and sacked the manager.

Despite mounting health problems Cullis took over at Birmingham City. But football had moved on and there was little hope for an iron disciplinarian who always wore a jacket and tie and never swore, punctuating his half-time tirades with 'flipping' and 'flopping' instead. He retired in 1970.

Kenny Dalglish

'He wasn't that big but he had a huge arse. It came down below his knees and that's where he got his strength from.' Brian **Clough**'s assessment of Kenny Dalglish's physique offers little suggestion of his achievements on the field. One of the greatest players the British game has produced, Dalglish won the League title eight times in 12 seasons at Liverpool as player and player-manager; the European Cup in 1978, 1981 and 1984; and the FA Cup twice.

Playing either in midfield or in a deep forward position behind a lone striker, Dalglish created as many goals as he scored. This was most notable in his partnership with Ian **Rush** at Liverpool during the early 1980s, one of the most productive the British game has seen. Lacking in pace but quick on the turn and physically very strong, Dalglish had the rare ability to perform effectively as a brilliant individualist within a rigid team structure.

A number of oddly personalized clichés tended to attach themselves to Dalglish the player. He was rumoured to be able to 'freeze' the play on receiving the ball in a promising area of the pitch, deference to his ability to pick the right pass quicker than the players around him. He was also the first player to attract the observation that 'the first yard is in his head', a reference to a lack of sprinting speed combined with good positional sense.

Dalglish was signed by Bob **Paisley** from Celtic for £440,000 in 1977, ostensibly as a replacement for Kevin **Keegan**, who had left for Hamburg. More instinctively talented than his workaholic predecessor, in time Dalglish would eclipse Keegan's achievements at Anfield, leading Liverpool to the League title in his first season, winning the

Footballer of the Year award in 1979 and again in 1983, when he also received the PFA Player of the Year award. The first player to score 100 goals in both the Scottish and English leagues, prior to his move to Anfield Dalglish had enjoyed a highly successful career with Celtic in his native Glasgow. Making his debut as an 18-year-old in 1969, he won four Scottish League championship medals, plus four Scottish Cups and one Scottish League Cup. He played for Scotland in three World Cups and won a record 102 caps, scoring 30 goals.

A successful career as a manager followed his retirement as a player. Dalglish is part of a small band – Herbert **Chapman** and Clough are the others – to have won the League title with two different clubs, although his achievements as a manager are frequently downgraded: at Liverpool he inherited a great team; and at Blackburn he spent an unprecedented amount of money in assembling a title-winning XI almost from scratch within four years of taking charge. Gloomy spells at Newcastle and Celtic (the latter as 'director of football operations') signalled the end of Dalglish's managerial career and a descent into golfing semi-retirement, enlivened by the occasional appearance as a laconic TV pundit.

Darlington

From 1999 until 2003 lower-division Darlington attracted a good deal of nationwide attention thanks to the antics of chairman George Reynolds, a former bank robber turned multi-millionaire fitted-kitchen magnate. Sporting a scrape-over hairdo of which Bobby **Charlton** would have been proud, the former resident of Durham jail was a one-man publicity machine.

Never at a loss for words, Reynolds involved himself in long-running and bitter disputes with regional journalists and fanzine editors, 'outed' a north-east DJ, sacked manager David Hodgson and then argued with him on radio phone-ins, claimed to be on the verge of signing Colombian star Faustino Asprilla and stood by while his wife hinted that his own players had deliberately thrown matches. Along the way he also moved the club from their old ground of Feethams (which they shared with Durham County Cricket Club) to a new purpose-built stadium on the outskirts of town.

The George Reynolds Arena, as it was named, cost £20m to build, boasted marble sinks, state-of-the-art lifts and 27,000 seats – quite a set-up for a perennially impoverished club with average attendances that rarely rose above the 5–6,000 mark. The drain on resources of the new ground inevitably took its toll. Shortly after Christmas 2003 the club went into administration.

Little in the previous history of the Quakers (members of the Society of Friends were prominent amongst the local worthies. It was Quaker businessmen who had been instrumental in building the Stockton–Darlington railway) hinted at the mayhem to come. Darlington FC was founded in 1883 and joined the newly inaugurated Northern League six years later. The club's best-known player in those early days was the goalkeeper Arthur Wharton, a talented all-round sportsman, who was also the first black footballer to play professionally in England.

Having won both the Northern League and the semi-professional North-Eastern League titles Darlington were elected to Division 3 (North) of the Football League for the 1921–22 season. Over the next 17 years they spent two seasons in Division 2 and applied for re-election once. After the Second World War things carried on in similar vein with the occasional highlight such as the 4–1 win over Chelsea in the 1957–58 FA Cup. Cyril Knowles – in 1984–85 – and Brian Little – in 1990–91 – both secured promotion to the then Division 3 for Darlington, the latter after leading the club to the Vauxhall Conference title the previous year following relegation from the Football League in 1988–89, but the club was never able to establish itself at the higher level. In total Darlington have spent just six seasons outside the bottom division of the Football League. In May 1999 George Reynolds arrived promising to change all that. Trailing dreams of Premiership football he delivered only financial ruin and it was left to a consortium of local businessmen and the Supporters' Trust to save the 120-year-old club from extinction.

Dixie Dean

By virtue of his goalscoring record alone, William 'Dixie' Dean is perhaps the finest centre-forward British football has produced. Scorer of 379 League goals in 437 games, 18 in 16 appearances for England, a record 60 in 39 games in a single season for Everton and 43 career hat-tricks, Dean also led Everton to the League title in 1928 and 1932, captaining the team with great energy and good humour. A muscular, supremely athletic man, Dean was a youthful prodigy at Tranmere Rovers, signing for the club at the age of 16. He made an immediate impression with his direct running, aerial ability – even though he was under six feet tall – and unusually powerful shot, an essential goalscoring weapon in the era of the heavy leather ball when few players were able to shoot successfully from distance.

Dean was also resilient. He survived the first of two career-threatening accidents when he was just 17, losing a testicle after a brutal foul by an Altrin-cham centre-half. Dean believed his assailant to have been a player called Davy Parks, whom he bumped into 17 years later in a pub in Liverpool. 'He sent me a pint across the bar,' Dean later recalled. 'I couldn't quite place the face for a time. But then I did. And I thumped him . . . they took him to hospital.' Never mind that subsequent reports have established that Dean's assailant was in fact a man called Molyneux.

He signed for Everton in 1925 for a reported £3,000, a huge fee for an 18-year-old, and from his first full season onwards he scored goals at a prodigious rate, interrupted only by his second major accident. In June 1926 Dean was involved in a head-on collision while out for a spin on his new Imperial motorbike with a girlfriend, narrowly avoiding death. Astonishingly he returned to action just four months later, scoring in a reserve game that drew 30,000 to Goodison Park. Dean was a handsome, gregarious man with a distinctive dark complexion. One of the explanations for his nickname is that 'Dixie' is a reference to black slaves in the deep south of America; the other is a corruption of 'Digsy', after Dean's habit of digging his hands into playmates during childhood games. Dean was a devotee of ballroom dancing and music halls and was well known locally for his carousing off the field. An occasional matchday task for the Everton backroom staff was the preparation of a pot of black coffee in order to assist their captain and centre-forward on to the field.

There have been suggestions that the change in the offside law to favour the attacking side contributed to the volume of goals Dean scored, as defenders struggled to adapt to the new laws. However, none of Dean's contemporaries can boast a comparable goal record, and the fact remains that he averaged almost a goal a game over nearly 500 matches, a feat of scoring unmatched in any era. Dean also played for Notts County and Sligo Rovers before retiring in 1940, after which he was landlord of the Dublin Packet pub for 15 years, before taking a job as a security guard at a Littlewood's warehouse in Liverpool. Dean died at Goodison Park in 1980 after watching Everton play Liverpool; a statue of him now stands outside the main entrance to the ground.

Derby County

Derby County have enjoyed a more fluctuating history than most. The fact that Derby won the League twice in four seasons during the 1970s under the guidance of first Brian **Clough** and then Dave **Mackay** may seem remarkable today; but it would have been almost as unexpected then, given that only three seasons previously the club was at the end of a 15-year stint in divisons 2 and 3. Successive promotions and relegations, plus the consistent threat of financial collapse, have been a major part of Derby's later history, during which they have still managed to keep up a record of consistent buoyancy in and around the top two divisions.

Formed in 1884 by members of Derbyshire County Cricket Club, Derby were one of the founder members of the Football League four years later. The club spent the next 20 years in the top division, and reached three FA Cup finals and a further ten semis between 1895 and 1909 without ever winning the competition. After a couple of Division 2 championships in 1912 and 1915 the Rams eventually claimed their first major trophy in 1946, winning the first post-war FA Cup competition with a side built around Raich **Carter**, Peter Doherty and Jack Stamps.

Twenty consecutive seasons in Division 1 ended with relegation in 1952–53, defeat at Stoke City in the penultimate fixture ensuring that Stoke escaped the drop while Derby finished bottom. Worse was to come, with relegation to Division 3 (North) for the first time two seasons later. Harry Storer led Derby to promotion almost immediately and the arrival of Brian Clough and Peter Taylor in 1967 preceded the most successful period in the club's history. Derby were promoted as champions in 1968–69 after winning their last nine games, and three seasons later the club finished top of the League for the first time in its history. The title was won by one point from Leeds United, and two other clubs. Clough had already taken his team to Majorca for an end-of-season holiday when news came through that the title had been won after Leeds lost at Wolves and Liverpool failed to beat Arsenal. Clough's team included Colin Todd and Roy McFarland in the centre of defence, winger Alan Hinton and centre-forward Kevin Hector. Hector would go on to make a record 486 appearances in two spells between 1966 and 1982.

Other players, such as Archie Gemmill and John McGovern, would eventually follow Clough to Nottingham Forest after his resignation over a dispute with the board over the manager's high profile in the media. The team that Clough built won a further championship under Dave Mackay in 1974–75, taking the title with just 53 points and despite losing 10 games during the course of the season. The good times didn't last, however. Two seasons later Derby were battling relegation and in 1979–80 they were relegated.

The 1980s were a strange decade for Derby. Financial difficulties and relegation to Division 3 in 1984 were followed by a resuscitation under the management of Arthur Cox and, from 1987, under the financial guidance of new chairman, media mogul Robert Maxwell. Cox led the team to successive promotions from Division 3 to Division 1, and a team containing Peter **Shilton**, Mark Wright and Dean Saunders finished fifth in Division 1 in 1989, three seasons after leaving the third. A yo-yoing ten years of promotions and relegation between the top two divisions followed, including a couple of top-ten finishes in the Premiership under Jim Smith, with a team comprised mainly of foreign imports, some of them successful, such as Stefano Eranio, who made nearly a hundred appearances after signing on a free transfer, and some less so: Fabrizio Ravanelli, a disruptive influence during a disastrous relegation season was nevertheless among the club's highest earners as debts of £30 million stacked up.

An internal restructuring and a promising academy structure point towards a more promising future for a team in a 'footballing town' that has, apart from a brief Clough-induced golden era, largely underperformed. Derby is a large place with few other obvious competitors for the attention of its supporters; rivalry with Nottingham Forest has been fierce at times, but Derby still claim a catchment area of support even in Nottinghamshire. With time and with sound financial management the club could play at a level to match its potential.

Doncaster Rovers

In October 2004, Doncaster Rovers celebrated their 125th birthday. That they were able to do so as a Football League club would not have seemed possible just six years earlier. Doncaster's relegation

to the Conference in 1997–98 – a season in which they didn't win any of their first 20 matches, used 45 players, and finished bottom by 15 points – was the final chapter in a traumatic saga. It began in 1993 when Ken Richardson, a businessman whose first venture into sport had led to a ban from the Jockey Club for running a racehorse under a false name, became the club's major shareholder and later its sole owner.

Richardson was never a director of Doncaster but installed various associates as chairmen and ran the team, organizing transfers and hiring managers – the club went through five, plus 12 coaches, in his time in charge. Shortly after Richardson's takeover, supporters were surprised to see Belle Vue, their ground since 1920, being offered for sale in the national press, even though it was owned by Doncaster Council on a 99-year lease. Two years later, two men were arrested for trying to burn down Belle Vue (fortunately, they tried to set fire to concrete and made so much noise in the process that the police were alerted). Richardson, who had responded to fans' criticisms by threatening to pull the club out of the League, was arrested in March 1996 and charged with conspiracy to commit arson. He was found guilty three years later. At Rovers' next match, away at Kettering, the tannoy announcer read out 'a message from the fans for a Mr Richardson who can't be here today' then played *Firestarter* by The Prodigy.

Doncaster Rovers were formed in 1879 when an 18-year-old railway fitter, Albert Jenkins, assembled a team to play a match against the Yorkshire Institute for the Deaf & Dumb. Having ditched their original blue shirts with a yellow St Andrews cross for the now traditional red and white, the club entered the FA

Cup for the first time in 1888 – losing 9–1 at home to Rotherham Town – and joined the Football League in 1901–02, finishing seventh in Division 2, still their best performance. Surprisingly, they lost a re-election vote a year later and dropped into regional football, where they stayed until 1920, barring one further League season in 1904–05, when they finished bottom with a record low total of 8 points having lost all of their 17 away matches.

The closest Rovers have come to recapturing the heyday of 1902 was in the 1950s. Belle Vue regularly saw crowds in excess of 20,000 as Doncaster completed eight successive seasons in the second flight under the leadership of Peter Doherty. Matt **Busby** took notice and was set to sign teenage striker Alick Jeffrey, only for the forward to break his leg playing for England Under 23s. Instead, Busby took Northern Ireland international Harry Gregg to Man Utd for £23,000, then a world record for a goalkeeper.

By 1959, following successive relegations, Rovers were back in the League's basement, to which they swiftly returned after promotions in 1966 and 1969. In the 1980s, Billy **Bremner**'s side also went up twice, in 1981 and 1984. Four years later, with the first team set for another relegation, Doncaster's youth side made it all the way to the FA Youth Cup Final – the lowest placed club ever to do so – beating Tottenham and Manchester City before losing to Arsenal. Several players from that team went on to a higher level, including central defenders Paul Raven (West Brom) and Rufus Brevett (Fulham and West Ham among others) but Rovers were unable to build on the foundations.

After five years of rebuilding in non-League football and heavy investment from new owner John Ryan, Doncaster rejoined the Football League in 2003, winning promotion from Division 3 in their first season back.

the Double

The fact that so few clubs managed to win the League championship and FA Cup in the same season was, until very recently, held up as proof of English football's fierce competitiveness. This, it was argued, contrasted with supposedly lesser leagues such as Scotland, where Doubles and even trebles were a frequent occurrence for the two or three dominant clubs. Preston ('The Invincibles') did the Double in 1889, the first year of the League, and Aston Villa followed in 1897. After that, various agonizing near-misses outnumbered the successes. Tottenham's feted team of 1961 and Arsenal's more prosaic 1971 squad proved that the Double was possible.

Among the might-have-beens were: Newcastle (1905 – lost in the Cup Final); Sunderland (1913 – lost the Cup Final to Villa, who were second in the League); Man Utd (1957 – lost the Cup Final to Villa after a brutal challenge on goalkeeper Ray Wood); and Wolves (1960 – lost the League title by a point to Burnley). Don **Revie**'s Leeds then turned Double near misses into an art form, suffering in various ways in 1965, 1970 and 1972. That last year, two days after beating Arsenal in the Cup Final, Leeds needed only a point at Wolves to secure the Double, but lost 2–1. Liverpool endured their own close call, losing the Cup Final to Manchester United in 1977, which would have given them a treble (with the European Cup). After finally cracking it in 1986 (when Everton were runners-up in League and Cup) they missed out again by the narrowest of all margins, thanks to Michael Thomas's last-minute goal that won the 1989 title for Arsenal at Anfield. But the spell was broken in the 1990s by Arsenal and Man Utd, who between 1994 and 2004 won five Doubles between them, including United's treble in 1999. The devalued currency of the Double is perhaps the starkest illustration of the concentration of power at the top of the Premiership.

drugs

The closest British football has come to a genuine drugs scandal is Rio Ferdinand's missed test in September 2003, for which he was banned for eight months and fined £50,000. Ferdinand claims to have 'forgotten' to meet up with the testers after training, going shopping instead and turning off his mobile so that nobody could contact him. So far this has been one form of corruption from which the sport has generally been free. A number of individual players failed tests in Italy during recent years and a whisper of lax testing practices in the UK has cast only a tiny shadow on this unblemished reputation. Drugs in football have been little more than a rumour until now; an occasional suggestion, never substantiated.

Generally, drugs fall into two categories. Those that make you better at your sport, and those that make you better at either dancing, eating ice cream or talking very quickly about yourself. Given their exposure to intense performance pressures, to quick and easy wealth, and to seedy hangers-on, footballers are probably likely to be equally tempted by both kinds of substances.

Performance-enhancing drugs are designed to promote healing after injuries, to enhance muscle build, or to increase the effects of training: stamina, explosiveness and speed of reaction. Such substances have long been a part of sport.

Strychnine and other primitive amphetamines have been used in athletics since the turn of the twentieth century. When it comes to testing procedures the football authorities have tended to follow the lead of the International Olympic Committee. This led to FIFA carrying out the first-ever official dope testing of footballers in 1966 at the World Cup in England. UEFA set up its own dope-testing committee in 1979, partly as a reaction to Willie Johnston failing a test for amphetamines (or 'pep-pills') at the World Cup in Argentina in 1978.

There is anecdotal evidence to suggest drug use among English footballers before doping laws were enforced. Former Manchester United goalkeeper Harry Gregg has admitted that stimulants were used in British football during the 1960s. Gregg admitted taking the amphetamine dexadrin – or speed – before every game, after which he would have trouble sleeping, often staying awake pacing his room into the early hours of the morning. 'I know for a fact there were things taken at that time at other clubs,' Gregg claimed. 'One famous international would put them on the towel in the dressing room and he would have two of them. He'd take one before the game. And if he wasn't playing as well as he thought he should be, he'd take the other one.'

A system of regular random tests was introduced in 1994 and has failed to reveal any great tendency towards substance abuse. This suggests either that footballers take far fewer drugs than the rest of the population, or that testing hasn't been particularly stringent. In 2003, 1,200 tests were carried out among English footballers for recreational and performance-enhancing drugs, testing taking place both in training and on match days. In Scotland testing is far less rigorous, and can only take place after a game. During 2003 there were only 42 random drug tests in Scottish football. Failed drug tests have so far only been for recreational drugs. To date, no Premiership footballer has ever tested positive for PEDs, and there have been about 50 positive tests out of over 7,000 for other substances. The most high profile of these was Chelsea goalkeeper Mark Bosnich's positive test for cocaine, which led to a nine-month ban from the game. This was followed by Romanian Adrian Mutu, also of Chelsea, who was sacked by the club in 2004 after apparently developing an addiction to cocaine.

However, a BBC survey in 2003 suggested far more widespread drug use. According to a sample of 700 footballers 5.6 per cent knew of a colleague who used performance-enhancers and 46 per cent knew of a colleague who used recreational drugs. Drugs testers have suggested collusion between players and clubs to prevent discovery. A club will be warned of the testers' visit the day before and on their arrival the testers can only select from the players present, the suggestion being that clubs will shield players suspected of having problems.

Dumbarton

Dumbarton won the first two Scottish titles after the League's formation in 1890, sharing the honour with Rangers in the inaugural season after a play-off game ended in a 2–2 draw. Having won their only Scottish Cup in 1883, and reaching five more finals before the end of the nineteenth century, the main glory years of 'The Sons' remain largely confined to the era of amateur football.

Formed in 1872 (on 'a wet Sunday afternoon', according to the club historian), they were founder members of the SFA, and make up the trio of clubs, together with Queen's Park and Kilmarnock, to have taken part in every Scottish Cup. After their sole Cup Final victory over local rivals Vale of Leven, they thrashed FA Cup winners Blackburn Olympic 6–1 for the right to be called Champions of Britain. Their two most capped players – striker John Lindsay and goalkeeper James McAulay, with eight and nine respectively – played for Scotland between 1880 and 1887.

The advent of professionalism in 1893 brought both financial trouble and a slump in performance. After finishing equal bottom of Division 1 with Leith Athletic in 1895 Dumbarton reverted to amateur status as they had no money to pay the players. The following season they finished bottom and were voted down to Division 2. Worse was to follow in the lower tier as they came last again in 1897 and were voted out of the League altogether, despite having reached the Cup Final.

Just as the town survived being burnt to the ground by James 'The Fat' in 1425, the football club returned to the League in 1906. The vagaries of a League without automatic promotion meant that as Division 2 champions in 1911 they stayed down, but were voted up two years later, despite finishing only sixth. Relegated in 1922 they remained in Division 2 for the next 50 years.

In the 1970s a limp breeze of success wafted through the evocatively named Boghead Park. Dumbarton took Celtic to a replay in the semi-final of the 1970–71 League Cup, going down 4–3 after extra time. The following season they were Division 2 champions, and survived two seasons in the top flight before missing the cut-off for the newly created ten-team Premier League. Players such as future internationals Murdo Macleod, Graeme Sharp and Ian Wallace came up through the ranks and were sold on, although an audacious attempt to sign Johan Cruyff in the early 1980s failed.

A single year in the Premier League in 1984–85 was followed by a slide to Division 3 and numerous changes in the club's ownership. In 2000 the side left Boghead Park, its home for 121 years, to relocate at 'The Rock' (or 'The Strathclyde Homes Stadium', as it's officially known), a new single-stand stadium at the confluence of the rivers Clyde and Leven directly beneath the imposing cliff that supports Dumbarton Castle. And so the club remains overshadowed by history.

Dundee

A history of Dundee FC, like one of popular British culture, is fixated with the 1960s, and a brief period when everything seemed possible. Unfortunately, those dreamy years of over-achievement have never seemed further away for a club that is now racked with financial uncertainty, another cross to bear for supporters starved of success in the 40 years since.

Dundee FC were formed in June 1893 after an amalgamation of two clubs, Our Boys and East End, and after six years of nomadic wandering they settled on their current home of Dens Park in 1899. The club grew quickly, attracting home crowds of up to 30,000 and capturing the Scottish Cup in 1910. After a losing appearance in the 1925 final, a gradual decline culminated in relegation for the first time in 1938.

However, it was the post-war period into the early 1960s that formed Dundee's golden age, beginning with a brace of League Cups in 1951 and 1952, a year which also saw a losing Scottish Cup Final appearance. This success was instigated by costly additions, yet it was a hand-reared squad that won the Division 1 Championship in 1961–62. Twelve of the fifteen playing staff were

groomed at Dens, and five would win international recognition including future Spurs legend Alan Gilzean. (A popular 1990s fanzine was entitled 'Eh Mind o' Gillie', *trans*. 'I remember Gilzean'.)

The following season 'The Dees', reached the European Cup semi-finals before succumbing to eventual winners AC Milan. Under inspirational captain Bobby 'The Sliding Tackle' Cox, now a matchday host, the Scottish Cup Final was again reached in 1964, before Dundee's brief spell of sustained prominence came to an end. There has not been a trophy won since, and boardroom shenanigans have regularly overshadowed on-field mediocrity. Then chairman Angus Cook provoked predictable outrage in 1992 when he mooted the possibility of purchasing neighbours Dundee United and merging the two clubs, whilst Canadian 'saviour' Ron Dixon displayed an unsuccessful obsession with incorporating an ice rink within Dens. Recently, notorious Italian lawyer Giovanni Di Stefano popped up temporarily to delight the media if no-one else.

The comparative success of United throughout the late 1970s and 1980s was a further endurance for Dundee fans, and meant the city's youth were swayed towards United, successful home and abroad whilst Dundee flitted between the Premier League and the First Division.

The mantle of the city's major club looked like being retaken in 2000–01 when Dundee installed Italian manager Ivano Bonetti and signed high-earning foreigners including former Argentinian World Cup winner Claudio Caniggia. What would later be called 'an experiment' ended disastrously in 2003 when the club entered administration with reported debts of £20m, which have been cut significantly since, but Dundee remain financially crippled and were relegated from the Premier League in 2005.

Dundee United

The history of Dundee United (born Dundee Hibernian in 1909) is one of an extended infancy, marked by financial concerns and neglible success, until the 1959 appointment of manager Jerry Kerr. Kerr established United in the Scottish top flight and delivered European football before becoming general manager in 1971 to make way for Jim McLean, who took the club to levels of achievement unthinkable for the Irish businessmen who founded Dundee Hibernian.

The name was a nod to the city's Irish community and an attempt to provide them with a focal point similar to Edinburgh's Hibernian and Glasgow's Celtic. However, the club had no sectarian undertones in selection or attempted appeal as the founders saw the need for widespread support to survive in the shadows of Dundee FC, an established club attracting crowds of up to 30,000.

In a show of defiance, the committee decided that their ground would be an existing pitch just 300 yards from Dundee's Dens Park home. In 1923, with initial concerns over finance and support unresolved, the committee recognized that the 'Hibernian' limited appeal. After Dundee blocked the choice of 'Dundee City', claiming the two clubs' correspondence would be mixed up, 'Dundee United' was settled on.

A couple of flirtations with Division 1 and a losing 1940 War Cup Final appearance followed, but United remained in comparative obscurity until Kerr's appointment. The former club captain recruited several Scandinavian players and preached attacking football that saw new converts converge on Tannadice. Within a year United were in Division 1 and, with the exception of 1995–96, they have been in the top division ever since.

The 1971 appointment of McLean, a 33-year-old coach at neighbours Dundee who would manage United for nearly 22 years, was an almost supernatural piece of talent-spotting by the board. The small, abrasive figure whose man-management often veered close to tyrannical, re-invigorated the youth system whilst overseeing United's installation as a leading Scottish club.

The League Cup was captured twice from four final appearances, whilst six losing Scottish Cup Final appearances provided excitement but left fans, or 'Arabs' (stemming from a 1963 game at Tannadice, played on a sand-covered pitch), pondering the existence of a 'Hampden Hoodoo'.

Three highlights shine brightest from the McLean years. Firstly, the capture of the League title in 1982–83, sweetly won with a victory at Dens Park. The following season saw an extraordinary run to the European Cup semi-finals, Roma defeating United 3–2 on aggregate. In 1986–87, an outstanding UEFA Cup run saw Terry **Venables**'s Barcelona despatched in the quarter-finals. United lost the final to IFK Gothenburg, 2–1 on aggregate.

Unsurprisingly, the 1980s' success has not been matched since, with the exception of the Hoodoo-busting 1994 Scottish Cup triumph under charismatic Serbian manager Ivan Golac.

Dunfermline Athletic

It must have been a particularly balmy evening on 2 June 1885 for the regulars of Dunfermline's Old Inn pub to decide to form a football club. Yet, when the hangovers cleared, the decision remained intact and Dunfermline Athletic was founded. That the highlight of the following 70 years or so was a change of kit to today's black and white stripes gives an indication of just how little tangible success was achieved other than the gradual growth of the fan base.

They would eventually have reasons to celebrate, starting with the 1958 appointment of Jock **Stein** as manager. Stein had followed his playing career with Celtic by taking the job of reserve-team manager but correctly concluded that his Protestant faith meant he would need additional achievements for the Celtic board to consider him for the managerial position. In Dunfermline he saw a club where he would have free rein, and he soon tasted success.

From near relegation, he led them to an astonishing Scottish Cup win in 1961. It was the start of a period of genuine achievement, with the decade seeing the club capture the Scottish Cup again in 1968 and enjoy seven European campaigns under Stein and his successors Willie Cunningham and George Farm. In 1961–62 they reached the quarter-finals of the European Cup Winners' Cup, and in 1968–69 the semi-finals of the same competition. Amongst the stars of that period was a bruising centre-forward named Alex **Ferguson**.

There followed a dip in fortunes that was as depressing as it was continual.

When Jim Leishman was appointed manager in 1983 they languished near the foot of Division 2, then Scotland's lowest. In his seven years at the helm, he brought them to the Premier League whilst delighting journalists with his propensity for issuing poems on the eve of vital matches. Leishman returned as manager in 2005.

The 1990s saw a yo-yoing between divisions until the arrival of Jimmy Calderwood, who formed a squad of uncompromising athleticism and took the Pars to a Scottish Cup Final in 2004. Despite defeat to Celtic, the victors' status as League Champions meant a return to Europe for Dunfermline after nearly 40 years. Calderwood left for Aberdeen, leaving Davie Hay to oversee a slump in the team's fortunes, including an exit from the UEFA Cup to Icelandic opposition, and increasing concerns over the club's financial health.

Less-attractive attention has been gained by the cash-strapped Pars volunteering to use an artificial pitch on trial in 2003 in return for a UEFA grant. The surface has failed to convince many of its worth, and was outlawed by a vote of the SPL in May 2005, a decision that has since been contested by the club.

early deaths

In the formative years at the end of the 19th century, when football was basically a cross between rugby and a gentlemen's kick-me contest, a number of deaths resulted from injuries sustained on the field of play. In the last decade of the century it was estimated by medical journalists that, taking rugby and football combined, just under 100 deaths had resulted through participation in these two new enthusiasms. As the game's rules were gradually honed and a referee was employed to administer them, fatalities became more infrequent.

Isolated tragedies continued to occur, however. In 1892, St Mirren's James Dunlop died of tetanus resulting from a cut received in a tackle. Four years later, Arsenal's Joseph Powell died when infection took hold after he broke his arm attempting a high kick on a sloping pitch. After a 1909 match, Hibernian's James Milne died from internal injuries. Most famously, in 1931, Celtic's 22-year-old goalkeeper John Thomson fractured his skull diving headlong at the feet of Rangers forward Sam English. Thomson died in hospital five hours later. On the brink of a great League and international career, he became a legend commemorated in a Celtic song that ends '. . . between your posts there stands a ghost, Johnny Thomson is his name'. In 1934, Gillingham's centre-forward, Sim Raleigh, collided with Paul Mooney, a Brighton defender, resulting in the former's death from a brain haemorrhage.

Many players died fighting in the First World War; Donald Bell, a Bradford defender, was awarded the Victoria Cross posthumously after he was killed at the Somme. During the Second World War a large proportion of footballers joined the Territorials or War Reserve Police, or became Army PT instructors instead of going to the front; but still 75 registered professionals were killed on active service.

Other untimely deaths have been attributed to a player's inherent medical condition. Arsenal's Bob Benson was the first such case in 1916. In the 1990s, David Longhurst of York City, Ian Bell, newly signed to Hartlepool, John Marshall, who had signed to Everton only the day before his death, and Manchester City's Marc Vivien Foe, who collapsed during a televised international between Cameroon and Colombia in June 2003, were all found to have serious but dormant cardiac conditions.

Several players have been struck by lightning in sudden storms. Spurs' brilliant inside-right John White, highly influential in bringing his team the Double in 1961, was struck by lightning and killed while playing golf on a London course in 1964. Oxford midfielder Peter Houseman, a member of Chelsea's 1970 FA Cup-winning team, died as a result of a car crash in 1977, and one of the first black England internationals, Laurie Cunningham, was killed in a car accident in Spain in 1989.

In the most reverberating tragedy of all, Manchester United lost eight of their team when their plane crashed at Munich airport in February 1958 trying to take off for the third time in poor weather conditions (see **Munich aircrash**).

More recently, Justin Fashanu, a highly talented but unsettled footballer, declared his homosexuality towards the end of his career, provoking an intense and erratic relationship with the British tabloid press. Some weeks before he was due to leave for a coaching post in the US, Fashanu, the first black player priced at £1m, hanged himself in an East London garage.

East Fife

It may seem hard to imagine now, but the Methil-based 'Fifers', founded in 1903 and League members since 1921, were one of the most celebrated clubs in Scottish football in the decade after the Second World War. The side also holds two unique Scottish football records unlikely to be broken for some time. They are the only Division 2 club to have won the Scottish Cup (in 1938), and are likewise the only team outside the top flight to have won the League Cup.

The latter success came in the remarkable 1947–48 season under the leadership of future Rangers manager Scot Symon, when East Fife were champions of Division 2 by 11 points, scoring 103 goals in the process. They lost to Rangers in the Scottish Cup quarter-final, but overcame the same opponents at the semi-final stage in the League Cup. In the final they drew 0–0 with Falkirk in front of over 52,000 fans, then won the replay 4–1, pulling in more than 30,000 for an afternoon midweek replay. Boasting five players capped by Scotland, including the hard-shooting Charlie 'Legs' Fleming, the side went on to lift the League Cup twice more in the following years – in 1949 and 1953 – and twice finished third in Division 1, their best-ever position. They were also Scottish Cup runners-up in 1950, to add to their losers' medals from 1927.

This purple patch overshadowed even their unlikely run to the Scottish Cup in 1938, when they beat Airdrie, Dundee United, Aberdeen and Raith on the way to despatching St Bernard's in the semi-final after a second replay. In the final they beat Kilmarnock 4–2 in a replay, with goalkeeper John Harvey winning a Scottish Cup medal on his debut for the club.

Success in the half-century after East

Fife's last League Cup triumph has been much harder to come by, and the reduced ambitions of a struggling Division 3 outfit are reflected in the 2,000 capacity of their new single-stand stadium at Methil Docks. On the plus side, the club announced in late 2004 that it now fully owned the stadium and had cleared the debts which had threatened its existence in the preceding years.

East Stirlingshire

In 2004 the very existence of Falkirk-based East Stirlingshire was in doubt as the club, formed in 1881 as Bainsford Britannia, looked like selling its stadium and relocating to nearby Grangemouth. With a volunteer coach, players on £10 a week and an unhappy playing record that saw them take just five points from the 2003–04 Division 3 campaign, ES gained widespread notoriety after losing 25 successive games, but little to reassure them that life would struggle on.

It wouldn't be the first time that the club has disappeared since joining the League in 1900, when they replaced Linthouse of Govan (whose catchment area encroached upon that of the mighty Rangers). In 1964 ES were bought by a Junior club in Clydebank and played in the League for one season at Kilbowie Park as ES Clydebank. The move was ruled illegal and 'The Shire' moved back to their home ground, Firs Park, while one year later Clydebank (now defunct) joined the Scottish League.

Falkirk is the smallest town in Britain to support two senior football sides, and ES have always come off second best to their bigger and more successful rivals. When they beat Falkirk at Firs Park in 1975 it was their first home success against the Bairns for 70 years. Over 4,600 saw the game. In 2004 a home game against Cowdenbeath drew less

than 700 on a day when spectators were allowed in for free, and many of those were away fans.

Bright spots in the club's history are few and far between. Striker Davie Alexander won two caps for Scotland (scoring once against Wales), but that was back in 1894, and they twice reached the Scottish Cup quarter-finals before the turn of the 20th century. In 1981 they surged to the same stage after knocking out Inverness Thistle and Cowdenbeath, but fell 2–0 to Celtic. East Stirlingshire's only honour was a 1932 Division 2 title. The following season they went straight back down.

Elgin City

When the rampaging Wolf of Badenach burnt down the town of Elgin and its cathedral in 1390 upon being excommunicated by the Bishop of Moray, he may also have razed all traces of imagination from the market town around the river Lossie. Only this would explain why the club's two nicknames – 'The City' and 'The Black and Whites' – are so uninspiring. 'The Wolves of Badenach' would surely have been more effective at terrifying opponents.

Elgin City FC, formed just over 500 years later in 1893, were at least effective in winning the Highland League – founded the same year, although Elgin didn't join until two years later – taking the trophy 15 times during just over 100 years of membership. This included a particularly dominant period between 1956 and 1970, when they were champions no fewer than nine times.

In its early Highland League years, however, Elgin struggled, briefly leaving the League on two occasions. In spite of this they nurtured a number of classy pre-First World War players such as R. C. Hamilton, who moved on to

Rangers and was capped 11 times by Scotland, and James Miller and John Mackenzie, who both likewise headed for Ibrox. But it wasn't until 1931–32, under Bert Maclachlan, that they took the Highland title.

In 1968 they enjoyed their greatest Scottish Cup run, reaching the quarter-finals after knocking out three League sides, including a third round 2–0 home defeat of Arbroath before almost 13,000 fans. They finally fell to Morton – at that time a relative powerhouse in Scottish football – by the odd goal in three. Other post-war Cup runs have ended more heavily, including two 6–1 defeats at Ibrox, although in 1960 they were narrowly pipped 2–1 by Celtic at their Borough Briggs home in the third round.

Upon gaining Scottish League status in 2000 alongside Peterhead, when the Premier League expanded to 12 teams and allowed the two sides into Division 3, the Borough Briggs stadium was upgraded with seats from Newcastle United's St James' Park, while grass banking was replaced with concrete terraces. Only the miserable perform-ances of East Stirlingshire prevented two bottom place finishes in their first three seasons, but in 2004–05 Elgin began to find their feet and finished in mid-table.

England

Buoyed by over-confidence or befuddled by self-doubt, the England team have staggered around the world playing foot-ball for over a hundred years. During this time the team has been in a state of almost constant confusion over its own abilities on the pitch and, in the last 30 years, the often unneighbourly behaviour of its supporters. The England team has been pioneering, reactionary, sports-manlike, thuggish, unlucky and cartoonishly inept. It has been both racially inclusive and, at times, a clearing house for various strains of unpleasant nationalism.

International football is a paradoxical business. On the face of it competition between countries should be cause for celebration. A presence at a major competition can be a moment of major historical importance for emerging nations. Not so for followers of England. Two things matter. How good are we? And will we win? Initial successes at any tournament are generally a signal for hysterical triumphalism. Defeat brings despair. Despite this burden of expec-tation England have tended to hover unspectacularly among the second rank of international teams. The FIFA world rankings have always been a question-able yardstick, but a best of fourth in December 1997, a worst of 27th in February 1996 and an average of around eighth sounds about right for England. The team has won the World Cup once, as hosts in 1966, the Home International Championship 54 times, and Le Tournoi de France in 1997 – their only triumph abroad.

England took part in the first official international football match, a 0–0 draw with Scotland in Glasgow in 1872. The game was organized by Charles Alcock, Honorary Secretary of the Football Association, who advertised in a sporting newspaper that a match would be played between 'the leading representatives of the Scotch and English sections'. A crowd of 4,000 turned out for what would be the first of a series of games between the two teams over the next ten years. It wasn't until 1908, when a side toured central Europe, that England first played against countries outside Britain. Rivalry with their northern neighbours is a distinctive feature of England's early history, as a team selected by an FA committee spent much of its time battling for parochial supremacy.

In more modern times, the history of any international team is bound up in its successes or failures at major tournaments. Despite steady achievement, for England international competition has been a largely painful and almost always disappointing experience. It took the Football Association 30 years to come around to the idea that the World Cup might be a tournament worth competing in. The English FA left FIFA in 1928, months before the Amsterdam congress at which Jules Rimet and Henri Delaunay finalized plans for the first ever World Cup in Uruguay. The British nations were offered guest spots at the tournament. All four declined and maintained an isolationist, wait-and-see policy throughout the 1930s as two further World Cups were staged in mainland Europe. By the time of the first post-war World Cup in Brazil all four British nations had rejoined FIFA, although only England travelled to take part in the tournament.

With pre-tournament qualification a shambolic affair – several teams withdrew at short notice, India because FIFA would not let them play in bare feet – England qualified easily and were much fancied at home. Led by their first proper manager, Walter **Winterbottom**, England became the fall guys in one of the biggest shocks in World Cup history, losing 1–0 to the USA in Belo Horizonte and exiting the tournament in humiliating circumstances. Not for the last time there was a great deal of hand-wringing over the inadequacies of the national team, with archaic training methods, insular tactics and a direct style of play blamed for the failure.

Four years later England took the same tactics, training methods and long-ball optimism to Switzerland, along with a team containing Stanley **Matthews**, Tom **Finney**, Nat **Lofthouse** and Billy **Wright**. They lost 4–2 to Uruguay in the quarter-finals, while Germany went on to beat Hungary 3–2 in the Final, signalling their own arrival as a footballing force, one that would soon emerge as a northern European World Cup superpower where England had notably failed. By the time of the 1958 World Cup England's resources had been weakened tragically by the **Munich aircrash**, in which Roger Byrne, Tommy Taylor and Duncan Edwards were killed. A young team containing Bobby **Robson**, Don **Howe** and the 20-year-old Bobby **Charlton** went out of a tough group at the first stage, despite a 0–0 draw in Gothenburg against eventual champions Brazil.

The 1962 World Cup in Chile was a disappointing tournament, notable mainly for the ferocity of the play and a rash of negative tactics. An England team featuring Charlton, Bobby **Moore** and Jimmy **Greaves** were knocked out by holders and eventual champions Brazil. England were outclassed in Vina Del Mar as Garrincha – who was to emerge as the star of the tournament – scored twice in a 3–1 victory. Again, questions arose over the nature of England's preparations. In Chile their regime included warm-up games alongside an expat middle-aged Australian millionaire. The tournament would be Winterbottom's last in charge of the team.

By the next tournament Alf **Ramsey** had managed to transform England into a team capable of beating the best in the world, admittedly in the process playing every game at Wembley and taking advantage of the helpings of good fortune afforded to most winners on home soil.

The European Championships were first staged in 1960, as a cup competition played home and away until the final stages. England performed well in 1968, reaching the semi-finals, something they would manage only once again in their history to date. They travelled to Mexico for the World Cup two years later as the only British nation to make the trip. In the rarefied air and June heat Ramsey's men would wilt in the quarter-finals against West Germany, having begun the tournament with arguably a stronger squad than four years previously.

The group stage did, however, produce perhaps England's greatest ever World Cup game, the 1–0 defeat to Mario Zagallo's peerless Brazil team of Pelé, Jairzinho and Carlos Alberto, a game that produced various incidents that have become canonized as iconic World Cup moments: Moore's perfectly balanced tackle on Jairzinho, Gordon **Banks**'s gymnastic save from Pelé's header and the fraternal shirt-swapping between Pelé and Moore at the end of the game. A rematch in the Final was keenly anticipated, but unfortunately English football was heading in another direction in 1970, propelled by the first of several high-level capitulations against West Germany, a 3–2 defeat in the heat of Leon after being two goals ahead. England failed to make it to the 1974 tournament, a stuttering qualification campaign coming off the rails at Wembley, where an underrated Poland team earned a 1–1 draw to eliminate the former champions. Ramsey resigned the following year.

The lowest period in England's international history followed as, under Don **Revie**, who left suddenly in order to take up a job offer in the Middle East, and Ron **Greenwood**, England remained on the outside of top-level international competition. They played in the 1980 European Championship but failed to progress beyond their group. At the Spain World Cup in 1982 Greenwood was manager of a talented team, including Bryan **Robson**, Ray Wilkins, Peter **Shilton** and the convalescent duo Kevin **Keegan** and Trevor **Brooking**. There was much optimism after an opening 3–1 win over France in Bilbao (Bryan Robson scoring what was then the World Cup's fastest-ever goal after 27 seconds), but Greenwood's men exited the tournament in the second round despite not losing a game, thanks to two goalless draws and an inability to convert chances.

England failed to qualify for the next European Championships, having lost surprisingly to an emerging Denmark team, Allan Simonsen scoring the only goal in a 1–0 victory for the Danes at Wembley that would signal the low point of Bobby Robson's time as England manager. Two years later at the 1986 World Cup in Mexico, Robson's team started poorly, but qualified for the next stage by way of a predatory hat-trick by Gary **Lineker** (tournament top scorer with six goals) in the 3–0 victory over Poland, followed by a 3–0 defeat of Paraguay. Diego Maradona then scored both goals – one infamous, the other sublime – in a 2–1 victory for Argentina in the Azteca stadium in the quarter-finals. His slaloming run past six England players remains one of the greatest World Cup goals. For all the furore over his use of a hand to palm the ball past Peter Shilton for his first goal, another couple of outings for the likes of Peter Reid, Steve Hodge and Terry Fenwick could not have compared with Maradona's feats in the final stages. England were squarely, if not fairly, beaten.

In 1988 England travelled to the European Championships in Germany with a formidable-looking team, containing John Barnes, Bryan Robson, Chris Waddle, Peter Beardsley and Gary Lineker. Within ten days they were out of the tournament having lost every game, the last two by 3–1 to Holland and the USSR. Despite this disappointment, at Italia 90 England enjoyed their most successful campaign ever on foreign soil as Robson's team reached the semi-finals before losing on penalties to Germany. Almost by chance the manager stumbled on a successful system, switching to a sweeper defence during the group game against Holland. Midfielders Paul **Gascoigne** and David Platt rose to the occasion alongside old hands Lineker and Terry Butcher. England topped a closely fought group by virtue of a 1–0 win over Egypt, and in the next round Platt sent them into the last eight, volleying a spectacular winner against Belgium in the last minute of extra time.

In the quarter-final England needed extra time and two penalties to see off the challenge of Cameroon, Robson's men winning 3–2 in one of the best games of a drab tournament. The semi-final against West Germany ended 1–1, Andreas Brehme scoring a fortunate deflected opener for Franz Beckenbauer's side before Lineker equalized late in the game. Inspired by Paul Gascoigne, who emerged as one of the players of the tournament, England pressed forward in extra time and hit the post twice, but the Germans held on and didn't miss a kick in the penalty shoot-out.

In 1992 there was yet another dismal performance at a European Championships, this time in Sweden. Graham **Taylor** had succeeded Robson after the World Cup only to see his team regress at an alarming rate. Suddenly England appeared to be bereft of talented footballers. Taylor's reign was characterized by short-lived selections, the manager seeming to take the view that form was permanent and class temporary. An undistinguished squad travelled to Sweden. Laden with energetic but limited midfielders and playing an antiquated long-ball game, Taylor led England to elimination at the first hurdle after a 2–1 defeat by the host nation. Failure to qualify for USA 94 meant that for the first time since before the Second World War there was no UK representation at a World Cup. For England a 2–0 defeat in Norway followed by a tense and slightly unfortunate loss to Holland in Rotterdam spelt the end. Taylor hung on a year longer before leaving his post.

The mood had changed dramatically by Euro 96, only the second major tournament England has hosted. However, euphoria at reaching the semi-finals was undercut by Terry **Venables**'s departure as manager. Venables had been popular with players, fans and press, but left the job to pursue a series of murky courtroom battles, clearing the way for the appointment of Glenn **Hoddle** – reportedly the only man approached who would actually take the job – and the winding down of Venables's own coaching career.

England qualified impressively for the World Cup in France, with a team built around Alan **Shearer**, Tony **Adams** and Paul Ince and fortified by youngsters such as Michael **Owen**, Paul Scholes and David **Beckham**. They finished second in their group behind Romania, and faced Argentina in St Etienne in the next round in what would develop into a classic World Cup encounter. With the scores level at 1–1 after two early penalties, Michael Owen scored the goal of the tournament, sprinting past two defenders from just inside the Argentinian half before finishing. Javier Zanetti levelled the scores, Hoddle's men fought on into extra time with ten men after Beckham was sent off for a flex of the ankle, and ultimately David Batty failed to convert from the penalty spot as Argentina won after a shoot-out.

Undermined by a strained relationship with players and press, Hoddle was sacked as England manager after some bizarre and ill-thought-out comments about the disabled during a press conference. Kevin Keegan was appointed in his place amid a largely contrived public clamour in the tabloid press. Keegan's England qualified for Euro 2000, beating Scotland narrowly in a play-off after fortunate results elsewhere. An ageing team exited dismally at the first hurdle. Within four months England had lost 1–0 to Germany in the final match played at the Empire Stadium, leading to Keegan's immediate televised resignation.

Almost five years of stability have followed under Sven-Göran **Eriksson**, England's first foreign coach. Immediate improvement, with World Cup qualification eased by the stunning 5–1 win against Germany in Munich, has been qualified by only steady achievement. A team based around David Beckham's long passing, Michael Owen's speed and finishing, and the defending of Rio Ferdinand and Sol Campbell promised much. But a disappointingly passive elimination at the hands of Brazil in Korea would become characteristic of the criticism of Eriksson's low-octane stewardship. Qualification for Euro 2004 was achieved easily, but the team failed to inspire, going out on penalties to the hosts Portugal. Characteristically, England failed to hold a lead after the departure of the injured Wayne **Rooney**, one of just a trio of players of genuine international class, along with Ashley Cole and Ferdinand, to have emerged during Eriksson's reign.

A decidedly friendly qualifying group helped England negotiate a more or less straightforward path to the 2006 World Cup. This was despite a historic 1–0 defeat at Windsor Park to a Northern Ireland team ranked 116th in the world, as well as gathering tabloid newspaper antipathy towards Eriksson. In January 2006 the manager duly announced that he would be leaving his post after the World Cup. In spite of this England once again travelled to a major tournament buoyed by an unquenchable optimism that star players such as Rooney and Beckham can live up to the occasionally hysterical expectation heaped upon them.

Hope, however, will continue to flourish. Despite a perceived devaluing of international football, with tournaments like the Champions' League stealing some of its thunder, as well as the recent glorified training game status of international friendlies, there will always be an England team, one that excites and frustrates in equal measures. But England are an unruly guest, one you don't want camped out in your town square. Every two years, in the good times, tournament cities across the world have either braced themselves for its arrival or given thanks for the presence instead of Norway or Ecuador. Despite this the England team holds a fascination even for people born outside its borders. England is a great footballing nation, if not on merit, then because of things like history and passion and enduring influence. In the modern era it has only ever briefly produced a national team truly worthy of this position.

Sven-Göran Eriksson

In January 2001 Sven-Göran Eriksson became the first foreign coach of the England national team. The Swede's subsequent record in the role should be seen in the context of the dismal nadir England had reached under his predecessor, Kevin **Keegan**, and the hysteria generated in certain quarters by the prospect of the national team being coached by somebody born outside its borders. 'I don't like a non-Englishman being in charge,' Terry **Venables** was quoted as saying after Eriksson's appointment, although his remarks might have been better interpreted as 'I don't like a non-Dagenham-born former board game designer and disqualified company director being in charge'.

Before his time with England Eriksson had been a successful manager in Sweden, where he won the UEFA Cup with Gothenburg, Portugal, where he took Benfica to the league title, and Serie A, where he had recently laid to rest a reputation for *almost* winning trophies by taking the league title with Lazio. 'We must dare to fail in order to dare to succeed,' he wrote in the strangely platitudinous *Sven-Göran Eriksson on Football*. Prior to Eriksson's appointment as manager, England had dared merely to be eliminated from Euro 2000 in farcical circumstances and then to lose at home to Germany in their opening World Cup 2002 qualifier. His appointment as England coach coincided with the national team's itinerant exile from Wembley. Eriksson's travelling England, built around the captaincy of David **Beckham** and a team selected after a meticulous whistlestop tour of every Premiership ground, proved an instant success. The new manager transformed what had been a jittery, tactically incoherent team into a calm, proficient unit, albeit an occasionally less than thrilling one. A significant aspect of his success was his transformation of Beckham into both the creative mainstay of the team and a tabloid-friendly England skipper. Under Eriksson, Beckham scored 12 goals in his first 26 internationals, as opposed to just one in his previous 36.

Qualification for the World Cup in Japan and South Korea was a significant triumph. The high points of the campaign were the improbable 5–1 away win in Germany, hailed at the time as the most impressive performance by any England team in the modern era, and the free-kick goal scored by Beckham at Old Trafford in the last minute of England's final qualifier against Greece to earn the point that took England to the World Cup. The latter certainly confirmed Eriksson's burgeoning reputation as a lucky manager. His record as England coach suggests otherwise. Under Eriksson England lost just one competitive international in three and a half years before defeats to France and Portugal on penalties during Euro 2004, the exception being the 2–1 defeat by Brazil in the quarter-finals of the World Cup in Shizuoka. Had England not fallen short against the world champions it is far from fanciful to suggest that they would have beaten Turkey and Germany and won the World Cup.

Like the Beatles selling American music back to Americans, Eriksson has been the most English of foreign coaches. A devotee of traditional 'direct' English football, and able to quote verbatim the statistical analysis of Wing Commander Charles Reep, Eriksson has never attempted complex tactical innovations. Pace in forward positions and quick, accurate long passing have been his approach, exemplified by the two central players of his reign, Michael **Owen** and David Beckham.

Disingenuously demure in his dealings with the tabloid press – traditionally the England manager's greatest adversary – Eriksson has so far disarmed potential critics with an opaque and at times unquotably bland public persona. Even an improbable love affair with Anglo-Swedish minor celebrity Ulrika Jonsson failed to detract from Eriksson's public popularity, based as it was in an unarguably sound set of results. A subsequent publicized affair with a secretary at the FA attracted greater censure.

An increasingly fractious relationship with sections of the press came to a head in January 2006 when a *News of the World* reporter posing as a wealthy Arab sheikh secretly filmed a meeting with the England manager on a hired luxury yacht in Dubai. Eriksson's comments about current England players, although largely uncontroversial, attracted widespread censure. Within a fortnight he had announced that he would step down after the World Cup in Germany, two years before the end of his contract. The least excitable of all recent England managers had seen his reign prematurely terminated by the standard red-top shemozzle.

Euro 96

There are two ways of looking at Euro 96. The first says that hosts England staged a well-organized tournament that was almost free of hooliganism; that home fans learnt to support their team in a patriotic rather than jingoistic manner; that football fever, to the soundtrack of 'Three Lions', held the country in thrall for a month; and that England played heroically and were unlucky to lose the semi-final on penalties to the Germans.

The second version propagates the view that the tournament was a bit of a washout – many stadiums had conspicuously empty swathes of seats because tickets were hugely overpriced (unless you were one of the several thousand lucky enough to be on a corporate beano), and because applying for tickets was both complicated and package-based; the football was largely forgettable; and that England played one good game and benefited from referees mysteriously disallowing perfectly legitimate opposition goals – Salinas for Spain in the 0–0 quarter-final that England went on to win on penalties and Kuntz for Germany in the semi (see below). The

truth is maybe somewhere in between. Indeed, there were few outstanding games, teams or individual performers, and the goals-per-game average was a miserly 2.06. The six quarter- and semi-final matches reaped a sole goal per game, with four of the ties being decided on penalties after extra time.

Nonetheless, England were involved in some of the tournament's more compelling moments, such as Paul **Gascoigne**'s brilliant solo goal against Scotland in the 2–0 group game victory, the 4–1 demolition of a divided and disillusioned Dutch side that saw England safely into the quarter-finals (but whose late slip allowing the Dutch to score meant Scotland's first-round exit on goal difference), and the exhilarating semi-final against Germany when, with the score at 1–1, Darren Anderton hit the post in extra time, and Paul Gascoigne was a slither away from connecting with a ball that crossed the face of the open German goal. Gareth Southgate missed in the penalty shoot-out, Andy Möller didn't, and Germany went through to the Final.

Their opponents were the Czech Republic, who had beaten the lacklustre French on penalties after a dire 0–0 draw in the other semi-final, at Old Trafford, and preceding that had ousted Portugal thanks to Karel Poborsky's spooned lob at Villa Park. They had also benefited at the group stage from Italian coach Arrigo Sacchi's decision to bench half of his first-choice players following an opening 2–1 win over Russia. The Czechs consequently beat Italy 2–1 and then sneaked through thanks to a last-minute equalizer in a 3–3 draw against Russia, the tournament's highest-scoring match. Meanwhile, Italy were held to a 0–0 draw by ten-man Germany and were eliminated.

The Wembley final was lively enough, with Patrik Berger scoring a penalty for the Czechs after an hour, and Oliver

Bierhoff equalizing with a header just four minutes after coming on as a substitute. In extra time the tournament's first golden-goal winner finally came by way of a half-hit Bierhoff shot that the Czech keeper Kouba could somehow only pat on to the inside of the post before it nestled reproachfully in the net. At least he had the decency to look embarrassed, and perhaps it was a fittingly anti-climactic end to a tournament where the German coach Berti Vogts stated prosaic-ally, 'I think we were the best team in the tournament and have been rightly crowned.' In fact it was one of those tournaments when anyone could have won, even Scotland.

Before the England v Germany semi-final, London's tabloid press had been at its war-invoking, xenophobic worst. How they must have had to swallow on their own insults and hatred as our smiling Queen (of German ancestry, of course) handed over the winners' trophy to the very model of Anglo-German concili-ation, Jürgen Klinsmann. Europe 1, Little England 0.

European Cup

There was a time before the Champions' League (not really a league, and not really competed for by champions), when UEFA ran a gloriously simple compe-tition. The title-winners of each European country would play in a two-legged knockout tournament to see who became champions of Europe, with the one-game final to be played at a neutral venue.

The idea was not UEFA's, but origin-ated from *L'Équipe* journalist Gabriel Hanot. Only when he initiated the compe-tition in the mid-1950s by bringing the representatives of a number of clubs together in Paris did the footballing auth-orities realize its potential. FIFA sanc-tioned the Cup with the proviso that

clubs could only play with the approval of their home associations, and that it should be managed by UEFA. In terms of prestige it quickly usurped the existing multi-national club competition, the Mitropa Cup, which was restricted to central European teams.

Sixteen teams competed in the first year, 1955–56 (England's entrant, Chelsea, didn't play on the advice of the Football League), and not all were league champions. The following year Manchester United became England's first team in competitive European play, falling to Real Madrid in the semi-finals, and it was the Spanish side who domi-nated the competition's free-scoring early years by taking all of the first five titles.

This culminated in the famous 7–3 win over Eintracht Frankfurt at Hampden Park in 1960 (Frankfurt themselves had beaten Glasgow Rangers 12–4 on aggre-gate in the semi-final). Madrid's stellar frontline of Alfredo Di Stefano (3) and Ferenc Puskás (4) split the goals between them in front of 135,000 fans. Two years later Puskás scored another hat-trick, against Benfica, but this time Madrid shipped five in return, two scored by Eusébio, confirming that the previous year's win over Barcelona had been no fluke for the Portuguese club.

After that a number of teams imposed their particular style on the competition for short periods. The counter-attacking Internazionale side of the mid-1960s made the previous goal-packed finals already seem a distant memory, and preceded the first British successes of Celtic (1967) and Manchester United (1968). The fluid Ajax side of Cruyff and Neeskens won the trophy three times in a row between 1971 and 1973, before Bayern Munich enjoyed a similar trio of triumphs, including a controversial 2–0 win over Leeds in the 1975 final, a game that saw crowd disturbances that led to

Leeds being banned from European competition for three years. The trophy then stayed in England for seven of the next eight years, Liverpool taking it four times, Nottingham Forest twice, and Aston Villa once. Five of these finals were won by a single goal to nil, while Liverpool's 1984 victory over Roma was decided on penalties after a 1–1 draw.

After English clubs were banned from Europe in the wake of the **Heysel disaster** low-scoring finals became the norm, with Steaua Bucharest, PSV Eindhoven and Red Star Belgrade all winning on spot-kicks after goalless games. Red Star's turgid 1991 encounter with Olympique Marseille became the final year that the competition was played as a straight knockout. It was a sad, if fitting, finale to what had once been a showpiece competition.

European Cup Winners' Cup

A cup competition to determine the champion winners of cup competitions may sound a superfluous concept, but it could be argued that the European Cup Winner's Cup was as pure a cup competition as they come. Not pure enough for UEFA, however, who axed it in 1999 after almost 40 years.

Glasgow Rangers reached the first final, in 1960–61, losing 4–1 to Fiorentina over two legs. The next year, 23 teams entered, and the final became a single-leg affair, Fiorentina this time losing to Atlético Madrid. Then in 1963 Tottenham became the first English side to win a European title, Bill **Nicholson**'s side hammering holders Atlético 5–1 in Rotterdam, with Jimmy **Greaves** and Terry Dyson both scoring twice.

No single side ever dominated the Cup Winners' Cup in the same way that clubs did the European Cup, but British sides

fared well, with West Ham, Manchester City, Chelsea (who beat Real Madrid at the second attempt at a time when draws were still replayed) and Rangers all holding the Cup aloft up to 1972. The following year Leeds United were thwarted by a suspect Greek referee, Michas, who failed to award them a number of clear decisions in their 1–0 defeat to AC Milan in Salonika. Michas was later suspended by UEFA.

One of the great things about the Cup Winners' Cup was that it offered teams from second-tier European nations, or second-tier teams from 'big' countries, a shot at glory. FC Magdeburg of East Germany beat AC Milan in 1974, Anderlecht of Belgium triumphed 4–2 over West Ham in 1976 (and won it again in 1978), while other less celebrated victors included Aberdeen, Mechelen, Dynamo Tbilisi, Sampdoria and Paris St-Germain.

Finals were generally less guarded affairs than the European Cup. Barcelona beat Fortuna Düsseldorf by the odd goal in seven in 1979, and only the Valencia–Arsenal game the following year ended 0–0, remaining the sole final decided on penalties. Manchester United announced English clubs' return to Europe after the **Heysel disaster** ban by defeating Barcelona 2–1 in 1991.

Ultimately, UEFA reacted to moans that the cup could not generate enough income for its participants, and in the wake of the burgeoning, bloated Champions' League the Cup Winners' Cup was killed off. Lazio won the final competition in a lively match at Villa Park, defeating Mallorca 2–1. National cup winners are now directed towards the UEFA Cup.

European Footballer of the Year

Like the World Cup and the European Cup, the European Footballer of the Year award was a French idea. In 1956 the magazine *France Football* asked selected journalists around Europe to vote for their player of the year and Stanley **Matthews** was the first recipient – as a result Blackpool are still one of only three English clubs to boast a winner, with Manchester United and Liverpool. Unlike the two great team competitions, it did not take France long to record their own winner, with Raymond Kopa in 1958 (Michel Platini, Jean-Pierre Papin and Zinedine Zidane have followed).

Kopa's success, in his first year at Real Madrid, hinted that the award would almost always recognize achievement in either the European Cup, World Cup or European Championships – since it is presented in December, it reflects the calendar year rather than the season. There were a few early exceptions, such as Dynamo Moscow's Lev Yashin in 1963 and Florian Albert of Ferencváros in 1967, and more recently Michael **Owen** (2001), whose Liverpool side won the UEFA Cup and England's two knockout trophies. Yashin was also exceptional in being the only goalkeeper to have won the award; only Dino Zoff (second in 1973), Ivo Viktor (third in 1976) and Oliver Kahn (third in 2001 and 2002) have come remotely close to emulating him.

Defenders have suffered similarly. Inter's Giacinto Facchetti was a close runner-up to Eusébio in 1965, Bobby **Moore** came second to Gerd Müller in 1970 and Franco Baresi chased Marco van Basten in 1989, but only the two great German converts from midfield to sweeper, Franz Beckenbauer (1972 and 1976) and Matthias Sammer (1996), have won.

Indeed, Beckenbauer can claim the greatest record of all in the award, for although Platini won in three straight years (1983–85) and Van Basten and Johan Cruyff also took the award three times, Beckenbauer finished in the top

five on a record ten occasions, including seven years in a row (1970–76).

Among English players, Kevin **Keegan** has been the most successful, winning in 1978 and 1979 while at Hamburg, while Bobby **Charlton** (1966) joined Matthews and Owen. Denis **Law** of Scotland and Northern Ireland's George **Best** won with Manchester United in 1964 and 1968 respectively, while John **Charles** (third in 1959) and Ian **Rush** (fourth in 1984) were Wales's best efforts. No player from the Republic of Ireland has ever finished in the top five. Kenny **Dalglish**, with perhaps Ferenc Puskás, Charles, Dennis Bergkamp and Bernd Schuster (who finished in the top three three times), might count himself among the unluckier players never to win.

Of England's clubs, behind Man Utd (three wins and eight in the top three), Liverpool (one win, one second) and Blackpool (one win) come six others who have had a player in the top three: Arsenal (Thierry **Henry**), West Ham (Moore), Wolves (Billy **Wright**), Fulham (Johnny Haynes), Newcastle (Alan **Shearer**) and Tottenham (Jimmy **Greaves**). Celtic's Jimmy Johnstone was third in 1967, while Gordon Strachan rode to fourth place in 1983 on the back of Aberdeen's European Cup-Winners' Cup triumph.

The chances of a player from a relatively small club featuring again have greatly diminished in recent years, although Theo Zagorakis of Bologna was an unlikely fifth in 2004 thanks to Greece's European Championships win. No team from eastern Europe has figured in the top five since Darko Pancev and Dejan Savicevic of Red Star Belgrade shared second place in 1991.

Despite the sometimes contentious nature of the voting – only a select group of journalists gets to vote and some have been known to favour their more obscure compatriots – the Ballon d'or (Golden Ball) trophy was certainly regarded as the highest individual honour for a European player until the 1990s. In recent years it has been challenged by FIFA's World Player of the Year (voted on by national team coaches since 1991) and undermined by the decision to allow non-European players at European clubs to become eligible from 1995. Of the first ten awards since then, three went to Brazilians and one to the Liberian George Weah. The influence of the big tournaments also reached a rather absurd peak in 2002, when Real Madrid's Ronaldo won on the back of a World Cup-winning performance, despite appearing only sporadically for his club.

Everton

Founder members of the Football League in 1888, no club has spent more seasons in the top division of English football than Everton, or achieved so much – nine League championships and five FA Cups – without ever truly establishing itself as the greatest team of a particular era. Nicknamed 'The Toffees' after Ye Ancient Everton Toffee House, situated close to the hotel where the club was founded, they came into being in 1878 as the football section of St Domingo's church social club, changing their name to Everton a year later. The Moonlight Dribblers (early teams trained late at night) won the League championship in 1891 and again in 1914, by which time they had also finished runners-up in the League six times, a spell of near-triumph that was a characteristic of the club in its early years; Everton won the FA Cup in 1906, but also finished runners-up three times by 1907.

The most successful period in Everton's history occurred just before the Second World War, and coincided with

the emergence of their greatest player, Dixie **Dean**, who was the key figure in their League championships of 1928 and 1932 (after winning Division 2 a year before, one of only four seasons spent outside the top flight). The team's precisely orchestrated style of play in this period inspired the nickname 'School of Science', which is still cited today though nearly always in a disparaging way. ('Don't talk to me about the "School of Science",' raged Liverpool manager Roy Evans after a particularly robust Everton team had got a point at Anfield in a 1995 League match.) Everton's 1939 championship team was possibly their best ever, with Tommy **Lawton** replacing Dean and Joe **Mercer** a key figure at wing-half, but both were released after the war and the club went into a steep decline, spending three seasons in Division 2 in the mid-1950s, though they did reach the FA Cup semi-finals in 1953.

During the 1960s one of the finest Everton sides emerged, managed by the taciturn Harry Catterick. Scottish forward Alex Young (later the focal point of an early Ken Loach drama, *The Golden Vision*) starred in the team that won the League title in 1963, took the FA Cup again in 1966 and, with the addition of midfielders Alan Ball and Howard Kendall, won the League championship in 1970. Goalkeeper Gordon West and centre-half Brian Labone, both capped by England, also played in all their trophy-winning sides during this period.

Everton's young title-winning team then fell away sharply, finishing in the bottom half for three consecutive seasons. A new team assembled by Catterick's successor, Billy Bingham, topped the table at Easter in 1974–75 but finished fourth, the four points dropped to relegated Carlisle costing them the championship. Gordon Lee took Everton to the League Cup Final in 1977, where they lost to

Aston Villa in the last minute of extra time in the second replay. The following season they finished third, with centre-forward Bob Latchford (who celebrated scoring by running a few steps then jumping and punching the air like a seven-year-old in the back garden) winning a cash prize for 30 League goals in the season.

Howard Kendall returned as manager in the early 1980s and, after a mediocre start that led to some of the club's lowest recorded crowds, constructed the greatest Everton team of modern times. Built around the goalkeeping of Neville Southall and a fine midfield of Kevin Sheedy, Paul Bracewell, Peter Reid and Trevor Steven, Kendall's Everton won first-division championships in 1985 and 1987 and the FA Cup in 1984 (when they also lost the League Cup Final in a replay to Liverpool). They lifted the club's only European trophy, the European Cup Winners' Cup, in 1985. However, even during their most successful period of modern times, Everton found themselves narrowly overshadowed by the achievements of their city neighbours Liverpool.

The rivalry with Liverpool, although not based in any regional city divide, has always been intense. On occasion it has been claimed that a sectarian footballing divide akin to that of Glasgow's Rangers and Celtic exists in Liverpool, with Everton the Catholic club, with attendant Irish connections, and Liverpool the more Scot-friendly Protestants. However, such a schism would seem to be based in the assumptions of a small minority of fans rather than any genuine historical or social affiliation. Nevertheless the rivalry between the two clubs has become more heated in recent times, perhaps owing in part to a shift among supporters of both clubs to living further away from the city centre, where previously they might have been neighbours. A tendency among a minority of Everton fans to cite the Euro-

pean ban imposed after the **Heysel disaster** as the impetus for the dissolution of their greatest modern team has not eased the relationship.

Recently Everton have succeeded in breaking a run of relegation-haunted Premiership seasons, the worst of which saw Mike Walker's team come back from two down at home to Wimbledon on the final day of the season in 1993–94 to win 3–2, and hold on to a place in the Premiership. Despite an FA Cup triumph under Joe Royle in 1995 this feat of escapology would be repeated in 1998 when, with Kendall returning briefly for a third spell in charge, Everton avoided relegation on goal difference on the final day of the season. This sparked delirious pitch invasions for the second time in five seasons as the club held on to its 45-year tenure in the top division by the narrowest of margins.

Under current manager David Moyes, Everton have enjoyed two successful seasons, finishing seventh and fourth, sandwiching a dismal 17th in 2003–04. The team struggled again at the start of 2005–06 but rallied to finish 11th. This period coincided with the emergence of the precocious youth team product Wayne **Rooney**, whose transfer to Manchester United for £27m at the age of 18 confirmed both the club's short-term financial survival, and their decline since being considered one of the 'big five' in English football during the 1980s.

Exeter City

Exeter City spent the first 70 years of their League existence meandering between divisions 3 and 4, before finally making it into Division 2 by default in 1992 after the creation of the Premiership. Two seasons at such a rarefied level seemed to induce a kind of vertigo, as within ten years the club had fallen out of the League, relegated to the Conference in 2003 after escaping a similar fate in 1995 only thanks to the 'inadequate facilities' of Conference champions Macclesfield Town.

Founded in 1904, Exeter turned professional in 1908 after a meeting of club members at the Red Lion Hotel. Exeter boast the distinction of having been Brazil's first-ever international opponents, taking on the team who would become five-time World Cup winners in Rio de Janeiro in July 1914 during a South American tour. Brazil won the game 2–0. The only major honour in the club's history remains the Division 4 championship in 1990, a ten-point procession that seemed to promise an era of unprecedented success.

However, the charge through the divisions failed to materialize and relegation in 1994 was followed by mounting debts and then a bizarre interlude as celebrity psychic Uri Geller headed up a consortium that took over the club. Geller promised not to use his paranormal powers to influence events on the pitch, and proved as good as his word as Exeter finished bottom of the League after his only season. They did, nonetheless, enjoy the benefits of morale-boosting visits from Geller's celebrity pals, Michael Jackson and illusionist David Blaine. The club have since been taken over by a supporters' trust and experienced one of their greatest days in January 2005 when they took Manchester United to a replay in the FA Cup having drawn the first match at Old Trafford.

Exeter's nickname, 'The Grecians', derives from a re-enactment of the Siege of Troy staged in 1737 at St Sidwell's just outside the city walls. St Sidwell's inhabitants soon become known locally as Greeks, gradually adapted to Grecians, a name naturally associated with the club after their ground was built in Sidwell Street.

extra time

When knockout matches finish level after full time, the usual first resort is extra time, consisting of two periods of 15 minutes when tired limbs and minds can lead a stalemate to become a goal feast. Or another stalemate. In 1968, the second European Cup Final to finish level after 90 minutes saw Manchester United convert a 1–1 draw with Benfica into a 4–1 win. But the first goalless 90 minutes in a World Cup Final, between Brazil and Italy in 1994, was followed by the first goalless extra time in a World Cup Final.

Extra time is not a new idea: the fourth and fifth FA Cup finals, 1875 and 1876, saw Old Etonians battle to 1–1 draws then play through goalless additional periods, before losing in replays. Wanderers became the first team to win the FA Cup in extra time against Oxford University in 1877. Old Etonians became the second team to lose in extra time, against Blackburn Olympic in 1883.

When extra time doesn't work, replays, especially in international tournaments, are not good options because of tight schedules. Nor are penalty shoot-outs felt to be satisfactory and, after a succession of matches settled that way, including that 1994 World Cup Final, golden-goal extra time was introduced, whereby as soon as a goal was scored the match finished.

This method settled the 1996 and 2000 European Championship finals, won by Germany and France. But the acrimony that followed France's winning goal, a disputed penalty, against Portugal in the 2000 semi-final led to a rethink and the introduction of the silver goal, whereby a team ahead at half-time in extra time are the winners. This rule decided the Greece v Czech Republic semi-final at Euro 2004, with what was almost a golden silver goal, with there being virtually no time left to restart the match.

FA Amateur Cup

Founded in 1894 as a reaction to the
FA Cup's domination by professional
teams, the FA Amateur Cup Final has
been contested by teams as diverse as
Middlesbrough, Bournemouth Gasworks,
Barnet, Wimbledon and Depot Battalion
Royal Engineers. In its early days it was
frequently the property of teams of
ex-public schoolboys such as Old
Carthusians and Old Malvernians. When
most of these teams deserted to stage
their own Arthur Dunn Cup, it was north-
east clubs such as Stockton, West
Hartlepool and Bishop Auckland that
came to the fore in the early part of the
20th century. The final between Stockton
and Eston United in 1912, played at
Middlesbrough, drew 20,000 spectators.

In 1974–75 the Amateur Cup was
renamed the FA Vase, as by this time
most of the clubs taking part were a long
way from being amateurs. In fact the
trophy had long been the property of
teams from two distinct geographical
regions, those of the Northern League
plus the Isthmian and other leagues from
the south-east. Outside these competitions, very few teams were considered
genuine amateurs and therefore eligible
to compete.

Crowd figures sometimes rose to
above 30,000 between the wars when
London sides such as Leyton, Clapton,
and Dulwich Hamlet – three times
winners in the 1930s, including a 7–1
thrashing of Marine in 1932 at Upton
Park – successfully challenged the
northern grip. It was after the Second
World War, however, that the competition really came into its own, pulling
capacity 100,000 crowds at Wembley for
five successive years in the 1950s.

The first final to achieve this was the
1951 clash between Pegasus, a team of
Oxford and Cambridge graduates, and

Bishop Auckland. Pegasus took the final 2–1. The Pegasus team contained many older players, their careers put on hold by the war, and the club's lifetime as a footballing force would be brief. The following year an all east London final between victors Walthamstow Avenue and Leyton was also a sell-out, before Pegasus returned for a final fling in 1953, whipping Harwich & Parkeston 6–0. The 1954 showdown between Bishop Auckland and Crook Town drew a total crowd of 192,000 over three games, including two replays at Newcastle and Middlesbrough, before Crook triumphed 1–0. Bishop Auckland's 2–0 beating of Hendon the year after was the last time Wembley sold out for the amateurs.

Since the competition's renaming as the FA Vase, spectator numbers have slumped, although the final was still played at Wembley up until its closure for rebuilding. It remains a very well-subscribed tournament – in 1999, 446 clubs entered the competition, leading to the creation of two preliminary rounds before the first round proper. Billericay Town are the FA Vase kings, having hoisted the silverware on a record three occasions.

It helps to be called 'Town'. Not only did Halesowen Town take the Vase in successive years in the mid-1980s, but from 1992 to 2001 ten successive winners from nine different non-cities – Wimborne, Bridlington, Diss, Arlesey, Brigg, Whitby, Tiverton (twice), Deal and Taunton – were all blessed with the moniker, and a generation of local newspaper sub-editors could draw on the headline 'It's Town for the Crown!'

FA Cup

For over a hundred years the FA Cup was considered the most important club football tournament in the world. This was more than just English insularity. The Cup was the first national football tournament anywhere, and the first to impose a unifying set of rules on its participants.

The competition may have diminished in importance in recent years, ranking behind even qualification for the preliminary stages of the Champions League for many Premiership managers, but it remains the bedrock of the modern game. The origins of the Cup must be seen in context. Up until the mid 19th century football matches tended to be played according to an ad hoc set of rules. A murky permissiveness prevailed. Captains would agree beforehand on whether to allow 'hacking' (i.e. vicious limb-threatening fouls) and handling of the ball.

Conforming to the FA's rules of the game – including the outlawing of hacking and the introduction of the handball rule – was a prerequisite for participation in the Cup. Among those willing to take their place in the Cup under these constraints, a rabble of public school dissenters went out and created something very different: rugby, a sport where hacking, handball and carrying a picnic hamper in the boot of your estate car are to this day actively encouraged. Football, meanwhile, was being led along a civilizing path.

The FA Cup was first staged in 1871–72. It was organized by the secretary of the Football Association, C. W. Alcock, and featured just 15 clubs. The first winners were the Wanderers, who beat the Royal Engineers 1–0 in a final staged at the Kennington Oval in London, also the scene of the first ever cricket Test Match in England. In its early years the trophy was won by a succession of southern amateur sides. Blackburn Olympic, in 1883, were the first northern team to win the Cup, ushering in an 18-year period of northern dominance. Before long the Cup Final had evolved into a great season-ending show-piece occasion. Crowds mushroomed as professionalism transformed the game. The 1913 Final at the Crystal Palace Stadium attracted more than 120,000 people and ten years later the **White Horse Final**, the first to be played at the new Empire Stadium at Wembley, drew a crowd of around 200,000.

The particular appeal of the Cup lies not just in its finals. A competition that ends in May is also an essential part of watching football in January and February, the third and fourth rounds breathing fresh life into the middle of the season. In modern times this has been the point at which clubs in the top two divisions join the competition, taking on the lower and non-League clubs who have made it through the first two rounds. Acts of giant-killing are rare but tend to stay in the memory.

In recent years it has become increasingly rare for smaller teams to lift the Cup. The last genuine surprise was Wimbledon's 1–0 Final victory over Liverpool in 1988, which also featured the first-ever missed penalty in an FA Cup Final, Dave Beasant saving John Aldridge's kick. Before that Sunderland's 1–0 victory over Leeds in 1973, Southampton's victory over Man Utd in 1976 and West Ham beating Arsenal in 1980 – the last time a club outside the top flight won the Cup – provided similar upsets. In terms of all-round competition the Cup enjoyed a golden era from the mid-1920s to mid-1940s. From 1927, when Cardiff City became the only Welsh club ever to win the FA Cup, to Wolves' victory in 1949, there were 14 different winners in 15 years of competition. These included the sole FA Cup-winning campaigns of Portsmouth, Derby and Charlton, which came in successive tournaments.

The Matthews Final of 1953 is perhaps the most famous of all FA Cup matches. Its legend resides not just in the game itself, in which Blackpool rallied from 3–1 down late on to beat Bolton 4–3. The occasion became a centrepiece to a year of national celebration as Britain emerged from the post-war austerity of the 1940s. Stan Mortensen's hat-trick remains the only such scoring feat in an FA Cup Final (although his first goal, a deflected shot, was initially thought to have been an own goal).

During the 1950s and early 1960s there was much talk of the Wembley hoodoo, as FA Cup finals were marred by a series of high-profile injuries although these were more likely to be caused by nerves and end-of-season weariness. The Cup Final has traditionally been a tense, closely fought affair and often a disappointment as a game of football. Every so often, however, a classic final comes along. In 1966 Everton came from 2–0 down to beat Sheffield Wednesday 3–2, with two goals from young Cornish striker Mike Trebilcock, one of many minor footballing names stitched into the history of the domestic game by their association with the Cup. In 1971 Arsenal won another classic Final, completing the League and Cup Double by beating Liverpool 2–1 after extra time with a memorable winning goal from Charlie George, who then unveiled the first-ever high-profile personalized goal celebration (a slow-motion backwards dive).

The 1970s was a golden era for the notion of the Magic of the Cup. During a time of general economic depression, 12 years without a World Cup finals appearance for the England team, and the beginnings of the grimmer aspects of hooliganism and the running down of stadiums around the country, the Cup provided much compensatory excitement. Sunderland's 1–0 underdog victory over Leeds United in 1973 was memorable, as was Liverpool's 3–0 defeat of Newcastle United the following year. The 1980s saw underdog triumphs for Wimbledon in 1988 and Coventry a year earlier. The most notable final of the decade was probably the all-Merseyside affair in 1989 that followed the **Hillsborough disaster** semi-final. Liverpool won 3–2 but the game was memorable more for the sense of grief inside Wembley.

During the 1990s the decline in the relative importance of the FA Cup began in earnest, helped on its way by the superlative marketing success of the Sky TV-sponsored Premiership. The Champions' League sharpened appetites within the game for European football, and for a revenue-chasing decade-long beano that seemed to leave the FA Cup lost somewhere in its wake. In 2000 Manchester United declined to defend the trophy after winning it the previous year, choosing instead to take part in an underwhelming Club World Championship competition in Brazil when the third and fourth rounds were due to be played. Such a decision would have been unthinkable even a decade earlier. However, the fact remains that any diminishing in the lustre of the world's oldest football tournament exists only at the very top of the scale. Sadly, with Arsenal, Manchester United, Liverpool and Chelsea winning 13 of the last 14 FA Cup finals, it seems that those clubs who value the FA Cup least will nevertheless continue to monopolize it.

FA Sunday Cup

In 1960 the FA allowed Sunday leagues to become affiliated to county associations, and four years later it even let them have their own national cup with a prestigious final venue. Which is why there are so many fat, middle-aged men in English pubs sitting at bars up and down the country spinning unlikely yarns about the time they played at Carrow Road or The Hawthorns.

In the first season, counties sent representative sides, but London beating Staffordshire over two legs was of little significance to anyone, so in 1965–66 clubs from Sunday league top divisions could enter. More likely-sounding Sunday teams – in this case Ubique United and Aldridge Fabrications – reached the final.

Now the fixture list has a poetry all of its own. While winners and losers may be of little importance to anyone but the players, their immediate families and the old man with the labrador who comes to shout at the referee, there's nothing like the sound of Codsall 440 versus Ruston Dorman to pique the ear of the amateur football enthusiast. Or Peterlee Moorcock v Lobster. Tabular-Beaufort v Ollis Transport Combined. And all on a Sunday too.

FA Trophy

This knockout national cup was introduced in the 1969–70 season for senior semi-professional sides, although it never quite captured the imagination of the non-League footballing public in the way that the Amateur Cup had once done. Indeed it was the Amateur Cup (which was replaced in 1974 by the FA Vase) that drew the bigger crowd at the end of the season, pulling in 33,000 compared with the 28,000 that came to see Macclesfield Town beat Telford United 2–0 at Wembley. The Challenge Trophy's record attendance – 34,842 for the 1991 final between Wycombe Wanderers and Kidderminster Harriers – still falls well shy of the many higher crowds that came to post-Second World War FA Amateur Cup finals.

Only two teams have so far completed the double of FA Trophy and Conference title-winners. In 1984–85, Wealdstone were the first side to take both contests (when the Conference was called the Gola League), under the managership of Brian Hall and with the help of the explosive-sounding Cordice brothers, beating Boston United 2–1. This was two years too early for automatic promotion to the Football League to have sweetened the triumph further. When the Martin O'Neill-led Wycombe Wanderers beat Runcorn 4–1 in 1993 they also took the Conference title along with FL promotion. Other dominant forces include erstwhile Football League members Scarborough, who picked the trophy up three times in five years during the 1970s, and the recently bankrupted Telford United, five-time finalists and three-time holders. Latterly, Woking racked up a treble of victories in three of the four finals spanning 1994 to 1997 (with former Chelsea veteran Clive Walker, once hailed as 'the new Pelé', approaching his career's end as a medal-winner in all three), while Kingstonian took successive titles across the turn of the century. Since Wembley reconstruction began, finals have been played at Villa Park.

Falkirk

Though it may pain a supporter to admit it, Falkirk could be the epitome of a nondescript, middle-ranking Scottish club. Their history might be long (they formed in 1876), but with the exception of a couple of Scottish Cup wins in 1913 and 1957 it's fairly uneventful, even if you include them making football's first £5,000 signing (Syd Puddefoot from West Ham in 1922) and hosting Britain's first televised floodlit match.

Generally they've bobbed between Scotland's top two divisions, and provided a few players for the national team along the way (their most capped player, full-back Alex Parker, was a member of the 1957 Cup winners before moving to Everton). Oddly though, the Stirlingshire club has been a regular home for Scotland managers during their playing days. Craig Brown played in Falkirk's navy blue, as did Alex **Ferguson** and his successor as Scottish boss, Andy Roxburgh, who formed a very successful strike partnership in the side that won promotion from Division 2 in 1971.

Having suffered the ignominy of being relegated in their centenary year, Falkirk underwent something of a renaissance in the early 1990s under Jim Jefferies without properly establishing themselves in the top flight. Relegated to Division 1 in 1996, they were promoted back to the Scottish Premier League in 2005. They reached the Cup Final in 1997 (losing to Kilmarnock, having beaten Celtic in a replayed semi-final) and the semis in 1998.

During the 1990s, any on-field success was matched by off-field shenanigans and mismanagement, and the club was placed in provisional liquidation in 1998. While a successful supporters' campaign kept the club afloat until it was bought, Falkirk's biggest problem remained their ground, Brockville Park – a site too small to allow redevelopment to meet SPL standards and, at the time, unattractive for retail development – which cost the club a play-off for a place in the SPL in 2000, and promotion after winning Division 1 in 2003. On both occasions, groundsharing proposals were rejected by the SPL.

Brockville was sold in 2003, allowing construction of a new ground to start, and after one season sharing with

Stenhousemuir the club moved to the Falkirk Stadium, in August 2004. The ground remains an odd structure – an impressive main stand will be flanked by an end stand designed purely to take the number of seats over the SPL minimum. However, there remains cause for optimism. Falkirk has its own training facility (a bit of a rarity in Scotland) and a focus on financial stability that should see them equipped to survive what might be a shrinking game.

famous people

There have been plenty of failed trialists and former apprentices who have gone on to become famous for doing something else. There are also plenty of urban myths about celebrities and football that have taken on increasing credibility with each retelling. Did Leonard Rossiter really try out for Everton as a schoolboy? Sadly it appears not, although he did once score every goal in an 11–0 victory for his school team. Sean Connery did have a trial for East Fife although not, as is sometimes reported, for Celtic or Manchester United (Matt **Busby** invited him but he was too busy performing in *South Pacific*). Rod Stewart did spend some time as an apprentice at Brentford, although he never got close to the first team. David Frost was able to consider a professional career with Nottingham Forest but opted for university instead.

Similarly, Des O'Connor was once on the books of Northampton Town, although his only appearances came for the reserves in the United Counties League. As Northampton club historian Frank Grand has recalled: 'It was just after the war and the club were giving trials to just about any young lad who came along.' Latterly O'Connor has played down his own talents: 'I played

wing and was very fast . . . unfortunately, I often forgot to take the ball with me.'

There seems to be something about comedians. Eddie Large and Stan Boardman were briefly at Manchester City and Liverpool respectively, Bob Mortimer had schoolboy trials for Middlesbrough and the actor Ralf Little was a trialist with Swindon and Millwall. Among musicians, Leyton Orient ran the rule over David Essex in 1962 and Robbie Williams was briefly involved with Port Vale at a junior level. Despite his professed fandom, he refused appeals to aid the financially stricken Vale until he was finally persuaded to invest in the club in 2006.

Perhaps strangest of all, the Duke of Westminster was a promising junior footballer and had trials with Fulham. The Duke was eventually forbidden to pursue a career as a footballer by his father, who was reported to be appalled by the sight of men 'kissing' one another during goal celebrations.

fanzines

From the mid-1980s football fans in the UK found a platform for their opinions through fanzines, small-scale publications that provided an alternative perspective on the game. The fanzine subculture began to develop after the **Heysel disaster** and **Bradford fire** of 1985, when football was shackled with an appalling public image and grew largely from the desire of fans to counter that image with their own views – not only on the serious issues that threatened football's future but also on the more quirky, trivial and even ludicrous aspects of being a fan.

Lurid and exaggerated press reports of fan violence would have led anyone who didn't attend matches themselves to think that stadiums were hazardous, potentially life-threatening environments, teeming with drunken maniacs. Contemporary press coverage of football was largely split between glossy magazines aimed at teenagers and the tabloid newspapers, devoted to sensationalist exposés of the sport's seamier side.

Two national publications, *When Saturday Comes* (*WSC*) and *Off the Ball*, were launched almost simultaneously in March 1986, though without any prior knowledge of the other's existence. Both aimed to establish contact with other fans who were dissatisfied with the way the game was run and written about – *Off the Ball*, based in Birmingham, folded after 16 issues; *WSC* still exists as a monthly. A rash of club-specific fanzines quickly followed.

Small magazines covering other subcultures, particularly punk music, had been in existence since the mid-1970s and the new football fanzines drew heavily on these in their appearance and attitudes. Most, however, were unaware of football's own forerunner. Beginning in 1972, a group of students at Cambridge University had published *Foul*, motivated, according to one of its writers, Chris Lightbown (quoted in *The Face* in 1987), by the fact that 'football had simply not assimilated any of the social or cultural changes of the sixties. It was in a complete time warp.' *Foul* lasted just four years – finished off partly by legal action from a tabloid journalist – but a number of its gripes, such as poor media coverage and the lack of creativity in the British game, were echoed by many of the fanzines that emerged in the late 1980s.

The growth of fanzines ran parallel with the appearance of politicized supporters' groups, whose principal task was to defend football and its fans from the sustained attacks of the government and, at times, its own authorities.

Margaret Thatcher's post-Heysel resolve to 'do something' about hooliganism led to a woefully misconceived plan, finally abandoned in 1990, that would have required spectators to produce identity cards in order to gain admission to grounds.

Between 1988 and 1990 the number of fanzines mushroomed from around 20 to over 200, most of them charting the fortunes of specific clubs from the perspective of the committed supporter. New computer technology meant fanzines could be produced cheaply and relatively professionally at home. Almost every club in the country had at least one, the vast majority of which were non-profit-making, produced on a monthly or bi-monthly basis, and sold only a few hundred copies, although combined sales over a season exceeded a million. Among the best were *The Almighty Brian* (Nottingham Forest), *AWOL* (the now defunct Meadowbank Thistle) and *The Absolute Game* (covering Scottish football in general).

The fanzine boom had subsided by the mid-1990s, after which websites and internet message boards became the focal points of fan activity, although many long-established titles are still published, including *Brian Moore's Head* (Gillingham), *When Skies are Grey* (Everton) and Bradford City's *City Gent*, the longest-running fanzine, having been in existence since October 1984. In the late 1990s, attempts were made to transpose the spirit of fanzine culture to television, with varied results. The best effort was BBC2's *Standing Room Only*, a half-hour programme mixing news features, comedy sketches and interviews. Subsequent fan shows, such as *Fantasy Football*, tended to dilute the political ingredients of the fanzine brew with aspects of 'lad culture', a celebration of some young men's obsessions with drinking, football and sex promoted by a rash of glossy mainstream magazines.

It is estimated that well over 600 football fanzines have existed at some point. Their influence has occasionally been direct and dramatic – such as the successful campaign by Charlton Athletic's *Voice of the Valley* to return the club to its home ground. But they helped even more significantly to bring about a cumulative shift in the perception of fans – by the media, government, football authorities and themselves – from social deviants to intelligent and active participants. Without the contribution of fanzines it is impossible to imagine such recent initiatives as Supporters Direct making any headway.

Sir Alex Ferguson

In terms of major trophies won, Alex Ferguson is the most successful manager in the history of British football. Characterized by a middle period of almost complete domestic domination, his tenure at Manchester United has now become doubly remarkable for its longevity. In 1999 he was the first working club manager to be knighted.

Ferguson was born in Glasgow in 1941. In his star-struck official biography, *Fergie*, Stephen Kelly suggests that Ferguson's birth in some way contributed to the defeat of the Nazi menace ('on New Year's Eve prime minister Churchill confidently told the Canadian parliament that "the tide is turning". Alex Ferguson was born that same day'). His upbringing in Glasgow was undoubtedly a tough one. Partly as a sop to his confrontational public persona, journalists are fond of referring to Ferguson as 'the former Govan factory shop steward', and during his time as an apprentice at a tool factory he did once lead his fellow workers out on strike over pay and conditions. An aggressive, cumbersome centre-forward, Ferguson played in the Scottish League for Queen's Park, St Johnstone and Rangers among others. Four disappointing years at Ibrox were most notable for the manner of Ferguson's departure, his having been made a public scapegoat for a 4–0 defeat by Celtic in the 1969 Cup Final.

In 1974 Ferguson was appointed to his first managerial job, at second-division East Stirlingshire. After four months he left for St Mirren, where he would eventually produce a set of players to take the club into the Premier Division. Oddly, Ferguson was sacked after his first season in the top flight, following allegations that he had paid trialists out of club money. Within days of leaving Love Street he had become manager of Aberdeen, where he would build his first great team.

Ferguson's Aberdeen intruded decisively on the Old Firm hegemony in Scottish football, winning the League title in 1980, 1984 and 1985, the Scottish Cup four times and, most famously, the European Cup Winners' Cup in 1983. The team that beat Real Madrid in the final contained Gordon Strachan, Alex McLeish, Mark McGhee and Eric Black, all of whom would follow Ferguson into management.

Ferguson then led Scotland to a disappointing first-round exit at the 1986 World Cup finals, having stepped into the breach after the death of Jock **Stein**. The same year Ferguson joined Manchester United, taking over in November after the sacking of Ron Atkinson, and embarking on an initial period of almost five years without a trophy. His greatest early achievement was to dismantle the notorious 'drinking club' founded around Paul McGrath, Norman Whiteside and Bryan **Robson**, a restructuring that preceded his first trophy, the FA Cup, won after a replay against Crystal Palace in 1990. Legend has it that Ferguson would have been fired had United not won the Cup that season. Either way, it proved a catalyst for a sudden run of success: the Cup Winners' Cup the next season, the League Cup the following year and then in 1992–93 a first League title in 26 years.

The League and Cup Double followed in 1993–94, after which a trophy-less season led to Ferguson reshaping his team and choosing instead to field a clutch of homegrown young players, among them Paul Scholes, Gary Neville, Nicky Butt and, latterly, David **Beckham**. Ferguson's most significant early signing, Eric **Cantona**, would lead this young team to another League and Cup Double, the beginning of a run that would extend to eight Premiership titles out of 11 seasons by the time Beckham left the club in 2003. In the middle of this orgy of success, during which United were transformed through an unprecedented marketing mobilization into the wealthiest club in the world, Ferguson achieved his greatest triumph, the treble of League title, FA Cup and Champions' League in 1999. Interviewed in the tunnel seconds after two goals in two minutes had turned the final in favour of his team, Ferguson could only mutter: 'Football . . . Bloody hell.'

Latterly, Ferguson has become embroiled in a series of public rivalries. A long-running antipathy towards various board members and shareholders has been part of his motivation for remaining at Old Trafford beyond his retirement plans for the end of the 2002–03 season. The much-vaunted 'mind games' which Ferguson has used to wind up fellow managers with occasional success have become an increasingly regular part of

his repertoire. He is credited with fatally disorientating Newcastle manager Kevin **Keegan** during the run-in to the 1995–96 season (Keegan's tearful televised 'I will love it if we beat them' tirade effectively signalling the end of his team's title ambitions). Recently Ferguson has found a sterner opponent in Arsenal manager Arsène **Wenger** and now, too, José **Mourinho** at Chelsea. The rivalry between the men has provided an absorbing postscript to the later stages of a managerial career largely forged out of a sense of galvanizing adversity.

FIFA

The Fédération Internationale de Football Association (FIFA) was founded in the rear of the headquarters of the Union Française des Sports Athlétiques in Paris on 21 May 1904. Among those present were two Frenchmen, two Belgians, a Dane, a Swede and – oddly perhaps – a representative of the Madrid football club. There was no British representation, despite the fact that the Football Association had been in existence since 1863. In a typically British stance towards European federalism the Football Association, under Lord Kinnaird, gave its cautious approval to the new body without actually expressing any interest in getting involved. Eventually, tired of waiting for British approval, FIFA's founding members went ahead with the formation of their umbrella organization for international football.

The founding tenets of the new body included: recognition of the national associations of its members; clubs and players to be forbidden to play simultaneously for different national associations; recognition by all associations of a player's suspension; the playing of matches according to the Laws of the Game as established by the English FA;

and the rule that FIFA alone was entitled to organize an international competition. England, Scotland, Wales and Ireland joined the new organization in 1905, and Daniel Burley Woolfall became the first English president of FIFA a year later. Under Woolfall's guidance FIFA stepped up its campaign for worldwide uniformity in the rules of the game. The British associations were to withdraw twice, for four years from 1918 in protest at other members playing matches against Germany and again ten years later over 'broken time' payments being made to amateur players. They returned in 1946.

The first Olympic football tournament was played (a pointer towards the World Cup) and won by England (not a pointer towards the World Cup). FIFA had expanded beyond Europe by now. South Africa joined in 1909, Argentina and Chile in 1912 and the USA in 1913, the same year that French was adopted as the organization's official language. Despite this, at the 1912 Olympics in Stockholm the new global sport was still viewed with some suspicion, and considered a spectacle rather than a competition.

FIFA's progress was interrupted by the First World War, which seemed set to scupper its expansionist agenda, and by the death of its president in 1918. During this period one man, honorary secretary Carl Anton Wilhelm Hirschmann, kept the ailing organization alive, corresponding intermittently with his members at his own expense from his offices in Amsterdam. The first post-war meeting was held in Antwerp in 1920. Among those present was Jules Rimet, a Frenchman who became FIFA's third president on 1 March 1921. Rimet would retire after the 1954 World Cup in Switzerland at the age of 80, having overseen the establishment of

FIFA as the world's dominant sporting body.

Rimet's dream of holding FIFA's own international tournament finally came about in Montevideo, Uruguay, in 1930. The first World Cup was a success, despite being dogged by late withdrawals and the growing economic crisis in Europe. Two further expanded World Cups followed, and after the Second World War FIFA reconvened in 1946 with 34 nations represented and Jules Rimet still at the helm.

The following year saw the return of all four British associations to FIFA and the staging of a benefit game in FIFA's honour between a British team and a Rest of Europe XI at Hampden Park, won 6–1 by the British.

The 1950 World Cup in Brazil was the first truly modern tournament, and a powerful statement of FIFA's global spread. Sir Stanley **Rous** became president in 1961 and oversaw a gradual, if conservative, expansion of an organization that still depended for its funding on the four-yearly jamboree of the World Cup. Under the Brazilian João Havelange, who took over from Rous in 1974, FIFA began to flex its global muscles, becoming involved in development programmes in Africa and in aggressively marketing itself and the game. Havelange oversaw the growth of FIFA's staff from just 12 under Rous to over a hundred, as the popularity of the game and its earning capacity were ruthlessly farmed. The 1982 World Cup saw 24 teams taking part, increased to 32 by 1998. FIFA, reinforced by football's position as the world's most popular sport, has since become a powerful quasi-commercial body.

In its official biography of Sepp Blatter, FIFA describes its current president as 'one of the most versatile and experienced exponents of international sport diplomacy', whatever that might be. Certainly Blatter finds himself head of one of the most powerful and widely spread non-governmental bodies in the world. Plenty of laudable initiatives are trumpeted by FIFA's prolific public relations department: the distribution of footballs and equipment in poorer parts of Africa; quasi-diplomatic intervention to enable the playing of matches between historically hostile nations; and lots of soft-focus publicity photographs of its apparatchiks shaking hands with other expensively suited apparatchiks. What FIFA might choose to do with this power, beyond propagating its own popularity and waging its own internal power struggles, remains to be seen.

Tom Finney

A number of locally born players became synonymous with certain clubs during the immediate post-war period. Wilf **Mannion** at Middlesbrough, Billy **Wright** at Wolves and Nat **Lofthouse** at Bolton being just a few examples. Preston's candidate was Tom Finney. Born less than a mile from the ground, Finney went on to be knighted, serve as the club's Life President, be depicted by a statue outside the stand which bears his name and have his image picked out in the seats which back on to Sir Tom Finney Way. Over 40 years after his retirement, Tom Finney remains the image and name most closely associated with Preston North End.

Finney joined Preston as a schoolboy, but war delayed his League debut until 1946, by which time he was 24. However, his talent was already well known beyond Preston. Naturally left-footed, his preferred position was on the right wing, where his talents were not confined merely to making goals for

others. A consummate dribbler, he was also a regular goalscorer and surprisingly good with his head given that he was of only average height. Finney's skills brought him into competition with Stanley **Matthews** for the right-wing berth for England, and a rivalry which never existed on a personal level was whipped up in the press. The fact that the two men played their League football for bitter Lancashire rivals only increased the debate. The situation was resolved when Finney was moved onto the left wing, where he performed equally well.

However, Finney was much more than a mere winger. His heading and scoring ability saw him move into the centre of the attack later in his career, with no diminishing of his impact on the team or the game. Such was Finney's versatility that he eventually played in all five traditional forward positions and ended his career in 1960 as Preston's all-time record goalscorer. In 14 seasons, he scored 210 goals for the club; in addition, he also recorded 30 goals for England from his 76 caps – another club record. His importance to the side was such that his poor performance in the 1954 Cup Final was widely seen as the determining factor in West Bromwich's victory. A one-club man, he was once offered a huge sum to move to Palermo in the Italian league, but in those more authoritarian days the club chairman's response of 'You're staying here' put an end to the matter.

Finney's personal and football merits can best be judged by the views of those who played with and against him. He and Matthews had a lifelong mutual admiration, whilst Lofthouse was always grateful for the number of goals Finney created for him and the two remain close friends. Perhaps the most telling opinion was that of former Preston team-mate and international opponent Bill

Shankly, who openly idolized Finney, calling him the greatest player he had ever seen. Asked once how a top star of the day compared to Finney, Shankly replied, 'Aye he's as good as Tommy – but then Tommy's nearly 60 now.'

floodlights

Floodlit matches have been a regular feature of the English football season for nearly 50 years, providing a midweek late-night counterpoint to the traditional Saturday afternoon kick-off. The introduction of floodlights during the 1950s and 1960s cleared the way for English clubs to compete in midweek European competition, and for the introduction of tournaments such as the League Cup. Initially an expedient of enlarging the fixture list, and later an essential part of the growth of televised football, floodlit matches generate a distinctive kind of excitement: the glow from the lights on the approach to the ground; the presentation of the game as evening entertainment to a crowd leavened by alcohol and by the end of the working day; and the spectacle of the lights themselves, initially towering pylons supporting a huge grid of bulbs, now more likely to be sleeker structures or mounted on the roof of the stadium.

The first floodlit football match took place at Bramall Lane in October 1878 between two scratch Sheffield teams, playing under lamps powered by portable dynamos. The match happened two years before the first floodlit baseball game was held in the US but, while baseball persevered with the experiment, the first major floodlit game in England only took place in 1956, Portsmouth facing Newcastle in a League game under the evening lights at Fratton Park. In between various experiments with lights were carried out, including suspending

lanterns across the pitch on wires, and the use of oil-fired lamps. Arsenal manager Herbert **Chapman** campaigned for the use of floodlights during the 1930s, only for the FA to introduce an official ban on floodlit matches that, for reasons that remain unclear, held until 1950.

With the fixture-clogging expansion of the Champions' League, the Big European Night Under Lights has become a slightly hackneyed notion in recent years, but it was only after a series of successful midweek floodlit friendlies against European teams during the 1950s that the FA decided to relax its embargo on floodlights. Soon they were commonplace, although early designs were often affected by electricity failure, shadows on the pitch (alleviated by making the lights higher off the ground) and by the time taken to actually switch them on. Gradually clubs upgraded their lights partly in response to the demands of colour television. Current FA Premier League guidelines demand that floodlights give at least an average illumination of 800 lux, the equivalent of a moderately overcast day.

In 1999 three men admitted planning to sabotage the lights during a Premiership match between Charlton and Liverpool at The Valley. It was claimed that the men were part of a Far Eastern betting syndicate that had already arranged for floodlight failures at two Premiership games during 1997. Under Eastern gambling rules a result stands in a game ending at any point after half-time, opening the door for a contrived electrical failure to finish a match when the score is favourable. Although a link between Far Eastern gamblers and the faulty lights has never been officially established, in both games the floodlights failed directly after one team had scored an equalizing goal.

Football Association

In 2000 the Football Association quit its Victorian HQ in Lancaster Gate and moved into a swish modern office block in Soho Square. The effect on the FA's notoriously long-winded and often shambolic administration of the game was not immediately obvious, but all the glass and steel certainly stirred up some of the organization's senior employees.

In 2004 an FA secretary, Faria Alam, revealed that she had had affairs with FA chief executive Mark Palios and the England manager Sven-Göran **Eriksson**. 'Sven admired my breasts,' Alam told the *News of the World*. 'He called them my mountains. He said he wanted to get his handies on my Andes.' Eriksson stayed on, but Palios – brought in, ironically, to steady the ship after a series of crises under his predecessor, Adam Crozier – was forced to quit after conspiring with his press chief to pass on details of Eriksson's affair to a tabloid in exchange for keeping his own relationship quiet. In its previous incarnation the FA had often been derided as farcical – never had that accusation appeared so literally true.

The Football Association was founded on 26 October 1863, when a group of army captains and representatives from diverse group of Home Counties clubs that included Crystal Palace, Kilburn, Crusaders, Kensington School and the War Office met at the Freemasons' Tavern in Great Queen Street, London. They were there to establish a set of universally accepted rules for a game that up until that point had been fractured into a wide assortment of parochial codes, at least one of which was clearly rugby.

Over the next 20 years the FA grew in strength largely through the efforts of a triumvirate of able if somewhat archetypal Victorian administrators: discipli-narian president Major F. A. Marindin (Royal Engineers), innovative secretary C. W. Alcock (Old Harrovians) and treasurer the Hon. A. F. Kinnaird, flamboyant ginger-haired skipper of the Old Etonians. Of the three Alcock was arguably the most important. It was at his suggestion that the FA Cup was introduced and he, too, who first proposed an international challenge match between England and Scotland.

From 1885 onwards the FA faced mounting problems as it struggled to adapt (or perhaps not to adapt) to the changing nature of the game. Professionalism, the foundation of the Football League and the increasing popularity of football around the world all created problems with which the administrators battled in a manner that ranged from the acute to the obtuse.

Arguably the most damaging in the long term was the short-sighted attitude taken to football abroad by Alcock's successor as secretary, Sir Frederick Wall. During the Edwardian era Wall swatted aside various attempts by Dutch and Belgians to institute an international tournament, dismissed a French proposal for a federation of European football associations out of hand and then gave a predictably frosty response when the splendidly named Count Carl van der Streten Ponthoy approached him to ask if the FA might send an English team to play in an international equivalent of the FA Cup.

Undaunted the Europeans went ahead on their own and founded FIFA. The World Cup followed. Stubbornly the FA continued its isolationist policy. They refused to send a team to the World Cup until 1950, would not enter Olympic football tournaments and initially forbade English sides from entering the European Champions' Cup. In so doing they surrendered England's pre-eminent position in the game and did untold long-term damage to the quality of football played at national and club level.

The battle with the Football League – effectively subordinate to the FA but at the same time richer and in many ways more powerful – rumbled on for over a century with neither side ever quite able to deliver a knockout blow. The ending was sudden and surprising. In 1992 the FA, guardians of grassroots football (it has responsibility for the whole of the non-League game, involving some 2,200 leagues and over 40,000 clubs), signed an extraordinary deal with Division 1 clubs to form a breakaway elite, the Premier League. It was a move that effectively concentrated football's real wealth into the hands of a few, condemning the lower-division clubs to penury.

Paradoxically, in hijacking the Football League's most lucrative members, the FA had also weakened its own position. The Premier League chairmen controlled the purse strings, and attempts by the FA to impose order on the game's increasingly rackety and corrupt financial system, via the inaptly named Compliance Unit, ended in inevitable and pathetic defeat. Caught up in a laborious and costly attempt to build a new national stadium at Wembley the FA ran into financial trouble and the progressive chief executive, Adam Crozier, who had led the move to Soho Square, was forced to resign because of his opposition to the clubs' proposal for reforms in the way the game was run. In order to establish itself once and for all as English football's top administrative body the Football Association had sold the game down the river and simultaneously shot itself in the foot.

football books

The history of football literature is not a glorious one. This could be because the sport simply doesn't lend itself to fiction; or perhaps because nobody who's any good at writing fiction has ever written much about football.

Books with a football theme first began to appear shortly after the First World War. These were aimed mainly at young boys and were often set in glowering public schools. As far as adult literature is concerned, only Arnold Bennett and J. B. Priestley of established novelists dipped into the football world for material. In his novel *The Card* Bennett observed that football had superseded all other forms of recreation in the Potteries region, particularly for the fanatical supporters of Knype (Stoke City) and Bursley (Port Vale). Leonard Gribble's *The Arsenal Stadium Mystery* (1939), a crime novel in a famous footballing setting, was made into a film that is still occasionally televised on dark Tuesday afternoons. After the Second World War football stories – increasingly formulaic tales of star strikers and young hopefuls – were churned out by many of the new children's comics.

In his 1968 novel *A Kestrel For A Knave*, later filmed as *Kes*, Barry Hines created a brilliant and enduring cameo of a school games lesson, which sees an overly competitive games teacher taking on the role of Bobby Charlton in an under-14s kickabout. There was more football in Hines's earlier novel *The Blinder*, with its central character a precocious young striker, roustabout and Angry Young Man. The authenticity of the football scenes can be partly attributed to Hines's youthful appearances in the Burnley 'A' team.

In the late 1980s authors such as Julian Barnes and Martin Amis started dropping the odd football passage into their work. Amis's rendering of fans' speech can be deemed either 'stylized' or 'clumsy', depending on your mood, but it still led away from the sex-and-soap stories that predominated in the early 1970s and 1980s – Jimmy **Greaves** being the co-writer of one such series with the *Jackie Groves* novels of 1979–81.

Fiction based on hooliganism began to proliferate in the 1990s, with the most famous of this genre arguably John King's trilogy *The Football Factory, Headhunters* and *England Away. The Football Factory*, which became a cult novel and film, is graced with a first line that Thomas Hardy couldn't have come up with in a hundred years: 'Coventry are fuck all.'

Other footballing literary works include J. L. Carr's *How Steeple Sinderby Wanderers Won the FA Cup*, a parody of tabloid journalese and modern management, and Jim Crumley's *The Goalie*, a novel based on the real-life figure of the author's grandfather, Bob Crumley, keeper for Dundee United and, subsequently, foot soldier in the Great War. Alongside these is Brian Glanville's enduring *Goalkeepers are Different*, the story of a young gloveman making his way in the professional game.

Of football non-fiction, Arthur Hopcraft's *The Football Man* (1969) stands out, Hopcraft was among the first football writers to make statements such as 'Football in Britain is not just a sport people take to, like cricket or tennis . . . it is inherent in the people.' Simon Inglis's comprehensive works on British football grounds are the best series of reference books ever produced about the game. Phil Soar and Martin Tyler's *The Story of Football* (1978) brings some of the richness of Greek tragedy to every historic turn and crucial match it describes.

Hunter Davies's account of a season at Tottenham, *The Glory Game* (1972), stands out as a rare example of real insight, allied to real feeling, allied to football. Published in 1992, *Fever Pitch* by Nick Hornby was a self-deprecatingly honest portrait of a fan ruled by his obsession. It was a surprise best-seller and many imitations followed. Of the mostly anodyne football autobiographies that litter the market, Len **Shackleton**'s *The Clown Prince of Soccer*, Eamon Dunphy's *Only a Game* and Tony Cascarino's *Full Time* are among a select few that give a genuine flavour of the professional game and the lives being led within it.

football films

Football films are rarely about football. There are relationship/football films, thuggishly violent bloke films with a football element, buddy movies with some football, comedy hamming by a famous soapstar in a football setting, the war/escape movie with some football scenes, the classic maverick-waster-finds-redemption films in a football setting and thriller/mystery/football films. It's a complicated genre.

While inter-war football fans would have queued overnight to watch the world premier of, say, *A Day in the Life of Clifford Bastin*, the first big film in the genre was actually called *The Arsenal Stadium Mystery* (Thorold Dickinson, 1939). It's a run of the mill thriller plot in which an amateur team plays a friendly against Arsenal and one of their players collapses and dies. A maverick inspector comes in to solve the case. It is a period curiosity if nothing else.

The football film about footballers has to overcome the problem that the interior life of the typical player is possibly not very interesting. Hence they tended to be presented as hard-drinking-maverick wasters finding redemption. The template for this was the Jackie Collins-penned *Yesterday's Hero* (Neil Leifer, 1979), in which a pre-Lovejoy Ian McShane (whose father, Harry, had been a player with Bolton and Manchester United among others) stars as a boozy has-been who tries to make one last comeback and scores the winner in the FA Cup Final. Almost 20 years later *When Saturday Comes* (Maria Giese, 1996) follows a similar trajectory – it's an absurdly scripted rags to riches tale of a Sheffield United fanatic played by glowering Sean Bean who gets his dream and turns out for the Blades (weirdly, captained by former Sheffield Wednesday stalwart Mel Sterland).

Football is often used as a metaphor for ordinary people attempting to live their dreams, achieve redemption or to escape. *Escape to Victory* (John Huston, 1981) takes this literally. Centred on a match in a prisoner of war camp, the film towers over the genre of football films like a wooden-voiced, badly acted colossus. It was even voted the best football film of all time in a poll conducted by UCI cinemas. From a fan's perspective, it may be rubbish but it's *our* rubbish, and features Pelé and a host of Football League stars acting their socks off alongside Michael Caine and a goalkeeping Sylvester Stallone (who confessed, 'To be honest, I hate the sport').

That same year saw another take on the football film. *Gregory's Girl* (Bill Forsyth) uses the game as a humorous way for the main character to get closer to the object of his affections (she can play, he's rubbish). Relationship issues, confusion and football as rite-of-passage are also at work in the Nick Hornby adaptation, *Fever Pitch* (David Evans, 1997). It's from a fan's perspective but really the film version is a romantic story about the three-way relationship between a man, a woman and an obsession. There might have been a more introspective film to be made from Hornby's book, but it certainly wouldn't have starred Colin Firth.

Around the same time that Hornby was reinvigorating the intellectual life of the football fan, there was also a parallel surge in books about hooliganism, a porn sub-genre that had flared briefly once before, in the early 1970s. The first notable hooligan film was *The Firm* (directed by Alan Clarke), a TV drama about a small gang starring the perma-snarling Gary Oldman. Then came *ID* (Philip Davies, 1995), in which an under-cover cop infiltrates a hoolie gang and ends up getting carried away with his new life. John King's *The Football Factory* only made it to the big screen in 2004 and features angry men supporting Chelsea and smacking everyone who doesn't. Pelé re-emerged as a film talent in the low-budget comedy *Mike Bassett, England Manager* (Steve Baron, 2001). Ricky Tomlinson plays a maverick who takes over the England manager's job when no one else want it, with moderately hilarious results (it came out just after Kevin **Keegan**'s reign). Finally, a new direction for the football film was hinted at by *Bend It Like Beckham* (Gurinder Chadha, 2002), which was a big international hit, replacing as it did ugly footballers with good looking actresses and throwing in an inspiring crossing-cultural-barriers storyline.

Until recently, football films have succeeded despite their overall mediocrity thanks to a certain kind of post-pub so-bad-it's good knowingness among their target audience. But in this age of football as a global brand, film executives might soon be insisting on a more believable football element. Expect to see a whole raft of films in the near future aimed at the new demographic of the interested semi-fan. Jude Law is probably working on his free kicks right now.

football games

Football games and other paraphernalia first appeared in the best department stores in the late 19th century as the game began to develop mass appeal. The Edwardian era saw the invention of action games such as Blow Football and bagatelle boards bearing the images of famous players. By the Roaring '20s the game of *Newfooty* (1929) had appeared, introducing for the first time the notion of flicking miniature players headlong into a ball.

The big breakthrough for football games came in 1947 with the emergence of *Subbuteo* from a shed in Tunbridge Wells. The game was marketed brilliantly by Waddington's, who demonstrated to young males its suitability both for competing with other young males and for collecting teams and accessories in a quietly obsessive manner. The popularity of *Subbuteo* (from *Subbuteo Falco*, literally 'Hobby Hawk') grew steadily through the 1960s and 1970s and the inaugural *Subbuteo* World Cup was held in 1987.

Waddington's also gave the nation *Table Football*, a game featuring inch-high plastic footballers naked from the waist up on a plush green cardboard pitch. To pass or propel the tiddlywink ball goalwards, you simply pressed down with the tiddlywink base of your nearest player and watched as the ball either skidded into the ridge on the pitch where it was folded away or looped up into your opponent's sweater. *Super Striker* was more sophisticated but less enjoyable, as it involved ushering the ball with painful deliberation into the vicinity of a forward, who would then have it placed carefully next to his kicking boot so that

the revolutionary technology of the game (you push his head down and he kicks it) could be activated. The introduction of diving goalkeepers could not save *Super Striker* from gathering dust beneath the beds of a thousand schoolchildren. *Super Soccer*, a game that created movement by having its little players attached to magnets, similarly disappeared very quickly from the national consciousness.

These more successful innovations aside, board games have generally done football a disservice. Alan Ball endorsed *Soccerama*, a game with a rules-to-pleasure ratio of approximately 50:1, while Bryan **Robson** tied his fortunes to *90 Minutes*, the format of which allows a randomness of action on the 'pitch' not seen since the great days of Wimbledon v Sheffield United in the late 1980s. *Wembley*, 'the thrilling cup-tie game', has a more recognizable structure. Players journey around a *Monopoly*-style board, buying teams and rolling dice (doctored according to which division the team plays in) to determine the winner of each tie. Not innovative perhaps, but a solid and wholesome indoor pastime.

Board games and action games have long now been submerged beneath the flow of computer-based football simulations, each new version of which consistently out-sells other genres of computer game. Even more popular than the simulation software are the management games. These allow you to buy, sell and pick your own team from a large pool of contemporary players from all over the world, then play to the formation of your choice. You can also train players, fine players, give out press releases and bawl at your expensively assembled side as they go down 1–0 at home to Stoke in the Carling Cup.

Football League

The English League is the oldest football championship in the world. It was conceived by William McGregor, a Scot and an Aston Villa committee member. Villa's success – they won the FA Cup in 1887 – and the large crowds drawn to their matches led McGregor to believe that there would be wide public interest in a regular set of fixtures between the leading clubs, following the league format already established by county cricket. McGregor convened a meeting of 12 professional teams in April 1888 – Accrington, Villa, Blackburn Rovers, Bolton Wanderers, Burnley, Derby County, Everton, Notts County, Preston North End (champions the first two seasons, but never since), Stoke, West Bromwich Albion and Wolverhampton Wanderers – who founded the Football League in time for kick-off the next September.

Nottingham Forest, who had been rejected as founding members, formed the rival Football Alliance a year later, but all the Alliance members were absorbed into the League in 1891, when it expanded to 16 teams and added a 12-team Division 2. After six seasons of 'test' matches – forerunners to the play-offs – to determine relegation and promotion, teams then went up and down automatically, although a side could still be elected in and out of a division.

The first team to dominate the league was Aston Villa, who lifted the title five times before the end of 1900. Herbert **Chapman** then led Huddersfield Town to three successive trophies in the 1920s and made Arsenal the most successful team the League had seen during the 1930s. By this time the League had grown to 88 teams across four divisions, having added a Division 3 (South) in 1920 (taking the first division of the Southern League, formed in 1894), and a Division 3 (North) a year later.

The third divisions added two clubs each in 1950, and in 1958 merged to become divisions 3 and 4, with four teams automatically moving between the two. Still only two sides went up from Division 3 to 2, and from Division 2 to 1. This was the era when Manchester United would make their name – between 1947 and 1968 they won the title five times and finished as runners-up on seven occasions. Wolves' claims to be a 'big' club are based on their trio of championships from the 1950s, and Tottenham nostalgists hark back to 1961, when Spurs' Double-winning team became the first since Aston Villa in 1897 to take both domestic trophies.

Nonetheless, the League was a lot more open to unlikely winners, reflected by title-winning teams like Burnley (1960) and newly promoted Ipswich Town (1962). As late as the 1970s, when Brian **Clough** led Derby County and Nottingham Forest to titles, the League was still an interesting competition to people outside London and Lancashire. This was just prior to the astonishing era of Liverpool dominance between 1976 and 1990, when they won the trophy ten times (with neighbours Everton also taking two titles) and set a template for monotonous triumph that was followed by Manchester United and, latterly, Arsenal in the Premiership.

Three points for a win was adopted in 1981, a move designed to encourage attacking football and subsequently intro-duced worldwide. In 1975 the League abolished goal average to separate sides with equal points, in favour of the more logical, not to mention fairer, goal differ-ence. Play-offs were introduced to determine the final promotion spot across all the divisions in 1986–87.

Automatic demotion of the bottom club to non-League football from Division 4 was initiated in the same year, and has since been increased to two teams.

The Football Association founded the breakaway Premier League in collusion with Division 1 club chairmen in 1992. In the years that have followed, the League's clubs have continued to suffer severe financial troubles, exacerbated by a collapsed television deal with ITV Digital in 2002. The League itself has suffered from a combination of identity crisis and inferiority complex in the shadow of the *nouveau riche*, super-hyped top flight, most recently streamlined to 20 teams and leaving the FL with 72 members and three divisions of 24 teams each.

Initially the League labelled its divisions 1, 2 and 3, with Division 1 competing for the League Championship trophy. In 2004 Football League chairman and former Conservative politician Brian Mawhinney – the latest in a long line of administrators to have blighted FL history – introduced the rebranding of the divisions as 'The Championship', League 1 and League 2, supposedly to emphasize the League's heritage. To the rest of us, however, fixtures like Scunthorpe v Rochdale will always mean fourth division. The League's heritage lies in the depth and longevity of its history. Monkeying around with its name only serves to diminish this.

football pools

You know when something new has caught on when people start betting on it. The earliest football matches invited informal gambling among spectators but it all got a bit more serious with the establishment of a league and an official fixture list. In 1909, the *Racing & Football Outlook* offered 5 guineas a week for any reader who correctly forecast six away wins, and when *The Umpire* magazine offered £300 for predicting the scores of six games a year later, the football pools in their current form were just around the corner.

The football pools ask entrants to correctly forecast drawn matches from a coupon of 49 English and Scottish games. Three points are awarded for a score draw, 2 points for a no-score draw and 1 point for a home or away win. If the best 8 selections (from 10 or 15 paid for) amount to a total of 24 points, the jackpot – a proportion of the pooled entry fees of all participating – is shared between all the winners. Smaller payouts can result from a score of 23 or 22 points.

Littlewoods Pools, which boasts much the biggest market share of the pools companies currently operating, was started by three Liverpudlian telegraphists in 1922 with a total investment of £150. The first pools coupons were sold outside Old Trafford, but only 35 of the 4,000 were returned unspoilt and John Moores (later chairman of Everton) quickly found himself going solo with the project. His faith was rewarded by the mid-1920s as the concept caught on and other pools companies started up, most notably Vernons in 1925 and Zetters in 1933. The first-ever Littlewoods jackpot was £2. Viv Nicholson, miner's-wife-turned-infamous-spendthrift, collected £150,000 in 1961, and, after her husband died in his new Jaguar, four more husbands in quick succession. If she won now, Viv would have to get through £3m in double-time.

Government legislation to stifle all forms of gambling in the 1930s was meant to include the football pools but public outcry forced that particular clause to be dropped from the Betting and Lotteries Act. A subsequent Private Member's Bill to abolish the pools was defeated. The Football League also attempted to smother the baby at birth by not publishing away teams until one day before the game, but clubs protested when attendances declined as a result and the sabotage was dropped.

The League finally got its hands on some of the pools companies' money when it was granted copyright in its fixture lists in 1960, forcing Littlewoods and the rest to agree to hand over 0.5 per cent of their takings. By 1973 the Football League had secured a 13-year deal with the pools companies worth £23 million. Since the 1960s, a significant proportion of money raised by the football pools has found its way, via the Football Trust, to teams at the poorest level of the game.

Before the National Lottery reared up in 1994, about 10 million pools coupons were collected in Britain every week. By 2003 this figure was down to 2 million, the large majority of which, as has always been the case, are from what sociologists call Social Class IIIM. Not only have the football pools lost several million skilled manual workers to the National Lottery, but it has also lost its place as the nation's pre-eminent fantasy gambling event. The question, on encountering a friend driving a brand new car, 'Win the pools, did ya?', is sadly losing currency to its upstart Lottery counterpart.

football quotes

The Famous Footballing Quote is now an industry in itself. Legends evolve, books are published, and sub-standard TV shows outlive their shelf life – all on the back of the football quote. Quotes tend to fall into three categories. The first of these, the Perennial Favourite, is usually attributed to an infamous figure from the recent past. Often recycled for the benefit of a new football fan keen to experience some of the game's authentic mythology, the longevity of such quotes springs from a misconceived notion of the footballer as roguish raconteur or romantic hero. Examples include George **Best**'s 'I spent a lot of money on booze, birds and fast cars. The rest I just squandered' and Frank Worthington declaring: 'I had 11 clubs – 12 if you count Stringfellow's.'

The genealogy of these types of sayings can be confusing. A memorable phrase is often attributed to more than one larger-than-life footballing figure. Like Christmas cracker jokes, they form a kind of T-shirt slogan oral tradition, the most commonly quoted of which is Bill **Shankly**'s 'Some people believe football is a matter of life and death. I can assure you it is much, much more important than that.' Shankly's words have since been misquoted, dissected, translated and waved above the Kop on a handpainted double bedsheet. An off-the-cuff remark to a journalist – Shankly was actually quoting Green Bay Packers coach Vince Lombardi – has become his defining utterance.

The second category of footballing soundbite, the Misunderstood Quote, is used to ridicule rather than to mythologize, and tends to be the preserve of the non-fan unfamiliar with the game's argot. So if Jimmy **Hill** is reported to have said: 'what makes this game so delightful is that when both teams get the ball they are attacking their opponents' goal', anyone who watches football will know exactly what he's talking about. Similarly, Dave Bassett's observation that 'you've got to miss them to score them sometimes' becomes less incoherent when you've seen some of the forwards in teams Bassett has managed.

The third and final category is the Amusing the First Time You Heard It Quote. It is generally a good thing that Ian **Rush** described playing for Juventus as 'like being in a foreign country', that Kevin **Keegan** once observed, 'I don't think there is anyone bigger or smaller than Maradona', and that Stuart Pearce revealed he could 'see the carrot at the end of the tunnel'. Just don't go on about it.

Footballer of the Year

The Footballer of the Year award was the idea of Charles Buchan, of *Football Monthly* fame, and was first awarded in 1948 after a ballot of the members of the Football Writers' Association. Stanley **Matthews** was the first winner and he took the award again in 1963, becoming one of only seven players to win it twice (and with by far the longest period in between). In the award's early days in particular, the voters showed a good deal of imagination in their choices. It wasn't until 1961 (Danny **Blanchflower**) that a player from the championship-winning side was chosen and it took another Double before that occurred again (Arsenal's Frank McLintock in 1971).

Since the winner is traditionally announced in April, it has tended to reward consistency rather than eye-catching performances in the title run-in or later stages of the FA Cup. The writers sometimes appear to have used the award to mark not just a player's outstanding season but his achievements over a whole career – such as Tony Book (1969), Ian Callaghan (1974), Alan Mullery (1975), Steve Perryman (1982) and Teddy Sheringham (2001). Mullery, by then of Fulham, is the only player to win while playing in Division 2. Only four goalkeepers have won, the first of whom,

Bert Trautmann (1956), is usually also recorded as the first foreigner to win, although Ireland's Johnny Carey took the award in 1949. A whole spate of foreigners have won in recent years (Teddy Sheringham and Frank Lampard are the only English winners since 1994), of whom David Ginola in 1999 was one of the more controversial – his Tottenham side finished 11th – although in fairness he was also chosen by his fellow players. Indeed, Tottenham have been remarkably favoured by the writers' opinions, having won the award no fewer than eight times, with seven different players, second only to Liverpool (ten times with eight players).

In 1974 the English PFA set up their own award, often known as the 'players' player', voted on by their members. Norman Hunter won the inaugural award and Terry McDermott was the first to win both awards in the same year, 1980. The PFA award has spared the blushes of clubs such as Aston Villa (Andy Gray 1977, David Platt 1990, Paul McGrath 1993) and Newcastle (Les Ferdinand 1996, Alan **Shearer** 1997), who have never won the writers' award – though not Sunderland, who still await either. Charlie Buchan himself would surely have won it on Wearside if someone else had had the idea 30 years earlier.

The PFA also honours the best young player of the year – Andy Gray won both junior and senior awards in 1977 – and gives out a somewhat predictable 'merit award', a practice copied by the Football Writers with their 'tribute award' since 1983. The PFA also instituted a fans' award for each division in 2001, adding to what has become a frankly over-crowded shelf of seasonal gongs – particularly in Thierry **Henry**'s house after he was chosen by the writers, the players and the fans in 2003 and 2004. After the death of Stanley Matthews in

2000 the Footballer of the Year award was renamed after him, although the trophy itself is still of an anonymous jinking player – the PFA's is more substantial, but not as evocative.

Over the last ten years foreign players have dominated the Scottish writers' award, created in 1965, and the PFA equivalent set up 12 years later. Among the eight players to have won both awards in the same year, Rangers' Brian Laudrup and Henrik Larsson of Celtic did two 'doubles' each, in 1995 and 1997, then 1999 and 2001 respectively.

footballers in advertising

When Stanley **Matthews** was filmed ferrying a ball around for a portly gentleman from Imperial Tobacco in 1947, it was at a time when little was known about footballers' private lives. 'Nimble-footed Stanley' was in the picture purely for his name: Matthews never once smoked a cigarette. In the advert's final shot of the portly gentleman proffering a cigarette, the hand that selects one in close-up is conspicuously not his. Elsewhere Dixie **Dean** stared out moodily from publicity photographs with a Carreras Club cigarette clamped between his lips without looking particularly contented. Like many of his colleagues in that era Dean collected a secondary income through lending his image to gentleman's products. Denis Compton looked a little breezier in posters for Brylcreem but the general tone of footballing advertisements was simply that these were footballers who through their prowess had become household names, and that was all everybody needed to know.

Something happened somewhere in the late 1960s and 1970s. A handful of footballers became genuine celebrities.

George **Best**'s 'El Beatle' phase was swiftly followed by his Chain of Boutiques phase. Kevin **Keegan** took the baton on with an ill-remembered pop career and a series of advertisements for Brut after-shave. Homoerotic subtext aside, the dressing-room scenes with Henry Cooper saw Keegan 'acting naturally', and appearing as something other than just a footballer in front of camera.

Footballers have become a sought-after commodity for advertisers across global markets, mainly because they tend to be instantly recognizable around the world. Players themselves are more conscious of their own image. They can send themselves up (Alan **Shearer** being boring in a McDonald's advert of 2000), invert expectations (Gary **Lineker** acting mean in the endless Walker's Crisps series) or turn their own failure into a comic selling point (Pizza Hut's 1996 effort featuring penalty-missers Waddle, Pearce and Southgate). Lately the trend has been to gang world famous players together in extravagantly expensive epics. The French influx into the Premiership has served to raise the standard of performance as first Eric **Cantona**, then David Ginola and Thierry **Henry** gave the impression of actually not being embarrassed by their thespian work. Ginola's work for L'Oréal wasn't as suave as his compatriots' perhaps, but did go some way to dispelling the memory of Jason McAteer lathering himself for a shampoo commercial.

Oddly, despite burgeoning budgets and complex choreography becoming the norm, one of the most memorable TV adverts of recent years was also the most basic. In 2003 Adidas promoted their boots by leaving the camera on while David **Beckham** and Jonny Wilkinson amiably took pot-shots with a round and an oval ball. The marketing people would call this Naturalistic

Performance Marketing. Stanley Matthews would call it Kicking the Ball around for the Fat Man.

foreign players

Foreign players were not permitted to play professionally in the Football League until 1978, when the authorities were obliged to submit to the Treaty of Rome, which permitted free movement of individuals within the European Community.

Prior to then almost all the overseas players active in England had been either Commonwealth citizens able to work in the UK without permits – there were 15 such players in the top two divisions in 1964 – or, earlier on, amateurs from Scandinavia. The latter included Danish international centre-half Nils Middleboe, who spent nine years with Chelsea from 1913 and Swedish striker Hans Jeppson who scored nine goals in 11 games for Charlton in 1950–51 before following many of his compatriots to a professional career in Italy. In the inter-war period, acts of parliament imposed stiff restrictions on foreigners seeking to work in the UK and the players' union, the PFA, intervened when football clubs attempted to sign overseas players on full-time contracts, notably when renowned Austrian goalkeeper Rudolf Hiden tried to join Arsenal in 1930.

There was a brief relaxation of the rules after the war when some UK-based foreign servicemen played for Football League clubs, while German goalkeeper Bernd ('Bert') Trautmann was an exceptional case: a former Luftwaffe paratrooper who joined Manchester City after being released from a prisoner of war camp in 1949, he went on to play in 508 League games and won an FA Cup medal in 1956.

The Scottish League accepted foreign professionals from the early 1960s, leading to a brief boom in Scandinavian imports. The majority came from Denmark and were signed by one club, Greenock Morton, whose most notable buy, goalkeeper Erik Sørensen, later became their manager. Occasionally English clubs tried to follow suit but were always rebuffed: having made an impression in the 1970 World Cup finals, Israeli striker Mordechai Spiegler played in pre-season games for West Ham but was denied a permit; after the next World Cup, Stoke City failed to get clearance for Argentine midfield star Carlos Babington despite his British ancestry.

The opening up of English football in 1978 extended beyond Europe, with clubs allowed to sign two players from other parts of the world. Three Argentinians were among the first to arrive: Tottenham's Osvaldo Ardiles and Ricardo Villa had been members of the victorious 1978 World Cup squad, but the third, Alex Sabella, had not been capped by Argentina at the time of his arrival at Sheffield United (who came close to buying the then 17-year-old Diego Maradona). At the request of the PFA, the criteria for admitting foreign players were tightened up shortly after Sabella signed – henceforth they would have to be 'established internationals' whose suitability would be judged by a panel including representatives from the players' union.

Spurs' duo were the first of the overseas wave to win FA Cup medals, in 1981, with Villa scoring the spectacular winner against Manchester City. In the same season, another pair of midfielders, Dutchmen Arnold Muhren and Frans Thijssen (the latter the first overseas player since Bert Trautmann to be voted Footballer of the Year) were integral to Ipswich's UEFA Cup-winning side. Liverpool's Danish midfielder, Jan

Mølby, was the only foreigner to play in title-winning teams in the 1980s, though several others were in sides winning promotion to Division 1, notably a trio of Yugoslavs in 1981: defenders Ante Rajkovic and Dzemal Hadziabdic with Swansea and goalkeeper Radojko Avramovic of Notts County.

With the wave of imports having subsided during the five years in which English clubs were banned from European competition (see **Heysel disaster**) the next foreign player to have a decisive influence on a championship-winning team was Frenchman Eric **Cantona**. A key player for Leeds United when they took the title in 1992, he went on to win the Premiership five times with Manchester United, alongside Danish goalkeeper Peter Schmeichel and, for most of that era, Russian winger Andrei Kanchelskis. Cantona was also voted Footballer of the Year in 1996, one of the five consecutive years in which an overseas player won the award, ending with Spurs' David Ginola in 1999.

In the late 1980s, the European Union removed the limits on the number of footballers from member states permitted to play for any club in another EU nation. This, coupled with the **Bosman** judgment of 1995, contributed to a substantial increase in foreign imports. Arsenal's consistent success after Arsène **Wenger** became manager in 1996 was built around overseas stars in midfield and attack, notably Marc Overmars and Dennis Bergkamp from Holland and Frenchmen Emmanuel Petit, Patrick Vieira, Thierry **Henry** and Robert Pires (the last two also voted Footballer of the Year). On Boxing Day, 1999 Chelsea became the first English club to field an entire team of foreigners; Old Firm derbies these days may feature no more than half a dozen Scottish players.

The major Premiership clubs now follow a policy of signing teenagers from abroad and bringing them up through their youth system, often via nursery clubs overseas (Arsenal and Manchester United both have 'feeder' teams in Belgium where young African players can acquire European Union passports more quickly than in the UK). On a typical Premiership weekend, British-born players make up less than 40 per cent of those on show. With domestic players' transfer values remaining high, lower-division clubs too have increasingly looked abroad for cheap reinforcements, a trend that may continue as the European Union expands.

Forfar Athletic

Forfar's 17th-century passion for witch-hunting has never quite been transformed into a love of football, and following its formation in 1885 it took the team 99 years to win its first senior honour, the 1984 Division 2 Championship. Since then the cupboard at Station Park has been further adorned with the inaugural 1995 Division 3 trophy.

'The Loons' have never played in Scotland's top flight. They were formed by the reserve team of Forfar's other side at the time, Angus Athletic. The nickname may have come from the second string being made up of younger players, 'loons' in the local parlance meaning 'lads'. A 1982 attempt to rebrand the team as 'The Sky Blues' happily proved unpopular with fans.

Forfar joined the new Division 2 in 1921 but were relegated to the short-lived Division 3 in 1925. When that division folded the following year, they were re-elected to Division 2 to replace the extinct Broxburn United.

When the Scottish League was restructured from two to three divisions in the 1970s, Forfar were against naming the divisions 1, 2 and 3 because of lingering bad memories from half a century before. Their other third-tier experience was a slightly happier one, when they came top of the post-war Division C in 1949 and reclaimed their spot in the division above at the expense of East Stirlingshire.

Two major Cup runs have taken them to domestic semi-finals, once in the 1977–78 League Cup, and once in the 1982 Scottish Cup. Both times they fell to Rangers, although in the latter tie they took them to a replay after the first game was drawn 0–0. Further 'almosts' include almost beating Dundee United in the 1987 Scottish Cup quarter-final (in the year United almost won the UEFA Cup), but they succumbed to a late equalizer and lost the replay, and almost gaining promotion to the Premier League in 1985, but they missed out by a point.

The club's ground, Station Park, would almost be close to a railway station if Lord Beeching hadn't closed it down in 1968.

former League clubs

The first club to leave the Football League were Bootle, from north Liverpool, who resigned after one season in Division 2 in 1892–93. Since then 40 have left without so far returning. There were ten ex-League clubs in the Conference in 2006–07, seven of whom had gone down since automatic relegation was instituted in the late 1980s. One of these, Halifax Town, has dropped out of the League twice with one promotion in between since 1993 – they also lost in the Conference play-off final in 2006. Oxford United returned to non League football in 2006–07 after 43 years in the League. Aldershot went out of business after leaving the League in 1992. After reforming at a low level and adding the suffix 'Town' they reached the Conference in 2003–04. Northwich Victoria

have been in non-League football since their two seasons in Football League Division 2, 1892–94.

Nine ex-League clubs have disappeared entirely: New Brighton Tower and New Brighton from the Wirral coast, Aberdare Athletic, Thames, Middlesbrough Ironopolis, Loughborough Town and three based in the Stafforshire brewery town of Burton – Swifts, Wanderers and United, the latter formed from a merger of the first two; Burton Albion, currently in the Conference, have no direct link to their predecessors. Maidstone United are the only club to have spent their League history as tenants of another team. Promoted in 1989 they groundshared at Dartford – where they beat Gillingham in the League's first Kent derby and reached a promotion play-off – before mounting debts forced them out of business after three seasons. They were reformed in the Kent County League Division 4 and have since climbed up several levels.

Two clubs, Wigan Borough and Leeds City, had successors formed within a year of the original club's collapse, though it took Wigan 47 years to get another full-time professional club between Borough folding in 1931 and Athletic's admission to the League. Several others reformed some time after the original club's disappearance – the current Bootle, now in the North-West Counties League, were set up in 1954; Glossop North End, from the smallest town ever to have had a League club, were re-created in 1992, a decade after folding. Accrington Stanley entered the League in 1921, 28 years after Accrington FC had dropped out; they disappeared after being ejected over unpaid debts during 1961–62 but started up again six years later. They were promoted to the League as Conference champions at the end of 2005–06. Two other East Lancashire teams, Darwen and Nelson, now play in the same competition as Bootle, having been out of the League for 106 and 74 years respectively.

The demotion of Gateshead, League members from 1919 to 1960, was probably the most contentious. Having finished third from bottom of Division 4 they had to apply for re-election for the first time since 1937, but were rejected in favour of Peterborough United from the Midland League. A successor club based at the Gateshead Athletic Stadium has played in the Conference since but is currently in the Northern Premier League. West Cumbria lost both its League clubs during the 1970s. Barrow were members for 51 years before being voted out in 1972 but have since won the FA Trophy and spent several seasons in the Conference. Workington fell much further after dropping out in 1977 but have revived recently and start 2005–06 in Conference 2 (North), two levels below the Football League.

South Wales clubs Merthyr Tydfil and Newport County (who reformed after going bankrupt in 1989) are still in the English pyramid system, having resisted pressure to join the League of Wales on its formation in 1992. Newport entered the League in 1932 to replace Thames, who are the most obscure club ever to play in professional football. Formed to play at a newly built greyhound stadium in West Ham, Thames were League members for just two years, 1930–32, and hold the record for the lowest attendance for a Saturday afternoon fixture, 469 against Luton Town during their first season.

forwards

A team without a great centre-forward can never really be great. Being a centre-forward is like being the lead singer in a band. No other position has such expectation heaped upon it or such an enduring mythology attached. The ideal centre-forward is moody and charismatic. He launches mistimed tackles at centre-halves and, in an ideal world, concusses himself by putting his head in 'where it hurts'. A good centre-forward will first and foremost allay the British footballing fear of being out-muscled, out-fought or out-run. After that everything else – such as skill, speed or goal scoring – is a bonus. Forwards bear the burden of being the only position on the field judged by their statistics. A goalkeeper's clean sheets are occasionally mentioned, but no-one really keeps count. For a forward your goal record is a major barometer of your worth.

Positionally, if not technically, a forward has over time become a more simple thing to define. The most successful forwards of the early days of organized football were usually known for their ability to shoot convincingly (see Steve **Bloomer**). The football itself was incredibly heavy, a stitched leather bladder bloated with water and mud. A player who could actually propel the ball powerfully towards goal was a vital member of any team. Even great forwards of later years such as Dixie **Dean** and Jackie **Milburn** were often praised by their contemporaries for their simple ability to strike a moving ball on a mudheap in a meaningful fashion. At the same time, the most skilful attacking players of early professional football tended to be wingers or inside-forwards.

The popularity of direct, long-ball tactics before and after the Second World War led to the evolution of a new style of attacking player. Under the old-fashioned WM formation, which featured wingers and inside-forwards, goals were shared out by up to five attacking players – Arsenal's Cliff **Bastin** scored 150 League goals cutting inside from a position on the wing. The new style of direct play demanded forwards with courage and strength. Nat **Lofthouse** entered popular football mythology as 'The Lion Of Vienna' after willingly undergoing a fearsome physical battering while playing for England against Austria. For a while Tommy **Lawton** became the epitome of the combative English centre-forward. Tall, excessively brylcreemed, able to leap vast distances and with a superhero-like antenna for confrontation, centre-forwards in the Lawton mould are still one of the British game's enduring archetypes. Emile Heskey's entire international career is based around this notion of 'physical presence' in the forward line. Heskey made a spectacularly well-received England debut against Argentina in 2000. The game was a 0–0 draw and he had few scoring chances. Crucially, however, he did run around a lot and eventually bundled over the aged Argentine defender Nestor Sensini so forcefully that he had to be substituted. On the strength of this Heskey was immediately hailed as the ideal man to replace the fading Alan **Shearer**.

Shearer himself has helped to prolong the appeal of the traditional centre-forward in the Premiership. His association with the north-east, an area of football's regional map inexorably bound up with great and popular number nines, provides a distinct umbilical link to the Lawton, Lofthouse, Dean, Milburn forward of legend. There are numerous other types of forward player, however, many of which have been at least as successful in British football as the bustling number nine. Jimmy **Greaves** and Gary **Lineker**, fast and clever rather than physically dominant, were perhaps the two most successful out-and-out forwards ever to play for England. Kevin **Keegan** and Peter Beardsley both had great success playing from deeper positions and creating goals for others as well as scoring them. In typically British fashion both made up for an absence of physical power with boundless scurrying energy.

In keeping with the game's development into a more athletic, less contact-based sport, the most successful forwards of very recent times have relied primarily on speed. Lineker, Michael **Owen** and Thierry **Henry** have all been known for their exceptional acceleration. A lack of excess pace is now seen as an obstacle in the development of a young forward, where once it would have been an absence of power or height. At the lower levels of the League scouts have targeted amateur sprinters with a view to turning them into pacy forwards.

One recent fashion has been for teams to play with a big man (wins headers) and little man (scuttles about behind him) combination. Niall Quinn and Kevin Phillips combined like this over several seasons for Sunderland, as did John Toshack and Keegan with spectacular success for Liverpool during the 1970s. Recently this sort of partnership has been updated into a deeper-lying creative forward combining with a more advanced and usually quicker striker to provide the rapier thrust, or with a massed five-man midfield taking it in turns to support a sole attacker. This is usually a physically strong player, such as Manchester United's Ruud Van Nistelrooy, an expert at holding on to possession while other players break to join him.

Irrespective of tactical fashion, and notwithstanding the rule changes that have tended to penalize aggressive aerial challenges or the demands of a more mobility-based style of football, British football will continue to provide a home for powerful centre-forwards. There will always be a place for the big man up front.

free kick

According to the laws of football, there are two types of free kick: direct, from which a goal can be scored in the opposition's net, and indirect, from which neither team can score. If the defending side puts the ball straight into their own net from any free kick, then a corner is awarded; if the opposition net direct from an indirect free kick, then a goal kick is awarded.

Leaving the laws aside, there are many other types of free kick. Quick free kicks are often the most controversial. There are short free kicks, wasted free kicks, training-ground free kicks, curled free kicks, blasted free kicks, promising free kicks and free kicks in David **Beckham**'s range (replacing the commentators' favourite, a free kick 'in Koeman territory' of the late 1980s and early 1990s).

Soft free kicks refer not to the force with which the ball is struck but the ease with which the victim of a foul fell over, or the folly of the person committing the foul for doing something obvious and/or unnecessary. Clear or obvious free kicks are usually those that have not been awarded.

Indirect free kicks are signalled by the referee holding his arm above his head until a second player has touched the ball. They are awarded for mainly technical offences – offside, picking up a back pass, obstruction and dissent that causes the referee to stop the game. Famous indirect free kicks include a blast from Stuart Pearce for England against the Netherlands at the 1990 World Cup, which Hans van Breukelen tried but failed to handle – had it brushed him a goal would have been given, but the ball went straight in.

Direct free kicks are awarded for intentional handball and a number of contact offences committed carelessly, recklessly or using excessive force. Unknown direct free kicks include the seven that David Beckham missed for England against Greece in a World Cup qualifier at Old Trafford in 2001, all overshadowed by the eighth, the one that he did score.

Fulham

Fulham is a club with a proud self-image which is proving difficult to sustain in the modern game. It is summed up by one revered word, 'Fulhamish', the club's old telegraphic address. As London's oldest professional club, it has a history stretching back to the founding of a church side, Fulham St Andrew's, in 1879. Appropriately the early, non-League years appear to have been conducted at a sedate pace, though inklings of later eccentricities were betrayed by the abandonment at half-time of an 1887 game against Millwall Rovers after the only three balls available had burst.

Following entry into the Southern League, Football League status was gained in 1907, significantly only two years after Chelsea was founded by the Mears family just a mile up the road. With the exception of a handful of seasons, the Fulham Road upstarts have been an over-shadowing presence ever since. Equally Fulham's failure to take advantage of their early start was reinforced by the transfer of local MP Henry Norris's considerable influence to the then struggling Arsenal, where he proved a major player in that club's move to Highbury and emergence as a force in Division 1 after the First World War.

Fulham's current position in the Premiership appears a historical aberration. Fifty of the 88 seasons contested to date have taken place in the second level. Nineteen have been contested in the third, only three in the lowest division – in the disaster years of 1994–97 – and the remaining 17 have been scrapped out amongst the elite. Hopes remain high that the club can defy gravity somewhat longer but the historical omens are not promising.

Ninth place in 2003–04 was the club's highest-ever finish in the top flight. Indeed, the only other top-half finish was in 1960, when Johnny Haynes was at the height of his career as England captain, assisted by the likes of England full-back George Cohen, midfielder Alan Mullery and Scottish striker Graham Leggatt. The 1960s were widely seen until recently as Fulham's golden age, when the image of a friendly club, occasionally blessed by the presence of real talent, was set in the public consciousness. However, the decade witnessed an increasingly desperate battle to stay up, with Haynes's powers declining and many of the better players being sold, as the club's finances became more precarious under the benevolent but less than efficient regime of comedian Tommy Trinder.

Although the 1970s saw general security in Division 2 and the club achieved its only appearance (in spite of six semis) in an FA Cup Final, the change in direction in the boardroom represented by rapacious businessmen Eric Miller and Ernie Clay led finally to the disastrous events of the late 1980s. After squandering a highly talented team, led to the brink of the top division by manager Malcolm Macdonald in 1983, the club faced near extinction in 1987 at the hands of property developers who attempted to bring about a merger with Queens Park Rangers.

Not many other sets of fans would hail Jimmy Hill as a saviour, but if it had not been for his sometimes clumsy but well-intentioned intervention at this time, the renaissance of recent years would never have been possible and Craven Cottage – their stadium since 1896 – which has been a battlefield amongst competing interests for nearly two decades now, would have been concreted over long ago. (Hill, who played nearly 300 games for the club in the 1950s, was on the board for ten years up to 1997.)

The position now of course is more complex. The Fulham self-image held dear by generations of fans looks increasingly unrealistic in the ruthless world of the Premiership, particularly at a club with as controversial a businessman as Mohamed Fayed at the helm. Moreover, expectations amongst many fans, after eight years of progress, are such that a retreat into the comforting shell of Fulhamish eccentricity is no longer likely to be enough.

full-back

In a standard British formation the full-backs occupy the defensive space on the left and right flank beside the two centre-halves. The attacking full-back is a relatively modern innovation. In the WM formation favoured before the 1960s full-backs would be expected primarily to defend. Stationed either side of a single stopper centre-half, their job was to mark a pair of specialist wingers, a duel fought almost exclusively in their own half. With the evolution towards a 4–4–2 shape and the gradual replacement of wingers with more conservative wide midfielders, full-backs were expected to patrol the entire flank from defence to attack while still tucking infield to support their central defence or midfield.

The full-backs in England's 1966 World Cup-winning team, Ray Wilson and George Cohen, were specialist defenders who played a hundred games between them without scoring a goal. Wilson won 63 caps for his country during a time when far fewer games were played and is regarded as one of the genuinely outstanding members of England's 1966 World Cup squad. Wilson is also one of the few international players to have had a post-football career an an undertaker.

Over time full-backs have tended to become more important as an attacking force. This has not been a traditional British strength. Between 1979 and 1988 Kenny Sansom played 86 times for England at left-back on the strength of his defensive play, rarely venturing forward to any effect. The modern full-back is expected to overlap, put in crosses and support his advanced midfielder at all times. Ashley Cole was an automatic choice at two major international tournaments before the age of 24, without ever having suggested any great mastery of defending, but providing the promise of a significant attacking thrust down the left-hand side.

The least conspicuous or glamorous position on the field when filled by a player with little attacking intention, a talented full-back can still become a major influence in any team. Stuart Pearce, perhaps the best-ever English left-back, provided both leadership and attacking threat. Pearce once scored 16 goals in a season for Nottingham Forest from full-back and provided a chest-beating presence under five England managers and a career of 78 caps. Similarly, Danny McGrain became a much-feted figure during his time at Celtic during the 1970s and 1980s, winning seven League championships and playing over 600 games for the club, as well as captaining his country and playing at two World Cups.

Full Members' Cup

The Full Members' Cup, championed by ex-Chelsea chairman Ken Bates, was set up in 1985 to try to fill the gap left by English clubs' ban from Europe in the wake of the **Heysel disaster**. Perhaps unsurprisingly, it proved inherently suspect, lasting just seven seasons under further aliases the Simod Cup (1987–89) and the Zenith Data Systems Cup (1989–92).

Entry was open to all clubs from the top two divisions, but Manchester United, Arsenal, Liverpool and Tottenham turned their noses up at it, while Everton competed just twice, losing in the final both times. In its first year just 21 clubs entered, although this rose to 41 by its final season. Gates were poor – only four non-final matches pulled more than 20,000 over the course of seven years – but the Wembley finals were well attended. The 1990 showdown between Chelsea and Middlesbrough drew over 76,000, which was more than came to the League Cup Final that year.

In fact, if the competition is remembered at all, it will be for its finals. In 1986 Chelsea edged Manchester City 5–4 (possibly both defences were exhausted after playing League games the day before), with Chelsea's David Speedie scoring the first Wembley hat-trick since Geoff **Hurst** in 1966. Then in 1989 Nottingham Forest beat Everton by the odd goal in seven. Chelsea and Forest both took the trophy twice, while the other three winners were Blackburn, Reading and Crystal Palace.

Bates claimed that the cup was an 'innovation' that would eventually be accepted as the League Cup had been. Yet even in 1985 the League Cup was starting to prove a second-rate draw for the top-tier clubs, and when English clubs were readmitted to Europe in 1990 the competition entered its death throes. When the ZDS sponsorship expired in 1992, so did the trophy.

Still, it lasted six years longer than the Super Cup, the other ban-inspired competition that attempted to fill the European void. The six teams that would have qualified for Europe faced off home and away in two groups of three during the 1985–86 season, followed by two-legged semi-finals and final. When Liverpool and Everton had no time to play the final it was held over until the following season, the Reds emerging as 7–2 aggregate winners. The cup presumably still sits in a quiet corner of the Anfield trophy room, the object perhaps of the occasional baffled inquiry.

full time

One of a referee's primary and least contentious functions is to act as time-keeper and to blow his whistle for the last time at the end of the match. Full time is reached once the designated length of the second half plus any added time for stoppages have elapsed, with one exception.

If in the final seconds of a game a team concedes a penalty then the spot kick is taken, even if full time in theory

passes before everyone is ready. In such circumstances, the ball must go directly into the goal or deflect in off the goal-keeper, woodwork or a combination of the two; the referee blows for full time before any follow-up is allowed.

Some managers keep a keen eye on any stoppage time and complain if the referee does not blow for full time at the moment they consider to be the correct one. These notions of when full time is due are usually earlier if their team are ahead, later if they are looking for an equalizer or winner. Few of these complaints are heeded, but in the 1930 World Cup Gilberto de Almeida Rego, a Brazilian referee, blew for full time six minutes early in the match between Argentina and France. The latter had just gone behind and, according to some sources, were on the attack when the mistake was made. After protest the game was restarted, but Argentina held on to win 1–0.

While players, officials, managers and fans can relax, celebrate or slump their shoulders when the referee blows up, in journalism full time is referred to as 'on the whistle'; this is the time that reporters are expected notionally to file their reports for the first editions and in news-paper offices heralds the storm after the comparative lull of the 90 minutes.

Paul Gascoigne

Paul Gascoigne has been described many times as a wasted talent. With the increasingly lurid biographical details that have accompanied his recent retirement from playing, it is tempting to see Gascoigne's successes as a player as monumental achievements in the face of adversity. The most impressive young player at the 1990 World Cup, Gascoigne had the talent to become one of England's most successful players of all time.

He had other things on his mind, however, such as his burgeoning alcohol dependence, lifelong bulimia, periodic cocaine addiction, depression, consistently terrible diet, a calamitous family life and successive serious injuries. That he achieved as much as he did is a testimony to the depth of his talent and his undimmed passion for playing the game, which would see him bustling around in the middle of the Gobi desert in China at the age of 35 just because someone had said they would give him a game (and half a million pounds).

Gascoigne was born in Gateshead in 1967. He joined Newcastle United as a short, pudgy apprentice in 1983, made his League debut against QPR at St James' Park two years later and went on to make 99 League and Cup appearances for Newcastle, scoring 25 goals. Gascoigne stood out as a precocious teenager, and even developed a fitful and cantankerous partnership with the Brazilian international Mirandinha during his final season at St James' Park. Despite being courted by Alex **Ferguson** over a move to Old Trafford, he signed for Tottenham Hotspur for £2m in July 1988.

The 1990 World Cup was a watershed in Gascoigne's career. Bobby Robson took him to Italy as a 'gamble' after a particularly impressive performance in a friendly victory over Czechoslovakia at Wembley. Playing in a five-man midfield, Gascoigne was England's best player against Holland, Egypt and Cameroon, when his incisive passing brought about two England penalties to turn the game. In the semi-final against Germany Gascoigne had the better part of a fierce midfield battle with Lothar Matthäus, the player of the tournament. Gascoigne would have missed the Final following his booking in the second half of the game, but television pictures of his tears after being shown the yellow card proved significant in helping to create a new and idiotically ubiquitous personage: Gazza.

Gazza-mania was as overpowering and as short-lived as the remainder of Gazza's time at his footballing peak. For a season after his return from the World Cup Gascoigne played some remarkable football, leading Tottenham to an FA Cup final, scoring memorable goals and continuing his fine form with England. He released a hit single with the group Lindisfarne, the terrible 'Fog on the Tyne'; he sold warehouses full of Gazza T-shirts; he appeared on *Wogan* and various other mainstream television programmes, at a time when footballers just weren't invited to do that sort of thing; and he agreed to advertise anything that was put in front of him.

With a record £5.5m transfer to Lazio looming, Gascoigne suffered a serious injury in the 1991 FA Cup Final, tearing apart the ligaments in his knee after launching himself into an adrenalin-fuelled lunge at Nottingham Forest's Gary Charles. Gascoigne would never be the same player again. Worse, this was the first public example of the frenzied self-destructiveness that would come to dog him in later years. After aggravating the injury further in an incident in a night club in October 1991, Gascoigne was out of football for sixteen months, finally

passing the fitness tests for his move to Lazio the following year. His time in Italy would be fractious, intermittently spectacular and blighted by further injuries. Immediately taken to heart by the Lazio fans for his passion as much as his skill, Gascoigne scored some great goals, including the winner in a Rome derby.

His Lazio career coincided with the start of Channel 4's live *Football Italia*, a programme that at times became something of a weekly documentary on his progress. His debut was marked by a banner which read: 'Gazza's Boys, We Are Here. Shake Your Women And Drink Your Beer'. Other memorable tributes included the banner at an away game that read: 'Paul Gazza, You Are Fat Poofta'.

There were moments of controversy too: the £9,000 fine for burping into a TV microphone, after which questions were asked in the Italian parliament; and the furore over Gascoigne's response when asked if he had any message for the people of Norway ahead of their World Cup qualifier against England ('Yes. Fuck off Norway'). In December 1993 he reported back after a Christmas break with a thigh strain suffered getting out of bed. Four months later he broke his leg in a freak training ground accident and spent another year on the sidelines. A move to Rangers led to a period of stability and perhaps the most successful spell of his career. In 1996 he was Scottish Player of the Season as Rangers won their eighth title in a row.

The other high point of Gascoigne's playing career came at Euro 96, where – under his favourite manager Terry **Venables** – he was part of the England team that reached the semi-finals before losing again to Germany on penalties. Gascoigne played superbly in the first half of England's opening game against Switzerland and then scored a brilliant second goal in the 2–0 victory over Scotland. He was close to a three-quarter-speed version of his very best against Holland and Germany; but already there were signs of decline. His celebration after scoring against the Scots – lying on his back while team mates squirted water into his mouth – was supposedly a gesture of defiance to those who had criticized his boozing on a trip to Hong Kong. Now it looks a bit more like a harbinger of sad times to come. In the semi-final Gascoigne was inches away from connecting with a cross to score a golden goal winner deep into extra time. One less daft injury, a couple of drinks refused and he might have made it.

Walter Smith's replacement by Dick Advocaat as Rangers manager signalled the end of Gascoigne's Ibrox career. He returned to England with Middlesbrough and helped them return to the Premiership under Bryan **Robson**'s managership. There was time for one last great performance for England, a masterpiece in ball retention against Italy on his former home ground in Rome in October 1997 during a 0–0 draw that guaranteed England's place at the World Cup. Months later, by now a knock-kneed and visibly frailer figure, Gascoigne was omitted from England's squad for France. Told to pack his bags by Glenn **Hoddle** during a squad trip to La Manga, he smashed a lamp and a chair in Hoddle's hotel room in his rage at the decision, injuring his foot in the process.

Spells at Everton and Burnley followed, as well as an ill-advised trek into the desert to play for Gansu Tianma. Within days of scoring a spectacular goal on his Chinese debut, Gascoigne had disappeared, turning up in an Arizona rehabilitation clinic. It's hard to predict what the future holds for Gascoigne, long separated from his wife Cheryl, whom he admitted beating. The launch of an auto-biography in 2004 – complete with cover portrait of its author looking like a crazed TV evangelist – saw him living in a flat in Gateshead with his ever-present companion Jimmy 'Five Bellies' Gardner.

geography

Professional football in England was a child of industrial Lancashire and the Midlands, and the patterns set in the 1880s have proved remarkably durable. The 12 founder members of the Football League were split evenly between the two (if you count Stoke as part of the Midlands) and no team south of Birmingham joined the League until Arsenal in 1893, when they were London's lonely representative among 31 other teams. Even by 1920, when Division 3 South was incorporated, there were just seven southerners among 44, all from London bar Bristol City. Indeed, if you take away Arsenal, the south's League record has been pitiful, with only seven championships to its credit, all but one in a mid-century burst (Portsmouth in 1949 and 1950, Tottenham in 1951 and 1961, Chelsea in 1955, Ipswich in 1962).

The Cup has been an entirely different matter. In the professional era no fewer than ten southern teams have won it and a further eight have been beaten finalists. Even Orient and Plymouth have reached the semis. Northern fans, of course, would say that simply confirms the reputation of southern teams as flighty and inconsistent (Arsenal always excepted), capable of one-off success but not in it for the long haul.

But the north's apparent dominance is far from the whole picture. For one thing, it does not imply any lack of enthusiasm for the game in the south – London clubs have frequently topped the attendance tables, despite their inferior results. Second, it hides more subtle regional variations. Yorkshire, for example, has produced only three champion sides (Leeds in 1969, 1974 and 1992) since the end of the 1920s. As for the fabled hot-bed of the north-east, Newcastle have been waiting for a title since 1927, Sunderland since 1936 and Middlesbrough have yet to trouble the scorers. In the south, too, some regions have notably underachieved, particularly Bristol and the south-west (not to mention London 'giants' such as Chelsea, and even spasmodically well-backed Charlton), while others have had unexpected golden eras, such as Ipswich and Southampton. Third, the fact is that Arsenal do exist, and their success hints at the reason for the south's more general failure.

Certainly it was disadvantaged at the start by the preponderance of northern teams. But by the 1920s at the latest, the traditional strongholds had already been threatened – Huddersfield, for example, overcame the strong appeal of rugby league to win their three League titles in 1924–26. In the first of those triumphs they edged out Cardiff, similarly challenged by rugby union, but a football power in the mid-1920s. The key to any club's success over an extended period is not its location, but a dominant personality at the helm: Herbert **Chapman** in the case of Huddersfield and then Arsenal; Matt **Busby** and then Alex **Ferguson** at Manchester United; Bill **Shankly** at Liverpool; Jock **Stein** at Celtic; Don **Revie** at Leeds; Brian **Clough** at Derby and Forest; and now Arsène **Wenger** at Arsenal.

Ipswich and Southampton could point to the influential reigns of Alf **Ramsey**, Bobby **Robson** and Lawrie McMenemy, but for reasons that may come down to nothing more than chance, the potentially dominant London clubs such as Chelsea, Tottenham and West Ham have never found such a commanding figure (with the brief exception of Bill **Nicholson**). And there are plenty of big northern and Midlands clubs who have similarly stumbled through recent decades, not least Manchester City and Wolves.

A club's location now seems less and less relevant to its chances of winning trophies. For a brief period in the 1980s, Division 1 was overrun with southern clubs – in 1987–88 12 of the 21 top-flight teams were from the south, plus Norwich. But the implausibility of clubs such as Luton, Oxford and Wimbledon (who all won trophies in that decade) challenging again is entirely due to their size and the inequalities reinforced by the Premier League, not their geography. Even colonizing Milton Keynes is unlikely to help.

Ryan Giggs

David **Beckham** may have courted more publicity, Gary Neville may have won more caps, but no player better represents the success of Manchester United under Sir Alex **Ferguson** than Ryan Giggs. The winger has won more trophies than any other player in the club's history, and was the first of 'Fergie's Fledglings', United's all-conquering youth team of the early 1990s, to break into the first team, in March 1991. He was credited with the only goal of the game against Manchester City in his first League start a few weeks later, although he never touched the ball (it was a Colin Hendry own-goal).

Giggs was born Ryan Wilson in Cardiff in 1973. His Welsh parents, Lynne Giggs and Danny Wilson, moved to England when he was seven – his father played rugby league for teams in the north-west. At nine, he was spotted by a Manchester

City scout and played in their school of excellence. Ferguson had heard City did not want him and visited his parents' home on his 14th birthday, when Giggs signed schoolboy forms with the team he supported. He captained England schoolboys but was never eligible to play for England. When his parents split up, he adopted the surname Giggs so that 'the world would know I was my mother's son'.

Ferguson banned Giggs, tipped as 'the new George **Best**', from talking to the press but the youngster's head was turned when his first season ended with a PFA Young Player of the Year award, a multi-million pound boot deal with Reebok, and celebrity girlfriends that included Dani Behr and Davinia Taylor. All that changed after a day-out with team-mate Lee Sharpe in Blackpool. Ferguson was tipped off at a charity dinner and stormed straight round to Sharpe's house. The sight of the shirtless beer-carrying teenager who opened the door sent him apoplectic: he burst in, indiscriminately clipped people round the ear, and threw everyone out. Giggs was not as fortunate as the two youth-teamers who hid in an upstairs wardrobe: he was caught by his boss, and received the 'hair-dryer' treatment for the first time.

It did the trick: Giggs did not go the way of Best, or Sharpe, but got the youthful excess out of his system. Giggs had already won two Premiership titles and one FA Cup when a young Beckham was on loan at Preston. When the other Fledglings broke into the side, Giggs was already the elder statesman of the team, coping with the adulation of a reported 2,000 fan letters a week (6,000 on Valentine's Day). Giggs has benefited from his Welsh heritage too. Though the youngest player to represent his country, aged 17 years and 321 days, he has never played

at a major international tournament and has had regular breaks between seasons.

Manchester United magazine readers voted Giggs's winning goal against Arsenal in the 1999 FA Cup semi-final replay as United's best-ever goal. He scored an even more important goal that injury-hit season, a last-minute equalizer in the Champions' League semi-final first leg against Juventus, which helped United reach the final and complete the treble. Giggs was criticized for having a testimonial in 2001, given that he was already a millionaire, and was booed the following season. That changed when his recurring hamstring problem improved thanks to a special training routine and the conversion of his Porsche to an automatic. His performances in December 2004 were as good as any in his career.

Ryan Giggs has never received the credit he deserves, perhaps because United fans take his consistency for granted. Giggs is within sight of Bobby **Charlton**'s all-time appearance record of 606 games: breaking that would be a fitting end to a glittering career.

Johnny Giles

Like his contemporary, George **Best**, Johnny Giles was a world-class player who missed out on playing in a World Cup finals but made a major contribution to his club's success in domestic and international football. Born in Dublin in 1940, Giles began his League career as a right-winger with Manchester United, winning an FA Cup medal in 1963. Shortly after, however, he fell out with Matt **Busby** and in keeping with the United manager's habit of not selling players to Division 1 rivals, was offloaded to Leeds in Division 2.

Leeds were promoted at the end of that season and Giles soon switched over to the left side of midfield, quickly developing a formidable partnership with Billy **Bremner**. The latter became Leeds captain but Giles's range of passing and tactical nous made him equally influential, though his unshowy style meant that he was never a particular favourite with the Leeds crowd. Many opponents rated him the toughest player in a famously combative team, and, unlike the more hot-headed Bremner, one with a knack for committing fouls that escaped the attention of the referee.

During his time at Leeds, Giles won two League championships, an FA Cup, a League Cup and two Fairs Cups and came close on several other occasions. He scored 150 goals in all competitions for the club and as their main penalty-taker for a decade missed only three of 50 spotkicks. His team-mates had expected him to be named manager when Don **Revie** left to take over England in 1974 and Giles was one of many within the dressing room who did not welcome the surprise appointment of Brian **Clough**, previously a severe critic of Leeds's rather clinical approach.

Giles became manager of West Brom in 1975 and led them to promotion from Division 2 in his first season before returning home as part-owner of Shamrock Rovers; within a few months he also took charge of the Republic of Ireland international side, a position he held for three years. He had a second spell at West Brom, with brother in law Nobby Stiles and former Leeds colleague Norman Hunter as his assistants, but left after a year in 1985 with the team near the foot of Division 1. He is still involved in football as a newspaper columnist and an often acerbic pundit, alongside the equally forthright Eamon Dunphy, on RTE's football programmes.

Gillingham

Inspired by the success of the Royal Engineers team based at Chatham, the Medway area in Kent was fertile territory for aspirant football clubs in the late 19th century. Originally known as New Brompton, Gillingham were founded in 1893 by a group of Victorian gentleman with links to the successful Excelsior club. New Brompton bought a plot of land on Gillham Road for £600, which would subsequently become the Priestfield Stadium. The club changed its name to Gillingham FC in 1913 and seven years later became a founder member of Division 3. There followed an undistinguished period as Gillingham consistently finished near the bottom of the League.

Five applications were made for re-election, the last of which, in 1938, was refused. Following their demotion the Gills went on to enjoy a successful spell in the Southern League followed by a period of liquidation after the Second World War, before winning re-election to the League in 1950 as Division 3 was enlarged from 22 to 24 teams. Gillingham's sole honour remains the Division 4 title won in 1964, a triumph that included a record run of 52 unbeaten home matches under the tutelage of manager Freddie Cox, whose team of defensive battlers edged out free-scoring Carlisle on goal average.

Gillingham narrowly avoided relegation to the Conference in 1989 after beating eventual bottom club Halifax 2–0 on the final day of the season. They almost went out of existence in 1995 before current chairman Paul Scally took charge of the club, eventually providing enough money to construct three new stands and build a team that would take the Gills to new heights. In 1996 Tony Pulis oversaw promotion from Division 3, though he was later involved in a long-running legal dispute with Scally over the circumstances of his dismissal. Further success followed as Peter Taylor led the club into Division 1 in 2000, the Gills coming from behind to beat Wigan Athletic 3–2 in extra time, a year after they had lost on penalties at the same stage to Manchester City.

In fact, the last ten years have been the most successful in the club's history, incorporating five consecutive seasons in Division 1 and an FA Cup run in 1999–2000 which saw Taylor's men defeat Premier League Bradford City and Sheffield Wednesday before losing to Chelsea in the quarter-finals. Taylor's successor, Andy Hessenthaler, was player-manager for over four years until stepping down during 2004–05 to be replaced by Stan Ternent, who oversaw a dramatic last-day relegation. Commentator and lifelong fan Brian Moore served as director of the club for a while before and during this successful period, giving his name to the Gillingham fanzine *Brian Moore's Head Looks Like The London Planetarium*, which – true to say – it did.

Brian Yeo is the club's all-time top scorer with 135 goals between 1963 and 1975, and a domestic Golden Boot-winning 31 in 1973–74. Capped once in 1925, goalkeeper Fred Fox remains the only Gills player to represent England. Ireland international Tony Cascarino played for the club in the mid-1980s, part of an exciting team managed by Keith Peacock, which included maverick Northern Irish winger Terry Cochrane, remembered for blowing his nose on the corner flag, leaving the field during a game to sit in the stand and, once, scoring spectacularly from 45 yards against Bristol Rovers. In recent times striker Mamady Sidibe has been capped by Mali.

goal difference

Teams that are level on points in league competitions must often be separated to determine final placings. Though there are many methods – with an increasing emphasis on head-to-head records between teams in international competitions – goal difference, the gap between goals scored and conceded in all or a set selection of games, is the commonest.

It was introduced into English League football in 1975. Before that date, goal average was used. Under this system, the ratios of teams' goals scored and conceded were compared. In most cases, this was a mathematically complicated way of achieving the same outcome as would occur today. The exception was that if teams were level on goal difference, then the one that had scored and conceded fewer goals would have a better goal average. In 1924, Cardiff finished level on points with Huddersfield at the top of Division 1. Their goal differences were the same and under the modern method Cardiff would have won the League on goals scored. But under goal average Huddersfield won the first of their three consecutive titles and Cardiff are yet to win one.

goals

The winner of a game of football, if any, is the team that has scored more goals when the final whistle is blown. This is the only approved method of settling games at most levels and even cup ties settled by penalty shoot-outs are still listed as draws – a ruling that improves the won–drawn–lost figures of three England managers. A goal should be awarded when, in the absence of any infringements, the ball has crossed the goal-line. This simple stipulation has caused confusion, with some people confused by the term 'crossed' and unsure whether a ball has to be entirely behind the goal-line. It is unknown whether such people regard a ferry that is three-quarters or nine-tenths of the way from Dover to Calais as having crossed the Channel, and get wet as a result.

All goals are of equal value, except when teams finish level on aggregate in some two-legged cup ties, in which case away goals are more valuable. In 1984 Queens Park Rangers became the first team to lose a UEFA Cup tie on away goals after holding a four-goal first-leg lead. Having beaten Partizan Belgrade 6–2 in the first match, they went out of the competition following a 4–0 defeat in the return.

Own-goals are worth the same as goals scored by a player in the opposition's net, though are rarely noted with a player's name attached beyond the initial match report. However, in 1998–99, David Ginola was named Footballer of the Year despite his League goals total for Spurs only overtaking that of Liverpool's Jamie Carragher in May, the defender finding his own net in both that season's meetings of the teams.

George Graham

George Graham was a good player who became a great manager. His title-winning Arsenal teams of 1989 and 1991 have come to represent both the best qualities and the obvious limitations of a particular era in the recent history of English football. Graham was appointed Arsenal manager in 1986, the first year of the ban on English clubs playing in European football following the **Heysel disaster**. Between the beginning of the ban and the start of the Premiership English football was as geographically isolated as it ever had been since the

1950s. Tactically, the game became a high-speed long-ball duel, with teams compressed between symmetrical offside traps.

During this period Graham's Arsenal won two League titles, based around the miserly defending of Lee Dixon, Nigel Winterburn, Tony **Adams** and Steve Bould, and the aerial attacking talents of Alan Smith and Niall Quinn. The Arsenal offside trap was ingrained through rigorously one-dimensional training methods. In 1990–91 Graham's team conceded just 18 League goals.

A former Scotland international, Graham was an elegant central midfielder with Aston Villa, Chelsea, Arsenal – where he was part of the 1970–71 Double-winning team – Manchester United and Crystal Palace. He began his managerial career at Millwall in 1982, after five years as a youth coach at Crystal Palace and QPR. It was as much for his reputation as a disciplinarian as his success in Division 2 that Arsenal appointed Graham manager following the departure of Don **Howe**.

Graham immediately set to work imposing standards of dress, behaviour and training ground enthusiasm, as well as sticking rigidly to the Highbury wage structure. Success came quickly, a League Cup victory in 1987 followed by the astonishing 2–0 victory over Liverpool at Anfield in 1989, Michael Thomas's last-minute goal bringing the club its first League title since 1971. Thomas was one of a clutch of fine young players brought through by Graham in his first few years in charge, including David Rocastle, Tony Adams and Paul Merson.

There were obvious limits to his methods, however. Arsenal were the first Champions of England to re-enter the European Cup. A 3–1 defeat at Highbury by a vastly superior Benfica team signalled not just the end of their run in the competition, but in retrospect seems like a watershed in Graham's own managerial career. The first leg, a 1–1 draw in Lisbon, had probably been the high point of Graham's reign as Arsenal manager. A double of FA Cup and League Cup followed in 1993, Graham's men beating Sheffield Wednesday both times, and a European Cup Winners' Cup victory in 1994, when Alan Smith's goal was enough to defeat Parma. It had been a smash and grab victory, however, and would prove to be Graham's last trophy as Arsenal manager.

After the revelation that he had received £425,000 in 'unsolicited gifts' related to transfer dealings, Graham was sacked by Arsenal in 1995 and banned from all football for a year. He returned to manage Leeds United briefly and also Tottenham, where he won another League Cup in 1999; but Graham's time seemed to have passed, leaving him to take up a secondary career as an eloquently dour television pundit.

Jimmy Greaves

Jimmy Greaves has existed in several guises. First, as a prolific and elegant goalscorer for Tottenham Hotspur, Chelsea and England. Then as a drawlingly opinionated television pundit, one half of the strangely successful Saturday lunchtime pairing of Saint and Greavsie, and a man always on the verge of giggling at his own (never very funny) jokes. And throughout this as the first high-profile professional footballer to admit publicly to being an alcoholic, supposedly driven in part by his omission from Alf **Ramsey**'s World Cup team of 1966 at the quarter-final stage in favour of hat-trick hero Geoff **Hurst**.

Greaves began his career at Chelsea,

where he scored a Division 1 hat-trick as a 17-year-old and then became the first man to score a hundred League goals before the age of 21. After an unhappy spell at AC Milan, he returned to England, signing for Spurs for £99,999. During his first season at the club he top-scored with 22 goals and helped Spurs retain the FA Cup; in the next two seasons he scored 35 and 37 goals, this last an all-time Spurs record, and in total he was Division 1's top scorer six times between 1958 and 1969 and remains the only player ever to head the list for three consecutive years. A nine-year career at Spurs was followed by an unsuccessful spell at West Ham, where Greaves began to struggle with the **alcohol** problem that would precede his successful return to prominence as a pundit and newspaper columnist.

Greaves was a popular player, an elegant mover and a scorer of spectacular goals. He was known for his skill with the ball at his feet, great acceleration and a powerful left-footed shot. On his debut for Tottenham he scored a hat-trick that included a bicycle kick that is still considered by some to be the most memorable goal ever scored by a Spurs player. He had a remarkable record of scoring on debuts, doing so for Chelsea, Milan, Tottenham, West Ham and for both England Under-23 and the full team. In fact, Greaves remains arguably England's greatest-ever goalscorer. His record of 44 goals in 57 matches is unsurpassed among players with a significant goal total (Gary **Lineker** scored four more goals but from 80 matches).

Had he not fallen out of favour with Alf Ramsey during the 1966 World Cup Greaves would have set an unsurpassable mark beyond Bobby **Charlton**'s 49-goal record: his final appearance for the national team came in 1967, when he was just 27. Despite its early start and early finish, Greaves's playing career is still remarkable both for its statistical feats and for the reverence in which his skills as a goalscoring inside-forward are still held by supporters of Chelsea and Spurs.

Greenock Morton

Morton's fortunes have waned since the now defunct *Soccer Monthly* magazine declared them in February 1980 to be the team that 'strike fear in the hearts of the Old Firm'. At the time 'The Ton' were enjoying a brief period at the heights of the Scottish Premier League. Since then they've been as far down as Division 3, while in 2000 fans and the local council had to defeat the attempts of an archetypally megalomaniac chairman, Hugh Scott, to shut down the club and sell its Cappielow ground to a supermarket chain.

Formed in 1874 as Greenock Morton FC, the latter part of the club's name either came in tribute to the town's provost between 1868 and 1871, James Morton, or, more romantically, because its founders played around the area of Morton Terrace, close to the Cappielow ground by the Clydeside shipyards that the club moved into in 1879.

The side turned professional in 1893 and became members of the Scottish League, achieving promotion to Division 1 at the start of the 20th century. They beat Rangers 1–0 in the 1922 Scottish Cup Final, their sole success in this competition.

Morton have a good record in yielding talent that moved on to greater things. Its most renowned star was the maverick, diminutive Billy Steel, who made his debut for Scotland against England at Wembley in 1947 with a 'dramatically brilliant' performance, according to reports. Shortly after, he was chosen for a Great Britain side that played the Rest of the World, and a fine solo goal ensured he was sold that summer to Derby for £15,500. Two years later, goalkeeper Jimmy Cowan's performance for the Scots in their 3–1 win at Wembley earned similar rave reviews. Capped 25 times, he was also Morton's number one in 1948 when they took Rangers to a Scottish Cup Final replay that they lost by a single goal. Both games attracted over 130,000 fans.

Later sales included Joe Harper to Aberdeen and future Scottish regular Joe Jordan to Leeds in 1970, a move said to have scuppered Morton's chances of progressing in the Texaco Cup. After beating West Brom 3–1 on aggregate in the first round, a Jordan-less Morton lost to Wolves. The club's only European fixture took them no further than London – they lost in the first round of the 1968–69 Fairs Cup 9–3 over two games to Chelsea.

Hal Stewart it was, though, who had rescued the club in 1962 when Cappielow was almost sold for real estate development. He bought a majority shareholding and appointed himself manager, then in the following years took the team to two Division 2 championships, two Scottish Cup semi-finals, and a League Cup Final, losing 5–0 to Rangers. He was also the first Scottish manager to sign players from Scandinavia, starting with goalie Erik Sørensen from Denmark, famously billed on the team sheet before his debut as 'Mr X'.

Since then the club has had to be content with picking up three Division 1 championships and one title each in Divisions 2 and 3. The latter was won in 2003, before 8,500 fans and the club's new chairman, Douglas Rae, whose company had taken over the team a couple of years before to save it from extinction.

Ron Greenwood

The joke West Ham fans like to tell about Ron Greenwood is that he was more helpful to the England team when he was in charge of the Hammers than when he became national coach 16 years later. They are half right: three West Ham players were part of England's 1966 World Cup-winning side and though Bobby **Moore** was already a star in the making when Greenwood joined West Ham in 1961, Geoff **Hurst** and Martin Peters were five years from playing international football.

Greenwood, born in Burnley in November 1921, earned one England 'B' cap as a centre-half. He signed terms with Bradford Park Avenue in 1945, moved to London in 1949 and never left. He played for Brentford, Chelsea and Fulham and coached non-League Eastbourne United before he was appointed Arsenal assistant manager aged 37. By then he had worked as an England youth coach and graduated to the Under-23s. He made Moore captain of both sides, marking his reputation as a coach with an uncanny eye for spotting leaders on and off the pitch.

Greenwood established his reputation after he became the first man with no previous West Ham connection to coach the club in 1961. Again he appointed Moore – then a teenager – captain, and broke the English transfer record signing Johnny Byrne from Crystal Palace. The transfer looked ill-judged until Greenwood converted Hurst from a wing-half into a forward, and the Byrne–Hurst partnership rained goals. Within three years, West Ham won the first major trophy in their history, the 1964 FA Cup. Greater success came the following season, when the Hammers beat 1860 Munich at Wembley to win the European Cup Winners' Cup with Greenwood pioneering a counter-attacking style previously unpopular in England.

Greenwood fell out with Moore before the World Cup and refused him a move to Spurs after it. The pair clashed again in 1971 when Moore was caught drinking before an embarrassing FA Cup defeat to Blackpool. Greenwood went on to reject an approach from Derby for Moore and a young Trevor **Brooking**, who both stayed to help West Ham finish a best-ever sixth place in 1973.

After making Billy Bonds captain in place of Moore (another great appointment), Greenwood suggested that his former captain John Lyall should take over the first team and he became general manager in 1974. The same season, the outspoken Don **Revie** had become England coach but he walked out for a lucrative move to the UAE with the side on the verge of elimination from the 1978 World Cup qualifiers. The FA did not want to risk appointing another maverick, so overlooked Brian **Clough** in favour of the more conservative Greenwood.

Greenwood demanded that the England youth teams get top coaches, who included future England bosses Bobby **Robson**, Terry **Venables** and Howard Wilkinson. After the disaster of 1978, Greenwood restored England to a competitive level, but in the 1980 European Championships in Italy defeat to the hosts – against the backdrop of rioting fans – prevented further progress. Hopes were not much higher for the 1982 World Cup in Spain, with qualification only sealed with a last-match win over Hungary. Three wins in the first group phase increased expectations before draws to West Germany and Spain cost England in the second phase. Greenwood retired after the tournament, and was the only English coach after Sir Alf **Ramsey** to end a World Cup finals tournament with an unbeaten record. He died in 2006.

Gretna

When Gretna FC joined the Scottish League in 2002 to replace the newly defunct Clydebank they fulfilled all the criteria for Scottish lower-division football – a tiny ground, low crowds and low expectations. Gretna was built between the wars as a neighbour to Gretna Green to house workers at the nearby munitions factory, but when 'The Black and Whites' were formed in 1946 they hardly exploded onto the Scottish football scene. They lasted just one year in the Dumfriesshire Junior League before looking south instead, the same year they moved to the 2,200-capacity Raydale Park.

Whereas Berwick Rangers are famous for being the only senior English team to play in the Scottish League, Gretna were perhaps less notorious for being the only Scottish team to play in England, where up until 2002 they had been performing with little distinction in the Northern Premier (Unibond) League. Prior to that they had done better in the Northern League, whose Division 2 they'd entered in 1982 after three and a half decades in the Carlisle and District League, and whose first division they won back to back in 1991 and 1992 before being promoted to the NPL (are you still with us?).

While playing in England they made the first round of the FA Cup twice, both times losing to Lancashire opposition. In 1992 they held Rochdale at home before going down 3–1 in a replay, then two years later lost 3–2 at Bolton after leading 2–1 with 11 minutes to go. In the Scottish Cup Gretna already has a bogey team – in their first two years competing they fell both times to Clyde.

That Gretna were granted senior status in Scotland ahead of a number of more strongly supported Highland League teams came as something of a surprise, but they finished their second season in 2004 in a respectable third position after going full-time. The next season they began to rack up the kind of scores against long-standing League members that usually come amid decades of struggle, swatting the hapless East Stirlingshire 8–1, and then scoring six at Albion Rovers, with two in reply, the following weekend in late 2004. At the end of the season they were promoted to Division 2 with 130 goals and 98 points. Another promotion followed in 2005–06, together with an appearance in the Scottish Cup Final, where they were beaten on penalties by Hearts.

Grimsby Town

There exist two significant items of trivia in relation to Grimsby Town FC. The first is now well known by most quiz-night enthusiasts – that the club has never lost at home (it plays in neighbouring Cleethorpes) but the second one usually ruffles the most dedicated student of the game. To the question, 'What was Old Trafford's highest-ever attendance?', the answer would be '76,962, Wolves v Grimsby Town, March 1939, FA Cup semi-final.' Wolves won, of course, as did Arsenal at Leeds Road three years earlier in Grimsby's other semi-final appearance, but the facts lie at the heart of the strange paradox that is Grimsby Town.

Nowadays, mentions of the club generally occur within the context of the irritating phrase, 'No disrespect to the likes of your Grimsbys' – meaning that along with your Rochdales and your Darlingtons it is not the sort of place you would wish to visit on a cold winter's evening. You might come away with the three points, but the phrase implies that there is no glamour attached to the visit, no joy. Indeed, so incensed did a group of Grimsby supporters become with the constant appearance of this phrase in the media during the 1990s that they compiled a list of its every occurrence and the people guilty of using it. They did this because although the club has not exactly set the League alight, they have been around since 1878, have spent 14 seasons in the old Division 1 and have managed two FA Cup semi-finals. Perhaps a little more respect is therefore required.

Of course, Grimsby is singularly unglamorous, and this fact now stands proudly at the core of the club's image. The town is for ever redolent of fish, despite the fact that very few trawlers ever come within miles of its docks these days. But it remains one of the country's harder no-nonsense places, geographically isolated with a curious cut-off mentality that this engenders. The dwindling hard-core who still trundle through the rusting turnstiles of Blundell Park prefer tough, committed performers and are suspicious of any fancy stuff.

Founded as Grimsby Pelham back in 1878 they got off to an inauspicious start, losing their first two games. Twenty years later they built the Blundell Park ground, where they still play today. The scorer of the first goal on its hallowed turf was one J. W. Cockshot, but the club nevertheless made it to the top flight by 1901, hanging in there for a couple of years before plummeting down to the old Division 3 (North) by the early 1920s. But happier times were just around the corner and between 1929 and 1948 the town enjoyed its sepia glory days, a cloth-capped utopia to which it has never really returned. Legends such as the prolific Joe Robson, Pat Glover and the England international midfielder Jackie Bestall took Grimsby to fifth in Division 1 in 1934–35, their best-ever finish.

Such status as they had among that generation seems now to belong to some other space–time continuum. When they were relegated after the war, Bill **Shankly** briefly held the managerial reins before the club declined and fell to its 1969 nadir – finishing next to bottom of Division 4. There have been some bright moments since – a fine Division 4 championship won under the charismatic Lawrie McMenemy (later an FA Cup winner with Southampton), fifth position in the old Division 2 in 1984, a double-winning visit to Wembley in 1998 for the Auto Windscreens Shield and Division 2 play-offs, and an unlikely win at Anfield in 2001 in the Worthington Cup – all things to be cherished in the current patchy landscape of financial difficulties, with the taxman a regular visitor and administration looming darkly. Defeat in the League Two play-off final in 2006 was followed by the unexpected departure of manager Russell Slade.

grounds

When football ceased to be a street game it moved into public parks and the private 'meadows' of land-owners. By the 1880s the dimensions of the pitch had become more standardized and there was a need to enclose it off from the growing number of encroaching spectators. The opportunity to charge them was not lost on clubs, even amateur ones, either. 'Meadows' were still occasionally used *in extremis* and one Football League match took place in a field behind a vicarage (Loughborough v Port Vale, 1900).

The early football grounds usually featured a wooden grandstand, for the committee members, posh supporters and the ladies, terracing for the rest – more often made of turf or cinders and old railway sleepers rather than stone or concrete – and a surrounding fence bearing enamel advertising boards.

The enormous growth in the popularity of football between 1885 and 1915 drove the first wave of stadium-building. Everton and Newcastle were among the forerunners of the new era, raising the capacity of Goodison Park to 40,000 (1895) and St James' Park to 60,000 (1906) respectively. Aston Villa, another great club of the Edwardian era, even had plans to raise the capacity of Villa Park to 120,000 – larger than any ground in England has ever seen – though not as large as the old **Hampden Park**, Glasgow, which set an all-time British attendance record of 149,415 in 1937.

In the bygone era grounds were noted more for their capacity than their facilities. Capacity meant literally the physical capacity to contain human beings in no matter what state of discomfort, as this participant in the record attendance at Reading's old Elm Park ground in 1927 relates: 'The packed terraces were good to see though one wondered whether all the folks felt as nice as they looked. Personally, I should choose a density per acre that permitted the occasional lighting of a cigarette.'

The development of grounds (or stadiums as they have largely been termed since 1990) has been driven by the twin needs to maximize revenue and to respond to series of disasters – Ibrox 1902 (see **Ibrox disasters**), Bolton 1946 (see **Burnden Park disaster**), Ibrox 1971, Bradford City 1985 (see **Bradford fire**) – that befell spectators in over-crowded and unsafe circumstances. The **Hillsborough disaster** of 1989 in which 96 Liverpool fans were crushed to death marked a genuine turning point in the history of British stadiums. As Lord Justice Taylor remarked in his report, 'it is a depressing and chastening fact that mine is the ninth official report covering crowd safety and control at football grounds'. His central safety recommendation was to abolish terracing and make all professional grounds all-seater stadiums within ten years.

The **Taylor Report** was controversial and anti-traditional. Fifteen years later there is still some terracing at Football League clubs and a campaign for 'safe standing' continues. But the Report has without doubt dramatically changed the face of the game and the composition of its crowds (older and more middle class than before), and inspired a new generation of safer stadiums with greater comforts, better sight-lines and new facilities like concourse TVs and big-screen playbacks of match action. Since the Taylor Report, 26 of the 92 League clubs had moved to a new stadium by the start of 2005–06 while many others had changed out of all recognition.

British football fans have a serious sentimental attachment to their club's home ground and are strongly resistant to the 'economically beneficial' idea of ground-sharing with another team, as happens in municipally owned stadiums in Europe. Fans may have helped build or fund the building of the ground or its stands years ago or love its unusual individuality; Wrexham used to have the balcony seating from a cinema above an end terrace while Exeter had a bank of flowers alongside the touchline. From 1985 onwards Simon Inglis captured the attraction of this quirkiness with a series of best-selling books about football grounds. For those seriously interested in the phenomenon the term and hobby of 'ground-hopping' has been invented and there is also a club for those who have seen a match at all 92 League grounds, called, not surprisingly, The 92 Club.

In the early days of League football the results showed a disproportionate, almost irrational, level of home advantage. In 1903–04 57 per cent of League matches resulted in a home win. By 2003–04 the proportion had fallen to 45 per cent as a greater professionalism emerged and the old idiosyncracies of notorious slopes, vituperative paddocks and atmospheric cow-sheds disappeared from the game.

By the 21st century the ground was no longer somewhere to play football once a fortnight and keep the groundsman's equipment. It has become, to use the 1980s dream word, a 'multi-purpose' venue. Not only is first-class rugby played on a dozen football grounds, but the stadiums themselves can encompass restaurants, hotels, bowling alleys and conference centres, and some are even licensed as venues for marriage ceremonies.

The top clubs' stadiums are tourist attractions in their own right with attendant guided tours and museums. Throughout, British and European football 'standards' are enforced upon a club's grounds and facilities which determine at how high a level the club can compete. A vicar's back field will no longer do even if they have only got 11 men, same as you.

half-time

The break midway through the match is a chance for players to suck on an orange segment when they are young or debate, in a calm manner, what went right or wrong when they are older. Managers have a last direct chance to assert their game plan to players who have disregarded it and can also revise formations if it is the plan itself that has been at fault. Or, in the case of Ruud Gullit at Chelsea, you can take a shower while 2–0 down to Arsenal, to be found by coach Graham Rix banging one fist repeatedly against your forehead while the other hand holds a team sheet for the second half featuring only two defenders.

Half-time can be an irritating interruption if the game is going well, for players and fans alike, though for the latter it can provide a welcome opportunity to take on – or dispose of – refreshment. Heading for the facilities, whether refreshment or toilet, can ensure you miss any badly thought-out half-time entertainment. At its most harmless this can consist of a penalty shoot-out contest for local kids or ageing players, while the latter may also be deputed to conduct a raffle draw. Worse ideas have included pop groups, notably the Shamen at Arsenal, giant inflatable wrestlers, police dogs jumping through hoops of fire, and, at Rushden, the Dr Martens Rupert the Bear Impersonators Brass Band playing the theme to *Hawaii Five-O*. At Villa Park on 13 December 1998, the half-time interval had to be extended to 40 minutes following an injury to a parachutist who crashed into a stand roof and fell to the ground. Aston Villa had been losing 2–0 but after the extended break went on to win 3–2. The parachutist has since started a family with the nurse who looked after him.

Hamilton Academical

The second part of Hamilton's name, unique in senior football, comes from the club's origins. The Accies were formed in 1874 by the rector and pupils of the local school. Based in a town on the fringes of Glasgow, the team in red and white hoops had their most successful period in the years immediately prior to the Second World War, when they were a fixture in the old Division 1, their best season a fourth place in 1934–35. After the War the club slipped into the lower reaches of the old Division 2.

Before their rise under the cigar-smoking, pigeon-fancying manager John Lambie in the 1980s, the club's main claim to fame came in 1971, when, in a bid to arrest a decline that seemed terminal, they became the first Scottish club to recruit players from Eastern Europe. Three Polish internationals brought the club much interest from the national press, but little respite from their slump.

Hamilton's only cup successes came in 1991 and 1992, when a team including their most capped player, Canadian international defender Colin Miller, claimed back-to-back Challenge Cups, the trophy contested by the teams outside the Premier League. The latter season ended with Accies missing promotion to the top flight by goal difference. It was the closest they were to get in over a decade as they slumped through the leagues and left Douglas Park, their home for over 100 years.

Hamilton began the 2004–05 season in Division 1 for the first time since they moved into a new stadium in 2001. It ended a seven-year period of tenancy at Partick Thistle's Firhill stadium and Cliftonhill, home of Albion Rovers. Like Clyde, Airdrie United and Falkirk in the same league, they appear to have been buoyed by their new home, in this case appropriately called the Ballast Stadium on its opening.

Although they began the season with survival in mind, the long-term aim will to be replicate the achievements of the mid-1980s, when the Accies twice won Division 1 and enjoyed two brief flirtations with the big boys, their single-season stays the only time they have been in the top flight since League reconstruction. Although the team stuggled in the League, they did claim a notable Cup victory, winning 1–0 at Rangers in the Scottish FA Cup in 1987 courtesy of a goal by a full-back with a distinctly unheroic name: Adrian Sprott.

Hampden Park

The famous 'Hampden Roar' of the Scottish national stadium has long been diminished since the stadium became an all-seater with a reduced capacity playing host to a Scotland side that has free-fallen woefully down the FIFA rankings, and to perennial amateurs Queen's Park and their average home gate of around 300.

Built in 1903, Hampden Park was the third incarnation of the Queen's Park home ground. By 1873 the side had been playing at no fixed venue for six years, but then secured rental of part of the Queen's Park Recreation Ground from Glasgow City Council. They named the pitch after Hampden Terrace, an imposing row of terrace flats close to the ground which themselves had been named after John Hampden, reportedly a general in Cromwell's army during the English Civil War.

Ten years later the club were told to move because a planned railway line was projected to cross the pitch, so a second Hampden, with two stands, was opened 500 yards away in 1884. As the club could never secure more than a five-year lease, they were always on the lookout for a permanent home, and in 1903 left the ground to Third Lanark, who renamed it Cathkin Park and played there until their demise in 1967. The ground still exists today as a public pitch with sections of overgrown, ramshackle terracing.

Hampden mark III was ready to move into that year and was inaugurated when Queen's Park beat Celtic 1–0. The stadium, designed by Archibald Leitch, benefited from its location in a natural 'bowl', so the terracing could be built on solid foundations. Already by 1909 major renovations were necessary when a riot followed a Celtic v Rangers Cup Final replay – the fans had expected extra time when the scores were level after 90 minutes, but when the players left the field and didn't return, they wrecked and set fire to turnstiles, fences and barriers.

As a venue for major internationals and Cup Finals, Hampden began to draw massive six-figure crowds, with a record 149,415 cramming in to watch Scotland play England in 1937, and over 146,000 watching the Scottish Cup Final between Celtic and Aberdeen the same year. The ground's most memorable game, however, involved no home side, when 130,000 mainly Scottish spectators watched Real Madrid demolish Eintracht Frankfurt 7–3 in the 1960 European Cup Final.

By the 1970s the grand old stadium was crumbling, and barely surviving on facilities that were half a century old. After the Tory government reneged on a deal to upgrade the ground in the early 1980s, it looked for a while like Queen's Park would be forced to sell the ground and move next door to Lesser Hampden, a small adjacent stadium built in the 1920s on what had been a farm.

It took another decade before enough funding was scraped together to convert Hampden into a 52,000 all-seater, completed in 1999. Recognition for the modernized stadium came in the form of a UEFA 5-star grading and the 2002 European Cup Final between Real Madrid and Bayer Leverkusen. It's only a shame that the Scottish national side can no longer play football good enough to fill it.

handball

The conjoined twins of football and rugby were finally separated in 1863. The chief point of contention among the two games' first rule-makers, along with hacking, was handling the ball. At a famous meeting at the Freemason's Tavern, London, in 1863, the 12 founding clubs of the Football Association agreed that catching the ball was fine, in order to make a mark and take a free kick, but running around carrying the ball was definitely not acceptable.

At this point the handling and hacking fraternity decided to turn their back on the game and started playing with their own ball. In 1866 the last rugby elements were purged from the game; catching the ball was outlawed and the forward pass became legal with the advent of the new offside law. By 1869, even touching the ball was disallowed and the last remaining hand fetishists were ushered from the game. Goalkeepers were banned from handling the ball outside their areas in 1912 (they were previously allowed to handle in their own half only) and the handball rule as we know it today was complete.

To many the word 'handball' will conjure up an image of Diego Maradona punching one past Peter **Shilton** at the 1986 World Cup. In truth, the golden age of the handball was by then long past. Since deliberate handball to stop a goal-bound shot became an automatic sending-off offence, the most we can hope for now from defenders is a clumsy flailing of the arms in the penalty area while attempting to block or head away a cross, followed by a predictable ball-to-hand/hand-to-ball debate in the studio.

Prior to that, defenders would habitually dive full-length on the goal-line to palm the ball away to safety. The apotheosis of this was the full-length dive and parry employed by Norwich defender Mel Machin in the 1975 League Cup Final. It didn't prevent his team losing to the resulting penalty, but it lingers in the memory as one of the last examples of the spring-heeled deliberate handball, now lost to the game.

Hartlepool United

Hartlepool United hold the record for the most successful applications for re-election to the Football League. The club finished in the bottom slot in the bottom division on 14 occasions (and escaped on goal difference a couple more times), but avoided the drop every time. Quite how Hartlepool managed to pull off their escape act so often has never been fully established, though the allegedly lavish hospitality laid on for visiting club and FA officials is often cited by the followers of less fortunate clubs such as Gateshead, Workington and Bradford Park Avenue, all of whom were cut adrift over the years despite having better records than the team from the Victoria Ground.

Hartlepools United was formed as a professional club in 1908 and took the plural form from the two local boroughs it represented, Hartlepool and West Hartlepool. Struggling financially right from the start, partly at least because of the rival attractions of local rugby union club, Hartlepool Rovers, Hartlepools' difficulties were exacerbated in 1916 when a Zeppelin dropped bombs on the

Victoria Ground, destroying the main stand. After the armistice Hartlepool petitioned Berlin for £2,500 compensation, but despite persistent requests the German government was unmoved. Further bomb damage to the stadium the next time hostilities broke out suggested a vendetta.

Hartlepools was elected to Division 3 (North) in 1921, the same year as local arch-rivals Darlington. Despite the presence of managers such as former British Army heavyweight boxing champion Jimmy Hamilton and Bill Norman, who reacted to his players' claims that it was too cold to train by stripping naked and rolling in the snow, little progress was made either on or off the field until the mid-1950s, when Fred Westgarth several times took the team to the brink of a first-ever promotion.

In 1965 Brian **Clough** arrived for his first taste of football management (and discovered that his predecessor had been keeping bantam cockerels in the main stand). Along with Peter Taylor, Clough built a capable side then in 1967 decamped for Derby, taking Pools' midfielder John McGovern with them. The following year Hartlepools finally struggled out from the bottom division for the first time. The club celebrated by dropping both the 's' and the United from their name. After nearly a decade of terrace grumbling the appendage was eventually restored in 1977.

Hartlepool last applied for re-election in 1984, but since automatic relegation into the Conference was introduced their fortunes have mysteriously improved. In recent years the management skills of first Chris Turner and then Neale Cooper and the financial stability created by the club's Norwegian owners have transformed the team. After promotion from Division 3 in 2003 they achieved their highest League finish the following season, losing in the play-offs, where they were beaten again in the 2005 Final by Sheffield Wednesday. The team were relegated to League Two the following season.

Hartlepool United made headlines of a different sort in 2002 when the club's mascot, H'Angus the Monkey (a reference to the local legend that Poolies once lynched a monkey after mistaking the unfortunate simian for a French spy), was elected mayor of the town. H'Angus, or at least the man who filled his suit on matchdays, Stuart Drummond, ran on a ticket of free bananas for local schoolchildren, but once in office reneged on the promise, citing financial constraints.

heading

The skill of heading is not as old as the game itself, as the earliest players barely headed the ball at all. In the 19th-century dribbling game, in which a player was judged offside if he was standing ahead of the ball, passing was a purely incidental aspect of football. However, with the development of the passing game and the changes in the offside law to reward lofting the ball forward at every opportunity, heading suddenly became an extremely effective and desirable skill.

While the game's creative playmakers are still cloaked in a specious mantle of intellect and artistry, the persistent header of the ball is more likely to be categorized as a game, determined fellow with a low brow. This is evidenced by the Scottish, Irish and Northern English colloquial epithet of 'head-the-ball', denoting a disturbed individual or nutter. The great headers of the ball, of course, rise above such stereotypes. Tommy **Lawton** was rumoured among his contemporaries to be able to put top-spin on the ball when he headed it. In 399 matches for Everton, Dixie **Dean** scored approximately half of his 349 League

goals from headers. Dean's aerial powers, also legendary, were more tangible. His party trick was to jump on to a billiards table from a standing position.

There are many different types of header. There are the bullet header executed by the courageous centre-forward and the flying header (includes the flying-header own-goal, the apotheosis of which was Everton left-back Sandy Brown's screamer against Liverpool). Then there are the defensive header (always accompanied at set pieces by the hoarsely bawled 'A-waaaaaaay!' from the back four's designated shouter), the cushion header to a smaller and better placed colleague and the 'little eyebrows', a near-post flick-on from corners or long throw-ins.

Despite this versatility, the header remains to many purists the poor man's deft back-heeled lay-off. Brian **Clough** declared that football was a game played on grass – although he wasn't particularly bothered when Trevor Francis nodded home the winner in the 1979 European Cup Final.

The dangers of heading the ball used to be confined to the cuts players received from connecting with the ball's laces. However, in 2002 the coroner at the inquest into former England striker Jeff Astle's death commented on the 'repeated small traumas to the brain' resulting from Astle's long service to WBA as a target man during the 1960s and 1970s.

Mercifully, the modern football no longer absorbs water as the old heavy leather ball used to, thanks to a special polyurethane preparation of the surface. Partly because of this it seems likely, thankfully, that the American innovation of a soccer skull cap to be worn specifically for heading the ball will never be widely adopted.

headlines

Football has always lent itself to rhetoric. Chants, songs, aphorisms, one-liners and even graffiti are all part of the lore of the game. Periodically newspaper headlines have caught the mood, the best of which have entered the footballing vernacular of their own accord.

Memorable football headlines tend to fall into two categories: the slyly punning epithet; and – more unique to the game – the lyrical headline with its echoes of the terraces. Harold Evans, in his book *News Headlines*, writes that 'simplicity and impact' are the essence of a good headline. 'It must be a clear signal; economical in editorial, production, and reading time.' It's hard to imagine what Evans would have made of the *Sun*'s 'SUPER CALEY GO BALLISTIC CELTIC ARE ATROCIOUS', above a report of Inverness Caledonian Thistle's Cup defeat of Celtic. Only football offers such creative latitude: the pointless corralling of a Mary Poppins catchphrase, and the loopy brilliance of the pun, which already sounds like a terrace song. Similarly, a local newspaper welcomed Dwight Yorke's fellow Trinidadian Stern John to Nottingham Forest with the jaunty 'IT'S UP TO YOU NEW YORKE'.

The everyday staple of football headline writing has long been the strangled pun on a player's name: 'SHEAR BLISS' (Alan **Shearer** scores a goal); 'SHERI ON THE ROCKS' (something unfortunate happens to Teddy Sheringham); 'DUMI TO THE RESCUE' (Ilie Dumitrescu signs for Spurs). Occasionally the pun-friendly name and unusual circumstances coalesce to relate something more memorable: 'QUEEN IN BRAWL AT PALACE' appeared in the *Guardian* after Crystal Palace player Gerry Queen got himself in a spot of bother during the 1970–71 season. And 'WAITING FOR GODDARD' appeared when the West Ham forward was threatening a return from injury.

Occasions of national footballing disaster have tended to call forth their own memorable one-liners. The *Sun* began its campaign to evict Graham **Taylor** from the England manager's job with its infamous 'SWEDES 2 TURNIPS 1' headline after Taylor's men had lost to the hosts at the 1992 European Championships. The use of new technology to graft a photo of Taylor's head on to a sketch of a turnip opened up a new fashion for cartoon imagery, reaching a notable low point with the *Daily Mirror*'s palpitations before England's Euro 96 semi-final against Germany: 'ACHTUNG SURRENDER' screamed the front page, exhorting Terry **Venables**'s team – in the form of Stuart Pearce and Paul **Gascoigne** wearing First World War army helmets – to 'BLITZ FRITZ'.

The paper was chastised for its cheerless jingoism, but the *Mirror*'s inane posturings reflect the bleaker side of the football headline, the tendency to use the bold caps of the back page to trumpet cretinizing generalizations in the name of football. The *Sun*'s coverage of the aftermath of the **Hillsborough disaster** spawned possibly the nadir of all such footballing headlines. Under the banner 'The Truth' – managing in two words to be sensationalist, offensive and wrong – the paper parroted a series of claims made by the South Yorkshire Police Force about the behaviour of Liverpool fans. Censured by Lord Justice Taylor in his final report on the disaster in 1990, and burnt in piles by angry Liverpudlians, the paper remains a pariah in parts of Merseyside.

There have, however, been more cheerful mistakes made than this. The *New York Post* announced the transfer of one of the US's biggest stars with the

headline 'JOHN HARKES GOING TO SHEF-
FIELD, WEDNESDAY'.

Hearts

With a history touched by tragedy and
success, and a position as the perceived
establishment club of Scotland's capital,
Hearts should be seen as a dignified institution in Scottish football. Recent years
have seen infighting and financial turmoil
more associated with fledgling operations
than a club with 131 years of history.

Heart of Midlothian (named after the
dance hall frequented by the founders)
formed in 1874 and settled into their
current Tynecastle home in 1886, joining
the Scottish League four years later.
League titles and Scottish Cup wins were
garnered in that initial period, including
the only Scottish Cup Final ever to be
played outside Glasgow, a 3–1 win over
city rivals Hibernian at Logie Green in
1896, yet the club's identity was to be
marked by events far from home. Upon
the outbreak of war, the entire Hearts
playing staff volunteered for service and,
in doing so, led thousands of followers to
do the same. Seven players were killed
with several others never recovering
from their experiences, and the annual
remembrance service at Tynecastle is a
sombre affair.

The inter-war period saw a consolidation of Hearts' large support, but the
peak of the club's achievement was not
to arrive until the 1950s, starting with the
1956 return of the Scottish Cup. The
League followed in 1958 and 1960 and
the League Cup on four occasions for a
side captained by the irrepressible Dave
Mackay. In 1964 Hearts needed to
avoid a two-goal defeat to Kilmarnock in
their match to take another championship, but they lost 2–0. Decline followed,
culminating in three relegations during
the late 1970s and early 1980s before the

1983 promotion that brought Hearts back
into the top division, where they have
remained.

In 1985–86, a fine side, starring striker
John Robertson and future manager
Craig Levein at centre-back, came within
a whisker of winning the League but lost
at Dundee on the final day of the season
while rivals Celtic won away and so took
the title on goal difference. A demoral-
ized team lost the Scottish Cup Final to
Aberdeen a week later. Although no
silverware was forthcoming during this
period, Hearts fans (or 'Jambos' – Jam
Tarts/Hearts) had the considerable
consolation of 22 consecutive League
games without defeat against Hibernian.
Off the field, Hearts owner Wallace
Mercer soon grabbed some headlines
of his own when he unsuccessfully
attempted to purchase Hibs and merge
the two clubs.

A trophy finally arrived in 1998 when
former player Jim Jefferies led the club
to a 2–1 defeat of Rangers in the Scottish
Cup Final, with jubilant scenes in Edinburgh the following day as the cup was
paraded through the city. Jefferies was
replaced by former captain Craig Levein
in 2000, who achieved high League
finishes and European qualification before
departing for Leicester City in 2004.

The irony was that such achievement
had been gained against uncertainty
caused by the club's ever-spiralling debt.
It seemed that no measure was too
desperate for the club's board to
consider, especially when it was revealed
in 2004 that they were considering
playing a one-off home fixture in
Australia. Selling Tynecastle and renting
Murrayfield, Scotland's rugby stadium,
on match days was another possibility
that was unsurprisingly greeted with fury
by supporters.

Salvation appears to have arrived in
the shape of Lithuanian banker Vladimir

Romanovs, but his dismissal of manager John Robertson in 2005 was not a popular move. Despite a promising start to the season Robertson's replacement, George Burley, also left the club in October 2005. Burley was replaced by surprise choice Graham Rix. Four months later Rix was sacked, despite keeping the club on track for a first ever appearance in the Champions League qualifying round. Under Lithuanian manager Valdas Ivanauskas, Hearts went on to finish second in the League and won the Scottish Cup, beating Gretna on penalties.

Thierry Henry

Thierry Henry is one of the finest attacking players to appear in British football during the last 20 years, and probably the most exciting foreign player to emerge in this country. Signed by Arsène **Wenger** in 1999 as a speedy but peripheral left-winger after a difficult season in Italy with Juventus, Henry has been transformed at Arsenal. Henry still has astonishing speed and acceleration, but has evolved into a central striker with every attribute: trickery on the ball, precise finishing, shooting power, the vision to create goals for others, free-kick expertise, stamina, a scoring record that matches any other top striker, and an ability to lead his team-mates from the front.

More than this, Henry is the ultimate modern player. Media-literate and bilingual, he is the first world-class foreign player to come to maturity in the Premiership rather than be brought over as the finished item, a model of fitness and healthy living off the field and an embodiment of the cultural and social changes at Arsenal under Arsène Wenger during the late 1990s. Even Henry's success has been greeted in a particularly modern fashion. Talk of his being perhaps the greatest forward ever to play

in England is premature and excitable, a response to the heightened volume and televised hysteria of the Premiership, and a failure of judgement born out of witnessing a rare and spectacular kind of talent in his physical prime.

Born in Les Ulis in France, Henry trained at the national football academy at Clairefontaine before making his professional debut with Monaco, in the same team as David Trezeguet, who would later become his long-term striking partner in the national team. Henry's move to the Premiership saw him play as a central striker for the first time, and after eight games without a goal after making his debut he finished the season with 31, including a run of scoring in nine games in a row.

That year Henry scored three times as France won Euro 2000, followed by almost 50 goals in the next two seasons as Arsenal took the League title. Another 90 in his next two seasons plus the Player of the Year Award in both 2003 and 2004, and second place in the 2003 and 2004 World Player of the Year polls, the best showing by a Premiership player since the award was inaugurated in 1991, confirmed Henry as the most influential player in English football since the turn of the decade. By now continually linked with a move to either Spain or Italy, he was to be a key figure in a further League title for Arsenal in 2004 and an FA Cup win the following year. After Arsenal's defeat to Barcelona in the 2006 Champions League Final, Henry ended speculation about his future by announcing that he would be staying put.

Heysel disaster

On 29 May 1985, 39 people were killed and 454 injured in the stands at Heysel Stadium just outside Brussels. The disaster occurred before the European

Cup Final between Liverpool and Juventus, when a concrete retaining wall collapsed under the weight of a crowd of supporters who were fleeing from violence between fans of the two sides.

Subsequent investigations concluded that the decrepit 1930s stadium was unsuitable to hold such a major sporting event, and the authorities were heavily criticized for their poor organization ahead of the game. UEFA had allocated one end of the ground to Liverpool supporters, but left a section of it for 'neutrals'. Called Block Z, this area was separated from the Liverpool fans by a flimsy fence made of chicken wire. Inevitably, many Juventus fans had bought tickets for Block Z from local Belgians and tension between the two sets of poorly segregated supporters grew as the ground filled up – in part precipitated by violence after the previous year's final between Liverpool and another Italian club, AS Roma.

Fighting and missile throwing had started about an hour before the scheduled kick-off time, but local police seemed unable to bring it under control and the wall collapsed when fans fled from onrushing Liverpool supporters. Thirty-eight of those who died were Italian, one was Belgian.

The game itself eventually went ahead after an 85-minute delay, with the ground authorities fearing even more violence if it was cancelled. Neither team had much appetite for the match, however, as riot police continued to patrol the perimeter track and Juventus fans attempted to invade the pitch. Juventus won the largely meaningless match with a penalty scored by Frenchman Michel Platini. On British television the commentary alternated between descriptions of the play and the rising death toll. Only West German TV took the decision to drop transmission.

In the aftermath, the English FA immediately withdrew all English clubs from European competition. UEFA followed suit, imposing a blanket ban which lasted for five years, with Liverpool having to wait a further year. Initial blame for the events at Heysel was laid squarely at the feet of the fans, or football hooligans, as they were universally described. But partly thanks to the efforts of the newly formed Football Supporters' Association, a different story gradually began to emerge, highlighting the inadequacies of the stadium, the organization and the Belgian authorities. Indeed, officials at Liverpool FC had complained to UEFA about the stadium and their ticket allocation weeks before the game, but were ignored.

The stadium was later demolished and rebuilt as the Stade Roi Baudouin in time for the 2000 European Championships, but no major inquiry was ever held into the causes of the disaster, although both clubs and cities have made efforts to heal the wounds. In May 2000, for example, the bells in Liverpool's municipal buildings pealed 39 times and a plaque was unveiled paying tribute to the victims; Juventus flags and scarves are often still carried by Liverpool fans at Anfield, where a ceremony commemorating the dead was held before the clubs' Champions' League quarter-final match in 2005.

Along with the tragedy of the **Hillsborough disaster**, Heysel has come to be seen in subsequent years as one of football's turning points – its 'Year Zero'. Ten years later, it was possible to argue that the 39 deaths at Heysel were not simply caused by hooliganism – though the violence clearly played its part – but were a product of the ignorance and complacency of UEFA and the Belgian police. What's more, watching football was no longer seen as the peculiar pastime of a violent youth sub-culture, and no-one needed to explain why they were a football fan.

Hibernian

A Scottish football club created by a city's Catholic hierarchy to give their menfolk a constructive pastime and the Irish population a focal point? Not Glasgow Celtic, but Edinburgh's Hibernian Football Club, whose formation in 1875 came 13 years before their Glasgow rivals. Of the 130 years since, it was in the late 1940s and early 1950s that Hibernian enjoyed their Golden Age.

Hibs's base in Leith only became part of Edinburgh in 1924, and that despite a plebiscite voting 80/20 against the move. 'Sunshine in Leith', a stirring piece by The Proclaimers (the bespectacled crooners join Irvine Welsh and Dougray Scott as Hibs's celebrity supporter contingent), is the booming anthem of Easter Road, the stadium that sits in the heart of this fiercely autonomous area of Scotland's capital.

An early decision to ensure that only Catholics could play for the club was soon abandoned, and Hibs settled into an unremarkable existence – they won the last of their two Scottish Cups to date in 1902 – until that memorable spell following the Second World War. The achievements, principally three League titles in six years, stand up to anything attained by a non-Old Firm club in the history of Scottish football.

The pin-ups of those glorious years were the famous forward line, dubbed 'The Famous Five', namely Gordon Smith, Bobby Johnstone, Eddie Turnbull, Lawrie Reilly and Willie Ormond. In 1955 they spread their fame internationally, as Hibs became the first British club to enter European competition when they reached the semi-finals of the inaugural Champions' Cup. They have played in Europe 16 times since, including a run to the semi-final of the Fairs Cup in 1961.

The Hibs side of the early 1970s, dubbed 'Turnbull's Tornadoes', after their former Famous Five manager, upheld the attacking traditions of the earlier generation. A team containing seven players who were to win Scottish international caps beat Celtic to win the 1972 League Cup and, less than a month later, hammered city rivals Hearts 7–0. The win is remembered to this day, not least when the current captain, locally born Ian Murray, chose a recent derby to have the year '1972', shaved into his hair. The club were to be League runners-up for the next two seasons but have not done better than one third-place finish since, and spent two seasons in Division 1, in 1979–80 and 1998–99.

An unsuccessful bid in 1990 by Hearts chairman Wallace Mercer to merge the two clubs saw Sir Tom Farmer purchase Hibs and ensure their survival. A year later, Farmer joined some 50,000 others in a victory march down Edinburgh's Princes Street after a League Cup Final win over Dunfermline. There have been two lost Cup Finals since, yet it is in the installation of Tony Mowbray as manager in the summer of 2004 that Hibs fans have seen the strongest signs of hope. The young, attacking team led by Murray have attracted multitudes of followers back to Easter Road as they threaten to remind older supporters of the flair of the past.

Jimmy Hill

Like a sporting Forrest Gump, Jimmy Hill has been present at almost every major staging point in the evolution of English football during the last 40 years. By the time he retired from playing at the age of 33 after a serious knee injury, Hill had already embarked on the most significant achievement of his career. In his capacity as chairman of the Players'

Union he initiated the strike action that would ultimately result in the abolition of the maximum wage for footballers. Hill threatened to bring the game to a complete halt in the winter of 1961 unless the £20-a-week ceiling was abolished. Fulham team-mate Bobby **Robson** has described how the 'very eloquent' young Hill, an inside-forward with Brentford and Fulham, had managed to attract a 100 per cent ballot backing for the strike, even enlisting the potent support of the 'Wizard Of Dribble', Sir Stanley **Matthews**.

After a successful spell as manager of Coventry City, Hill began his television career. As Head of Sport at London Weekend Television, and later ITV's Deputy Controller of Programmes, he faced a mountainous task. When he started at LWT commercial television had no broadcasting rights to live sport at all. ITV were desperate to compete and before long Hill was introducing the *World of Sport* to such televised treats as log-chopping and off-road cycling. In a groundbreaking piece of broadcasting he then put together a legendary hand-picked punditry panel for ITV's coverage of the 1970 World Cup. Buoyed by his World Cup coup, Hill soon had ITV wrangling with the BBC over the amounts paid to screen domestic football (which still totalled just half a million pounds as late as 1978), thereby helping to introduce the notion of competition among TV companies producing an alternative – if unreliable – stream of revenue into the English game.

Hill returned to Coventry City as managing director in 1974, where he became the first of English football's celebrity chairmen. Already a larger-than-life figure – known in sections of the press as 'the beatnik with a ball' – Jimmy set a blueprint for a new breed of publicity-drenched club director. And

from Carlisle's Michael Knighton to Peter Ridsdale at Leeds, they've buzzed about football ever since. The nadir of Hill's spell as chairman of the Sky Blues came in 1981, when his attempt to make Highfield Road the country's first all-seater stadium ended in disaster, as hooligans ripped up the seats and used them as missiles. Hill left the club two years later but a seed had been planted, and within 25 years of Hill's initiative standing terraces would vanish from the top flight of English football.

Like the man who split the atom, Jimmy gave football the chance to make choices; bad ones as it turned out. Abolishing the salary cap: obviously a good idea. As long as you don't go and spoil it by paying Benito Carbone £2m a year, like Sheffield Wednesday. TV companies competing to broadcast football: what could be better? Hardly Jimmy's fault they ruin everything 20 years down the line by overstretching their shallow-pocketed paymasters. As for running a club with unchecked ambition from the top down: another excellent idea. But try explaining that to a Leeds United fan.

Hill certainly leaves a unique legacy to a game he has served uniquely – as player, union official, manager, chairman, pundit, linesman (he once took up the flag in a League match at Arsenal after one of the officials had injured himself) and member of the parliamentary Football Work Permit Review Panel. It is in this capacity, as a footballing everyman, the hot-dog seller in the background of all the biggest scenes, that Jimmy Hill will survive. His achievements, circumscribed by the kind of vanity that makes a man stick it out for over 600 appearances on *Match of the Day*, opened doors for others to tiptoe through. And then kick over a table or two once they were inside.

Hillsborough disaster

On 15 April 1989, 96 people were crushed to death and 170 injured at an FA Cup semi-final between Liverpool and Nottingham Forest at Hillsborough stadium, the home ground of Sheffield Wednesday. It was the greatest loss of life ever at a British football match and shocked the football world into bringing about some of the most radical changes in the game's history, changes which have revolutionized stadiums and stadium design; shifted outdated perceptions of football fans; and changed the way football is financed, policed and watched.

For many football supporters it was a tragedy waiting to happen. There was nothing special about Hillsborough; like many grounds, it was a potential death trap. The deaths occurred because of severe overcrowding in one section of the ground, and the failure of the police and ground authorities to control the flow of spectators and ensure their safety.

A huge crowd had travelled to watch the game and in the minutes before kick-off the Leppings Lane enclosure became packed with Liverpool supporters. As more and more tried to enter, those at the front were crushed against the perimeter fencing which, at first, stewards refused to open. Many were asphyxiated while others scrambled to escape by climbing the fence or being hauled into the upper tier. The match was abandoned after six minutes, although not before live television pictures had shown the tragedy unfolding. Within minutes the watching public witnessed bodies being laid out on the grass and carried away on make-shift stretchers hastily constructed from sections of advertising hoardings.

At first, some national newspapers, notably the *Sun*, alleged that drunken football 'hooligans' were behind the disaster, blackening the newspaper's name on Merseyside to this day. The official inquiry (see **Taylor Report**) concluded that 'operational errors' were the main cause of the disaster, and demanded many basic reforms to the way crowds were managed and grounds designed, and called for better relations between the police and football supporters.

With the finger of blame pointing at the police, some parents of Hillsborough victims began a campaign to convict the senior police officers in charge on the day, alleging they had ignored video evidence of the overcrowding before any deaths occurred. The Hillsborough Family Support Group also claimed many families were poorly treated by police when trying to identify bodies.

The police in turn tried to blame drunkenness and initially claimed the fans had forced open a gate. Ironically, many of the supporters who died were at the front and would have been among the first in the ground, eager to get a good view, and therefore least likely to have been drinking. Also, it emerged later that Chief Superintendent David Duckenfield himself gave the order for the gate to be opened, despite claiming shortly after the game was stopped that the fans had broken it down.

Despite Taylor's interim report in August 1989 condemning 'a failure of police control', the police immediately tried to avoid liability – at first seeking an out of court settlement, and then influencing the coroner, Dr Stefan Popper, to take blood-alcohol samples from the victims and highlight these at the inquest. In August 1990, the Director of Public Prosecutions ruled that there was insufficient evidence to prosecute South Yorkshire Police, Sheffield Wednesday

FC, the city council or the ground's engineers.

In November 1990, the coroner ruled that no evidence at the inquest would be heard about events after 3.15pm, and in March 1991 the inquest returned a 9–2 majority verdict of accidental death. Duckenfield retired later that year, avoiding internal police disciplinary charges. In 1998 a 'judicial scrutiny' of new evidence, ordered by the Home Secretary, Jack Straw, concluded that there was no basis to reopen the case.

To date, no-one's been convicted or prosecuted for the disaster, and members of the victims' families feel like they've never had justice. One thing's for sure, for all football fans, the word Hillsborough will never again refer simply to an area of Sheffield or a football ground.

Glenn Hoddle

Glenn Hoddle has lived through several different incarnations during his football career. As an elegant central midfielder for Spurs, Monaco, Swindon, Chelsea and England, he was considered the most talented Englishman in his position during the 1980s. Hoddle had a languid air. He lacked a dominant physical presence, but he could pass a ball with unusual accuracy over short or long distances. He also had excellent control of the ball, the ability to shoot from distance and expertise at set-pieces.

He scored 88 goals in 378 League appearances for Spurs and won FA Cup winners' medals in 1981 and the following year, when he scored the decisive penalty in a replay against QPR. During his time at Spurs, Hoddle also found time to record a hit single with Chris Waddle, released under the disappointingly humourless name 'Glenn and Chris'. 'Diamond Lights' reached number 12 in the charts in 1987, and Hoddle and Waddle appeared on *Top of the Pops* in a haze of dry ice, wearing suit jackets with the sleeves rolled up.

During his playing career with the national team as much attention was paid to what Hoddle couldn't do – tackle, win headers and run around like Bryan **Robson** – as to what he could. He played 53 times for England and scored a spectacular volleyed goal at Wembley on his debut, but he never really settled, often finding himself dropped as a scapegoat when things went wrong. 'The average Englishman is a very limited player,' Hoddle declared on leaving Spurs to play for Monaco in 1987, where he was feted by the footballing press, winning the Foreign Player of the Year award in 1988.

Unfortunately, Hoddle's parting remark also illustrates the downside to his appeal as a player: the lack of personal charm that has undermined his subsequent career as a manager. Returning to England in 1991, he had a successful spell as player-manager at Swindon before leaving to oversee the first stirrings of Chelsea's transformation into a cosmopolitan playing force. Hoddle took the club to the FA Cup Final in 1994 before leaving to succeed Terry **Venables** as England manager.

At the time he was not the FA's first choice, and his popularity would slip further with press and administrators after the 1998 World Cup, where his reputation for tactical acumen was undermined by divisive management of his players, including heavy-handed treatment of those excluded from the squad. He also invited ridicule by insisting on contact with his preferred faith healer, the infamous Eileen Drewery, and fostered his quackishness with a bizarre association with Uri Geller and by publicly espousing his own form of evangelical spirituality.

Hoddle was sacked from the England job after a media-led furore over strange and ill-thought-out comments regarding disabled people during an interview. He resurrected his managerial credibility at Southampton before moving to Spurs, where mediocre results were combined with further unpopularity on the training field and yet more tales of Hoddle's lack of patience with players less skilled than himself. He was sacked from the Spurs job in 2003, returning to management with Wolverhampton during 2004–05. Hoddle also has an infuriating habit of saying 'them' when he means 'those' or 'these' – someone really should have a word with him about it.

Home International Championships

The oldest international competition began in the 1883–84 season after the football authorities of Scotland, Wales, Northern Ireland and England met in 1882 to draw up a single set of game rules while forming the International Football Association Board. That body still exists today and is still dominated by the same four countries, outlasting even the tournament they created, which was finally scrapped 101 years later in 1984.

At the meeting the four associations not only agreed on the uniform laws of the game, but also to create an annual championship between the four British nations. Once the most prestigious international tournament of all, it fell victim to the ever-burgeoning demands of the fixture list as both Scotland and England jettisoned Northern Ireland and Wales in favour of lucrative internationals against more prestigious opposition.

The games were usually played throughout the season, climaxing with the England v Scotland fixture in spring, but from 1969 the games were all staged in one week at the season's end, supposedly because more players would be available from their clubs. This may have been the tournament's death knell. At the end of an exhausting season, neither fans nor players had much appetite for yet another repeat of Scotland v Wales, and only the world's oldest international game – the England v Scotland fixture that had started in 1872 – seemed to draw much attention as attendances dwindled. Once the Home Internationals ceased in 1984, however, the annual north–south joust survived only five more years, but ceased after too many English hooligans used it as an excuse to head to Glasgow to bang heads together.

Of the 89 tournaments, Wales won the tournament outright seven times, and Northern Ireland three, while England and Scotland were far ahead with 34 and 24 wins respectively. Because until 1979 titles were decided only on points, and not goal difference, 20 titles were shared, and on one occasion, in 1955–56, the four nations split the honour after they all finished even on three points apiece. In 1980–81 there was no winner because England and Wales both refused to travel to Belfast owing to civil unrest.

In 1949–50 and 1953–54 the championship was used to decide World Cup qualifiers, with the top two teams going to the finals. How Scotland would love now to have the opportunity they passed up in 1950 – finishing second, they opted to stay home from the Brazil tournament. Over two seasons from 1966 to 1968 they missed out again as the two championships together decided a single qualifier for the European Championship. England pipped them nine points to eight.

Nonetheless, the games between the two provide some of the happiest stories in Scottish football history, including the 5–1 victory in 1928, when the 'Wembley

Wizards' tore England apart in London, and the 3–2 win on the same ground in 1967 just nine months after England had been crowned world champions there. Less auspiciously, Scottish fans marked a 1977 Queen's Silver Jubilee Year win by invading England's home field, breaking the goalposts and ripping up the turf. All aimed at celebrating Her Royal Majesty's longevity, of course.

Scotland also suffered some terrible hidings down the years, including a 7–2 defeat in 1955 and a 9–3 hammering in 1961 that marked the second and final cap for Celtic goalkeeper Frank Haffey and the start of Wembley as a cursed place for Scottish goalkeepers. The career of Rangers' Stuart Kennedy never recovered from his shipping five in the 1975 defeat on a day when he seemed more intent on hugging the posts for comfort than stopping goals. Still, the fixture is more missed by Scottish than English fans, perhaps in memory of the days when Scotland at least had the chance of winning *something*.

hooliganism

In the heyday of hooliganism, in the 1970s and 1980s, the words 'football' and 'hooligan' were more readily connected than 'football' and 'fan'; in the eyes of the media and much of the public, to be one was to be the other. So great was the moral panic at times that football hooliganism has prompted numerous changes in public order laws, created a whole new sub-culture of academic research, and spawned a seemingly never-ending stream of ageing hoolies' hackish memoirs.

Football hooliganism was first identified as a serious social problem in the 1960s. Yet it has a much longer history stretching back to the earliest organized matches in the mid 19th century. As far

back as 1846, for example, fans were read the riot act at a match in Derby and two troops of dragoons were called in to tackle disorder. Pitch invasions were common from the 1880s and reports of the first professional games regularly talked about gangs of 'roughs' causing trouble, attacking and stoning referees and visiting players. The absence of visiting fans at the time meant fighting between supporters of rival teams was rare, though this was later to become the defining image of football hooliganism.

Football between the wars was more 'respectable' as the game attracted huge crowds, and there were few reports of trouble right up until the late 1950s. Football violence did not disappear, though, and in the early 1960s – alongside the rise of rock'n'roll, the birth of the teenager and growing concerns about youth behaviour – hooliganism began to attract closer scrutiny. As tension between youth styles – Teddy boys, mods and skinheads – was superseded by violence between rival fans, football became the arena for fighting and disorder.

It was in the 1960s, too, that hooliganism first became more organized as fans took on the kind of match-day alliances and territorial allegiances later cemented by the 'bovver boys' of the 1970s, and the firms, crews and Casuals of the 1980s. As fan rivalries formed and reputations grew, the purpose of playing away became as much about taking your opponent's end as snatching a lucky point.

Judging from some of the literature, football grounds in the 1970s and 1980s were like war zones, as were the streets and pubs around them. Newspapers carried reports of smashed-up trains and fights at service stations as opposing hooligans ran into each other as they criss-crossed the country. Some academics suggested much of the violence was ritualistic and territorial, but people did get killed and many were badly injured. The hardest of the hard core formed 'firms' with distinctive names – West Ham's Inter City Firm and the Chelsea Headhunters were among the most notorious.

Hooliganism went international too as English teams played in European competitions and fans followed them around the continent. Ultimately, following the **Heysel disaster** of May 1985, English clubs were banned from Europe. In the meantime, the 'English disease', as it became known (although organized violence occurs in many football cultures), spread to the national side and has been associated with England ever since.

The combination of violence and groups of largely white, working-class young men also attracted the far right, and in the late 1970s and early 1980s hooligan crews at clubs like Leeds and West Ham involved members of the National Front and British National Party. Combat 18, the BNP's more violent offshoot, was also linked to Chelsea and England.

By the late 1980s, heightened security and a huge police presence at matches meant most serious confrontations took place outside grounds and even away from the stadiums altogether. Sometimes these were planned and prearranged to avoid the police. In time, however, with a change in youth culture, and the gradual slide of the casual style into the rave scene, hooliganism began to decline. This was accelerated by the **Taylor Report** which precipitated all-seater stadiums and CCTV. In 1991–92 around 5,000 arrests were made at all Football League matches; by 2001–02 there were 3,000. In 2001 only 7 per cent of Premier League fans thought hooliganism was increasing and only 19 per cent witnessed any incidents; far more complained about ticket prices and kick-off times.

Not that hooliganism disappeared completely. Crowd disorder is more common at lower League grounds, and violence between rival Premier League fans does still take place away from matches. In January 2001, for example, firms from Leeds and Manchester United fought outside Rochdale en route to their respective games at Manchester City and Bradford. And trouble involving England fans has continued to cause outrage in the media – at the 1998 World Cup in France, for example, and the 2000 European Championships in Belgium. In Europe, too, it can still be an issue – in April 2000 two Leeds United fans were murdered in Istanbul, and later that year Arsenal fans and Galatasaray fans clashed at the UEFA Cup Final in Copenhagen.

No doubt the intense media interest in hooliganism over the years has served to amplify the phenomenon and its influence. Yet with libraries' worth of books on the subject, and at least five pieces of legislation enacted to deal with the offenders, football hooliganism has certainly been a significant part of the modern game.

Don Howe

'It was like finding Miss World was free and asking for a date,' remarked Bristol Rovers manager Bobby Gould on appointing Don Howe as his assistant in 1986. The footballing Miss World, in heavy-rimmed glasses and brown porkpie hat, Don Howe has also been called 'the best coach of association football in the world' by former FA technical director and Svengali of the long-ball game, Charles Hughes.

For 25 years Don Howe was the most revered training-ground guru in English football. He was a hugely influential assistant to Bertie Mee, manager of the

Arsenal team that won the Double in 1971, and coached the England team for 15 years under three different managers, taking in the World Cups of 1982 and 1986. Renowned as a defensive coach nonpareil, Howe is credited with helping to popularize the distinctively English style of play of the 1970s and 1980s, whereby players 'pressed' the opposition in all areas of the pitch, attempting to stifle attacks by playing an offside trap based around a rigid 4–4–2 formation.

Howe is also credited with devising the more technically astute aspects of the 'direct football' regime in place at the FA during his time in the vanguard of English coaching. His success as coach at Arsenal during the 1970s and late 1980s and as assistant to Gould when Wimbledon won the FA Cup in 1988 was based around rigid defence and a mastery of carefully rehearsed set pieces. Howe was also responsible for popularizing such innovations as the long throw-in flicked into the path of an onrushing midfielder – the move with which Bryan **Robson** scored for a Howe-coached England team after 27 seconds of their opening game of the 1982 World Cup.

A talented right-back in his time with West Bromwich Albion (for whom he made over 350 appearances) and later Arsenal, Howe played for England at the 1958 World Cup in Sweden and the 1962 Finals in Chile and went on to win 23 caps before injury ended his career prematurely in 1966. In a life spent largely on the training field, Howe has worked at all levels of the game, most notably coaching his local Isthmian League side Newbury Town while also working with the England team. Howe was less successful during spells as manager at West Bromwich Albion and Arsenal, when he became notorious for an overly cautious, excessively defensive approach.

Throughout his coaching career Howe displayed an underlying fetish for the rigidly marshalled defence and the arm-raised one-out-all-out offside trap, a discipline that seems at best essentially English, and at worst an anachronism from a particularly bleak period in English football's history.

Huddersfield Town

The textiles centre of Huddersfield was a rugby stronghold in the late 19th century but has had a rich, if chequered, footballing history since Huddersfield Town was formed in 1908 to play at the newly built Leeds Road ground.

Two successful seasons in the Midland League led to election to the League's Division 2 in 1910 but moderate early success failed to avert a flirtation with extinction just nine years later, when the club came within days of merging with Leeds City. £1 'shares' in the club were bought by fans – the equivalent of a week's wage in the local mills – and Huddersfield were saved. From this crisis, however, the club emerged stronger and the 1920s saw unparalleled success.

Under the management of authoritarian football visionary Herbert **Chapman**, poached from Leeds in 1921 when relegation looked a certainty, Town won three consecutive League titles from 1924 to 1926, the first side to achieve such a feat. Inside-right Clem Stephenson, with the club nearly three decades as player and manager, and forward Billy Smith, the holder of the club's appearance record and the first player to officially score directly from a corner, were among the stars of the team that also appeared in four FA Cup Finals. They won one Cup – the 1–0 extra-time success over Preston North End in 1922 considered one of the worst finals ever played – and finished second in the League on two occasions. Chapman was not in charge when Town claimed the historic third title. While his new side, Arsenal, were embarking on their own championship run in the 1930s, Huddersfield went into a decline that culminated in relegation to Division 2 after 32 years in the top flight in 1952.

A period of stagnation in the 1960s was characterized by the now Division 2 club's being unable to hold on to a swathe of talent, including England full-back and eventual World Cup winner Ray Wilson – who as a reserve team midfield player had famously refused to play full-back until he realized it meant a first-team start – and a short, slight Scot who made his debut aged 16, the proceeds from his sale to Manchester City, a then British record £55,000, funding what became known as the Denis **Law** floodlights. Barely a year later, two of the structures were destroyed in fierce gales. The side bounced back, briefly, thanks to the formation of the most celebrated striking partnership the club has seen, the 'Old Firm' of outside-forward Vic Metcalf providing the ammunition for the majority of marksman Jimmy Glazzard's 142 goals, a club record held jointly with 1920s striker George Brown.

The 1970 Division 2 championship was secured in some style thanks to players of the calibre of future England defender Trevor Cherry and the irrepressible Frank Worthington, but relegation hastened their exit and heralded a quarter-century of Huddersfield climbing up and slipping down the variously named lower divisions. The Terriers, so named after a club mascot Yorkshire Terrier had been adopted in the late 1950s, hit rock bottom when recording a lowest-ever League finish of 15th in the old Division 4 in 1978. Four promotions

and three relegations over the course of the next quarter-century mean Huddersfield are back in the third tier of English football but at a new home since 1994. The Galpharm Stadium, formerly the McAlpine Stadium – the first of a raft of post-**Taylor Report** developments – was voted building of the year by the Royal Institute of British Architects in 1995.

The return of former player Peter Jackson for a second spell of management and a dramatic Division 3 play-off win in 2004 by virtue of a penalty shoot-out have renewed hopes that this former giant may yet be woken from its heavy slumber.

Hull City

The start of the 2004–05 season saw Hull City celebrating 100 years of, it has to be said, almost unrelenting mediocrity. Most people know the trivia: Hull is the biggest city never to have hosted top-flight football and the Tigers (named for their yellow and black strip) have never made it to a major cup final. Nevertheless, the last few years have seen good times for City supporters: a chairman with deep pockets, big-name signings, a £43 million stadium with large crowds and two promotions in successive seasons between 2003 and 2005.

Formed in 1904, Hull City began by playing friendly matches. Victories over such luminaries as the Coldstream Guards persuaded the club to take the plunge into professional football and, on 2 September 1905, they beat Barnsley 4–1 in their first-ever Division 2 match. The club had staged their early home matches at the Boulevard, home of rugby team Hull FC, but were refused permission to play League matches there. This was the beginning of a mutually antagonistic relationship which is still played out in the local press today.

Playing at the Circle, in the shadow of their present KC Stadium, Hull made a solid start to life as a League club, achieving what is still their highest League position in 1909–10. Having led Division 2 for most of the season, City went into their last match with Oldham needing only a draw to go up. They had previously thrashed Oldham 4–0 at the Circle, but still contrived to lose, missing out on promotion by three-tenths of a goal.

Throughout their history Hull City have imbued in their fans pride and frustration in equal measure. And 1929–30 proved to the most archetypal of all seasons. An awful League campaign saw the Tigers plummet to their first relegation whilst simultaneously embarking on what is still their best-ever FA Cup run, all the way to the semi-final before a controversial replay defeat to Arsenal, the aftermath of which saw the referee summarily banned by the FA for his handling of the game.

The post-war years brought a move to Boothferry Park, which was to remain the club's home until 2002. Huge crowds came to see veteran England striker Raich **Carter** and his team-mates win the Division 3 (North) in 1948–49 (in the same season they drew a club record 55,000 for an FA Cup tie with Man Utd) but the Tigers couldn't manage better than seventh place in the higher division prior to relegation in 1956.

The next decade saw the legendary strike duo of Chris Chilton and Ken Wagstaff score nearly 400 goals between them for a team that again achieved little other than promotion from Division 3 in 1966. The club then more or less stagnated until the turn of the century, dropping into the basement division for the first time in 1981. The fortunes of the team were sometimes an irrelevance, with financial problems overshadowing events on the pitch, and increasingly disen-

chanted supporters fighting bitterly with a succession of boardroom incompetents. The Needler family had owned the club since the 1940s but, against a back-drop of mounting debts and falling support, sold out to former tennis star David Lloyd, who lost a lot of money and thoroughly alienated supporters before calling in the receivers.

Lloyd was succeeded by two Yorkshire businessmen, Nick Buchanan and Stephen Hinchliffe, who were soon the subjects of an FA and police fraud investigation. Boycotts, demonstrations, receivership and lock-outs eventually led to the arrival of Adam Pearson as chairman. He has overseen the transformation of Hull City from a debt-ridden club flirting with the Conference into a profit-making crowd-pulling machine. Now all he has to do is win something.

Hungary 53

No match has acquired greater symbolic significance in English football history than the 6–3 defeat suffered at Wembley against Hungary on 25 November 1953. It is remembered as the day England's superiority complex was shattered by their first defeat against a foreign country on home soil, causing the English game to re-evaluate outmoded traditions and suddenly begin to see itself as a pupil rather than the master. As with most such legends, it is only partly true. For a start, England had already lost at home to the Republic of Ireland, 2–0 at Goodison Park in 1949, though while it is rude not to acknowledge that achievement, it had no long-term footballing significance.

More to the point was that the writing had been on the wall for more than 20 years before 1953, in fact ever since the spread of the game after the First World War and the 1925 change in the offside rule had unleashed a flood of tactical and technical ideas across Europe and South America. England's first away defeat (Home Internationals excepted) had come as early as 1929, 4–3 to Spain in Madrid, which was followed in regular succession through the 1930s by victories for France (by as much as 5–2 in 1931), Hungary, Czechoslovakia, Austria, Belgium, Switzerland and Yugoslavia. But England maintained a psychological hold at home, which disastrously delayed the realization that others had moved far ahead.

It should have dawned in 1932 against the Austrian *Wunder*-team at the height of its powers – the forerunner in so many ways of Hungary a generation later. But England got away with a lucky 4–3 win at Stamford Bridge. It might have come against the world champions Italy in 1934, but they chose to spark a brawl instead of a match and lost the 'Battle of Highbury' 3–2.

After the war, a famous tour by Russian club Moscow Dynamo briefly opened a few eyes to the value of combination passing, running off the ball and simple technical innovations such as pre-match warm-ups. Defeat against the US and Spain in the 1950 World Cup was too far from home to sink in. In 1951 a last-minute penalty by Alf **Ramsey** saved a 2–2 draw against Austria at Wembley. And only a month before the Hungary debacle England had rescued a scandalous 4–4 draw after being outplayed by the Rest of Europe in the match to celebrate the FA's 90th birthday.

So it fell, appropriately, to the best side of the era to teach England its lesson (and the other British teams for that matter, although psychologically the pain was all England's). Captain Billy **Wright** said later he had expected to win, if for no better reason than that 'We had been conditioned always to expect to win at Wembley.' But Nándor Hidegkuti put Hungary ahead in the first minute and they were 4–1 up after half an hour. Most observers agreed England were flattered by the final score, an impression confirmed when they travelled to Budapest the following May and were hammered 7–1.

What did the Hungarians have that England did not? In short, flexibility. England were trained to play by numbers, literally expecting their opponents' shirt numbers to follow the old 2–3–5 pattern (even though the number 5 had been converted to a defender since the days of Herbert **Chapman**). So when Hungary's number 9 Hidegkuti (the centre-forward in English thinking) dropped deep, it baffled his marker, Blackpool's Harry Johnston, and the rapid interplay of Hungary's forwards, Sándor Kocsis and Ferenc Puskás above all, made mincemeat of the covering full-backs.

Of course, Hungary had outstanding players – if one moment has served as the emblem of the match it is Puskás's outrageous drag-back that left Billy Wright thundering helplessly towards the goal-line as the chunky Magyar whacked in the third goal. But the lessons they taught were more about mentality, technique, fitness, tactics and even equipment – they wore more modern, lighter boots than England's clod-hoppers – than natural brilliance.

If English observers did not understand this for themselves, they were lucky to have an observer on hand – Willy Meisl, the brother of *Wunder*-team coach Hugo, whose brilliant book *Soccer Revolution* (1955) spelled it out from the standpoint of a sympathetic outsider (Meisl worked as a journalist after arriving in England as a refugee). 'Isolation, insularism, obstinate resistance to any reforms, refusal to break with outdated methods from training to tactics, from selecting internationals to educating talent had put us ten light-years behind,' Meisl wrote. On tactics he correctly forecast that 'the future will be fluid', even anticipating the rise of the ball-playing goalkeeper.

Did England and the other home nations learn? Well, yes and no. The press who acclaimed Wolverhampton Wanderers as 'club champions of the world' when they beat Honvéd in a friendly the following year obviously needed further persuasion from the results of the European Cup, a competition their foolish claim helped to initiate. Others took better notes, such as Alf Ramsey, who played his last international that foggy afternoon. His 1966 triumph showed what flexible, innovative tactics could do when combined with fitness, preparation and – another Hungarian demonstration – a single man in charge (Gusztáv Sebes in their case, who moulded the 1953 team).

Yet still England tended to copy the obvious manifestations of the Hungarians' approach, such as the low-cut boots and the deep-lying centre-forward – Don **Revie** was an early exponent at Manchester City – rather than adopting their broader openness to innovation. As a result they still failed to move with the times, which led to similar Wembley humiliations in the age of 'total football' at the hands of West Germany (3–1 in 1972) and Holland (2–0 in 1977), not to mention successive World Cup failures. England's prevailing insularity was not finally broken until the 1990s, with the return to European club competition after the **Heysel disaster** ban and the huge influx of foreign players into the Premiership.

Above all Hungary 1953 changed England from a country with a footballing superiority complex to one that suffered violent mood swings, from absurd over-confidence to coruscating self-flagellation. Worse, perhaps, for the Hungarians themselves it created an impossible ideal to live up to, a shadow too great for any of their subsequent teams to escape.

Sir Geoff Hurst

Geoff Hurst remains the only player to score a hat-trick in a World Cup Final. In the process he became the custodian of the most treasured and obsessively replayed moment in English footballing history; and a name for ever synonymous with red-shirted England players hoisting the Jules Rimet trophy in July sunshine at the Empire Stadium. A powerful centre-forward in the classic English mould, Hurst was also a lucky footballer, one who took advantage of being the right man in the right place. His status as an English sporting hero owes as much to the instincts of his managers at club and national level as to his own determined and occasionally inspired performances for West Ham and England.

Born in Tameside in 1941, Hurst made his debut for West Ham in 1959 as an eager but slightly clumsy left-half. Identifying his goalscoring potential at a relatively late stage, Hammers manager Ron **Greenwood** subsequently converted him into a centre-forward. Hurst would go on to make 411 League appearances for the Hammers, scoring 180 goals and establishing himself as the club's greatest-ever forward. Powerful, two-footed and surprisingly quick, he also played professional cricket in the early 1960s, appearing in one County Championship match for Essex.

A part of West Ham's FA Cup-winning team of 1964 and European Cup Winners' Cup success a year later, Hurst scored 40 goals in 1965–66, earning a surprise late call-up to Alf **Ramsey**'s 1966 World Cup squad. He had made his debut against West Germany only five months previously and was considered a fringe player, cover for the forward pairing of Jimmy **Greaves** and Roger Hunt. Ramsey decided to take a gamble on him halfway through the tournament, replacing the prolific but injured Greaves with a player with only one England goal to his name. Hurst responded, heading the winner in the quarter-final against Argentina and keeping his place in the starting XI for the rest of the competition. His luck kept pace: not only was his hat-trick in the Final indebted to the controversial decision by an Azerbaijani linesman that his close range shot from Alan Ball's pass had crossed the line after bouncing down off the bar; but his iconic third goal – Hurst, cheeks puffed, lifted off the ground by the force of his own shot – was made possible by Weber's 90th-minute equalizer for West Germany, and subsequently by 22 minutes of increasingly carefree defending as Germany sought another equalizing goal.

Although he went on to play 49 times for his country, scoring 24 goals in total, and completed 13 years' service with West Ham before leaving for spells at Stoke City (30 goals in over a hundred appearances), West Bromwich Albion and Seattle Sounders, Hurst had already made his indelible mark. A spell in management followed, firstly at Telford and then at Chelsea – acrimoniously in the end: his dismissal from Stamford Bridge would end up with club and ex-manager slogging it out in the law courts.

Subsequently Hurst coached in Kuwait for a couple of years before pursuing a career in nostalgia-fuelled motivational speech-making, returning to the international stage in 2000 to play a part in England's doomed World Cup 2006 bid. No matter; the red number 10 shirt Hurst wore during the 1966 World Cup Final was bought recently for £80,000 at auction. He will remain an overwhelmingly potent figure: a symbol of English football's greatest triumph – and a reminder of 40 years of anti-climax ever since.

Ibrox disasters

Ibrox Park, home of Rangers, has been the scene of two major football disasters with nearly 70 years between them. In 1902, 26 people died and 517 were injured at a Scotland–England match. Six minutes into the game several rows of wooden planks in the recently rebuilt western stand gave way under the pressure of the swaying crowd, causing hundreds of spectators to plummet 40 feet to the ground. Players on both sides helped carry the injured to medical help. When the game restarted it carried on around posses of policemen running across the pitch to keep the crowd in check. The match was played to its end, albeit halfheartedly, and the result was quickly expunged from the records. A replay was staged at Villa Park to raise money for victims of the world's first recorded football disaster.

In January 1971, 66 people were killed at an Old Firm derby game as a consequence of overcrowding in the stands. Supporters leaving the ground turned back when they heard the crowd react to a late goal being scored. Some became jammed at the top of the staircases, with many falling backwards as a result and crushing those further down. At the time the death toll made this the worst tragedy in British football history. It led, ultimately, to the Safety of Sports Grounds Act 1975, which imposed limits on UK ground capacities and introduced a licence system for stadiums.

injuries

Injuries have always been a major part of footballing life. At any given time most players will be 'carrying' some kind of ailment, often nursed along by physiotherapy or pain-killing injections. Ailments tend to divide into two types:

stress injuries from prolonged over-exertion or strain; and impact injuries suffered by breaking, tearing or otherwise momentarily over-extending a bodily part. Leg injuries, unsurprisingly, are most common. Broken toes and ankles, while serious, remain preferable to damage to the knee or recurrent problems with strained hamstrings, both of which can end or seriously shorten a career.

Broken legs are common, but have a surprisingly good rate of recovery. In 1999 Celtic striker Henrik Larsson suffered a horrific double break of the leg that briefly left half of his shin flapping at right angles inside his sock; two years later he won the Golden Shoe for finishing the season as Europe's top goalscorer. In 1964 Spurs midfielder Dave **Mackay** famously stayed on the field despite suffering a broken leg; as did Stuart Pearce, who, after breaking his left leg in a tackle playing for West Ham against Watford in 1999, stayed on until half-time in an attempt to 'run it off'. Similarly, former German soldier and Second World War POW Bert Trautmann kept goal for Manchester City in the closing stages of the 1956 FA Cup Final with a broken neck.

Injuries can be a very public affair. During the 1980s part of the fascination of watching England captain Bryan **Robson** centred around how long he could manage to stay on the field before indulging in some heroic piece of self-mutilation. The dramatic recurrence of a long-term shoulder injury during the 1986 World Cup was front-page news. Domestic accidents have frequently intruded into the catalogue of footballing injuries. In 1964 Tottenham and England midfielder Alan Mullery strained his back while cleaning his teeth, causing him to miss a tour of Brazil. More recently Rio Ferdinand damaged a knee after sitting

for four hours watching television with his legs up on a coffee table. Goalkeeper Dave Beasant famously sliced open his toe trying to catch a bottle of salad cream that had fallen out of a cupboard in his kitchen. 'My natural instinct was to catch it but I couldn't,' Beasant revealed afterwards, presumably suffering a moment of intense déjà vu.

Goalkeepers have always tended to attract freakish injuries. This is probably to do with the fact that they spend a lot of time throwing themselves around on the ground. In 1998 Barry Town goalkeeper Andy Dibble threatened Carmarthen Town with legal action after being hospitalized with chemical burns suffered diving on the Richmond Park turf, which had been sprinkled with lime. Even more unfortunately, Brentford keeper Chic Brodie was forced to retire from the game after an incident with a stray dog during a League game against Colchester United in November 1970. The dog had been allowed to scamper about the field of play for several minutes before sending Brodie flying as he bent down to pick up a back pass, shattering his kneecap. In 1997 Liverpool reserve keeper Michael Stensgaard's Anfield career was ended by a dislocated shoulder suffered while putting up an ironing board.

Certain injuries have always been more fashionable than others. In the 1970s players' knees were susceptible to cartilage injuries, since supplanted in the treatment room vocabulary by the 'cruciate ligament'. In the run-up to the 2002 World Cup the metatarsal bone entered the national consciousness after a tackle by Deportivo La Coruña's Aldo Duscher fractured David **Beckham**'s toe. Soon United team-mate Gary Neville had also broken his metatarsal, and the injury has remained popular since. Some time in the mid-1990s 'shin splints' appeared on the scene, as have such recent cutting-edge 'niggles' as the strained adductor muscle (formerly 'thigh strain'), the fractured scaphoid (another Beckham upgrade – formerly 'broken hand') and the first formal appearance in football of the late 20th-century plague, depression (previously known as 'stop moaning and get on with it').

In 2002 AC Milan became the first European club to try out biomedical software that promises to predict when players are likely to become injured, using statistics and a personal profile – possibly pre-empting serious injuries by spotting problems early on. Which all sounded very helpful, until the firm producing it revealed that the software is 'over 70 per cent accurate' – not actually that much of an advance on a layman's assessment of Michael **Owen**'s chances of feeling a twinge of the hamstring before the end of the season.

injury time

At the end of each half, the referee should add on such time as has been lost to a variety of stoppages, including substitutions and deliberate timewasting or the ball being lost in the crowd. However, the fact that such added time is often caused by delays for treatment – especially in the days before players were hastened off the pitch – gave it its popular name. For many years, the precise amount of injury time was a secret known only to the referee and perhaps the linesmen. Today, the information is more widely disseminated, first, using hand signals, to the fourth official and then to the players and crowd via the boards used to indicate substitutes' shirt numbers.

The number shown is supposed to be the minimum number of minutes of added time to be played. In close games,

when fans dare not take their eye off the action, this leads to cries of 'How many minutes? How many minutes?' by those who missed the board, at grounds where the PA announcer does not relay the information. Some managers, notably Sir Alex **Ferguson**, consult their own stopwatches and often take issue with the time allowed, which is deemed to be too long if their team is winning and not enough when they need to score. The system has, however, diminished the whistling from the crowd, which is designed to persuade the referee to call time.

internet

Football on the internet is a giant Tower of Babel, a huge seething dustbin of gossip, rumour, rant, news and inexhaustible statistics. Since the mid-1990s the game has found expression on the internet in various forms. The first of these was the individual fan site. At their best fan sites reflect that aspect of the web, the freedom for individuals to communicate on any subject unrestrained by intermediaries, that led so many people to get excited in San Francisco coffee houses during its early years. The best fan sites tend to be an arm of an existing club fanzine, or an extension in spirit of the fanzine culture that emerged in print during the 1980s.

Direct action by supporters – usually against either club directors or the threat of financial meltdown – has been made much easier by the growth in popularity of football on the web and by the relative cheapness of hosting a site. The campaign by Brighton fans to persuade the government to approve planning permission for the club's new stadium has relied on a huge web-based mobilization of supporters.

The internet has also given birth to

innumerable bedroom shrines to both club and player, usually a mishmash of inner monologue, photos, opinion and lies.

In recent years official team sites have tended to become uniformly drab, particularly those run by the ubiquitous Premium TV, who have managed to acquire the rights to publish the majority of official League club sites. Reading like a taciturn match-day programme, these official sites contain little more than the stark mundanity of player profiles, syndicated match reports, an approved and mercifully brief interview with a player, and lots of banner and pop-up advertising.

Some official sites are still surprisingly amateurish, including Manchester United's, which remains primitive in both design and content. Despite their blandness, official club websites have changed fundamentally the way in which clubs communicate with their supporters. Tickets are now available online, sometimes exclusively so, and press releases and official club information are often published solely through the club site.

There is a vast amount of daily football news on the internet. The need for fresh content to boost traffic has elevated what was previously minor – hamstring strains, suspensions, denials of denials regarding transfer tattle – into bold-type headlines. Sites such as the BBC's and *Sporting Life*'s now provide instant football news 24 hours a day, much of which is distinctly homogenized, having been lifted from the same agency news wire. Meanwhile, every administrative body in world football now has its own official website. UEFA.com operates in a UEFA-centric football universe: the Champions' League is minutely reported and its history is thoroughly trumpeted. FIFA.com operates to promote the power base of its shadowy master,

providing personal messages from Sepp Blatter himself and a broad range of propaganda stories from around the world, designed to illustrate exactly how Blatter and his associates are saving the world through football-related junkets.

Most of all, the internet has given us football statistics. Football statistics on the web are the last great wilderness. There is no end to the wealth of scores, players, matches, tables and potted careers available. Some statistics sites are reliable and meticulously maintained. Soccerbase can be trusted, as can the many England national team sites that continue to document every England game ever played.

Other stat sites are an extension of the bedroom shrine phenomenon: crankish, one-eyed and devotedly unreliable. On the other hand, at some heady point during the dotcom boom somebody thought it would be a good idea to enter every single League match ever played into a series of otherwise very average fan sites: the Footymad franchise, which now covers every British League club. A simple click of the mouse tells you that on 18 March 1922 Halifax Town lost 5–1 away to Wrexham, leaving them 18th in Division 3 (North).

Inverness CT

Caledonian Thistle's 1994 entry into Scottish League football initially appears as a natural solution to an obvious problem. The Scottish League was expanding, and the anomaly of a region roughly half the size of Scotland as a whole not having a representative in the nation's professional set-up was overdue some form of adjustment. For a century, Highland League teams had been denied a place in the national leagues on the grounds of travelling distance. This, surely, was the chance they had been waiting for.

Except things weren't that simple. First of all, Caledonian Thistle didn't exist when the Scottish League clubs decided that one of the new Division 3 places be awarded to a team in the Highland capital. Instead they disclosed privately to Caledonian FC and Inverness Thistle FC that a merged 'Inverness United' would be successful. The subsequent 1993 joint application hid a background of acrimony between the two clubs as well as infighting within the respective camps. In particular, a set of rebel 'Caley' fans protested even after the SFL had deemed the bid successful and Caledonian Thistle FC played their first League fixture in August 1994.

The difficult birth of the club, particularly in the merging of the two existing teams' assets and the need to re-attract the local business community, meant that manager Sergei Baltacha achieved a mid-table finish that opening year with little resources. His replacement Steve Paterson arrived with plans approved for a new stadium and momentum building from the local community, helped by the soothing addition of 'Inverness' to the club's title in 1996.

Paterson's seven years at the helm would see ICT rise to Division 1, gaining local support and national attention along the way. This would arrive memorably on the night of Tuesday, 8 February 2000, when they travelled to Parkhead and defeated Celtic 3–1 in the Scottish Cup. At this point a part-time Division 1 team, Paterson's men struck one of the most famous victories in Scottish football history, and cost Celtic head coach John Barnes his job.

Two years later, Paterson led his men to victory at the Tynecastle home of SPL side Hearts by a similar scoreline, again

in the Scottish Cup. This liking of cup competitions did not disappear with Paterson's defection to Aberdeen in December 2002. His replacement, John Robertson, oversaw two consecutive runs to the Scottish Cup semi-finals as well as the capture of the Scottish Challenge Cup in 2003–04.

That season had a far greater source of celebration, when ICT held their nerve on the final day of the season to defeat St Johnstone and win the Division 1 title. Ten years after their inception, the club had delivered top-level football to the Scottish Highlands, an incredible achievement. An enforced six-month match-day rental of Aberdeen's Pittodrie ground did not dampen spirits, and ICT are now back home at the refurbished Tulloch Caledonian Stadium and winning their fight to maintain their SPL status under player-manager Craig Brewster.

Ipswich Town

For a club that only joined the Football League in 1938, Ipswich Town have had an extremely varied and occasionally very successful history. Ipswich Association FC was formed in 1878 at a town hall meeting, with local MP and brewey magnate T. C. Cobbold installed as president. Ipswich remained an amateur club for nearly 50 years, winning the Southern Amateur League four times and the Suffolk Senior Cup 12 times, including three times in four years between 1905 and 1908. They finished seventh in Division 3 (South) in their first League season. A 1–1 draw with fierce local rivals Norwich at the start of their second season was followed the next day by the declaration of war and the suspension of League football.

On resumption of the League, Ipswich spent eight further seasons in Division 3, followed by promotion as champions in 1954. At the beginning of the 1960s they achieved the remarkable feat of promotion to Division 1 followed by the League title in their first-ever season in the top flight in 1962. Alf **Ramsey**'s team beat Arsenal and Aston Villa in dramatic circumstances in the final week of the season to seal the League championship. The team cost a mere £30,000 in total and contained just one player with international caps, striker Ray Crawford. Ramsey would leave the club the following season to manage England and within two years Ipswich were back in Division 2 after remaining bottom of the table from October to the end of the season.

Ipswich regrouped and, under Bill McGarry, won their fifth divisional championship in 15 years to return to Division 1, with Ray Crawford top scorer on his way to a club record of 203 League goals. The appointment of Bobby **Robson** in 1969 proved the impetus for the most successful period in the club's history. By the time Robson left in 1982, like Ramsey to take up the England job, Ipswich had spent 13 consecutive seasons in Division 1, while also winning the FA Cup in 1978 and the Texaco Cup in 1973, competing in the UEFA Cup seven times (and winning it in 1981), and finishing runners-up in the League in 1981 and 1982.

This remarkable run of success was built around Robson's ability to bring on home-produced players, mostly from the north-east and Scotland, including youth-team graduates Kevin Beattie, Eric Gates, John Wark and George Burley. During Robson's reign Dutch midfielders Arnold Muhren and Frans Thijssen became two of the first high-profile foreign players to succeed in English football. The peak of Ipswich's success under Robson came in 1981, with a UEFA Cup win, second

place in Division 1 and Thijssen being voted Footballer of the Year, with John Wark taking the PFA's award.

Robson's departure, and that of captain Mick Mills after a club record 741 appearances, coincided with a sudden decline. By 1986 Ipswich were back in Division 2, since when they have maintained a steady oscillation between the top two divisions, leavened by a Division 2 championship in 1992 and a fifth-place finish in the Premiership in 2001, with George Burley voted Manager of the Year. The following season Ipswich were relegated and Burley sacked, a strange decision given the club's record of managerial stability. In recent years they have continued to produce good young players, including Kieron Dyer and Richard Wright, both of whom were sold for club record fees of £6m. Having endured a financial crisis after dropping out of the Premiership in 2002, Ipswich have been revived by manager Joe Royle, whose young side have settled in the upper reaches of Division 1.

Irish League

The story of football in Ireland began in Belfast, a city with many of the ingredients for a vigorous club culture: an industrial base, close links to other football cities (above all Glasgow) and a ready-made fan rivalry along religious lines. However, unlike in Glasgow, that rivalry and the wider political conflict in Ireland have proved too deadly to keep within the bounds of football stadiums. As a result Northern Ireland has been deprived of some of its strongest clubs, been denied regular contact with potential opponents in the south and had to watch as support leaches away to Scotland and England.

Belfast's industrial prominence

(particularly shipbuilding) and the ties of its predominantly Protestant population to England and Scotland gave it a head start as the centre of football in late 19th-century Ireland, not least because this was also the time when the Gaelic Athletic Association had begun to spread its own games, and its anti-soccer ideology, through the south and the Catholic areas of the north. The Irish Football Association was formed in the city in 1880 and the Irish Cup first competed for the following year – Moyola Park defeated Cliftonville 1–0 in the final (which remained the highlight of the club's history until the Division 2 title was secured in 2002).

Until the political division of Ireland in the early 1920s the IFA governed the whole island, but northern clubs were utterly dominant throughout that period. Until 1901 the Irish League (as it became) was known simply as the Belfast and District League and at times comprised as few as four teams. Gradually other centres emerged, first among Belfast's Catholic population with Belfast Celtic (who joined the League in 1896), then Derry (Derry Celtic in 1900) and finally Dublin (Bohemians in 1902 and Shelbourne in 1903). But no team outside Belfast won the League until Glenavon of Lurgan in 1952.

In the first half of the 20th century three clubs established themselves as the predominant forces: Belfast Celtic, Linfield and Glentoran. Between 1910 and 1951 they won every title between them bar one (which went to briefly blazing Queens Island in 1924). By the end of that period, however, Belfast Celtic were no longer in the League, withdrawing after their players were attacked by Linfield fans who invaded the pitch during a match at Windsor Park on Boxing Day 1948. Celtic, based in west Belfast and drawing their support largely from the Catholic population (to a ground that held 50,000), had been the natural rivals for Protestant Linfield, who subsequently became the best-supported and most successful team in the north, though also the most staunchly Loyalist.

But the competition as a whole suffered from Celtic's withdrawal, and was further diminished when Derry City pulled out for similar reasons at the height of the Troubles in 1972 (later to join the southern League of Ireland). Since then Cliftonville have become the club of some Belfast Catholics at their aptly named ground, Solitude, but while the atmosphere between their fans and those of the largely Protestant clubs may be just as poisonous, they have never managed to emulate Belfast Celtic's prowess on the pitch.

Among the other clubs who have occasionally made their mark on the Irish League or Cup – or the proliferation of smaller tournaments that have pock-marked the province's history – are the current powers Portadown, Distillery (also forced from their Belfast ground during the 1970s), Crusaders and Coleraine. Far down the list of trophy-winners come Ballyclare Comrades, but in stubbornly preserving their name they surely deserve some kind of medal for defying the tide of political history.

Northern Ireland's small population always made it unlikely that their teams would reach high international standards, even without the added complications of political violence. On only two occasions have their teams reached European quarter-finals, and both were in the days when it was possible to get there by winning two ties against moderate opposition. In 1966–67 Linfield went out creditably by only 3–2 on aggregate against CSKA Sofia in the European Cup (perhaps fortunately eliminating the possibility that they would meet Glasgow

Celtic in the semi or the final), while in 1973–74 Glentoran succumbed 7–0 over two legs to a Borussia Mönchengladbach side near its peak.

In recent years Northern Irish football has suffered from the decline in the fortunes of the national team and the increasingly stark contrast between its modest facilities and playing standards and those of the Premiership and Scottish Premier League, with attendances dropping to alarming levels. On the positive side, the mix of players in the League has become more cosmopolitan (including local Catholics at all clubs, southerners and more exotic foreigners) and the recent innovation of a cross-border tournament gives some hope that football may eventually benefit from the easing of violence and moves towards a peace settlement.

Isthmian League

The Isthmian League that kicked off its first season in 1905 contained a curious agglomeration of players, including ex-public schoolboys from The Casuals and London Caledonians against the decidedly more proletarian representatives of Clapton and Ilford. No championship trophy was awarded, the prestige of winning being considered sufficient. Much has changed in the intervening 100 years but the League uniquely encapsulates football's original class-based attitudes, a place where Corinthian ideals and working-class pragmatism met to forge an uneasy but long-lasting alliance.

By 1920 the Isthmian League was established as the premier amateur competition in southern England. During the inter-war years it comprised 14 clubs that rarely altered. Entry was by invitation only and infrequently offered; the rejected were asked to look elsewhere. In response a plethora of Hellenically

inspired leagues emerged; Athenians, Corinthians, Delphians, Spartans and others attempted to emulate the senior league's success. Eventually the Isthmians would be forced to accommodate these upstarts but between 1919 and 1939 viewed them with suitably Olympian disdain.

The League's clubs did have enviable records, winning the FA Amateur Cup a record 30 times prior to the competition's demise in 1974. Seven Isthmian clubs also reached the fourth round proper of the FA Cup in the post-war era. The most notable performances involved Leatherhead, two goals up at Leicester before losing 3–2 in 1974–75; Harlow Town, who did defeat Leicester before losing 4–3 to Watford in 1979–80; and Woking, 4–2 winners at West Brom in the third round, then beaten 1–0 at Everton in 1990–91.

Many clubs commanded substantial support. Dulwich Hamlet were able to build a 30,000 capacity stadium in 1931 through fundraising and member subscription only. The inaugural match, a regular League fixture, was attended by 16,200 in October. Unfortunately, Nunhead, the opposition at Champion Hill that day and perennial pre-Second World War powerhouses, did not reappear in 1945, and neither did founder members London Caledonians. The same year also saw the aristocratic Corinthians – who played most matches on an invitational basis only – amalgamate with The Casuals to form perhaps the last bastion of pure amateurism in English league football: Corinthian Casuals.

In truth the Isthmian League's exclusivity was beginning to work against it. Post-war affluence and mobility led to the decline of some clubs and the rise of others. The Isthmians could no longer claim automatic superiority among other, suspiciously professional-looking, senior amateur sides. Between 1953 and 1963, in order to maintain their elevated status, the League expanded to 20 teams, absorbing eight ambitious newcomers from the Athenian League. In 1964, in the members' bar of Hitchin Town, one of the new clubs, the secretary publicly admitted making illegal payments to players. The press had a field day. Within a decade 'shamateur' football in England ceased to exist and the glory days of the Isthmian League were over.

A 30-year period of continuous reorganization and realignment followed, accompanied by diminishing fan interest. The Isthmian League eventually swallowed the Athenian League, which, in turn, had devoured several smaller leagues. Today, sponsored by the stationers Ryman, it comprises 60 clubs divided into three divisions; they contribute to steps three, four and five in non-League football's 'pyramid.' In spite of its diminished status, the League can claim a fair share of recent non-League notables: Canvey Island, the re-formed Aldershot and every footballing romantic's favourites – AFC Wimbledon. These clubs, however, are passing through on their way to bigger and brighter futures, or so they hope; the Isthmian League is merely a stepping stone, not an end in itself.

Meanwhile, behind the Old Spotted Dog pub, Clapton's players trot out on a Saturday afternoon to the cheers of about 30 spectators in the stands and thousands more echoing through the past century – for them it seems unlikely there's a similar way out.

Alex James

Alex James was the chief on-field inspiration for Arsenal's domination of the English League during the 1930s. Born in Mossend, Lanarkshire in 1901, James escaped a life in the local steelworks by signing for Raith Rovers, before moving south to Preston North End in 1925. Having led Scotland's fabled 'Wembley Wizards' in their 5–1 demolition of England in 1928, James was courted by many top English teams. A year later he signed for Herbert **Chapman**'s Arsenal, induced by the incentive of a lucrative side-career as 'sports demonstrator' in Selfridges.

With James providing the crucial link between defence and attack in Chapman's innovative WM or 3–2–2–3 system, Arsenal won five League titles and two FA Cups during the following decade, with James only absent for the last League championship of 1937–38. To give an idea of James's importance to the club, he was on the losing side only 36 times in 200 appearances between 1930 and 1937. Perhaps even more unlikely, James – a notorious night owl and in his time a sharply dressed protoype of the footballing celebrity – was given special dispensation to stay in bed until noon on match days by the famously autocratic Chapman.

James was known as a quick thinker with an incisive eye for a pass and a bewildering body-swerve. The body-swerve was especially mystifying to defenders who had supposed they were marking a stocky little chap with unusually stumpy legs. In fact, James's famous baggy shorts were a response to a *Daily Mail* cartoon of him which he chose to take a step further, a long-running visual joke of the period.

James had a reputation for falling out with managers. One summer he went on a one-man wildcat strike so that he didn't have to tour abroad with Arsenal during the close-season. It was said that the only man who knew Alex James's worth more than Herbert Chapman was Alex James, but the statistics bore him out. The more he played for Arsenal, the more they scored. James was the first modern player in the sense that he had licence to roam the pitch rather than stick rigidly to a formation, and his confidence and consistency were key to the success of an Arsenal team that utterly dominated its era. He retired from football in 1937. His greatness had been etched on to the public consciousness and his status as the game's first 'star' was demonstrated when *The Times* published his obituary – the first time it had ever marked the passing of a working footballer.

Roy Keane

Roy Keane was the finest midfield player of his generation: the dominant person-ality in the Manchester United team that won the Premiership title seven times times between 1994 and 2003, and Foot-baller of the Year in 2000. Keane's career has been remarkable for its unstinting competitive intensity. Lauded for his achievements in leading United to 12 major trophies in ten years and for his unspectacular but remarkably effective midfield play, Keane's single-mindedness has also brought him notoriety as a combative and sometimes overly aggressive opponent.

As a promising junior footballer in Cork, Keane wrote to every first-division club (except Manchester United – 'I thought I had no chance') requesting trials and was turned down by every one. Considered too small as a youth, Keane took a job lifting beer barrels to help build up his strength and credits a spell as a child boxer with teaching him about physical conditioning. Aged 18 Keane was spotted playing for Cobh Ramblers in Cork by a Nottingham Forest scout and signed by Brian **Clough** for £20,000. Four years later, after 114 League appear-ances and a losing FA Cup Final against Spurs in 1991, he signed for Manchester United for a British transfer record £3.75m, having been part of Brian Clough's 'too good to go down' Forest team, relegated from the Premiership in his final season as manager.

At Old Trafford, Keane blossomed into one of the finest central midfielders in Europe, initially in defence. During the mid-1990s Keane became the dominant midfield force in English football. His driving midfield play – winning the ball in defensive situations and driving forward in support of an attack – and relentlessly unforgiving attitude towards his team-mates were a major source of inspiration in United's League and Cup Double-winning years of 1994 and 1996.

After being made club captain at the end of the 1996–97 season, Keane seriously injured his cruciate ligament chasing down a loose ball against Leeds in September 1997 and was out of football for nearly a year. The incident would have a seismic effect on his career: the following season a rejuvenated Keane led United to the greatest season in any domestic club's history, a treble of League title, FA Cup and Champions' League. Keane produced the definitive display of an inspirational career against Juventus in the semi-final of the Champions' League as he scored a crucial goal in leading his men to victory from a 2–0 deficit at the Stadio Delle Alpi.

Unfortunately the injury also brought the worst out of Keane, who appeared to have spent much of his recuperation brooding over comments made by Leeds player Alfe-Inge Haaland while he lay injured. On their next meeting, at Old Trafford in 2000, by which time Haaland was with Manchester City, Keane launched a horrific, deliberate high challenge at the Norwegian's knee. He describes the incident in his autobiography: 'I'd waited long enough. I fucking hit him hard. The ball was there (I think). Take that, you cunt. And don't ever stand over me again sneering about fake injuries.'

Keane was banned for five games and fined £150,000 by the FA after the publication of his book, which, to add to a tumult of interest in his off-field difficulties, appeared shortly after his decision to retire from international football just before the start of the 2002 World Cup. Keane played 58 times for the Republic of Ireland from 1991, appearing for Jack **Charlton**'s team at the 1994 World Cup. However, a high profile falling-out with Ireland manager Mick McCarthy led to Keane being expelled from the Irish party shortly before the opening game of the tournament and flying home amid widespread condemnation. New coach Brian Kerr has since persuaded Keane to return to the international squad.

Having gone from goalscoring midfielder to right-back to dominant central force, the following season Keane again reinvented himself after a serious hamstring injury as a more restrained orchestrator in the middle of the field, lying deeper and letting others dictate the tempo of a game, and in the process winning a seventh Premiership medal.

Keane's departure from Old Trafford was characteristically brusque. After a cooling of his relationship with Alex Ferguson and a minor furore over comments made about team-mates in an interview with MUTV that was never broadcast, he signed for Celtic in December 2005. Injury restricted him to just eight league games during the remainder of the season, too few to qualify for another league medal.

Unapologetically aggressive and occasionally a painfully isolated figure off the field, Keane has repeatedly demonstrated that a commitment to victory which borders on a minor psychosis often tends to be a part of sustained footballing success.

Kevin Keegan

Also known as Mighty Mouse, Special K, Super Kev and, during his early days at Liverpool, Andy McDaft (explanation: 'I wore flares so wide I couldn't see my shoes'), Kevin Keegan was one of the most successful players English football has ever seen. Ron **Greenwood** once described Keegan as 'the most modern of all modern footballers'. He was also the first post-modern footballer: the first British sportsman to exploit successfully the commercial nexus between sport, celebrity and pop culture; and the first reigning European Footballer of the Year to have a solo UK hit record – 'Head Over Heels' (B-side: 'Move On Down') reaching number 31 in the summer of 1979.

Born in Armthorpe in Yorkshire, Keegan began his playing career at Scunthorpe United, making 141 appearances for 'The Iron' as a wide midfielder before moving to Bill **Shankly**'s Liverpool for £35,000 – a fee Shankly later described as 'robbery with violence'. Signed as a fringe player, Keegan made rapid strides under Shankly and went on to play a major role in three League championships, an FA Cup triumph, two UEFA Cups and, famously, victory in the European Cup in 1977. He was voted Footballer of the Year in 1976, and played 63 times for England between 1973 and 1982. Transferred to SV Hamburg in 1977 for a British record £500,000, he was voted European Footballer of the Year in 1978 and 1979 – a title he still held when he returned to England to play for Southampton in 1980. A promotion-winning season at Newcastle followed before his retirement in 1983 and seven years of golfing purgatory on the Anglo-Spanish Riviera.

To an extent Keegan's frequently tearful managerial spells at Newcastle, Fulham and Manchester City – together with a spell in charge of the England team that included a disastrous Euro 2000 campaign and the shattering 1–0 defeat by Germany in the last game played at Wembley – have obscured the phenomenal impact he made as a player. Captain of England during the national team's darkest period, Keegan alone provided a dusting of glamour. As a player he was said to lack the natural talents of various contemporaries; Brian Glanville once described him as 'the epitome of the fine self-made player'.

Through a combination of the unstinting dedication he showed on the pitch and a vigorous pre-Thatcherite speculative ambition, he became the most recognizable footballer in the world after his move to Hamburg. Bubble-permed and irrepressible in KK-branded Shetland wool V-neck, flared polyester slacks and stack-heeled boots, he was the face of Brut aftershave, a high-profile ambassador for Patrick Boots, 'Super Kev' in a series of BP adverts; and finally, in a statesmanlike postscript, the only football manager ever to have played a televised game of head tennis with a serving Labour Party leader. He exchanged 27 consecutive headers with Tony Blair in front of the nation's media on Brighton beach in 1995.

kick-off

A match starts – or restarts after a goal – with a kick-off from the centre spot. The ball must be kicked into the opponents' half, and is in play once it has travelled a distance equivalent to one rotation. As with all set-pieces, pre-rehearsed kick-off routines are common, although no-one has yet devised a successful means of translating the kick-off into a threatening attacking manoeuvre.

During the 1980s English coaches developed a fairly standard kick-off based around a long punt from the edge of the centre circle out towards the left wing, where a designated rangy midfielder would be haring along the touchline hoping to flick the ball infield towards the oposition penalty area – a method adopted by Graham **Taylor**'s England team during its most 'direct' period. At one point there were even rumours that the routine was being used as a cover for a spreadbetting sting involving unnamed Premiership players: place money on the timing of the first throw-in during a game and then immediately hoof the ball out of play from kick-off. At the other end of the scale Brian **Clough**'s more enterprising Nottingham Forest teams would often charge en masse towards goal from kick-off in a rush of dribbling and one-twos.

FIFA recently amended the laws of the game so that a goal can be scored directly from kick-off, although the combination of circumstances that might lead to this happening is not easy to envisage. To date the record for the quickest goal scored from kick-off belongs, unofficially, to Colin Cowperthwaite of Barrow, who is reputed to have scored after only 3.58 seconds of play against Kettering Town in 1979 in the pre-Conference Alliance Premier League. Various players share the official League record of six seconds for the quickest goal from the start of a game, including most recently Keith Smith for Crystal Palace against Derby in December 1964.

However, the kick-off remains essentially a functional thing: the fairest way of starting or restarting the game, usually enacted by a simple shuttling of the ball back into defence. By way of variation, members of the royal family have in the past occasionally condescended to take the kick-off in major cup finals – although whether the royal personage ever opted to hoof the ball in the direction of a sprinting left-winger is not recorded.

Kidderminster Harriers

Kidderminster Harriers first came to national attention in 1993–94, a season

of unprecedented success for the club but one which ended in frustration. After winning their first Conference title, Harriers were unable to take their place as the first Worcestershire club in the Football League as a result of the facilities at their Aggborough ground failing to meet the required standard.

Three stands had been redeveloped during the club's decade in the Conference but the one side that hadn't been touched cost them a League place. As a fan subsequently commented, 'Northampton's three-sided ground with three derelict stands was deemed to be better than our four-sided ground with one derelict stand. Or was it something to do with funny handshakes?' Stadium redevelopments had been further delayed by the team's best-ever FA Cup run that saw them beat Birmingham City away in their first-ever appearance in the third round, then knock out Preston North End before succumbing to West Ham.

Another good run in the Conference in 1997 ended in disappointment with a runners-up spot behind Macclesfield. Three years later, in his first season in charge, former Liverpool and Denmark midfielder Jan Mølby led the club to the Conference championship and promotion to the Football League at last. Many long-term supporters were dismayed at the club's subsequent jettisoning of their distinctive red-and-white-halved shirts for plain red, a move that has coincided with a dramatic slump in their fortunes.

Kidderminster Harriers were initially formed as an athletics club, hence the name, before concentrating on football in 1886. Three years later they joined the Birmingham & District League but had little success until back-to-back championships in 1938 and 1939. The club moved over to the Southern

League twice to little effect. Only after they joined the smaller West Midlands League in the 1960s did they become established as one of the leading non-League clubs in the region. Players such as brothers Brendan and Peter Wassall, who hold the club's appearance and goalscoring records respectively, helped them to four championship wins, including three in a row from 1969 to 1971.

Ten years after a return to the Southern League, a second-place finish in 1983 led to promotion to the Alliance Premier League (now the Conference) and the most important appointment in the club's history, with Graham Allner taking over as manager. He was to be in charge for 15 years and had an immediate impact, taking the side to two Welsh Cup finals, the first in the centenary season of 1985–86 in which striker Kim Casey set a club record in scoring an extraordinary 73 goals in all competitions. The Harriers then took the FA Trophy in 1987, with a replay victory over Burton Albion; further finals followed with defeats against Wycombe Wanderers in 1991 (before a Trophy record crowd of nearly 35,000) and Woking in 1995.

Mølby left in 2002 to take over at Hull but returned a year later to help keep the club from being relegated. In 2004, with Harriers struggling near the foot of the League, he left the club again to be replaced by Stuart Watkiss. The club returned to non-League football at the end of 2004–05.

Kilmarnock

Kilmarnock's position as the pre-eminent football force in Ayrshire, a sprawling blend of town and country on the western coast of Scotland, has never been in serious doubt since the club's birth in 1869. However, any national success has been spread thinly throughout their history, despite sustained spells in the top division and a sizeable fanbase.

The formation of 'Killie' occurred when a group of local cricketers decided they needed to fill their time during the winter months. The primitive form of football they played was so divorced from that practised today that, when their ground was named, the chosen title was Rugby Park. However, when the Scottish League was formed four years later in 1873, the experimental cricketers reluctantly fell into line and the football club became a founding member.

Like the majority of Scottish clubs outside the Old Firm, it was to cup competitions that Kilmarnock were forced to look for the prospect of silverware, which would arrive in 1920 with the capture of the Scottish Cup after a victory over Albion Rovers. A further win in 1929 was even more impressive with Rangers defeated by a Killie side including their most-capped player, full-back Joe Nibloe.

The next 30 years saw four more finals reached and lost, as the club flitted between divisions and suffered the occasional financial scare. Support fluctuated similarly, but those that stuck by the club were given an astonishing reward in 1964–65 when Kilmarnock won the Scottish League title. Their challenge had been expected to fade throughout the season and, visiting Hearts on the final day two points behind the hosts and needing a two-goal victory to dislodge them, they had been expected to finish plucky runners-up. However, a 2–0 win saw scenes of jubilation that continued for several days in Kilmarnock. That same season the club staged a remarkable comeback in a

European Fairs Cup tie against SV Hamburg. Trailing 3–0 from the first leg, they went a goal down in the return at Rugby Park before rallying to take the tie 5–4 on aggregate.

With title-winning manager Willie Waddell departing for Rangers, the old pattern reasserted itself, Killie again yo-yoing between the divisions until promotion into the Scottish Premier League in 1993 under Tommy Burns.

The board matched this upturn in fortunes by undertaking some much-needed renovation of Rugby Park, which by 1995 was an 18,000 all-seater stadium, one of the largest of its kind in Scotland. This work has meant the club have battled subsequent financial constraints since, yet they have remained ensconced in the Premier League and followed a Scottish Cup win in 1997 with several lofty League finishes. The board have recently voiced fresh concerns about the club's financial outlook but the team remains competitive under Jim Jefferies, the longest-serving manager in the SPL.

Denis Law

Sir Matt **Busby** claims in his autobiography, *Soccer at the Top*, that Denis Law was the first player in British football to salute the crowd when he scored a goal. Yet when the Aberdeen-born Scot scored his most notorious strike at Old Trafford he was playing for Manchester City, and he walked back to the centre circle in a trance, arms firmly by his sides, as his happy team-mates mobbed him.

The goal, scored on the last day of the 1973–74 season, was typical of 'The King': effortlessly improvised and cheeky, it was an audaciously nonchalant back-heel scored late in the game. It was also Manchester United's last match before relegation to Division 2 for the first time in 37 years. Law, unwanted by new boss Tommy Docherty, who was trying to rebuild the team, had moved across town, but it was clear his heart still lay with the club he'd helped to become champions of Europe and darlings of England.

United's success under Busby in the 1960s and subsequent decline in the early 1970s was mirrored by the presence of Law, who was one component of the legendary and lethal attacking triumvirate completed by Bobby **Charlton** and George **Best**. In the early 1960s he went from Huddersfield Town, where he'd made his debut at 16 in 1956, to brief spells at Manchester City and Torino, before Busby paid £115,000 for him, 'the most expensive signing I ever made'.

Busby had given him his first cap at 18 when briefly in charge of Scotland, then later brought him to United because 'he was the quickest-thinking player I ever saw. He had the most tremendous acceleration. He leapt Olympian heights. He headed the ball with almost unbelievable accuracy. He had the courage to take on the biggest and most ferocious opponents. His passing was impeccable.'

In his first season he helped United take the 1963 FA Cup, scoring 23 goals in 38 games. In 1964 he was voted European Footballer of the Year, and in 1965 and 1967 he helped his side become champions. Although he missed the 1968 European Cup Final victory over Benfica though injury, he set a Scottish goal-scoring record with 30 goals in 55 games, a milestone he shares with Kenny **Dalglish** (who needed 102 caps to equal Law's tally). Overall in English League play he scored 217 goals in 458 appearances, including 171 in 309 games for Manchester United, plus another 65 goals in European and domestic cups.

Law had a temper too, and admitted to Busby that he couldn't help but retaliate to the defenders who tried to control him by foul means. Injuries slowed him down as his career progressed, although he was still called up to the Scotland squad for the 1974 World Cup in Germany at the age of 34, playing in the 2–0 win over Zaïre. By then he'd already retired from club football – scoring the 'relegation' back-heeled goal against his old club depressed him so much that he quit.

laws of the game

One reason why football became so popular was that its rules were codified early and simply, and its governing bodies resisted the temptation to tinker with them too much for more than 100 years. For 20 years after the founding of the FA in 1863, the rules evolved rapidly from the original amalgam of the various public school versions. But a modern observer would certainly recognize the football played after 1891, when the introduction of the penalty kick settled the last significant source of disputes about what the laws should be (arguments

about their interpretation, of course, would persist for ever).

The most important decision that set football apart from the other nascent codes was taken at the 1863 meeting and baldly stated in rule 9 of the 14 adopted: 'No player shall carry the ball.' That did not yet mean that no player could handle the ball – until 1870 they could make a 'fair catch' and retreat from the mark to take a free kick, as in Australian Rules today. But it did mean there was no need for any cumbersome mechanism (such as a scrum) to prevent the ball becoming permanently lodged at the bottom of a heaving mass of bodies once a ball-carrier had been tackled. Moving the ball only by foot also meant goals were relatively scarce and made it difficult, as today's TV statistics confirm, for one side to dominate possession or territory completely. That in turn gives a technically inferior side a much better chance of overturning their 'betters' in football than in any of the handling codes, a precious but entirely unintended consequence of those very early decisions.

In 1867 came another crucial moment, the adoption of the modern offside law (although initially with three players required between the attacker and the goal). Before that it was simply forbidden to pass the ball forwards, which is why dribbling rather than passing was the skill prized above all in the early days – nothing to do with toffee-nosed individualism versus the 'cooperative' working men's passing game, as is often claimed. After that came a succession of milestones as the professional era emerged: goal kicks (1869); teams of 11-a-side, with only the goalkeeper allowed to handle (1870); corners (1872); free kicks (1873); and the modern throw-in (1882), a Scottish tradition – in England one-armed hurling was allowed.

That 1882 ruling, at a meeting which

also standardized other peculiarities – such as insisting on a fixed crossbar rather than a tape – paved the way for international matches without endless wrangles over the laws, a development confirmed four years later by the formation of the International Board, still the game's law-making body.

In the 20th century rule change was mercifully much slower, but two innovations stand out, both intended to encourage the attacking side. In 1925 the offside rule was changed so that the number of players required between the attacker and the goal became two, instead of three. This was in response to the increasing sophistication of defenders, typified by Newcastle's Bill McCracken, in setting the offside trap. The rule change sparked a brief bonanza for strikers, with Middlesbrough's George Camsell (59 goals in 1926–27) and Everton's Dixie **Dean** (60 the following year) smashing all League records. But inevitably tactics were adjusted to cope, above all by Herbert **Chapman**, who deployed the first purely defensive centre-back – author Martin Tyler has called Arsenal's 4–0 win at West Ham in October 1925, the first time Chapman tried the system, 'perhaps the most significant result in the history of the game'.

The second change did not come until 1992, when goalkeepers were barred from picking up back-passes, a change which certainly increased the pace of the game, not to mention the number of comic incidents. Goalkeepers have been messed around by rule changes more than most, being required to stand still on their line for penalties from 1929 (misguidedly altered by the 'dancing' concession of 1997) and take only four steps with the ball from 1982 to 1997 (subsequently altered to a six-second limit).

Other recent changes have related mostly to disciplinary effects of foul play, such as the automatic red card for bringing down an attacker faced by only a single defender – what might be termed the 'Willie Young law', since the Arsenal defender's desperate hack on West Ham's Paul Allen in the 1980 FA Cup final was so often cited as a typical 'last man' offence. Other players have written their footnotes into the Laws in more imaginative ways than Young, McCracken or Notts County's William Gunn (of cricket bat Gunn & Moore fame), whose huge one-armed throws were outlawed by the 1882 ruling.

The free-kick rules were clarified when Coventry's Ernie Hunt volleyed in against Everton in 1970 after Willie Carr had flicked the ball up between his ankles – a move subsequently ruled as a double touch. Everton were the beneficiaries of an even stranger goal in 1924, immediately after the rule had been changed to allow players to score direct from a corner. In a game against Tottenham at White Hart Lane, Sam Chedgzoy simply dribbled past nonplussed defenders from the corner flag and put the ball in the net – the rulemakers had carelessly forgotten to mention that the player could not touch the ball twice. After heated argument, the goal was allowed to stand, but the law was quickly amended.

Tommy Lawton

'Once upon a time there was a lad of sixteen and a half who earned himself the distinction of being the youngest centreforward ever to play in a Football League game. On his second senior side appearance he scored two goals.' So begins Tommy Lawton's introduction to his own *All Star Football Book*. The cover of the book features a drawing of Lawton in typical pose: three feet off the ground, lumpy brown boots made out of tractor tyres on his feet, and a single strand of Brylcreemed hair dislodged as he heads an enormous brown medicine ball towards a distant goal. 'Can you imagine the pride with which my young heart was bursting?' Lawton asks. 'Of course you can.'

Lawton was playing for Burnley at the time. He made his debut in 1936, moving to Everton shortly afterwards and first played for England two years later. One of the finest centre-forwards English football has ever produced, Lawton was lined up to replace the great Dixie **Dean** as Everton's number 9 and played a key role in the club winning the last League championship before the Second World War. After the war he played for Chelsea and later joined Notts County for a record £20,000, a move that aroused a certain amount of curiosity as he was only 28 at the time and had chosen to drop down to Division 3. His appearance is said to have added 10,000 to the home gates. He still managed to captain England while he was there, the only Division 3 player ever to do so. Lawton played the last of his 23 games (22 goals) for England in 1948. In all he scored 231 goals in 390 League appearances. Spells in management at Brentford and Kettering Town followed, before he retired from the game to become a pub landlord.

Ruthlessly strong in the air, Lawton was a classic English number 9, and in the last years before the war he was probably the most celebrated player in British football. Besides his *All Star Football Book*, Lawton was a pioneering beneficiary of early player celebrity endorsements, lending his name and likeness to such innovations as the autographed 220-piece Tommy Lawton jigsaw. He died in 1996 and his ashes are currently being kept at the National Football Museum at Preston.

LDV Vans Trophy

Put simply, this knockout cup gives teams in the two lowest English League divisions the chance to win a trophy at Wembley or, latterly, the Millennium Stadium. Its identity is, however, far more complicated than that. At the time of the first competition in 1984–85 the old Division 3 and 4 teams were known as associate members because they only had four Football League votes between them, as opposed to the 'full' League members in Divisions 1 and 2, who had a vote each. It only existed as the Associate Members' Cup for that first season, and has since gone through half a dozen sponsors.

The tournament evolved from the short-lived Anglo-Scottish and Texaco Cups of the 1970s into the Football League Group Cup in 1982 and the Football League Group Trophy in 1983. Its generic, unsponsored name is now, officially, the Football League Trophy, but no one apart from a couple of Football League employees actually knows this. Once sponsorship had been secured for the 1984–85 competition, a Wembley final became the incentive for clubs to take it more seriously. Since then it has four times been a Trophy (Freight Rover, Sherpa Vans, Autoglass and now the LDV Vans), once a Cup (Leyland DAF), and once a Shield (Auto Windscreens).

The early rounds were at first organized into regional mini-leagues, but now it is a straight knockout, competed for in north and south, with the winners of the two regional finals competing for the trophy, or cup, or shield. or whatever. Since 2000 a number of sides from the Conference have also taken part, starting at eight and now increased to 12.

Bolshier clubs looking for promotion to the top two divisions have been known to field under-strength teams to show they consider the competition beneath then, and attendances are notably low for the first rounds.

However, the final stages have been far more successful at capturing public imagination as fans realize that no matter how difficult it is to remember the competition's name, it still represents the rare chance to win an honour in a huge stadium. When two well-supported teams in Wolves and Burnley reached the final in 1988, the result was a 2–0 win for the Midlanders and a crowd of over 80,000. Twice-winners are Port Vale, Stoke City, Birmingham City, Blackpool, Wigan Athletic and Bristol City.

League Cup

The League Cup was created almost by accident. In the late 1950s Football League secretary Alan Hardaker devised a plan to halve the slide in attendances, which had begun to fall away after the post-war boom. He proposed to reduce the number of clubs in each division to 20, the idea being that this would create a larger proportion of 'meaningful' matches involving promotion and relegation issues. Clubs would be compensated for the loss of several home fixtures by a new cup competition to be played in midweek. The League club chairmen rejected the restructuring of the divisions but decided to keep the cup.

After initially being shunned by the major clubs, the League Cup partially succeeded in gaining prestige during its peak in the 1970s and 1980s, but has since once more become an also-ran in the crowded fixture list, its very existence the subject of perpetual debate. The first competition in 1960–61 attracted only 46

of the 92 League clubs, and although they included Manchester United, the event was ignored by reigning champions Spurs and the previous season's League runners-up, Sheffield Wednesday, along with other big clubs at the time such as Wolves and Arsenal. The Cup's priority was reflected in the fact that its two-legged final between Aston Villa and Division 2 Rotherham could not be completed until the following season, Villa running out 3–2 winners.

The competition's detractors had further ammunition when the 1962 end-game was fought out between Division 2 Norwich and Rochdale of Division 4, Norwich winning 4–0 overall. The competition limped on through the mid-1960s without the major clubs, but then the League introduced a Wembley final with the lure of a place in the Fairs Cup (later the UEFA Cup) for the winners in the 1966–67 season. Journalist Brian Glanville previewed that year's final between West Brom and third-division QPR by describing the competition as 'that mammoth irrelevance', but conceded after the game that 'as pseudo events go, it wasn't half bad'. QPR came back from a 2–0 half-time deficit to win 3–2 before 97,000, and the competition came of age. The only snag was that, as they were a Division 3 side, UEFA would not let QPR compete in the Fairs Cup.

That the big sides began to take the Cup seriously is clear from the following season's line-up, with Leeds topping Arsenal 1–0 in a dull encounter. The next season Arsenal returned to be defeated again, this time more famously by Division 3 Swindon, who won 3–1 in extra time thanks to two goals by Don Rogers. Several 1970s finals stand out, such as Stoke's 2–1 victory over Chelsea in 1972 to take their first senior trophy, Manchester City's 2–1 defeat by Wolves in 1974, and their return in 1976 to beat

Newcastle by the same scoreline thanks to Dennis Tueart's eye-catching overhead kick winner. Nottingham Forest began a successful run in 1978 by beating Liverpool 1–0 in a replay, and then by trumping Southampton by the odd goal in five a year later. Sell-out crowds of 100,000 had now become the norm for the Wembley finals.

Forest's 1–0 final defeat by Wolves in 1980 ushered in a period of dominance by Liverpool, who took the trophy four successive times without complaining that the League Cup was interfering with their simultaneous success in the European Cup. They remain record winners with seven trophies, although Forest won two more, including a scintillating 3–2 victory over Luton in 1989, the last truly engaging final. Aston Villa have also lifted the trophy on five occasions.

Although Manchester United boss Sir Alex **Ferguson** yearly states that he wants to win the competition, his fielding of youth and reserve teams for League Cup ties from the mid-1990s onwards slightly undermines his claim, and the 1992 title remains United's sole success in this arena. Arsenal, Chelsea and several other Premier League sides have also taken to regularly fielding second-string elevens, leading to diminishing crowds, interest and respect for the title, especially as its constantly changing sponsors (six in all since 1982) have sown confusion as to the competition's identity.

Despite threats from UEFA, however, the League Cup still holds the carrot of a European place, and for a number of sides such as Tottenham and Middlesbrough, it has lately represented their best chance of both silverware and a shot at European competition.

Leeds United

Always at their best in a battle, Leeds United have enjoyed two distinct periods of success since the club's foundation in 1919. Also known as 'The Peacocks' and latterly 'The Whites', the club was created out of the ashes of the defunct Leeds City, who, under the management of Herbert **Chapman**, had been found guilty of making illegal payments to players and expelled from the League. The new club entered Division 2 in 1920 and spent the next 40 years oscillating gently between the top two divisions.

Barring a Division 2 title in 1924 and the emergence of John **Charles** during the 1950s, they achieved very little, beyond a steady series of promotions and relegations, before the appointment of Don **Revie** as manager in 1961. Over the next ten years Leeds were transformed into the most powerful footballing force in the country. Revie forged his team's enduring characteristics of fierce competitiveness and utter professionalism, qualities that would on occasion lead to accusations of physical intimidation on the field of play.

Under Revie, Leeds won the Division 2 title in 1964 and through the efforts of players such as Jack **Charlton** (club record 629 League appearances and Footballer of the Year 1967), Billy **Bremner** (Footballer of the Year 1970), and Norman Hunter (PFA Player of the Year 1973) proceeded to finish as either League champions or runners-up seven seasons out of ten from 1965, also reaching the FA Cup Final four times, but winning just once.

In fact Leeds's record during this period is notable for the amount of times Revie's team almost picked up trophies. Having progressed to the final stages of 17 competitions they won just six major honours, including two European Fairs

Cups, during their peak years. In 1970 Leeds threatened to win a then unprecedented treble of European Cup, League championship and FA Cup, only to fall at the last in all three competitions: defeat in the semi-final of the European Cup, second place to Everton in Division 1 and a Cup Final loss to Chelsea. During this period battles between Leeds and Chelsea took on a wider significance (grim northern aggressors versus metropolitan playboys) that seemed to crystallize the enduring public perception of Revie's team.

In homage to the great Real Madrid side of the 1950s Revie had changed the club strip to all white early on in his career at Elland Road and at times, through players such as Johnny **Giles** and Eddie Gray, Leeds did indeed perform with some of the panache of the great 'Meringues' of Di Stefano and Puskás. This was perhaps most notable during the 7–0 televised destruction of Southampton in 1972, during which Leeds players teased their opponents by keeping the ball with a series of backheels and flicks ('It's almost cruel,' crowed the television commentary, 'every man jack of this Leeds side is taking it in turns to put on a show').

Revie left the club in 1974 to begin an undistinguished spell in charge of the England team. Leeds had won the League that season and a year later reached the final of the European Cup, losing 2–0 to Bayern Munich in a game remembered more for rioting by Leeds fans which led to a three-year suspension from European football. Ultimately the game signalled the end of an era: Revie's team was dismantled and a period of unprecedented success dissolved into one where the club became better known for the violent behaviour of some of its followers. Twice in four years Leeds suffered the ignominy of attracting one of

the great managers – Brian **Clough** in 1974 and then Jock **Stein** in 1978 – only for the new boss to leave the club after, in each case, exactly 44 days in charge. Clough was sacked and Stein left to manage Scotland.

Following a sequence of eight seasons in Division 2, Leeds finally returned to the top flight under the guidance of Howard Wilkinson in 1990, and two years later Wilkinson's team won the last ever old Division 1 title. The loss of key players such as Gordon Strachan, Lee Chapman and Mel Sterland – plus the cut-price sale of Eric **Cantona**, who would become one of the most influential players in the early years of the Premiership – contributed to Leeds's 17th-place finish the following season. In 1996 Wilkinson was sacked by the club's new owners, Caspian, although the youth system he put in place still produced players such as Alan Smith, Ian Harte and Paul Robinson, who would prove instrumental in David O'Leary's exciting young team reaching the semi-finals of the Champions League in 2001.

Unfortunately O'Leary's initial gains failed to translate into lasting success as serious financial mismanagement of the club's playing staff helped to create a crippling debt of over £100m. Chairman Peter Ridsdale sacked O'Leary and then resigned himself, leaving the club, relegated in 2004, to pick up the tab as a series of new managers set about the business of building a Leeds United that might be able to bloom once again in the enduring shadow of the Revie era. In 2006 they were beaten in the Championship play-off final by Watford.

left foot

'Don't never let nobody tell you that these here lefthanders is right,' observed baseball pitcher Jack Keefe in Ring

Lardner's legendary sporting tale *You Know Me Al*. Outlawed for a while by the Catholic Church and supposedly regarded by Zulus as an affliction curable only by repeated scaldings, in football being a leftie occupies a more venerated position. This is due to simple rules of demand and supply, which dictate that left-footed players are always going to be a precious commodity. Ideally a football team would have an even split of left- and right-sided players, but in practice only about one in ten people favour the left. In fact research conducted by psychologists at the University of Aberdeen during the 1998 World Cup determined that 80 per cent of the 216 players taking part in the survey were predominantly right-footed.

Perhaps because of this rarity value left-footed players have tended to attract favourable stereotypes. References to a 'cultured' or 'educated' left foot are commonplace. Arsenal midfielder Liam Brady is one of many players to become known for possessing an erudite left foot. Two of the greatest players of all time, Diego Maradona and Hungarian legend Ferenc Puskás, were exclusively left-footed: Maradona is famous for juggling a golf ball, while Puskás was revered for his ability to do keep-ups with a bar of soap in the shower ('His left foot was like a hand,' observed Real Madrid team mate Francisco Gento). All of which conforms to the mythology of the left-footer as a uniquely tricksy performer; no great right-footed player has ever been known for his household-object-juggling skills. The left-footer is often characterized as erratic and artistic – with the exception of left-footed full-backs (Julian 'The Terminator' Dicks, Stuart 'Psycho' Pearce or Mark 'No Nickname to Speak of But Sent Off 12 Times' Dennis), who have tended to adopt more of a hardman role.

The recent dearth of high quality left-footed English players has become a *cause célèbre* for the national team. During his first two years as England manager Sven-Göran **Eriksson** selected 16 different players on the left side of midfield, only one of whom (Wayne Bridge, a defender) was actually left-footed. The lack of left-hand-siders has been made all the more noticeable by the tendency for English players to be one-footed: the left foot merely a 'swinger', or 'only used for standing on'. The FA coaching manual produced by long-term technical chief Charles Hughes makes no mention at all of either left- or two-footedness, which might go some way towards explaining why British football no longer produces genuinely two-footed players of the quality of George **Best** or Tom **Finney**.

In fact the University of Aberdeen's research into the subject concluded that all players are potentially two-footed, but many are restrained by an innate fear of attempting something unusual or unfamiliar – a condition not unknown in the English game. Assessing the passing and shooting of players at France 98, the researchers found that, under pressure, players performed equally well with both feet. Similarly, in his book *Soccer for Thinkers* former Manchester City manager Malcolm **Allison** warns that relying on one foot leads to players being unable to visualize certain parts of the field, which are 'blanked out' in their mind's eye. The logic seems simple enough: the best players tend to use both feet.

Leicester City

Leicester have spent much of their largely unremarkable existence bouncing between the top two divisions – never quite producing a side good enough to win major honours, yet never quite sliding down to the third tier. Since their birth in

1884 as Leicester Fosse the club has produced and nurtured a number of talented players, but unlike supporters of their two east Midlands rivals – Derby County and Nottingham Forest – Leicester fans have never enjoyed a glory period to sustain them through leaner times.

Leicester Fosse were formed by former pupils of Wyggeston Boys' Grammar school and held their first fixture in a private field close to Fosse Road. The club's first professional, Harry Webb, was signed in 1888 from Stafford Rangers, for two shillings and sixpence a week, and its first 'non-friendly' fixture was held in 1891, when Fosse joined the Midland League. When the Leicester Corporation closed its Mill Lane ground, the club moved to Filbert Street, destined to be its home for the next 111 years.

Leicester were elected to Division 2 of the Football League in 1894 and in their first season recorded a club record 13–0 victory over Notts Olympic in an FA Cup qualifier. They secured promotion to the top flight for the first time in April 1908 but were immediately relegated. A 12–0 defeat to Nottingham Forest in 1908–09 prompted an enquiry, which revealed the players had been out the day before celebrating the wedding of former team-mate 'Leggy' Turner – it was not the last time Leicester players would be caught up in scandal.

Leicester Fosse was replaced by Leicester City in July 1919, the new name marking the Leicester borough's elevation to city status. The 1920s were Leicester's best years as the shrewd Scot Peter Hodge fashioned a team capable of topping Division 1, in September 1926, and finishing runners-up in 1929. Hodge also signed some of City's finest players, including Adam Black, who made 528 appearances, and Arthur Chandler, whose 273 goals is still a club record.

This period produced Filbert Street's record crowd (47,298 for an FA Cup match against Spurs in 1928) but also saw Leicester attract the lowest League attendance ever: just 13 for a match against Stockport County. Actually there were about 2,000 present for the game at Old Trafford, but it was the second part of a double-header (the first involving Man Utd and Derby) and only the few additional spectators were counted.

True to tradition, City were relegated in 1935, bounced back again before the war, but then slipped back to Division 2. In 1949, the Foxes reached their first Cup Final, inspired by future Leeds and England manager Don **Revie**, but lost 3–1 to Wolves. The 1950s were the Arthur Rowley era as the striker scored 265 goals between 1954 and 1958, steered Leicester to their fourth Division 2 title, and set a League record of 434 career goals. The Filberts' longest unbroken spell in the top flight came between 1957 and 1969, thanks partly to the keeping of World Cup winner Gordon **Banks**. They also reached three FA Cup Finals – in 1961, 1963 and 1969 – and captured the League Cup, beating Stoke in the 1964 final.

Jimmy Bloomfield's flamboyant 1970s side are fondly remembered. Including Keith Weller, Frank Worthington and Alan Birchenall (who later became the club's half-time raffle man), they reached the FA Cup semi-final in 1974, losing to Liverpool. The skilful Worthington was noted as a crowd-pleaser and lover of the high life, while Weller hit the headlines for playing in a pair of white tights in a televised match.

The yo-yoing resumed in the late 1970s and continued throughout the 1980s, a period which saw the rise of local lad Gary **Lineker**. Leicester fans finally celebrated something approaching sustained success in the mid-1990s, when Martin O'Neill's disciplined but glitter-less side finished in the top ten of the Premier League in four successive seasons and won the League Cup in both 1997 and 2000.

Peter Taylor briefly took Leicester to the top of the Premier League in October 2000, luring unsuspecting fans into a false sense of security. Twelve months later Taylor had been sacked; in April 2002 City were relegated; and by October 2002 the club, now based at the unfortunately named Walker's Stadium, entered administration, only to be saved by a Lineker-led consortium in February 2003.

Managed by Micky Adams, the club scrambled back to the Premier League. Relegation struck yet again in April 2004, but not before three first-team players had been arrested in Spain on rape charges (they were later acquitted). Adams left after a bad start to the 2004–05 season to be replaced by Scotsman Craig Levein, who lasted barely a year.

Leyton Orient

Leyton Orient – geographically squeezed between West Ham, Arsenal and Tottenham, and regularly patted on the head as 'everyone's second-favourite team' – are in fact one of the oldest clubs in the capital. The O's began life in 1881 as the Glyn Cricket Club, established by former members of Homerton College, a teacher training college for the Puritans. The club didn't get down to the business of playing football until 1888, when players decided they wanted something to do in the winter.

So Orient Football Club (named after a newly launched P&O ship by an employee of the company, player and committee member, Jack Dearing) was born. Snob value caused them to change their name to Clapton Orient in 1898 – Clapton was seen as a desirable area at the time – and name-tweaking was to become a regular habit.

The club moved to the sizeable Mill-fields Road ground in 1900, and election to the Football League followed in 1905. The O's started as they meant to go on: they finished bottom of Division 2 in a season beset by financial difficulties. The following season they blazed a trail for Manchester United 93 years later by not bothering to enter the FA Cup, claiming that they needed to concentrate their meagre resources on League struggles. Fortunes improved in subsequent seasons, and in 1913 Orient joined forces with Spurs to protest against Arsenal's move to Highbury from Woolwich, seeing the arrival of new neighbours as an impediment to their progress.

Orient suffered their first relegation in 1929 and the crippling cost of rent on the Millfields ground, owned by a greyhound syndicate, finally forced the club to vacate the stadium the following year. After a spell at nearby Lea Bridge Road, and two League games at Wembley in November 1930, the club were on the move again in 1937, moving a mile or so east to Leyton Amateurs' ground at Brisbane Road, where they remain. After the war, the club were renamed again, as Leyton Orient.

In 1949 Alec Stock was appointed manager, heralding one of the best periods in the club's history. Good FA Cup runs were followed by promotion in 1956, the O's galloping to the Division 3 (South) title and scoring 106 goals in the process. Things got even better at the start of the next decade when, under Johnny Carey's stewardship, the club were promoted to the top flight for the only time. Relegated straight away, by the end of 1966 they'd slipped back to Division 3 and into another near bankruptcy.

The club survived and changed its name again (to plain Orient), and the appointment of Jimmy Bloomfield as manager laid the foundations for a rather more successful 1970s, including a last-game near-miss on elevation to the top flight in 1974. More fondly remembered from this decade are the runs to the sixth round of the FA Cup in 1972 and the semi-finals in 1978. Victories over Chelsea in both campaigns were high points of a decade in which the likes of Laurie Cunningham, Peter Kitchen, John Chiedozie and Glenn Roeder became O's legends.

But relegation in 1982 was followed by another in 1985 to give the club their first ever taste of fourth-level football. Four years and another name change later (Leyton Orient again, 1987) they scrambled back up through the play-offs. A drop back to the fourth tier, in 1995, was inevitable after the financial crisis brought on by chairman Tony Wood losing his coffee business in the horrific Rwandan genocide.

Into the breach came sports promoter Barry Hearn, amid a flurry of promises that have become more modest by the season. He took the club out of debt and has since stabilized the finances and modernized the ground (the trade-off for which is a reduced capacity and blocks of flats at each corner of the ground). Fans were worried that the O's were turning into an archetypal bottom-division club – until they were promoted on a dramatic final day of the 2005–06 season.

Lincoln City

Lincoln City are mostly remembered for two reasons. The Imps – named after a tiny devilish sculpture high up on a pillar in the city's Cathedral – still hold the record for the most League points in a season, and in 1987 became the first Football League side to be automatically relegated to non-League football.

These two landmarks are closely linked to the two most prominent managers of recent history at Sincil Bank. A youthful Graham **Taylor** led an attacking Lincoln team to the 1975–76 Division 4 title with 74 points (only Sunderland have levelled it, their tally of 105 in 1998–99 equalling Lincoln's record under the old two-points-for-a-win system). Five-figure crowds were commonplace to watch a team featuring the colossal Percy Freeman up front and the domineering captain Sam Ellis at the back.

When Lincoln went down to the Conference 11 years later, they called back Colin Murphy for a second spell to take them straight back up to League football. During his first stay in the early 1980s Murphy, notorious for his sense-less and garbled programme notes, had also led Lincoln up to Division 3, where in 1981–82 they missed out on promo-tion by one point after drawing with Fulham 1–1 at Craven Cottage in the season's final game (Fulham went up instead). Supported by disappointing crowds of around 4,000, the team only managed sixth the following year, and arguably the strongest Lincoln team ever – built around Trevor Peake, Gordon Hobson, Steve Thompson, George Shipley and Glenn Cockerill – went its different ways. The players moved up to the higher divisions, while Lincoln soon moved back down.

Formed in 1884, Lincoln entered Football League Division 2 in 1892 from the Football Alliance. They were relegated out of the League in 1908, 1911 and 1920, but each time bounced back in a single season by winning the Midland League (twice) and the Central League. Founding members of Division 3

(North) in 1921, they were three times champions (in 1932, 1948 and 1952), but life in Division 2 was short-lived until the last title. They survived there nine seasons under Bill Anderson before going down twice in a row to Division 4, where they stayed until Taylor revitalized the club in the 1970s. Not since 1887 have Lincoln reached the FA Cup fifth round, where they progressed thanks to two byes before losing 3–0 to Glasgow Rangers.

The club has survived a series of financial crises throughout its history, leading to the sale of the ground in 1982 to the City Council, and its repurchase in 2000 – by which time it was an all-seater, 10,000-capacity stadium – at a knock-down price to be used as collateral. The sale of players such as Darren Huckerby to Newcastle and Gareth Ainsworth to Wimbledon has also helped keep the club afloat.

The most recent money troubles, in 2002, led to the club being taken over by a Supporters' Trust, which runs the club on a tight budget while upholding a greater sense of community. City made the Division 3 play-off final in 2003 and 2005 under folk-hero manager Keith Alexander.

Gary Lineker

Gary Lineker is the only Englishman ever to win the Golden Boot at a World Cup finals. He was also the only player to top the Division 1 scoring charts at three different clubs, and – after an untypically happy three-year spell at Barcelona – one of the most successful English foot-ballers at a foreign club. Blessed with speed, athleticism and an unusual calm-ness in front of goal, he was a definitive English example of the kind of centre-forward play that is almost impossible to describe without resorting to cliché: a

penalty box predator, a man with a nose for a chance, an eye for goal and a sixth sense for a yard of space. At his best Lineker was the epitome of all these striking stereotypes.

He began his career at Leicester City in 1978, initially as a right-winger, before converting to centre-forward as City were promoted to Division 1 two years later. In 1982–83 he scored 26 goals, leading to an England call-up the following year and a £1.1m transfer to Everton in the summer of 1985. It was at Goodison Park that Lineker's talent really blossomed. In the 1985–86 season he scored 30 League goals, won both Foot-baller of the Year awards, and went on to become top scorer at the Mexico 86 World Cup, scoring six times as Bobby **Robson**'s team reached the quarter-finals. Lineker's year was capped by a £2.75m move to Barcelona, where he would score 44 goals in 99 games and win the Spanish Cup in his second season (his first medal as a player) before suffering one of the few lean spells of his career, owing in part to a bout of hepa-titis. He reinvented himself as a right-winger for a while under the guidance of Johan Cruyff, from which position he laid on the first goal in the final as Barcelona won the 1989 European Cup Winners' Cup.

Lineker signed for Tottenham Hotspur for £1.2m in 1989 and was leading scorer in Division 1 in his first season back, before scoring four times at the Italia 90 World Cup as England fell at the semi-final stage. Two years later he retired from international football after the European Championships; his late substi-tution during England's defeat by hosts Sweden – with Graham **Taylor**'s side desperate for a goal and Lineker himself just one short of Bobby **Charlton**'s inter-national record of 49 – signified the begin-ning of the end for Taylor's troubled regime. A spell in the nascent J-League with Grampus Eight was cut short by a series of foot injuries, and in 1994 Lineker retired from playing at the age of 34.

His record is unique: 236 goals in 431 League appearances; second on the all-time England international scoring list (in 1992 he missed a penalty against Brazil that would have equalled Bobby Charlton's record); three major Player of the Year awards; an OBE and two honorary MA's; and a FIFA Fair Play Award in 1990, testimony to an almost anachronistic ambassadorial presence on and off the field and to another great – and increasingly unlikely-sounding – Lineker achievement of never having been booked. Since retiring he has embarked on a successful career as a broadcaster, becoming the BBC's foot-balling frontman. Perhaps owing in part to his retirement at a time when players were only just beginning to earn significant amounts of money, Lineker has also allowed himself to be lured into such cul-de-sacs as the lad-culture nadir of the dismal TV quiz show *They Think It's All Over*, and a series of increasingly inane junk food advertising campaigns. However, his leading role in the successful financial resuscitation of his hometown club Leicester City during the 2002–03 season suggests that the legacy of his post-playing career may amount to something greater than the unhealthy indignity of Salt'n'Lineker.

Liverpool

Despite the recent dominance of Manchester United and Arsenal, Liverpool remain English football's most successful club. In an 18-year period between 1973 and 1990 Liverpool won 11 League titles (finishing second every other season except one) as well as three FA Cups, four League Cups, four European Cups, two UEFA Cups and a European Super Cup. This is a period of unmatched – and probably unmatchable – domination.

Liverpool's sustained success during this period is remarkable for other reasons too. Arsenal had a period of supremacy during the 1930s; Manchester United achieved much under Matt **Busby** and Don **Revie**'s Leeds United had been the most consistent team in the country prior to Bill **Shankly**'s third League title win in 1973. But such single-minded domination had never been seen before.

Shankly and his successor Bob **Paisley** built their championship teams cheaply. These were the days before home teams kept all of their gate receipts, and well before television revenue had transformed the spending power of the larger clubs; there was always something home-grown about Liverpool's success. Players were bought young and transformed into stars. Kevin **Keegan**, a dominant force under Shankly for five years during the mid-1970s, cost £35,000 from Scunthorpe. Ray Clemence was bought for £15,000 from the same club. Phil Neal signed from Northampton for £65,000, and still shares the record for most Championship medals won. Alan Hansen, perhaps the club's greatest-ever defender, was bought for £100,000 from Partick Thistle. Kenny **Dalglish** cost a British record £440,000 when he signed from Celtic and duly went on to become arguably the most influential player in Liverpool's history.

Similarly, much was made of the Anfield 'boot room', the under-stairs broom cupboard in which the coaching staff gathered for over 40 years in order to plot League titles and European campaigns over a pot of tea. Shankly instigated a tradition of tactical discussion, which was carried forward by Paisley, Joe Fagan, Roy Evans and Reuben Bennett among others. The boot room was demolished in 1993 to make way for ground improvements.

Oddly, it was the club's home ground, Anfield, that provided the motivation for the founding of Liverpool Football Club. Its original tenants were city rivals Everton. However, Everton fell out with their landlord, John Houlding, in 1892 and left for good. Houlding formed his own club in order to fill the ground. Liverpool have had an intense and passionate rivalry with Everton ever since, some of the most memorable derby games coming in the mid-1980s, when the clubs were the dominant football forces in the country.

Liverpool played their first League game in 1893. Early teams were largely made up of Scottish players. The first of many Scots to captain successful Liverpool teams, centre-half Alex Raisbeck joined from Stoke in 1898 and went on to play 340 games over 11 years, helping the club to two League titles. Irish goalkeeper Elisha Scott was considered the finest in the country during the inter-war years, making 467 appearances for Liverpool over eighteen seasons and playing a key role in the League Championship victories of 1922 and 1923. Scott had a very public rivalry with Everton forward Dixie **Dean** during the 1920s, so much so that the story circulated of the two meeting in a Liverpool street: Dean nodded politely, at which point Scott threw himself to the ground to save an imaginary header.

Albert Stubbins, a record £12,500 signing from Newcastle, proved a prolific goalscorer in a later championship-winning side, playing alongside Scottish international Billy Liddell, one of the finest British players of his generation

and a two-footed goalscoring winger to rank alongside Stanley **Matthews** and Tom **Finney**. Liddell's retirement in 1961 dovetailed with the first stirrings of the Shankly revolution at Anfield. Bill Shankly had been appointed manager in 1959 with the club in Division 2 and at the lowest point in its history. Shankly brought about a revolution in personnel, methods and expectations. Promotion in 1962 was followed by the League title two years later and the club's first-ever FA Cup in 1965. During this period the Liverpool Kop, known for their songs and their support of the team, began to develop. The Kop, named after Spion Kop, the site of a battle during the Boer War, had been built at the Anfield Road end of the ground in 1906 to house the vast new following acquired during the club's second League championship victory. At its peak it housed 27,000 spectators, although this was steadily reduced by health and safety legislation.

Liverpool have had several great strikers. Ian St John was the first popular star of their modern era, his name one of the first great chants to emerge from the Kop. Around the same time Roger Hunt was becoming the club's record goalscorer, reaching 100 goals for the club in only 144 games, although his eventual tally of 201 would later be surpassed by Ian **Rush**. Keegan, Dalglish and latterly Michael **Owen** have kept up the tradition of fine, and occasionally home-nurtured, forward talent.

The enduring image of Liverpool's most successful period is probably the European triumphs. The European Cup came to Anfield four times in the space of seven years, and the finals remain the highlights of the club's history: a 3–1 win in Rome against Borussia Mönchengladbach in 1977; a 1–0 win against Bruges at Wembley the year after, with Kenny Dalglish scoring a coolly taken winner;

the 1–0 win against Real Madrid in Paris in 1981; and the extraordinary penalty shoot-out against Roma on their home pitch in 1984, when Bruce Grobbelaar pulled silly faces in goal and did his 'spaghetti legs' routine as Roma's penalty-takers lost their nerve.

The following year Liverpool would be back to defend their trophy in the Final, this time in the Heysel Stadium in Brussels against Juventus. The deaths in the crowd that evening of the **Heysel disaster** led to a five-year European ban for English clubs, extended to six for Liverpool. During that period the club would also endure the **Hillsborough disaster** in 1989, a further blow that traumatized not just manager Kenny Dalglish, who left the club in 1991, but the city itself.

Dalglish's departure brought Graeme Souness back to the club as manager. It was an unhappy period. Souness signed a lot of players and sold a lot amid a general feeling of transition and unrest; but the only trophy was an FA Cup win in 1992. After three years Souness was replaced by Roy Evans, who created a stylish but ineffectual Liverpool team, his reign coinciding with the rise of the 'Spice Boys': a prominent coterie of young players, among them Steve McManaman, Robbie Fowler and David James, who seemed to be more interested in foppish off-field activities than in returning the club to the prominence of previous eras. Evans was joined in joint managership by Gérard Houllier in 1998 and replaced altogether by the Frenchman a year later.

Six years of steady progress brought a treble of FA Cup, League Cup and UEFA Cup in 2001, and saw the emergence of players such as Owen and Steven Gerrard, before Houllier's departure in 2004. A direct style of play, a series of unsuccessful signings and visible relief at reaching the qualifying stages of the Champions' League proved to be not enough at a club where unparalleled successes have created almost unmatchable expectations.

Subsequently success has come in an unexpected rush. Liverpool won the Champions' League in 2005, under the guidance of Houllier's successor, Rafael Benitez, and with a team made up largely of players signed by the Frenchman. Surprise winners of the competition, not least because they had to come back from 3–0 down at half-time to beat Milan on penalties, Liverpool were allowed to defend the trophy the following season although they had finished outside the qualifying positions, in fifth place, in the Premier League. Only time will tell whether a fifth European Cup can usher in another period of sustained success, but the team won another trophy in 2006, beating West Ham on penalties in the FA Cup Final.

Livingston

Despite only playing their first league fixture on 11 November 1995, Livingston seem to have lived a lifetime in the ten years since. Indeed, with a current financial outlook that would kindly be described as bleak, any lengthy extension to that meagre existence is far from assured. Along the way, there has been promotion through the leagues, a third-place finish, a Cup victory, European football and boardroom intrigue.

In 1974, Ferranti Thistle, an Edinburgh works team, decided to switch to the Meadowbank athletics stadium and were admitted to the Scottish League under the name of Meadowbank Thistle. Despite a hardcore support of only a few hundred, the club went close to promotion to the Scottish Premier League in 1987–88, finishing four points behind Division 1 champions Hamilton, but they had dropped back down into the lower leagues within five years. In the early 1990s, chairman Bill Hunter launched plans to move the club ten miles west of Edinburgh, to the new town of Livingston, where there was a burgeoning community that he felt would embrace a professional football team.

From that point to Livingston's opening fixture in 1995–96 the bid to relocate proceeded to a backdrop of supporter unrest. Hunter was advised by police to stay away from home fixtures as abusive chants rang round the Meadowbank grandstand, and a mine-field of administrative and funding issues was negotiated before the club changed its name and moved to the Almondvale Stadium in Livingston, built by the local council. Some Meadowbank supporters, meanwhile, switched to following a local non-League club, Edinburgh City.

Livingston attracted a growing local interest as they progressed gradually up the leagues under Ray Stewart initially and then the experienced duo of Jim Leishman and Davie Hay. Promoted to the Scottish Premier League in 2000–01, the next year saw Livingston attain the incredible achievement of third place and a subsequent short foray into Europe. The years since have shown a gradual decline both on the pitch and in the club's financial footing, with the highly notable exception of a League Cup Final victory over Hibernian in 2003–04. Davie Hay, by now sole manager, was replaced with his assistant Allan Preston just three months later by an Irish consortium that bought the ailing club in controversial circumstances.

Preston would last just a matter of months himself before being replaced by former Rangers captain Richard Gough. New manager Paul Lambert, who took over in the summer of 2005, was unable to keep the nation's newest club in the top division from which they were relegated with just 18 points in 2005–06. Off the field, the owners face a demanding task just to keep Livingston in existence as Almondvale sees a decreasing number of locals willing on the team they welcomed to their city just 11 years ago.

Nat Lofthouse

One of the great forwards of his era, Nat Lofthouse spent his entire playing career in the employ of his home town team, contributing more to the image and fortunes of Bolton Wanderers than anyone else to emerge from the club. Remembered as an exemplar of a physical, barging football that would exceed the game's rules if played today, Lofthouse was possessed of more than just a talented shoulder. Direct but not without style, his fast attacking achieved a club record 255 goals from 452 League matches – while 33 England caps saw him take what was then a record-equalling 30 goals for his country.

Signed by Bolton while still a school-boy, Lofty made his debut in 1941 aged only 15. He scored twice on his first appearance (a 5–1 drubbing of neigh-bours Bury) and sustained a prolific goal rate over two decades. Netting in every round of the 1952–53 FA Cup (though losing to Blackpool in the final), Loft-house was Division 1's leading scorer in 1955–56. He struck 12 goals in the first nine games of the following season, and in 1958 captained Wanderers to FA Cup victory over Manchester United. Although he bagged both of the Final's goals, his second – for which he charged United goalkeeper Harry Gregg, and with him the ball, past the line – remains a bone of contention between the two teams half a century on.

Recognized at international level in 1950, through his endeavours for England Lofthouse had, within two years, earned himself a heroic nickname. In the course of bagging the winner in a 3–2 victory over Austria, he ran half the length of the pitch, shucking defenders and eventually colliding with the keeper with such vigour that he knocked himself out. For his courage and concussion, he was dubbed 'The Lion of Vienna' – a sobriquet that lives on in the furry form of Wanderers' present-day mascot, Lofty the Lion.

After failing to recover from a severe ankle injury, Lofthouse retired from playing in 1961. He went on to serve Bolton as coach, then manager (on three separate occasions: 1968 to 1970, 1971 and 1985) but – famously mild-mannered – felt disinclined towards leadership, preferring his eventual ambassadorial role of club president.

Along with Tom **Finney** and Fulham's Johnny Haynes, Lofthouse can be numbered among the select group of players who, through remaining so loyal to one team that they become emblematic of it, attain a far broader reputation.

long-ball game

Wing Commander Charles Reep has been called many things. Journalist Brian Glanville once described him as a member of a 'band of believers and acolytes', the archangel of 'a fanatical credo, a pseudo-religion', wedded to the ideas of Football Association coaching director Charles Hughes. After his death in 2002 the *Journal of Sports Sciences* settled for recording that Reep was the first 'professional performance analyst of football'. His detailed shorthand notes provided a comprehensive set of match data and featured such future classic soundbites as 'over 80 per cent of all goals result from moves of three passes

or less' and '60 per cent of all goalscoring moves begin 35 yards from an opponent's goal'.

Reep trained as an accountant before joining the RAF. After the war he would record the exact time he first implemented his notational system at a professional football match – 3.50pm on 18 March 1950. Three years later the national team suffered the greatest shock in its history, losing 6–3 to an overwhelmingly superior Hungarian side at Wembley. Reep shared the mood of national humiliation, but not the general prognosis that traditional English methods were outdated. Almost 30 years later he published an article in the *Times* entitled 'The Great Magyar Myth Exploded', in which he claimed to have 'all the relevant facts and figures' necessary to demystify the Hungarian team's apparent complete technical superiority. The urge to debunk footballing complexities was a force behind much of Reep's work. Among his published articles are the jaunty 'This Pattern-Weaving Talk Is All Bunk!' (1961), the po-faced 'Skill And Chance In Association Football' (1968) and the downright aggrieved 'Are We Getting Too Clever?' (1962).

Shortly after the Hungarian demolition, Reep met Wolves manager Stan **Cullis**. Cullis wanted his help in devising a style of play that would borrow from the Magyars while reaffirming the 'wholly English' principles of 'direct passing'. The Cullis/Reep methodology met with immediate success as Wolves defeated Hungarian champions Honvéd 3–2 at Molineux in December 1954 and went on to win the League title twice during the 1950s.

However, with the advent of the flair-friendly 1960s, and against a background of World and European Cup triumphs, there seemed little demand for a statistically robust analysis of why George **Best** really ought to stop holding on to the ball and ideally get his hair cut too.

It would take ten years of World Cup humiliation for English football to turn to Charles Reep again. Sensing a sea change in tactical thinking, Reep contacted Watford manager Graham **Taylor** in 1980. Before long the ex-Wing Commander was providing match-by-match performance analysis as Taylor's no-nonsense Hornets marched towards the top of Division 1. Utterly swayed by Reep's theories, Taylor would remark after England's World Cup exit in 1982 that 'possession and patience are myths. Goals come from mistakes.' Within six months Reep was working with Charles Hughes, soon to become Director of Coaching at the FA and the staunchest advocate of the direct-football mantra of the time. The findings of Reep's 30 years of notebook-scribbling and pocket-calculator-bashing permeate both Hughes's FA coaching manual (reprinted 11 times since 1980) and his more theoretical *Winning Formula* (1990).

Reep's influence began to dwindle with the approach of the Premiership and the increasingly cosmopolitan spread of domestic players and coaches. However, there would be a bizarre final call to arms for the octogenarian ex-Wing Commander. In 1993 he was flown to Oslo as guest of honour of the Norwegian FA for a World Cup qualifier against Graham Taylor's England. In a bizarre footballing tableau, Reep watched as Egil Olsen's Norway, schooled in his own long-ball theory, out-muscled an England XI marshalled by the man responsible for resurrecting his methods nearly 15 years earlier.

In some ways Charles Reep's influence at the highest level is as great as ever. Humiliating defeat at Euro 2000 led to perhaps the third great crisis of confidence in the recent history of domestic football. 'I don't think you can question our commitment – but you can question our ability to pass a football,' remarked head coach Kevin **Keegan**. And so English football did what it always does in times of crisis – go back to basics. 'The continental teams have conned us into believing the way we play has no chance. They have made us ashamed of our own style,' explained Graham Taylor during TV pundit duties at Euro 2000. Taylor knew what was coming. In time for qualification for the 2002 World Cup the England team would be led by a Swedish pragmatist, who would announce at a press conference three months before Charles Reep's death: 'if you look at the statistics in big club games or internationals, more than 80 per cent of goals are scored with fewer than five passes.' Now who does that sound like?

Luton Town

Formed by the local council in 1885, Luton had three seasons in Division 2 at the turn of the century, but otherwise remained non-League until the creation of Division 3 in 1921. Five years after their formation, however, they had employed the the first professional player in the south of England, striker Frank Whitby being paid five shillings a week. The club soon gained the nickname of 'The Hatters' after the town's hat industry. The Hatters became nearly-men until promotion thanks to Joe Payne's 55 goals in 1936–37. The season before, Payne scored ten goals in Luton's 12–0 win over Bristol Rovers, in the reserve centre-half's first game up front. Luton later converted Malcolm Macdonald from defender to prolific striker, while 1960s goalkeeper Tony Read also enjoyed a season as a forward.

By 1955–56, Luton were in Division 1. The club's only FA Cup Final came in

1959, a 2–1 defeat to Nottingham Forest. That season, player-manager Syd Owen became the only Luton man to win Footballer of the Year, but he was also 37, highlighting an ageing side. By 1965–66, Luton were in Division 4. Nine years later, they were back in Division 1, albeit for one season. In between, Graham French gave a new definition to 'mercurial winger' when he served two years in prison over a shooting outside a pub. Returning straight to the first team on his release in 1972, he was never the same player. The club were managed for part of this period by Alec Stock, the inspiration for Ron Manager. Stock, often in ill-health after having been hit in the back by a bazooka shell during the Second World War, summed up his attitude as 'Train, play, laugh and never let those three mix.'

David Pleat, an injury-prone winger as a Luton player, guided the club to Division 1 by blooding youngsters such as Brian Stein and Ricky Hill. Both played for England and, in 1985, England's strike force in a 2–0 defeat against France was Stein and Luton glamour boy Paul Walsh. After Pleat, Luton lost managers for the oddest reasons. John Moore got a record finish in Division 1 of 7th in his sole season, but didn't like the attention. Ray Harford: won the Littlewoods Cup against Arsenal in 1988, sacked for not smiling enough. Jim Ryan: the last manager to keep the Hatters up, fired for being rude to the chairman's wife.

That win over Arsenal had every cliché: Luton strolling into a 2–0 lead, pegged back to 2–2, young second-choice keeper Andy Dibble rounds off fine stops by saving a penalty, and Stein gets the winner in the final minute. But Arsenal were most neutrals' favourites thanks to Luton's plastic pitch and the ban on away fans at Kenilworth, imposed by chariman David Evans, who, despite being an arch Thatcherite MP, at least spent a lot of money on the team.

Relegated in the final season of the old Division 1, Luton's record signing Lars Elstrup threatened in pre-season to retire unless he was allowed to go home to Denmark. Odense thus got him for just £250,000. Two years later, Elstrup changed his name to Darando after joining the Wild Goose cult and was arrested for flashing in a town centre.

By 2001–02, Luton were back in the basement, getting promoted under Joe Kinnear. At the end of the following season, Kinnear was sacked by new chairman John Gurney. During his six weeks in charge, Gurney threatened to change the name of the club to London Luton FC and build a Formula One race-track around a new stadium, and replaced Kinnear with Mike Newell in a dubious Manager Idol vote. Having guided the team to the League 1 championship in 2004–05, however, Newell is the club's most popular manager in years.

Macclesfield Town

Macclesfield Town were relegated for the first time ever as recently as 1998–99. The season began with a home defeat to Kevin **Keegan**'s Fulham, the club's first loss at their Moss Rose ground in nearly two years; they went on to finish bottom of League Division 2. It was the first setback after a decade of success unparalleled in Macclesfield's history.

'The Silkmen' – nicknamed from the weaving industry that was the town's main employer – began 1997–98 as the Football League's newest members having just won the Conference. Heavily tipped to go straight back down, they were to be unbeaten in the first 23 matches, of which 19 were won. They finished second, with no home defeats and derbies against Manchester City to look forward to (both were lost, the match at Maine Road watched by over 31,000).

The architect of the club's rise was former Northern Ireland international Sammy McIlroy, who had taken over in 1993 after Macclesfield just avoided relegation from the Conference, to which they had been promoted from the Northern Premier League six years earlier. McIlroy had an immediate impact, taking the club to the championship in his first season but Moss Rose, their home since 1891, failed to meet the League's grounds criteria. They followed this up with a fourth-place finish and 3–1 Wembley win over neighbouring Northwich in the FA Trophy final. The following year the Silkmen again won the Conference and were allowed to replace Hereford in the Football League.

A football club was formed in the South Cheshire town in 1874. They went bankrupt in 1897 but a local amateur team, Hallefield, adopted the name 'Macclesfield' and joined the Manchester & District League in 1900, regularly finishing above Newton Heath, who went on to become Manchester United. After the First World War, the club joined the Cheshire League, remaining there until 1968, when they entered, and immediately won, the Northern Premier League.

Macclesfield appeared on *Match of the Day* the previous year, losing controversially to Fulham in the FA Cup third round, a dubious penalty helping the home side to win 4–2. The 7,002 who saw Spennymoor United beaten in the previous round is still Moss Rose's record attendance. Macclesfield retained the NPL title and then won the first-ever FA Trophy in 1970. The club struggled for most of the decade, however, and even finished bottom of the NPL in 1978–79, at a time when there was no automatic relegation into lower leagues. After steady improvement through the 1980s, the Silkmen went up from the Northern Premier League in 1987 on the back of a 22-match unbeaten run.

Since Sammy McIlroy's departure in 2000 the club has had five managers. The most recent, Brian Horton, oversaw a run of four wins in their final seven games that saved Macclesfield from a return to the Conference at the end of 2003–04 and took them into the play-offs the following year.

Dave Mackay

There is a famous photograph of Dave Mackay, chosen to represent him when he was inducted into the Scottish Football Hall of Fame, snarling as he grabs the collar of Billy **Bremner**, who has his arms out wide in supplication. Mackay says he dislikes the picture as it makes him look like a bully although he was never sent off in his career. The back-

ground to the incident, in a Spurs v Leeds match in 1966, provides some mitigation: Bremner had aimed a kick at the left leg that Mackay had broken twice in the preceding three years.

'He would storm into things with his bloody chest out and that Scottish brawn,' said Spurs manager Bill **Nicholson**, but although ferociously competitive, Dave Mackay was equally valued for his passing ability and, especially in his early days, a flair for scoring important goals. He began with his local club Hearts in 1952 and helped turn them into one of the strongest teams in Scotland: champions in 1958, plus winners of the Scottish Cup and two League Cups over a five-year period.

Moving on to Spurs at the end of the decade, Mackay formed a strong half-back partnership with Danny **Blanchflower** in the side that won the Double in 1961 and the FA Cup again the following year; the first of his leg breaks meant that he missed the European Cup Winners' Cup Final of 1963. Mackay won 22 Scotland caps but they were spread over nine years after his international debut in 1957 – a result, it is said, of Scottish selectors' bias against the 'Anglos' who tended to carry the can for defeats.

Within a year of captaining Spurs to another FA Cup Final victory in 1967, he moved down to Division 2 with Derby County. Their manager Brian **Clough**, at 33 a few months younger than his new captain, would rate Mackay as his best-ever signing. Derby won promotion in 1969, Mackay sharing the Footballer of the Year Award with another veteran, Tony Book of Manchester City.

On retiring in 1971 Mackay had brief spells in management at Swindon and Nottingham Forest before unexpectely returning to Derby as Clough's replacement. Champions in 1972, the club were now in disarray with supporter protests and players threatening strike action over the manager's departure, which was blamed on the board. Derby didn't win a match in Mackay's first four months in charge, during which the BBC (Bring Back Clough) campaign was in full swing. To general surprise, they took the title again in his second full season, 1974–75.

However, with striker Francis Lee the only regular player brought in by Mackay, the spectre of the former manager hung over his achievement; he resigned from Derby in 1976 after a tabloid had claimed his sacking was imminent. After a year at Walsall, Mackay spent nine lucrative years coaching in the Middle East before returning to manage Doncaster Rovers in 1987, after which he had a short spell at Birmingham City before retiring in 1991.

magazines

Football magazines are almost as old as the game itself. *The Goal*, 'the Chronicle of Football', covered the 1873–74 season before folding, while the authoritative *Athletic News* was almost the unofficial mouthpiece of the FA in the late Victorian era. But it was player-turned-journalist Charles Buchan who first came up with something like the modern-day football magazine in 1951. As more or less the only source for serious writing on the game, *Charles Buchan's Football Monthly* enjoyed huge sales in the early 1950s, with well over 100,000 readers each month absorbing lengthy articles on the championship race, tantalizing information on far-off wizards like the 'Magic Magyars', and the innovation of full-page colour photographs of star players.

By the 1960s, it had competition: *Jimmy Hill's Football Weekly*, a similar proposition but, as the name suggests, weekly and – as the name also suggests – horribly earnest and joyless. The more popular *Goal*, launched in 1968, was a fairly staid but very successful mix of news, opinion and interview, boasting 'Bobby Charlton's Diary' (a football diary that is, rather than pages of agonized self-analysis and ramblings about girls), the immensely complicated 'Jack Potts' Pools Guide' and, in a nod to feminism, 'The Girl Behind The Man': glamorous at-home shots of players' miniskirted wives, plus intriguing background information ('Valerie keeps busy when Ron is away by doing embroidery'). For the adult fan who took his football perhaps too seriously there was the fact-drenched *Soccer Star* and the *Football League Review*.

For the football-obsessed boys of the 1970s and 1980s, *Shoot!* (which began in 1969 and eventually absorbed its stablemate *Goal*) was the new bible, a snappier, shinier affair packed with features like 'League Ladders' (move cut-out paper tabs representing various teams up and down a bit of cardboard with slots in it), 'You Are The Ref' ('The ball bounces down off the underside of a pigeon and into the goal – what do you give?'), blatantly ghost-written 'celebrity' columns and, best of all, the same perversely trivial Q&A sessions long endured by pop stars: a selection of memorable 'Miscellaneous Dislikes' would include 'arrogance and dancing' (Frank Barlow, Sheffield United – not a John Travolta fan), Joe Corrigan's nemesis, 'women who smoke', and the very specific *bêtes noires* of Bristol City's Keith Fear – 'dirty hands, people who know very little but talk a lot, *Mr & Mrs* TV show'. The doyen of football magazines until the 1990s, *Shoot!* was rivalled only by *Match*, another glossy weekly which seemed to have been founded on the principle that *Shoot!* was a little too in-depth and text-heavy.

The football boom of the 1990s

produced a flurry of new titles, including quasi-fanzines like *The Onion Bag*, as well as a slew of expensive glossies. The revamped *Goal* was a non-starter, while *Total Football*, the BBC's *Match of the Day* magazine and the irreverent, teen-focused weekly *90 Minutes* lasted longer but petered out amid general lack of interest. The only real success story was *FourFourTwo*, a lavish and self-consciously laddish monthly (its founding editor had become interested in football during the 1990 World Cup – 'I said to myself, "Hey, this lager louts' game is fun!"') just intelligent enough to appeal to teenagers and students, but sufficiently bland to ensure ongoing cooperation from Premiership clubs and sportswear firms. The great survivor of the market is *World Soccer*, which dates back to the days of Charles Buchan and still satisfies those of a more internationalist bent.

For most British men of a certain age, however, nothing will ever top *Roy of the Rovers*. Set in a make-believe football world that was simultaneously sanitized (sex, booze and bad language were out) and absurdly dramatic (players found it difficult to leave Britain without being kidnapped or having their plane hijacked; managers thought nothing of hiring goons to cripple the opposition centre-forward; star signings would routinely discover disgruntled benchwarmers cutting the brake cables on their car), the comic bore little relation to life, but its alternative reality provided football with some enduring clichés – 'real Roy Of The Rovers stuff' – as well as a host of immortal characters like Mighty Mouse the 25-stone winger, Colin-Hendry-a-like Highlander Hot Shot Hamish, and mountainous 'Hard Man' Johnny Dexter. Even the rotation of the same 'Football Funnies' over a 30-year period (boy in hat and rosette sits in front of giant matchstick – Dad: 'What are you doing,

son?' Boy: 'I'm watching the big match') could not dim its magic.

managers

In the sport's earliest days, football managers rarely – if ever – concerned themselves with what happened on the pitch. Tactics and training were of little consequence, and many wouldn't have had the time for such things anyway. Most of those first League clubs had their origins in cricket, and all followed the organizational template of the summer game. Secretary-managers were voted in by committee, kept their head down, did what they were told and stayed in the job for years, busy balancing accounts and totalling up gate receipts.

Things started to change after William Sudell was appointed manager of Preston North End. Sudell enthusiastically filched players and tactics from Scotland and took a blackboard into changing rooms to explain systems. Sudell's reward for the Invincibles' 1889 Double win was a stint as League treasurer (he was later sacked and imprisoned in 1895, caught siphoning off funds from his struggling mill employers to pay his PNE players).

It was a time for solid, stout types: Jack Addenbrooke's 30 seasons at Wolves (1885–1922) is still a record, just pipping John Nicholson at Sheffield United with 29 (1899–1932). Not that there was any money in it – the more ambitious headed overseas to try their luck in the burgeoning European leagues; Willy Garbutt enjoyed some success at Genoa in 1912, all the while complaining it was impossible to make a living in England. Shortly afterwards, Fred Pentland introduced the wonders of 'pass and move' to anglophile Basques at Athletic Bilbao; like Garbutt, he enjoyed a freedom to work exclusively with his players, without having to worry about committees or bill-paying.

The modern age of management began with Herbert **Chapman** at Arsenal. The first manager to become a symbol of his club, Chapman understood the value of good relations with the media and positioned himself as a buffer between his players and the boardroom. The old secretary-hybrid had pretty much died out by the beginning of the 1930s, although Everton didn't get around to appointing a manager until 1939 (when secretary Theo Kelly had his duties extended) and Fred Everiss managed to hang around at West Brom until 1948, having arrived at the Hawthorns in 1920.

The new breed advanced in time with the game's growing commercialism, becoming manager-coaches, responsible for team selection and transfers. Sir Matt **Busby** thrived in such an atmosphere, setting up **scouting** networks and building teams. Busby, along with Liverpool's Bill **Shankly**, became a public figure, an increasing point of focus; managers were fast becoming bigger personalities than their players. Malcolm **Allison** worked with Joe **Mercer** to great effect at Manchester City, while in north London the Bertie Mee–Don **Howe** partnership guided Arsenal to the 1971 Double. Like Bob **Paisley** after them, Mercer and Mee were modest men, echoes of the past, happy to let their partners hog the limelight. They appeared ever-more archaic in the face of the publicity-happy Allison and his sparring partner on ITV's World Cup panels, Brian **Clough**.

Together with Don **Revie** at Leeds, Clough developed Chapman's 'player's manager' model – encouraging a combative 'us and them' attitude that was anti other clubs (and managers), anti-media and, increasingly, anti their own

chairmen and directors. When the 1960s generation of footballers began to enter management, the likes of Terry **Venables**, George **Graham** and Ron Atkinson were just a few years older than their senior players. They cemented the player–manager relationship, reinforcing a canteen culture that protected their boys from the real world.

Sir Alex **Ferguson** is the bridge between two eras, his phenomenal success with Manchester United a product of, and flag-waver for, the new world of the Premier League. Ferguson married old-school sensibilities with a multinational playing staff, and was careful to distance himself from plc politics. His longevity (together with Dario Gradi at Crewe) is the exception to the rule: the high-pressure life of a modern manager has seen average 'life expectancy' in the job falling to just 18 months.

Arsène **Wenger**'s arrival at Highbury gave Ferguson something else to kick against, the urbane manner and international background of the Arsenal boss showing up the insular old ways of the English game as his entertaining side swept to victory. After 2003, Chelsea's newly acquired millions broke the two-club hegemony; the west Londoners' aggressive marketing practices apparently extending to the proposed branding of Portuguese manager José **Mourinho**. The bond between manager and player is now stronger than ever – Jack Addenbrooke would not approve.

Manchester City

According to the business seminar thinking that dominates so much of modern football, Manchester City are the sort of club that should no longer exist. By all survival-of-the-fittest logic, a team that is trophy-less since 1977 and shares a city with a global super-brand should have long since gone the way of eight-track cartridges. Yet, by drawing strength from their marginalized position, and recruiting amongst Mancunians with an antipathy towards United's corporate power, Manchester City have defied market logic and claimed an important place in the landscape of British football.

They began 123 years of life in south Manchester as West Gorton St Marks in 1880, becoming Manchester City, via Ardwick FC, in 1894. Though they managed their first FA Cup win a decade later, League football saw them start as they meant to go on, switching divisions regularly despite the efforts of early hero Billy **Meredith**, who was allowed to join neighbours United in 1906, having been one of 17 players suspended for receiving illegal payments. The move to their new home at Maine Road in 1923 after a fire at their Hyde Road ground did nothing to halt the inconsistency.

The 1930s would be the first great decade, bringing the FA Cup in 1934 and the League championship in 1937. They were top scorers in the following season – and got relegated, earning them the first of many entries in the annals of foot-balling comedy. The post-war period that began with City sharing their home with the bombed-out United would see more ups and downs. There would be another Cup success in 1956, whilst the 57–58 season saw them achieve the unique feat of scoring and conceding more than 100 goals.

The Bell/Lee/Summerbee era of the mid-1960s to the mid-1970s would be the club's most successful (see Joe **Mercer**) and account for most of its modern nostalgia business. The fans enjoyed a second League championship, two domestic cups, a European trophy and, of course, relegating United, at least in the popular memory if not in fact. Denis **Law**'s back-heeled goal that brought

City's 1–0 win at Old Trafford in April 1974 promoted a pitch invasion by home fans hoping to have the game abandoned – but other results meant that United would have gone down even if they had won the derby.

Unfortunately, chairman Peter Swales had plans for building on this success and making the club a major power – in other words, overtaking United. His obsession resulted in a disastrous period of wild overspending by 'character' managers, notably the returning Malcolm **Allison**, and after almost two decades of stability relegation came on the last day of the 82–83 season thanks to Luton's winning goal in the 86th minute.

The dismal 1980s did end on a high with an epochal 5–1 derby win in 1989, and consecutive top six finishes at the start of the 1990s under Peter Reid seemed to suggest better times ahead. However, a dip in form caused the ever-impatient Swales to sack Reid, finally triggering a major revolt by fans and an ugly struggle that saw former star Francis Lee, now a millionaire businessman, sweep to power on a wave of popular support.

It was a move Lee would regret. Debts spiralled out of control and a managerial tag-team (four bosses in five seasons after Reid) took City down to the third tier for the first time in their history in 1998. Despite the prodigious talents of Georgian midfielder Georgi Kinkladze, the fans' loyalty in adversity and brief hipness from the connection with celeb-rity fans the Gallagher brothers, City became football's easiest punchline. Lee's comment that if there were 'cups for cock-ups' then City's trophy cabinet would be full became the title of a book about the club's history.

With a new board in place City fought their way back to the Premiership under Joe Royle, but relegation in 2001 saw yet another managerial change. The arrival of Kevin **Keegan** (who departed in spring 2005) brought promotion, consolidation and even occasional derby wins, but the periods of chaotic inconsistency that many thought inevitable from such a meeting of minds ensured the fans didn't get too complacent. The move away from Moss Side to a strikingly modern new stadium in 2003 may have dented the gritty wrong-side-of-town image but their unpredictability seems harder to lose. However, after the nightmares of the 1990s, just to have come through their toughest tests and lived to tell the tale is cause enough for optimism.

Manchester United

From its earliest days a whiff of sulphur has hung, both literally and metaphorically, around Manchester United, making the red devil on the club crest a particularly fitting emblem. Founded in 1878 as Newton Heath by railway workers, the club's inaugural Football League match in 1892 was shrouded in steam from passing locomotives. A move to Bank Street in Clayton merely replaced steam with the diabolical stench from the 30 chimneys of the Albion Chemical Works and a pitch so boggy that a record 14–0 victory was declared void after complaints about its condition.

The 'Heathens' staved off bankruptcy in 1902, thanks to the tireless efforts of captain Harry Stafford, who recruited local brewer John Davies when he inadvertently bought Stafford's St Bernard dog at a fund-raising bazaar. The name Manchester United was adopted, chiefly to stop visiting teams from turning up at the old ground, and a new manager, Ernest Mangnall, appointed. Mangnall transformed the club's fortunes in 1906 after an impish coup, which secured (at a knockdown price) the pick of the players

who had been banned in perpetuity from playing for its more successful neighbour, Manchester City, after an illegal-payments scandal. One of these was the City captain, the 'Welsh Wizard' Billy **Meredith**. United promptly won the League championship in 1908 (the denuded City finishing third) and in 1911, as well as the FA Cup in 1909. This golden period ended when Mangnall left to manage City in 1912.

In 1909, two decisions were made which were fundamental for the history of football and for the future prosperity of Manchester United. Its players, dubbing themselves 'The Outcasts FC', refused to renounce their membership of the outlawed Players' Union, thereby securing its existence. Secondly, Chairman John Davies invested the then enormous sum of £60,000 in a new stadium. His choice of site, on the Trafford Park industrial estate, named after its aristocratic former owners, the De Traffords, was inspired. Though one side (in an echo of the club's roots) was flanked by a railway line, the other three were unencumbered, allowing for future stadium rebuilding and easy access.

The team failed to do justice to their magnificent surroundings at Old Trafford for the next 40 years. United dubiously avoided relegation in 1915 because of a match against Liverpool which had been fixed, but it was only a temporary reprieve. The 1920s and 1930s saw the club yo-yo between the top two divisions. In 1926, manager John Chapman was suspended by the FA 'for improper conduct', the details of which remain mysterious to this day. After 26 goals were conceded in the first five games of the 1930–31 season, the supporters' club organized a boycott of the home tie against Arsenal to little avail. United escaped a drop to Division 3 (North) in the final match of the 1933–34 season at

Millwall's Den and were welcomed home by a crowd of 3,000 delirious fans at Manchester's Central Station.

The Devils' second guardian angel, James Gibson, bought off the bailiffs, who at one point stood at the turnstiles to impound gate money, with a financial guarantee in 1932. After Luftwaffe bombs meant for the nearby Salford Docks (Manchester is, surprisingly, a port, hence the devil on the crest lurks under a ship) destroyed much of the ground in 1941, the club was run from the offices of Gibson's cold-storage business. Football did not return to Old Trafford until 1949, and a six-foot bush sprouted in the centre circle.

United's saviour was to be a 34-year-old, demobbed, ex-Scottish international and City player, Matt **Busby**, the manager who gave Old Trafford an international reputation for glamour and style. Busby managed three great United teams, winning the FA Cup in 1948 (while based at City's Maine Road) and the League title in 1952 with the first. His decision to defy FA recommendations and enter the newly formed European Cup with his second team, the 'Busby Babes', had unforeseen and far-reaching consequences.

The Babes, who swept to two consecutive League titles in 1956 and 1957, passed into legend when eight of them, including the incomparable 21-year-old wing-half Duncan Edwards, died when their plane crashed (see **Munich aircrash**). Busby recovered from his grave injuries to win two championships and an FA Cup, then the European Cup in 1968 with a team for ever associated with the trinity of George **Best**, Denis **Law** and Bobby **Charlton**, all three of whom won the European Footballer of the Year award. In 1965, United gave birth to the changeling of corporate hospitality at football, building 55 executive boxes into the new United Road stand.

Though Busby was a dignified figure, his respectable replacements struggled, while the less saintly have tended to do better. Wilf McGuinness went bald and Frank O'Farrell ended a promising managerial career attempting to deal with the wayward genius Best and build a new team. (Beset by internal strife, the club were relegated to Division 2 in 1973–74 under O'Farrell's successor, Tommy Docherty, who brought them back, revitalized, after one season.) The taciturn Dave Sexton was never forgiven for buying striker Garry Birtles, who scored just 11 goals in 58 League games after arriving from Nottingham Forest in 1980. Docherty and Ron Atkinson, flamboyant and outspoken, won FA Cups (in 1977, then 1983 and 1985 respectively) but not the League title, and United's continued failure, despite the obvious talents of players like Bryan **Robson**, became a long-running joke.

After a shaky start, with mostly disappointing League finishes offset by victories in the FA Cup in 1990, the European Cup Winners' Cup a year later and a League Cup in 1992, Alex **Ferguson** ended the '26-year wait' in 1993. The abrasive Scot went on to revive the Busby tradition by dominating the first decade of the Premiership (eight titles by 2004) and winning a historic treble in 1999 which included the Champions' League, his team built around the home-grown 'Fergie's Fledglings' and inspired (until 1997) by the demon king, Eric **Cantona**. Meanwhile the massive North Stand, which dominates the skyline, boosted Old Trafford's capacity still further, while ruining the pitch.

In the 1990s, as United became a PLC and its success and wealth grew, along with its support patently not all born in Manchester, so its domestic esteem has sunk, becoming a symbol of the evils of commercialism, encapsulated by the acronym 'ABU' ('Anyone But United').

By the summer of 2005 the club had

suffered an unexpected consequence of its own rampantly successful housekeeping: a stock market buy-out by the US financier Malcolm Glazer. United supporters, alarmed at Glazer's aggressive ticket price hikes and the burden of debt he has brought to the club, have vociferously resisted his ownership. Suddenly, and particularly after a trophy-less season in 2004–05, United's future looks uncertain.

Wilf Mannion

Wilf Mannion was an inside-forward gifted with such sublime skills that his England team-mate Tom **Finney** said, 'It was as if he had been sent down from heaven'. A brilliant dribbler and an incisive passer he also had a powerful shot and his record of 11 goals in his 26 internationals is testimony to his finishing ability. Scoring though was not what Mannion was about. His job, as he used to say, was to 'provide the bullets' for the centre-forwards – Micky Fenton at Middlesbrough, and Tommy **Lawton** for England.

The man nicknamed 'The Golden Boy' was born in South Bank on the outskirts of Middlesbrough a few weeks after the end of the First World War. He was signed by Boro from local side South Bank St Peter's in 1936 and made his League debut, aged 18, during his first season. It was a good team to play in, featuring as it did England left-back George Hardwick, Scotland skipper Bobby Baxter and the excellent Fenton in a line-up that was arguably the best the town ever had. The Second World War came just as Mannion was starting to establish himself as one of England's major talents. It robbed him of what would have been the peak years of his career and emotionally it may be that he never fully recovered from the effects of

military service. Unlike many other footballers Mannion turned down the offer of a place as an army physical training instructor and instead joined the Green Howards infantry regiment. He was evacuated from Dunkirk and fought in the Italian campaign. When he returned to Britain in 1946 he was so physically drained by his experiences that many who saw him believed he would never play again.

He did, brilliantly at times, notably for Great Britain against the Rest of the World at Hampden Park in 1948, but his post-war career was overshadowed by a bitter dispute with Middlesbrough. The draconian rules binding footballers to clubs, the maximum wage and the treatment of players as second-class citizens by the chairman and FA officials incensed him. In 1948–49, 40 years before Jean-Marc **Bosman**, Mannion staged a four-month solo strike in an attempt to force Middlesbrough to allow him to move to Oldham. In the end poverty forced him back to work and it wasn't until 1954, aged 36, that he was finally allowed to go to Hull City. The bitterness lingered and shamefully Middlesbrough denied the club's greatest-ever player a testimonial until the 1970s.

A feisty man with a strong sense of his own worth, Mannion was once asked what it had been like to play alongside the legendary Middlesbrough centre-forward George Camsell. Camsell had hit 325 goals in 418 League appearances for the Boro, 59 in the 1926–27 season alone. 'I'll tell you something about George,' he replied. 'He was ruddy useless. Couldn't trap a bag of cement.' He scored a lot of goals, the interviewer protested. 'Oh aye,' Mannion responded with a dismissive wave, 'he could score goals all right.' Such were the extravagant gifts of the Golden Boy that he regarded putting the ball into the net as a distinctly minor talent.

Mansfield Town

Sitting in the heart of a coal-mining and textile region and surrounded by the countryside of Sherwood Forest – hence the nickname 'The Stags' – Mansfield Town's history reflects that of the community in which it is based. The club can trace its origins back to 1861, when cotton entrepreneur H. J. Greenhalgh established a club for his employees utilizing land on his factory complex which became known as Field Mill. As the modern club plays on this same piece of land, Field Mill could lay claim to being one of the oldest football grounds in the world.

Mansfield Town evolved out of another local club, the Wesleyans, who had been formed in 1897. They moved to Field Mill in 1919 following a sharp piece of business, the previous tenants' lease having lapsed during the War. In 1929 the Stags travelled to Highbury for a fourth-round FA Cup tie, the first time the club had got so far in the competition. They lost 1–0, but the publicity generated by the team's performance helped secure election to the Football League at the seventh attempt in 1931.

Mansfield had a comfortable existence in the lower leagues and managed the odd Cup foray, including a record attendance of 24,500 against Nottingham Forest in 1953, but they did little to trouble the national press until 1964, when Stags players were among those involved in a fixed-odds betting scandal and trial. Five years later, Mansfield were in the FA Cup semi-final draw after a delayed quarter-final tie against Leicester. That match was lost 1–0 but the 3–0 victory in the previous round over West Ham ranks as one of the best results in the club's history.

The mid-1970s were the club's best era to date. In 1975 Dave Smith's team won the club's first championship, pipping Shrewsbury to the Division 4 title. Two years later, under Smith's successor, Peter Morris, Mansfield were promoted to Division 2 for the first time. The team slid straight back down, but contributed to one of the best televised matches of the season, a 3–3 draw with Tottenham on a rain-soaked pitch. The Stags had been denied victory at White Hart Lane in December by a missed penalty. In the return they held a 2–1 lead at half-time before Glenn **Hoddle** levelled from the spot. Mansfield were ahead again in the 85th minute with one of the great comedy goals – a visitors' attack floundered in the mud, the ball was punted downfield, Spurs keeper Barry Daines rushed out of his area but sliced his clearance horribly, allowing Dave Syrett to shoot into an empty net. In the final minute, as the sun shone for the first time all day, Hoddle curled in a free kick for 3–3.

Not until the arrival of Ian Greaves as manager in 1984 did the fortunes of the club improve again. At this time they also acquired the nickname of 'Scabs' from rivals in Yorkshire as the effects of the miners' strike hit the terraces. Promotion in 1986 was followed the next year by a Freight Rover Trophy success at Wembley, when goalkeeper Kevin Hitchcock saved penalties successively with his left and right foot. After the game Hitchcock attributed this to his size 10½ boots, later to become the title of Mansfield's first fanzine.

After a decline in the late 1980s and early 1990s the club was put up for sale and was bought for £1 in 1993 by Keith Haslam. By the end of the decade, Mansfield were in danger of folding as Haslam's attempts to secure a property deal on land around Field Mill faltered.

Thankfully, by 2001 the stadium's redevelopment was completed, with promotion following the next season. The Stags dropped straight back to the basement division but finished 2004 with a play-off final defeat on penalties. A few months later, manager Keith Curle departed in mysterious circumstances that became the subject of a court case.

mascots

Loathe them, hate them, or simply find them slightly annoying, mascots are currently a strongly entrenched feature of the match day experience in British football. Almost every professional club has a mascot, usually a furry-suited local 'character' dressed up as a figure related to the club's nickname or crest. Wolves have Wolfie the Wolf, Manchester United have Fred the Red and Arsenal have the Gunnersaurus, a dinosaur. In general, little attempt has been made to replicate the true behaviour of the animal being represented. A real stag, for example, would not have to readjust its head every time it took a penalty in a pre-match kick-in.

Mascots became particularly popular during the 1990s, part of the 'lively, family-orientated' atmosphere promoted at Premiership grounds and later in the Football League, a notion of marketing, brand promotion and selling small figurines to children, encouraged by the gaggle of marketers and product-floggers who litter the modern game.

Exactly how many millions of pounds have been lured into football by the presence of a sweating unemployed actor in an animal-suit has never been established. What is beyond doubt is that the unchoreographed antics of various off-message club mascots have become a part of the modern lore of the game. The profession appears to attract a particular kind of local exhibitionist. Cyril the Swan of Swansea City was fined £1,000 by the Welsh FA for bringing the game into disrepute after running on to the pitch to hug a goalscorer, the most famous instance of its new mascots' code of conduct being brought to bear. Hercules the Lion of Aston Villa was sacked from his job after making inappropriate advances towards Miss Aston Villa, while Wolfie of Wolverhampton and Bristol City's City Cat were involved in an on-pitch match day brawl.

The annual Mascot Grand National has been the subject of much back-slapping jollity. The race is run in costume over 100 metres and is also, for some reason, screened by Sky Television. During the 2003–04 season the *Guardian* ran a weekly column written by various club mascots, a showcase for various cats, dogs and snakes to talk about their strictly localized importance and exactly how good with children they really are.

Match of the Day

'A special welcome to those new viewers who have been won over by the World Cup – we hope you will go along and watch your local team as well as watching *Match of the Day*. And in response to your many requests, I will explain some of the more technical points of the game as we go along' – Kenneth Wolstenholme, introducing the first *Match of the Day* of the 1966–67 season: now sounding archaic to the point of comedy.

Ken's avuncular tone was probably justified, though, as it was only in the aftermath of the 1966 World Cup that watching football on TV became a part of British life; this was the first *Match of the Day* on BBC1 (televised football having been for the previous two seasons the province of new 'minority' channel

BBC2, and even then only once 2's controller David Attenborough had persuaded the League it wouldn't impact too badly on attendances as the viewing figures were so low), and the first to be watched by a substantial audience, many of whom would have been new to the muddy violence of the English Division 1.

It was a couple of years before the show settled into its groove. The advent of colour TV obviously made a huge difference, and in 1973 the BBC poached a new presenter from LWT, trailing the swoop in *Radio Times* as the 'Catch of the Year', such was their excitement. Out went smirking, gurgling David Coleman; in came Jimmy **Hill**. It was during Hill's tenure that *Match of the Day* became a kind of sporting *Blue Peter*: squeaky-clean, a little patronizing and horribly earnest, but such a national treasure that nobody gave a damn. Since *MOTD*, along with ITV's *The Big Match*, offered the *only* televised football of the English League season, it could hardly help but become the definitive football show, but objective scrutiny of the 1970s archive reveals something less thrilling than memory might suggest.

At the time, the sheer practical issues of installing cameras and cable at tatty British grounds meant that televised matches had to be chosen weeks in advance, making it impossible to follow the sides currently in form, or even to guarantee that the night's games would be entertaining – many times the nation would settle down to highlights of two 0–0 draws, Bob Wilson at his news desk informing us breezily that, elsewhere today, Manchester United and Spurs fought out a 6–5 thriller. Those who bristle at the garrulous likes of Hansen and Lawrenson should take a moment to recall how things used to be done: Jimmy Hill introducing the clips, talking us through slo-mo replays himself,

offering his unchallenged opinions, and pausing only for a self-congratulatory chuckle before moving on to the next game. In an era when most matches still weren't filmed at all, Hill became disliked for his omnipresence as well as his smugness – it must have seemed as though the game itself was his personal fiefdom.

Finally, Jimmy was put out to pasture in favour of the self-parodic smoothie Des Lynam, and later Gary **Lineker** (a shrewd choice, since neither a stint on a lamentable sports quiz nor a string of nauseating crisp adverts can undo an Englishman's love for the man who equalized against Germany in a World Cup semi-final). Sky Sports, of course, were already revolutionizing both the style and the sheer volume of football coverage in Britain, but *Match of the Day*'s formula remained unchanged – ultimately, on a Saturday night, even those with access to such digital riches want to watch a summary of the day's games, knowing they will have been, for the most part, far too boring for any neutral to endure their full 90 minutes. After ITV's theft of the rights to Premiership football highlights in 2001, and the untrammelled misery of three seasons of their own crass effort *The Premiership*, the return of *Match of the Day* in the 2004–05 season (albeit now positively foaming with its own sense of importance, and the extent to which it had become an institution) was very welcome.

Sir Stanley Matthews

'The Wizard of Dribble', 'The King of Soccer', 'The Maestro', 'The First Gentleman of Football', '*Der Zauberer*' (German for 'The Magician'), Stanley Matthews remains arguably the most entertaining attacking player the British game has seen. The first footballer to be knighted for his performances on the field, the oldest player to have played in Division 1, and a paragon of the Corinthian ideals of humility, good sportsmanship and physical prowess, Matthews's 30-year playing career encompassed 698 League appearances, the Player of the Year Award in 1948 and again 15 years later, a European Footballer of the Year Award and an International Fair Play Committee Award for Services to Sport, recognition of the fact that as a player he was never once booked or sent off.

Born in the Potteries in 1915, the son of a boxer known as 'The Fighting Barber of Hanley', Matthews made his professional debut for Stoke City in 1932. He played for England two years later aged 19, the first of 54 caps over 23 years, and quickly established himself as the star attraction of an exciting young pre-war Stoke side – so much so that when he requested a transfer in 1938, after falling out with the club, an estimated 4,000 people assembled at the Kings Hall in Stoke to demand that his services be retained at any cost.

A slight, wiry figure stationed close to the touchline at outside-right, Matthews developed a unique attacking style. Even opponents familiar with his repertoire of tricks and feints struggled to cope with his explosive speed – often from a distinctive standing start – and his legendary body swerve, described by Matthews himself as something that 'just comes out under pressure'. As Danny **Blanchflower** later remarked: 'you usually knew how he was going to beat you, but you couldn't do anything about it'. Matthews was renowned for his crossing ability – his talent lay in creating chances for others.

He did, however, score a hat-trick in a 5–4 victory against Czechoslovakia for a depleted ten-man England team after moving to inside-right at White Hart Lane in 1937 – an evening match played in the days before floodlights, the second half of which took place in almost total darkness. All three of Matthews's goals that night were scored with his left foot, the last of them – the winner – a shot that emerged out of the gloom to strike a surprised Czech defender on the shoulder and deflect into the net.

In May 1938 Matthews was a member of the England side cajoled into giving the Nazi salute before playing the German national team in Berlin. Beneath a giant portrait of Hitler, Matthews went on to give one of his finest displays, tormenting his marker Muenzenberg as England beat their hosts 6–3. During the war Matthews played a few times as a guest for Blackpool, where he and his wife Jean had opened a small hotel and, having failed to regain his place in the Stoke side after injury, he signed for Blackpool in 1947 for £11,500. He was the inaugural Footballer of the Year at the end of his first season, going on to lead Blackpool to defeat in the FA Cup Finals of 1948 and, 1951, and finally victory in 1953, the only major team honour of his career.

Matthews moved back to Stoke in 1961, helping them gain promotion to Division 1 two years later, before receiving a knighthood in 1965 while still a player, just a few days short of his 50th birthday. On his retirement at the end of the season he became manager of Port Vale, remaining in the job for three years before resigning after becoming embroiled in a minor scandal over illegal payments to young players.

Matthews stood out as the most exciting player in domestic football over two decades during which the game developed into a mass spectator sport. He was the major draw for what are still club record crowds of 51,380 at the Victoria Ground in 1937 and 38,098 at

Bloomfield Road in 1955, and played in front of the record attendance for an England international, 149,415 against Scotland at Hampden Park in 1937.

Legends have tended to spring up around him: the Matthews Final of 1953; the Matthews personality, a kind of pre-modern courtly sporting chevalier; his fearsome reputation as a ball-player, described as giving him the beating of a full-back before he'd even taken to the field; and his fabled ascetic physical conditioning, incorporating solo training runs on Blackpool beach, a range of customized breathing exercises learned from his boxing father, and a rigidly teetotal lifestyle. Indeed, so weighty is Matthews's reputation that discussions of his playing career often remark upon the significant absences from his achieve-ments: the solitary FA Cup winner's medal; 54 England caps – compared to 76 appearances by his contemporary and positional rival Tom **Finney**; and accusa-tions made throughout his career of being too maverick a talent, too slow to release the ball, and not scoring enough goals (just 71 in the League over 24 seasons).

However, his legend survives any such attempts at revisionism. When he died in February 2000 at the age of 85, Matthews was described by England captain Alan **Shearer** as being 'synony-mous with English football' – a solecism perhaps, but an insight nonetheless into the qualities that Matthews's name has become emblematic of: craftsmanship, robust humility, and a single-mindedness that borders on the crankish; all qualities essential to the blend of modesty, dedi-cation and longevity that constitute an English ideal of sporting excellence.

mavericks

It's long been a truism that League foot-ball in the 1970s was for the most part a grim game, enlivened largely by the unashamed flair of the mavericks, a group of players whose vision of how football should be played – and what constituted an acceptable social life – stood directly at odds with the English football establishment, in the grand tradition of George **Best**, the modern game's first rebel. There's some truth in it, and there's little doubt that players like Rodney Marsh, Frank Worthington, Peter Osgood, Stan Bowles and Charlie George (and, among several in the lower divisions, Reading's legendary Robin Friday, who died before he was 40 after a professional career lasting just four years) were manna to those grown tired of the defensive game, its thuggery and its sheer boredom.

In some cases, they were a little more cultured than their counterparts: who, for instance, would suspect that the seem-ingly blockheaded Marsh, sacked by Sky in 2005 for joking about the tsunami disaster, originally dreamed of being a fine artist ('I started out trying to paint like Matisse, Gauguin, Dali . . . I was an artist and I still am')? But in the main, their appeal was ideal for the *Clockwork Orange* generation: long locks, attention-seeking sideburns and fancy-dan tomfoolery on the ball, but a school tough's hostility to authority, an unpreten-tious and usually insatiable passion for birds, booze and betting, and an arro-gance which (when it came off) was auth-entically entertaining.

The mavericks' main bone of conten-tion is that they were rarely picked for the England side by the managers of the time. But it has to be said that few of these stellar talents ever excelled when given the chance at international level. Peter Osgood, England's in-form striker at the time of the 1970 World Cup, is right to moan at being excluded in Mexico in favour of the less effective Jeff

Astle (as he says, he would never have missed Astle's chance against Brazil); Charlie George surely deserved more than 60 minutes in a friendly; and anyone but an England manager could have found room in a humdrum midfield for the gifted Alan Hudson (two caps in 1975).

But Marsh was, for a while at least, an England regular, during which time the national side hardly covered itself in glory, and Tony Currie, too, earned caps well into double figures without ever doing anything particularly memorable in an England shirt. It's impossible to know whether this was indeed the result of overbearing and overly defensive tactics, or whether – whisper it – these players simply weren't as good as Gunther Netzer, Gianni Rivera, Michel Platini, or any of their other foreign peers, all of whom managed to light up international competition pretty effortlessly.

And how much did the mavericks actually achieve? Best, of course, won almost every gong going as a club player, including European Footballer of the Year. Surely it can't just have been near-sightedness that prevented this award ever finding its way to Frank Worthington? Frank was courted by Liverpool in the early 1970s, a move which collapsed when he failed a medical – whether his eminently watchable skills would have added welcome flash to the side, or just slowed down the sweeping passing moves which brought them their success is highly debatable. Rodney Marsh, signed in 1972 by Malcolm **Allison** to pep up a Manchester City side on the verge of glory, instead famously disrupted the rhythm of the team and arguably cost them the title. After missing Chelsea's 1970 Cup victory through injury, Hudson won nothing in the rest of his career.

Hearing the after-dinner stories once

again – the birds, the booze, the missed training, Worthington getting out of his broken-down car in the middle of the street, and walking off despite the ensuing traffic snarl-up because 'it's the club's responsibility to sort these things out' – it's easy to suspect that one or two of these players were not, in fact, precursors to Eric **Cantona**, but the spiritual fathers of self-regarding wasters like Kieron Dyer.

maximum wage

The maximum wage was an absolute and universally observed cap on what professional footballers could earn from the game. It was endorsed by the Ministry of Labour and acted as a ceiling on salaries and bonuses across every division of the Football League in England and Wales for over 60 years.

Following the legalization of profession-alism in 1888 there was rapid and uneven inflation of players' salaries in the English leagues. The first professional footballers were paid around £2 a week in wages and bonuses. This rose to £7 to £10 a week for the Liverpool players who won the Division 1 championship in 1900–01. However, the maximum wage was introduced in 1901–02, with the initial figure set at £4 a week. This rapidly became the standard for an experienced first-team player's wages in the top division, with salaries below this graded according to seniority.

The wage cap was reviewed in 1920 and a complicated sliding scale intro-duced, restricting initial wages to £5 a week rising annually by £1 to a maximum of £9. Unfortunately for the budding Ferrari owners and mock Tudor mansion dwellers of the day, this maximum was then reduced over the next few years: to £8 and £6 during the close season just two years later. Within this clubs were allowed to increase slightly the wages of players elevated to the first team and reduce those dropped from it, creating a standard system of performance-based pay. Throughout all of this there was no maximum wage in Scotland, although with only the largest clubs able to pay their players well there was little need for one.

After the Second World War, with the PFA in more militant mood, the maximum wage was raised steadily, reaching £15 in 1951 and £20 in 1958. During this period some high-profile English players went to play in Italy to take advantage of the greater wealth on offer. Jimmy **Greaves** endured an unhappy spell at Milan, John **Charles** won three Italian championships at Juventus after signing for a British record £65,000 in 1957, and England forward Gerry Hitchens spent eight years in Serie A with four different clubs.

Friction between the players' union, the Football League and the Government came to a head in the early 1960s under the PFA chairmanship of the charismatic Jimmy **Hill**. After a series of heated meetings involving Hill and League secretary Alan Hardaker, a players' strike planned for the following Saturday was called off in return for immediate abolition of the wage cap. In 1961 the maximum wage for footballers was £20 a week. After Hill's victory on behalf of the PFA, Fulham's England captain, Johnny Haynes, became overnight the first £100 a week player.

Some clubs continued to operate an unofficial ceiling on earnings even after the end of the maximum wage. Manchester United kept a strict control over salaries into the 1970s, while Arsenal maintained a formal wage structure even into the first few seasons of the Premiership, although this has now been effectively abandoned in the face of spiralling revenue and the need to keep star players. In the current climate of hyper-inflation – with players such as Roy **Keane** and Rio Ferdinand able to command wages of up to £90,000 a week – it seems fitting that the question of a maximum wage has again been raised.

A wage cap would offer a working solution to many of the game's most obvious problems: financial mismanagement, the alienating effect among supporters of following a multi-millionaire football team, and the increasing dominance of a small elite of wealthy clubs. In professional rugby league there is an agreement that no more than a certain percentage of a club's turnover can be spent on wages, with the salaries of individual players within this to be decided by the clubs themselves. Despite concern from many outside the game and the vast debts being accumulated by clubs throughout the divisions, British football has shown no inclination to introduce a similar protective measure.

In any case such a move would probably be in contravention of European labour laws, and would certainly be contrary to the general post-Thatcherite submission to market forces. There will never be a maximum wage in football again. For Premiership footballers the sky, or at least every last penny of the latest BSkyB broadcasting deal, remains the limit.

Joe Mercer

'I never wanted this bloody job in the first place'. So said Joe Mercer introducing his first team meeting as England caretaker manager after the departure of Sir Alf **Ramsey** in 1974. In fact, Mercer must have been delighted to be involved with the national side at the age of 60, but to have made a public display of the fact would have been contrary to his unassuming, genial personality. A natural optimist, free of the introspective gloominess which seems to afflict many managers, Mercer seemed to represent all that was decent in English football.

His managerial reputation rests on a brief but resoundingly successul period at Manchester City. Mercer's team was shaped by his assistant, Malcolm **Allison**, who developed an all-out attacking style that brought promotion in the duo's first season together in 1965–66 and the League title two years after that. They went on to win two domestic cups (a famous picture captured Mercer delightedly doffing his trilby to City fans at Wembley after they had beaten Leicester to win the FA Cup in 1969) and the European Cup Winners' Cup before Allison manoeuvred himself into the manager's seat. Unlike the much older Mercer, he was to prove crucially unable to take a detached view of the players' faults and strengths.

Born in Cheshire, the son of a footballing father, Joe Mercer had been a highly successful player, winning a championship as a spindly-legged wing-half with Everton in 1939 and the League and Cup following a switch to central defence with Arsenal after the war – he was voted Footballer of the Year at the age of 36 in 1950. However, prior to his arrival at Maine Road, he had experienced mixed managerial fortunes with Sheffield United and Aston Villa, taking both down from Division 1, though he did win the League Cup with the latter in 1961. The move from playing career to manager's office had hardly been seamless, with Mercer busying himself in his grocer's shop before the summons came from Sheffield United in 1955.

An astute bit of business by Jimmy **Hill** led to Mercer's appointment as general manager of Coventry City in 1971. He stayed there until his entertaining Indian summer with the England squad, where he gave opportunities to several flair players including Frank Worthington, Martin Dobson and Keith Weller. The partnership with Jimmy Hill was renewed on the BBC's 1974 World Cup panel, where he revealed a considerable, though by no means unique, talent for mispronouncing 'Cruyff'.

A director at Coventry until 1981, Mercer stayed out of the limelight after his England stint, aside from the occasional TV appearance when an old colleague died – he was sitting next to one of his and his father's old teammates, Dixie **Dean**, when the latter had a fatal heart attack at Goodison Park in 1980. His own death ten years later was marked by lavish tributes for 'Uncle Joe', a gent of the old school.

merchandise

It was estimated in 1999 that £15m worth of football memorabilia was in private hands across Britain. While most of that figure is taken up by programmes, it's a testament to the ever-growing market in club merchandise, where anything that can have a club badge stamped, engraved or otherwise marked on it as official product of the football club is priced up for sale in megastore-sized club shops.

It used to be much simpler. All clubs seemed to sell throughout the 1960s and most of the 1970s were badges, pennants and scarves, which were also available in town centre sports shops and via mail order ads in football magazines. The two-colour 'bar' scarves reached a peak of popularity in the late-1960s, Liverpool's Kop and other large terraces regularly turning into a mass of waving wool (three-colour scarves were soon introduced by Manchester United, adding black to their red and white). 'College' scarves with stripes across the length of the fabric were briefly popular as were otherwise useless 'silk' affairs with tassles, often to be seen fluttering out of car windows. Of late these have made a slight return after years of being used exclusively to denote football fans in television commercials.

Nevertheless, scarves will now always play second fiddle to replica shirts, which started appearing towards the end of the 1970s, disappeared for most of the next decade apart from on aspiring hooligans, and re-emerged with a vengeance after the 1990 World Cup. Now fans are able to catch up on their own club's history through vintage shirt designs, chiefly sold through mail order and direct to club shops by the likes of TOFFS – The Old Fashioned Football Shirt Company. Badges have also made a comeback in recent years, not least as TV cameras will always pick out any fan wearing what used to be called a beanie hat covered in club pins.

Supporters used to design their own headgear for special occasions like Cup Finals but the three-foot-high top hats and bonnets shaped like the FA Cup have been superseded by club-branded jester hats and afro wigs in team colours, also sold, alongside pirated copies of club scarves, by vendors who set up trestle tables near grounds on matchdays. Some would say that there is no finer sight in football than a gaggle of middle-aged men in XL replica shirts and two-tone wigs trying to hold back the tears after their team has lost a crucial match.

Ambitious clubs diversified into leisurewear around the turn of the 1990s but it took Manchester United to properly set about transforming a small marketing division into football's first hugely successful brand. In 2001, their turnover from official merchandise alone

was £19.2m. This attracted most attention through the annual unveiling throughout the mid-1990s of a new United kit, always followed by a chorus of disapproval from parents resigned to forking out up to £40 for the latest shirt. In 2003 United, Umbro, JJB Sports and the Football Association were among the companies fined by the Office of Fair Trading for operating a cartel to keep the cost of replica kits artificially high, since when prices have remained relatively stagnant, albeit still a huge mark-up on the levels of a decade ago.

On a wider scale, though, where their branded golf balls and octagonal glasses led, everyone else followed in due course and now you can't move in club shops for tat, from baby bibs and embossed toilet paper to financial services. That's not a joke, by the way – Manchester United offer a range of financial services in conjunction with the Bank of Scotland. They're not alone in doing this, although they may be unique in tying interest rates to club performance, offering bonuses to savers on Champions' League qualification.

Billy Meredith

As a sinuous, dribbling winger, gifted with exceptional balance, speed and a powerful shot, Billy Meredith was a central figure in the successes of both Manchester clubs in the first two decades of the twentieth century. During his unusually long career, spanning nearly 30 years, he became one of the biggest stars of Edwardian football, and was an outspoken advocate of players' rights and a staunch union man.

Born in the Welsh mining village of Chirk in 1874, Meredith worked as a miner from the age of 12 until he was 20. After a brief spell with Northwich Victoria, he signed in 1894 for Ardwick

(soon to be Manchester City), contributing 29 goals when they won the Division
2 championship in 1899. His brilliant
individual goal secured victory in the
1903 FA Cup.

Meredith was a hugely popular player,
instantly recognizable because of his
heavy Victorian moustache, bandy legs
(often exaggerated by cartoonists) and
habit of chewing a toothpick during the
game. However, he signed for rivals
Manchester United in 1906, following a
major scandal. Aston Villa captain Alex
Leake claimed that Meredith offered him
a £10 bribe to throw a crucial game.
Meredith's subsequent bitter dispute with
the club's management for not making
good his wages triggered an investigation by the FA which resulted in the
dissolution of the City team.

When Meredith, aged 34, returned to
football in January 1907 after 18 months'
suspension, the new Manchester United
player received a hero's welcome, and
played an integral role in United's
meteoric rise, winning two Division 1
titles in 1908 and 1911, as well as the FA
Cup in 1909. Nicknamed 'Merrylegs', in
tribute to his mesmeric dribbling, he even
had his own catchphrase, 'Meredith,
we're in', which supporters borrowed
from a Fred Karno sketch about bailiffs.

Rarely injured, he attributed his
longevity to a special diet, rarely drinking
or smoking, as well as a regime of hot
baths, massage and regular applications
of 'dog fat', a mining machinery
lubricant.

While at United, Meredith revived the
Players' Union and was one of the
'Outcasts FC' who threatened to strike
when the FA attempted to outlaw
membership in 1909. A fiercely patriotic
Welshman he won 48 caps for Wales, a
remarkable total given the infrequency of
internationals at that time. He fell into
dispute with United and finally engineered a free transfer back to City in 1921.
His swansong two FA Cup appearances
in 1924 when he was 49 attracted huge
publicity, and in retirement he became
one of the grand old men of northern
football, though never losing his taste for
controversy.

Sadly, when he died in 1958 aged 83,
he was destitute and kept a battered old
suitcase underneath his bed filled with
caps and medals, scant reward for a
player of whom the Manchester United
programme once said, 'Had he lived in
earlier years he would have been the
subject of an epic poem, and been immortalized with Achilles, Roland and the
Knights of the Round Table.'

Middlesbrough

When Middlesbrough left their old
Ayresome Park ground and moved to the
all-seater Riverside Stadium at the start
of the 1995–96 season, chairman Steve
Gibson, who had helped rescue the club
after it went into receivership in 1986,
summed up Boro's history as '120 years
of mediocrity'. He was exaggerating, but
not by much. Boro had never finished
higher than third in the League; never got
beyond the quarter-finals of the FA Cup,
or the semi-finals of the League Cup. Like
many fans, Gibson saw the move to the
new stadium as a chance to draw a line
under failure. He succeeded, but it took an
investment that amounted to £1m for
every year of the club's existence.

Middlesbrough football club was
founded at a tripe supper in 1876 as an
offshoot of the town's cricket club. Boro
were one of the founder members of the
amateur Northern League and twice – in
1895 and 1898 – won the FA Amateur
Cup, on the latter occasion in spite of the
fact they were not allowed to play home
ties on Teesside owing to a smallpox
epidemic. After the demise of Teesside's

original Football League club, Ironopolis, Middlesbrough turned professional and were elected to Football League Division 2 in 1899. Six years later they made national headlines when they became the first club in history to pay a four-figure transfer fee for a player, spending £1,000 to bring centre-forward Alf **Common** from Sunderland. Common soon left – prompting suggestions that the move was some kind of financial dodge – but Boro were still good enough to finish third in Division 1 in 1913–14 and might have expected to improve on that had not the Great War intervened.

A similar pattern was played out in the 1930s with Middlesbrough gradually forging a powerful team that included the England captain, George Hardwick, inside-forward Wilf **Mannion** and one of the most formidable goalscorers in the British game, George Camsell, whose tally of 59 goals in a single season has been bettered only by Dixie **Dean**. Boro finished seventh in 1936–37, fifth in 1937–38 and fourth in 1938–39. Three games into the next season Hitler invaded Poland. When football recommenced after the Second World War, Boro's pursuit of success was undermined by a series of bitter disputes between the directors and the team's stars. Two of the best players Teesside has ever produced, Mannion and Brian **Clough**, left in acrimonious circumstances and, amidst accusations of match-rigging, the club entrenched itself in Division 2.

The arrival of Jack **Charlton** as manager in 1973 stirred Ayresome Park from its torpor and Boro returned to the top division after just one season under the former Leeds centre-back. It was a position they maintained until 1982, when relegation coupled with falling gates precipitated the financial crisis that would eventually lead to the club being declared bankrupt. As manager Bruce

Rioch took training sessions with the remaining players in a local park, Steve Gibson – the son of a local steelworker who had made a fortune from container shipping – put together the consortium that eventually rescued the club.

Over the next decade, as Boro bobbed up and down between the top two divisions, Gibson's influence at the club slowly increased until he became its sole owner. It was Gibson who oversaw the move to the Riverside Stadium, who secured the services of manager Bryan **Robson** and his successor Steve McClaren, and financed transfer deals that saw Brazilian footballer of the year Juninho and Juventus forward Fabrizio Ravanelli pulling on the club jersey.

More frustration was to follow for Boro fans, however. In the 1996–97 season, thanks to the brilliance of Juninho and Ravanelli's goals they reached the final of the FA Cup and the League Cup only to lose both and then get relegated – a feat unique in English football history. Another appearance in the League Cup Final the following season also ended in defeat, but on this occasion supporters could at least console themselves with promotion back into the Premiership.

Despite the set-backs Gibson has continued to invest heavily in the club and it was his name the supporters chanted at the Millennium Stadium in 2004, when goals from Joseph-Désiré Job and Boudewijn Zenden secured a 2–1 victory over Bolton Wanderers in the Carling Cup Final to put an end at long last to Boro's long, long wait for major silverware. Boro reached the UEFA Final in 2006, but were beaten 4–0 by Sevilla.

midfielder

Midfielder is the only position whose name describes where a player stands rather than what he does. Defenders defend. Attackers attack. Goalkeepers keep goal. Midfielders don't midfield. So what do they do? Football has come up with various answers. Players are occasionally described as 'the complete midfielder'. In British football this term has been applied to Roy **Keane**, Steven Gerrard, Bryan **Robson**, Graeme Souness and Martin Peters: midfielders who could attack decisively, defend effectively or simply pass well enough to retain possession in the middle.

More commonly midfielders are given different roles. A 4–4–2 formation will usually accommodate a defensive midfielder, a more attacking central midfielder and two wide players. Prior to the fashion for 4–4–2, the old fashioned WM formation saw the middle of the pitch occupied by two wing-halves, with occasional incursions from two attacking inside-forwards. Controversially at the time, England won the 1966 World Cup playing with wide midfielders rather than wingers (three of whom were tried and discarded in their group matches), and subsequently a robust and fairly inflexible four-man midfield has become the tactical norm.

The defensive midfield player is integral to this. Also known as the 'anchorman', the 'ball-winner', the 'holding player', or among opposition supporters as 'dirty git with two left feet', the defensive midfield player is in the team to make tackles and to provide a screening presence in front of his defence. The position could be seen as an evolution of the wing-half. In the modern game a defensive midfielder will concentrate on covering the ground, tracking opposition midfield players and providing a snarlingly physical presence. Nobby Stiles and Billy **Bremner** are among the most effective to have played this role. The best players in this position

in recent times have included Roy Keane, Patrick Vieira and Paul Ince, all of whom were also able to make occasional attacking forays. This is obviously much easier to do when you're playing for Manchester United or Arsenal.

The attacking midfielder has licence to support the forwards when his team has possession. Players such as Paul Scholes and David Platt, who scored 22 times for England from midfield, have been known for their ability to advance from a deep position at just the right moment to seize on a pass or a loose ball. This is a very British type of attacking midfield play, based not on possession football, but instead on the assumption that the ball will be knocked down, flicked on and generally fumbled around with in attacking areas.

Modern wide midfielders are expected to track back and double up with their full-back in defence. Manchester United's success during the late 1990s was bolstered by the energetically versatile flank play of Ryan **Giggs** and David **Beckham**, two of the most defensively diligent wide men of recent times. Before their near-extinction in the 1980s and 1990s, and notwithstanding their recent renaissance in the Premiership, orthodox wingers were one of the most thrilling sights in football. Traditional wing play is a specialist but also very simple position. The winger stays wide, receives passes from the centre and takes play forward with the aim of beating his marking full-back and delivering a cross from close to the byeline, the angle that is considered hardest to defend.

Wingers such as 'Jinking' Jimmy Johnstone of Celtic, Stanley **Matthews**, Tom **Finney** and the young John Barnes would develop a range of tricks to defeat their marker. This, along with their physical proximity to the crowd, helped to make the winger perhaps the most popular position as well as one most likely to encourage gratuitous showmanship. In a game increasingly averse to risk or experimentation the periodic disappearance of wingers is hardly surprising. Despite this, recent seasons have seen the stirrings of a wing revival at the highest level, in particular through Chelsea's successful use of Damien Duff and Arjen Robben as solely attacking wide players.

On the whole midfielders need a bit of everything. They need to be able to pass, tackle, shoot and head. Above all, in British football at least, they need to be able to run.

Jackie Milburn

There are two statues of Jackie Milburn: one in his birthplace, Ashington, the other in Newcastle, the city with which he became synonymous. The bond between Newcastle and 'Wor Jackie' is legendary. He never played for another English team and scored 200 goals in 397 League and Cup appearances. Despite his standing as a footballer he remained shy and modest in public, once bringing the house down at St James' Park at the reception for the 1951 FA Cup winners when he affected a strange 'posh' voice at his turn at the microphone. England team-mate Tom **Finney** thought he had an 'inferiority complex – he never thought he was as good as he was', despite the fact that Milburn was quite clearly adored by fans and feared by opponents for his incredible speed, change of pace and shooting ability.

Milburn was born into an established football lineage. Jack Milburn the first was a goalkeeper for Northumberland in the early days of the organized game, and since that time there had been a famous local Milburn in football through the generations (including Cissie, mother of Bobby and Jackie **Charlton**). Jackie Milburn was born in 1924 and was spotted as a schoolboy by Newcastle United. Invited to a trial game at St James' Park, he scored a second-half double hat-trick in borrowed boots against the first team.

Milburn was still working as a fitter at the local colliery when he became a St James' regular, playing at inside-right and on the right wing for United. He was given the number 9 shirt for a match in October 1946 and, despite his misgivings at the prospect, went out and scored a hat-trick. Despite being an unselfish player he scored prolifically for Newcastle. Somehow he played only 13 times for England, despite scoring ten goals in the process, and his international career was tainted by his brief participation in the ill-fated World Cup trip to Brazil in 1950. Compensation was to follow on the home front. He won the FA Cup with Newcastle in 1951, 1952 and 1955, in the first game scoring two – including one of the great Wembley screamers – and in the last heading United ahead after 45 seconds, which remained the fastest Cup Final goal for 42 years.

After retiring as a player following a brief spell with Irish League club Linfield, Milburn suffered a short and punishing tenure as manager of Ipswich, before returning to the north-east to become a successful football writer covering the whole region (but with the inside-track on his old club). Before his 1967 testimonial he was characteristically worried that no-one would turn up. As it happened, 46,000 crowded into St James' Park for the midweek game. When Milburn died in 1988, the city of Newcastle stopped its business to line the streets in tribute to the team's greatest-ever goalscorer.

Millennium Stadium

Cardiff's Millennium Stadium is perhaps one of the most surprising success stories among the rash of new football grounds built during the 1990s. It was a surprise mainly because the stadium, in its previous guise as Cardiff Arms Park, had been primarily used for rugby for most of its life, although the Welsh national football team played there between 1896 and 1910 (almost all their home games before then were at Wrexham) and again from 1989 onwards. The Arms Park itself had been entirely reconstructed between 1968 and 1984, but lacked the modern amenities considered appropriate for any big stadium, let alone a national monument, by the mid-90s.

So the Arms Park became the Millennium Stadium in time for the 1999 rugby World Cup, a transformation that came remarkably cheaply at £130m considering it involved turning the pitch through 90 degrees and building a 73,000 capacity stadium with all mod cons, including a sliding roof, the first of its kind in Britain and the biggest in the world at the time of its construction.

It was a huge gamble for the Welsh Rugby Union, but they were rewarded for their boldness as the fiasco of Wembley's proposed reconstruction unfolded. The last FA Cup Final at the old Wembley took place in 2000 (Chelsea beating Aston Villa 1–0 in an appropriately grim match) and the Millennium Stadium stepped into the breach the following year for Liverpool's more vivid 2–1 win over Arsenal, the first final played away from Wembley since 1922, other than the 1970 replay between Chelsea and Leeds. Since then Cardiff has also staged the League Cup Final, the play-off finals, the Football League trophy (under the names of its sponsors) and Welsh national team matches.

The first football match played in the stadium was a friendly between Wales and, of all countries, Finland, on 29 March 2000. Jari Litmanen scored the first goal in front of a crowd of 66,000 and Nathan Blake was the first Welshman to find the net, albeit his own one, as the Finns won 2–1 (with Ryan **Giggs** on target at the right end).

While there was a certain amount of nostalgic grumbling when the Cup Final left Wembley, the stunning setting of the Millennium Stadium quickly made that seem absurd. It has been blighted with a succession of feeble contests in the FA Cup (the first final held there was the only one between 1993 and 2005 when both teams scored), but the view, the atmosphere and that intangible sense of occasion that great stadiums inspire have all been embraced by fans accustomed to the dire state of the old Wembley. Welsh fans even saw their team rise unexpectedly from the doldrums with the backing of the Millennium Stadium crowd to the heights of a near-miss Euro 2004 campaign that included a 2–1 win over Italy in 2002. In the same year they also beat Germany and drew with Argentina in friendlies at Cardiff.

Many will regret it when the finals return to Wembley after 2006. The WRU certainly will, and the stadium's future will be more uncertain without its regular football visitors. But contrary to the doubts of the Wembley diehards (few of whom watched from outside the press box) and leaving aside the inevitable promotional flim-flam that now blights all big football events, the Millennium Stadium has done the game a favour by showing how a cup final should be held.

Millwall

Millwall are the most urban of all London football clubs. Based at the Den in Cold

Blow Lane and latterly at the New Den, a new stadium in the club's traditional catchment area between New Cross and Bermondsey, Millwall have always had a reputation for competitiveness on the field and for an abrasiveness among their home crowd. This was exacerbated during the 1970s when a violent element, apparently attracted less by the club than by the chance to cause trouble, became associated with Millwall's core support.

Millwall is an inner-city club, an important part of an area of London that has been bombed, rebuilt, impoverished and repopulated with successive waves of immigration. In many ways the club's problems reflect the sharp end of some of the difficulties experienced in any major modern city; and the recent, often successful, work of the club's administrators, under one time chairman Theo Paphitis, to change the atmosphere in and around the ground and to encourage peaceable support from all parts of the local community is a reflection of the best efforts made to tackle these problems.

Founded in 1885, Millwall were originally known as Millwall Rovers and then Millwall Athletic, and in their early days fielded a team made up of workers from a local jam and marmalade factory. The club won its first trophy, the East End Cup, in 1887 and moved to the Den in 1910, before joining the Football League in 1920. Millwall have never been a successful club. The first 45 years of the club's League existence were divided up by a series of promotions and relegations between the bottom two divisions. In the 1920s and early 1930s they managed to finish in 14th place in Division 2 three seasons in a row.

Successive promotions in 1964 and 1965 took a team managed by Billy Gray and featuring legendary full-back Harry Cripps and Irish international midfielder Eamon Dunphy, into the modern Division 2 for the first time, where they stayed for nine relatively fruitful seasons. Gray didn't last long in the job, however, becoming one in a long line of short-lived managerial residencies at the Den. Between 1933 and 1989 Millwall had 17 managers; over the same period West Ham had just four.

Between 1964 and 1967 the club enjoyed a remarkable run of 59 successive games without defeat, and it was around this historically daunting home form that Millwall's only real period of success was built during the late 1980s. With the Den at its most formidable, and with the club's fans in the middle of the worst period of notoriety, a team built by George **Graham** and taken on by John Docherty finally reached Division 1 in 1988, and in 1989 even topped the League briefly.

Graham unearthed Millwall's finest-ever player, Teddy Sheringham, who would go on to become both the club's greatest-ever goalscorer with 93 League goals and the most successful ex-Lion in terms of trophies won and international caps (over 50 for England). Sheringham's big-man-even-bigger-man partnership with Tony Cascarino, leavened by a few seasons of a pre-Wimbledon John Fashanu, together with no-nonsense midfielders such as Terry Hurlock and Les Briley, were central to Millwall's tactic of success through physical intimidation.

After two seasons in the top flight the club were relegated and returned to the old routine of promotion and relegation between the lower divisions. In 2004, building on promotion under Mark McGhee that took the club close to the play-offs for a place in the Premiership, player-manager Dennis Wise led the Lions to their first ever FA Cup Final and into Europe for the first time in the UEFA Cup. The Lions lost to Hungary's Ferencváros in the first round.

A take-over by the entrepreneur Peter De Savary in November 2005 coincided with a shift in the club's fortunes. 'Within five years we want to be one of the top 15 clubs in the country,' De Savary told reporters. Within five months they were heading the wrong way again, down into League One for the 2006–07 season.

Montrose

Montrose is renowned for attracting huge crowds. Unfortunately for the town's old but uncelebrated football team the crowds are made up of pink-footed geese, up to 40,000 of which migrate every November to the adjacent land-locked two-mile square lagoon known as 'The Basin'.

The Basin causes a 'rich' odour to pervade the port town's air, and could well be a factor in having distracted Montrose from winning any senior honour until they lifted the 1984–85 Division 2 championship, 106 years after they were formed. The team at least boasts an imaginative nickname – 'The Gable Endies' are named after the town's houses that were built gable end to the street by 18th- and 19th-century merchants who had been influenced by European architecture.

On another international front, only two Montrose players have ever been capped by Scotland, and strangely enough both played in the same game, a 3–2 defeat of Northern Ireland in 1892. Alex Keillor, who had won an earlier cap, scored the opening goal for Scotland, and lined up alongside team-mate Gordon Bowman. Neither were selected again, although both moved on to play professionally.

Montrose didn't join the Scottish League until 1923, and only then as founder members of the short-lived Division 3. They were readmitted to Division 2 in 1929 when Bathgate and Arthurlie both folded, and after closing down for the Second World War were allowed in again for the 1955–56 season when Division 2 was expanded from 16 to 19 clubs. They finished bottom, shipping a massive 133 goals.

Cup success has been short but occasionally sweet. In 1973 Montrose reached the Scottish Cup quarter-final, falling 4–1 to Dundee in front of a record 8,983 at their Links Park home. In 1975–76 they made it again, going out to Hearts in a second replay, while the same year they beat Hibs over two legs to go a stage further in the League Cup, falling to Rangers 5–1 in the semi-final after leading 1–0 at half-time.

Lack of cash has been a typically perpetual problem for Montrose, and crowds over 500 are rare these days unless the visitors are ancient rivals Arbroath. Nonetheless, in 2004 the club celebrated its 125th anniversary. Like the town's odour, it has endured all human endeavours.

Bobby Moore

Bobby Moore was not a footballing prodigy as a child, nor did he go through his professional and personal life without the odd mistake. Those facts explain his enduring popularity as much as the events of 30 July 1966, the day he captained England to World Cup success.

Robert Frederick Moore was born in April 1941, on the night German bombs destroyed the most famous landmark in his birthplace, Barking. He won little recognition at school but at 14 joined West Ham, where centre-half Malcolm **Allison** took him under his wing. By the time Ron **Greenwood** was West Ham manager in 1961, Moore was a regular and a surprise selection in England's 1962 World Cup squad. Nine months later, after just 12 England games and aged 23, he replaced Jimmy Armfield as England captain.

Leadership suited him but his relationship with Greenwood began to unravel when no West Ham representative attended Moore's presentation for the country's Footballer of the Year award on the eve of the 1964 FA Cup Final. Still, the Hammers won the Cup and the following season the European Cup Winners' Cup. But Moore had not forgotten his snub, and allowed his contract to expire in June 1966. He was forced to sign a month's extension just to make him eligible for the World Cup.

Moore's composure was tested in the aggressive quarter-final against Argentina and he spent the morning of the final consoling his discarded room-mate Jimmy **Greaves**. In the final against West Germany, Moore set up Geoff **Hurst**'s first goal and last, sealing a 4–2 win. He even remembered to wipe his hands before accepting the trophy from the begloved Queen. 'I was more worried about getting the mud off than getting hold of the World Cup.'

Moore was just 25 at the time and no-one expected that to be the last major trophy he won. He was propelled into being an iconic figure, a drinking-buddy of the PM, Harold Wilson, and an overnight model for Ford and Bisto, and aftershave, swimwear and shirt companies. He was the perfect advertising tool, representing honesty, reliability and success. Unfortunately the latter was in short supply for the rest of his career.

He was still skipper for the 1970 World Cup in Mexico, despite being accused of stealing an emerald and diamond bracelet in Bogotá just before the tournament. Moore was arrested and detained for four days but the case collapsed during a reconstruction when it emerged Moore's tracksuit had no pockets. He starred in the draw with Brazil, but England lost to West Germany. The following season, Moore was suspended by West Ham for drinking after a curfew. He was dropped from the national side by the time England missed qualification for the 1974 World Cup.

After 16 years at West Ham, Moore moved to Fulham and lost the FA Cup Final (to West Ham) in his first season. He spent two summers in the North American Soccer League before Elton John reneged on a deal to appoint him Watford coach – luckily as it turned out, as Moore proved a managerial disaster at Oxford City and Southend. He moved into the media after a series of business ventures collapsed. Ten years after meeting his second wife, Stephanie Parlane-Moore, he died of colon cancer on 24 February 1993, aged 51. Moore bore his illness like he lived his life: with modesty, dignity and charm. He only made his two-year illness public nine days before he died. The bronze statue of him outside West Ham's ground is a minor memento to one of England's few true sporting heroes.

Motherwell

Only the most ardent followers of Motherwell would claim that the club ever managed to sustain a period of genuine challenge to the ruling clubs of Scottish football before recent times. Formed in 1886, the club with the distinctive amber and claret kit won national trophies (the League title in 1932, the League Cup in 1950 and Scottish Cup in 1952) but never really attracted significant interest outside Lanarkshire, an area of Scotland dominated by heavy machinery, leading to the 'Steelmen' nickname.

Excitement arrived in the team formed under Bobby Ancell in the ten years following his 1955 appointment. Amongst the 'Ancell Babes', who attracted large crowds and worried the Old Firm without landing any major trophies, was one Ian St John long before he became a television fixture. The 1970s had their share of glamour in the Texaco Cup, in which the 'Well defeated Spurs in front of a full house at Fir Park, and in 1975–76 a side inspired by prolific centre-forward Willie Pettigrew came fourth in the inaugural season of the Scottish Premier League.

Yet it was the 1984 appointment of Tommy McLean as manager that saw Motherwell enter a period that offered stability and the belated suggestion that the club truly belonged amongst the nation's elite. McLean's elder brother, Jim, had just led Dundee United to the European Cup semi-final as Scottish champions and his no-nonsense management style was mimicked by his equally uncompromising sibling. A high-profile meeting between the two was perhaps predestined and it arrived in the Scottish Cup Final of 1991.

Arguably the most memorable day in the club's history was dubbed 'the family final', both for the competing brothers and for the welcome occasion of two provincial sides competing in the national final, without the presence of the Old Firm and the sectarian edge offered by the latter. In one of the best Scottish Cup Finals in recent times, Motherwell triumphed 4–3 in extra time with starring performances from former Rangers winger Davie Cooper and goalkeeper Ally Maxwell, who spent the final spell clutching cracked ribs.

Two years later, McLean led Motherwell to a third-place Premier League finish before departing for Hearts. His successor was Alex McLeish, who further elevated the club to second in his first season in charge, leading to a European campaign that culminated in defeat to a Borussia Dortmund side that took a liking to 'Well midfielder Paul Lambert. Four years later, he would play in their European Cup Final victory over Juventus.

Recent years have seen the club rocked by financial administration, brought on by a period of speculative spending that failed to attract either the on-pitch success or inflated crowds that had been predicted. However, the ship has now been settled and former England captain Terry Butcher counfounded expectations by leading his young team to decent League finishes and a League Cup Final meeting with Rangers. Butcher left to work in Australia in May 2006.

Mourinho, José

Everything about José Mourinho's brief managerial career seems to have been speeded up. In just five full seasons as a top level coach Mourinho has won two Portuguese League titles, the Portuguese Cup, the Champions League, the UEFA Cup, the League Cup and the English Premiership twice. Two ruthlessly efficient seasons in England, backed by Roman Abramovich's petro-dollars, have seen Mourinho create a deceptively enduring aura of domestic dominance.

Perhaps this meteoric progress has something to do with his circuitous early career. Mourinho was born in Setubal, Portugal, in 1963, the son of goalkeeper Félix Mourinho, who was capped once by Portugal. The younger Mourinho never pursued a career as a professional player, but developed a taste for management after helping his father to prepare reports on his opponents. After studying for a degree in sports science he taught physical education in several schools while also gaining the relevant coaching badges. Having worked as Bobby Robson's interpreter at both Sporting Lisbon and FC Porto, Mourinho followed the former England manager to Barcelona, where he later stayed on to assist Louis Van Gaal after Robson's departure.

After becoming, in his own words, 'more like a critic than an assistant coach' to Van Gaal, he left in 2000 to become manager of Benfica. Two years later, as Porto manager, Mourinho set about building his first great team, considered by many the finest in the history of Portuguese football. He kicked off his first full term as a manager with the treble of league, cup and UEFA Cup. The following season brought another league title as well as a surprise Champions' League victory, a campaign that saw Mourinho's team lose just once, to Real Madrid. Porto also memorably knocked out Manchester United, Paulo Sergio's late equalizer inspiring Mourinho, in overcoat, gloves and scarf, to sprint along the Old Trafford touchline punching the air wildly.

Mourinho moved to Chelsea in the summer of 2004. The level of compensation paid to Porto made this effectively the first genuine transfer involving a manager – something entirely in keeping with the high-profile persona Mourinho would continue to develop during his time in charge at Stamford Bridge. 'I'm not one who comes out of a bottle. I'm a special one,' he announced at a press conference shortly after arriving in England, and the quote has stayed with him. Willingly courting the press, while at the same time appearing utterly disdainful of his publicity duties, Mourinho is the first superstar manager; the first, in post-inflationary times, to rival his players in terms of salary and endorsements; and the first manager to grace the style section of your weekend paper, as well as both back and front pages. Mourinho's urbane style, his looks and sartorial élan are all an important, and carefully maintained, part of his rare ability to motivate the modern footballer.

Beyond the cultivation of his own magnetic personal qualities, Mourinho doesn't bring any great technical innovation to his job. He has a fondness for business practices such as PowerPoint presentations instead of the traditional chalkboard, and a tendency to stay in constant touch with his players through memos and motivational messages, often by email or text. He also understands the value of delegation. His backroom staff is peopled by various experts in the fields of fitness, physiology and statistics, rather than the usual dyed-in-the-wool football-through-and-through types. Outside of this Mourinho has no revolutionary tactics in his armoury, or Arsène Wenger-style dietary control freakery (players are left to eat sensibly of their own accord). His managerial style is rooted in his own high profile, a willing lightning rod for the kind of press attention that often weighs heavily on players, a certain bookish thoroughness with tactics, and a happy habit of making dramatic and game-changing substitutions.

At his current rate of progress the next three years could see Mourinho achieve almost anything – win the Champions' League trophy outright, find himself helicoptered away to manage Real Madrid, NATO or the Martian national team, or possibly even disappear from view as quickly as his career has mushroomed into life. The English experience of

Mourinho has been a whirlwind seduction. Chelsea fans, at least, will be hoping for something a little more lasting.

Munich aircrash

On 6 February 1958 the plane carrying Manchester United's famous 'Busby Babes' crashed on take-off at Munich airport. The last game played by this brilliant young side was a 3–3 draw with Red Star Belgrade in Yugoslavia, a result that took them into the European Cup semi-finals for the second successive year. Their last domestic fixture against Arsenal, which ended 5–4 to United, is often cited as one of the greatest-ever games of football. The team had won the League championship the two previous seasons and had entered European competition against the wishes of the Football League. In the current League standings they were four points behind leaders Wolves in their chase for a hat-trick of championships.

Even the greatest tragedies are sometimes preventable. After stopping in Munich to refuel, two failed attempts had been made by the pilots to take off from the snowbound airport. Instead of electing to see the night out in Munich, the decision was made to try to get back to Manchester that night as the problem with the first two aborted take-offs had been put down to fuel surge, a common failing of that aircraft type. At just after 3pm, with the snow falling fast, the third attempt was begun. Just as they passed the point at which the flight could be safely aborted, the pilots noticed they were starting to lose velocity. The plane dipped, left the runway and ploughed through the perimeter fence, across a road and into a house. The fuselage was split in half and seven players – Mark Jones, Geoff Bent, Tommy Taylor, Bill Whelan, Roger Byrne, David Pegg and Eddie Colman – died in the wreckage. Just before the final attempt to get airborne, David Pegg had moved his position to a seat at the back of the plane with Mark Jones, Tommy Taylor, Eddie Colman and Duncan Edwards, where he thought it would be safer.

Of the 43 passengers on board, 23 were killed. Eight of the dead were journalists, including the former Manchester City and England goalkeeper Frank Swift. United also lost their trainer, chief coach and secretary. Bill Foulkes and Harry Gregg somehow emerged conscious and relatively unscathed, returning to the mangled plane to help the others. Teammates Bobby **Charlton**, Ray Wood, Dennis Violett, Ken Morgans, Albert Scanlon, John Berry, Jackie Blanchflower and Duncan Edwards all survived the initial impact and were rushed to hospital. Edwards, the phenomenally gifted 21-year-old who had already won 18 England caps and two championship medals, died there 15 days later after slipping in and out of consciousness and finally into a coma. Matt **Busby** was badly injured and only given a 50–50 chance of living. He and the remaining hospitalized players did recover but Blanchflower (brother of Tottenham's Danny) and Berry never played again.

Somehow, amid the grief and confusion back in Britain, the club managed to scrape together a team to play Sheffield Wednesday in the next round of the FA Cup. The programme team sheet for the game showed 11 blank spaces for the United team. The makeshift side beat Wednesday 3–0 and proceeded to reach the FA Cup Final where survivors Charlton, Violett, Foulkes and Gregg were bolstered by reserves. There was to be no miraculous outcome that year. United were beaten 2–0 by Bolton and ended the season in ninth place in the League.

The subsequent success of a second team of 'Busby Babes', culminating in the European Cup victory over Benfica in 1968, is still a significant factor in the club's singular character and its world-wide support today.

music

Almost without exception football records are terrible, some ranking among the worst indignities ever inflicted on the human ear. Over the last half-century footballers have often gone into record-ing studios, usually in celebration of an achievement such as a promotion or a cup win, to prove emphatically that they are unable to sing in time or hold a note.

'Man Utd Calypso' was one of the earliest such recordings, in the 1950s, followed by Leeds's own calypso effort delivered in a dreadful cod-Caribbean accent by crooner Ronnie Hilton, backed by a players' chorus. Rangers' 'Every Other Saturday' (1964) was arguably the first decent song; Celtic then brought out their own eponymously titled tune, which set the standard for 11 lads round the microphone belting out a cheery little number of self-praise. In this vein was Chelsea's 'Blue is the Colour', which made the Top Ten in 1972, yet some-thing in the innocence of the melody and words has made it a classic of the genre. 'Good Old Arsenal' (written by Jimmy **Hill**) celebrated that team's Double season of 1970–71 and is still occasionally heard among older members of the crowd at Highbury.

Spurs, however, are the leaders in the field. Beginning with 'Tip Top Tottenham' after their own Double season of 1961, they followed up in 1967 with an album, *The Spurs Go Marching On*, featuring squad members roughing up a selection of round-the-piano stan-dards. The next decade saw 'Nice One

Cyril' (a paean to full-back Cyril Knowles adapted from the punchline of a bread commercial) worm its way into the common consciousness, before the club entered a purple patch when the tradition for FA Cup Final songs coincided with their regular appearance at Wembley. With Chas & Dave they won over the weaker elements of the population with 'Ossie's Dream' (Argentinian playmaker Osvaldo Ardiles contributing a pitch-perfect mispronunciation solo in the middle) and continued the theme the next year with another song that, while unmemorable, did definitely rhyme 'Tottenham' with '(no-one to) stop them'.

The England World Cup squad got to number 1 with 'Back Home' on a wave of optimism before the 1970 World Cup finals. An entire album was recorded, feat-uring among other things a duet between Alan Ball and Emlyn Hughes ('Everton and Liverpool get together at last') on 'Make Me an Island' and Gordon **Banks**'s 'Lovey Dovey', described in the sleevenotes as 'your actual "reggae" music'. For the most part the musicians who worked on these albums were journeymen session players but occasion-ally famous people got involved – Ray Davies of the Kinks wrote an unreleased song for George **Best** while Rod Stewart recorded 'Olé Ola' for Scotland's 1978 World Cup campaign, which was joined in the Top Ten by comedian Andy Cameron's 'We're on the March with Ally's Army' (with its famous refrain, 'We'll really shake them up when we win the World Cup').

Amidst the howling mediocrity, New Order made a proper song – 'World In Motion' – with the 1990 England World Cup squad and the Lightning Seeds' Ian Brodie supplied the music for comedians David Baddiel and Frank Skinner's 'Three Lions' for Euro 96. Like the duo's *Fantasy Football* programme, the song is not to everyone's taste, but with the refrain 'Football's Coming Home' it became instantly popular with England fans and remains so, despite being cheekily adopted by German supporters when they won the tournament.

Other efforts of note in this field include 'Come On You Reds' (Man Utd's 1994 chart-topper with Status Quo), Glenn **Hoddle** and Chris Waddle's soppy disco ballad 'Diamond Lights', Paul **Gascoigne**'s up-tempo, down-market version of Lindisfarne's 'Fog on the Tyne' and 'Daydream Believer (Cheer Up Peter Reid)' – a minor hit for Sunderland, who neglected to record a song about their manager which was popular with rival fans – 'Peter Reid Eats Bananas with His Feet'.

Finally, if the Football Association should ever decide that the national game needs an official theme tune, they should look no further than 'I Like Football', a furiously paced ukulele rave-up by George Formby-soundalike Alan Randall in which he reels off the names of all 92 League clubs, mispronouncing 'Gillingham' with a hard 'g' and pausing for breath before 'Queens Park Rangers'.

Newcastle United

Newcastle United have enjoyed a number of successful spells down the years without ever quite fulfilling the potential Tyneside's proverbial love of football has given the club. Despite one of the largest supports in the country 'The Toon' have only ever once truly been a dominant force in the English game.

Newcastle upon Tyne's only professional football team was founded in 1892 when Newcastle East End moved from their original ground in Heaton to the St James' Park site left vacant by the disbanding of archrivals Newcastle West End. Proposals for the name for the new club included Newcastle City and Tyne & Newcastle Rangers, but Newcastle United was the one finally approved by the FA. United joined Division 2 of the Football League at the start of the 1893–94 season. They were promoted four years later. Initially local fans were hostile to the newly formed club, but the indifference was overcome and 70,000 supporters turned up at St James' Park in 1901 to watch the derby with Sunderland.

The Edwardian era proved to be the greatest period in the club's history. A Newcastle side that featured the Irish full-back Bill McCracken (usually credited with inventing the offside trap) won the League championship three times and appeared in five FA Cup Finals (though only one ended in a United victory). The team was captained by Colin Veitch, who as well as being a brilliant half-back was also a keen amateur actor, a leading member of the Fabian Society and close friend of George Bernard Shaw.

After the First World War, Newcastle continued to be one of England's strongest sides, winning the FA Cup for the second time in 1924. In 1925 the

Tynesiders bought the great Scottish centre-forward Hughie Gallacher from Airdrie for £5,500. The hard-drinking, combative and troubled Scot, who three decades later would commit suicide by throwing himself in front of a train in Gateshead, scored 23 times in his first 19 appearances. The following season he hit 36 in 38 matches and Newcastle won the title for the fourth and so far last time. Gallacher left for Chelsea in 1930 – allegedly because he needed the signing-on fee to settle debts – and though Newcastle won the FA Cup again in 1932 the team was on the slide and at the end of the 1933–34 season they were relegated.

After the Second World War Newcastle made a concerted effort to return to Division 1 and spent over £50,000 on new players, including three forwards, Roy Bentley, Charlie Wayman and the mercurial Len **Shackleton**, who scored six goals on his St James' Park debut but stayed for only a year. By the time he left, however, United were well on the way to promotion.

Jackie **Milburn** had by then become a fixture in the team at centre-forward. Born in Ashington, Milburn was fast enough to have run in the Powderhall Sprint and, like his relative Bobby **Charlton**, possessed a thunderous shot. He was the star in a Newcastle side that won the FA Cup three times between 1951 and 1955 and in all scored 200 goals for the club in slightly less than 400 appearances. Since the victory over Manchester City at Wembley in 1955 Newcastle have won just one trophy, the Fairs Cup in 1969. An FA Cup Final appearance in 1974 promised much, but the Magpies' star forward, Malcolm 'Supermac' Macdonald, failed to perform and the team were hammered by Liverpool. Three further Wembley appearances have likewise ended in defeat.

During the late 1980s, following years of a lack of investment and the selling of some fine home-grown players (amongst them Chris Waddle and Paul **Gascoigne**), the club lurched toward bankruptcy and in 1992 came within seconds of relegation to Division 3. The investment of local Thatcherite entrepreneur Sir John Hall and the management of former England captain Kevin **Keegan**, who had ended his playing career at St James', revived Toon's fortunes.

In 1995–96 Keegan's resurgent Newcastle seemed certain to land the Premiership title when they held a ten-point lead over closest rivals Manchester United going into the New Year. The manager had built a reputation for swashbuckling football and now instead of consolidating by investing to shore up his side's creaky defence he bought the brilliant but wayward Colombian striker Faustino Asprilla. Newcastle finished second.

Keegan responded by breaking the British transfer record to bring in another forward, Alan **Shearer** from Blackburn. The England captain was Newcastle-born and as a teenager had been a ball-boy at St James' Park, but he had been rejected by United as a youngster after a trial at which he was allegedly forced to play in goal. Shearer led the line brilliantly, but though Newcastle recorded a memorable 5–0 home victory over Manchester United early in the season it was plain that events of the previous year had taken their toll on Keegan, who duly resigned as manager.

Kenny **Dalglish** replaced him. Under the Scot, Newcastle finished second in the Premiership without ever truly threatening to lift the crown and their pragmatic style of play failed to appeal to a crowd that had enjoyed the attacking mayhem of the Keegan years. Dalglish was fired. His replacement Ruud Gullit promised, in a much-repeated quote, to bring 'sexy football' to Tyneside but didn't and, after 18 months and a bitter dispute with Shearer, resigned. Sir Bobby **Robson** took over from the Dutchman. The former England boss was a lifelong Newcastle fan, but despite his passion for the club and further huge investment in players, silverware continued to elude Newcastle and Robson too was sacked shortly after the start of the 2004–05 season. His successor, the relentlessly combative Graeme Souness, failed to win over supporters and was sacked in February 2006 after 16 months in the job.

newspapers

In his book *The People's Game*, James Walvin wrote, 'Until the rise of TV, newspapers, for the best part of a century, proved a key player in the history of modern football . . . Even the present-day spate of newspapers and magazines devoted wholly or in part to football was paralleled by a late-19th century wave of popular footballing journalism . . . using the printed word to excite interest in the game, to foster loyalties to chosen teams, to lavish adoration on particular players, and, of course, to make money from the sale of printed copy.'

From the earliest days of the professional game newspapers were football's information service, producing sports supplements and cheap weekly additions with news of fixtures, results, venues and transport for the game's new fans. Even before the advent of 'evening specials' and 'pink' papers – sport supplements rushed on to the streets within minutes of full time – newspapers were publishing results from matches around the country, pasting them up in local press office windows as soon they arrived via the new telegraph system.

Even between the wars, when their dominant position in shaping the

professional game's growing public image was challenged by the emergence of broadcasting, newspapers and football fed off each other. At first newspapers resisted the live radio broadcasts and results services that began in the 1930s, but in the end radio and newspapers complemented each other as even paying supporters wanted to read about the game they had just watched. Newspapers' primary role was far more seriously challenged by television, whose encroaching influence on the sport began in the late 1950s, an impact which has quickened with each passing decade.

After the Second World War, a new kind of sports journalism emerged, especially at the *News of the World*, the *Sunday People* and the *Daily* and *Sunday Express*. Adding features to their usual match reports, these papers aimed to expose corruption in the game and the conservatism of the authorities, as well as focus on players' lives and personalities. There was also a change in the so-called 'quality' papers, as writers such as Geoffrey Green, Brian Glanville and Hugh McIlvanney became influential commentators on the game, helping to raise football's status and give it an intellectual veneer.

Not surprisingly, however, the most dramatic changes in newspaper coverage of football occurred in the last 20 years, mirroring the resurgence of the game during 'the modern TV age'. As recently as the late 1980s it was still possible to read a national daily paper from cover to cover without seeing more than a few paragraphs about football. Even on Sundays and Mondays, broadsheets carried reports on only the top two or three weekend fixtures, and simply listed the other results, often without mentioning the scorers' names. While other European countries, such as Italy, France and Spain, had national daily papers dedicated to sport, weekday broadsheets in Britain had only one or two sports pages.

The massive increase in football coverage – partly prompted by greater exposure on television and the emergence of high-quality colour printing – began in the early 1990s, when papers started to produce special sports supplements, at first attached only to Monday editions of papers such as the *Guardian* and *The Times*. Now broadsheets and tabloids have large football sections every day. Coverage of so-called minor sports has been squeezed out or, in many tabloids, has disappeared altogether outside the Olympics or major tournaments. In the national press, at least, football has no close season.

The nature of the coverage has changed too. Football reporting is no longer about the matches; it relies on interviews, personalities, issues, disputes, the murky world of the football business, transfer gossip, managers' rows, takeover deals and all the rest. Even match reports are not merely reports any more. As writers assume their readers have seen or heard much of the action their copy is more a commentary on the 'talking points' surrounding a match, of which there are always plenty. In a print-world parallel to the TV panel, papers also carry a 'colour piece', a columnist's opinion, a fan's eye view and an 'expert' analysis of the game by a former player or manager. And then there are the reams of statistics on every aspect of the game, from team line-ups to goal:game ratios, passing indexes and player ratings.

With the rise and rise of TV football, British papers have had to adapt their coverage of the game. They may not be the only information service any more, but they're still hugely influential in moulding football's image. The national press in particular has played a major role in demonizing football supporters, building up and knocking down many a star player, and reinforcing a variety of crude national stereotypes. With the modern media's emphasis on making the news as much as reporting it, newspapers are the first repository for football's rumour-mongers, players' agents keen to fuel transfer speculation.

Whether such saturation coverage is good for the game, whether it merely responds to public appetites or feeds them, are moot points. One thing's for sure, though: even in the world of cable TV and instant internet news, newspapers continue to 'excite interest', 'foster loyalties', 'lavish adoration', and 'make money'. To paraphrase Walvin, millions still take part in the sport, 'at a distance, through the printed word'.

Bill Nicholson

Bill Nicholson's status as a managerial great was secured when his free-flowing Tottenham Hotspur side lifted the first League and Cup Double of the modern era in 1960–61. Further trailblazing successes, particularly in Europe, cemented his reputation as a pioneer. Nicholson did not win as many titles as the likes of Sir Alex **Ferguson**, Sir Matt **Busby**, and Bob **Paisley** but he remains a pivotal figure in the modernizing of the insular culture of post-war British football.

Nicholson was born in Scarborough in 1919. His association with Tottenham began in 1936, when he signed as a schoolboy, and would go on to span eight decades. In a playing career interrupted by war, his sole honour aside from a solitary England cap was the League championship – Tottenham's first – in 1951. This was engineered in the main by manager Arthur Rowe, and

Nicholson became a disciple of Rowe's innovative 'push-and-run' style.

Appointed as manager in 1958, his first game was a 10–4 home win against Everton, a precursor of what was to come, as Spurs carried all before them with a flair and style hitherto not seen in England. The side's achievements also defined the 'glory glory' image of Tottenham as the great entertainers; a label that has arguably hindered as well as inspired subsequent teams.

Nicholson, aided by coach Eddie Baily and assistant manager Harry Evans, advocated a deceptively simple playing style that hinged on having players throughout the side who were comfortable in their use of the ball. An advocate of employing maxims that his players could readily execute – 'if not in possession, get into position' being a prime example – his philosophy of fast, accurate passing and movement was a forerunner of the approach adopted by Arsène **Wenger**.

Nicholson's astuteness in the transfer market was also fundamental to his success. He made a series of crucial signings, chiefly in bringing in the fiercely competitive Dave **Mackay** to complement the elegant skill of Danny **Blanchflower**. Jimmy **Greaves**, the most prolific and natural English goalscorer of the 1960s, was another key signing, and his arrival helped Spurs to the semi-finals of the European Cup in 1962 and the European Cup Winners' Cup in 1963, the first European trophy won by a British club.

Spurs won the FA Cup again in 1967, plus two League Cups and another European trophy, the UEFA Cup in 1972. By then, however, Nicholson was becoming increasingly disenchanted with the game, particularly the rise of hooliganism, and he resigned shortly after Spurs lost the 1974 UEFA Cup Final, a match blighted by serious disorder.

As chief scout and then life president, Nicholson continued his association with Spurs until his death in 2004. He was awarded the CBE but missed out on a knighthood, a source of grievance for Tottenham fans but an omission that did nothing to diminish his standing as the club's central figure.

non-League

Non-League football is as old as the game itself. The first FA Cups were competed for by amateur teams in the days before professionalism was legalized and the Football League was founded. Now the term is taken to mean the whole pyramid of semi-professional and amateur leagues that exist below the 92-team, four-division professional structure of English football. That is, non-Football League or Premier League. The year after the Football League was formed in 1888, the first five non-League competitions began: Birmingham and District League, the Lancashire League, the Midland League, Football Alliance and the Northern League. More quickly followed, and by 1903 there were 42 county football associations running local amateur play.

In 1907, after years of dissent over rules and registrations, amateur football split with the FA and formed its own ruling body, the Amateur Football Defence Federation, later the Amateur Football Association. However, in 1913 the professional and amateur bodies reconciled and have worked together ever since. The AFA changed its title to the Amateur Football Alliance, and came to be represented on the FA Council. It still runs competitions for public school and university old boys sides, and the London Financial League with fixtures such as Dresdner Kleinwort Wasserstein v Mount Pleasant Post Office.

The post-Second World War period is seen as non-League's best era, with large crowds drawn by famous names like Bishop Auckland and Walthamstow Avenue, but 'shamateurism' increasingly became an issue – amateur clubs were known for giving out generous backhanders to attract players, even from teams who were officially semi-pro. In 1974 the legal and administrative distinction between amateurs and professionals was finally abolished and all footballers simply became 'players', making everything above board and giving teams and players greater freedom of contract.

Now that all non-League players could play in the same competitions, the stage was set for the pyramid system, and the Alliance Premier – later to become the Conference – was founded as the top semi-pro league, fed by the Southern and Northern Premier leagues (and, later, the Isthmian), themselves supplied by their lower divisions and regional leagues. Now that there is automatic promotion between the fourth professional division and the Conference, any non-League club in England theoretically has the potential to become Premier League champions.

In 2004 semi-professional football was reorganized with the creation of two north and south divisions below the Conference and a consequent downgrading of the three main feeder leagues. Whether the restructuring will be of general benefit to the non-League game remains to be seen.

Northampton Town

Formed in 1897, Northampton Town were founder members of Division 3 in 1920, their early years having been spent mostly in the Southern League. Nicknamed 'The Cobblers' after the shoe factories that were the town's biggest employers, the club were based at the three-sided County Ground – the open side led on to the pitch used by the county cricket team – from their inception until a move to the council-owned Sixfields Stadium in 1996. The County Ground's cricket connections had a long-term problem for the football club. Officals from Northants CCC ran the trust that administered the stadium and refused permission for stands to be erected on the open side, save for one match – an 8–2 FA Cup loss to Manchester United in 1970 – when a temporary structure was put up.

Playing in the county colours of claret and white, Northampton's first 40 years in the League were uneventful, with one relegation and no promotions, the most memorable match being an FA Cup defeat at Arsenal in 1951 watched by 72,000. All that changed, however, with the appointment of Dave Bowen as manager in 1959. Bowen had begun his playing career at the County Ground before moving on to Arsenal and had starred for Wales during their run to the World Cup quarter-finals in 1958. Under him the club set a record (subsequently matched by Swansea City) for the quickest journey from Division 4 to Division 1 and back again.

Promoted from the bottom division in 1961, they had returned by the end of 1968–69. That single season in the top flight, in 1965–66, hinged on one game at the end of April, when relegation rivals Fulham won 4–2 at the County Ground and stayed up by two points; Northampton's 33 points was the most won by a relegated team under the two points for a win system. Bowen (who was also Welsh national coach for seven years from 1964) became general manager after the drop into Division 3 in 1966–67, taking charge of the first team again two years later to little effect – the club had to face re-election for the first time in

1972. Bowen stayed on as secretary until 1982 and is credited with discovering several players who were sold on to bigger clubs, including Phil Neal and John Gregory. It was said that Bowen always tried to meet prospective signings at motorway service stations, before they got to see the three-sided ground.

The next manager to have a major impact at Northampton was Graham Carr, whose team were Division 4 champions in 1987 with a record 99 points and 102 goals scored. The attacking trio of Trevor Morley, Richard Hill and Ian Benjamin were promptly sold, however, and the club plunged downwards again. An FA Cup defeat of Coventry City in 1989–90 was the only bright moment before a slide into adminstration in 1991 which led to the youth team playing first-team fixtures.

This proved to be the catalyst for the formation of the first-ever supporters' trust which helped saved the club from extinction. The next season Northampton needed to win at Shrewsbury to avoid dropping out of the League altogether – two down at half-time they rallied to win 3–2. They were to finish rock bottom of the League the following year, being saved this time by Conference champions Kidderminster's failure to bring their ground up to League standard.

Manager Ian Atkins revived Northampton in the late 1990s, taking them to two Wembley play-offs. Promotion to Division 2 was achieved when Swansea were beaten 1–0 in the last minute; the next year they lost by the same score to Grimsby in front of 42,000 Cobblers fans, 37,000 of whom disappeared before the next game. Now owned by property developer David Cardoza, who has promised major improvements to Sixfields, Northampton prospered in the upper reaches of League Two before achieving promotion in 2005–06.

Northern Ireland

Putting to one side its dismal recent record, the history of the Northern Ireland national team is one of occasional but compelling over-achievement. Northern Ireland has a population of just over 1.5 million, a quarter the size of London. It has no professional league and, understandably in the circumstances, no history of success in European club football. Despite this Northern Ireland have appeared at three World Cup finals, won the Home International Championships three times, and produced a succession of players who have excelled in the English leagues.

Northern Ireland made their first appearance at the World Cup finals in Sweden in 1958. A well-drilled team, containing Danny **Blanchflower**, Billy Bingham and Harry Gregg, made a huge impression with their levels of fitness, organization – all set-pieces were meticulously rehearsed – and team spirit. They beat Czechoslovakia twice and drew with West Germany on their way to the knockout phase before losing 4–0 to France. It would be 24 years before Northern Ireland competed again at a major finals. At the 1982 World Cup in Spain, however, they were once again the surprise team of the tournament. Bingham, back as manager now, made 17-year-old Manchester United midfielder Norman Whiteside the youngest player ever to appear at the World Cup finals, while journeymen forwards Gerry Armstrong and Billy Hamilton emerged from worthy service in the English League to earn unlikely acclaim as a partnership on the biggest stage. Armstrong scored the winner as Northern Ireland beat the hosts 1–0 – the greatest result in their history and one of the best ever by a British team overseas – before losing

4–1 to France in the decisive match of the second-round group.

Sustaining the very brief illusion of a new and fruitful dawn for Northern Irish football, the national team also qualified for the 1986 World Cup in Mexico. This time Bingham's team went out in the first round, but not before Pat Jennings had won the last of his record 119 caps, a 3–0 defeat to Brazil the final game of a 22-year international career. Besides George **Best** – both men made their international debuts in the same game, against Wales in 1964 – Jennings is the only world-class player Northern Ireland have produced in the past 40 years. Best remains the finest player never to compete at an international tournament. He made only 37 appearances for his country and in November 1972 was forced to withdraw from the squad for a game against Spain after receiving death threats from the IRA. Similarly, 30 years later Celtic midfielder Neil Lennon, a Catholic, would announce his retirement from international football after receiving sustained abuse from home spectators during international matches at Windsor Park.

Around the same time Northern Ireland suffered their worst-ever patch of form, a goalless run of 13 games from the 4–1 defeat to Poland on 13 February 2002 to another defeat by the same score to Norway on 18 February 2004. Recent times have not been kind to Northern Ireland, including a slump to 122nd in the FIFA world rankings in December 2003. Despite this there have been signs of a mini-revival under manager Lawrie Sanchez, whose team beat England in a World Cup qualifier in September 2006 – their first victory over the English in Belfast since 1927.

Northern League

The Northern League is the world's second-oldest football league. It was founded in 1889 for amateur clubs based in north-eastern England, an area that encompassed Northumberland, Durham and the North Riding of Yorkshire (though teams as far afield as Sheffield have taken part).

Despite the incredible financial problems created by the north-east's economic dependence on the coal industry (Northern League club Langley Park once folded because they could not raise enough money to pay for a match ball), the Northern League flourished. Its teams were a dominant force in the FA Amateur Cup, with Bishop Auckland winning the trophy a record ten times and appearing in a further eight finals and the League produced many players who went on to success in the professional game including Raich **Carter** (Esh Winning), Bob **Paisley** (Bishop Auckland), Brian **Clough** (Billingham Synthonia), Chris Waddle (Tow Law Town) and Gary Pallister (Billingham Town).

Perhaps the Northern League's greatest moment came in 1954, when two Northern League teams, Bishops and archrivals Crook Town, contested the Amateur Cup Final. The match at Wembley finished 2–2 after extra time and it took two replays – at St James' and Ayresome Park – to finally settle it in Crook's favour. The Football Association seems to have viewed the success of the north-eastern teams with some suspicion. Official publications, such as Geoffrey Green's centenary history, refer to 'the greater will to win of the northern teams' as the reason they overcame southern opponents. Few in the region doubted that this was a veiled reference to 'boot money', the illegal payments made to amateur players, and it may be this – combined with traditional metropolitan bias – that accounted for so relatively few Northern League players being picked for the English amateur team.

Certainly the Northern League had had its fair share of scandals over covert professionalism. The most damaging of these was the 'Crook Town affair' of 1927–28 that saw 341 players suspended for accepting illegal payments. The truth was that such payments were relatively rare. The north-east had its own semi-professional league, the North-Eastern League, for those who wanted or needed to make money from the game. As one Bishop Auckland player from the 1930s recalled, 'There was money there if you asked, but most of the team had decent jobs so they didn't bother.' The amateur distinction was finally abolished in 1974.

In the 1980s, when the FA formed its non-League pyramid, the Northern League decided to opt out for financial reasons. The effect of this decision was the defection of many of the best and biggest clubs, including Bishop Auckland, Blyth Spartans and Spennymoor United. Eventually the Northern League did join the pyramid albeit at a much lower level than its administrators had originally been offered.

Though its clubs have continued to do well in national competitions (Tow Law Town, Whitby and Whitley Bay have all made recent appearances in FA Vase finals), in the past 20 years the League itself has suffered owing to a variety of social factors from vandalism to televised matches. As the chairman of the Northern League, Mike Amos, has observed, 'It is hard to persuade people to come out on a freezing wet night to watch Evenwood Town play West Auckland when ITV is showing Manchester United versus Barcelona.' Teams such as Willington and Crook who once played regularly in front of several thousand fans now draw only a few dozen spectators, while clubs such as Shotton Comrades would be delighted even with that.

Northern Premier League

The Northern Premier League (NPL) was formed in 1968 by clubs from five leagues covering an area from Northumberland to the Midlands. The aim was to improve the standard of competition among semi-professional teams in the northern half of the country and increase their chances of being elected to the Football League.

In the event, only one NPL club, Wigan Athletic in 1978, was voted directly into the Football League before the formation of the Conference a year later. Meanwhile, four of the clubs voted out of the League in the 1970s dropped down into the NPL: Bradford Park Avenue, Barrow, Workington and Southport. Aside from Wigan, three other founder members have moved into the Football League since direct promotion from the Conference began in 1987: Scarborough, Boston United and the NPL's first winners, Macclesfield Town. Lincolnshire club Gainsborough Trinity were the only continuous members from the NPL's inception until the restructuring of non-League football in 2004.

Two NPL clubs have reached the fourth round of the FA Cup, Stafford Rangers in 1974–75 and Northwich Victoria two seasons later, in both cases having beaten League opposition in the three previous rounds. Altrincham nearly matched Stafford's run in the same year, holding Everton to a 1–1 draw in the third round before losing the replay. The NPL dominated the early years of the FA Trophy, providing nine of the tournament's first ten winners up to 1978–79, after which seven of its members were among the 20 clubs who formed the inaugural Conference. Burscough in 2003 are the only NPL club to have won the Trophy since then, though Leek Town reached the final while in the NPL's second level, Division 1, in 1990.

Seven NPL champions failed to be promoted to the Conference because their grounds didn't meet the standard required, while Colne Dynamos, champions in 1989–90, had the fastest rise and fall of any non-League club in modern times. Newly promoted, and with full-time professional players, they won the NPL by a record margin but were summarily closed down by their owner because the Conference rejected his plan to groundshare while their modest stadium was brought up to scratch.

The league was sponsored first by Multipart in 1985–86 and since 1994 has carried the name of sealing products company Unibond. Following the creation of the Conference second divisions in 2004, the NPL has been downgraded to form part of the third level of non-League football. The subsidiary Division 1, formed in 1987, is supplied by three feeder leagues: the Northern League, the North-West Counties League and the Northern Counties East.

Norwich City

Norwich City Football Club was conceived in the Criterion Café in White Lion Street, Norwich on Tuesday, 17 June 1902, by two Victorian school-teachers, Robert Webster and Joseph Cowper Nutchey. Despite lacking the dense urban population of the traditional footballing heartlands, Norwich have survived as a professional club for 100 years, a history enlivened by occasional cup-chasing feats, periodic financial meltdowns and a tradition of stylish attacking football.

Wearing blue-and-white-halved shirts and calling themselves 'The Citizens', Norwich played their first fixture – a friendly against Harwich & Parkeston – in September 1902 at the club's Newmarket Road ground, a venue still used by local schools for hockey and rugby matches. The Citizens were admitted to the Norfolk and Suffolk League in 1902, where in their first season they would begin an enduring rivalry with neighbouring Ipswich Town. In 1904–05 Norwich won the league, but were later found by an FA commission to be a 'professional organization', and banned from taking part in the Amateur Cup. At a public meeting at the Agricultural Hall in Norwich in March 1905 a motion was passed to accept professional status and the club were subsequently admitted to the Southern League.

By 1907 the newly styled Canaries had adopted their distinctive yellow shirts with green collar and cuffs, and they would earn promotion to the Football League in 1920, two years after going into liquidation and being reformed as a new entity. Born-again, they won the Division 3 (South) title in 1934 and moved to current home Carrow Road the following year, having spent nearly 20 years at the Nest, a bizarre arena situated in a former chalk pit and bounded on one side by a cliff face that rose up just a yard from the touchline. Gradually the Nest had begun to crumble around the edges, with various chalk-slides and near-misses for players and fans: during the club's final season at the ground players were warned to beware of falling rubble when taking corners.

The 1950s saw Norwich enjoy some notable Cup successes, beating Liverpool at Carrow Road in 1950–51 and, famously, Arsenal at Highbury in 1953–54. However, bankruptcy loomed once again in 1957 after the club had installed a set of cripplingly expensive floodlights. A public appeal fund was launched, rapidly reaching its £25,000 target and inspiring the team to its most successful season thus far in 1958–59: Terry Bly scored 29 goals as Division 3 City reached the semi-finals of the FA Cup, beating Matt **Busby**'s Manchester United along the way. A League Cup win followed in 1962, and ten years later Norwich finally reached Division 1 under the guidance of the stern Ron Saunders, later a League title winner with Aston Villa.

The 1970s at Carrow Road were dominated by the reign of the charismatic John Bond, who led the club briefly to the top of Division 1 in 1979. This was one of many exhilarating moments during Bond's time as the Canaries consolidated their reputation for free-flowing attacking football, based around such players as Ted MacDougall, Phil Boyer and former World Cup-winning veteran Martin Peters. In 1985 under manager Ken Brown, Norwich won the League Cup for the second time, beating Sunderland 1–0 at Wembley, only to suffer relegation the same season and see their place in the UEFA Cup disappear in the wake of the **Heysel disaster**.

By 1992, however, the club would have a new chairman in Robert Chase and a new manager in Mike Walker, and would find itself a founder member of the Premier League. Walker's Norwich enjoyed a remarkable first season, challenging for the title until April before eventually finishing third. This was followed by an exuberant UEFA Cup campaign, in the course of which the Canaries became the first English team to win at Bayern Munich's Olympic Stadium, Jeremy Goss's volley sealing a 2–1 victory. Walker's men went out in the next round, Dennis Bergkamp scoring both goals in Internazionale's 2–0 aggregate win. However, troubled times followed as Walker left the club, relegation loomed and yet

another fight for financial survival ensued.

Chase was eventually bought out by a new board, which included celebrity chef and long-standing Canaries fan Delia Smith who, with her husband Michael Wynn Jones, would ultimately become majority shareholder and the public face of the club hierarchy. Under Nigel Worthington, Norwich's sixth manager in as many years, the club were promoted to the Premiership in 2004, then relegated on the last day of the following season.

Nottingham Forest

Nottingham Forest began in 1865 as a shinney team, playing a form of hockey in caps of 'Garibaldi Red', the colour adopted by an Italian republican movement. During a meeting in a local pub, a J. S. Scrimshaw proposed the club switch to football, and Forest are the second-oldest of the clubs that are now professional .

From the beginning, Forest were one of the most innovative of the fledgling clubs. They became the first team to play in shinguards (in 1874, albeit worn outside the socks), took part in a game where the referee used a whistle for the first time (1878), and introduced the classic 2–3–5 formation during the 1870s that endured for nearly 90 years. When two former Forest players moved down to London to work on the railways and joined the works team, they wrote to their old club for assistance. Forest duly mailed off a bundle of red shirts and white shorts to the London side, who were known as Woolwich Arsenal.

Forest were refused entry to the Football League in its inaugural year of 1888, having to make do with a spell in the Football Alliance. They joined the League in 1892, and beat Derby County to win the FA Cup six years later, just after moving into the City Ground on the south bank of the Trent, where they remain to this day. It was the last major trophy they were to win for 60 years; by the outbreak of the First World War they were bottom of Division 2 and applying for re-election. The inter-war years saw Forest rebounding between the two divisions. Despite being able to draw attendances of close to 5,000 in a two-team city, they always seemed to be mired in financial strife.

By the end of the 1940s, Forest reached their lowest point to date, being relegated to Division 3 along with neighbours County. However, double promotions saw them in the top flight by 1957; two years later they won the FA Cup, beating Luton 2–1 after being a man short for much of the game, losing Roy Dwight (first goal-scorer and Elton John's uncle) to a broken leg. Forest had one exceptionally successful season in the next decade, finishing as League runners-up and FA Cup semi-finalists in 1966–67. But injuries the following season to winger Ian Storey-Moore and key midfielder John Barnwell exposed the side's weaknesses and began a slide into Division 2 mediocrity in the shadow of Derby County and their (at the time) widely disliked manager, Brian **Clough**.

On 6 January 1975, the tables turned. Clough, after a disastrous spell as Leeds boss, joined Forest and immediately cleaned out the squad, drafting in favoured staff and players from his previous clubs. By 1977, the club was promoted to Division 1 by the skin of its teeth and the following season tore through the top flight. They beat Liverpool after a replay in the League Cup Final, began an undefeated run of 42 games (a record until Arsenal broke it in 2004), and took the League title with consummate ease. The next year they won the European Cup, beating Liverpool along the way, while also retaining

the League Cup and finishing second in the League.

Although their grip on the League and domestic cups started to slip in 1980, Forest had enough in the tank to win the European Cup again, defeating Kevin **Keegan**'s Hamburg 1–0 in Madrid. However, the purple patch ended when Clough's influential assistant Peter Taylor departed at the beginning of the 1980–81 season. Forest spent the 1980s cementing a reputation as a club that was impossible to dislike: attractive, passing football, likeably bonkers manager, occasionally popping up to tweak the tail of the 'Big Five' and win the odd minor trophy. A glorious run in the UEFA Cup in 1983–84 saw them overturn Celtic and PSV Eindhoven before losing in dramatic fashion in the semis to Anderlecht.

In 1988, Forest lost to Liverpool in the FA Cup semi-finals. In 1989 they lost again to the same opponents at the same stage, but hardly anyone remembers the score; it was a replayed match in the wake of the **Hillsborough disaster**. They eventually made it to the final in 1991, and it seemed like the end of an era; Clough, after winning the one trophy that had eluded him throughout his managerial career, was sure to retire. Thanks to a Paul **Gascoigne** tackle on Gary Charles that would have guaranteed a red card were it not for the fact that he was stretchered off himself and a Des Walker own-goal in extra time, Forest were denied and a seemingly troubled Clough stayed on. It was to be the beginning of the end for Forest.

Clough eventually retired at the end of the Premiership's inaugural season, but the club was relegated, which cost them dear. Save for a brief revival that took them to third place in 1994–95, Forest have until recently been either too good for the second tier, or not good enough for the Premiership, constantly nurturing quality players and then being forced to sell them on to bigger clubs. Their latest manager, Gary Megson, briefly a player under Clough, was appointed in 2005, but they succumbed to relegation. Megson left after a poor run the following season.

Notts County

Notts County have never been a particularly successful club, but they do hold several English League records. Among these are the most relegations (14) and a claim to being the oldest football club in the country, a version of Notts County having been organized in 1862 before its formal founding at the George IV Hotel in 1864. The club has been most notable in recent times for its financial problems. In October 2003 a less welcome record was set when County became the English League club to have spent longest in administration, the directors having conceded control over its finances in June 2002.

County were founder members of the Football League in 1888, and have been present in every League season since, spending time in all four divisions (but never the Premiership) without ever winning the League title. County also won the FA Cup in 1894 as a Division 2 team. More Division 2 championships followed in 1897, 1914 and 1923, the latter two after the club's move in 1910 to current home Meadow Lane. In 1923, two years before the change in the offside law to encourage more goals, County topped the division despite scoring just 46 goals in 42 matches, keeping 23 clean sheets in the process.

County have a long history of fluctuation. After 16 consecutive seasons in the top flight between 1897 and 1913 they embarked on what would become a typical run of seven promotions and relegations in 15 seasons. Relegated from the top division in 1926 County didn't return until 1981, when they were taken up by Scottish manager Jimmy Sirrel, a man with the gnarled look of a music hall comedian and probably the most popular figure at the club since Tommy **Lawton**'s spell as a player in the 1940s. The team struggled against the drop in each of their three years but did at least beat neighbours Forest twice, including a 2–0 win at the City Ground in 1982.

Back-to-back relegations in 1984 and 1985 were followed by successive promotions leading to a return to the top flight in 1991. Relegation the following year would be the spur for what has been the most difficult period in the club's history. An Anglo Italian Cup success in 1995 and a Division 3 title three years later, when the team lost only five games all season, couldn't disguise the serious financial problems that were jeopardizing County's future.

With debts already mounting following the prolonged £8m redevelopment of Meadow Lane, the real problems began in 1999 with the purchase of the club by a group headed by American Albert Scardino, a former Pulitzer Prize-winning journalist and formerly one of Bill Clinton's press aides. Overspending and a crippling wage bill led to a record 534 days in administration, followed by the threat of expulsion from the League.

County are entrenched in the bottom division of the League, though the Supporters' Trust now has a 30.2 per cent share in the consortium that controls the club and a director on the board. Instability at the top has tended to be a consistent feature of the club's history. Since 1927 there have been 39 managerial changes at Meadow Lane, with the team commanded by, among others, Tommy Lawton, Larry Lloyd, Neil Warnock, Howard Kendall and Sam Allardyce.

County's famous black and white stripes will live on even if the club goes out of existence. Juventus abandoned their original pink shirts after an English player, John Savage, was sent home to find replacements. He returned with replicas of Notts County's shirts.

offside

Along with handball and fouls, offside is
part of a holy trinity of football rules
without which the game would be unreco-
gnizable. With no offside, football would
be a shapeless free-for-all, something
similar to Gaelic football, with the ball
constantly punted forward in search of
goal-hanging attackers. Creative
attacking play would disappear, and the
world outside football would be full of
unemployed studio pundits and
redundant linesmen.

Of all the major rules, offside is the
most unobtrusive. Often referred to, by
those who don't know what they're referring to, as an obscure or learned rule,
offside is in fact a very pragmatic way of
ensuring the game maintains a recognizable structure. In basic terms a player
will be offside if, when the ball is played
or he is about to receive it, there are
fewer than two opponents between him
and the opposition goal, with the proviso
that a player cannot be offside in his own
half, or from a throw-in, or if he is behind
the ball. Bolstered by this rule, the
defending team can decide where the
game will be contested, pushing forward
in a line and forcing the attacking team
to construct a move in possession of the
ball that will defeat both defenders and
the need to stay onside.

The first major change to the offside
rule since the early days came in 1925,
when the number of players required
between a forward and the opposition
goal was reduced from three to two. This
was in response to fears that the game
had become overly dominated by
defence. In fact, the history of the offside
law reveals football's administrators in a
constant battle to loosen its tyranny over
attacking players and generally spice the
game up with a few more goals.

During the 1924–25 season 1,192

goals were scored in the English Division 1. The year after, with the new rule in place, 1,703 goals were scored. The immediate beneficiaries were strikers such as George Camsell, who scored 59 goals in 1926–27, and Dixie **Dean**, who beat Camsell's record by one goal the following season. Herbert **Chapman**'s Arsenal used innovative tactics to turn the new laws to their advantage, in the process winning five League titles in eight years. Chapman's use of the 'stopper' centre-half in defence and development of a direct attacking style of play through a dominant centre-forward still influences the way the game is played today.

It was another Arsenal team, George **Graham**'s League champions of 1989 and 1991, who embodied the most extreme example of another aspect of the offside laws: the offside trap. During the 1980s it was common to see Division 1 teams 'compressing' the game into a small space around the halfway line, and responding to attempts to break through this well-drilled line with immediate appeals to the linesman to raise his flag for offside. Relying on hours of practice at keeping a straight line, and on a general lack of attacking players with the wit and timing to break through this trap, the tactic generally succeeded in stifling the game. The finest exponents were Arsenal's League champions of 1989 and 1991. Captain Tony **Adams**'s raised right arm appealing for offside is one of the most memorable images of the last few seasons of the old Division 1.

Recently, FIFA has begun to tinker with the laws again, once more looking to make it harder for defenders to use offside to stifle attacking play. Recent innovations include the rule that attackers are onside if they are level with the last defender, followed by the requirement for 'daylight' between an attacker and his marker before he can be flagged.

Guidelines introduced in 2004 specifying such vagaries as 'active areas', and once again requiring that a player be 'interfering with play' before being deemed offside, served only to confuse the situation and led to some bizarre tactical innovations in the Premiership. Strikers such as Ruud van Nistelrooy began to loiter deliberately offside in order to avoid a marker, while Sam Allardyce instructed his Bolton players to charge back out of offside positions, often stationing them on the posts of their opponents' goal at free kicks. As a result, the laws relating to offside have rarely been so widely puzzled over.

Old Firm

Why the 'Old Firm'? The answer is Scottish football in microcosm: the nickname was adopted in the early 20th century largely because of the financial benefits gained by a visit of either Celtic or Rangers.

Virtually from their inception, Celtic and Rangers dominated Scottish football. There have been blips along the way, but they have proven to be temporary transfers of power, and normal service has soon resumed. Today, no team outside the two Glasgow giants has won the Scottish Premier League since Aberdeen in 1984–85 and the gap in both on- and off-field resources between the Old Firm and chasing pack is ever-widening.

Being ensconced in a duopoly is always likely to provide friction, yet the acrimonious relationship between Celtic and Rangers runs far deeper. The sectarian nature of the rivalry (to keep it simple, Celtic lean on Roman Catholic roots, Rangers similarly embrace a Protestant image) has made the fixture one of the most enticing in world football. However, it can also be accurately said that it is one of the more unattractive sights and sounds in modern British society.

A special Old Firm game in the wake of the Ibrox disaster of 1971 is perhaps the only example of a genuine coming together of the two clubs. As early as 1909 there was a riot at Hampden between supporters after a Scottish Cup Final replay and as recently as 1999 Parkhead saw one of the most eventful Old Firm games of all time. Referee Hugh Dallas was struck with a coin as chaotic scenes on the pitch and in the stands resulted in subsequent games being confined to early-afternoon kick-offs.

Both clubs have launched their own measures in an attempt to lessen the bigotry on such open view amongst their supports, yet success has been limited. And while both tacitly allow an element of sectarianism to continue unchecked, mindful of their financial revenues, that is likely to remain the case. The Scottish parliament has made plenty of noise about intervening, yet this bluster has yet to be converted into action.

For several years, both Celtic and Rangers have been eyeing a transfer to the English Premiership and the greater riches that the more high-profile league would offer. They claim to be financially stifled by the SPL, resulting in their failure to make serious inroads in Europe. However, their advances received a lukewarm reception at best and it has to be wondered just how much the English league needs two teams that continue to display such a blatant sectarian edge.

Oldham Athletic

Many football supporters like to blame a world war for having affected their team's chances of success. Oldham fans have a stronger case than most. In 1915, the Latics needed one point from their final two games, at home to Burnley and

Liverpool, to be crowned Division 1 champions. Both were lost and the title went to Everton. When football resumed, Oldham's moment had passed; the club were relegated in 1923, and it would be 69 years before the town witnessed top-flight football again.

A football club called Pine Villa was founded in Oldham in 1895 by the landlord of the Featherstall and Junction Hotel. The present name was adopted four years later and they were elected to the Football League in 1907, having just taken up residence at the famously wind-swept Boundary Park. Six years after their relegation from Division 1, and having led the table for most of the season, the club missed promotion after taking just two points from their final five games. In 1935 they dropped into Division 3 for the first time in their history. A lengthy period of flitting between the bottom two leagues followed, broken up by the club's sanctions-busting tour of Rhodesia in 1967, an initiative organized by then chairman Ken Bates.

The Latics' ascent began under the astute Jimmy Frizzell, a Scotsman who spent a decade as a player before becoming manager in 1970. Oldham won promotion from Division 4 in 1971, as well as monopolizing the 'Ford Sporting League', a competition for all 92 League clubs that awarded points for goals and subtracted them for bad behaviour. The sponsors' demand that the £70,000 prize money should be spent on ground improvements led to the construction of a Ford stand at Boundary Park. Another promotion followed under Frizzell in 1974 after which they spent 16 years as a solid Division 2 side, crowds holding up despite being within an hour's drive of several big clubs either side of the Pennines.

Oldham could have returned to the top division in 1987 under Frizzell's successor, Joe Royle, but lost out in the first-ever Division 2 play-offs. They got there eventually for a three-year spell between 1991 and 1994, and reached the Littlewoods Cup Final in 1990, losing 1–0 to Nottingham Forest. There were also two narrow FA Cup semi-final defeats to neighbours Manchester United, the first in controversial circumstances in 1990 after a shot from Nick Henry was deemed not to have crossed the line; and the second dramatically lost after a spectacular late equalizer by Mark Hughes in 1994, a moment that would ultimately signal the decline of the fine team assembled by Royle.

On Easter Monday 1994, Oldham had lost 3–2 at Old Trafford in a dress rehearsal for the following week's FA Cup semi-final. Exactly four years later, fans staged a sit-in protest after a 1–0 home defeat by Wycombe in Division 2 that left the club facing a third demotion in four years. Blame for the Latics' decline was directed at their major shareholders, the brewery J. W. Lees. In the early 1980s they had provided a loan to pay players' wages but then waived the £70,000 they were owed and instead took over a recently built supporters' club and sports complex plus four years' free shirt sponsorship. Lees provided no further financial assistance, their only contribution to the Royle years being the launch of 'Wembley lager' in 1990.

They sold up in 2001 to an IT entrepreneur, Chris Moore, who spent generously, then threatened to close the club down after taking heavy losses on the stock market. Manager Iain Dowie kept the penniless Latics up before leaving for Crystal Palace; since his departure, the team have recorded another notable FA Cup success, beating Manchester City in the third round on an exceptionally blustery Pennines afternoon in 2005.

Olympics

The British public have had a disparaging opinion of Olympic football for many years, mainly because they had no representatives involved. This was not always the case. At the 1900 Olympics in Paris, football was an exhibition sport and its major proponents, England, sent amateur club side Upton Park as its representatives. They promptly beat France 4–0. Football was a main event in London in 1908 when just six teams entered, including France A and B, after Hungary and Bohemia withdrew. The 'United Kingdom' team thrashed Sweden 12–1 and Holland 4–0 before seeing off Denmark 2–0 in the final to win the first football gold medal.

With British football having a head start on most other countries, it was little surprise when 'England' beat Hungary (7–0), Finland (4–0) and Denmark (4–2) to win gold again in Sweden in 1912. The standard of football elsewhere in Europe – the game was yet to be established worldwide – was indicated by Germany beating Russia 16–0.

By the next Olympiad at Antwerp in 1920, football had caught on all over the globe and professionalism was challenging the amateur ethic. The British again entered a purely amateur team but after their shock 2–0 defeat to Norway (ironically, also all amateur) in the first round the FA stormed off, claiming 'British amateurs have been playing against professionals of other countries; we shall never again take part in Olympic football'. The FA stood by their word and withdrew from the 1924 Paris games and, despite pleading, also missed the Amsterdam event four years later, both won by Uruguay. Other countries felt they had to pay players for taking weeks or even months off work to play – 'broken-time payments' – while the

English amateurs refused to consider such a thing.

With broken-time payments banned for the 1936 Olympics, the FA decided only three weeks before the tournament to send a team, and got help from the Scottish, Welsh and Northern Irish FAs to form a 'Great Britain' side. After beating China 2–0, GB were defeated 5–4 by Poland. The extravagant and futuristic facilities in Berlin astonished the Brits but did Germany no favours: they were sent home in disgrace by an onlooking Hitler – the only football match he ever attended – after a shock second-round defeat by Norway.

For the London Olympiad in 1948, Manchester United manager Matt **Busby** coached the British team that scraped past Holland and France before a 3–1 semi-final defeat by Yugoslavia at Wembley; Britain then lost the bronze medal match 5–3 to Denmark. GB's amateurs were embarrassingly defeated by Luxembourg in the first round in Helsinki in 1952, while the 'shamateurs' of Yugoslavia and the emerging Hungarians reached the final.

Having lost 5–3 on aggregate to Bulgaria in a qualifier for 1956, GB were reinstated when Hungary refused to travel to Melbourne. The Bulgarians proved their superiority when they hammered the English – the other home nations had refused to send players – 6–1 in Australia. Britain's last appearance to date at an Olympic finals came four years later in Rome where they scraped past Chinese Taipei 3–2, lost 4–3 to Brazil and drew with Italy, 2–2. Teams assembled from amateur leagues, notably the Isthmian and Northern, continued to play in Olympic-qualifying matches until Britain withdrew for good. Their final home match, a 1–0 win over Bulgaria in 1971, was watched by 3,000 at Wembley.

The IOC now wants a full inter-national tournament while FIFA – fiercely protective of the World Cup – insists that the Olympic football remain a minor event by restricting it to Under-23s (plus a compromise of three over-age players). With the European Under-21 competition acting as the qualifying tournament, the home nations would have to unite at that level first, an unthinkable move. However, with London bidding for the Olympics in 2012, noises are already coming from organizers as to how, as hosts, GB could get an automatic entry and a team featuring the best young players in Britain could be fielded for the first time ever.

other football codes

Despite the snobbishness that many followers of the various football codes exhibit towards the others, it is clear that they all derive from a common origin. All these codes are based in the preindustrial folk games that were tamed and codified in the 19th century, mainly (but not exclusively) by English public schools.

Myths about the origins of footballing codes have remained remarkably persistent. Rugby, for example, was certainly not 'invented' by William Webb Ellis at Rugby School in 1823; nor does the origin of Australian Rules football have anything to do with Gaelic games. The first rules for the Australian game were laid down in 1859 and derived from an amalgam of English public school versions of football: its leading pioneer, Thomas Wills, had been at school at Rugby. Australian Rules has a good claim to be the oldest of the surviving codes and to preserve the nearest example of what those early free-form games must have looked like (not to mention the oldest surviving club, Melbourne, formally founded in 1859).

The main split between the codes that

were to spread internationally came with the formation of the Football Association in 1863, which built on rules set down in Cambridge 17 years earlier. By 1870 the FA had made the decisive break that would define the game by outlawing handling of the ball, except by one designated player, the goalkeeper. Clubs and public schools that preferred to keep handling (and, initially, hacking) came together to form the Rugby Football Union in 1871.

While soccer (derived it's thought from the word 'association') spread rapidly downwards socially and outwards along Britain's trade routes, rugby became the winter game of the public schools at home and the colonies with substantial white populations – New Zealand, South Africa and the eastern states of Australia, where the local version of football had not yet prevailed. That class split was cemented in 1895 (mirrored in 1907 in Australia) by the further fracturing of rugby into professional and amateur versions.

Another tributary from rugby led to the United States, where Yale University came over to Harvard's version of the handling game in 1876. By the end of the century the distinct rules that would become modern American football were clearly present. Finally, another new code came into being in Ireland, in a classic act of 19th-century nationalist 'invention of tradition'. Supposedly based on ancient forms of football, the Gaelic game was codified after the formation of the Gaelic Athletic Association in 1884 as a hybrid of soccer and rugby (its hurling counterpart, however, did have much more credible local roots).

Gaelic football quickly grew in popularity and became what it had been intended to become – the cultural vanguard of Irish nationalism. But the diehards of the GAA who still refuse to allow soccer to be played on their pitches on the grounds that it is a 'foreign' game find themselves on the same shaky ground as British football fans who despise the term 'soccer'. There is no single code that can rightfully claim it is the one, true football. The truth is that all football, whether in San Francisco, Melbourne, Dublin or even Rugby, ultimately belongs to the same family.

The Oval

Although much more famous as a cricket venue, the Oval in south London played host to momentous football occasions in the 19th century. In 1872 it staged the first FA Cup Final, in which Wanderers beat the hot favourites Royal Engineers 1–0 in front of 2,000. In the first few years of the competition it was also the venue for the semi-finals. The ground, home to Surrey County Cricket Club, was chosen largely because Charles Alcock, the secretary of the Football Association and driving force behind the Cup, was also the secretary of Surrey.

The final stayed at the Oval until 1892 (with one diversion to west London's Lillie Bridge in 1873), but after 25,000 people had turned up to see West Brom beat Aston Villa, the cricket club decided enough was enough. The Oval was also the venue for England's first five international matches at home (four against Scotland, one against Wales) between 1873 and 1879.

After that regional grounds came into their own – England's first home game elsewhere was at Blackburn in 1881 – but the Oval hosted five more, the last a 3–2 defeat by Scotland in 1889. Regardless of the attitude of the cricket club, the awkwardness of staging football on such a large playing surface would have quickly become intolerable as crowds rapidly increased. In recent years the

Oval has again staged football, but of the Australian Rules variety, which has always shared cricket arenas on its home turf.

Michael Owen

Michael Owen is a unique footballer in many ways. Very few British players have made a similar impact at such an early age. Owen became the youngest player ever to score for England with his goal against Morocco in a World Cup warm-up game in 1998. Then at France 98 he provided one of the most memorable images of the tournament by scoring a spectacular solo goal against Argentina in Saint-Etienne.

Owen's unusually early success is in part a reflection of the way the game has developed in England since the start of the Premiership. By the time Owen made his debut for Liverpool in 1996 he was already a cultishly recognizable figure, a feted and photogenic youngster in a game suddenly hungry for youth and talent. In a previous era the teenage Owen would have scarcely been a target for media attention, but his time as the most gifted young player of his generation at the FA School of Excellence in Lilleshall had been widely gossiped about and written up. Within a couple of years he was already hosting his own *Soccer Skills* programme on national television.

At the age of 26 Owen's career has evolved through several distinct phases. After his early successes his progress stalled. Repeated hamstring and pelvic injuries restricted his development, although during his sporadic appearances for Liverpool and England he continued to score goals at an excellent rate. His record for Liverpool was very good: 158 goals in 297 games in a side that continually relied on him to win tight games.

After a difficult couple of seasons, the most productive period of Owen's career to date coincided with the high point of Gérard Houllier's reign as Liverpool manager. In 2001 Owen enjoyed an amazing purple patch, beginning with two late FA Cup Final-winning goals against Arsenal, goals in Liverpool's first-ever Champions' League campaign and a hat-trick in the 5–1 World Cup qualifier win against Germany in Munich. A remarkable six months finished with Owen winning the slightly surprising accolade of the youngest ever European Footballer of the Year. His period in possession of the title would be a difficult one, with more injuries and a prolonged loss of form for the first time in his career. Entering a new phase of his footballing existence after the 2002 World Cup, Owen spent his pre-season working in the gym to build up his leg and pelvic muscles. The result is a different style of player from the teenager known for his raw acceleration. Owen is stronger now, and trusts more to his composure, movement and prowess in the air to score goals.

For England, Owen has succeeded Gary **Lineker** and Alan **Shearer** as the latest centre-forward to set off on a quest for Bobby **Charlton**'s record 49 England goals. Owen does have some notable international achievements: a 100 per cent record of scoring in all tournament knockout games he has played in; participation in four major tournaments by the age of 25; and a habit of scoring important goals in big games.

Despite an opaque and highly coached media manner, Owen has earned a secondary fortune from commercial endorsements. This has been spent in some occasionally unusual ways: a house and car for members of his close family, all in the same street; and, at one stage, a gambling habit that was much trumpeted in the popular press after allegations that England players had frittered away vast sums playing cards on the team bus at the 2002 World Cup.

In 2004 Owen signed for Real Madrid, moving on to Newcastle United a year later. An oddity of Owen's career remains that – almost uniquely among feted goalscorers – he has never formed a notable partnership with a fellow forward for either club or country. His big-man/little-man double act with Emile Heskey remains the next best thing. Despite his occasional air of youthful world-weariness, there remains much for Owen to achieve.

Oxford United

While there has been a club called Oxford United only since 1960, its origins can be traced back to 1893, when a local vicar and doctor held a meeting in the Britannia Inn in a village just outside Oxford to create Headington United. For the next half-century the club was happy to compete in the local county leagues. Shortly after the Second World War their ambitious president, Vic Couling, took the calculated risk of turning Headington professional; and in 1949 they secured the final place in the newly expanded Southern League by a single vote.

The team flourished, so much so that 1953 saw them achieve the double of the championship and the Southern League Cup. Throughout the 1950s Headington pursued their twin objectives of acquiring Football League status and of changing their name to Oxford United; and when the FA finally agreed to the latter the team responded with successive Southern League championships, making them the natural choice in 1962 to replace the defunct Accrington Stanley in Division 4.

Progress for the club continued to be rapid. Captained by Ron Atkinson they became the first Division 4 team to reach an FA Cup quarter-final. The following year saw them promoted to Division 3, and in 1968 they were champions of that division. Despite clinging on to their Division 2 status for eight years, Oxford's modest crowds at the Manor Ground, their base since 1925, put a brake on their ambitions; and the club hit such serious financial problems in 1981 that it faced closure until publisher Robert Maxwell intervened. His aborted scheme to merge Oxford with Reading as the 'Thames Valley Royals' – it would have been the first merger of League clubs since before the First World War – meant he would never win the trust or affection of supporters. However, in the years he spent as chairman, with Jim Smith as manager, Oxford won the Division 3 and Division 2 championships in successive seasons – an unprecedented feat.

Throughout the mid-1980s Oxford became notorious giantkillers, especially in the League Cup. The compact Manor Ground provided an irresistible setting for the TV cameras in search of upsets; and time after time the team obliged, with Newcastle, Leeds, Arsenal and Manchester United (twice) departing vanquished.

For three seasons under Jim Smith's successor, Maurice Evans, Oxford survived in the top division, the goalscoring instincts of John Aldridge and Dean Saunders compensating for an often porous defence; and they also achieved a stylish 3–0 Wembley victory over QPR in 1986 to win the League Cup. Robert Maxwell's purchase of Derby County foretold the end of the euphoria. While other Maxwells continued for a while to run the club (Saunders was dutifully shipped off to Derby), it was clear the family's priorities lay elsewhere. Debt-ridden, Oxford slipped back down the divisions, with only a short-lived promotion from the (renamed) Division 2 lightening the gloom.

In 1999 there was another financial crisis and another 11th-hour saviour, Firoz Kassam, who not only kept the club alive but also negotiated a long-awaited move to a new stadium, modestly named after himself. By the time Oxford occupied their (three-quarters completed) new home in 2001 they were back in the bottom division of the League, their immediate future secured but their glory days a fading memory. In 2006 they were relegated to the Conference.

Bob Paisley

Bob Paisley is the most successful manager in the history of English football. During his period in charge of Liverpool from 1974 to 1983 the club won the League title six times, the European Cup in 1977, 1978 and 1981, the UEFA Cup in 1976 and three League Cups. Despite this, Paisley remains strangely un-feted outside Anfield, and is often characterized as the beneficiary of the groundwork laid by his more flamboyant predecessor, Bill **Shankly**. In brown overcoat and flat cap, publicly taciturn almost to the point of embarrassment, as a manager Paisley's strong point was tactical analysis. He bought successfully – key signings included Kenny **Dalglish**, perhaps Liverpool's greatest-ever player, Alan Hansen and Ian **Rush** – and quietly accumulated more substantial major honours than any manager before or since.

Born in 1919 in Hetton-le-Hole in Durham, Paisley began his football career as a tenacious and attacking left-half with Bishop Auckland in 1937, and was signed by Liverpool manager George Kay just before the outbreak of the Second World War. During the war Paisley served with General Montgomery's Eighth Army 'Desert Rats' and was part of the allied force that liberated Rome. Returning to the Italian capital with Liverpool for the European Cup Final in 1977 he memorably remarked on passing the Colosseum: 'the last time I drove down here I was sitting on top of a tank'.

Paisley was a regular in the Liverpool team that won the first League title after the war and went on to become club captain. After his retirement in 1954 he considered going back to his teenage trade of bricklaying, but accepted the offer of a backroom job at Anfield, having taken a correspondence course in physiotherapy.

The arrival of Bill Shankly at Anfield in 1959 brought a huge change in fortunes for the club and also an intensifying of Paisley's role with the first team. His speech to the first team on Shankly's retirement in 1974 ('they're giving me the job even though I didn't really want it') may have been typically downbeat, but his achievements surpassed those of the man credited with rebuilding the club. A shy and publicly very modest man, even at the height of Liverpool's success Paisley retained the public appearance of a man who had just popped out to buy a newspaper, as Mark Lawrenson recalled of his first meeting with his new manager: 'I had on my best suit, shirt and tie. When I got in the car I saw that Bob was wearing slippers and a cardigan. I couldn't believe it. They'd just won the European Cup and there was this fellow, who everyone in football thought was an absolute god, driving me to the ground in his slippers and cardigan.'

Partick Thistle

Partick have long provided a little light relief from the intense and often ugly rivalry of the **Old Firm**, with whom they share the city of Glasgow. In 2002 a teen-ager was in court charged with breaking into the club's Firhill stadium and stealing £21,000 worth of match tickets, which he later discarded. 'You are clearly not a Harry Wragg,' said the sheriff invoking one of the club's more colourful nicknames before sentencing. More commonly known as 'The Jags', Partick's other nickname, 'The Maryhill Magyars', underlines the affection with which they are regarded in the city.

Partick had spent a total of ten seasons in the Scottish Premier League after being promoted from Division 1 in

1975–76 (Alan Hansen made his name in their yellow and red shirts before joining Liverpool), but by the end of the 1990s they became the first of a wave of clubs to visit the brink of extinction. Only a supreme effort from their supporters saved the club. The mobilized fan base began the Save the Jags group, which mutated into Scotland's first supporters' trust and now guarantees the supporters a powerful place on the Partick board.

That close call came as Partick flirted with relegation to Division 3. Their financial recovery coincided with a charge through the divisions. In three heady years, Thistle were in the SPL and, against all odds, avoided finishing at its foot at the end of season 2002–03. If they had, they would not have been relegated, as the stadium of Falkirk, the Division 1 champions, did not meet SPL criteria. It is a typically ironic twist, then, that saw Thistle relegated the following season when the League changed its rules to allow groundshares. Inverness, the new Division 1 champions, relocated temporarily to Aberdeen, and Thistle went down. They fell further, to Division 2, at the end of 2004–05.

Partick had joined the Scottish League in 1893, 17 years after their formation. They won the Scottish Cup in 1921, and recorded their best-ever win in the same competition ten years later, thrashing Royal Albert 16–0 in a first-round match, but their finest hour came with a League Cup win over Celtic in 1971. The team they beat was the all-conquering side of Jock **Stein**, the team that had won the European Cup and would record nine consecutive League championships. The Partick line-up that won 4–1 after going four up before the break included the club's most capped player, goalkeeper Alan Rough, who made all but two of his 53 appearances for Scotland while with the Jags.

partnerships

In 1974 Kevin **Keegan** and John Toshack took part in a televised experiment designed to establish once and for all whether their on-field striking partnership at Liverpool was in fact telepathic. Sitting back to back, the two players were asked to study different-coloured pieces of card and then to transmit to one another, using only the power of the mind, the colour of the card they were looking at. Unexpectedly, Toshack guessed right four out of five times.

The incredible results were screened as part of a Granada documentary, but not before Toshack had shared with his partner the secret of his paranormal deductions. He had been able to see the colours Keegan had been 'sending' to him across the room reflected in a camera lens.

Despite their lack of paranormal powers, Keegan and Toshack remain one of the most widely revered footballing double acts. They also had a rare longevity as a pair: partnerships that enjoy any prolonged success are extremely scarce.

Changes in tactics and formation have increasingly brought the partnership to the fore. The five-man forward line, where two inside-forwards and two wingers operated around a central striker, has given way in the last 40 years to the more rigid 4–4–2. Under this system there is more emphasis on players operating in pairs: two strikers, two central midfielders, two centre-backs, and on the flanks a full-back and wide midfielder operating in tandem. Covering the right flank during their time together at Manchester United and in the England team, David **Beckham** and best mate/man Gary Neville formed one of the most effective partnerships in the recent history of British football, so much so that Neville's extended international career (he currently has 80 caps) can be attributed in large part to his understanding with the England captain.

Central defensive partnerships have stood out at times: Alan Hansen and Mark Lawrenson performed effectively together for Liverpool during the early 1980s; the heavyweight pairing of Steve Bruce and Gary Pallister were dominant for Manchester United in the Premiership for several seasons, less so against craftier continental opposition (witness their bewilderment at the movement of Romario and Hristo Stoichkov during a 4–0 defeat at the Nou Camp in 1995). And at Highbury a back four permed from Lee Dixon and Nigel Winterburn at full-back, with Tony **Adams** and one of either Martin Keown or Steve Bould in the centre, performed with a crushing parsimoniousness for over ten years.

Nevertheless, the most celebrated footballing partnerships have tended to be in attack. Ian **Rush** and Kenny **Dalglish**, again at Liverpool, formed a fearsome attacking pair, this time following the crafty playmaker/pacy poacher model, and exemplifying the simple disciplines of perceptive running and accurate passing. In this sense partnerships, like team spirit, are an illusion created by success. Teddy Sheringham, known for his rare ability to pass and link attacking play, has been credited with forming uncanny attacking partnership with practically every forward he has ever been paired with. Even during his formative years at Millwall, Sheringham's partnership with the lumbering Tony Cascarino was locally feted, while at international level his understanding with Alan **Shearer**, particularly around the time of Euro 96, at which the duo scored seven of England's eight goals, was widely celebrated.

Sheringham even managed to form an effective partnership at Manchester United with Andy Cole, during a period when the two players refused to speak to each other. This was in strict contrast to United's other successful attacking partnership of recent times, between Dwight Yorke and Andy Cole. Cole and Yorke's brief romance – it lasted, in effect, just one treble-winning season – was another rarity, a footballing partnership that involved friendship off the field, the two sharing a series of lurid sexual escapades meticulously documented in the tabloids. Partnerships, like everything else in football, are a matter of pragmatism, a winning formula stumbled upon and retained only for as long as they succeed.

passing

Passing, like calculus and wearing thin clothes in the cold, is a Scottish idea. Previously, the English public school game favoured the dribbling approach in which one of many forwards ran with the ball as far as possible until such time as he was dispossessed and the baton was taken up by the next player.

From Scotland came the theory that just as much ground – if not more – might be gained through the simple expedient of switching the ball amiably between team-mates and running onto something they called 'a pass'. With teams, mainly from the north of England, gaining success through the shifty employment of Scottish professionals, the dominance of the public schools faded and, with it, their style of play. Passing became popular, professionalism was legalized in England and the phrase 'pass and move' prepared to be born. To combat the new, improved way of trans-

ferring the ball towards goal, two other new ideas were introduced: defending and being onside while ahead of the ball.

Despite the fact that Britain has produced so many fine passers of the ball – Alex **James**, Wilf **Mannion**, Glenn **Hoddle**, David **Beckham** and the like – the language of passing in the domestic game is resoundingly conservative. Phrases such as 'back door!', 'get rid!' and 'easy ball!' dominate at grass-roots level and well over a century in there appears to be no adventurous alternative such as 'difficult ball!' to encourage the subtle and surprising reverse pass behind a flat back four. Indeed, foreign opposition are often mocked for trying to 'pass it in' when apparently bewitched by the beauty of their passing patterns on approaching goal.

The geometry of football is the secret knowledge of the great passer and the short, stabbed pass has always been far more damaging than the more spectacular showboating of the curled crossfield effort (or 'Hollywood ball' as Ron Atkinson used to say). However, the ways of passing are many and complex. It is well reported, for example, that Stanley **Matthews** would put top-spin on his crosses to delude the keeper into coming for a ball he could never get while your Mortensen, **Milburn** or **Lawton** stole in to head home. Of course, Stanley Matthews's passes were purposeful and not meant personally. On the other hand, towards the end of their 7–0 drubbing of Southampton in 1972, Leeds's Billy **Bremner** performed one of the cruellest televised passes when he executed a spooned flick-on from the heel area that was technically half-pass, half-curtsey.

penalty kick

A penalty kick is awarded during a game when a defending team commits an offence inside its own penalty area: usually either a foul or a handball. In fact a penalty kick can be awarded for any one of the 14 offences that can lead to a direct free kick – although, in practice, penalties awarded for a goalkeeper picking up the ball instead of taking a free kick or for a defender making insulting gestures towards an opponent are relatively rare.

The kick itself is a single strike at goal from the penalty spot. As the kick is taken only the goalkeeper and the player taking the kick are allowed within 9.5 metres of the ball, the distance from penalty spot to the arc at the edge of the penalty area. The kicker can only touch the ball again after a kick has either been saved, missed or scored, or – in the unusual circumstances of a scuff towards the corner flag or a gust of wind stopping the ball dead – once another opposition outfield player has touched it.

The penalty-taker must always be clearly indicated to the referee before a kick can be legitimately taken. Passing the ball from the penalty spot was only outlawed in 1982, after Ajax's Johan Cruyff exploited a lacuna in the laws to score the most bizarre goal from a penalty ever: having run up to take the kick, Cruyff laid the ball sideways to the onrushing Jesper Olsen, who then played it back to Cruyff to score from two yards.

The penalty kick was introduced 20 years after the first official codification of football's laws, and was initially a controversial development, with some amateurs deciding to interpret the rule as a slur on their sportsmanship. For a long time Corinthian Casuals retained a club rule that all penalties awarded must be deliberately shot wide of the goal, while their own keeper was instructed to stand to one side at opposition spot kicks.

The first-ever penalty goal in the Football League was scored by J. Heath of Wolves against Accrington on 14 September 1891. In those days goalkeepers were allowed to advance up to six yards off their line, although this rule was soon abolished. Attempts have been made recently to curb the tendency of goalkeepers to jump forward off their goal line at penalty kicks. Goalkeepers are required to remain on their line until a kick has been taken, but they can now indulge in any distracting movements they like as long as forward motion is not involved.

There are various ways of taking a penalty. The kick can be rolled into the corner, in the style of Eric **Cantona**, who tended to wait for the goalkeeper to move first before choosing his side; or it can be blasted in a premeditated direction in the style of Alan **Shearer**. Occasionally the cheeky dink straight down the middle makes an appearance, as perfected by Dwight Yorke and Paolo Di Canio, and as first unveiled by Czechoslovakia's Antonín Panenka, who scored with a delicate chip over the top of onrushing German goalkeeper Sepp Maier to win the 1976 European Championships for his country.

Penalty awards are often controversial. The potentially rich rewards of falling over in the penalty area have led to occasional instances of diving. This is often described as a recent addition to the English game, possibly something imported by foreign players. However, the most notoriously prolific earner of penalty kicks remains former England international Francis Lee, who scored a record 13 times from the spot for Manchester City in 1971–72, after earning most of the penalties himself (and a new nickname, 'Lee Pen').

Goalkeepers who specialize in saving penalties are rare. Ipswich's Paul Cooper is perhaps the most famous example. Cooper saved a record eight out of ten penalties faced during the 1979–80 season.

penalty shoot-out

Penalty shoot-outs are a unique part of football. At no other stage is the game finished but also in progress; and in no other scenario is it reduced to a single, staccato kick of the ball. The phrase 'somebody had to be the villain' is employed by commentators at no other time. And goalkeepers have never had it so good when it comes to prancing around on their line, making scary faces, disputing the turfing of the penalty spot and generally demanding that people pay attention to them.

The shoot-out is used to decide a drawn game in a knock-out tournament or any competition where a replay is not available. Both sides take five penalties, each by a different player. Once the ball has been saved or has hit the post (players are not permitted to score from rebounds) it has been missed. If the teams are level after five, both continue taking penalties on a 'sudden death' basis.

It is often said that penalty shoot-outs are 'a lottery', but this is not the case. A lottery is dictated by random chance, while scoring in a penalty shoot-out requires courage and skill. Players with excellent technique are far less likely to be distracted by the additional pressure. England supporters may feel unlucky to have seen their team exit major tournaments after a penalty shoot-out on four separate occasions in the past 15 years. But in each case – Germany twice (1990 World Cup and Euro 96), Argentina

(1998 World Cup) and Portugal (Euro 2004) – they lost out to a team with more proficient basic skills. At Euro 2004, in particular, it was no great surprise to see a Portugal team with visibly superior mastery of the ball succeed at what is, after all, a very simple piece of technique.

Penalty shoot-outs were first used in Britain in the 1970 Watney Cup. The first shoot-out ever staged was won by Manchester United after a 1–1 draw in the semi-final against Hull City. A variation on the penalty shoot-out, known as 'the shoot-out' was introduced in the USA in the late 1970s. Instead of taking penalties, players were allowed five seconds to dribble from close to the centre circle and beat the goalkeeper. It didn't catch on. In 1982 the penalty shoot-out was introduced at the World Cup finals for the first time and has since become a standard feature of all major tournaments throughout the world. Eight European Cup/Champions' League finals have been decided on penalties, beginning with Liverpool's win over Roma in 1984, while Tottenham's defeat of Anderlecht in the same year is one of four UEFA Cup Finals to have ended the same way. Numerous play-off finals and the 2001 Worthington Cup Final (Liverpool 5 Birmingham 4 after a 1–1 draw) and the 2005 and 2006 Cup Finals have also been settled by a shoot-out.

Penalty shoot-outs remain the only sensible method yet devised to decide a drawn game. Crucially, a shoot-out is perfect for television. It provides instant excitement and dramatically see-sawing moments of triumph and failure, all tied up in a ten-minute slot. From a scheduling point of view, the shoot-out is the most television-friendly segment of any football match. Even if for this reason alone, penalty shoot-outs will continue to lurk in the background of every major tournament.

Peterborough United

Peterborough United can call on a large catchment area throughout east Cambridgeshire, but the club's once healthy gates are falling. In part this is because many locals are originally from elsewhere and support other teams – after Peterborough was designated a New Town 30 years ago, there was a wave of migration from across the south-east encouraged by a TV campaign featuring Roy Kinnear as a Roman Legionnaire talking about 'The Peterborough Effect', later the name of the club's first fanzine. More recently, some regular supporters have been alienated by the often turbulent regime of manager-owner Barry Fry which saw the club cling on to a place in Division 2 with increasing desperation.

Peterborough's football club first became known as 'Posh' during the 1920s, after the manager was quoted as saying that he was looking for 'posh players for a posh team'. However, the current Peterborough United was not founded until 1934 following the demise of a similarly named club two years earlier. There followed 26 years in the semi-professional Midland League, including one infamous year when the fixtures were completed in June owing to bad weather, with the 1950s being the most successful. During this time Posh won the league on a regular basis, but kept getting turned down for League membership in the annual re-election vote.

Finally, in 1960, Peterborough gained entry to the Football League at the expense of Gateshead. During that first season they stormed to the Division 4 championship with Terry Bly scoring an incredible 52 League goals – still a record for any division below the top flight – in a total of 134. Four seasons later they had their best ever run in the FA Cup,

beating Arsenal in the fourth round before losing to Chelsea in the last eight; the following year the club reached the semi-finals of the League Cup, losing to West Bromwich Albion.

Disaster struck in January 1968 as the Football League decided that the club should be demoted at the end of the season for offering illegal signing-on fees and win bonuses, ironically including a 7–1 thrashing at Sunderland in the 1966–67 FA Cup fourth round. This left Peterborough with 27 meaningless matches to play; they lost almost an entire first-team squad as a consequence but bounced back to win the Division 4 title in 1973–74 under the stewardship of ex-Manchester United and Republic of Ireland player Noel Cantwell.

Peterborough went down again five years later and didn't get back until 1991. Then a play-off victory the following season took them from Division 3 to Division 1 thanks to the renaming that followed the creation of the Premier League. The same season the team – managed by popular ex-player, later chairman, Chris Turner – also knocked Liverpool out of the League Cup at London Road before losing to Middlesbrough in a quarter-final replay.

Barry Fry, outspoken former manager of Barnet and Birmingham among others, took over in 1996. Soon he passed on the reins to a local businessman, Peter Boizot, founder of the Pizza Express chain, who became chairman while Fry concentrated on running the football side – not very effectively as Posh went down in his first year in charge. (Boizot, a charming man but not the most worldly, supplied orange squash for the away supporters until told he couldn't by the police for safety reasons.)

The flamboyant Fry went through a dozen assistants in the next six seasons, threatened to walk out only a week after gaining promotion in the play-off final against Darlington in 2000, and later claimed that he had received a death threat and feared for his life following a comment on an unofficial website. In 2003 he took charge of the club again, but London Road is now owned by his friend, property developer Colin Hill. The ground is rent-free for the next ten years or until a new owner comes along, when it must be negotiated.

A large squad's wages and diminishing crowds suggest a new owner is going to come sooner rather than later, but will there be anything to own? After fighting relegation for three seasons, the club finally dropped into the bottom division at the end of 2004–05.

Peterhead

Although football had been played in Scotland's easternmost mainland town for a couple of decades prior, one of the Scottish League's newest recruits was officially formed in 1890. One year later they made Recreation Park their home for the next 106 years.

In 1997 they finally moved from the town centre venue – predictably sold to a supermarket chain – to the smart new Balmoor Stadium, which now boasts two stands, executive boxes and terracing at either end. The change helped clinch Scottish League status in 2000 when the SPL expanded by two clubs, allowing both 'The Toons' (Peterhead is known locally as 'The Blue Toon', and the team play in the same colour) and rival Elgin City to move across from the Highland League into Division 3.

Peterhead had joined the Highlanders in the 1930s after 30-odd years in the Aberdeenshire League. Their most successful team played under Percy Dickie, winning the title three times in four years in the late 1940s, but after that

they lifted the trophy only twice more, in 1989 and 1999. During the latter year they not only racked up a 17–0 hammering of Fort William, but set a new record for the least number of goals conceded in an HL season.

Although cup success has been limited to regional competitions, in 2001 Peterhead progressed to the Scottish Cup quarter-final after victories over Whitehill Welfare, Cove Rangers and Morton, and a walkover against the bankrupt Airdrie. It was another new-breed upstart – Livingston – who put an end to the port town's dreams with a 3–1 defeat. In 2005, they were promoted from Division 3 as runners-up to Gretna.

PFA

The Professional Footballers' Association was founded as the Association Football Players' Union in 1907 at the Imperial Hotel in Manchester. The PFA is the footballers' trade union, set up to protect and promote the interests of professional players in England and Wales. Among its initial aims was the abolition of the retain-and-transfer system and maximum wage.

The PFA threatened its first players' strike in 1908 in a dispute over its plans to take action over players' grievances directly through the courts, but it wasn't until after the Second World War that a more militant union began to achieve its first serious concessions, with reforms of the transfer system and the restrictions on earnings beginning to take hold. It took the campaigning skills of Fulham player and union chief Jimmy **Hill** in the early 1960s to force the hand of the Football Association and the Ministry of Labour, a successful legal challenge and a concerted threat of strike action bringing about immediate changes in both earnings and employment rights.

The PFA awards, among them Player of the Year, Young Player of the Year and divisional teams of the year were introduced in 1974. In recent years the PFA has offered an advisory service to players, similar to that offered by a professional player's agent, and has expanded its traditional services, among these offering legal aid, helping with financial assistance and providing a point of contact for unemployed players.

In 2001 the PFA received a 95 per cent backing for strike action from its members in a dispute over television income. PFA chief executive Gordon Taylor had questioned the allocation of television income among professional clubs, which saw £500m centred on the 20 Premiership clubs and £100m on the remaining 72. A strike was narrowly averted, with the PFA's action bringing a compromise offer from the Premier League, the Football Association and the Football League.

The strike brought to light the increasingly unusual status of the PFA. No other union can ever have had such a broad profile among its membership, representing as it does the alienated multimillionaires of the Premiership and players at Division 3 clubs whose careers among the professional ranks are under constant threat. A union created during the days of the maximum wage, and at a time when footballers were a largely powerless group of employees, has had to adapt to represent the huge shift in power at the top end of the scale between clubs and players. The insecurity of the profession has contributed to maintaining the PFA's solidarity. Despite the discrepancy in earnings, there remains a fraternity among professional footballers, born out of the fragile nature of a playing career, the possibility of career-ending injury and the vicissitudes of management changes, player clear-outs and the inherent brevity of any footballing life.

pitch invasions

The term 'pitch invasion' has come to describe any incident of one or more members of the general public stepping on to the field of play while a football match is in progress. Pitch invasions tend to fall into one of four categories: the streaker; the lone angry nutter; the post-match end-of-season we've-just-avoided-relegation free-for-all; and the hooligan rumble, thankfully largely a thing of the past.

Given that every day of the week for nine months of the year somewhere in the UK a football match is played in front of a bi-partisan crowd, on-field violence and security problems are remarkably rare. Perhaps for this reason, the more momentous pitch invasions of the past tend to be remembered with affection. The **White Horse Final** in 1923 remains a part of football's rattle-shaking Golden Age. The most famous pitch invasion in a televised cup final came in 1966 when balding Everton fan Eddie Cavanagh hurtled ecstatically across the Wembley turf, with several policemen trailing behind, after his team equalized against Sheffield Wednesday having been two goals down. A couple of months later several spectators ran on in the final moments of the World Cup Final between England and West Germany thinking, wrongly, that the final whistle had been blown.

More notoriously, at a vital end-of-season game between Leeds United and West Bromwich Albion in 1971 a goal scored by Albion's Jeff Astle from an offside position inspired a violent invasion of the pitch by irate Leeds fans and most of the club personnel (including manager Don **Revie** carrying a blanket).

The incident was given added poignancy by Barry Davies's unusually rabble-rousing television commentary: 'And Leeds will go mad! And they have every right to go mad!' Pitch invasions happened with increasing regularity during the decade, notably in April 1974 when fans of relegation-threatened Manchester United swarmed on at Old Trafford after neighbours City had taken a late lead that some believed would send United down.

During the 1980s nadir of hooliganism in and around football stadiums, the pitch invasion was seen in its most sinister form. After an FA Cup tie at Luton in 1985 a group of spectators in the Millwall end rampaged on to the pitch, throwing ripped up plastic seats and engaging in a pitched battle with mounted police. Similar incidents around the country led to the introduction of unbreachable iron perimeter fences, intended to pen potential invaders in the terraces; with tragic consequences, as it would turn out, after the utterly avoidable events at Hillsborough in 1989 (see **Hillsborough disaster**).

The pitch invasion has been the subject of increasing censure by the game's administrators, not just as a menace to the safety of players and officials, but to the sanctity of the stage itself. This is partly because of the dangers posed by groups of excitable people running around an enclosed square of grass; and partly a response to the isolating effects of the recent phenomenon of player celebrity. There is a sense that a pitch containing 22 millionaires who regularly appear on national television must be protected at all costs from the intrusions of the public. The Birmingham City fan who ran on to the pitch to confront Aston Villa goalkeeper Peter Enckelman in 2002, after the Finn had miskicked embarrassingly to gift a goal to City, received a life ban from St Andrews and was gaoled for four months. This may be a reasonable punishment; but the two-year ban imposed on a Crystal Palace supporter in 2000 for dancing on the pitch to celebrate a goal suggests that preserving the sanctity of the playing area can be taken too far.

pitch markings

Like the bunny slipper and map of the London Underground, the markings on a football pitch are a design classic, so ingrained into the common consciousness that merely the sight of a freshly lined park pitch will induce paunchy old men to jog over and stare themselves into a dream.

In the pre-dawn of football there was anarchy and no markings whatsoever. The very earliest rules refer vaguely to boundary flags but in those unregulated days these were treated as so much bunting. Marking a pitch out would have been anti-social as games were played on public ground. This began to change when proper clubs sprang up with their very own grounds, making it possible to paint white lines all over the place with impunity. Although there is no reliable date for the introduction of boundary lines, we must assume they appeared soon after the first serious competition, the FA Cup, was instigated in 1871.

The next thing needed was a centre spot, so that a game could commence, and then a circle of ten yards' radius around it so that the player who went to kick off wasn't instantly mobbed by the opposition. Again at the behest of the new Football Association, the goals shrank from, in some places, the entire width of the pitch to a tiny 8 yard model at the centre of the goal-line. The year 1887 was a busy one in which the halfway line and the one-yard arc at cornerflags were added, plus two adjacent semi-circles of six yards' radius around the goalmouth. The latter, the forerunner of the six-yard box, was either kidney-shaped or mammary in aspect, depending on your point of view.

When the penalty kick was introduced in 1891, two lines – 12 yards and 18 yards from the goal-line – were drawn the width of the pitch. Offences occurring anywhere between the 12 yard line and the goal-line incurred a penalty. It was not until 1902 that the pitch markings we still use today were introduced, with a penalty 'box' beginning 18 yards out and stretching 44 yards wide, itself containing a straightened 'goal area', 20 yards wide and six yards deep. Finally, in 1937, the Europeans persuaded the British to adopt a fussy little arc at the edge of the penalty area to ensure everyone was ten yards from the penalty spot.

plastic pitches

Of all the various gimmicks, moribund innovations and exercises in corner-cutting devised throughout the history of the British game, the plastic pitch is perhaps the least lamented. Intended both as a solution to the rain and frost of a British winter and as a means of gener-ating revenue by staging various non-footballing events on non-match days, the plastic football pitch was modelled on the Astroturf surfaces produced in the US in the 1960s and favoured during the North American Soccer League mini-boom of the late 1970s.

The first synthetic pitch in British foot-ball was laid at QPR's Loftus Road in 1981. Frost-proof and mud-free, unfortu-nately Rangers' Omniturf pitch also provided a rearing tennis ball bounce, terrifying carpet burns and a knee-jarringly hard surface. Despite Oldham, Luton and Preston following suit, the

plastic pitch failed to convince and by 1988 Loftus Road had reverted to grass. Preston's Deepdale was the last to revert to an organic playing area, in 1994. In due course plastic pitches were outlawed under Premier League guidelines, reflecting a sense among spectators that this, somehow, just wasn't right: green-grocer grass; men in trainers; and the death of the divot, the ten-foot mud-bound sliding tackle and the ball that takes 'a bit of a bobble' before being shanked into the crowd. Innovations such as undersoil heating and improved drainage took the sting out of the drive to develop a convincing artificial surface, although the fact remains that currently even the lushest footballing turf tends to contain a mix of artificial fibres to toughen up the live grass alongside it.

Moreover, plastic pitches may be staging a comeback: ten games at the 2003 Helsinki Under-17 World Champion-ships, including the final, were played on one of the new generation of artificial pitches. And the high-sided stands at grounds such as Old Trafford have tended to block out essential turf-friendly influences such as wind and rain, requiring pitches to be relaid once or even twice a season, and leading to speculation that an artificial pitch of sufficient quality might be a viable alternative. Recently, to a chorus of disapproval among fellow Scottish clubs, Dunfermline installed a state-of-the-art plastic pitch, taking advantage of grants being offered to further experiments with artificial playing surfaces.

play-offs

Martin Lange has given thousands of foot-ball supporters reason to shed tears of joy or despair at some point since the late 1980s. For he was the man who suggested the play-offs, the end-of-season extravaganza that has been with us now for 19 seasons and has involved 85 different clubs, from Maidstone to Chelsea and almost everywhere in between. Brentford chairman Lange was one of three representatives from lower league clubs who attended meetings called to discuss proposals for a 'Super League' put forward by the chairmen of the best-supported Division 1 clubs. It was as part of the Heathrow Agreement – the result of a meeting at the Post House Hotel, Heathrow, on 18 December 1985 – that Lange's play-off proposals appeared.

At a time when the bigger clubs were demanding a greater share of League revenue, Lange saw promotion play-offs as a means of rekindling supporter interest in the lower divisions, thereby bringing the clubs much-needed extra income. The play-offs remain with us today because they have met, and argu-ably exceeded, these expectations. Since 1985–86, the last season without play-offs, attendances across the lower three divisions have more than doubled. It is difficult to deny that Lange's innovation has been at least partly responsible for such a dramatic increase.

It is little wonder supporters have accepted the play-offs with enthusiasm, since they have invariably produced extraordinary levels of drama, epitom-ized by an astonishing number of crucial late goals. This began in the play-offs' debut season when Peter Shirtliff's two strikes in the final ten minutes of extra time against Leeds kept Charlton in the top flight (for the first two seasons each divisional play-off involved the team that had finished just above the relegation places plus three from the lower league). Of course, a sudden-death contest determining a club's fate for the whole of the following season inevitably leads to heightened emotions, the fall-out from which has offered ammunition to oppon-

ents of the play-off system. Occasional crowd trouble certainly threatened its future at one point, but violence is now rare and the emotional strain tends only to be seen in the paranoid ramblings of beaten managers, of whom Sam Allardyce and Trevor Francis have been splendidly entertaining examples in recent years.

Since only three clubs from 12 can succeed each season, tales of woe outnumber those of success. For Preston and Ipswich, the disappointment has been the greatest, with a record six unsuccessful attempts. No other clubs have tackled the play-offs so often without reward. Brentford are close behind, however, and it was perhaps inevitable that they would endure some of the most painful experiences at the hands of their former chairman's brain-child. Having failed in all five attempts at the play-offs, how the club's fans must wish that Lange had kept his thoughts to himself.

The play-offs have generally been good to Swindon. Along with Burnley and West Ham, they hold the record for the biggest points deficit to be overcome by play-off winners (12), and have an impressive three victories from five attempts overall, though the promotion earned by the second of those successes in 1990 was famously denied them as the League punished their financial misde-meanours. Crystal Palace, though, are the undisputed play-off masters. Four times they have taken part; on each occasion they have made the final, and only once have they failed to win promotion.

The play-offs are not without their detractors, and even their staunchest supporter would concede that fairness is compromised in the attempt to seduce the public. By the end of the 2005–06 season, of the 60 teams that have finished in what were previously automatic-promotion positions, only 26 have won through the play-offs. While that is regrettable, the fact that the money generated through striving for and taking part in the play-offs has undoubtedly kept some clubs alive is a strong defence. In the modern game, a financially successful innovation has its future guaranteed and so the play-offs will be around for some time to come, frustrating and delighting an increasing number of supporters along the way.

Plymouth Argyle

Plymouth's football club had no home for its first season of 1886–87 and played its first matches as away fixtures. They began life as Argyle Athletic Club, the etymology of the unique suffix explained variously through the club's proximity to the Argyll and Sutherland army regiment, the Argyle Tavern where its founders regularly met, or a local street named Argyll Terrace.

The club was formed from the pub talk of a Mr Pettybridge and a Mr Grose, the latter winning the argument as to which of them would become the first captain. Eventually they acquired a ground in the Mount Gould area of the town, finally settling at their present location, Home Park, in 1901, two years before turning professional in the Southern League. With their new status, the club gave itself a new name – Plymouth Argyle. They had an immediate taste of success in their first match, a 1–0 win at West Ham, and went on to win the Southern League Championship in 1912–13.

In 1920 Plymouth were admitted to the Football League and finished 11th in their first season in Division 3 (South), a season which saw their average attendance rise to nearly 13,000, a significant increase in local interest from the 4,000 that turned up for their first home game

in the Southern League. Until the arrival of Yeovil in 2002, Plymouth were the only League members to wear green as a first-choice colour. They became the nearly men of Division 3 (South), finishing second an agonizing six times in the seven seasons prior to finally achieving promotion as champions in 1929–30, by which time around 20,000 people were turning up regularly at Home Park to get their annual fix of disappointment. (The club's support has always spread across Devon and west into Cornwall.)

After the war, in which the town and Home Park were badly damaged by bombing, Argyle had long periods in Division 2, punctuated by occasional relegations. Highlights were two runs to the League Cup semi-finals, a 1973 victory over Pelé's touring Santos team (who wanted their appearance fee in cash beforehand) and a fine promotion in 1974–75 on the back of goals from Billy Rafferty and Paul Mariner – marked by the release of a club song, the opaquely titled 'Promotion'.

In 1983–84, Plymouth became only the sixth team from Division 3 to reach the semi-finals of the FA Cup, beating Derby County in a quarter-final replay with a goal direct from a corner before losing 1–0 to Watford. Two years later they were back in Division 2 with a team featuring one of the most popular players in their history, Liverpool-born striker Tommy Tynan, who scored 126 goals in three separate spells with the club.

Multi-millionaire Dan McCauley took control in the 1990s and installed Peter **Shilton** as manager, although too late in the 1991–92 season to prevent the club's slide into the old Division 3. Three years later, distracted by a widely publicized gambling addiction, Shilton resigned in the season Plymouth were relegated to the bottom division for the first time. A Wembley play-off victory under Neil

Warnock in 1996 proved to be a false dawn; the club slumped to their lowest-ever League position three seasons later. With Argyle under new ownership, Scottish manager Paul Sturrock oversaw the ascent back up the League. By the time of his departure for an ill-fated stab at top-flight management with Southampton in 2004, Argyle were assured a place in the newly named Championship. With a newly developed ground, Plymouth ought to be in a strong position from which to attempt their most serious bid yet for the top division.

policing

As with so many aspects of modern football, the **Hillsborough disaster** transformed the nature of policing at football matches. The fact that both fans and the official inquiry blamed the police for such a complete failure of crowd safety put the spotlight on police attitudes to football and its followers in a way that had never happened before.

It was not the first time a major incident at a football ground had raised the issue of the policing of football matches. The Short Report into overcrowding at the first Wembley Cup Final in 1923 concluded that 'the police should be responsible for all matters appertaining to the preservation of law and order and that concerning the arrangements for the convenience of the public the ground authority should be responsible.' And after 33 supporters were crushed to death at Bolton in the **Burnden Park disaster** in 1946, the Moelwyn-Hughes Report recommended that one police officer should be present for every 1,000 spectators at all English football grounds – presumably to ensure their safety, not merely to prevent trouble.

However, although there were at least eight official inquiries into ground safety before Hillsborough, the law and order agenda has dominated football policing. For at least two decades before Hillsborough the focus of policing was on preventing hooliganism and crowd control amounted to a strategy of 'pack them in and watch them carefully'. To the police, all fans were potential trouble-makers to be controlled, not paying spectators whose enjoyment and safety needed to be ensured.

Going to a football match in the 1970s and 1980s could be a bit like entering into a heavily guarded prison – with strictly segregated supporters penned in by perimeter fences and watched over by lines of heavy-handed bobbies. Away supporters were patrolled in a near military exercise, as ranks of police officers marched fans to and from stadiums, shunting them through alien towns and on to guarded trains, and setting up road blocks to stop their coaches miles from the ground.

Not suprisingly, relations between fans and police were often hostile and sometimes violent: fans felt they were treated like animals; the police saw them as hooligans, and therefore barely human. By the late 1980s, fanzines were peppered with complaints of mistreatment by police officers, and even John Stalker, former deputy chief constable of Greater Manchester Police, admitted that 'some police officers use Saturday as the day they are let off the leash'.

The **Taylor Report** backed up these comments, saying that 'there are reports that, at some grounds, some police treat supporters, especially away supporters, with a measure of contempt. When this happens it unfortunately sours the attitude of the supporters towards all police.' It called for 'friendly police and supporter relations' and made numerous recommendations aimed at improving the standard of policing at games.

Gradually, things changed. The fences came down, the police introduced football liaison officers to work with supporters' groups, and crowd safety was at least talked about, if not actually ensured. The Home Affairs Committee report on 'Policing Football Hooliganism' in 1991 called for lower profile policing and higher profile stewarding; better liaison between police, football authorities and fans; and moves towards desegregating rival fans where possible.

Meanwhile, as the focus of concern moved away from English grounds and on to supporters of the England team, the police's fight against hooliganism became more 'sophisticated'. A 1986 Metropolitan Police report concluded that 'traditional policing had its limits when dealing with hooligans', marking the introduction of new 'intelligent' tactics, such as the use of undercover officers, CCTV and video cameras, police spotters and the ill-conceived, politically motivated and quickly abandoned idea of a football fans' identity card.

A centre for collating information about hooligans, drawn from intelligence officers attached to all 92 League clubs, was established in 1989, and subsumed into the National Criminal Intelligence Service at Scotland Yard in 1992. Its database of football supporters, and use of banning orders to prevent known hooligans travelling abroad, has become notorious – not least for the number of innocent fans who have been caught in its snare.

As trouble at games declined, the number of police used at matches decreased. Now, about 5,000 officers police football each Saturday at an annual estimated cost of £22m. Clubs usually pay the full cost only of officers inside grounds, with those outside paid for by the local police authority. Between 25 and 100 officers are now employed at Premier League games – down threefold from the mid-1980s, as stewards and private security firms have taken on more responsibility for crowd control inside grounds, closely watched from the police control room.

According to the NCIS, 25 per cent of matches were completely police-free in 2003–04, and arrests were down 10 per cent on the previous season to fewer than 4,000, a rate of 0.01 per cent, despite the highest League attendances for 34 years – and 57 per cent of these were outside grounds.

Not that football policing has suddenly become unproblematic. Critics of anti-hooligan measures argue that CCTV and banning orders are an abuse of civil liberties. And fans still encounter some of the old heavy-handedness. One travelling Everton fan wrote in 2002: 'Travelling is bad enough. When you have to go through a policing system which might have been formulated at Gestapo, NKVD, CIA or MI5/6 headquarters then you have to seriously question whether any of it is worthwhile.'

politics

It has taken a surprisingly long time for British politicians to learn to love football, given its powerful hold over the emotions of so much of the population. Representatives from local councillors up to prime ministers have often allowed themselves to be associated with particular clubs in a ceremonial way (even Margaret Thatcher was installed as an honorary vice-president of Blackburn Rovers, no doubt to her bemusement), but it took the near-death of football in the 1980s and its rebirth in the 1990s to draw national politics much more tightly into the game's administration and culture.

For much of its pre-industrial history football was viewed with suspicion by Britain's rulers, largely because of its potential for social disorder and serious injury to young men who might be needed for more organized warfare. Edward III tried to ban it (and other 'useless and unlawful games') from London in 1349 because he thought it was distracting men from practising archery. Several other monarchs followed suit, as did the Puritans, who naturally objected to football on the grounds that it was fun.

The organized version of football that emerged in the second half of the 19th century aroused much less alarm at the highest levels – in fact, if they thought about it at all most politicians would undoubtedly have shared the view of the churches that it was better for the industrial working classes to spend their Saturday half-holiday at the football rather than organizing anything more seditious or immoral.

It was only with the outbreak of the First World War that football became a serious political issue. The regular season was played out in 1914–15 against a backdrop of fierce criticism of football's supposed disloyalty in parts of the press (rugby had immediately ceased all matches), though these tended to ignore the phenomenal success of the FA's recruiting campaign for the trenches – nearly half a million men signed up in 1914 alone through football organizations. When war came again the football authorities were quick to call a halt after only three games of the 1939–40 season (sadly for Blackpool, who had won all three), but were then encouraged by the government to construct wartime competitions on the most credible basis possible, to help maintain morale.

Apart perhaps from the presence of royalty at the Cup Final (a tradition since 1914), this was the first significant sign that those in power felt they could make political capital from the attraction of football. Before that, and particularly in the turbulent 1930s, the game must have seemed only a potential minefield. In 1935 the government had faced down protests from the trade unions and Jewish groups over the visit of Germany to play England at White Hart Lane; three years later came the notorious Nazi salute when England played in Berlin. Both situations offered nothing but trouble from a political point of view.

After the war the memory of the way Hitler and Mussolini had used sport, as well as its importance to the new communist regimes of eastern Europe, helped keep British governments at arm's length from football. Even when England won the World Cup in 1966 the Labour prime minister, Harold Wilson, was barely visible: the relationship between the team and the nation was mediated only by royalty (Bobby Moore wiping his hands on his shorts before receiving the trophy from the Queen) and by Kenneth Wolstenholme. Four years later Wilson rashly called an election for June, during the Mexico World Cup, and, some have argued, paid the price at the polls for England's quarter-final defeat a few days previously.

For the next 15 years England had neither a team nor fans that any politician would risk hitching their name to even in Wilson's tentative fashion. By the time of the **Heysel disaster** in 1985 English fans (and, above all, England fans) travelling abroad had become a politician's nightmare. Heysel meant the government finally had to get involved at a policy level rather than trotting out platitudes about national shame and bringing back the birch and/or national service.

Inevitably, Thatcher's response was to treat football as a law and order issue, all but ignoring the need for a broader safety culture at matches so graphically illustrated by the **Bradford fire** of the same year. In the short term this meant giving the police more or less free rein in crowd matters; eventually football supporters were to be controlled at a national level by an identity card scheme. Some aspects of such a scheme were implemented at Luton Town to exclude away fans, under the auspices of its chairman David Evans, one of Thatcher's backbench MPs.

The compulsory national identity card scheme was bitterly opposed by fan groups and many others (even the police were ambivalent), but it was finally introduced as part of the Football Spectators Act of 1989. However, the **Hillsborough disaster** of the same year, and the **Taylor Report** that followed it, destroyed the prevailing mentality on football crowd control and the identity card scheme was swiftly abandoned. With the election of Tony Blair's Labour government in 1997 football's relationship with politics took altogether new directions. By that time the 90s boom had made football an obviously attractive partner to be seen with for a populist government obsessed with youth and such nebulous concepts as 'Cool Britannia'. Even in the last years of the Conservatives football had become an acceptable passion – the prime minister John Major and his accident-prone Sports Minister David Mellor made much of their attachment to Chelsea. And whereas once Michael Foot's support for Plymouth Argyle had been marked down as one more sign of doddery eccentricity, now New Labour notables fell over themselves to make public their football allegiances, in particular Blair's press secretary Alaistair Campbell (Burnley), his first

Home Secretary Jack Straw (Blackburn) and Sports Minister Tony Banks (Chelsea).

Campbell was even said to have finalized Rupert Murdoch's backing for Labour at the 1997 general election when he bumped into the *Sun*'s editor Stuart Higgins at a game between Burnley and Brentford. Blair himself was famously photographed playing head tennis with Kevin **Keegan** and skylarking with Alex **Ferguson**.

So much for what football could do for the government. In return, the game got a decidedly mixed response. On hooliganism, efforts have concentrated on the imposition of banning orders to stop troublemakers travelling abroad, a policy which makes some uneasy on grounds of civil liberties, but which has been more effective and less controversial than the Tories' identity card proposals. On a more mundane, but possibly more telling, level, Labour has continued the Conservatives' disastrous policy of allowing (or even encouraging) schools to sell their playing fields, with obviously negative results for grass roots participation.

Labour's most high-profile effort on behalf of fans was the establishment in 1997 of the Football Task Force, under the less than unanimously popular chairmanship of David Mellor, which reported two years later. Its somewhat feeble remit encompassed recommendations on how to eliminate racism, improve access to grounds for disabled fans, encourage 'equitable' and 'fair' policies on tickets, prices and merchandise, and reconcile issues raised by the flotation of clubs on the stock market. Some unexpectedly positive long-term benefits emerged from the Task Force recommendations, in particular the concept of supporters' trusts, but many fans felt it reflected New Labour's desire to be seen to be doing

something in response to their grievances, rather than their genuine desire to
tackle any of the game's powerful vested
interests. The FA, the Football League
and the Premier League produced a
minority report on the fourth and most
critical strand of the Task Force recommendations, opposing the other
members' calls for greater regulation of
commercial activities.

Labour has since lost some of its appetite for football, particularly since the
appalling mess of England's bid to stage
the 2006 World Cup. The hugely disproportionate power in the game acquired
by the top clubs, the Premier League and
the TV companies has made it almost
inconceivable that government would
attempt to regulate their activities in any
meaningful way. Substantial intervention
in football is much more likely to come
through European Union legislation, as
with the **Bosman** ruling, than from any
initiative by the British government.

On the other hand, football has at least
shaken off its pariah image, which has
helped to open doors at less rarefied
levels of government. Certainly there is
more to be gained for smaller clubs and
their fans by cultivating good relationships with local councils (which played a
crucial role in the 1980s battles over
stadiums in London, in particular) than in
seeking the ear of national leaders.
Labour under Blair has found that identifying with football is no simple way to
foster its appeal to the voters. Nevertheless, the game occupies such a vast
space in the media and the popular
imagination that politicians can no longer
ignore it, let alone disdain it as Thatcher
did. If England were to win the World
Cup again any time soon, it is hard to
imagine the prime minister would not be
on the open-topped bus in Trafalgar
Square.

Pools Panel

The Pools Panel is a truly English institution – a product of a country obsessed
not only with football, but also with
bingo and the weather. Springing forth
out of the chaos of the freezing winter of
1962–63 – when one tie in the third
round of the FA Cup was postponed 22
times – the Panel took charge of the
nation's need for a reliable made-up
results service, ensuring that whatever
the weather the people of Great Britain
could still sate their urge to gamble on a
vast spread of totally unpredictable football results.

Defying the blizzards and frozen sea-
fronts, the original Pools Panel of Gerald
Nabarro MP (chair), George Young, Ted
Drake, Tommy **Lawton**, Tom **Finney**
and former ref Arthur Ellis sat for the first
time on 26 January 1963. In the early
years the Panel met in the Connaught
Rooms in central London, from where
the BBC would screen a live announce-
ment of the results of the venerable
guess-merchants' deliberations. These
days the Panel spend Saturday afternoons debating QPR's away form in the
relative hardship of a solicitor's office in
Liverpool.

Prospective members of the Panel are
vetted and vetoed by the main football
pools companies, Littlewoods, Vernons
and Zetters, two officials from whom are
present at all times during meetings. The
current line-up is Gordon **Banks**, former
Newcastle and Scotland midfielder Tony
Green and Roger Hunt, who has the
casting vote if there is a difference of
opinion.

When games they've adjudicated on
have subsequently been played the
results show that the Panel have got it
right 40 per cent of the time. And so they
ought to, because it's a full-time job these
days. The Panel used to meet whenever

25 or more matches were called off, but now they spring into action whenever any Saturday game is cancelled or moved, and also cover the Australian season during the English winter – all on a good salary with full expenses.

Which sounds a bit like winning the pools if you're a retired ex-pro with a supply of pencils and a copy of the *Sky Yearbook*. And you don't even have to pose in the paper with a big cheque.

Port Vale

It is popularly believed that Port Vale was founded in 1876, by workers from local pottery factories, but this date and the precise provenance of the club name has long been a matter of debate. The club's name derives from the 'Port Vale', a valley in which lies the Trent and Mersey Canal, and a number of port villages, factories and wharves, near Burslem, in what is now Stoke-on-Trent. The club has played at six different grounds, all within about one mile of Burslem, its main catchment area being the northern part of Stoke-on-Trent and environs. From 1884 to 1909 the club was known as Burslem Port Vale.

Vale came to local prominence as a non-League team, particularly in the FA Cup, and were elected to the Football League in 1892 as founder members of Division 2. The club's history is permeated with financial difficulties; in 1907, they were wound up and taken over by a local non-League side, but returned to the Football League in 1919, when Leeds City were thrown out of Division 2 because of illegal payments and Vale were elected to take over Leeds's fixtures.

Port Vale's current ground, Vale Park, was opened in time for the 1950–51 season. Construction had been slow owing to post-war demand for materials,

as rebuilding of homes and factories took precedence and the plan to build the 'Wembley of the North' never came to fruition. The first of the club's two periods of relative success came within a few years: in 1954, Vale reached the semi-finals of the FA Cup, and were promoted as Champions of Division 3 (North).

Stanley **Matthews** is possibly the most famous person to be associated with Port Vale. Matthews was general manager from July 1965, and team manager from May 1967 until his resignation in May 1968, a short reign which saw Vale fined and briefly expelled from the Football League in 1968 for financial irregularities.

The Vale's longest-serving employee was defender Roy Sproson, who played 837 matches between 1950 and 1972, and was manager from 1974 to October 1977, when he was sacked. There then followed a succession of five unsuccessful managers in two years, but out of this period of instability came something good: in December 1979, former Southampton player John McGrath took charge and made John Rudge his assistant.

John Rudge succeeded McGrath in autumn 1983 to manage Vale through their second boom period. In 1988–89, Port Vale were promoted to the old Division 2 for the first time in 32 years, remaining at that level for three seasons; they were promoted again in 1994, a year after winning the Autoglass Trophy Final. In 1996 the club achieved their highest League position for over 50 years, eighth place in what is now the Championship and in the 1990s finished above rivals Stoke City on five occasions, a feat not achieved for nearly 40 years.

Rudge had a talent for finding good players, and then selling them on at a profit to balance the books; Robbie Earle, Mark Bright, Andy Jones, Ian Taylor,

Steve Guppy, Gareth Ainsworth and Marcus Bent were among those who went on to greater things. Bent was Rudge's last signing, bought just three days before he was sacked, leaving a transfer profit of £5m after 843 matches in charge over 15 years.

Brian Horton took over, and after being relegated Vale lifted the LDV Trophy again in 2000, then spent a year in administration before missing out on the promotion play-offs on goal difference in 2003–04.

Portsmouth

'Nothing in the history of football can compare with the phenomenal rise and extraordinary performances of our club,' said Portsmouth boss Frank Brettell in 1899, at the end of the club's inaugural Southern League season. Twenty wins from 28 had seen Brettell's club, founded on 5 April 1898 from the ashes of leading amateur outfit Royal Artillery, finish runners-up behind Tottenham. It was three-and-a-half seasons before Pompey surrendered their unbeaten record at Fratton Park – still the club's home – and one which visiting fans will say seems hardly altered since the last days of Queen Victoria's reign. Brettell's promise of greatness has typified Pompey's story in the 108 years since the club turned professional.

Every so often – particularly in 2003–04 under the management of Harry Redknapp, which brought a highest top-flight finish (13th) since 1956 – the club has flickered spectacularly into life only for bad management, bad luck or a spectacular combination of both to take its toll. Following steady progress after entering the Football League in 1920, Pompey were the first club south of London to reach the top flight, in 1926–27. FA Cup success in 1939, a 4–1

hammering of much-fancied Wolves, saw the Blues hold the trophy for seven wartime years. Both teams were injected with supposedly performance-enhancing monkey glands. Manager Jack Tinn, in a smart bit of kidology, suggested the Wolves signatures on a ball handed around the dressing room before the game looked a bit shaky.

Buoyed by the presence of Britain's finest forces talent on their doorstep, Pompey's 'Iron Men', under 'Bowtie' Bob Jackson, won back-to-back championships in 1949 and 1950 (the club celebrated the first title by giving each player a £10 shopping voucher). England wing-half Jimmy Dickinson – 764 games and not one booking – Len Phillips, Peter Harris, Duggie 'Thunderboots' Reid and Jimmy Scoular were the bedrock of Pompey's success. But mediocrity soon set in and demotion to Division 2 in 1958–59, and the third flight two seasons later, heralded a dire period – in eight seasons they finished no higher than 15th in Division 2 before another relegation in 1975–76. So bad were the club's fortunes at that time, the 'SOS Pompey' appeal was floated to save the club.

A slow climb back after relegation to the basement in 1977–78 began when Scotsman Frank Burrows took the club up in 1979–80, in front of regular crowds in excess of 20,000 – unheard of in Division 4. Bobby Campbell attained Division 2 status for them as champions in 1982–83 before Alan Ball, at the third attempt, took the club back to the summit in 1987, just for one year. A revival looked on the cards again in the early 1990s, when Jim Smith's exciting young side, boasting Darren Anderton, reached the FA Cup semi-final in 1992, only to become the first to lose at that stage on a penalty shoot-out after two draws.

More heartbreak followed 12 months

on. Despite Guy Whittingham's club record-breaking 42 goals, West Ham won promotion to the Premiership on total goals scored. The club's subsequent slump was aided by the Department of the Environment, who rejected plans for a new ground at a public enquiry in 1994. Smith's departure, and the increasing ill-health of chairman Jim Gregory, paved the way for a sorry slide into adminis-tration in the club's centenary season during which Terry **Venables** had a brief spell as chairman while gates dipped below 7,000.

Serbian Milan Mandaric, previously involved with football clubs in the USA, France and Belgium, took over in 1999. A succession of managers, none of whom lasted a full season, typified the early years of his reign before Redknapp – with the popular Smith back as his sidekick – took Pompey back into the top division in 2002–03. The potent mix of big-name cast-offs, journeymen pros and young blood that clinched the Division 1 title continued to work in the Premiership: an impressive late surge of six wins and three draws in the final ten games banishing any relegation fears. But Redknapp's departure after a very public falling out with Mandaric in November 2004 cast a lengthy shadow. Redknapp's replacement, Alain Perrin, departed in November 2005, to be replaced in turn by Redknapp himself, back from a spell with neighbours Southampton. Another round of relegation-haunted wheeling and dealing duly followed. Cynics will claim that, whatever the personnel, Pompey's ability to make a sow's ear out of a silk purse remains undimmed by time.

post-football careers

Many of today's pros will never need to work again. But it wasn't always this way. The sad truth is that relatively few footballers make much of themselves after they finish playing. Such a rare and lucrative talent as footballing skill tends to be nurtured during adolescence to the detriment of everything else, and when the short career is over, our heroes are often stumped for a next move.

There are exceptions: Liverpool's Craig Johnston will have made more from inventing the Predator boot than he ever did from playing, Mike Channon is now a successful racehorse trainer, and Eric **Cantona** seems happy enough playing gay pirates in French arthouse films. For those garrulous cheeky chappies of the 1960s and 1970s, like Tommy Docherty, Peter Osgood, Rodney Marsh and Jimmy **Greaves**, after-dinner speaking was a natural progression – after all, if no one was paying them, they'd have spent the entire evening telling those same stories anyway. And from there, it was a short step to radio and television (we have these people to thank for the opening of the floodgates that led eventually to a TV football culture so in thrall to ex-pros that millions now spend their Saturday nights tolerating the thoughts of Peter Schmeichel).

But for most players who finished their careers without a nest egg, and had neither the inclination nor the character for management, life after football would be exactly the kind of grim slog they were trying to avoid by playing in the first place. Becoming a publican has always been the cliché, a route taken by (amongst many others) Peter Lorimer, Ian Callaghan, Jim **Baxter**, Ian Storey-Moore, Alan Sunderland, Terry Naylor, Steve Lynex, Kenny Burns . . . all the way back to 1930s heroes Cliff **Bastin** and Dixie **Dean**.

Those preferring the workaday life to the temptations associated with the pub could always follow the examples of

Martin Peters (insurance broker), Kevin Hector (postman) or Jon Sammels (driving instructor). Escape to sunnier climes is an option too – canny tricksters Charlie Cooke and Gordon Hill both became soccer coaches in warm parts of America, Eddie McCreadie set up a painting-and-decorating firm there, while former Fulham goakeeper Peter Mellor maintains swimming pools in Florida. Conversely, Leeds goalie David Harvey was drawn to the chilly isolation of farming in the Orkneys.

Wolves' Peter Knowles retired at the age of 23 in order to make himself useful by knocking on doors in the Black Country on behalf of the Jehovah's Witnesses (inspiring Billy Bragg's 'God's Footballer'), while Mike Summerbee became bespoke shirtmaker to the stars, but sadder stories are more common. For Everton defender Sandy Brown, scoring a famous own-goal in the first Merseyside derby televised in colour was bad enough, without knowing that he'd end up in a Peek Frean's factory in Blackpool.

Spurs' Nigerian international John Chiedozie might have had some fun running a company that distributes bouncy castles, but it's unlikely you could say the same for Allan 'Sniffer' Clarke (travelling salesman of extractor fans), Garry Birtles (a fish salesman prior to becoming a Sky pundit) or Fulham's Welsh striker Gordon Davies (who took up the enviable post of ratcatcher). And there must surely be a place in every football fan's heart for erstwhile Liverpool goalkeeping hero Tommy Lawrence, last heard of working the night shift at a wire factory in Warrington.

pre-match meal

Food has always been a controversial subject in football. The pre-match meal was once the only occasion during the season that a footballer's dietary habits would come under any great scrutiny. Steak and chips, egg and chips, and roast beef have all been favoured at various stages in the game's development. Bill **Shankly** is reported to have abandoned his player's strict pre-match steak diet in the early 1960s, after which meat was absolutely prohibited at lunchtime on a match day; this even extended into Shankly sending 'spies' along on train journeys to away games to monitor whether players were loading up on ham rolls from the buffet trolley.

Dietary fads have come and gone at regular intervals in the game's recent history. Even the traditional half-time cup of tea has now fallen out of favour with nutritionists, who prefer (even above water) specialist 'sports' drinks containing phosphates and other salts that encourage rehydration. Fish has been generally mistrusted as a pre-match meal, particularly shellfish and the footballer's favourite, scampi. One Division 1 manager became so determined that his players should eat no more than a single bread roll at pre-game lunches that he developed a habit of counting the rolls before and after a meal and demanding to know who had eaten any missing extras.

As notions of sensible nutrition have infiltrated the professional game, so the importance of the pre-match meal has declined. Just as the custom of midweek team drinking has given way to the idea that, actually, it's never a good thing for the constitution to drink 12 pints of lager very quickly and dance in a circle in a nightclub, so the importance of continually monitoring a footballer's diet has taken hold. Footballers now aim to eat a carbohydrate-rich diet most of the time, with extra protein after a game or a heavy training session. Fat should be minimized, particularly the night or morning before a game as it is notoriously hard to digest. The ideal footballing breakfast involves whole wheat cereals, skimmed milk, fruit, yoghurt and lots of fluids.

QPR manager Ian Holloway employed ex-army fitness instructor Scott Rushton for the 2003–04 season. Rangers players would eat a pre-match meal of cereals, pasta, scrambled eggs and fresh fruit at 11.30 in the morning, with the pre-match meals just a question of topping up what players have lost from the liver overnight. Rushton also revealed that during breaks in Holloway's team talks he filled the silence by 'firing out instructions such as "stand up, keep your legs moving and keep your brains lively . . . some sharp runs, turns and power jumping when you get outside, come on lads!"' Which is enough to put anyone off their penne rigate.

Like so many other things in football, food is tied up with superstition. Alan **Shearer** famously revealed during his Blackburn days that he always ate 'chicken and beans' before a game and most players have a favoured lucky meal. Nigel Winterburn's poached eggs on toast survived even the Arsène **Wenger** dietary revolution at Highbury, and pre-match meal favourites were a regular feature of Football League programmes during the 1970s and 1980s. In his autobiography Jimmy **Greaves** describes 'heading off to Moody's cafe in Canning Town where we would order our pre-match meal of roast beef and Yorkshire with all the trimmings or pie and mash followed by blackcurrant crumble and custard'. Greaves then recalls how players always ate steak before a game because they had been told it gave you energy. He describes Gordon **Banks**'s pre-match meal of 'a large steak with peas and both boiled and roast potatoes, followed by a large bowl of rice pudding'. All of which

makes Banks's sudden food poisoning at the 1970s World Cup finals less of an enduring mystery.

Premier League

Younger viewers of Sky TV might be forgiven for thinking that the history of football began in 1992, the year that Rupert Murdoch's channel negotiated a lucrative TV rights deal with the newly founded FA Premier League. Its pundits are prone to talking of 'Premier League records' as if 100 prior years of Football League history had never happened. So a ten-year-old may think that Alan **Shearer** is the greatest English goalscorer of all time, while Dixie **Dean**'s 60 goals for Everton in 1927–28 have apparently become a statistical irrelevance.

The best sides in the Premier League – which broke away from the Football League under the auspices of the Football Association on the initiative of club chairmen looking to increase revenue and dump the burdensome poorer brothers of the lower divisions – have certainly generated record amounts of cash. Few of them, however, have spent it wisely, and a team such as Leeds United has managed to rack up huge debts, by attracting and rewarding overpaid players, to go from Champions' League semi-finalists in 2001 to Football League strugglers just over three years later.

The Premier League has ushered in the era of improved stadium facilities, saturated television coverage, multitudes of foreign players of varying pedigree, increased crowds paying astronomical ticket prices, and a championship that only three teams, at most, have a realistic chance of winning. Only Blackburn Rovers, in 1995, had won the Premier League up until 2004 besides Manchester

United (eight times) and Arsenal (three). Since then, a Chelsea side pumped up with millions from Russian oil 'entrepreneur' Roman Abramovich, have also taken the title twice.

Teams promoted from the Football League often struggle to survive and go straight back down, with burnt out shipwreck cases like Barnsley, Bradford City and Sheffield Wednesday falling down the League and possibly wishing they'd never set eyes on the much-hyped, top-flight nirvana. The best that most teams can aspire to is a UEFA Cup place or the kind of mid-table steadiness achieved by teams like Charlton Athletic and Tottenham 'Big Five' Hotspur (ironically former Spurs chairman Alan Sugar was one of the prime movers behind the Premier League). As attendances begin to stagnate in the face of predictable results and over-priced tickets, the clubs who drooled at the sight of television cash may eventually need to melt down the troubled golden cash cow they thought was football's future.

Preston North End

Preston North End are inextricably linked with their most famous post-war player Tom **Finney**. Finney's retirement in 1960 marks the division between a successful era of regular top-flight football and a subsequent period of sustained decline, which has only recently shown signs of finally being reversed.

A cricket and rugby club was founded in Preston in 1863 and took up football around 16 years later. Affiliated to the Lancashire FA, they were the pre-eminent team in the years before the establishment of the Football League. Achievements such as the record 26–0 FA Cup win over luckless Hyde in 1888 – a game they were winning just 4–0 after half an hour – and other regular double-figure scores saw North End christened 'The Invincibles'. Towards the end of their most dominant period Preston were still good enough to win the first two League championships and finish runners-up in the next three seasons; they also won the FA Cup in 1889 without conceding a goal, thus recording the first ever Double.

Soon after, the emotions of North End fans resembled a rough day at Blackpool with alternating relegations and promotions for several years either side of the First World War, until the status of the club was regained in the mid-1930s. Great players such as Alex **James**, Bill **Shankly**, George Mutch and the Beattie brothers continued the club's Scottish tradition. An FA Cup was won in 1938, a year after a defeat in the Final.

The appearance of the magical Finney after the war marked a third golden age, as the rivalry with Arsenal was renewed. To this day, old men grow misty-eyed when they see the club president arriving for a game; his 76 England caps are as proudly remembered as any recent triumphs. Finney was supported by the likes of Tommy Docherty, Charlie Wayman and Tommy Thompson, but despite the talent available the only tangible reward for the last great Preston team was a losing FA Cup Final medal in 1954. Following Finney's retirement, the club entered a period of decline which lasted over 40 years, though they did at least reach the FA Cup Final as a Division 2 team, losing 3–2 to West Ham in 1964.

Preston's fortunes were revived by divisional championships in 1996 and 2000, the latter under David Moyes, who also took them to a Division 1 play-off final against Bolton in 2001. Sixteen years earlier the club had reached its lowest ebb. Relegation to the bottom division for the first time in 1985 was immediately followed by the deeper ignominy of re-election. The 2,007 who attended a midweek League match played on a Tuesday afternoon, because the floodlight pylons had been condemned and demolished, saw the club reduced to picking a substitute who had been dragged from his shift at a local factory (to which he had to return after the match ended).

For those fans who turned up (with their own brushes) to paint the ground, the three new stands at Deepdale must have seemed particularly impressive. The unveiling of a statue of Tom Finney in 2004, replicating the famous 'water splash' photograph of 1956, not only celebrates the history of Preston North End but also holds out a suggestion that some taste of former glories might one day return. In 2005 the team were one match away from a return to the top level, losing the Championship play-off final to West Ham.

programmes

The programme has been a distinctive part of watching a football match ever since the first single-sheet prototypes were produced in the late 19th century. Programmes have tended towards a hybrid of local advertising sheet and official club magazine, boasting team sheets, news and such staples as 'Manager's Notes' and 'Player Profiles' (standard questions: favourite TV programme; car driven; and preferred (a) food and (b) drink). What is considered to be the first ever match day programme was produced in Scotland in December 1815 by a Mr Scott, who distributed a commemorative poem among the crowd of 2,000 gathered to watch Selkirk take on Yarrow.

Early programmes remained little more than a collage of team sheets and crude

advertisements until the 1950s, which saw the gradual introduction – pioneered by clubs such as Chelsea and, later, Coventry City – of more sophisticated magazines. Programmes began to feature potted biographies of visiting teams, a weekly managerial comment and photographs of recent matches. Outside the top division production values remained simple and the contents of the programme closer to a local newspaper. Leyton Orient's programme for their Division 3 (South) clash with Ipswich Town on Thursday, 3 May 1956 begins with the words 'Hallo friends', and contains little more than 'Notes from the Supporters' Club' and a rambling editorial brimming with familial tributes to everybody connected with the club. During the late 1950s Crystal Palace introduced a small booklet format, which was adopted by, among others, Ipswich Town – a breast-pocket-sized Ipswich programme from 1965 (price: 6d) comprises 20 pages, of which 12 are devoted solely to adverts ('Home and Away – It's a Mini').

The programme for Chelsea's Fairs Cup home match against AC Milan in February 1966 contained the first use of colour photography, although it would be 15 years before colour photographs became standard in programmes. Between 1966 and 1974 the *Football League Review (The Official Journal Of The Football League)* was inserted into every club programme in the English League. The *Review* was a detailed, well-produced collection of columns, interviews, League information and colour photographs, usually far superior in quality to the sheath of line-ups, box adverts and laconic manager's notes that surrounded it. It was also the official mouthpiece of the Football League; an April 1968 issue contains a column that begins with the words: 'May I remind readers that the Football League is one of the best-run bodies in sport anywhere in the world', and sample features include an editorial on the devastating effects of decimalization on English football (references to 'the 5.5 metre box') and an article playing down the attraction of televised football.

By the time production of the *Review* ceased, programmes had borrowed from its text-heavy, journalistic format and the standard match programme contained a series of regular newspaper-style features, among them player profiles, 'on this day . . .' flashbacks and spot-the-ball competitions. Perhaps in response to the growth of fanzines in the mid-1980s, programmes eventually became longer and more detailed, closer in appearance to an official club magazine. Less formal too: in recent times managers' programme notes have been used variously as a personal soapbox, a means of responding to supporter discontent or – during Trevor Francis's final season as manager of Crystal Palace – as a means of explaining why you punched your substitute goalkeeper Alex Kolinko in the face during the previous League game. The programme notes of Chelsea's Italian manager Claudio Ranieri attained a certain internet-fuelled cult status, based on his distinctive idioms: 'We scored fantastic second and third goals, great football, toot, toot, toot, forward passing. I like when we play this well.'

But for most supporters there tend to be two approaches to programmes. The first involves compiling a vast archive spanning at least 100 years, each programme jealously guarded in its own airtight vacuum pack and occasionally auctioned off at exaggerated prices. Programmes are the most widely collected form of football memorabilia, with prices tending to depend on rarity: a programme from the 1938 FA Cup Final between Preston and Huddersfield

('Centre neat fold – otherwise superb') changes hands for £475, £200 more than a programme ('Mint Condition') from the 1966 World Cup Final. The second approach to programmes – and by far the more common – involves buying one, rolling it up and leaving it on the train on the way home.

promotion/relegation

Promotion and relegation are not the only ways of shuffling a pack of competing teams, but until recently few fans would have considered anything else remotely fair or likely. Unlike the franchise system of US sports (businessmen waving wads of cash to bring teams to their town), changes to the composition of the League have been decided, almost without exception, on the pitch.

Promotion arrived along with the founding of the Football League's 12-team Division 2 in 1892–93. In that first season three promotion places were decided by a single 'Test match' between the top three in Division 2 and the bottom three in Division 1. It began inauspiciously. Sheffield United and Darwen went up in place of Accrington and Notts County. But Newton Heath (Man Utd in embryo) – who had finished well adrift at the bottom of the first – survived by overcoming Small Heath (later Birmingham), who had finished top of the second. That dubious outcome set the tone for the Test matches, which were abandoned after six years in favour of a simple two-up, two-down system.

That formula was extended over the next 75 years or so, with the addition of two further divisions after the First World War. It was still harder to go up to or down from Division 1, as the promotion places remained at two even when the top two divisions expanded to 22 teams each. The ladder was pulled up altogether at the bottom of the League, with the imposition of an election system weighted heavily in favour of the existing League clubs. Otherwise, fair promotion was the rule, with the notorious exception of Arsenal, who talked their way into the enlarged Division 1 in 1919 despite finishing fifth in the second in the last season before the interruption of war.

Changes to this system began with the move to three-up, three-down between the top two flights in 1973–74. After that came the revived play-offs in 1986–87 and direct relegation from Division 4 the same year. More recently the Football League has seen changes to the number of teams in each division, the increase in promotion places from the Conference from one to two in 2002–03 and finally the Wimbledon/Milton Keynes affair, which to many fans symbolized the acceptance of a franchise system by the back door.

Some teams have more experience of this kind of thing than others. Their first demotion in 1893 was a sign of things to come for Notts County, who have been promoted or relegated more times than anyone else. Their relegation to the newly renamed League Two in 2004 took them to 26 (including a record 14 relegations). Others can recall single occasions of infamy. West Brom would have gone up on goal average in 1909 if they had scored just once more during the season. During their 2–0 win at Blackpool in November 1908, a scoring shot had rebounded from the unusually tightly strung net, but the ref failed to give a goal, believing it had hit the bar. Manchester City contrived to be relegated from Division 1 in 1938 with a positive goal average – they lost on the last day, while four other teams on the same points all won.

At least City have been back since. Blackpool's last season at the second level, 1977–78, ended in a run of 11 games without a win that left them one point behind no fewer than seven other teams (of whom six had a worse goal difference). Torquay United were famously saved from going down to the Conference on the final day of the first season of direct relegation, when they scored in time added on after defender Jim McNichol had been bitten by a police dog. And in 1994–95 Reading became the first team since 1897 to finish second at the second level but fail to win promotion, thanks to the cut in Premier League numbers that year.

Several clubs charged through the divisions in both directions in the 1970s and 1980s, in what may prove to have been the last hurrah of the League's much-prized mobility. Watford finished second in the League in 1983, only five seasons after leaving Division 4; Wimbledon bounded from the fourth to the first between 1983 and 1986; Bristol City left the first in 1980 and did not stop falling until they reached the basement two years later; and Swansea experienced a stomach-jolting decade, hiking from the fourth to the first and back again between 1978 and 1986.

In the modern era, as the financial gaps between all divisions widen, such odysseys seem much more unlikely. Since the beginning of the Premiership at least one club promoted from the division below has gone straight back down in each season.

pubs

Football is intimately bound up with the drinking, serving and manufacture of alcohol. Pubs have provided the social centre for both clubs and supporters from the earliest days of organized football in Britain. In fact, the majority of current League clubs were either formed in or around a pub, or owe some aspect of their origins to the brewing industry. During the late 19th century pubs were where people met to talk about the game and to organize or administer the first formal teams. Soon pubs were offering score updates and match results on Saturday afternoons, and an organizational hub for travelling groups of supporters.

Many clubs have at some stage been partly owned by pubs, or rescued from financial collapse by breweries. It was a brewer, John Davies, who rescued Newton Heath from ruin in 1902 and named them Manchester United, distributing shares among his fellow brewery directors. Oddly, even through the club's successful period under Sir Matt **Busby** and into the 1980s alcohol has been strongly bound up with Manchester United, with players at the club being notoriously hard-drinking, from George **Best**'s obvious problems to the Old Trafford Drinking Club of Norman Whiteside, Bryan **Robson** and Paul McGrath.

Of those clubs not founded in or around a pub, many were born out of the pub's exact spiritual opposite, the Temperance Movement. The Football League's first chairman, William McGregor, was an evangelical abstainer, and Charles Sutcliffe, the League's founding secretary, was cut from a similarly sober god-fearing cloth. In 1873 the Scottish Football Association was brought into being inside the Dewar's Temperance Hotel in Glasgow. The founding fathers of Scottish football would have scarcely warmed to many of its subsequent sponsors – among them Bell's, Tennents and Whyte & Mackay.

Socially, there is still an intimate bond between pubs and both football players and supporters. The retired player turned pub landlord is a familiar figure, with many ex-footballers also finding work in other parts of the brewing industry. Similarly, from the earliest days of migratory football support pubs have been a vital part of the travelling fan's experience. Many city pubs have become synonymous with a particular local club, either through location or tradition, such as the Strawberry in Newcastle, the Stanley Park (commonly known as 'The Blue House') near Goodison Park and the Corner Pin next to White Hart Lane.

Pubs and breweries continue to be major sponsors of football. This has been the case since the early days of the Football League, with the habit during the 1930s of painting an entire stand roof with the vast logo of a particular brand of beer. In the 1960s a television commercial featuring Bobby **Moore** and Martin Peters buying a drink with their wives in a mahogany-and-chandelier saloon bar encouraged people to stop off at their local pub – any local pub – and have a drink ('drop in at the local'). By the 1980s breweries were one of the most enthusiastic of early shirt sponsors, and in recent years the Worthington Cup, the Carling Premiership and the Tennents Cup have proved to be lucrative investments for their sponsors.

The inherent pub culture in British football has also been associated with some of its bleakest moments. The widespread regulation of alcohol in and around football grounds has certainly been a factor in controlling violence at matches. Similarly the alcoholic ex-pro is a recurrent figure, possibly a casualty of the social drinking among players. Football teams tend to drink competitively, a habit encouraged for a while by some managers as a kind of social glue to promote 'team spirit'. Recent fashions for sensible nutrition have seen drinking clubs identified as likely to be detrimental to performance on the field. The transformation at Arsenal is the most obvious example of this, crystallized by the club captain Tony **Adams**'s struggle with alcoholism: a club which would previously encourage players to spend their evenings drinking together is now the market leader in minutely controlled dietary intake.

pundits

Jimmy **Hill** pioneered televison punditry when he put together an 'expert panel' for ITV's coverage of the 1970 World Cup. Assembled in one room were a group of the biggest mouths and egos in the game: Brian **Clough**, Malcolm **Allison**, Derek Dougan and Pat Crerand were among the guests. The television audience loved the panel's heated, even frenzied, debates and a similar group assembled for ITV's 1974 campaign (Hill, now at the BBC, contributed to a slightly less flashy rival panel including Lawrie McMenemy and Joe **Mercer**). From that time it became impossible to watch a match on television without being exposed to the views of at least two ex-players at half-time.

The problem is that, since those heady 1970s days, we've got more televised football and fewer interesting pundits. Expert analysis became increasingly less passionate and more deftly packaged. From the mid-1980s to mid-1990s, Ian St John and Jimmy **Greaves** cornered the market in straight-man, funny-man analysis in *Saint & Greavsie* on ITV, while the BBC adopted a self-consciously understated style which began with the increasingly twitchy Jimmy Hill on *Match of the Day* and evolved into the debonair *sang-froid* of Des Lynam and, subsequently, Gary **Lineker**. During the latter part of the 1990s, Hill began playing up to his image as bumptious

buffoon and appeared to be invited on BBC panels ostensibly to act as the stooge of first Terry **Venables** and Lynam, then Lineker and Alan Hansen.

Nowadays, the style is for the host to ask a leading question which steers the reliable ex-pro into fetching back the only answer possible, rather like a dog with a stick. Martin O'Neill will occasionally scare Lineker with his combination of intense staring while being asked a question and intense unpredictability when answering, and Gordon Strachan can be aggressively sarcastic, but mostly there is nothing edgier than Alan Hansen lounging back in his chair and saying 'dismal'. The opinion, largely coming from ex-footballers and current or resting managers, is of one type and from one angle – it is only very rarely that television makes use of football journalists or supporters. Radio, notably BBC Radio 5 and Talk Sport, use both regularly and its coverage is more representative and less cliché-ridden as a result.

There are still some highlights that stand out from the cliché-filled dross: Hansen's 'You can't win anything with kids' during 1995–96 when a young Manchester United won the Double; Ruud Gullit's 'sexy football' (he only said it once, you know, it wasn't a catch-phrase); Martin O'Neill telling pop super-star Robbie Williams that he'd done very well for a chap with no talent during the 1998 World Cup coverage; 'Big' Ron Atkinson's variable success in getting his self-made football patois into common usage ('early doors' and 'little lollipop' have been well assimilated; 'he couldn't head a bus queue' and 'giving it the little eyebrows' are still bubbling under somewhat).

It's worth remembering that all punditry – Andy Gray's frenzied tactical acumen, Jack **Charlton**'s inability to identify individual foreign players, Bobby **Robson**'s gnomic incoherence, Barry Venison's shirts, Ally McCoist's cheeky smirk – all of it can be cooked up and boiled down into one phrase, patented by the super-earnest Garth Crooks: 'Football is football: if that weren't the case it wouldn't be the game it is.'

Queen of the South

The town of Dumfries acquired the alias Queen of the South in 1857 when a local poet, David Dunbar, coined it during his campaign to be elected to Parliament. Queen of the South was selected as the name of a new club formed from several existing local sides in 1919. They are the only team given a name check in the Bible, during the Old Testament tale of the Queen of Sheba, proving that Mr Dunbar was a man who knew his scriptures.

At the other end of their history, Queens are enjoying one of the most successful periods: 2002 saw them win Division 2, only the second championship win in 83 years, and also the Challenge Cup, a knockout competition for lower league teams. Since then they have remained in Division 1 and punched above their weight, even after losing their manager, John Connolly, to St Johnstone as a result of his success in Dumfries. Since promotion from Division 2, Queens have edged towards a return to the top flight of Scottish football for the first time since 1965.

However, for consistently competing with the best in Scotland the club still looks back to the immediate pre- and post-war era. Between 1934 and 1959 Queen of the South spent just one season below the top division, finishing fourth in 1934 and sixth in 1956. In 1948–49 their striker Billy Houliston earned three caps for Scotland and remains the club's only full international, although former Carlisle midfielder Chris Balderstone turned out for the club in the late 1970s shortly after having played cricket for England. Among the several other English players to have starred for Queens, the most fondly remembered is goalkeeper Allan Ball, who played 819 competitive matches for the club over 19 seasons from 1963.

During Queens' golden period, their finest hour in the Scottish Cup was a 1950 semi-final against Rangers, which they lost in a replay. The first match, which resulted in a 1–1 draw, was played in front of 55,000. Palmerston Park, Queen of the South's home since its inception, has a capacity of 6,412 and houses Scotland's tallest floodlights at 84ft.

The club's nickname, 'The Doonhamers', comes from the way that Dumfries folk referred to their hometown while working away from it ('doon hame').

Queen's Park

The Queen's Park club motto is *Ludere causa ludendi* – 'to play for the sake of playing'. Founded in 1867 by students and white-collar professionals, they remain the only senior amateur club in either England or Scotland.

'The Spiders', or 'The Hoops', won the Scottish Cup ten times between 1873 and 1893 and provided the bulk of the players for the first Scottish national teams. But their influence was just as great off the field as they wrote their own set of rules at a time when there was no unified code for the game, introducing innovations such as half-time, free kicks and crossbars. It was under the Queen's Park rules that the first international game between Scotland and England was played in Glasgow in 1872. The Scotland team was made up entirely of Queen's Park players, who played in their blue club colours that remain Scotland's first-choice kit. The club, however, changed to black and white hoops the following year.

Queen's Park distinguished themselves in England as well. After five years of haphazard fixtures, they were invited to take part in the first FA Cup in 1872, and given an exemption until the semi-final

because of their travel costs. They drew 0–0 against Wanderers, but had to concede – they couldn't afford to stay around for a replay, and the final had been scheduled for the next day to save money. They later reached the final in successive years in 1884 and 1885, both times falling to Blackburn Rovers.

The club is the sole survivor of the Scottish FA's eight founding 1873 members, and in 1890 opposed the formation of the Scottish League because they said it would usher in professionalism and strangle a lot of the smaller and weaker clubs (six of the League's founding members had duly gone under within a decade).

In 1900, however, after finding that the big-name opponents were increasingly too occupied with League play to stage exhibition matches, they finally joined Division 1, despite remaining resolutely amateur. In 1903 they moved to the new (and third) Hampden Park that remains both their home and Scotland's national stadium. Their best days were already over, and no player would again approach the club record 14 Scottish caps won by legendary full-back Watty Arnott in the previous century. Left-winger and future Wembley Wizard Alan Morton, otherwise known as 'The Wee Blue Devil', left the club in 1920, inevitably for Ibrox.

For a long time the Spiders stayed in the top division mainly thanks to the lack of automatic relegation, and the special treatment they were given owing to their standing in the game. In 1922, when such reverence was no longer granted, they went down to Division 2, although they bounced straight back as champions, and even finished fifth in Division 1 in 1928–29, scoring 100 goals. In 1933, they could still pull a club record crowd of 97,000 for a second-round Scottish Cup tie with Rangers, but this was also

the last year when the club's amateurs –
Bob Gillespie and Jimmy Crawford –
represented the national side.

They put together another strong team
right after the Second World War, but
when professional salaries were re-established they declined once more. Queen's
Park's only successes since their last
season at the top level in 1957–58 have
been the nurturing of a young player and
future manager called Alex **Ferguson**; a
Division 2 title in 1981; and a Division 3
championship in 2000 (followed by
immediate relegation). Why they continue to play Division 3 fixtures in the
52,500-seater national stadium in front of
a few hundred fans is anybody's guess,
as the quirky, adjacent Lesser Hampden
– where they played while Hampden
Park was renovated in the 1990s – is far
better suited to lower league football.

Some concessions have now at last
been made to the modern game: former
pros can play for the club as long as
they're not paid, and a full-time coach
has been in place since 1998.

Queens Park Rangers

Queens Park Rangers were founded in
1885 through a merger of two north-west
London youth teams, Christchurch
Rangers and St Jude's. After turning
professional in 1899 the club joined the
Southern League, and then moved to
current home Loftus Road in 1917 after a
nomadic early existence that included a
spell at the 60,000 capacity Park Royal
stadium. In 1920 QPR were one of the
founder members of Division 3; six years
later the club colours were changed for
the fourth and final time to the current
blue and white hoops.

Despite a Division 3 (South) title in
1948, Rangers had to wait until 1968
before winning promotion to Division 1
for the first time. It was Alec Stock's

appointment as manager in 1961 that
signalled an upturn in the club's fortunes.
The signings of Spurs striker Les Allen
and then Rodney Marsh from Fulham in
1965 provided the impetus for successive
promotions, as champions of Division 3
in 1967 and runners-up in Division 2 in
1968. In 1967 the club also won the
League Cup, beating West Bromwich
Albion 3–2 having been two goals down,
QPR's only major tournament victory to
date.

These were tempestuous years for the
club. An acrimonious proposal for a
merger with Brentford was abandoned
after mass protests by both sets of
supporters. For Rangers this was
followed by immediate relegation from
Division 1. Stock's team finished
1968–69 with 18 points, then the lowest-
ever points total for a 42-game season in
the top division, failing to win a game
from November to April and bringing
about his resignation as manager.

In 1973 Rangers were back in the top
flight, this time for six straight seasons,
incorporating a second-place finish in
1976. Dave Sexton's team featured
several internationals, including Phil
Parkes, Frank McLintock, Gerry Francis
and Stan Bowles, and is generally
regarded as the finest QPR XI ever
assembled. Rangers were unbeaten at
home all season, but lost out on the title
by the narrowest of margins, Liverpool
scoring three times in the last 13 minutes
of their last game against Wolves to take
the League by one point.

In 1977 Sexton left for Manchester
United and two seasons later Rangers
were relegated, despite receiving
£550,000, a record for a goalkeeper, for
Phil Parkes from West Ham. In 1980 star
striker Clive Allen (son of Les), who had
scored a hat-trick on his debut, was sold
to Arsenal for £1.5m, the same year that
Terry **Venables** became the club's new

manager. Venables oversaw the installation of Loftus Road's plastic pitch, with the help of which Rangers reached their only FA Cup Final, losing 1–0 to Tottenham after a replay in 1982. A season later, Venables's team won Division 2 by ten points to begin a spell of 13 consecutive years at the top level.

Under Jim Smith, Rangers lost 3–0 to Oxford United in the final of the League Cup in 1986. A year later inspirational chairman Jim Gregory sold the club, sparking a brief furore as fan action prevented a projected west London merger with Fulham, which would have created something called Fulham Park Rangers. In 1992 a QPR team containing England internationals Les Ferdinand and Paul Parker finished fifth in the top division, making Rangers London's top club for the second season in six years.

However, friction between manager Gerry Francis and the board led to his departure in 1995. Bleaker times were around the corner: in 1996 Rangers went down, ushering in an era of board room reshuffles, financial profligacy, relegation to Division 2 in 2001 and near-extinction after going into administration in 2002. Under the management of the voluble Ian Holloway, QPR not only regained their financial equilibrium but won promotion back into the Championship in 2004.

racism

In 1991, the issue of racism in English football was finally confronted on the sports pages of the national press. The catalyst was a nationally broadcast television programme entitled 'Great Britain United', which compared the experiences of the current generation of black footballers with those of their pioneering predecessors during the 1970s, the first decade in which many had made a major impact on the sport and suffered from widespread racist abuse from the terraces.

The programme-makers sought the views of Ron Noades, chairman of Crystal Palace, where Afro-Caribbean players made up roughly half the first-team squad. He complimented black footballers on their skills but questioned their organizational abilities – 'you also need white players in there to balance things up and give the team some brains and some common sense'. Noades's remarks were delivered with the serene confidence of a man not used to being contradicted and he professed astonishment at the uproar they caused. After considerable effort, the players' union, the PFA, succeeded in prising a public apology from Noades, but his views were indicative of the myths that continued to blight English football even when evidence to the contrary was clearly presented every weekend. An outlook widely popular among those born before the sun set on the Empire was that black players were fast and skilful but shied away from physical contact and were temperamentally unsuited to leadership; useful foot soldiers but not really officer material.

The increase in the numbers of black players turning out for professional clubs during the 1970s was matched by the growth of racist taunting among spectators. A black player in possession of the ball would be greeted by a chorus of monkey noises, and abusive songs and chants. Extreme-right political groups, such as the National Front and the British Movement, began selling racist literature outside stadiums, and their banners, often Union Jack flags daubed with slogans, were seen at several football grounds across the country, notably in east London, Lancashire, West Yorkshire and the West Midlands.

Despite the abuse, by the early 1980s professional clubs in most major cities had a number of black players. Liverpool was an exception. It has a substantial black population, established as long ago as the 18th century when the city, then a busy port, played a vital role in the trade triangle between England, West Africa and America, yet by the end of the 1980s only two players from the community had ever played for the two clubs (Howard Gayle with Liverpool in 1980–81, Cliff Marshall for Everton in the mid-1970s). Furthermore, until 1987, when Liverpool acquired England international forward John Barnes, neither they nor Everton had ever bought a black footballer from elsewhere, though both have signed numerous black players since.

In the late 1980s, a number of fans' groups began to tackle the terrace racism. Leeds fans created a group called Leeds United against Racism and Fascism and succeeded in getting a ban placed on the sale of racist literature outside their team's stadium. Millwall, whose home in the London docklands had been a fertile recruitment area for the extreme right in the past, went to considerable lengths to reshape the club's image. In the early 1990s the Football Supporters' Association instigated a national campaign against racism among fans, eliciting the support of many club fanzines and publishing an anti-

racist fanzine of its own, called *United Colours of Football*.

The football authorities were slower to act, but a national campaign was started in 1993 by the Commission for Racial Equality and the PFA. First called 'Kick Racism out of Football' it recruited prominent players to act as figureheads and persuaded clubs to put up anti-racist banners at grounds. Since changing its name to 'Kick It Out', the campaign has continued working with clubs, players, fans, communities and schools to highlight prejudice. It has been instrumental in starting a Europe-wide campaign against racism in football, and organizes an annual 'Kick It Out week of action'. The law has also been used. The **Taylor Report** recommended that racist abuse at football matches be made a specific offence and this was given effect by the Football (Offences) Act (1991) which made it an offence to 'take part at a designated football match in chanting of an indecent or racialist nature'.

As a result of these efforts – and wider changes in British society – racism in football is clearly less crude and prominent than in the late 1970s and early 1980s. It is not uncommon now for more than half the players in a League team to be of Afro-Caribbean background, although there are still very few black managers (fewer than a dozen have been employed by League clubs over the past 20 years), and despite the efforts of 'Kick It Out', racist abuse is still an occasional accompaniment to watching a football match in the UK.

radio

Those who campaigned bitterly against the live broadcast of matches on TV throughout the 1970s and 1980s might have learnt something from the experience of radio, which met similar heated opposition from the press, clubs and the football authorities in the 1920s. As TV ultimately proved that it could do more to encourage live attendance than discourage it, so radio brought the game into innumerable households and stimulated the football imagination of millions.

Although technically possible much earlier, radio had to wait until 1927 to begin its long and fruitful relationship with the game. On 1 January the BBC became a public corporation and was granted the right to broadcast sporting events. Two weeks later it covered an England v Wales rugby match and on 22 January Henry Blythe Thornhill Wakelam (a former rugby player) was at Highbury to relay Arsenal's match against Sheffield United to the audience. Later that year George Allison, subsequently Arsenal's manager in succession to Herbert **Chapman**, made the first live broadcast of the FA Cup Final, Cardiff's historic 1–0 win over his future charges.

Before that first match at Highbury, the *Radio Times* helpfully printed a diagram of the pitch divided into eight squares, and as Wakelam described the play his co-commentator interjected with the number of the square the ball was in. This experiment, which continued for some years, is believed to have popularized, if not initiated, the phrase 'back to square one'. The *Manchester Guardian* wrote approvingly that 'it was fairly easy to visualize what was actually happening and the cheers and the groans of the spectators help considerably the imagination of the listeners'.

It is this dual source of information – the commentator articulate but detached, the crowd inarticulate but partisan – that has given radio coverage an appeal that persists even in the days of frequent live televised matches. While football was more frantic than cricket, whose relationship with radio eventually became even

closer, its ebb and flow still lent itself well to both description and analysis – unlike tennis or athletics, when the action is often too compressed to be effectively conveyed.

England, perhaps, has no single emblematic broadcast from the heyday of radio – certainly none to match the frenetic emotion of Germany's 1954 World Cup Final win over Hungary, whose legendary broadcast by Herbert Zimmermann became a best-selling record. The radio voice most closely identified with football to a modern audience is that of James Alexander Gordon, who has read the classified results on BBC radio at 5pm every Saturday from 1972. With the *Sports Report* signature tune, 'Out of the Blue', his distinctive Edinburgh tones have defined the weekend ritual for those on their way back from matches and those at home – not to mention millions of expatriates and foreigners plugged in through the World Service.

It was the reading of the scores rather than live match commentaries that gave radio its initial impetus, not only for devoted fans but also for the millions of people whose interest in football was largely confined to the pools coupon. While other sources of information and other forms of betting have undermined that relationship, the tradition of the 5pm reading has survived, even as 'Football League, Division 1' has come to mean something quite different and even if half the games are no longer played on Saturdays.

Radio had two other trump cards that maintained its sway even after television began to initiate its own 5pm ritual. One, at least until the arrival of the mobile phone, was the development of pocket-sized receivers which could be comfortably carried to the match. While the scores may arrive in numerous technologically sophisticated ways now, none has so far matched the excitement and uncertainty of the live reporter struggling to be heard against the backdrop of a raucous crowd. The other was the innovation of car radios, which made it the only possible medium for those who travelled to and from the match that way.

Radio also prospers thanks to its most obvious limitation (a lack of pictures), in that it gives room for those idiosyncratic reporters who use words in original or eccentric ways. Love them or hate them, neither Stuart Hall nor Jonathan Pearce has the same impact on television. More recently, its profile has again been raised by the seemingly insatiable craze for football phone-ins on both BBC and commercial radio, hosted by provocative (or plain irritating, according to taste) presenters such as David Mellor, Alan Green and DJ Spoony. As with the fanzine movement of the 1980s, in hindsight it seems extraordinary that no-one before had thought to exploit the shared culture of football fandom in this way, however uninspiring some of the results may be.

Raith Rovers

A TV sports presenter, commonly believed to be David Coleman, once declared that 'they will be dancing on the streets of Raith' after the Rovers won an important match. In fact, there's no such place. The club's home is the linoleum-manufacturing town of Kirkcaldy in Fifeshire; they take their name from the Laird of Raith, who owned the land on which the team first played, at a ramshackle venue called Robbie's Park, in 1883. They moved to their current ground, Starks Park, eight years later.

The club, who play in the Scottish international colurs of navy blue and white, have experienced one purple patch in

their 123-year history, under the management of Jimmy Nicholl in the mid-1990s. Inspired by the fledgling skills of current Scotland internationals Stevie Crawford and Colin Cameron, Raith were Division 1 champions in 1994–95 and secured their first major trophy, beating Celtic in a dramatic League Cup Final. Current manager Gordon Dalziel scored to make it 2–2 in the dying moments of normal time and keeper Scott Thomson sealed victory by saving from Celtic captain Paul McStay in the penalty shoot-out. In the following season's UEFA Cup, Raith lost 2–0 at home to mighty Bayern Munich in the first leg of their tie but held a 1–0 half-time lead in the return before losing 2–1. After two seasons in the top flight, the loss of key players allied to crippling financial problems saw the club slip back into lower-league penury in 1997.

Raith returned to the limelight in 2004 when, desperate for investment, the directors accepted an offer from Claude Anelka, erstwhile football agent and brother of sulky striker Nicolas. Unfortunately Anelka's insistence on taking over the day-to-day coaching of the team resulted in unmitigated disaster. He was only in charge for around three months but it was enough time to cement the team at the bottom of Division 1, from which they were relegated in 2005.

League members from 1902, Raith were runners-up in the 1913 Scottish Cup and the 1949 League Cup. Their most capped international, David Morris, played six times for Scotland in the 1920s, though the club also nurtured Alex **James** and future Rangers star Jim **Baxter**, regarded by many as Scotland's best-ever player. Raith's last spell in the top division before the Jimmy Nicholl era came in the late 1960s with a side including midfielder Ian Porterfield, scorer of Sunderland's winner in the

1973 FA Cup Final, and Gordon Wallace, voted Scottish Footballer of the Year in 1968 even though the team finished just one place above the relegation area.

Sir Alf Ramsey

Leeds striker Allan Clarke was picked to play for England by Alf Ramsey. On his first international trip abroad Clarke spent his time joking around with other players at the back of the team aeroplane. After a while Ramsey walked down the aisle and stood listening. 'Enjoying yourself Allan?' he asked. 'Yes, Alf, great, thanks.' 'Well you don't. fucking enjoy yourself with me,' came the reply. This sounds about right. Ramsey wasn't really one for enjoying himself. After his Ipswich Town team had won the League title, the club owners, the Cobbold family, threw a lavish party. Ramsey was the only member of staff not to attend. He was busy scouting at a youth team game.

There is a famous picture of Ramsey on the England bench at the World Cup Final in 1966, taken just as Geoff **Hurst** scores his final goal in the 4–2 victory. While the rest of the party leap into the air, goggle-eyed with excitement, Ramsey is still seated, his chin in his hands, wearing the expression of a man who's just been told he'll have to wait another half-hour on the platform at Clapham Junction. Later, as the final whistle blew, he told trainer Harold Shepherdson, 'Sit down and behave yourself, man.'

This unnatural reserve was collateral to Ramsey's success. He may have been England's only World Cup-winning manager, a man who reinvented the role of national team coach, and before that a prodigiously successful club manager, but the style of his achievements created a highly unusual public persona. Ramsey

was a true original, a self-made man in the plainest sense.

It was in his voice that this came across most clearly. Ramsey's accent was a nightmare of strained elocution. After one early press conference with England the *Observer* correspondent wrote: 'he is more careful of his aspirates than his answers', and Ramsey's pretensions are easily mocked. While on duty with England he once told a restaurant car steward, in clipped tones, 'No, thank you, I don't want no dinner.' Asked in a radio interview where his parents lived he replied, 'Dagenham . . . I believe.'

This awkward persona had its roots in something vital to Ramsey's success. In private he spoke of the need within the FA to show himself as able as any member of the officer class committee men who had traditionally been in charge of the team. If there was a battle being waged with his superiors it was won by Ramsey. On his appointment the unpopular and parochial International Selection Committee was immediately abolished, opening the way for a system where only the manager would have a say in team matters or selection.

The son of a straw dealer, Ramsey was raised in east London. As a young man he refused to work at Ford's Dagenham car factory and was set to become a grocer before signing for Portsmouth in 1939 as a tough-tackling full-back. During the Second World War Ramsey served as a quartermaster and played for forces teams before joining Southampton when professional football resumed (somewhere along the line he knocked a couple of years off his age). In 1950 Arthur Rowe brought him to Tottenham for £21,000, a record fee for a full-back.

Rowe made a deep impression on Ramsey and it was at Spurs that he began to develop his managerial ambitions. He got his chance with

Ipswich in 1955. Ramsey's success there has been overshadowed by his achievements with England, but it bears repeating. A side sometimes called 'Ramsey's rustics' in the press won the Division 2 title in 1961, playing an unusual midfield formation without wide players, a blueprint for the 'wingless wonders' of the 1966 World Cup. A year later Ipswich took the League title at the first attempt. Ramsey was in pole position to become national team coach after Walter **Winterbottom**'s resignation that same year. There was never any doubt he would take the job. Geoff **Hurst** called Ramsey 'the most patriotic man I've ever met', which is probably saying something. During his playing days Ramsey had been capped 32 times, often as captain. His last appearance came in the devastating 6–3 defeat by Hungary at Wembley in 1953; he also played in England's other great post-war defeat, the shock 1–0 loss to the US in Belo Horizonte at the 1950 World Cup.

Ramsey was the first England manager to take sole charge of team affairs. He was also the first manager to develop a notably spiteful relationship with the press. Ramsey hated being around journalists, partly because of his unease among what he saw as educated men. In one of his early press conferences he declared, 'I believe England will win the 1966 World Cup.' This was a brave prediction. Despite a 5–2 defeat to France in Ramsey's first match, by the end of 1963 England were on the rise, drawing with world champions Brazil and winning 4–2 in Czechoslovakia and 8–1 in Switzerland. Ramsey was utterly dedicated to his task. In preparation for the 1966 World Cup players were instructed in everything from diet and sleeping patterns to how to clip their toenails correctly. During pre-tournament basketball games at the training camp in

Roehampton Ramsey bruised and winded several of his own players. He looked on approvingly as Jack **Charlton** and Nobby Stiles came to blows.

Ramsey created a totally committed party of players with an utterly ruthless team spirit. Hurst has also described the England players' affection for their manager. After victory at the World Cup Final, the single achievement that would earn Ramsey both his knighthood and a unique status among his peers, he left his team to celebrate alone on the pitch before congratulating them all with great warmth in the safety of the dressing room. The World Cup victory would be Ramsey's high point.

An exit at the quarter-final stage in the 1970 tournament was followed by failure to qualify for 1974, his team falling at the qualifying stage after a bungled 1–1 draw against Poland at Wembley. Ramsey left the job on 3 April 1974, two days after a draw with Portugal in Lisbon. A short spell as manager of Birmingham City followed, but Ramsey didn't stay long in football. He spent his retirement in Suffolk and died in 1999.

Rangers

As with their great rivals, Glasgow Celtic, any history of Rangers must look beyond the emphatic domestic trophy haul to study the club's health in relation to its Old Firm rival, and the periods when it threatened to make a sustained impact on European football.

Peter and Moses McNeil, Peter Campbell and William McBeath are the four men credited with the formation of Rangers in 1873. Teenager Moses suggested the name 'Rangers' ('Glasgow' is not part of the club's offical name) after spotting it in an English rugby football annual, and he would go on to be Rangers' first ever international as well as playing in their first Scottish Cup Final, a defeat to Vale of Leven in 1877.

Rangers arrived at their current Ibrox home in 1899 but success proved elusive, such was the dominance of Celtic in the years up to the First World War. However, the 1920s and 1930s would see a shift in power between the two that would, in turn, alter the balance of Scottish football. William Wilton and then the legendary Bill Struth led Rangers to 16 League titles in 21 years. It is a startling statistic, and one that Struth delivered through a regime that could kindly be described as authoritarian. He was said to watch the arrival of his players at Ibrox from his office window. If any had dared to walk with hands in pockets, they would be summoned to undertake the journey again in a manner more fitting for a Rangers player.

A post-Second World War loosening of their hold on the League title – the club won 'only' 12 championships in the next 30 years – was softened by European adventure. The 1960 European Cup semi-final and 1961 European Cup Winners' Cup Final were both lost, as was the European Cup Winners' Cup Final of 1967, defeat to Bayern Munich coming just days after Celtic had won the European Cup. The hoodoo was banished in the European Cup Winners' Cup Final of 1971–72. The travelling Rangers fans in Barcelona's Nou Camp saw two goals from maverick winger Willie Johnston secure a hard-fought 3–2 victory over Dynamo Moscow, but their over-exuberance led to chaotic scenes after the final whistle. As the Spanish police restored order with batons on the pitch, Rangers captain John Greig received the trophy in a small room within the stadium in front of a few officials.

What made the win more poignant was that it came a little over a year after the **Ibrox disaster**, of 2 January 1971, when 66 home supporters died as steel

barriers on a staircase gave way while the crowd left the ground. This acted as the catalyst for the regeneration of Ibrox into an all-seater arena well ahead of its time. Yet it was only after the appointment of Graeme Souness as player-manager in 1986 that a team would arrive to match the exalted surroundings.

Souness and new chairman David Murray recognized that major investment was required in the playing staff and, backed by Murray, the manager looked to England for salvation. The European ban on English clubs helped Rangers attract Trevor Steven, Terry Butcher and others and the capture of the Scottish Premier League in 1988–89 was the first instalment of a nine-in-a-row sequence that equalled the record of Jock **Stein**'s legendary Celtic team.

Walter Smith, who stepped up from assistant when Souness left for Liverpool, oversaw the final six of those wins and also led the team to within a game of the 1993 European Cup Final. Since his departure, Dutch coach Dick Advocaat and Alex McLeish have both produced treble-winning teams. After Celtic's purple patch under Martin O'Neill, their city rivals seemed set to wrest the initiative back with a second League title in three years in 2004–05. But the team only finished third in 2005–06 and MacLeish departed.

Reading

Founded in 1871 Reading are the oldest of the current League clubs in the south of England. Founder and secretary Joseph Sydenham engineered a short and unimaginative fixture list which included playing the local grammar school four times in the first six matches.

This may have prompted the emergence of Reading Hornets in 1873. The Hornets were both rivals and allies, sharing the same pitch and many of the same players. In 1877 the two fused together under the more established banner of Reading FC and a brief halcyon period ensued. In 1878 the club moved to an enclosed ground with pavilion and 'ladies' tent', extended the range of fixtures to include some leading London sides and by 1881 were recognized by the FA as one of the 'principal' clubs in the land along with Aston Villa, Blackburn Rovers, Old Carthusians and a dozen others.

But then – as football elsewhere took off with the advent of passing, professionalism and grandstands – Reading retreated to a stiff amateurism and a hedge-lined ground in a remote part of town. The club barely survived into the 1890s but its old reputation held good when the Southern League was formed in 1894. Reading were elected as founder members. Poor form in the first season and the lingering painful memories of an 18–0 FA Cup defeat at Preston (the latter had cannily worn studs to help them through the Deepdale mud) finally drove the football-loving public of Reading to overthrow the old amateur regime in 1895 and turn the club professional.

The move to Elm Park followed in 1896 and Reading returned to Lancashire in 1901 to beat Bolton to reach the FA Cup quarter-finals. In this era Elm Park hosted an FA Cup semi-final and Holt and Smith from the Reading defence represented England. 'The Biscuitmen', so called after the local Huntley & Palmers factory, returned from a 1913 tour of Italy acclaimed as the finest foreign team ever to play there.

So finally joining the Football League in 1920 was something of an anti-climax. Reading won Division 3 (South) in 1926 and reached the FA Cup semi-finals the next year. However, the promise of establishing a long-term position as a 'bigger' club was ended by relegation in 1931 and

the half-century of frustration and mediocrity that followed. Frustration lay in finishing second or third seven times in the next 15 seasons, in the days of 'one-up one-down'. Promotions from Division 4 under Charlie Hurley (whose most lasting act was to choose the club's new nickname – 'The Royals') in 1976 and Maurice Evans three years later did not alter the big picture. Mediocrity over a 30-year period had led, by 1983, to the chairman trying to sell the club to Robert Maxwell's Oxford United.

The foiling of this 'merger' unleashed fresh energy. Within five years Reading, under Ian Branfoot's guidance, had set a record for most wins from the start of a season (13), climbed two divisions and won the Simod Cup at Wembley in front of nearly 62,000. Glory days lasted about another six weeks before relegation back to the third tier. At death's door again in 1990 Reading were saved by millionaire John Madejski, who brought stability and wealth that was the envy of many lower-division rivals. In 1998 the club moved to an all-seater stadium with conference centre, academy dome, all mod cons. Following promotion in 2002 it established itself in the second tier then, under Steve Coppell, achieved promotion to the Premiership with two months to spare in 2005–06. Attendances are at record levels with a prosperous catchment area spread across several southern counties as well as the growing town itself. Not quite one of the 'principal' clubs yet but, at last, back on its promising early path. Unlike Old Carthusians.

re-election

For much of the last century, the Football League was a distinct entity, a private members' club. The reason was re-election. Rather than the system of promotion and relegation that the four Football League divisions operated between themselves, any top non-League club aspiring to become one of the 92 had to wait for a member to be kicked out.

At the end of every season, the 44 Full Members (clubs in Divisions 1 and 2) and the Four Associate Members representing the bottom two divisions, were presented with a ballot comprising the four clubs who finished at the foot of Division 4 and a number of non-League clubs, sometimes more than 20, who were applying for League membership. Each representative of an Associate Member had to vote for the four clubs they wished to see in the League for the following season. For some it was an annual humiliation. Several Southern League clubs, notably Nuneaton, Bedford and Chelmsford, routinely put themselves forward for many years in a row without polling more than a couple of votes at a time, while Cambridge City also persisted in standing even after their neighbours, United, had been elected in 1970.

Having to apply for re-election may have been embarrassing (it even happened to the first-ever Football League champions, Preston North End, in 1986), but for over 50 years it was mostly nothing to worry about, unless you came from a small, northern coastal town. The one factor that influenced member clubs' vote more than any other was how much it cost to play the short-listed clubs. If they were an expensive 400-mile journey away or more, they were on rocky ground. The size of crowds was also taken into account at a time when gate money was shared.

So, out went the hugely unfortunate Gateshead (replaced by Midland League champions Peterborough in 1960), Barrow (replaced by Hereford on a second ballot in 1972 two years after being in Division 3), Workington (who had replaced another northern coastal club, New Brighton, in 1951, dropped in favour of Wimbledon in 1977), and South-port (five years after winning Division 4 they were out, Lancashire neighbours Wigan Athletic supplanting them in 1978). Also dismissed in 1970 were the hapless Bradford Park Avenue, who had been bottom of the pile for three successive campaigns and were replaced by Southern League champions Cambridge United.

After the formation of a national semi-professional league, the Alliance Premier League in 1978, only one non-League club stood for nomination each year but it was still to no avail. The only aspirants who came close were the first champions of the new league, Altrincham. They polled one vote fewer than Rochdale in 1979 because representatives of two clubs, Grimsby and Luton, who had promised to support them, failed to vote at all.

Finally, the League conceded that the closed shop they were running was unfair and anti-competitive. Re-election was replaced by one-up, one-down in 1987 (although it was still conditional on the Conference champions having facilities deemed to be of League standard), with eight-time re-election candidates Darlington subsequently making the drop but bouncing back. Since then – and a change to two-up, two-down from 2002–03 – none of the perennial strugglers have slipped out of the League, with Hartlepool (re-elected 14 times), Roch-dale and Crewe (ten each) all surviving and sometimes thriving.

referees

According to the laws of football, 'The decisions of the referee regarding facts connected with play are final.' Once, there were just players. The arrival of officials in the mid-1860s denoted football's transformation from a game into a sport, because the introduction of competition and, later, professionalism demanded an independent arbitrator. Before, disputes were settled by a discussion between the captains; imagine Roy **Keane** and Patrick Vieira, say, trying to agree about anything.

Today, many in the stands believe that they have a better view of proceedings than the referee; in the early days, they had a near-equal view, the official not leaving the sidelines for the pitch until 1891. For the previous 25 years, he had merely intervened in disputes between the two umpires, one in each half, usually nominated one by each team. They became the linesmen, today's assistant referees, and at all serious levels of the game neutrals, too.

The referee's responsibilities today include enforcement of the rules and maintaining the safety of the players. Neither is a straightforward task. Most players and managers, never mind fans and journalists, rarely pick up a copy of the laws of the game; nor are many concerned about the accuracy of decisions provided that they go in their team's favour. And while player safety can include such simple decisions as telling players to remove jewellery, it also includes judging the fitness of the pitch; abandoning or postponing a match is rarely a popular move.

It is often said that the sign of a good referee is that you don't notice him. This can be nonsense: if players step out of line then the referee's obligation is to intervene and if he fails to do so he may not be noticed but he will have failed in his duty. However, some officials appear to thrive on notoriety, arguably to the detriment of the sport. Clive Thomas, the Welsh referee who blew for full time as the ball was on its way into the net for a potential winning goal in a match

between Brazil and Sweden in the 1978 World Cup, is one such. He still appears in the tabloid press from time to time today; away from the game, he was chosen to become high sheriff of Mid Glamorgan for the year commencing March 2005.

There are other ways for referees to make a name for themselves that endures long after their careers in the middle. Sir Stanley **Rous** became a senior official in the 1920s and refereed the 1934 FA Cup Final, but was elected secretary of the Football Association that year then served as president of FIFA from 1961 to 1974. Arthur Ellis, on the other hand, officiated in three World Cups – 1950, 1954 and 1958 – and the first European Cup Final in 1956, then became the adjudicator on *It's A Knockout*.

The highest accolade a referee can receive is to be selected for a World Cup Final. Three English referees have handled this match, the most recent being Jack Taylor, who officiated in 1974 and, in the absence of Sir Alf **Ramsey**'s team from the tournament, was England's sole representative. The final started well for Taylor: he pointed out the absence of corner flags, delaying kick-off for several minutes, then correctly awarded the Netherlands a penalty in the first minute. His subsequent award of a penalty to West Germany was more controversial and helped them to a 2–1 win.

Taylor's English predecessors were George Reader (1950, Brazil 1 Uruguay 2, last game of final pool) and Bill Ling (1954, West Germany 3 Hungary 2). Aside from these three, the most distinguished English referee is probably Ken Aston, who refereed the infamous Battle of Santiago between Chile and Italy in the 1962 World Cup then helped run the refereeing committees at the 1966 and

1970 World Cups, and invented red and yellow cards.

Aston's invention at least made part of the referee's life simpler. The hardest part of the job, made worse by increasing scrutiny from television pundits armed with slow-motion replays and multiple angles, is that while mistakes by players are usually quickly forgotten, any error by an official is seized upon. A sign of the times is that, following attacks on the houses of referees, the home town of officials in Scotland is no longer published.

The worst crime a referee can be accused of is bias, whether through favouritism or corruption. Though the former is usually just the bleating of a losing team, sadly there have been many examples of the latter, from the bribing of officials in European Cup ties exposed in the so-called 'Lobo–Solti affair' of 1973 when it was alleged that Juventus bribed a referee to favour them in a European Cup semi-final against Derby County, to the case of German referee Robert Hoyzer, who confessed in 2005 to fixing matches.

referee's kit

In the early days of amateur football, the referee's equipment consisted solely of a handkerchief, the waving of which was only mildly effective when it came to stopping play. The alternative of shouting 'Foul!' could also go unnoticed on a blustery day. Referees responded by taking up an instrument recently adopted by the police: the pea whistle. A company called Hudson and Co. began producing the 'Acme Thunderer', a specialist sporting whistle first used by football referees in 1878.

Early referees wore robust outdoor clothes, but nothing that would have them mistaken for an athlete. As the pace of the game increased referees began to wear long shorts and by the start of the First World War the official and his linesmen generally turned out in a black jacket or blazer with a white shirt open at the collar. Some continued to wear neckties right up until the 1930s. After the Second World War referees' kits became smarter and more technologically complex (the white collar on the black 'blouse' was detachable, just like a vicar's). Truly short shorts didn't appear until the 1970s, however.

With the advent of the Premier League in 1992, referees were given green pin-striped shirts, possibly to emphasize the brash corporate environment of the Premiership. Yellow and red cards had been introduced by the Football League in October 1976. They were withdrawn briefly in 1981, but are now a permanent part of the referee's arsenal. Currently the professional ref walks on to the pitch armed with pens and pencils, notebook, whistle, spare whistle, watch, stopwatch, red card, yellow card, a coin for the toss-up, match report card, vibrating device on his arm to alert him to an assistant's raised flag and – for effecting swift repairs to playing equipment – a pen-knife.

replays

Despite pressure from Arsène **Wenger** and Sven-Göran **Eriksson**, the FA has rejected calls in recent years for cup replays to be scrapped because of fixture congestion. Part of its reasoning is that such occasions are part of the 'fabric and the romance of the competition'.

This is no overstatement; the replay, with the visiting team getting to host the second game, was written into the first agreed rules of the FA Cup, as instigated by Charles Alcock in 1871. The fourth and fifth FA Cup Finals went to replays, with Royal Engineers overcoming Old Etonians 2–0 in the second game in 1875 and The Wanderers seeing off the same opponents 3–0 in the 1876 replay. There have been 15 replays of the FA Cup Final up to 2005, with three consecutive replays needed between 1910 and 1912 and again between 1981 and 1983, while not a single replay was required in any of the finals played between 1912 and 1970. The first-ever replayed game of football was the 1873–74 cup tie between Sheffield and Shropshire Wanderers, with Sheffield going through on the toss of a coin after the replay was also drawn. The same season Clydesdale and Third Lanark were the first teams to come back and try again in the Scottish Cup.

While clubs could see the profit through their turnstiles from playing two or more games, the replay wasn't always welcomed by working men unable to afford tickets and transport. Tottenham Hotspur of the Southern League became the first and only non-League team to win the FA Cup, beating Sheffield United in the replayed final of 1901, although few United fans witnessed it as the Lancashire & Yorkshire rail company refused to provide cheap tickets for a second match. When Celtic and Rangers drew the 1909 Scottish Cup Final, many fans expected extra time. As it became obvious this wouldn't take place, rumour spread that the draw had been staged to bring in extra revenue. A pitch invasion followed and the stand and pay-boxes were set on fire.

In 1953, Chelsea needed four matches to see off West Bromwich Albion in the fourth round and had to play their fifth-round match three days later. This would have been luxury for Beith, who had to play four replays to finally defeat Broxburn in the Scottish Cup in 1909, with the last three played on con-secutive days. Beith lost 3–0 to St Mirren in the next round, a game played the day after the fourth Broxburn replay.

Stoke needed five matches to beat Bury in the third round of the 1954–55 Cup and, in the next round, Doncaster also took five to see off Aston Villa. The record, however, goes to Alvechurch, who beat Oxford City 1–0 in the fifth replay of an FA Cup fourth-round quali-fying match in 1971. The total of 11 hours spent over one result will never be beaten. The FA killed off the second replay in 1991, introducing instead penalty shoot-outs at the end of first replays. Rotherham were the first team to benefit from this rule that same year, beating Scunthorpe on penalties in the first round.

retain-and-transfer system

The abolition of the maximum wage in 1961 is generally held to be the moment when the power balance between clubs and players began to swing in favour of the employees. But the scrapping of the retain-and-transfer system, which went hand in hand with the wage case, was at least as important in moving football towards a world where players, or their agents, call the shots on transfers.

Like the maximum wage, the retain-and-transfer system had at least partly honourable intentions, namely the survival of the smaller clubs and the preservation of healthy competition throughout the League. The minnows feared that the free movement of players and a free market in their wages would lead to domination of the League by a very small number of elite clubs. But like other attempts to keep clubs on a relatively even keel, such as the draft in American sports, retain-and-transfer also had iniquitous consequences for the individual players.

It was initiated with the rise of professionalism in the late 1880s to limit the poaching of players, which had become rampant. Players could be signed on for only one season at a time. At the end of each season, the clubs listed the players they wanted to keep and those available for transfer. No player could leave a club without its consent, except by appealing to the League. If he turned down the club's offer of wages and the League refused to step in, he was left with no other option but to quit football altogether. Despite the vehement opposition of the players' union to the system, particularly in the turbulent years before the First World War, it survived essentially un-touched until the George Eastham case of 1963.

Eastham, of Newcastle and England, fell out with his club and asked for a transfer. They refused and the League declined to intervene – as a result Eastham spent a year out of the game. Backed by a determined PFA fresh from its victory over the maximum wage, he took legal action against the system his lawyer described in court as being 'like the bartering of cattle' and 'a relic of the Middle Ages'. Justice Wilberforce of the High Court agreed. Eastham, by then transferred to Arsenal, won the case on 4 July 1963, and the old system was declared an unreasonable restraint of trade.

The arguments remained the same throughout the decades the system was in place. In 1952 a committee appointed by the Ministry of Labour found that changing the system would mean 'star players would tend to be concentrated with a few rich clubs, and thus the

general standard of League football would decline'. They were half right.

Don Revie

As a player Don Revie was frequently described as 'scheming'. This may in itself have been enough to earn him the post of Leeds United player-manager when the club were struggling near the bottom of the old Division 2 in March 1961. In fact, Revie was offered the role as an afterthought while a club director was writing him a letter of recommenda-tion for the manager's job at Bournemouth.

On the pitch Revie had been successful as a scheming attacker at Leicester and later as the deep-lying centre-forward (copying the role of Hungary's Hidegkuti) in Manchester City's 'Revie Plan' as City won the FA Cup in 1956. The year before, Revie had been voted Footballer of the Year. He ended his playing career at Leeds, where, as the team hovered above the drop to Division 3, he was able to start putting his coaching ideas into practice.

By the time Revie left Elland Road to take up the job of England manager in 1974 Leeds were the most feared and disliked team – and arguably the most successful – in the Football League. Legend has it that Revie paid a visit to Matt **Busby** in his first weeks as Leeds boss to get advice on how to be a good manager. Busby told him: 'treat your players well . . . and never lie to them'. Revie went back to his team, persuaded the highly influential Bobby Collins to take back his transfer request, and guided Leeds to safety with a 3–0 win at Newcastle in their final match. Three seasons later they were Division 2 cham-pions and the following year, 1965, they ended runners-up in the League. The club finished in the top four for the next ten seasons, only slipping to ninth in 1974–75, the season Revie left.

With Collins sidelined through injury, Revie paired Billy **Bremner** with Johnny **Giles** in midfield and the Leeds blend of skill and disciplined aggression began to take shape. They were seen as a negative, cynical team for much of Revie's tenure. This was not entirely unfair. Leeds's first League title in 1968–69 was won with 16 of their games containing only one goal. Revie would instruct his team closely on how best to negate their opponents' strengths. Allan Clarke, a clever and prolific striker, admitted to creating the odd goal for himself through the expedient of discreetly ankle-tapping defenders just as they were about to make a back pass.

Revie had the Leeds kit changed from blue and yellow to Real Madrid white, and dominated his players to the extent that Norman Hunter, Billy Bremner, Johnny Giles and colleagues spent most of their Friday evenings in the early 1970s contesting bingo and carpet bowls. The Revie way became ingrained in players, staff and fans, inspiring a crushing momentum on the pitch – as, among others, Chelsea (beaten 7–0 in 1967) and Southampton (7–0 in 1972, a televised display described by Barry Davies as 'cruel') – could testify.

Revie's Leeds won the League title twice, the FA Cup once, the League Cup once and the Fairs (later UEFA) Cup twice. Among these triumphs was a fair dose of controversy and pure bad luck: the 'offside' WBA goal of 1971 that cost Leeds the title, the last-day defeat to Wolves when they only needed a draw to finish top, the apparently biased referee in the European Cup Winners' Cup Final of 1973 and the Montgomery double save in the 1973 FA Cup final against Sunderland.

Revie and Leeds went downhill after they parted. Revie lasted three underwhelming years as England manager before slipping off to Dubai to earn himself a vast amount of money and, for some, the label of 'traitor'. Allegations of bribery attempts during his time at Leeds had surfaced before he died of motor-neurone disease in 1989. He left Leeds United with a back-breaking legacy of greatness, one which dogs players, managers and chairmen to this day.

rivalries

The reason why the word 'derby' came to mean a close rivalry, usually geographical, is not entirely clear, although it most likely relates to the very local rivalry of the ancient Shrovetide game played at Ashbourne in Derbyshire. More important than its origins is the fact that the concept, and indeed the word, is understood everywhere that football is played – *el derbi, le derby, Das Derby, il derby* – and the great rivalries have helped to fuel the development of all the world's successful leagues.

There can be many reasons for animosity between two teams, but the most common is certainly geography. Of the big European leagues, only Spain has traditionally understood its biggest *derbi* to be between two teams from different cities – Real Madrid and Barcelona – although such is the recent dominance of Arsenal and Manchester United in England that their matches have come to overshadow their traditional derbies. (Holland, with Feyenoord and Ajax, also has a long-standing intercity rivalry that dwarfs any local feeling.)

The fiercest derbies arise where another element is added to geography and the roughly equal standing of two big-city rivals. In Glasgow and Edinburgh it is religion, or at least the tribal identity initially shaped by religious differences. In north London it is history, for Tottenham fans still cannot forgive Arsenal for queering their pitch with their move from Woolwich in 1913 and highly dubious promotion immediately after the First World War.

In England and Scotland, it so happened that the size of the cities and the timing of football's growth left several centres with two more or less evenly matched clubs: Glasgow, Edinburgh, Dundee, Liverpool, Manchester, Birmingham, Nottingham, Sheffield, Bristol, even Bradford (perversely, since it was also an important rugby league city). Many other smaller industrial towns were so close that no sooner was a club born than it immediately looked to its neighbour to settle local scores on the pitch. Away from the industrial north, mutual isolation could also foster a certain amount of spite, as between Ipswich and Norwich.

The web of rivalries that developed for each club – with its nearest club of similar size, with a much smaller or larger local challenger, with perennial opponents from another part of the country – has changed subtly over the years as the fortunes of each club has waxed and waned, but in principle they have remained. Perhaps the greatest shift has been in the balance of the big Lancashire derbies, where previously dominant Manchester City and Everton were firmly relegated to the status of underdogs in the second half of the 20th century.

Manchester United's recovery from the **Munich aircrash** of 1958 (indeed, it became part of the mythology that turned them into a 'national' club) stands in stark contrast to the fate of Torino, whose dominance of their city and of Italian football was usurped by Juventus after a catastrophic aircrash wiped out their team in 1949.

Being parochial by their nature, the beauty of derbies is that they need no external context to maintain their needle. No matter what division they are in, or how unimportant the points, a match between Blackburn Rovers and Burnley, or between Cardiff and Swansea, or even Lincoln City and Boston, will always have an edge. Indeed it is often when nothing more is at stake than local pride that matches tend to descend into violence on or off the pitch. Clubs that do not have 'natural' derbies seem to feel the need to create one, such as the intensity between Chelsea and Leeds (both lacking a mutually satisfying derby opponent) that grew initially from the 1970 FA Cup Final, or between Crystal Palace and Brighton since their 1970s promotion tussles.

Derbies in the showpiece finals of English football have been astonishingly rare (unlike the regular Scottish final clashes between Celtic and Rangers, of course). It took until 1967 for two London sides to meet in the FA Cup Final (Chelsea and Tottenham), and though others have done so since, the 'true' London derby (Arsenal v Tottenham) has never got further than a semi-final. Liverpool and Everton met in the 1986 and 1989 finals (and the League Cup Final in 1984), but the only other final to feature a big-city derby was Birmingham v Aston Villa in the 1963 two-legged climax of the then low-key League Cup. The Midlands have provided the nearest thing to a true derby in the FA Cup Final, too, other than the two Merseyside affairs (Villa and West Brom met three times in the 19th century and Nottingham Forest defeated Derby in 1898), but the last was in 1931, when West Brom beat Birmingham 2–1.

In recent years it has become fashionable for the biggest clubs to claim that they have somehow 'outgrown' their traditional local derby, so that Manchester United's most highly charged game of the season is no longer against City, but against Liverpool or Arsenal (or soon perhaps even against Real Madrid or Milan). Naturally that serves only to inflame their city rivals further, but the day may not be far off when the biggest League derbies are devalued by the 'resting' of star players in the same way that the League Cup and the FA Cup have been. All the more reason, then, to savour the minor classic derbies in the lower leagues, where the passions may be parochial and at times nasty, but at least are not created for the benefit of television viewers.

Sir Bobby Robson

Bobby Robson's career as a player and manager is remarkable for its longevity, and for the many different eras within the game that he has embraced. Robson was born in Langley Park, County Durham, in 1933. He had a successful playing career as a right-half at West Bromwich Albion and Fulham and played for England at the 1958 World Cup. Despite his success as a player, Robson has been most influential as a manager, in which profession he has spent more than half his life.

Robson took his first step into management at Vancouver Whitecaps in 1967, staying in Canada for a year before becoming manager of Fulham in 1968, where he lasted less than a year. His first significant success came at Ipswich Town. Between 1973 and 1982 Robson's Ipswich finished outside the top six in Division 1 just once and competed in Europe eight years out of nine. They also won the FA Cup in 1978, the year the manager famously told his players to 'stop Sammy Nelson' (the unassuming Arsenal left-back) in the Final, having identified the diffident Nelson as the main source of the Gunners' attacking play. A UEFA Cup triumph followed in 1981, with a 5–4 aggregate victory over AZ 67 Alkmaar.

Robson was appointed England manager in 1982 in succession to Ron **Greenwood**, and remained in the job for eight years, during which time he took England to three major championships and was frequently portrayed in the media as tactically confused and excitable to the point of eccentricity.

The low point of failure to qualify for the 1984 European Championship was followed by the high of relative success at the 1986 World Cup. In Mexico, Robson's team started badly with a 1–0 defeat to Portugal. A turning point came with the radical rejigging of the team for its third match against Poland, including the introduction of Peter Beardsley for the less subtle Mark Hateley.

As with the sudden tactical switch to playing Mark Wright as a sweeper in the 1990 World Cup, in 1986 there were rumours around the England camp of player revolt and of decisions made by committee. England beat Poland 3–0, Gary **Lineker**, who scored 35 goals under Robson's international management, getting a hat-trick. They were eventually eliminated in the quarter-finals with a creditable sense of injustice after being outplayed by Diego Maradona, but handed the genuine grievance of an illegally converted first goal. Robson eventually left the England job with his reputation enhanced by success at the 1990 World Cup, a team containing the youthful Paul **Gascoigne** and David Platt going out on penalties in the semi-final in Turin.

Robson managed PSV Eindhoven, winning the Dutch league twice and overseeing the signing of the 17-year-old Ronaldo from Cruzeiro in 1994, and also worked with Sporting Lisbon and Porto in Portugal, and with Barcelona. His time abroad was much like his stint as England manager: mildly successful, although apparently more by good-natured inspiration than any great technical mastery. Robson returned to England in 1999 to take over at Newcastle United. During his time at St James' Park the club avoided possible relegation in his first season and competed in the Champions' League twice, as Robson oversaw an era of spiralling debt and brattish off-field behaviour among his players with some creditable if qualified success. He was sacked in 2004 at the age of 71, a scapegoat for the underachievement and off-field excesses of his players. Robson returned to football as assistant manager of the Republic of Ireland in 2006.

Bryan Robson

Bryan Robson was an energetic, combative central midfield player, known among excitable tabloid newspaper editors as Captain Marvel. During a highly successful career with Manchester United and England, whom he captained 63 times in an international career of 90 caps and 26 goals, Robson was renowned for his tackling ability, forward runs and goal-scoring prowess. Chest-beatingly committed to the cause, and perpetually flirting with serious injury as his surprisingly fragile physique absorbed the rigours of his all-action style, in retrospect Robson also seems like an embodiment of the traditional strengths and weaknesses of a domestic game that has often prized athletic zeal above all else.

Robson began his career at West Bromwich Albion in 1974, and was part of the progressive Albion team managed by Ron Atkinson during the late 1970s. He followed Atkinson to Old Trafford in 1981, signing for Manchester United for £1.7m, a British transfer fee record. By the time Robson retired 12 years later he had made 457 appearances for United and scored 97 goals, winning the FA Cup three times, the Cup Winners' Cup in 1991 and the Premier League title twice. Both League championships came at the tail end of Robson's career. After a decade during which Robson had led the way in attempting to inspire a series of underachieving United teams, the veteran skipper's dotage coincided with the opening acts of Alex **Ferguson**'s success at Old Trafford. Robson left Old Trafford to become player-manager at Middlesbrough in 1994, presiding over a madcap era that included relegation from the Premiership and two cup finals all in a single season, and overseeing such high-profile signings as Juninho (good) and Fabrizio Ravanelli (not quite so good). He left his post at the Riverside in 2001, unsuccessfully managed Bradford City in 2003–04 and is now with West Brom.

It was as a buccaneering England captain that Robson found his enduring incarnation. He made his international debut against the Republic of Ireland in 1980 and went on to play at three World Cups, scoring what was then the fastest goal in World Cup history after 27 seconds of his opening World Cup game against France in 1982. In 1986 the recurrence of a shoulder injury against Morocco was deemed front-page news as the talismanic captain found himself forced out of the tournament. Oddly enough, exactly the same thing happened in Italy in 1990. Even more unexpectedly, in both cases England performed much better without their inspirational midfielder. Coincidence perhaps, but the suspicion remains that Robson the player – committed almost to the point of self-parody – represented an apotheosis of a particular kind of fist-clenching Englishness, and fist-clenching Englishness doesn't win many tournaments.

In an era that also produced the languidly gifted but largely mistrusted Glenn **Hoddle**, Robson led an England team struggling energetically with its own inadequacies, becoming in the process the ultimate manifestation of a footballing ideology that prizes above all else perpetual motion and direct play. Given an environment receptive to complementary footballing qualities – alongside a Hoddle, rather than a Peter Reid or a Steve McMahon – Robson had the talent to have achieved even more.

Rochdale

Since forming in 1907, Rochdale have laid claim to some inauspicious records: fewest wins in a season (two, 1973–74); lowest post-war League attendance (450 v Cambridge United, in February 1974), most goals conceded in a season (135, 1931–32). They've finished bottom of the Football League on six occasions and spent all but five seasons of their League tenure in the lowest division.

Of their 34 managers, 23 departed within two years and 16 never worked in that capacity again after leaving the club. The most famous name to have played for Rochdale is Harry Potter, a full-back in the early 1950s, though three fathers of famous sons have turned out in the 'Dale's blue and white: Alan Ball Snr, plus Charlie Hurst and Terry Owen, fathers of Sir Geoff and Michael respectively.

The town, originally famed for its prodigious manufacture of cotton, is 12 miles north of Manchester, at the foot-

hills of the Pennines, which are visible from the ground should the need to ponder arise. Over the years locals have traditionally travelled out to support United, City or the other bigger nearby clubs (League attendances have fallen below 1,000 on 31 occasions). Rochdale joined the League in 1921–22, when it had its major restructure, establishing Divisions 3 North and South. Before this the club had journeyed around various minor northern leagues with only one outstanding moment: on 10 January 1920, they put up a hearty performance against Arsenal at Highbury in the FA Cup, leading 2–1 at half-time before eventually losing 4–2. 'Dale's two goals were scored by Harry Mellalieu, who later became a comedian, sharing stages with the town's most famous daughter, Gracie Fields.

Rochdale spent a season in Division 3 when the lower leagues were reorganized in 1958–59 but finished bottom, having failed to win a single away match. This was followed immediately by the best period in their history. Led by Tony Collins, the League's first black manager, Rochdale were the first club from the lowest division to appear in a major cup final, losing 4–0 over two legs to Norwich City in the 1961–62 League Cup. Their League form improved steadily and in 1968–69 they secured their one and only promotion with a team starring winger Dennis Butler, tiny midfielder Billy Rudd and Cornish striker Reg Jenkins, whose fearsome shots could allegedly rip the net. Five seasons later they were back down and in a parlous state. Whip-rounds were held in pubs across the town and players said to be little above pub league standard became first-team regulars. Only the generosity of the club chairman, springs-magnate Freddie Ratcliffe, kept the club in business.

Several miraculous escapes under the re-election system saw Rochdale limp into the 1990s with a team that was, at last, becoming proficient and solid within its own division. The once ramshackle ground, Spotland, has improved too, with three sides completely rebuilt. In 2001–02 Rochdale celebrated two firsts – reaching the play-offs (losing out to Rushden & Diamonds) and having players capped, with Patrick McCourt and Lee McEvilly appearing for Northern Ireland in the same match against Spain.

Wayne Rooney

At the age of 20 Wayne Rooney was already a global star. He is also the youngest-ever goalscorer for England, and after his £27m move from Everton to Manchester United the second most expensive British player in football history. Despite this, his career has barely begun. Very little can be predicted about his longevity in the game, his ability to enjoy prolonged success or even – despite a few opaque public appearances – what he's actually like.

Notwithstanding the desensitizing effects of the hype and hard sell of modern football, Rooney's talent is startling. After making a superb full England debut as a 17-year-old in the 2–0 European Championships qualifying victory over Turkey in 2003, he scored nine international goals in his first year as an England player. Then, after joining Manchester United in the summer of 2004, he scored a spectacular Champions' League hat-trick against Fenerbahçe on his injury-delayed debut for the club. Rooney is a completely natural footballer. Powerfully built, well-balanced and seeming low to the ground despite being 5'10" tall, even as a 16-year-old he had an intimidating physical presence. Playing as a striker or in an attacking midfield position, he has superb control, vision, shooting power and an ability to perform on the big occasion.

The urge to compare Rooney to the greatest players of the past has overwhelmed even experienced managers. After his successful appearances at Euro 2004, where he scored four times against Switzerland and Croatia, Sven-Göran **Eriksson** compared Rooney's impact to that of the similarly 17-year-old Pelé at the 1958 World Cup. The Fenerbahçe coach, Christoph Daum, said Rooney could be 'the player of the century', George **Best** called him 'the complete player . . . as good as anything you've seen', and Wimbledon champion Serena Williams described him as 'a sweetie' during England's run to the the quarter-finals of Euro 2004.

Rooney was a familiar whispered topic of conversation among Everton fans long before his debut for the club in August 2002. His spectacular performances for Everton's FA Youth Cup finalists of 2001–02 made him one of the most talked about young players in the country. From the start, Rooney has appeared utterly unfazed by the pressure of expectation. After scoring his first senior goals against Wrexham in the League Cup while still a 16-year-old, he announced himself in the Premiership with the spectacular long-range strike against Arsenal at Goodison Park two weeks later. The goal demonstrated the completeness of his talent: instant control of a bouncing ball, awareness of the space in front of him, quick feet to manoeuvre the ball and then an extraordinary dipping side-footed shot beyond the England goalkeeper David Seaman.

In truth, Rooney's Everton career never had time to live up to its astonishing start. Injuries and loss of form, combined with manager David Moyes's reluctance to over-burden a teenager, restricted Rooney to 40 starts in Premiership games and 15 goals over two years. In 2003–04 he played well in patches, scoring several crucial goals in a relegation-threatened campaign, but also spending time out of position on the right wing and missing games through suspension. Several rash tackles led to unhelpful comparisons with the young Paul **Gascoigne**, another prodigiously talented, occasionally reckless player from a poor background. There is no real comparison. Even at his best Gascoigne always appeared to be slightly out of control, in thrall to his own trapped and destructive energy. On Rooney's better days he appears calm and focused. At his worst, although less so in recent times, he has the petulance of a teenager.

Unusually, Rooney's talent has flowered in the England team rather than at the levels below. He scored his first international goal away to Macedonia in a Euro 2004 qualifier in September 2003 and has since become the dominant force in Sven-Göran Eriksson's team. He was one of the players of the tournament in Portugal in 2004. After Rooney left the field in the quarter-final with a broken metatarsal, England lost both momentum and a 1–0 lead against the hosts. It's no exaggeration to suggest that, had he not been injured, they would probably have been favourites to win the competition at that stage.

A strange summer followed for Rooney. Weekly stories emerged in the tabloid press of his visits to prostitutes in Liverpool the previous year, causing some much-publicized soul-searching over his relationship with fiancée Coleen McLoughlin. In the middle of this he signed for Manchester United, completed his recovery from injury and began his Old Trafford career in spectacular style. The future for Rooney would seem to be wide open. He has prodigious talent, a resilient physique and a place in the starting XI at one of the biggest clubs in the world. Success doesn't always follow in such circumstances. But British football has rarely, if ever, seen a young player progress so meteorically. Either way, it should be fascinating to watch.

Ross County

In 1994 Ross County fans were celebrating the Dingwall club's long-overdue admittance into the Scottish Football League – a momentous occasion even if it did mean entering the national set-up at the lowest possible tier. Ten years on and the same fans are beginning to grumble at the team's inability to make the step up from the lower leagues to the SPL.

Unreasonable expectations, one might think; however, the problem for the club is that the achievements of bitter foes Inverness Caledonian Thistle are the benchmark to which County managers have to aspire. The two clubs both graduated from the Highland League to the Scottish Football League at the same time and the pair have shared roughly the same path since then. Unfortunately there is a perception among County fans that their club is regarded as the junior partner in the duo.

This feeling of inadequacy and resentment has reached a peak in recent times owing to Caley Thistle's landmark feat in 2004 of becoming the first Highland team to compete among Scotland's elite. County's achievements are unremarkable only by comparison. During their 65 years of Highland League membership, between 1929 and 1994, County notched up three Championships, four League Cups, two Qualifying Cups, four North of Scotland Cups and eight Inverness Cups. For years the top Highland clubs – including County – had been lobbying for an opportunity to compete at a national league level.

This persistence finally paid off in 1994, when the Scottish League decided to expand its membership to 40 clubs. It took County a few years to settle in the League, but under former Rangers, Aston Villa and Aberdeen midfielder Neale Cooper they eventually escaped Division 3 in 1999. This emancipation from the murky depths of Scottish football's dead zone was immediately followed by promotion to Division 1, where the club has remained ever since, with veteran gaffer Alex Smith replacing Cooper in 2002.

Rotherham United

Formed in 1925 by a merger of clubs called Town and County, there have been a surprising number of footballing firsts in Rotherham United's history. Another forerunner, Rotherham Club (who disappointingly changed their name from Lunar Rovers) were the first team to score a penalty, against Darlington St Augustine's. A hundred years later 'The Millers' (named for their ground, Millmoor) would become the first team to win an FA Cup tie settled by penalties, 7–6 against Scunthorpe after the replay finished 3–3 after extra time, beating Exeter City to the record by ten minutes.

Rotherham contested the first League Cup Final in 1960–61 with Aston Villa, losing 3–2 on aggregate in extra time. Their next Cup Final appearance was in the Auto Windscreens Shield in 1996 (see **LDV Vans Trophy**), where a 2–1 victory over Shrewsbury Town became the first lower league cup final to be shown live on television. The supporters won a prize too, being crowned the first, and only, winners of the BBC's Kop Choir competition in 1969–70 with a trip to Milan for the European Cup Final as a reward.

Rotherham have never played in the top flight, their nearest being a third place in Division 2 in 1954–55, when they needed to beat Liverpool 16–0 on the final day and fell 11 goals short, only winning 6–1. The club went down in 1968, returning 12 years later as Division 3 champions with Ian Porterfield as manager, and Ronnie Moore a talismanic striker. Surprisingly, Porterfield then left to manage Sheffield United in Division 4 and the club acquired a new chairman, Anton Johnson (formerly of Southend United), who led them into administration with debts of £750,000, despite their having been in the black when he arrived. Johnson even loaned money to Derby County so they could pay their players' wages: that season Rotherham went down and Derby stayed up.

Ken Booth, owner of the country's biggest scrap business – his yards surround Millmoor on three sides – took over as chairman in 1986, finally stepping down at the end of 2004 when fans' group Millers '05 took over. Relegation to Division 3 in 1997 heralded the return of Ronnie Moore, this time as manager, on the back of a fans' campaign. Three years of consistent improvement in Division 3 led to promotion in 2000. A year later Alan Lee's last-minute winner against Brentford on 28 April 2001 ensured another promotion.

From 1997 to 2003 Ronnie Moore improved Rotherham's average attendance, League position and squad every single year, despite running a club on a minuscule budget. His most expensive signing, £150,000, equalled the club record – set in 1980. Moore was seen by supporters as having been almost solely responsible for keeping the club in Division 1 for four years, and there was little criticism of him during a desperate relegation season in 2004–05 in which they took 20 games to record a first win.

Surprisingly, he stepped down in February 2005 after unsuccessful contract talks with the new owners. In 2006 the club narrowly avoided relegation to League Two and began the following season with ten points deducted as punishment for having gone into administration.

Sir Stanley Rous

Knighted in 1949, Sir Stanley Rous was the last president of FIFA before it embraced a commercial outlook. His successor, João Havelange, who ousted Rous in 1974, said at the end of his term in office, 'When I came to FIFA, we had 20 dollars in the bank. Now we have four billion.' Amazingly, given the British associations' on-off relationship with FIFA in its first half-century, Rous was the third English president, following Daniel Burley Woolfall (1906–18) and Arthur Drewry (1955–61).

Born in Watford in 1895, Rous played as a goalkeeper in amateur football in East Anglia before the First World War, but a wrist injury encouraged him to take up refereeing. A compulsive organizer by nature, he invented the diagonal system of controlling a game that became standard and later promoted the use of yellow and red cards, first introduced at the 1968 Olympics, although he believed they should only be used where there was a language barrier and were otherwise 'humiliating' to the players. He refereed 36 international matches as well as the 1934 FA Cup Final and in that same year was appointed secretary of the FA in succession to Sir Frederick Wall, despite having no serious football administrative experience (he was a teacher in Watford at the time). It was a haphazard process that put Rous on the path to the top job in world football. He claimed the crucial factor in the inter-view was that his knowledge of lip-reading allowed him to communicate with the FA president, Sir Charles Clegg, who was deaf. Among the candidates he defeated was 'an unknown man wearing lavender gloves and a high-wing collar'.

Rous would stay at the FA until 1961, the year he took over as head of FIFA following the death of the Grimsby fish merchant Drewry. As a member of the International Board he helped reformulate the laws of the game in 1938 (the last significant revision until 1997) and then oversaw the return of England to FIFA in 1946. He and Drewry together successfully pressed for the decentralization of FIFA into regional confederations, which led to the establishment of UEFA in 1954. Rous was a progressive and an internationalist by the standards of the FA at the time, although no one would call the period between the 1930s and 1950s one of radical change in England's football administration. He was inordinately proud of his role in setting up the cumbersome Fairs Cup as a competition run by and for the clubs, and bitterly opposed its takeover by UEFA in the late 1960s.

As FIFA president Rous proved reactive rather than dynamic, failing to appreciate the implications of the newly independent former colonies for football's politics, or to capitalize on the technology that made the World Cup a potential television goldmine. Rous's FIFA alienated Africa in particular, both by denying the continent a guaranteed place in the finals, which led to the boycott of the 1966 tournament, and by its indulgent attitude to South Africa and Rhodesia. He also fell out with the Soviet Union (and the large bloc of countries whose votes they influenced) over their refusal to play the second leg of their World Cup qualifying tie against Chile in

the Santiago stadium where General Pino-
chet's opponents had been rounded up
and tortured after the coup against President Allende in September 1973. Rous
stuck rigidly to the mantra of 'keeping
politics out of sport', by which he meant
not offending anyone in power – as FA
secretary in 1938 he had helped
persuade England players that giving the
Nazi salute in Berlin was a harmless diplo-
matic gesture.

These shortcomings – not to mention
the fact that by then Rous was almost 80
– proved crucial when Havelange's slick
leadership campaign surprised him in
1974, winning the support of the
developing nations to eject him from the
presidency and shifting the balance of
power in world football away from
Europe for the first time. After his election Havelange offered to name the new
World Cup trophy the Rous Cup (Brazil
having claimed the Jules Rimet in
perpetuity), but Sir Stanley declined 'as I
do not believe such major trophies
should bear individuals' names'.

Always meticulously dressed (with
trademark white cuffs protruding from
his jacket), Rous was one of the last of
the old school, a genuine football man,
incorruptible but largely innocent in the
world of business, and incapable of
shaking off the patrician habits of the
Empire. Brian Glanville waspishly said he
gave the game integrity, but was nevertheless 'an authoritarian figure and a
ghastly snob'.

Rous suffered a stroke at the 1986
World Cup finals in Mexico and died a
few weeks later in England, aged 91. He
was remembered briefly in a very
different Rous Cup, which initially took
the place of the Home Internationals in
the 1980s, and more permanently in the
Rous Stand at Watford's Vicarage Road,
although he had little formal connection
with the club.

Ian Rush

Whippet-thin, pale and unswervingly
moustachioed, Ian Rush was the cutting
edge of the Liverpool front line of the
1980s. Rush was one of the finest goalscorers of the modern game and an
essential component in one of the
greatest teams the game has seen. In an
era of all-British Division 1 line-ups,
muscular direct play and unflatteringly
tiny satin shorts, Rush was a star player
without an attitude.

His reputation was built around hard
work and the sheer volume of his goals –
209 in 332 games during his two spells at
Liverpool, including 32 League goals in
1984, when he won the European Golden
Boot. Rush spent his 90 minutes perpetually on the move, skinny elbows
pumping, unrelenting in his hustling of
defenders. Mathematical rather than
artful in his finishing, he tended to score
when it mattered most, including a
record five goals in FA Cup Finals, a
then-record 20 in Europe, and 23 goals in
24 derby games against Everton.

Signed from Chester for £300,000 in
1980, Rush took a while to settle at Liverpool, a shy young man at the most
successful club in Europe. After finding
his feet in his second season he won
championship medals in 1982, 1983,
1984, 1986 and 1990, the FA Cup three
times, the League Cup five times and the
European Cup in 1984. His partnership
with Kenny **Dalglish**, the creative force
to complement Rush's pace and rapier
touch, remains one of the most revered
in British football history. Rush played for
Wales 73 times, scoring 28 goals, and
along with Mark Hughes and Neville
Southall of the same generation remains
one of the finest British players not to
have played in the finals of an international tournament.

Liverpool sold Rush to Juventus for a

record £3.25m in the summer of 1987, but his time in Turin was unhappy. Rush failed to settle or learn the language and is famously – and apocryphally – quoted as observing that being in Italy was 'like living in a foreign country'. He was loaned back to Liverpool after one traumatic season, and then returned permanently, scoring a further 142 goals in 332 games during the second half of his Anfield career.

An unaffected character off the pitch, Rush's on-field appearance remained unaltered throughout the length of his career. Rush might be ten years older than when you first saw him play, but nothing in his appearance or grooming habits would confirm or deny this; all that changed was the cut of the kit on his back. Fitful spells at Leeds, Newcastle, Sheffield United and Wrexham followed his departure from Liverpool, where he returned as a coaching assistant after retiring as a player. Rush was recently manager at his first club, Chester City.

Rushden & Diamonds

Rural south Northamptonshire at the end of 1991–92 season. Max Griggs, multimillionaire owner of the Dr Martens footwear brand, is approached to sponsor a non-League club, Irthlingborough Diamonds, based in a town with a population of 6,000. Instead, Griggs suggests a merger with their bigger rivals Rushden Town (formed in 1889), who were playing in Division 2 of the Southern League.

Although based in a town a quarter the size of Rushden, the Diamonds had had more success in recent times. They twice reached the semi-finals of the FA Vase in the 1980s, while Rushden were usually dumped out in the early rounds, and they had good facilities for a club at their

level, being the first in the United Counties League to install floodlights. Irthlingborough's Nene Park ground was developed to a level deemed acceptable for the new club to start the 1992–93 season in the Southern League Midland Division. The new era began with the visit of Bilston Town in front of 315 spectators. The Midland Division title was won the following year and the impressive development of the ground continued. Boosted by striker Carl Alford, signed for a non-League record fee of £85,000, manager Roger Ashby's team won the Southern League title and a place in the Conference in May 1996 with a nervous 3–2 win over Merthyr Tydfil watched by 4,500. The club also reached the first round of the FA Cup, losing 3–1 to Cardiff.

Under Ashby's successor, Brian Talbot, Football League status was gained at the end of 2000–01, just nine years after the club's formation (Irthlingborough residents have had to get used to the regular media references to the club simply as 'Rushden'). Diamonds' historic first League goal was scored by Warren Patmore, a proven Conference goalscorer poached from rivals Yeovil. Another club record was set in a 7–1 defeat of Cardiff in the LDV Vans Trophy. A successful first year, buoyed by a post-Christmas goalscoring spree by Jamaican international Onandi Lowe, ultimately ended in disappointment, with defeat to Cheltenham in the play-off final at the Millennium Stadium. The next season, however, Diamonds overturned Hartlepool's 12-point lead and won the Division 3 title with a draw on the last day of the season against the long-time leaders.

For much of 2003–04 it seemed that the club was secure in a mid-table position. But the Griggs Group were facing harder times in the footwear world. The football club, it was decided, had to be run as a business, not a hobby. Max Griggs may have thought Division 2 status was safe when he withdrew his involvement, but manager Brian Talbot and the high wage-earners on the playing staff also departed with bewildering speed and the club slithered to relegation with just one win in their last 14 matches. The exponential growth in attendances needed to replace Max's Millions has not materialized but the Diamonds have a legacy of a fine ground and good training facilities. However, they were relegated to the Conference at the end of 2005–06.

satellite television

'A myth has grown up that football should strive to be entertaining. Sport is not entertainment.' While he was manager of Leeds United, Howard Wilkinson did what he could to put his own words into practice. Unfortunately for him it was in a losing cause. These days football is *light* entertainment: a prime-time ratings-driver, an advertising honeypot and an important part of any TV schedule.

Sky Sports has twice paid over a billion pounds to retain its live Premiership broadcast rights. As a landmark of how deeply entwined with television the national game has become, Murdoch's billion is salutary. As late as 1978 the total amount paid to screen domestic football was just half a million pounds. In the last 20 years the game has turned itself inside out for television. Players, clubs, competitions, stadiums and the demographic of those who can actually afford to watch – even on screen – have altered fundamentally. Football supporters, at the top end at least, are being remodelled into the equivalent of a studio audience, a seated chorus of edited applause. Twenty years ago *When Saturday Comes* seemed like an appropriate name for a football magazine. These days it's tempting to ask: when Saturday comes – what? Only one day to go before 'Super Sunday'? Meanwhile, bloated almost beyond recognition and utterly dependent on the revenue fix that was once no more than a shot in the arm, football continues to hang on to the rising balloon.

In 1979 the former Prime Minister, Harold Wilson, warned that the UK was about to be struck by 'a foreign cultural invasion through the satellite'. In fact it would be nine years before the invasion began in earnest. Government plans during the 1980s to give five satellite frequencies to the BBC failed, partly through lack of funding and perhaps also owing to apathy caused by the absence of a serious rival broadcaster to threaten the corporation's hegemony. The first signs that this might be about to change came in 1986, when the Independent Broadcasting Authority advertised for tenders to run the domestic satellite frequencies. British Satellite Broadcasting (BSB) emerged victorious. BSB had gambled on its knowledge of dish technology. A new Luxembourg-based TV service would soon be launched from the rival Astra satellite, but current thinking was that to pick up the signals in the UK would require an unmanageably huge dish. BSB had reckoned without Rupert Murdoch. In 1988 Murdoch announced that he would shortly begin broadcasting his unlicensed Sky service to the UK from the Astra satellite. Sky were transmitting on the widely overlooked Pal system which, unlike BSB's D-Mac technology, only required a small and easily-fitted dish. Via the unlikely route of an unofficial Luxembourg-based piece of space hardware, the most rapid of English football's revolutions had begun.

BSB fought back with the 'squarial', a small antennae-like aerial, hailed as preferable to the far weightier dish. The company spent millions on new programmes, but stopped just short of capturing the rights to the Football League. Sky launched first, in February 1989, BSB in March 1990. Both companies lost money at an alarming rate, with Sky's losses, at one point up to a staggering £10m a week, threatening the future of the whole News International operation. In 1990, with the battle for control of the skies between BSB and Sky TV at its most feverish, camera-shy media mogul Murdoch took

the unusual step of paying a surprise visit to the home of Sky's millionth UK subscriber. Looking a lot like *The Simpsons*' Mr Burns, Murdoch smiled for the cameras with one arm around the shoulders of a family of five torn from their expensively assembled tea-time viewing to stand outside in the cold next to a laconic billionaire.

This was truly a fight to the end. With both parties' future in doubt the two companies announced a merger in November 1990, to become British Sky Broadcasting, or BSkyB. Or eventually just Sky. The new company traded as Sky, most BSB staff lost their jobs, the squarials were ditched and the majority of BSB programming was cancelled. Football survived, and would become absolutely bound up with the success of BSkyB.

The Big Deal arrived in May 1992. Amstrad owner Alan Sugar's behaviour at the meeting of Premier League chairmen on 18 May 1992 has been widely documented. The chairmen were meeting to vote on the destination of the new TV rights deal. The least damning accounts of Sugar's role describe the Spurs chairman phoning BSkyB executive Sam Chisholm from the meeting to leak the details of ITV's £224m bid, before instructing Chisholm to 'blow them out of the water'. Sky now had the right to show Premier League games twice weekly for the next five seasons, with their bid partners, the BBC, showing highlights. Why would Sugar do this? Because his company, Amstrad, had a deal in place with BSkyB to provide the dishes should they win the contract. Chisholm duly offered more, and in a moment of laughable propriety Sugar then offered not to vote on the deal, but was persuaded to do so by his fellow chairmen. The Sky bid was accepted by 14 votes to 6, Sugar's own vote ultimately proving crucial to the required two-thirds majority.

With dishes spreading like a giant fungus across the land, catching the tail wind of football's cash-driven, post Italia 90 popularity (see Paul **Gascoigne**), the game itself began to change dramatically. Between 1993 and 1999 the wage bills of Premiership clubs rose by 266 per cent. The relationships between player and club and player and fan would never be the same again. New skills were required. How do you motivate a dressing room full of extremely wealthy young men? How does a teenager cope with being given £40,000 a week? Satellite television certainly didn't have any answers. But it did still have an awful lot of money to give away. The Sky deal allowed two live games to be shown a week, which would have to be broadcast on Sunday, Monday or Tuesday. This required Sky to reschedule games to fit its timetable, another decisive moment in the changing relationship between television and the professional game.

By 1995 Sky had bought the rights to live Football League and League Cup matches for £25m a season, as well as the rights to live Scottish football, creating an effective financial monopoly of British football. Digital services became available in 1998, offering better reception for cable and satellite viewers, as well as hundreds more channels. At the same time there were others after a piece of the satellite dollar. For a while Norwegian stations showing live Premiership games on a Saturday afternoon were screened in pirate pubs up and down the country.

Only slightly higher up the evolutionary scale, in February 1999 ITV agreed a £250m four-year deal for exclusive live Champions' League rights. The hope was that football could do for the subscription figures of its pay TV operation ONDigital what the Premier League had done for Sky. In a desperate attempt to save this semi-invisible digital project, the network then rebranded the monkey-fronted venture as ITV Digital and launched the ITV Sport Channel, paying £315m for the rights to screen Football League games. This would implode disastrously as ITV Digital collapsed in March 2002, still owing £178.5 million to the Football League.

The Scottish Premier League tried to launch SPL TV, their own channel, but that was blocked by the Old Firm, who felt they could exploit their greater pulling power elsewhere. The BBC stepped in and picked up live matches for two seasons at a bargain price. Irish channel Setanta, who already provided Rangers and Celtic with their club channels, paid a large sum for a three-year deal from the start of 2004–05, with ITV picking up the highlights package.

Currently English football is still utterly in thrall to satellite television. Sky's interactive service has brought a new and undreamed of level of saturation: watch every Champions' League tie on a Wednesday; then via *Football First*, spend the night in front of extended highlights of every single Premiership game. This is a feast of Mr Creosote proportions. Sky Sports have super-sized us. No, no more football. Not even a wafer-thin highlights package. We really might burst.

Meanwhile the government has promised to switch off analogue terrestrial signals between 2006 and 2010. BskyB claims to have 'more than 17 million viewers in seven million households'. Things are changing quickly and they might not be finished yet. There are now more than 2 million broadband connections in the UK and the Premier League wants a slice of the action. The current media rights deal offers separate broadband rights packages to internet companies for the first time. Somehow it's hard to get too excited about watching football on the internet, just as it's difficult to imagine a more remote way of experiencing a match.

In the middle of all this football is being transformed from a social activity into an alienating, individual pursuit. The satellite dish divides: watch from your armchair, select your match and your camera view. It's there whether you want it or not, shoehorned in between soaps and game shows, and even into the ad break. With the help of Sky Sports 1, 2 and 3, Sky Sports Extra, Sky Premiership Season Ticket, British Eurosport and Five's willingness to screen a bunch of bus drivers having a kickabout if no one else has already bought it, it's now possible to watch someone playing someone else somewhere in the world 24 hours a day. Football has not only come home. It's gone and put its dirty great feet up on your sofa.

schools football

Although football has the public school system to thank for its existence, it is the state schools that have produced the vast majority of Britain's footballers. Despite not being in the elementary school curriculum until 1906, football had been organized for schools in many British towns since the 1880s. The oldest surviving schools' football competition in the world is believed to be the Wix Shield, competed for by the secondary schools of Hertfordshire and Luton since 1901.

Many cities were already playing representative games when a group of teachers came together to form a national body in 1904 – the English Schools' Football Association, chaired by Football League founder William McGregor – to administer schools football in England and Wales. Among the founder members were London, Northampton, Nottingham, Birmingham, Liverpool, Derby, Sheffield, Bradford and Bolton.

The first national competition set up by the ESFA was the trophy for district associations (towns' representative sides), in 1905. As with the FA Youth Cup, the English Schools Trophy became hugely popular, with five-figure crowds commonplace at the latter stages; most districts played home games on their local Football League ground. As more competitions were invented for senior teams, interest in the schools games diminished, although four-figure attendances are still the norm at most finals. Thanks to thousands of teachers volunteering their time for free, the ESFA now run national competitions for every age group from Under-11 to Under-18, with small-sided games, girls, individual schools, districts and counties all catered for.

While the number of competitions has risen, the ESFA's flagship team – England Schoolboys Under-15s – was removed from its control in 1998 as part of Howard Wilkinson's FA Charter for Quality, which also saw club academies take the best talent and prevent many boys from playing schools football. Wilkinson, a former teacher, decided that young talent would be better nurtured by the professional clubs and the FA were keen to take the prestigious England Schoolboys team under their wing.

Many future stars have featured in England Schoolboys teams since the first game against Wales at Walsall in 1907. Among them were Stanley **Matthews**, Raich **Carter**, Len **Shackleton**, Johnny Haynes, Duncan Edwards, Bobby

Charlton, Terry **Venables**, Martin Peters, Peter **Shilton**, Trevor **Brooking**, Ray Wilkins, Ryan **Giggs** (born Wilson, who captained the side before playing for Wales), Jamie Redknapp, Joe Cole and Jermain Defoe.

Initially England only played the Home Nations in the Victory Shield but expanded their international programme to play regularly against the likes of Germany, Brazil, the Netherlands and Switzerland. Crowds for the two annual Wembley fixtures peaked at 90,000 and were rarely below 30,000. The Under-15s' record goalscorer in a season is Michael **Owen** for his 12 goals in eight games in 1994–95, although Rod Thomas scored the most overall with 15 in a record 18 appearances from 1984 to 1986. England's biggest wins came when they beat Northern Ireland 11–0 in Lurgan in 1995 and Ireland by the same score in Sheffield in 1970. Their biggest defeat was 6–0 to West Germany in Berlin in 1967.

All records are unlikely to be broken as the FA's version of England Schoolboys is now competing at Under-16 level. The ESFA concentrate their international efforts on the Under-18 team, consisting of the best sixth-formers and college students, whose alumni are less famous but who still produce on average two future professional players per season.

scoring feats

In the time before defending was invented, one of the earliest to assume the role of prolific goalscorer was Walter Tait of Burnley, who, on 15 September 1888, scored the first ever hat-trick in the Football League, away at Bolton on the second-ever football Saturday.

The term 'hat-trick' was almost certainly pilfered from cricket, where a bowler getting three wickets in successive balls would be awarded a commemorative bonnet by his club for apparently doing the impossible, in the way that the music-hall conjuror would pull a rabbit from his hat. There is, however, a breakaway school who point to the tradition of football fans passing round a cap, which was filled with coins and handed to their three-goal hero on the charabanc home. Purists, incidentally, argue that a proper hat-trick involves three goals scored specifically with each foot and the head.

Two years after Tait, William Townley won immortality as the first scorer of a hat-trick in the FA Cup final in Blackburn's 6–1 tonking of The Wednesday. Some months prior to this, Nick and Jimmy Ross had made their mother very proud by scoring alternating hat-tricks on three successive Saturdays for Preston. In terms of consistency, whey-faced assassin Steve **Bloomer** top-scored in Division 1 five seasons out of eight for Derby between 1896 and 1904.

Chelsea's George 'Gatling Gun' Hilsdon had the most impressive start to a career – five goals on his debut in 1906 against Glossop and, the following season, a double hat-trick past Worksop Town. John Southworth was the pioneer of the double hat-trick in England, introducing the rare feat in 1893 for Everton against West Brom; although John Petrie had scored 13 for Arbroath against Bon Accord in 1885 and probably didn't even mention it when he got home. The king of debut scoring, however, must be Jimmy **Greaves**, who hustled one in during his first games for Chelsea, England Under-23s, England, AC Milan, Spurs and West Ham. Greaves also managed six hat-tricks for England and scored 357 times in 517 League games, with 100 goals before his 21st birthday.

Denis **Law** deserves a mention for 171 goals in 309 games for Man Utd and 30 Scotland goals in only 55 international appearances, while Swedish striker Henrik Larsson was the most prolific goalscorer in modern times in the Scottsh League, with 173 goals in 221 League games for Celtic from 1997 to 2004.

The mid-1930s was a good time for solo performances. Arsenal's Ted Drake, his injured knee strapped, hit seven past Aston Villa in 1935. 'Bunny' Bell ran in nine for Tranmere against Oldham in the same year, the opposition presumably lulled into a false sense of security by his non-threatening nickname. Joe Payne then scored ten times for Luton in the 12–0 defeat of Bristol Rovers in 1936 – and Payne was only playing because of an injury crisis. The following year, Scottish goalkeepers got lucky when Jimmy McGrory, scorer of 410 League goals for Clydebank and Celtic at a rate of more than one a game, retired. Bournemouth's Ted MacDougall pioneered the modern-day triple hat-trick in 1971, putting nine past Margate in the first round of the FA Cup.

Dixie **Dean** of Everton will probably always hold the record for most League goals in a season, scoring his 60th in the last ten minutes of the last match of the 1927–28 season (40 of them had been headers). Dean finished his career in 1937 with 379 goals in 437 games, but still fell over 50 short of Arthur Rowley's record tally of 434 goals between 1946 and 1965 for Fulham, West Brom, Leicester and Shrewsbury Town.

Many will recall the young David **Beckham** scoring from inside his own half against Wimbledon, but others have scored from even further out. Although usually not on purpose. Keepers who have embarrassed their counterparts at the other end with goalscoring clearances include Pat Jennings for Spurs in the 1967 Charity Shield, Peter **Shilton** for Leicester in the same season, Bristol City's Ray Cashley in 1973–74, Steve Sherwood ten years later for Watford and Steve Ogrizovic for Coventry in 1986–87. Switching from distance to speed, James Hayter, appearing as an 84th-minute sub for Bournemouth against Wrexham in 2004, completed a hat-trick in 140 seconds. In top-flight football, Robbie Fowler had a funny five minutes for Liverpool in 1994, scoring three in 4 minutes, 30 seconds past Arsenal's David Seaman.

British club record scorers remain Arbroath with their 36–0 humiliation of Bon Accord (actually a cricket team that turned up by mistake) in the first round of the 1885 Scottish Cup. We can assume this result very much annoyed Dundee Harp, who beat Aberdeen Rovers 35–0 on the same day and had presumably been expecting to go down in history.

Preston North End's 26–0 drubbing of Hyde is the FA Cup record thrashing. Celtic have the Scottish League's top-flight record with an 11–0 drubbing of Dundee in 1895, while, in the English League, Newcastle United can dwell proudly on their 13–0 defeat of Newport County.

Scotland

According to the official FIFA rankings, in November 2004 Scotland were the 71st best international team. This put them one place behind the Democratic Republic of Congo, twenty places behind Uzbekistan and marginally ahead of Burkina Faso. This is poor progress indeed for one of the participants in the first-ever international football match, after which they would have been rated, however briefly, at least in the top two.

Scots have historically been over-achievers, instrumental as players or managers in nearly all of British club football's greatest triumphs. Many early Football League clubs were made up almost entirely of Scots, hired en masse by agents who trawled the Highlands armed only with nets, ropes and tiny expense-related bribes. More recently the great Manchester United, Leeds and Liverpool teams of the 20th century tended to have a bedrock of fine Scottish players.

The first great Scotland team emerged in the 1920s. A generation of skilful and often free-spirited Scottish players that had illuminated the English League – including Alex **James** of Arsenal and Hughie Gallacher of Newcastle and others – reached a notable peak with their 5–1 defeat of England at Wembley in 1928. Strangely, and also tellingly in a history littered with isolated fine performances, the 'Wembley Wizards' XI that day would never play together again in an international.

An abundance of skilful footballers, and, latterly, an abundance of players who can run around a lot, has never translated into any great success for the national team. During the 1960s and 1970s, notably, Scotland could select from a formidable playing roster. Despite a lack of progress at major tournaments, the Scots' record against England in particular, and against other major European teams, remained very good. The 3–2 victory over the English world champions at Wembley Stadium in 1967 – a game dominated by the attacking skills of 'Slim' Jim **Baxter** – led to some Scots proclaiming their team the best in the world. However, this does overlook the fact that they lost their next two games against the USSR and Northern Ireland without scoring a goal.

Scotland's record at tournaments is one of creditable qualification followed by repeated failure. First-round exits, on the back of embarrassing results against minor nations, are a recurrent feature. Scotland took part in a World Cup for the first time in 1954, going out at the first hurdle after a 1–0 defeat to Austria and a 7–0 annihilation by reigning champions Uruguay. Another first-round exit followed in Sweden in 1958, after which Scotland failed to make an appearance until the 1974 finals in Germany, when they were the only home nation to make the trip. True to form, they caught the plane home at the first opportunity, although a team managed by Willie Ormond and containing Billy **Bremner**, Kenny **Dalglish** and Peter Lorimer was unlucky to go out on goal difference after finishing third, unbeaten and level on points with group winners Brazil.

Four years later Scotland were again the UK's only World Cup representative. A buoyant squad travelled to Argentina under the guidance of the excitable Ally ('I'm a winner') McLeod, and spurred on by not one but two top ten World Cup hit singles. Backed by a squad as talented, particularly in midfield, as most in Europe, McLeod convinced the Scottish press that his team were among the favourites to bring back the trophy. In the event the most confident Scotland team ever to leave home would return the most vilified. 'Let them worry about us,' McLeod told his team before their first game against Peru. With the training camp already beset by rumours of late nights and heavy drinking, Scotland were easily beaten 3–1.

This was followed by a traumatic 1–1 draw with Iran, after which Willie Johnston was sent home after testing positive for the stimulant Fencamfaminthen. A gripping 3–2 victory over Holland, capped by Archie Gemmill's brilliant solo goal, wasn't enough to prevent them going out early once again. This would be repeated at the World Cups of 1982, 1986, 1990 and 1998. Most of these involved defeat to Brazil and some form of goalkeeping disaster, notably Alan Rough's disconsolate performance in the 4–1 defeat to the team of Socrates, Falcão and Zico in 1982.

Scotland had to wait until Sweden in 1992 to qualify for the finals of the European Championships. Andy Roxburgh's team lost to Germany and Holland on its way to a first-round exit, although in the process Scotland did manage to field seven players whose names began with 'Mc': McKimmie, McStay, McPherson, McCall, McCoist, McClair and McAllister all started against the Germans. Four years later the Scots were back for their only other European tournament foray to date. Euro 96 remains most memorable for their mistreatment at the hands of England. The 2–0 defeat at Wembley was made no easier by Gary McAllister's missed penalty with the score at 1–0, or by the fact that only the late goal scored by Patrick Kluivert in England's 4–1 victory over the Dutch, with Wembley already celebrating, prevented the Scots from progressing to the knock-out stages for the first time in their history.

In recent times Scotland have swapped agonizing first-round exits for agonizing failures to qualify for anything at all. Absence from Germany in 2006 completed four major tournaments in a row without Scottish participation. Over the last ten years the talent pool has shrunk dramatically, corresponding with an almost total falling off of Scottish players appearing regularly for English Premiership clubs. In many ways the problems facing Scottish football are similar to those in England. Scotland has a lack of outdoor space and playing fields, exacerbated by the dying off of the Boys' Brigade and district youth teams that had provided a ready-made finishing school for young players.

Scottish teams throughout the top division are heavily staffed with well-paid foreign imports, a culture change that has done nothing to improve domestic standards or the success of Scottish clubs in European competition. At a time when even getting a couple of Scots in the Celtic first XI is considered an achievement, it's quite clear that Glasgow will never again produce anything close to a home-grown European champion XI, as it did in 1967 (see **Celtic**).

Currently the future looks highly uncertain for the Scottish national team, particularly in light of the bleak three-year managerial reign of former Germany coach Berti Vogts, replaced by Walter Smith in 2005. The emergence of a fresh crop of players capable of competing at the highest level of club football is a prerequisite to any return to the standards set, if sporadically, by players such as Billy Liddell, Denis **Law**, Jimmy Johnstone and Graeme Souness.

Scottish FA Cup

The Scottish Cup was directly inspired by its English counterpart. It was founded on the same day as the Scottish FA in 1873, and the £56 silver and gold trophy – purchased through club donations – turned out to be a canny purchase as the cup is still in use today. Scotland's first team, Queen's Park, won the first three trophies, which was followed by a hat-trick of wins by Vale of Leven, and then a further trio of victories for the founding fathers of Hampden Park.

The early years of the competition were also marked by a string of protests and controversy. In 1879 Vale of Leven and Glasgow Rangers drew 1–1, but Rangers petulantly refused to show for the replay because they were so incensed at a decision to disallow them a second goal. Vale of Leven lined up for the replay, rolled the ball into an empty goal, and took the Cup. Two years later Queen's Park beat Dumbarton 3–1 in a replayed game after Dumbarton had protested about their 2–1 defeat in the first. Then in 1884 Vale of Leven asked to be excused from the final replay against Queen's Park because one of their defenders, J. Forbes, had died. The SFA granted them a postponement, but then they tried to have the game put off again because two players were ill and three were 'indisposed'. Queen's Park were awarded the trophy with Vale of Leven's 1879 award over Rangers cited as a precedent.

In 1889 Third Lanark had to beat Celtic twice to take the Cup when the first game was ruled invalid because of the playing conditions, while Celtic beat Queen's Park 5–1 in 1892 after winning a 'mutually protested' first game 1–0. Quite why Celtic protested about a game they had won is unclear, but the trend for Parkhead's paranoia about refereeing decisions is clearly not a recent phenomenon.

Things began to settle down to the customary pattern of Old Firm dominance in the 20th century – there have been 15 Rangers v Celtic finals in all. The most infamous, in 1909, resulted in neither side winning when fans rioted in protest at the lack of extra time after a drawn replay, unaware that the rules stipulated extra time only after a drawn *third* game. After the damage caused to Hampden and the city, both sides refused to take further part.

In light of the prevalence of the big Glasgow two, perhaps the most surprising Scottish Cup statistic is that Rangers once went 25 years without winning it (1903–28, including six Final losses). They have also been on the receiving end of the competition's biggest shocks – in 1921 they lost to a makeshift Partick Thistle side, having lost only once in 42 games through the whole League season. Thistle were so blighted by injuries that their 40-year-old coach, ex-Celt Jimmy McMenemy, had to turn out at the last minute and help lead Partick to its sole Scottish Cup triumph by a goal to nil.

Rangers were knocked out of the Cup 1–0 by Berwick Rangers in 1967 in what was generally agreed to be the competition's greatest upset, at least until Celtic lost 3–1 at home to Inverness Caledonian Thistle in the 1999–2000 competition.

Celtic took part in many of the most famous finals. In 1931 they were 2–0 down to a strong Motherwell side with eight minutes to go, but pulled back to 2–2 thanks to a last-minute own-goal, then won the replay 4–2. In 1961 they lost 2–0 in a replay to Jock **Stein**'s upstart Dunfermline side, a victory that launched the ex-Celt's stellar managerial career. And in 2002 they fell to an injury-time winner from Peter Lovenkrands that saw Rangers take a thrilling final by three goals to two.

Motherwell and Dundee United had gone two goals better when the Lanarkshire side edged a seven-goal game in extra time in 1991. East Fife, meanwhile, remain the only Division 2 team to take the Cup after their 1938 downing of Kilmarnock in a replay. Celtic and Rangers (33 and 31 Cups respectively) far outstrip the next most-titled teams – Queen's Park (ten), Aberdeen and Hearts (both seven).

Scottish fans at Wembley

England against Scotland is the oldest international football fixture, one that has been contested 110 times (England shading it with 45 wins to Scotland's 41). By the 1930s, Scottish fans had come to look upon the Wembley fixture as a biennial party in the capital.

This enthusiasm came to a head in 1977. It had been a long, hot June day in an era when a show of high emotion from soccer tribes was viewed indulgently by the footballing authorities and, more tellingly, 'tinnies' were still allowed into the ground. In a less-than-memorable match, Gordon McQueen and Kenny **Dalglish** had scored for Scotland, with Mick Channon converting a penalty for England as a late consolation. At the final whistle, thousands of Scotland fans invaded the pitch in order to congratulate their heroes and to goad their hosts with a show of mass triumphalism. The two teams having squirmed away to the safety of the tunnel, the fans busied themselves with tearing up patches of turf as souvenirs, and climbing on top of the goalposts in order to wrench the crossbars joyously to the ground. The Metropolitan Police had somehow not been trained for this eventuality and, despite the arrests of over 130 Scots, at least £20,000 of damage was visited on the Empire Stadium.

There was an immediate ban on alcohol and an introduction of barrier fencing inside football grounds, but incidents of a more violent kind continued to accompany the fixture over the subsequent years until, in 1989, the two FAs agreed to abandon it. When the two sides met again at Wembley in 1999 in the play-offs for the 2000 European Championship, over 1,000 uniformed police offers were on duty in and around Wembley Stadium for the second leg. Despite losing 1–0, England won the tie 2–1 and progressed at Scotland's expense. And yet again thousands of good-humoured Scottish fans couldn't be persuaded to leave the stadium for over an hour after the game.

Scottish Football Association

'Scottish football is sick, but the sickness is like alcoholism,' wrote the late but revered football journalist John Rafferty in *The Scotsman*. 'Until the disease is admitted no remedial measures can be taken. The administration – top heavy with lightweights intoxicated by power – is reluctant to admit the obvious, and disturbingly complacent about the state of the game today.'

Rafferty's indictment was printed in 1971, before Scotland qualified for the World Cup on five successive occasions, and things have clearly gone downhill since. It's not difficult to guess how he'd judge the current administration that oversees a national side with a dearth of quality players, and little prospect of any to come, and a national league structure that remains both fragmented and fragile despite 130 years in which to get it right.

The SFA was formed on the initiative of Queen's Park, which called a meeting to form the administration and founded the Scottish Cup on 13 March 1873 at Dewar's Hotel in Glasgow. In addition, Clydesdale, Vale of Leven, Dumbreck, Third Lanark, Volunteer Reserves, Eastern and Granville attended the meeting, and Kilmarnock joined by mail. At last some order was brought to the Scottish game after centuries of what was termed 'rowdy kickabout', with several Scottish kings in the 15th century having attempted, by Parliament, to ban 'the fute-ball'.

After ten years the SFA boasted 133 member clubs, including one in Newfoundland. In fact the body exhibited an early missionary zeal in trying to spread football to distant parts of the world such as Canada, the USA and Australia, to convert clubs and players from rugby. Initially this met with some success, and the SFA's first secretary, William Dick, died in 1880 with what was said to be a worldwide reputation.

In the 1880s, however, the SFA spent much of its energies resisting professionalism (which it labelled 'this evil') and missed out on instigating a league in Scotland because it was already too unwieldy an organization covering the interests of too many varied parties. Celtic, who joined the SFA in 1888, was the first team run as a proper business, and knew that professionalism was inevitable. Clubs formed the Scottish League in 1890 and professionalism was legalized three years later, and in many ways the SFA's been lagging behind ever since.

It wasn't until 1954 that the SFA appointed a part-time manager to the national team, and even then they did it in a half-hearted manner because they thought a committee could run an international team the same way they ran a club. Andy Beattie, Matt **Busby** and Jock **Stein** were all frustrated by the obstructive ways of the governors, and as late as 1966 the post was advertised as a job 'which might suit those with other business interests'. Only in 1967 did it finally appoint a full-timer, Bobby Brown, and not until Tommy Docherty took over four years later was a manager listened to on team matters concerning travel and training.

In recent years the SFA has, as it did in the 1950s, undertaken a number of coaching schemes across the country at all levels, and after a couple of decades

when it looked like the national stadium was ready to crumble and be bulldozed into history, they finally managed to oversee the rebuilding of Hampden Park. The lack of a unified structure that would incorporate the Junior League into a national pyramid, and the failure to tackle, or even discuss, the unhealthy stranglehold of Rangers and Celtic over Scottish football, mean that the legacy of the Queen's Park amateur philosophy still blights the sport in Scotland, which is as lacking in direction as it was when Rafferty delivered his damning verdict almost 35 years ago.

Scottish League

When Scottish sides followed their southern neighbours by founding a competitive league in 1890 they did so without the greatest team in Scottish football, Queen's Park. Had the staunch amateurs not objected to the idea of a league, which they rightly predicted would usher in professionalism and cause many clubs to go under, then perhaps the history of Scottish football would not have been so utterly dominated by their Glasgow neighbours Rangers and Celtic.

The truth is that when the League was formed – by Abercorn, Cambuslang, Celtic, Cowlairs, Dumbarton, Hearts, Rangers, St Mirren, Third Lanark and Vale of Leven – many sides were already surreptitiously paying their players to stop them heading for the professional game in England. In 1893 professionalism was inevitably legalized in Scotland and still Scottish club football suffered for decades from its best players being poached by English teams.

The amateurs' objections weren't wholly principled. The League's birth deprived them of the lucrative friendly games that had allowed them to survive and thrive. By 1900, Rangers and Celtic had already begun to exert their interminable grip on the domestic game. Rangers shared the first-ever title, with Dumbarton, after a deciding play-off game ended in a draw. Dumbarton won again the following year, with a brace of titles for Hearts and one each for Hibernian and Third Lanark interrupting Rangers' and Celtic's success until the latter's 1905 championship.

This sparked off a period of Old Firm control, with only Motherwell's 1932 trophy taking the title from either Glasgow side up until Hibernian won it again in 1948 (the Edinburgh side took three of its four titles between 1948 and 1952). The 1964–65 season, when Kilmarnock won its sole championship, remains the only year that both Celtic and Rangers finished outside the top three. Hearts enjoyed a fleeting maroon patch by winning twice in three years between 1958 and 1960.

A second division had been added, in 1893, and automatic promotion was introduced in 1921. A third division starring luminaries such as Dykehead, Clackmannan and Lochgelly United survived just three years – from 1923 to 1926 – owing to small crowds and long distances. After the Second World War there was a brief Division 'C', but it wasn't until League reform in 1975 that a third tier became permanently established. The 18-team Division 1 became the streamlined ten-team Premier League, with 14 teams each in Divisions 1 and 2. It was hoped that semi-professional Division 2 sides who had shunned promotion for fear of failure and immediate relegation would now be keener to climb to the new Division 1.

For a while the new format seemed to make Scottish football more competitive.

Celtic had won nine titles in a row under Jock **Stein** up until 1974, but in the six seasons between 1980 and 1985 the championship was shared between Aberdeen (thrice winners), Celtic (twice) and Dundee United. Since then the Glasgow duopoly has exclusively re-established governance of the honours, with Rangers equalling Celtic's nine-in-a-row record between 1989 and 1997.

The League underwent further restructuring in 1994 with the creation of a Division 3, while in 2000 the Premier League expanded to 12 teams, complemented by the gradual addition at the bottom end of newcomers such as Peterhead, Elgin City and Gretna. With the bulk of support and money at Ibrox and Parkhead, though, Scottish club football remains moribund as the Big Two buy up the best players, or buy expensive recruits from abroad. Bored themselves with the competition, or lack of it, the Old Firm from time to time threaten to move, either to English football or a mythical European Super League. Some think this would mean the death of Scottish club football. Others think it would be the ideal way to make a new start.

Scottish League Cup

Inevitably won by Rangers tons of times (24), and Celtic slightly less tons of times (13), the Scottish League Cup may seem as interesting to non-Scots as a day-trip to Peebles, but the competition does at least boast a history of high-scoring finals and the sporadic unexpected victor.

Unlike its later English cousin, the Cup was a popular event from the start, riding on the coat-tails of the post-war football boom after existing during the Second World War as the Southern League Cup, which had been founded to boost the fixture list of the 16 clubs still running at the time. Inaugurated in 1946–47, it thrived for its first 15 years as the sole domestic competition not wholly dominated by the Old Firm.

With the League replenished to two divisions, teams played in mini-leagues of four against clubs from their own division, so that half the teams qualifying for the competition's quarter-final, two-leg knockout stages were from the second division. In only its second year, East Fife became the first and only second-division side to win the trophy (as they had done the Scottish Cup in 1938), beating Falkirk in a replay. They went on to win it twice more during the early years, as a first-division side, while Hearts, Dundee, Motherwell and Aberdeen shared the Cup around with Rangers and Celtic.

The 1960s saw some massive crowds as Celtic and Rangers began to win with the usual regularity. In 1963–64 almost 106,000 saw Rangers beat second-division Morton 5–0, while two years later Celtic beat Rangers 2–1 before a record gate of 107,609. This was the second year of Celtic's 14 consecutive appearances in the Final, including five successive wins from 1966 onwards, followed by four successive defeats. Having beaten Rangers 7–1 in the 1957–58 final, they also put six past Hibernian, twice, including a 6–3 victory in 1974–75 when Joe Harper scored a hat-trick for the losing side.

That long sequence also included one of Scottish football's biggest-ever shocks – Partick Thistle's 4–1 victory over Celtic in the 1971–72 final (Partick were 4–0 up at half-time). And between the 1975 victory over Hibs and its 1998 toppling of Dundee United, Celtic only won the trophy once, ceding power to Rangers, who racked up numerous wins in the 1980s and 1990s.

By this time the Cup had become knock-out only after various meddlings with the format which, combined with crowd restrictions after the **Ibrox disaster** in 1971, had caused a slump in interest during the 1970s. Rangers and Aberdeen produced a brace of exciting finals in 1987 and 1989 (Rangers won both, the first on penalties after a 3–3 draw touted as one of Hampden's best-ever finals), and Celtic were again victims of an upset when they lost to Raith Rovers on penalties in 1994–95 after a 2–2 tie. Rangers' 4–3 defeat of Hearts in 1995–96 also caught the eye.

Even though the incentive of a European place for the winners was recently withdrawn, the Cup has survived and throws up the odd chance of glory for an outside team. In 2001–02, Ayr United made a rare final appearance, losing 4–0 to Rangers, and two years later Livingston beat Hibernian 2–0 in a rare non-Glasgow final.

There's been one further change in response to Scottish footballing trends. Previously the Final was played before Christmas, sometimes as early as October. Now it's played in the spring, long after all Scottish clubs are safely out of Europe.

Scottish non-League

Despite years of talk about reform, Scottish non-League football still boasts no English-style pyramid system. Two sets of leagues exist independently of each other – the 'senior' non-leagues affiliated to the Scottish FA (the Highland League, the East of Scotland League and the South of Scotland League) and the regional Junior leagues, run by the Junior League FA, whose teams have their own national cup competition and do not enter the Scottish Cup. Although a number of Highland League sides have recently graduated to the Scottish League, there is no automatic promotion between the SL and non-League football.

The 'Juniors' are not determined by age, but by the fact they are not seniors, and are seen as staging posts for players on their way up, although former professionals can regain Junior status. District leagues began in the 1890s, and lasted until League reform in 1968 saw the forming of six regional leagues. These were restructured again in 2002 to cover the three regions of East, North and West, each having its own Super League with lower feeder divisions, some of them regionalized.

In Junior football's prime in the 1920s there were over 450 clubs in Scotland, many of them associated with local industries, especially mining. Today there are fewer than half that, with increasing numbers of struggling clubs in dilapidated grounds going under, although old and successful clubs such as Larkhall Thistle (founded 1878), Bonnyrigg Rose Athletic (1890) and Dundee North End (1896) continue to play and, to some extent, succeed.

The main event for Junior clubs, though, has always been the Junior Cup, first staged in 1887, when Fairfield beat Edinburgh Woodburn 3–1 at Argyle Park in Govan. Its record winners are Auchinleck Talbot, who have triumphed six times, including five trophies between 1986 and 1992, and who are the only team to win it three times on the trot. In the late 1940s and early 1950s the final attracted huge crowds to Hampden, including a record 77,650 for the clash between Petershill and Irvine Meadow in 1951. The final is still shown live on Scottish TV, although it's no longer played at Hampden. The competition was immortalized in Robin Jenkins's 1954 novel *The Thistle and the Grail*,

following the fortunes of fictitious Drumsagart Thistle.

The Highland League, founded in 1894, is seen as the strongest non-League level of Scottish football, with Elgin City and the Inverness trio of Clachnacuddin, Caledonian and Thistle dominating over the 20th century and causing several upsets in the Scottish Cup. But the League was weakened when Caledonian and Thistle merged in 1994 and entered the expanded Scottish League, soon to be followed by Elgin and Peterhead in 2000.

The East of Scotland League was founded in 1928, and its most frequent champions have been Whitehill Welfare (14 titles) and Gala Fairydean (nine). The South of Scotland League began one year later, and aside from the Stranraer 'A' side (14 titles) its most prominent teams have been Threave Rovers, St Cuthbert Wanderers and Tarff Rovers (seven each). The 2001 competition was never completed because of the outbreak of foot and mouth disease.

scouting

A mysterious, amorphous figure, rumoured to appear briefly at the back of the stand on even the most freezing non-League night, the football scout has been a part of football lore, and an essential component of the professional game, for over a hundred years. Scouts are employed by clubs to keep a constant register of footballing talent – the young, the promising, those who have somehow managed to slip through the net – in a particular region. An experienced scout will become an expert on the most fruitful clubs, teams and competitions in their geographical zone.

Even the smaller professional clubs tend to employ up to 15 scouts, while larger ones will have as many as 50 on their books, many of them full-time employees. The scout will identify those players at lower levels who might conceivably have a chance of making it at a higher level, or travel to watch those who have already been 'spotted' by others, and provide a detailed report on all aspects of the player's technique, physique and, increasingly, personality and lifestyle.

Occasionally a scout will unearth a genuine find. Jack Hixon will for ever be known as the man who discovered Alan **Shearer**. The Southampton scout spotted the 14-year-old future England captain playing for Wallsend Boys' Club on Tyneside. But more often the lot of the scout is to cover all the bases, to keep a steady procession of young and soon-to-be-disappointed youngsters heading in the direction of the professional game, and to reassure clubs that the really big fish – whether he actually exists or not – doesn't get away.

Partly out of necessity professional scouts are rarely well known, even within the professional game. One of the most famous was Bob Bishop, Manchester United's chief scout in Northern Ireland for nearly 40 years before his retirement in 1987. During his time Bishop helped discover George **Best**, Norman Whiteside, Sammy McIlroy and many others. But such high-profile success is rare, and likely to become even rarer with the recent shifts in the way in which clubs, particularly in the Premiership, nurture young talent. The growth of academies and youth programmes that tend to concentrate on a select few identified at an early age has already cut the number of players entering the professional game through the traditional scouting route, with the scout replaced by the youth development officer or junior academy coach as the first point

of contact between club and young player.

Whether academies develop into a more successful method of nurturing talent remains to be seen; the cost of train fare and expenses for an anonymous-looking man in a raincoat to visit a few hundred non-League games every season, and if he's lucky spot the odd promising young Dwain, Wayne or Jermaine, has to be balanced against the gamble of providing a few years' coaching and pastoral care for a generation of youngsters who might well disappear from the scene at the end of their internship. Scouting has provided the professional game with an all-seeing eye for over a hundred years. Like many such invisible presences the scout, with his notebook and flask of tea in the rain at Wealdstone on a Tuesday night, may only be missed when he's gone.

Scunthorpe United

Known as 'The Iron' in reference to the steel industry that used to be the town's major employer, Scunthorpe United were founded in 1899 through an amalgamation of local teams, chief among them Brumby Hall. After another merger in 1910 the club became known as Scunthorpe and Lindsey United – a name they kept until 1958 before dropping the Lindsey on gaining promotion to the old Division 2 for the first and only time.

Scunthorpe were admitted to the Football League in 1950 after playing a role in the successful campaign to increase the number of teams in the League, since when – outside that six-year spell in Division 2 – they have spent all but eight seasons in the basement division. The best-ever Scunthorpe side finished fourth in Division 2 in 1960–61, thanks largely to the goals of Barrie Thomas, who scored 31 in just 24 games (still a club record) before being sold to Newcastle.

Other famous players include Jack Brownsword, who played in the club's first-ever League game, and its record defeat – 8–0 against Carlisle on Christmas Day 1952 – and who would go on to make a record 657 appearances; and the England cricketer Ian Botham (currently a vice-president of the club), who played 11 League games as a centre-half between 1976 and 1984. Scunthorpe have never fielded a current international, although they are renowned for their successful ex-players: Kevin **Keegan**, who played 141 times for them before going on to become European Footballer of the Year twice; and goalkeeper Ray Clemence, later capped 61 times by England.

Scunthorpe can claim to have begun the recent trend for clubs to relocate to out-of-town stadiums, having left the Old Showground for brand-new Glanford Park in 1988. The first League stadium with a cantilever (i.e. pillarless) stand, the Old Showground hosted the club's record attendance, 23,935 for the visit of Portsmouth in the FA Cup fourth round in January 1954, and was Scunthorpe's home when they won their only major honour, the Division 3 (North) title in 1958.

Under the stewardship of manager Brian Laws and shipping magnate chairman Steve Wharton (one of the richest football club owners in the country), Scunthorpe have become a model of lower-league excellence in recent years. Perhaps the greatest single day in their history to date was 29 May 1999, when a goal from long-serving Spanish midfielder Alex Calvo-Garcia beat Leyton Orient in the Division 3 play-off final, in front of 13,000 travelling Iron fans – a fifth of the town's population.

Chelsea manager José **Mourinho** graciously conceded that his team didn't deserve their 3–1 win over Scunthorpe in the FA Cup third round in January 2005 and he was right – Scunthorpe were the better side. Laws's team won promotion from League Two in 2005.

the season

To judge by the complaints at the start of each season, you would think football had been steadily encroaching on the summer holidays ever since some golden era when games began in September and were finished by April. In fact, it has been common for the League season to start in mid-August and finish in early May for most of the post-war period. Even the very earliest seasons of professional football took a form that would be easily recognizable today. The first round of League games was on Saturday, 8 September 1888 (also the day Jack the Ripper killed his second victim) and the 12-team League season ended in March, but friendlies and other matches continued even then until the end of May.

While the season has not extended that much at either end, its internal structure has become much more complicated thanks largely to two innovations which first made their mark in the 1950s: floodlights and television. Floodlighting made midweek competitions much more feasible, first the European Cup and Fairs Cup, both beginning in 1955, then the Cup Winners' Cup and, in England, the League Cup in 1960–61. Tuesday and Wednesday nights also became the regular occasion for FA Cup replays and postponed League matches.

The accepted weekly schedule of games on Saturdays and Wednesdays began to crack when live football was first shown on Sundays (and briefly on Friday nights) from 1983, and crumbled altogether after the arrival of pay TV in the 1990s, which has shunted games to almost every conceivable day of the week and time of the day. Perhaps the last barrier came down in 1994 when UEFA scheduled regular UEFA Cup matches for Thursdays so that the Champions' League could have Wednesdays to itself (and later spread its vast bulk over two days).

While the European tournaments have intruded mightily on the traditional structure, other elements have survived. The FA Cup, after some disastrously misguided fiddling at both ends, has been restored to what many would see as its proper place in the calendar, with the third round on the first Saturday in January and the final after the last round of League matches. The Charity/Community Shield opens the season as it has done since 1959. Before then it had often been played in September or October, and until 1927 was more regularly a season-ender in May.

While players and managers still complain about the hectic schedules over Christmas and Easter, they do at least now have Christmas Day off – the last full programme was in 1957, although the tradition of the same two teams playing each other in successive games over the holiday period persisted into the 1960s. The clamour for a winter break, which would be the most drastic interruption to the schedule ever envisaged, has been growing much more insistent in recent years. If it succeeds the top players will finally have the chance to rest, or possibly to tour a warmer country selected by the club's marketing department.

While club football has expanded alarmingly in some areas (particularly the Champions' League), it is the number of international fixtures that have done more to extend and distort the season. The summer tournaments have grown

(the World Cup from 16 teams to 24 and then to 32; the European Championship from eight to 16), and the qualifying tournaments even more so. They have been bloated by the addition of 15 or so European countries after the break-up of the Soviet Union, Yugoslavia and Czechoslovakia and UEFA's willingness to welcome associations that are barely countries (Faroes, San Marino, Andorra) and countries that stretch the definition of Europe to its limits (Israel, Kazakhstan). The domestic calendar has become pockmarked and ragged around the edges as a result of the number of internationals, and it is the conflict between club and country that seems likely to inflict further change on the increasingly uncertain seasonal rituals.

season tickets

The proportion of supporters buying season tickets for their club's home games rose dramatically in the boom period of the late 1990s. The increase began with the trio of repercussions that followed the **Taylor Report**: all-seater stands, new stadiums and the birth of the Premiership.

In the years before the Premiership most fans simply paid cash over the turnstiles and entered even the biggest grounds in the country. As late as 1993, passers-by could wander into the Warwick Road End at Old Trafford and watch the last 15 minutes or so of Alex **Ferguson**'s championship-chasing team for free. Within a couple of years, Manchester United became the preserve of only those wealthy enough to purchase a season ticket the previous summer to guarantee them a seat.

With all-seater stadiums came the need for fans to secure their place in the ground and most games became all-ticket. For regular fans, buying tickets for every home game was an avoidable hassle. Season tickets also offered the only guarantee that you would be able to sit with your friends and family all year. As the cost of match day tickets rose, so did that of season tickets, to such an extent that some Premiership clubs were charging over £1,000 for one in 2004–05, Chelsea even having the audacity to charge their supporters more for a season ticket than it would cost to buy individual tickets for every match. The club justified it by reminding fans that they had a reserved seat for every game and would never miss out.

Discounts have become more sophisticated and bargains can be had by fans prepared to pay up front at the end of the previous season but this is before they know which players are being bought or sold. Year after year clubs announce 'record season ticket sales' even if their average crowds are falling. With 93 per cent capacity in the Premiership in 2004–05, there are few tickets available on match days. Many previously dedicated fans, who cannot afford season tickets, have given up trying to get their hands on what are known in the US as SGTs (single-game tickets).

One negative effect of season ticket mania is dismal attendances at many cup ties. With most clubs no longer including cup ties in season tickets, crowds have plummeted in the early rounds of the League and FA Cup. With 40,000 seats to sell for their FA Cup ties with Scunthorpe and Birmingham in 2005, Chelsea even resorted to radio campaigns to remind fans that tickets were available.

Many clubs also find walk-in crowds dwindling in bleak mid-winter until attendances are down to virtually season ticket holders and away fans only, but with 20–30,000 guaranteed bums on seats, most Premiership clubs have little to worry about.

sendings off

It is only relatively recently that players being sent off has become a regular feature of the game. In 1963 Jimmy **Greaves** became only the second Tottenham player ever to be dismissed, while in 1972 *Goal* magazine were still able to draw attention to Nottingham Forest's barely credible record of not having had a player sent off since before the Second World War.

By contrast Roy **Keane** has been sent off nine times in his career, while Arsenal accumulated a remarkable 50 red cards during Arsène **Wenger**'s first six years in charge. Clearly, something has changed: either players are at least a hunded times worse behaved than in previous eras; or standards of refereeing have become neurotically demanding where once they were laughably permissive.

Certainly, there seem to be more ways of being dismissed these days. FIFA's **laws of the game** currently list seven offences worthy of a straight red card, including such favourites as denying an 'obvious goalscoring opportunity' by foul means, violent conduct, and offensive language or gestures. Similarly, there are seven categories of yellow-card offence, infringement of any two of which will bring a sending off. Significantly not one of these seven offences – from leaving the field of play without the referee's permission to delaying the restart of play – relates to the traditional free-kick territory of fouls and handball. It is in the areas of encouraging good sportsmanship, speeding up the passage of the game and promoting attacking play that discplinary sanctions have been most noticeably tightenened.

Len Shackleton

Never was a journalistic sobriquet so merited. Len Shackleton was the 'Clown Prince of Soccer', a man dedicated to beating his opponent and giving the crowd as much pleasure in the game as he derived from it.

Born in Bradford in 1922, 'Shack' joined Bradford Park Avenue and scored 166 goals in his six years. After the Second World War, Shackleton picked up his career in 1946 with Newcastle United, scoring six goals on his debut as the Magpies crushed Newport County 13–0. After only 18 months at St James' Park, he was signed by Sunderland for a then record fee of £20,050. Shackleton didn't seem encumbered by high-fee anxiety and went on to score 101 goals in 348 games for Sunderland, especially impressive as he was no out-and-out forward but spent most of his career at inside- or outside-right.

His sense of humour was as legendary as his ball skills. When his autobiography came out in 1956 it was the first of its genre to talk honestly and openly about the game rather than perpetuate the idea that football was a game played by heroes, managed by gentlemen. It still stands out proudly from the safe, anodyne autobiographies of the 21st-century footballer and one chapter in particular, an empty page beneath the title 'The Average Director's Knowledge of Football', was characteristic of his imperviousness to authority.

During his playing career Shackleton regularly displayed verbal and visual wit to enliven training sessions and matches. One of his favourite tricks was to take a throw-in and bounce the ball off the nearest defender straight back to his own feet. At other times he was known to distress already vulnerable full-backs by executing one-twos with the corner flag.

On one famous occasion at Highbury, with the home team 2–1 down and just five minutes remaining, Shackleton dribbled into the Arsenal penalty area, stopped, stood on the ball and pretended to comb his hair while looking at his watch.

Being a true maverick, Shackleton wasn't very popular with the FA and this almost certainly accounts for his paltry five England caps. One selector, asked to supply a reason for this insult, replied, 'Because we play at Wembley Stadium, not London Palladium.' Making a mockery of one of England manager Walter **Winterbottom**'s tactics lectures by asking what side of the post Winterbottom wanted them to hit the ball will not have helped Shackleton's cause.

His one weakness was his individualism in a time when the emphasis on team cohesion had superseded the romantic game. Even Shackleton's greatest fans admitted that some of the things he did with the ball were not strictly relevant to the passage of play or the end result. Forced to retire through injury in 1957, Shackleton launched a career as an uninhibited football writer for two national newspapers. He died near his home in Grange-over-Sands after suffering a heart attack in 2000.

Bill Shankly

Thirty years after his retirement, Bill Shankly's reign as Liverpool manager remains a uniquely vivid interlude in the history of the domestic game. No other football manager before or since has attracted such an evangelical cult of personality, both among supporters of the club and in the wider culture of the game: wisecracking, passionate, political and defiantly a man of the people, the process of mythologizing surrounding

Shankly's time at Anfield began the moment he took charge of the club, with the stated aim of creating 'a team that's invincible; so that they'll have to send a team from Mars to beat us'.

Shankly's achievements stand on their own merits. After winning promotion from Division 2 as champions his radically reconstructed team took the League title in 1964 and 1966 and the FA Cup in 1965. After a seven-year hiatus without a trophy Shankly's second great Liverpool team won the League title and UEFA Cup in 1973 and another FA Cup a year later, laying the foundations for 15 years of almost total domination of domestic football, a period that would also include four European Cups.

Shankly was the youngest boy of a family of five brothers and five sisters. All four of his brothers played professional football in England or Scotland, Bill to the highest level, winning an FA Cup medal with Preston North End in 1938 and five Scotland caps before taking his first job as a manager with Carlisle in 1949. Spells at Grimsby, Workington and Huddersfield followed. When he was appointed manager of Liverpool in 1959 the club had been in Division 2 for five seasons and, in his own words, 'it was a shambles of a place. The team wasn't very good and the ground was run down.'

Shankly's first game in charge was a 4–0 home defeat against Cardiff City. The Liverpool side that day included Ronnie Moran and Roger Hunt, both subsequent members of a title-winning team, but within two years Shankly had dispensed with 24 of the players he inherited. Crucially, however, he kept on the backroom staff, including Joe Fagan, Bob **Paisley** and Reuben Bennett, men who would remain as part of the fabled 'boot room' throughout the club's subsequent success.

Outspoken in the media in a way no manager had been before, Shankly developed a uniquely partisan, soundbite-friendly public persona. His talent for aphorisms and comic put-downs has assured him an enduring place in the verbal lore of the game, as the man who said, 'This city has two great teams – Liverpool and Liverpool reserves,' and who introduced big defender Ron Yeats to the press by saying, 'Come and take a walk around my new centre-half.'

Thirty years previously Herbert **Chapman** had developed the notion that a manager could, by stealth, exercise absolute power at almost every level of a football club, and Shankly cheerfully threw himself into the role: a tyrannical, affectionate Jimmy Cagney of a manager, single-minded to the point of parody, the abrasive celebration of his own achievements always part of a greater mythologizing of the club itself and its supporters. Throughout Liverpool's success Shankly managed to retain a powerful attachment to the club's support and the people of the city, as a story told by Liverpool winger Peter Thompson demonstrates:

'It was a quarter to three on match day at Anfield and there was no sign of Shanks. Suddenly, he came in. His shirt's torn, tie undone, jacket hanging off, hair all over the place. "What's happened, boss?" "I've just been in the Kop with the boys." He'd gone in with 28,000 of them and they'd been lifting him shoulder high, passing him round, and he loved that.'

Shankly retired suddenly in 1974 and died seven years later. Immensely influential, venerated among Liverpool supporters like no other manager in football history, he remains one the game's most vivid voices.

Alan Shearer

In his autobiography, *My Story So Far*, Alan Shearer reveals that his teenage nickname was 'Smoky'. 'It had nothing to do with my speed or scoring ability,' he cautions, before the reader can become overly excited by this news. 'It was because of my love for smoky bacon crisps. I couldn't get enough of them.' Along with the revelation that Shearer 'seemed to get on quite well' with his future wife Lainya when they met for the first time, this qualifies as a startling public intimacy for a man who has managed to maintain a veneer of remarkable blandness despite being one of the most famous footballers in the country for over a decade.

In his prime Alan Shearer was a very exciting footballer. An aggressive, direct centre-forward, he had the rare distinction for a British player of being considered, around the time of Euro 96, among the best in the world. A succession of serious injuries – and the subsequent loss of speed and mobility – altered his style of play significantly in the lead-up to his international retirement in 2000. The determination to keep playing has prolonged the existence of this secondary Shearer: a grappling target man engaged in a constant trading of free kicks with his marker. Along with regular but bafflingly dull appearances as a pundit for the BBC, the later Shearer has tended to obscure the image of the dynamic earlier model.

Shearer's achievements reflect not just his abilities, but his single-mindedness: sixth on the all-time England international scoring list with 30 goals from 63 games; Footballer of the Year in 1994 (Writers' award) and 1995 (PFA award); Golden Boot winner at Euro 96; captain of his country at the 1998 World Cup and Euro 2000; and awarded the Premiership 'Ten Seasons' individual award for the best player during the first decade of the Premiership.

He was born in Gosforth, Newcastle, where he played for Wallsend Boys' Club – other famous old boys include Peter Beardsley, Lee Clark and Michael Carrick – but began his professional career at Southampton. He scored a hat-trick on his debut at the age of 17 against Arsenal in April 1988. 'I just ran around for a while flapping my arms about,' he later said, a goal celebration that he modified later to one raised arm.

His record at Southampton was unexceptional: 23 goals in 118 League games over four years. It was enough to earn him a £3.6m move to Blackburn Rovers, where he would play the best football of his career, scoring 112 goals in 138 League games and 34 during the Premiership-winning campaign of 1994–95. Shearer signed for Newcastle for a world record £15m in 1996 and has overtaken Jackie **Milburn**'s all-time scoring record of 200 career goals for his home-town club. To an extent Shearer's career has been shaped by his refusal, twice, to sign for Manchester United, the second time after having a series of covert meetings with Alex **Ferguson**. He eventually decided to join Newcastle following a clandestine rendezvous with Kevin **Keegan** in a pub (both men wore sunglasses and baseball hats) and after mulling over his decision at a Bryan Adams concert in Huddersfield.

Shearer may have won more medals if he'd moved to Manchester, but his place in the enduring affections of the Newcastle support is secure. In the last five years two Newcastle managers, Ruud Gullit and Sir Bobby **Robson**, have been sacked days after losing a match for which Shearer had been controversially dropped. He retired at the end of 2005–06.

Sheffield United

Sheffield United FC were founded in 1889 by the committee members of Sheffield United cricket club, who intended to use the football team as a way of keeping its players' fitness levels up during the winter and maximizing revenue from Bramall Lane. The ground had formerly been the home of Sheffield Wednesday, but had been empty in the winter months since the original occupants' departure (the fourth side of Bramall Lane, previously a cricket pavilion, was enclosed as late as the 1970s). With many of the club's early players recruited en masse from Scotland, United joined the the newly formed Football League in 1892 – Wednesday were admitted the same year, but into the top division – and won promotion from Division 2 in their first season.

The club then embarked on the most successful period in its history, part of an uninterrupted forty years in the top flight. The Blades' only League title to date came in 1898. A year later United won the FA Cup for the first time (they would win it again in 1902) and the following season were pipped to the League title on the last day of the season by Aston Villa. Despite further FA Cup triumphs in 1915 and 1925, United would never again enjoy such sustained success, although the 1925 Cup-winning team – which featured their most-capped player, Northern Ireland striker Billy Gillespie – is perhaps the best celebrated in the club's history. The subsequent 75 years have seen the Blades win only two more major trophies, the championships of Division 2 in 1953 and Division 4 in 1982; a yo-yoing existence that has seen them either relegated, promoted or in the play-offs 21 times since 1932–33.

United experienced something of a revival in the first half of the 1970s, a team starring England international play-maker Tony Currie and robust striker Alan Woodward finishing sixth in the League in 1975. The same year a canti-lever stand was completed on what had been the open side of Bramall Lane but its spiralling construction costs were to be a drain on the club's finances into the 1990s. United were to be relegated the following season, during which manager Ken Furphy left, taking several players with him, to join Pelé's New York Cosmos in the North American Soccer League. In 1981 the club reached the lowest point in its history, going from top of Division 3 in late September to relegation – a penalty missed in the final minute of their last match would have kept them up and they finished with a positive goal difference – a period that coincided with a near financial meltdown.

Two promotions in three years followed as the club began a further rise though the divisions that would see them become one the of the founder members of the Premier League in 1992 under the management of Dave Bassett, who built a typically direct, physical United team around players such as Brian Deane and Glyn Hodges. The club lost to rivals Wednesday in the FA Cup semi-final in 1993, watched by over 76,000 at Wembley, and were to be relegated on the final day of the season that followed.

In the late 90s United's chairman of the time, Mike McDonald (by his own admission, a Manchester City supporter), met his Wednesday counterpart Dave Richards to discuss merging the two clubs, with the new entity to be set up in a stadium near the city airport. Local media coverage established that both sets of fans were vehemently opposed and the plan was hastily dropped. In 2006 the fiery Neil Warnock (who stirs strong emotions in his fellow managers, not all positive) led United to promotion as Championship runners-up, having previously taken the team to two FA Cup semi-finals and the Division 1 play-offs in 2002–03.

Sheffield Wednesday

Like their rivals Sheffield United, founded two decades later, the Wednesday Football Club was created in 1867 as a way of keeping players from a cricket club fit over the winter. The name comes from the fact that the cricketers, mostly self-employed cutlers, played on their half-day off in midweek. The fifth-oldest professional football club, they didn't officially become *Sheffield* Wednesday until 1929. Membership of the Football League came in 1892.

Forced to leave their first ground, Olive Grove, built on land owned by the expanding railway, Wednesday played their first match at Owlerton in 1899–1900. The location lead to a new nickname 'The Owls' (previously the club was known as 'The Blades'). Renamed Hillsborough, the stadium has since staged numerous international matches and cup semi-finals (see also **Hillsborough disaster**).

Promotion in their first League season was soon followed by the club's first League championship in 1902–03, repeated a year later, when they were undefeated at home. Wednesday again won the League for two years in succession in 1928–29 and 1929–30, striker Jack Allen being overlooked by England despite scoring 66 League goals in those two seasons. That would be their last championship to date, although a strong Wednesday side were runners-up to the Spurs Double-winners in

1960–61 and Trevor Francis managed the team to third place in the last season of the old Division 1.

Since their successful years, Wednesday have led a restless existence, appearing in the top three divisions. During a turbulent 1950s, which saw three relegations and four promotions, young striker Derek Dooley set a club record of 47 goals in all competitions despite not starting to play until October. The next season, 1952–53, he suffered a broken leg, contracted gangrene and had to have a life-saving leg amputation; a potential international career cruelly destroyed. In the 1960s three Wednesday players were involved in an illegal betting scam resulting in long bans – one, former England centre-half Peter Swan, returned to play for the club in the 1970s. After relegation in 1969–70, Wednesday reached an all time low six years later, avoiding the drop into the old Division 4 by one point in 1975–76 with crowds of 8,000 echoing around a ground that could hold seven times that number.

Jack **Charlton** lifted the club back into Division 2, the turning point being the 'Boxing Day Massacre' of 1979, when the Owls beat their cross-city rivals 4–0 in front of almost 50,000 (a Division 3 record). Howard Wilkinson took Wednesday back to the top flight using wing-backs, long before the term was popularized, and a swingeing offside trap at a time when the famous Arsenal back four were still practising co-ordinated arm raising. Relegated after a sudden bad run in 1989–90, they won promotion and the League Cup the next season under Ron Atkinson.

The club's record in the FA Cup echoes that in the League, with early wins in 1896 and 1907 (the teams featuring record appearance holder and goalscorer, Scottish international Andrew Wilson). Wednesday won the Cup for the last time to date in 1935 and lost one of the great post-war finals 3–2 to Everton in 1966. Founder members of the Premier League, the Owls played at Wembley three times in 1993. First up was the 'Steel City semi-final' at Wembley, when United were beaten 2–1. A side packed with internationals then went on to lose to Arsenal in both Cup Finals, Chris Waddle's Footballer of the Year award being scant consolation.

Arguably the club never really recovered from this double defeat: League form dropped off and expensive overseas signings, including Benito Carbone and Paolo Di Canio, flopped. Chairman Dave Richards, who presided over a period of massive overspending, somehow moved on to become chairman of the Premier League, an appointment compared to 'the captain of the *Titanic* being promoted to Admiral of the Fleet'. Relegated in 1999–2000 and again in 2002–03, the club were promoted back to the second level through the play-offs in May 2005.

Peter Shilton

Peter Shilton played for England a record 125 times between 1970 and 1990, and for a period during the 1980s he was considered by many to be the best goalkeeper in the world. Just over six feet tall and powerfully built, Shilton was a gruff but reassuring presence in goal, rarely making mistakes and on more than one occasion producing an inspired match-saving performance, notably away to Poland in 1989 in a game England needed to draw to qualify for the World Cup finals.

Perhaps the most remarkable thing about Shilton was his longevity. He made his League debut for Leicester in 1966 as a 17-year-old. His final League appearance came in 1997, for Leyton Orient in Division 3. In between he made a record 1,004 League appearances for 11 different League clubs. Strangely for a player of his stature Shilton never played for a big-city club, enjoying his most successful spell at Nottingham Forest in the late 1970s and early 1980s, where he kept goal during two European Cup triumphs and one League championship.

His international career started badly. In his first season of permanent occupancy in the England jersey after replacing his former Leicester club-mate Gordon **Banks**, Shilton played a major part in the goal that would prevent England from qualifying for the 1974 World Cup. Needing a win against Poland at Wembley, Alf **Ramsey**'s men could only draw 1–1, Poland's goal coming after a missed tackle by Norman Hunter on the halfway line led to a break-away and a shot by Gregorsz Lato that Shilton could only dive over the top of. Undaunted, Shilton went on to play at three World Cups, keeping his place in the team for the next 17 years, a spell interrupted only by a brief job share arrangement with Ray Clemence during the early 1980s.

Shilton had his eccentricities too. Known for his obsessive preparation, he was rumoured to have hung from the banisters at his childhood home in an attempt to develop longer arms. Later, he would resign as manager of Plymouth Argyle, after early successes were undermined by problems off the field, reportedly suffering from an addiction to gambling.

Intensely competitive on the field, obsessive in training and with a physique that was more muscular than cat-like, Shilton set a template for a certain kind of English goalkeeper: the bulky shot-stopper with a wide-angled physique and a foghorn voice. England goalkeepers are often remembered more for their mistakes than for their successes. A younger Shilton might well have had the spring to keep out Andreas Brehme's deflected shot in the 1990 World Cup semi-final. He was never known as a penalty-saver, and a different type of goalkeeper, a bigger man perhaps, might have got near one of the German penalty kicks in the shoot-out in the same game. These are churlish objections. Shilton had by then become an immovable monument in the England goal; and, on balance, perhaps the greatest ever to take on the job.

shinpads

The lowly shinpad has its roots in football's big bang, when the various disparate practitioners of the fledgling sport met in 1863 to try to hammer out a basic set of rules. The fall-out from the unresolved debate led to the dribbling contingent and the carrying contingent going their different ways. It wasn't handling the ball that caused the insuperable rift, however, but whether 'hacking' – the ruggedly direct tactic of kicking your opponent in the shins – should be allowed. The Football Association formed from that meeting outlawed hacking, but it was still in the blood of many of the young gentlemen and the habit wasn't to die out overnight.

The first wearer of shinpads was Sam Widdowson of Nottingham Forest in 1874. They were essentially protection against ex-hackers who forgot themselves at Widdowson's expense and mishaps – not actual fouls – because in the days when universities and public schools ran the game, it was considered that a gentleman would never commit a foul against an opponent knowingly. At that time teams played a dribbling game with eight forwards, which generally resulted in a series of genteel scrim-

mages as a crowd of players attempted to shepherd the ball towards goal while their opposite numbers endeavoured to shoo it away. Obviously browned off with being accidentally kicked in the endless melees, this same pioneer Widdowson is also credited with the invention of the new, radically defensive formation of 2–3–5.

John Radford, playing for Arsenal's first Double-winning side nearly a century later, took things a stage further. Playing in an era when the tackle from behind was both legal and commonplace and people like Ron 'Chopper' Harris and Billy **Bremner** were running around free, Radford possibly added several seasons to his career through the cunning expedient of inserting a second pair of shin pads down the back of his legs.

The first shinpads were bulky and heavy and worn outside the socks. Football took much of its early costume from cricket – flannel trousers and tasselled caps were worn by all – and the shinpads that protected the lower legs were originally a cut-down version of cricket pads, fastened likewise round the back of the leg with sturdy straps. Over the course of the last century they developed into smaller, lighter plastic affairs, with more ankle support and ventilation, but it is only recently that it actually became compulsory to wear them.

Even before they became a legal requirement, however, they were considered an important enough part of the kit for Bolton's trainer, when they arrived to play Middlesbrough in the 1940s without their shinpads, to rush out and buy 22 romantic paperback novels as last-minute replacements. This misadventure perfectly demonstrates the two chief functions of the shinpad: namely, to protect the player from injury, and be something either clean forgotten or impossible to find when in a hurry.

shirt numbers

Shirt numbers were first introduced as a limited experiment in 1928, Arsenal wearing them in a game against the Wednesday and Chelsea against Swansea. The practice did not become widespread until after the 1933 FA Cup Final, when Everton wore 1–11 (Dixie **Dean** becoming the first great number 9) and Manchester City wore 12–22. Numbering finally became compulsory in England in 1939, introduced as an aid to identifying players for referees and spectators. Scotland eventually followed suit, although Celtic initially resisted, before finally issuing their players with numbered shorts in 1960.

Aberdeen played the 1967–68 season with players' numbers on the front of their shirts before abandoning the experiment, while Don **Revie**'s Leeds played for a while with numbered sock ties. From the advent of the 4–4–2 formation in the mid-1960s until the adoption of squad numbers, the numbers on the shirts of a British football team usually lined up as follows: 1 goalkeeper; 2 right-back; 5 centre-half; 6 centre-half; 3 left-back; 7 right wing; 4 defensive midfield; 8 attacking midfield; 11 left wing; 10 forward; 9 centre-forward. Substitutes would tend to wear 12 and 13, although for a while many clubs would have number 12 and 14 shirts instead to avoid any risk of bad luck.

Shirt numbers have developed a certain potency, particularly at individual clubs where the number alone has entered club legend. Newcastle United have a slightly clichéd tradition of charismatic goalscoring number 9's, beginning with Jackie **Milburn** and continuing through Malcolm Macdonald and latterly the goalscoring exploits of Andy Cole, Les Ferdinand and Alan **Shearer** (Ferdinand wanted a 99 shirt when his new team-mate Shearer, signed from Blackburn, was given the 9). Liverpool, meanwhile, have a more recent tradition of creative number 7's, from Kevin **Keegan**, through Kenny **Dalglish** and Peter Beardsley. Nigel Clough's tenure as number 7 may have been undistinguished, but Steve McManaman wore the shirt for several seasons and the potentially inspirational Harry Kewell was handed it on signing from Leeds United.

The adoption of squad numbers in 1993 has specialized rather than diminished the power of the shirt number. Number 16 has been adopted by Roy **Keane**, otherwise a typical number 4. David **Beckham**'s number 7 was incorporated into his signature, his corporate logo and his tattoo collection before his move from Old Trafford. His choice of number 23 at Real Madrid was a conscious piece of myth-making, recycling the most famous number in US sport (basketball legend Michael Jordan wore 23) into a part of his own global branding.

shirt sponsorship

Shirt advertising was first permitted in British football in 1979, a decade or so after most other Western European countries. Cash-starved teams wasted little time in transforming themselves into ambulatory billboards promoting breweries, electronics firms, airlines, building societies, fast-food restaurants, on-line casinos, anti-smoking initiatives and the odd garden centre.

While Liverpool are widely regarded to have been the pioneers, splattering 'Hitachi' across their collective selves in 1979, they weren't the first British club to compromise themselves in this way. A few years earlier, Kettering Town had tested the FA's resolve by turning out for a Southern League fixture in jerseys which promoted 'Kettering Tyres'. When ordered to desist, they craftily altered the message to a more ambiguous 'Kettering T—', in vain, as it turned out: under the threat of a crippling fine, the remaining letters disappeared a few months later.

Liverpool and their Japanese sponsors were given a statutory 16 square inches of space to sell, in letters no more than two inches high (a regulation which would land Aston Villa in hot water a few years later when they exclaimed 'Mita Copiers' a little too loudly). Others would follow in rapid succession – but it would ·be another decade before clubs were allowed to wear sponsored shirts for televised games. Soon companies such as 'Hafnia' (freezers) and 'Talbot' (a short-lived brand of car) found them-selves as prominent a part of football as the professional foul and the offside trap.

For the bigger clubs the first shirt deals were worth a few hundred thousand pounds stretched over two or three years – a fraction of what a sponsor would pay today. But there was at least something of a financial case for them: for all their domestic and European success, Liver-pool's chairman claimed his club had earned a profit of just £71,000 in its last season of unadorned shirts. Today, spon-sorship is no longer a financial lifeline, just another attractive revenue stream. For some, it is far more attractive than others – the space on a Charlton Athletic or Blackburn Rovers chest will only ever earn a fraction of the £10 million per year Manchester United are said to command for theirs. Denying top-division clubs the opportunity to rent out this space would remove some of the tilt from an already heavily sloped playing field. So thou-sands of fans walk around in outfits which promote a brand of lager or a telecom firm just as loudly as their foot-ball team.

Sponsors' colours and names often clash violently with those of the club; not long ago Aston Villa fans saw their claret and blue competing with the bright purple and lime green of their sponsor, creating a colour combination rarely seen outside infant school art class. South-ampton's playing in shirts labelled 'Friends Provident' can't have struck much fear into the Saints' opponents. The more corpulent fans of Grimsby Town must have enjoyed wearing a replica strip bearing the phrase 'Food Giant'. These and other arrangements seem ill-advised, given the ferocity with which clubs now guard their 'image'.

shooting

'Keep your head down and over the ball. Kick the ball with the top of your foot, not the toe.' It's the first piece of coaching advice given to kids, aspirant strikers all. Astonishing, then, that so few pros seem able to shoot the ball regularly and powerfully on target. Did players really shoot better in the olden days? The statistics – many more goals per game, and centre-forwards who'd net 30 plus per season, every season, wearing the same old pair of boots – would seem to back up the nostalgics. Then again, black-and-white highlights reels rarely tend to show the parts where players blasted the ball artlessly into Row Z.

In the pre-modern age, footballs were heavier, especially when it was wet, and defences less packed, less conditioned and less disciplined. Yet still it could be that daily live TV coverage gives us the spurious impression that today's foot-ballers are, in the realm of finishing, more fallible and less ruthless than their predecessors.

The fan, meanwhile, is like that youngster at his first training session – they always opt for the shot, regardless of distance and angle. 'Have a go!' they yell. Then when the player's attempt curls miserably off target and trickles out of play somewhere near the corner flag they turn to their neighbour and demand to know why the hell he didn't pass. Apart from the rare goalkeeper's error, no on-field mistake will elicit as loud and frustrated a groan as the scuffed or miscued shot. So close to goal, yet so far off the mark.

Pity the poor player who by chance succeeds in belting one into the top corner from 30 yards. Sure, he gets his moment of incredulous glory. But for many years afterwards he'll be subject to a buzz of anticipation from the home fans when he receives the ball within shooting range. This buzz will inevitably cause him to stub his toe into the turf and fall over ignominiously.

There have nonetheless been reams of players in the history of the game who successfully mastered the skill, and not all of them were called Roy Race. In the 1970s Dutch midfielder Arie Haan seemed to score from outside the penalty area every time he played. Everton's Andy King did the same whenever his team was on *Match of the Day*. Latterly, Wayne **Rooney** looks set to inherit Alan **Shearer**'s mantle as the main man to reach the target with a reliably thundering accuracy.

For the more human players, however, it's time to master the ever lighter and more 'aerodynamic' playing equipment with a few extra hours at the training ground. Listen carefully now to what Arsène and Alex have to say. 'Keep your head down and over the ball . . .'

Shrewsbury Town

Old boys of the elite Shrewsbury School founded Shrewsbury Town in 1886. The prestige did not help financially, though:
it was a few years before semi-professional players turned out for 'The Town' and the hand-to-mouth existence has continued ever since. Gay Meadow, adjacent to the River Severn and invariably described as 'picturesque', became their home in 1910 thanks to the generosity of the local council. Floods put paid to many fixtures in that first season, a theme that has continued throughout the club's history. The Severn's proximity also led to a coracle being deployed to retrieve stray footballs, but this tradition stopped in the mid-1990s when the 'Coracle Man', Fred Davies, died.

Shrewsbury, also known as 'The Blues' or 'Salop' (the old name for the county of Shropshire), knocked about in various league competitions before being elected to the Football League in 1950. For a team with quite a short League history, they have been fortunate to have two successful eras. The first began with the arrival of Arthur Rowley as player-manager in 1958. Rowley was a bustling stereotype of the post-war centre-forward, with a fierce shot and a take-no-prisoners attitude to opposition goal-keepers. One story tells of a mis-hit Rowley shot that sailed out of the ground and landed in a coal wagon on a train passing near the ground, ending up in Newport, South Wales. Rowley set the League scoring record of 434 goals while with Shrewsbury, hitting 38 of his 152 goals for the club in his first season as the club finished champions of the newly formed Division 4.

In 1961 Shrewsbury reached the semi-finals of the inaugural League Cup, but despite being on the brink of promotion a couple of times ended up back in the basement division in 1974. A year later they gained promotion again and in 1979 the second golden era began. With player-manager Graham Turner in charge, and a change of kit from all blue to blue-and-amber stripes, Town stormed to the Division 3 title to compete at the second level of English football for the first time.

The club spent ten seasons in Division 2, then slipped gradually down, stopping to lose the Associate Members' Cup Final at Wembley along the way. By 2000 a win at Exeter City on the final day of the season was needed to prevent relegation from the League to the Conference. That disaster finally happened in 2003, but one season later Shrewsbury were back, winning the Conference play-off final on penalties.

Shrewsbury's future looks precarious – situated as they are in a small town in a sparsely populated county. There are plans to move to a new purpose-built ground on the edge of town, but with Shrewsbury having a reputation as a place that's resistant to change (more Tudor buildings still stand in the centre than in any other town in Britain), it's anyone's guess when that will happen.

songs and chants

Football songs, at least between the 1960s and the invention of the internet, have been the main means of communication (mostly abusive) between fans of rival teams and between fans and players. Communal singing at matches began in the music hall era, and one or two of those tunes still survive, most famously Newcastle's 'Blaydon Races'. Another of the oldest known fans' songs is Norwich City's 'On The Ball City'. Dating from about 1900, it runs to several verses and includes the exhortation 'have a little scrimmage', which would probably result in a free kick these days. Hymns were another early source of inspiration, whether officially sanc-

tioned – the first rendition of 'Abide With Me' at the Cup Final was in 1927 – or not.

It was in the 1960s that the football song as we know it today grew up, fuelled by the simultaneous rise of teenage pop culture and the increase in the number of travelling fans – songs of encouragement, celebration, threatened violence and simple 'us v them' played an important role in cementing the increasingly fierce group identity of the terrace regulars. At first pop was treated as an addition to the repertoire of songs to be sung 'straight', as can be seen in the footage of young Liverpool fans belting out 'She Loves You' at Anfield in 1964. But it wasn't long before the more quick-witted began to change the words to give the songs a more direct connection to the match.

The results have often been crude, racist and sickening, but also sometimes endearing and funny, and, perhaps more often than some would care to admit, an uncomfortable mixture. No event has been too appalling to be celebrated in song by rival fans, from the **Munich aircrash**, through the **Hillsborough disaster** to serial killer Harold Shipman (a keen Notts County fan, though songs mentioning him are aimed primarily at supporters from Greater Manchester, where most of his murders took place). No racial slur has been too gratuitous, no sexual allegation too unpleasant, no vilification of another city too grotesque to be left unsung. Yet football crowds can also be sentimental and generous, and even among the most hideously offensive songs and chants there is the relic of something worth having – namely, that the terrace songs were part of an organic football culture that was created by and belonged to the fans themselves. A late 1980s Manchester City supporters' song about striker Imre Varadi, in which he was rechristened 'Imre Banana', led directly to a brief national craze for taking inflatable objects to matches, following the lead of a City fan who brought along a blow-up banana to wave around in time with the song.

Songs with the simplest melodies and the most saccharine lyrics are best adapted for football purposes. Not only do they work well when sung by large crowds, but for some there is something enjoyably subversive about twisting an innocent sentiment into something much darker. That may help explain why the aggressive tides of punk, heavy metal and rap barely left a mark on the football repertoire, while Chicory Tip's 1972 hit 'Son Of My Father', Boney M's 'Holi-Holiday', Middle of the Road's 'Chirpy, Chirpy, Cheep Cheep' and Mary Hopkin's 'Those were the Days' found new life in a thoroughly different context. No doubt St Winifred's School Choir would have been appalled at the use some football fans made of their insufferably mawkish hit, 'I'm Only a Poor Little Sparrow'.

More inspirational even than the charts have been much older seams of music hall ('My Old Man Said Follow the Van'), musicals ('My Darling Clementine'), wartime favourites ('Bless 'Em All'), festive schmaltz ('Deck the Halls with Boughs of Holly', 'Winter Wonderland'), stirring political anthems ('The Red Flag', 'John Brown's Body'), folk favourites ('In My Liverpool Home') and even children's classics ('The Teddy Bears' Picnic'). Tunes from advertisements had a brief heyday (particularly British Airways' 'Fly the Flag' campaign in the early 1980s) and even an original football song, Scotland's 1978 World Cup effort, 'Ally's Army', proved a lasting influence.

A Spanish-tinged period in the 1980s ('Guantanamera', 'Que Sera, Sera') was followed by Italian influences more appropriate to arrivals from Serie A in the 1990s ('Volare', 'La Donna E Mobile'). Hymns, too, kept their currency, particularly 'Bread of Heaven', 'Amazing Grace' and, proving that the Church of England's modernizing efforts in the 1960s hadn't entirely gone to waste, 'Lord of the Dance'. Everton fans, showing a proper appreciation of their club's church origins, converted 'One Day at a Time, Sweet Jesus', to 'One Goal at a Time, Bob Latchford'.

Rarely, though, has a tune made it straight from the charts to the stadiums – one enduring exception was the Pet Shop Boys' cover of 'Go West', picked up by Arsenal fans for their trademark '1–0 to the Arsenal' from the early 1990s. But mostly fans stuck to, or even revived, old favourites as their club identifiers: 'You'll Never Walk Alone' at Liverpool; 'I'm Forever Blowing Bubbles' at West Ham; 'Blue Moon' at Man City; 'Delilah' at Stoke; and, perversely, at Crystal Palace 'Glad All Over', the biggest hit for the 'Tottenham Sound' of the Dave Clark Five in the mid-1960s.

When all-seater stadiums replaced terraces many feared it was the end of that elusive quality, 'atmosphere', and any musical inventiveness in particular. But in fact it has survived that and worse threats, such as the intrusion of video screens and ever-louder music inside grounds, even sometimes during the match. And, of course, songs and chants have been 'discovered', mined for material and to some extent tamed by the ever-rapacious football bandwagon since the early 1990s. In one telling example, the TV presenters David Baddiel and Frank Skinner were blamed for targeting the Nottingham Forest striker Jason Lee in 1996, whose haircut led to nationwide chants of 'He's Got a Pineapple on His Head' (to the tune of

'We've Got the Whole World in Our Hands').

The media's love affair with football produced new atrocities at the 1998 World Cup, when the *Sun* sponsored the brass band set up by Sheffield Wednesday fans to plod through wartime themes such as the 'Dambusters' march at England's matches. The ultimate absurdity in official attempts to sanction crowd participation was perpetrated by Premiership sponsors Barclaycard in 2003, who announced a competition to find the 'chant laureate', to be judged by the poet Andrew Motion. Probably they did not have in mind those veterans of the 1970s terraces who still cannot hear 'I Do Like to be Beside the Seaside' without mentally including a brusque suggestion for fans of West Brom, or whose instinctive response to 'Those were the Days, My Friend' is to add 'We took the Stretford End.'

Southampton

Southampton FC was formed in the St Mary's district of the city in 1885, opting for association football at a time when rugby was more popular in the south of England. Saints' fan base is drawn largely from the southern districts of Hampshire and Wiltshire and, aside from a few pockets of enthusiasm, it has never extended much outside these areas.

The team set up camp at The Dell, their first purpose-built stadium, in 1898 and at the turn of the 20th century achieved the first of four FA Cup Final appearances. A 4–0 Final defeat to Bury was followed by a further taste of the runners-up spot two years later, when they were overcome by Sheffield United after a replay. Featuring at right-back in their 1902 Cup Final appearance was all-round sportsman Charles Burgess Fry (an exceptional cricketer and athlete but in

truth an ordinary footballer), who later famously turned down the throne of Albania.

'The Saints', as they were now known, entered the Football League in 1920, came second in the new Division 3 in their first season and were promoted the following year. They remained at the second level for over thirty years, coming closest to promotion in 1948–49, when a side containing Alf **Ramsey** blew an eight-point lead with only eight games to go. A year later, Saints played in front of a largest-ever crowd for a Division 2 match, 70,302 at Spurs. (In 1953, The Dell became the first English ground to stage a competitive match under flood-lights – a Football Combination encounter with Spurs reserves.)

In 1955, with the team back in Division 3, former player Ted Bates took over as manager and the wheels were set in motion for the Saints' rise to the highest level. Bates built a team featuring locally developed talent in England winger Terry Paine and free-scoring Derek Reeves that returned to Division 2 in 1960 and reached the top division in 1966. Paine won the last of his England caps in that year's World Cup against France.

Paine was joined in the side by another local discovery, Martin Chivers, and new signing Welshman Ron Davies, who between them scored enough goals – 37 from Davies – to ensure Saints' survival in their first top-flight season despite a goals-against tally of 92. In 1969 the Saints made their first foray into Europe, courtesy of the scarcely fathomable rules of the Inter-Cities Fairs Cup. By this time Chivers had left for a then record transfer fee of £125,000 and been replaced in the side by another local, Mike Channon, later an England cap but now known as a horse-racing trainer.

Bates made way for Lawrie McMenemy in 1973 and the former

Coldstream Guardsman took Saints down in his first season. But this turned out to be a temporary setback – in 1976 it was third time lucky in the FA Cup Final, Bobby Stokes's 83rd minute goal being enough to defeat overwhelming favourites Manchester United. The next two seasons saw Saints reach the European Cup Winners' Cup quarter-finals and then return to Division 1 under the captaincy of Alan Ball.

There followed an exciting phase as McMenemy signed Kevin **Keegan** and assembled a side packed with internationals. They were title contenders in 1981–82 before defensive frailties and a lack of strength in depth put paid to the challenge. Two seasons on, they ended the season runners-up three points short of the title, and only a last-minute-of-extra-time goal denied them a place in the FA Cup Final.

Saints have never hit such heights, occasionally flirting with relegation until 2005 and regularly cocking a snook at the wealthier clubs who habitually take away the club's best players (such as Alan **Shearer**, whom they snapped up after he was overlooked by Newcastle). Fortunately Matt Le Tissier, perhaps Saints' best-ever player, resisted the overtures of others and remained commendably loyal to the club throughout his career. Le Tissier's goals out of nothing helped Saints keep their heads above water at a time when The Dell's capacity was just 15,000, before they said goodbye and returned to their roots at the new St Mary's Stadium. This and another FA Cup Final appearance in 2003 seemed to herald a bright new era – but regular managerial changes have hindered Saints' progress. The club were relegated from the Premiership in 2004–05, having employed three managers within the season.

Southend United

In 1906 a group of worthies gathered in the Blue Boar public house in Prittlewell (of which Southend was once the 'south end') to establish a football club to rival the local amateur side Southend Athletic. The team colours were chosen as blue largely because Athletic wore red. The team played on Roots Hall field, just over the road from the Blue Boar, turned professional and joined the Division 2 of the Southern League. In their second season the Blues went up. Harold Halse, 91-goal (yes, ninety-one) hero of the first season, moved to Manchester United and eventually played for England.

Wound up during the First World War, Southend reformed in 1919 and rejoined the Southern League, playing at the Kursaal Amusement Park on the seafront. The next year they were founder members of Division 3 (South), and remained there for 38 years, decamping from the amusement park to the Grainger Road Greyhound Stadium in 1934. George McKenzie became the club's most capped international at the end of the decade, playing nine times for the Republic of Ireland.

In 1953, work began on a new stadium at Roots Hall. In the years since 1914 it had been a sandpit and was now many feet lower. The new stadium, financed and built solely by the supporters' club, was unwisely handed over to the club in the 1960s. The club car park doubled as a venue for Roots Hall market and for most of the 1970s and 1980s Southend played their home games on Friday night – the market was given priority over the football on Saturdays. To rub it in, the legend 'Save as you spend at Roots Hall market Wednesdays and Saturdays' adorned the front of the main stand.

In 1966 Southend dropped to the bottom division for the first time but had an extraordinary FA Cup run two seasons later, when they scored 19 goals in two matches, beating Kings Lynn 9–0 in the first round then Brentwood 10–1 in the second. The Scottish striker who sounded like a comic hero, Billy Best, got eight of these goals and was to score over 100 for Southend, averaging almost one every two games. His striking partnership with Bill Garner propelled Southend to promotion from Division 4 in 1971–72 but Garner soon left for Chelsea and the club went straight back down.

In 1981 Southend went up again as Division 4 champions under the sound management of Dave Smith. His good work was soon undone, however, by Essex butcher, nightclub owner and self-styled 'football broker' Anton Johnson, who bought a majority shareholding and nearly ran the club into the ground before being arrested. Johnson's successor, Vic Jobson, was never liked by supporters either but he did preside over a promotion to Division 2, achieved by David Webb's team in 1990. The club spent three and a quarter hours of New Year's Day 1992 on top of the division but Webb departed in May after falling out with Jobson. His successor, Colin Murphy, only lasted a year but did sign Stan Collymore, probably the club's best-ever player, from Crystal Palace reserves.

Southend stayed up until 1997 under the self-promoting eccentric Barry Fry, succeeded by Peter Taylor and Ronnie Whelan, but it was all downhill for nearly a decade thereafter, enlightened only by Vic Jobson selling up. Six subsequent managers, including David Webb again, failed to lift Southend out of the bottom half of the bottom division but popular ex-player Steve Tilson revived the club, which he took to the LDV Vans Final in 2004 and 2005, the latter quickly followed by promotion through the play-offs. They went up again, as League One champions, in 2005–06.

Southern League

The Southern League began in 1893 as a professional rival to the Football League, which was initially restricted to clubs in the north. Several future League clubs were among the founder members, including Reading, Luton Town and Millwall. Tottenham won the FA Cup as a Southern League club in 1901, by which time the competition had begun to lose members to the expanding Football League (Spurs finally moved across in 1908). After the entire first division departed in 1920 to form the inaugural Division 3, the Southern League was padded out by Football League reserve teams and split into Western and Eastern divisions (there was also a short-lived Welsh Section).

Following the Second World War the League was reorganized as a semi-professional competition, gaining a second level, Division 1, in 1959–60. Prior to the abolition of the maximum wage, some Southern League clubs could offer more money than their League counterparts, attracting Tommy **Lawton** to Kettering and former Blackpool and England striker Stan Mortensen to Bath. In the 1970s, Jimmy **Greaves** came out of premature retirement to play in midfield for Barnet, but caused a game to be abandoned after he refused to accept a sending off for foul and abusive language. Geoff **Hurst** was the player-manager of Telford United, while Derek Dougan performed the same role at Kettering. Others who launched their managerial careers in the League include Herbert **Chapman**, Malcolm **Allison** and Ron Atkinson.

With new members filling the gaps created by departures to the Football League – Gillingham and Colchester (1950), Oxford United (1962), Cambridge United (1969), Hereford United (1972),

Wimbledon (1977) – the Southern League came to be seen as the country's strongest non-League competion prior to the creation of the Conference. The League still covers a wider area than its two counterparts, the Northern Premier and the Isthmian, with a membership stretching from the East Midlands to the south coast.

Since the introduction of automatic promotion from the Conference in 1987, five former Southern League clubs have moved up to the Football League – Barnet, Cheltenham, Kidderminster, Yeovil and Boston (the latter two having also played in the Isthmian and Northern Premier respectively).

Among the many SL clubs to have failed in applications to join the Football League the most notable were Merthyr Tydfil, previously League members for ten years from 1920, who won five Southern League championships in seven seasons between 1947–48 and 1953–54.

Aside from Tottenham's victory, Southampton reached the FA Cup Final twice as a Southern League club in 1900 and 1902 and the League provided a further six beaten semi-finalists up to 1912. In modern times, Colchester in 1948 and Yeovil a year later both got to the fifth round, and another eight Southern League teams reached the fourth round between the end of the Second World War and the creation of the Conference, Wimbledon being the last to do so in 1974–75. Hereford United only once failed to reach the first round of the Cup from 1948 until their election to the League in 1972.

St Johnstone

The only 'J' to feature in any team name in senior British football has its origins in the historical alias for the city of Perth, Saint John's Toun. In 1884 a group of cricketers playing under the name St Johnstone were looking for something to do in the winter and a football club was born. McDiarmid Park, the club's third home, was opened in 1989 and was Britain's first purpose-built 10,000 all-seated stadium. It is named after the farmer who donated the land, on the outskirts of the city, on which it was built after the antiquated but atmospheric Muirton Park, home to the Saints since 1924, was sold to a retail chain.

The revamping of the Scottish Premier League, in 1998, made such facilities mandatory and St Johnstone had every right to believe that they were a part of the good times that lay ahead, as they were in the middle of one of their most successful periods. Paul Sturrock had guided the club to their third Division 1 title in 1997 and season 1998–99 gave them only their second appearance in a major final, the League Cup, plus a third-placed finish in the rebranded top flight, Sandy Clark finishing the job started by Sturrock. On both counts, the club's achievements mirrored that of season 1969–70, when the manager was Willie Ormond – one of two Saints managers, along with Bobby Brown, who also coached the national side. These two campaigns gave the club its only shots at European competition, from which they emerged unbeaten at home after five fixtures, which included knocking SV Hamburg out of the Fairs Cup in 1970–71.

Saints were among the founder members of the Scottish Premier League in 1975–76 but were relegated in the first year (disastrously, with one point from 18 away matches) and spent only one of the next 15 seasons at the top level. St Johnstone were on the bottom rung of Scottish football as recently as 1986 and were relegated from the SPL in 2002, by which time Billy Stark had replaced Clark. When he failed to take the club back to the top flight, John Connolly, a winger in Willie Ormond's Fairs Cup team who later departed for Everton, took over (he was sacked in 2005). Other notable players include goalkeeper Sandy McLaren, capped five times for Scotland, Bobby Davidson, sold to Arsenal for £1,000 in 1935, and Ally McCoist, who was transferred as an 18-year-old to Sunderland for £400,000 in 1981.

St Mirren

For the first two years of St Mirren's history it was cricket and not football that was played in Paisley. They saw the error of their ways in 1877 and 13 years later they joined nine other clubs in the inaugural Scottish League, one of five founding teams still playing in the competition.

Love Street, their home since 1894, was shut down for two weeks during the 1908–09 season after a referee was pelted with ash for disallowing a home goal for offside. In the same match, William Key was sent off and picked up a one-month ban for entering the crowd and striking a supporter who had been abusing him.

'The Buddies', a nickname not just for the club but for all the residents of Paisley, Renfrewshire, have never finished higher than third, and have hit that mark twice, behind Celtic and Rangers in 1893 and behind Aberdeen and Celtic in 1980 (two members of the latter team, defender Iain Munro and goalkeeper Billy Thompson, are jointly the club's most capped Scottish players). Second-level champions three times, they were last in the Premier League in 2001, being relegated despite ending the season with a seven-game unbeaten run,

and have been mired in the midst of the ultra-competitive Division 1 since.

St Mirren have lifted the Scottish Cup three times, in 1926, with record scorer Davie McCrae scoring in a 2–0 win over Celtic, 1959 and 1987, the latest success arriving courtesy of an Ian Ferguson goal against Dundee United. Ferguson was sold to Rangers months later for £850,000 and most of St Mirren's best players achieved greatness after leaving Love Street. Archie Gemmill, Paul Lambert, Frank McAvennie and Gordon McQueen were all sold on before they graduated to the international side.

The same could be said of their most famous former manager. Alex **Ferguson** was sacked despite winning the Division 1 championship and establishing the team in the Premier League, after a bitter dispute with the St Mirren directors. He was picked up by Aberdeen shortly afterwards and would eventually sign three of his St Mirren players – Billy Stark, Peter Weir and Frank McDougal – during eight phenomenally successful years at Pittodrie.

Others joined the Buddies with their best behind them. Roy Aitken won only the last of his 57 caps with St Mirren. Steve Archibald was off the international radar by the time he signed, as was Victor Muñoz, who joined his former Barcelona team-mate for 21 games during season 1990–91, to date the only former captain of Spain to turn out for the club.

Jock Stein

In terms of achievements relative to resources, Jock Stein is the most successful manager in the history of British football. Stein was Celtic manager for 13 years from 1965, during which time his team won ten League titles (including a record nine in a row), eight

Scottish Cups, six Scottish League Cups and in 1967 became the first British team to win the European Cup. This last remains his greatest triumph. The team that beat Internazionale in Lisbon had cost just £42,000 to assemble and was basically a local Glasgow XI, with all the players born and raised in or around the city. 'John, you're immortal,' Bill **Shankly** famously told Stein immediately after the victory.

Midfielder Bobby Murdoch commented on the contrast between Celtic and Inter in the final: 'They were sleek and tanned like film stars. On our side there were quite a few with no teeth and we had blobs of Vaseline on our eyebrows to block the sweat. It must have looked quite funny.' Stein's 'Lisbon Lions' played relentlessly attacking football – what their manager liked to call 'Cossack charges'. They went one down to Inter after eight minutes but came back to win 2–1, Stevie Chalmers scoring the winner with five minutes left. Celtic reached the final again three years later, losing narrowly to Feyenoord, and were to be semi-finalists twice more under Stein, in 1972 and 1974.

Born in the Lanarkshire pit village of Burnbank, Jock Stein combined work as a miner – he was to be a keen supporter of the NUM during the national strike of the mid-1980s – with playing as a centre-half in amateur football before joining semi-professional Albion Rovers in the second division of the Scottish League, winning promotion with them in 1948. After a short spell with Welsh club Llanelli, he joined Celtic at the age of 28 in 1951. A regular in the team that won the club's first League and Cup Double in 40 years in 1954, Stein soon moved on to the Parkhead coaching staff before taking up managerial jobs at Dunfermline – with whom he won a Scottish Cup against Celtic in 1961 – and Hibernian. He

returned to Celtic towards the end of the 1964–65 season, when they won the Scottish Cup but finished a dismal eighth in the League.

Stein soon became known for his clever psychological management of his own players and the ability to undermine or out-think his opposite number, as in the League Cup Final of 1967, when three forwards switched from their usual positions; surprised opponents Dundee went on to concede two goals in the opening ten minutes. Stein unearthed and helped develop some of the finest Scottish players of any era, among them Kenny **Dalglish**, winger Jimmy Johnstone and full-back Danny McGrain. He was a shrewd operator in the transfer market, known for travelling huge distances to watch potential signings.

A serious car crash in Glasgow in 1975 dealt Stein's health a debilitating blow. He was absent for a season, during which Celtic failed to win a trophy for the first time in 12 years, and appeared to have lost his edge when he came back. After Celtic had struggled badly during 1977–78, finishing fifth and losing as many matches as they won, Stein was offered a new job as a 'working director' (basically a brush-off, it would have included running the Celtic supporters' football pools) but decided instead to accept an offer to work at Leeds United. Just six weeks into his new job, he left to become Scotland manager – he'd held the post on a part-time basis in the 1960s – taking them to the World Cup finals in 1982. 'The Big Man' died as he'd spent most of his life, suffering a fatal heart attack while in the dugout watching his Scotland team play Wales in a World Cup qualifier in 1985.

Stenhousemuir

One of the least successful teams in Scottish football history, despite some stiff competition, 'The Warriors' of Ochilview Park are living proof of the old Scottish epigram, 'They also serve who only stand and wait.' In 1996, at the age of 112, Stenhousemuir lifted its first trophy, the Scottish Challenge Cup (the competition for clubs not in the Scottish Premier League), when they beat Dundee United on penalties following a 0–0 draw.

Guided by legendary manager Terry Christie, a grammar school headmaster who always wore a dufflecoat on match days, Stenhousemuir had made bigger headlines in 1995, when they beat Aberdeen in the fourth round of the Scottish Cup by two Tommy Steel goals to nil. They succumbed 4–0 at home to Hibernian in the quarter-final. This was the first sniff of success for the small town near Falkirk (birthplace of comedy actor James Finlayson, the bald, moustachioed nemesis of Laurel and Hardy) since reaching the Scottish Cup semi-final in 1903, where they were beaten 4–1 by eventual winners Rangers.

The club's lack of ambition was highlighted in a 1926 bribery scandal, when it was claimed that the side did not want to be promoted because it was too expensive. Stenhousemuir goalie Joe Shortt had been approached at the train station in the neighbouring town of Larbert by the representative of a Glasgow bookmaker, and was offered £50 to 'let his side down' against Broxburn United. The goalkeeper reported the offer, and at the ensuing trial the defence counsel claimed the approach had been partly justified because the club did not want to be promoted anyway, on cost grounds. When quizzed in the witness box, the club secretary Malcolm Roughead would only say, 'That has not been settled by our committee.'

A later club secretary would prove much doughtier. In 1964 Jim Weir led the fight to save Stenhousemuir and four other clubs from an initiative by Rangers to cut the League from 37 to 32 clubs, arguing that Stenhousemuir's fixture was just as important as anyone else's at bringing in income from the football pools. After court action, Rangers eventually dropped the proposal.

Weir was sanguine about the club's eternal struggle to survive on low gates, and said in 1969 that local people 'may not take the trouble to attend matches, but they have done their utmost to keep the club in existence'. Bearing in mind the current bloated budgets and climbing deficits of the Old Firm, he also noted with canny prescience that clubs like Stenhousemuir could teach a few of the big clubs 'something about money management'.

stickers/cards

Footballers began to feature on cigarette cards, first introduced simply to stiffen paper packets, around the beginning of the 20th century. The rarest series, known as 'Cricket and Football Teams', was issued in 1902 by D. & J. Macdonald. The cards have a team group on the front and a fixture list on the back; no-one knows how many were issued as they're so rare – catalogued at £350 per card, they usually go for twice that when they appear at auction.

Cigarette card production was suspended in 1940 owing to paper shortages, and the leading cigarette companies agreed not to resume after the war, when rationing was still in place. Instead, footballers began to appear in sets produced by manufacturers of sweets and bubblegum. Typically, there would be a colour photograph of a player on the front with biographical information and quiz questions on the reverse. While bubblegum cards were swapped in school playgrounds, however, collectors had nowhere to keep them other than in piles held together with elastic bands.

A breakthrough was made in the 1967–68 season, when a publisher called FKS (a subsidiary of a Spanish company that had begun manufacturing football cards in the 1950s) produced the first card album to be widely sold in the UK, *The Wonderful World of Soccer Stars*. The paper stickers, which had to be glued into the albums, were sold in packets of six at newsagents; collectors could send off for missing numbers. The information on each player was provided by Jack Rollin, later the editor of the annual *Rothmans Yearbook*, in a distinctive style: there were 'custodians' in goal, centre-halves were frequently 'sturdy pivots', midfielders might 'probe from deep' and, best of all, Manchester City's rotund striker Francis Lee was a 'chunky raider'.

FKS's dominance in the UK market was challenged within a few years by the Italian publishing giant Panini, who pioneered the production of self-adhesive stickers. Panini broke into the UK via a company called Top Sellers in the early 1970s; the first Football League album published under their own banner appeared in 1977–78, featuring players from the top divisions of England and Scotland. FKS, reliant on the glue-in method, saw their sales decline and bowed out in 1983, after which Panini had the UK sticker market almost to themselves until the arrival of a company called Merlin in 1990.

The latter acquired the exclusive rights to the Premiership in 1993 which meant that Panini albums were no longer able to depict footballers wearing their official club colours. Instead, they had to make do with pictures of players in tracksuits, though they did at least produce three

collections for the Football League from 1995 onwards. Panini continue to publish albums in the UK for international tournaments, but are hampered by players having control of their image rights – Ronaldo, for example, withheld permission to be featured in the Brazil squad for the World Cup 98 album.

Recent trends hark back to the earlier days of bubblegum card swapping, with companies like Topps and Upper Deck producing series of glossy laminated trading cards containing holographic images and copious statistics about the featured players.

Stirling Albion

Significant historical encounters are more associated with the town of Stirling than its football club, William Wallace having defeated the English at the Battle of Stirling Bridge in 1297, and Robert the Bruce repeating the feat at Bannockburn just down the road 17 years later. But it was a different war that altered the destiny of the town's football history when in July 1940 a stray German bomb – reportedly one of only two that hit Stirling during the Second World War – destroyed Forthbank Stadium, the home of King's Park FC.

Prior to the war King's Park FC had been playing in Division 2 since admission in 1921, but only the Stirlingshire Cup, which the team won four times, troubled its trophy cabinet. King's Park played wartime football for a year until the bombing, but after the war, perhaps because of debt as well as the ruined ground, a new club, Stirling Albion, was founded and played in a new stadium, Annfield, close by the site of the crater-scarred Forthbank.

Uninspiringly nicknamed 'The Albion', but latterly known as 'The Binos', the new side regularly attracted crowds of

8,000 and gained promotion from the post-war Division C in 1947, and then two years later to Division A. In the following years they yo-yoed up and down between the first and second levels, being four times champions and twice runners-up of Division 2 between 1949 and 1965.

The closest the side came to a major honour was during the 1961–62 League Cup, when they were knocked out by Hearts in the semi-final at Easter Road after extra time. Celtic were edgy visitors to Annfield during this period, losing on five of their 11 League visits between 1950 and 1968. Off the field Stirling were years ahead of their time, proposing at the 1952 Scottish League AGM that the league should be expanded to 42 members to allow teams in the new towns of East Kilbride, Cumbernauld, Livingston and Glenrothes to exploit nascent catchment areas. The proposal was rejected and most of those potential fans probably ended up at Ibrox and Parkhead.

Since the 1960s they've contented themselves with the odd lower-league title or promotion, and making the news in 1971 for appointing Bob Shankly as manager at Annfield while his brother Bill was boss at Anfield. They also beat Selkirk 20–0 in the 1984–85 Scottish Cup, a 20th-century record in the competition, and were one of the few teams to install a plastic pitch in the 1980s, a condition of selling their ground to Stirling District Council and having to lease it back again. In 1993 they returned to a stadium called Forthbank, but this was a brand-new 'box-kit' set-up on the outskirts of town with a modest capacity of 3,800 that reflects the club's narrowed ambitions.

Stockport County

Heaton Norris Rovers was formed in 1883 by members of the Wycliffe Congregational church, although their first recorded game didn't take place until October the following year. To mark the formation of the County Borough of Stockport in 1890, the club was renamed Stockport County. The club gained admission to Football League Division 2 in 1900 and moved in to their current home, Edgeley Park, two years later.

Not re-elected in 1904, but readmitted when they won the title win the following season, County have remained a League side ever since despite a few close shaves in the 1970s. In the 19 years after relegation to the basement division in 1970, the team had to apply for re-election four times. Fourteen managers, including ex-internationals Mike Summerbee and Asa Hartford, were unable to rouse them. But this bleak era was followed by the best period in Stockport's history. The appointment of Uruguayan Danny Bergara as manager in 1989 was the catalyst. In the five seasons after his arrival, County achieved a promotion, four play-off finishes, and two Autoglass Trophy finals. Bergara, who had arrived in England as a coach in the 1970s after a playing career spent mainly in Spain, became the first foreign manager to lead an English club side out at Wembley.

He was to leave under a cloud, however, being dismissed in 1995 after an 'incident' with chairman Brendan Elwood at an official club function (Bergara won the subsequent unfair-dismissal hearing). Dave Jones was promoted from assistant, and built on what Bergara achieved – so successfully, in fact, that the 1996–97 season was the club's best ever. As well as gaining promotion from Division 2 in second place, Stockport reached the semi-finals of the Coca-Cola Cup, losing 2–1 on aggregate to Middlesbrough, having beaten three Premiership sides as well as Division 1 Sheffield United 5–2 on their own ground. They also reached the fourth round of the FA Cup, playing 67 games in total.

The team stayed in Division 1 for five years, achieving the highest-ever finish of eighth under Jones's successor Gary Megson in 1997–98 before being relegated after an abject 2001–02 campaign. Perhaps realizing that the good times were coming to an end, in 2003 Brendan Elwood sold the club and ground to Sale Sharks owner Brian Kennedy, in a deal which saw the rugby union side move to Edgeley Park, with County now tenants in their former home. The club were relegated back to the bottom division in 2004–05.

Stockport fans don't use the club's nickname 'The Hatters' (preferring the more prosaic 'County'), but the town was the centre of the hat-making industry for many years and England's only hat museum is based there. Despite such a claim to uniqueness, however, Stockport has struggled to be seen as more than a suburb of Manchester. The same is true, to a degree, of the football club – with much of City's support, especially, being drawn from the town. Even during the success of the 1990s, support hardly boomed, which served as confirmation that County will always exist under the shadow of the Manchester giants.

Stoke City

In 1959, Stoke City's board of directors made probably their best-ever decision, promoting coach Tony Waddington to manager. The man who once described football as 'the working man's ballet' was to preside over the club's most succesful

period. Two years later, Stanley **Matthews** returned to the home-town club he'd left for Blackpool in 1947. He helped Stoke back into the top flight in 1962–63, scoring the vital goal in a 2–0 home win over Luton.

By the 1970s, Waddington had built a sturdy Division 1 team with England's Gordon **Banks** in goal and several home-grown players in defence. In 1972, after two successive FA Cup semi-final defeats to Arsenal, Stoke secured a major trophy for the first time by beating Chelsea 2–1 in the League Cup Final. A group of supporters known as 'Potters' also reached number 34 in the charts with the song 'We'll be with You'. Stoke had two brief excursions in the UEFA Cup, including defeat on away goals to triple European Champions Ajax.

Stoke were founded in 1868 (although some say it was 1863) and became founder members of the Football League in 1888. They finished bottom of the table for the first two seasons. After failing to gain re-election, Stoke returned a year later, but this time only Darwen finished lower. Financial mismanagement eventually led to relegation in 1907, and the following year a bankrupted club resigned their Football League membership.

A new Stoke club was set up in 1908 and they rejoined Division 2 in 1919. They were back in the top flight in 1922 for one season but were down in Division 3 (North) by 1926. That stay was also brief, Stoke winning the title by five points at the first attempt, by this time with the word 'City' added to the name. They would not drop so low again for 63 years. In 1933 a young team built around 18-year-old Stanley Matthews won the second-division title by one point from Tottenham.

In the first post-war League campaign, manager Bob McGrory's team were favourites for the title going into the last few matches but Matthews, who had been looking for a new club for a while, had his transfer request agreed with three games to go and left. Stoke lost their final fixture at Sheffield United when a win would have given them the title, and finished fourth.

In January 1976 the Tony Waddington era began to unravel when the roof was blown off the Butler Street Stand. The massive costs incurred were mostly met through player sales, notably Jimmy Greenhoff to Manchester United and Alan Hudson back to Chelsea, turning Stoke into one of the classic 'selling clubs' of recent times. Between 1923 and 1977 the club had employed four managers with an average of 12 years in the job. Since 1977, 15 people have had the job on a full-time basis averaging less than two seasons, a roll-call that eventually led the club into Division 3.

In 1992 Lou Macari won the Autoglass Trophy and a season later the first Division 2 title before leaving for Celtic. Back after a year, he took the team to a play-off semi-final place in 1996, the closest the Potters have been to a return to top-flight football. The following year they left the Victoria Ground, their home since 1878, for the Britannia Stadium.

Since then, Chris Kamara got three months on the way to relegation in 1998, Gary Megson lasted slightly longer until an Icelandic consortium purchased the club in 1999, appointing their own manager, Gudjón Thórdarson, who brought promotion back to Division 1 in 2002. Steve Cotterill passed through for 13 games on his way to Sunderland. His successors, Tony Pulis and Johan Boskamp, have broken the average for recent years and, by consolidating in the second tier, appear to have achieved Stoke City's par League position.

Formed from six towns, Stoke is the smallest city in England to have two Football League teams. The Potters' traditional fan base is in Longton, Fenton and Stoke itself, whilst Burslem and Tunstall are more associated with rivals Port Vale. Hanley (the city's main centre and birthplace of Matthews) tends to be split between the two.

Stranraer

Although formed in 1870 from an amalgamation of teams, Stranraer FC did not represent the port town in the Scottish League until 1949, when they were admitted to the south-west section of the post-war Division 3 (the 'C' League) that consisted mainly of Eastern League teams and reserve sides. Up until then, its remote location meant that transportation logistics excluded them from senior football, even as they racked up regional trophies like the Tweedie Cup and the Galloway Shield.

After a variety of venues, the club bought Stair Park in 1907, but it wasn't until the 1930s and beyond that they played regularly in the Scottish Cup. Honorable defeats at home to Rangers in early 1948, and at Motherwell the season after, helped raise the club's profile to secure League entry and ensure that the ground has remained Scottish football's most southerly, and possibly least desired, location, with most of its football traffic provided by Old Firm fans from Ireland passing through on their way to and from Glasgow.

The club won Division 2 titles in 1993–94 and 1997–98 and were champions of Division 3 in 2003–04, followed by another promotion in 2005 – though they were relegated straight away. They also took the Scottish Challenge Cup (the competition excluding Premier League sides) in 1997. However, the club is said to be the oldest senior side in the world unrepresented at international level. Also, for most of the first century of its existence, it dispensed with the need for a team manager, with the side traditionally picked by the club's 12 directors on a Monday night. It was also the last Scottish club to completely install floodlights, in 1981.

An uncharacteristic surge in the 1968–69 League Cup ended at the quarter-final stage with a 10–0 aggregate loss to Dundee. In a history largely bereft of either glory or giant-killings, except for a defeat of the now defunct Third Lanark in the 1963–64 Scottish Cup, Stranraer fans have contented themselves by hating 'local' rivals Queen of the South, who play in Dumfries, 75 miles further east. Although Kilmarnock and Ayr are geographically closer, the birth of the rivalry can perhaps be explained by the fact that 'The Doonhamers' hammered Stranraer 11–1 in a 1931 Scottish Cup first-round tie, a score that still stands as the side's record defeat.

structure of clubs

Most football clubs created in the 19th century began as members' clubs run by an elected committee. Once professionalism was introduced they were reconstituted as limited companies with an unpaid board of directors, a chairman and a small number of shareholders. (Nottingham Forest were unique in remaining a members' club throughout most of the 20th century, including the period when they were European champions.) Both the Football Association and the Football League introduced regulations to protect sporting values, putting off any potential City investors.

In the public imagination boards of directors became football's equivalent of a debauched military junta. They were ridiculed by Len **Shackleton**, while Tommy Docherty once commented that

'The ideal board of directors should be made up of three men – two dead and the other dying.' Originally local benefactors made good, on the lookout for a bit of prestige, football club directors have always been strictly businessmen (as Freddie Shepherd and Douglas Hall of Newcastle once revealed in a notorious interview held in a Catalan brothel), the cigar-chomping flak-catchers, sitting in the posh seats with their own space prominently marked out in the car park.

Appropriately perhaps, a number of famous comedians have served as club directors, including Tommy Cannon at Rochdale, Jasper Carrott at Birmingham, Eric Morecambe at Luton and Norman Wisdom at Brighton. Most bizarre of all, the self-styled King of Pop, Michael Jackson, was an honorary member of the board at Exeter City during his friend Uri Geller's brief involvement with the club.

In 1981, the Football Association eased the restriction on directors taking a salary. For a new breed of businessmen taking up positions in the boardrooms it was a start, but not enough. Men such as Irving Scholar at Tottenham Hotspur were convinced that the socially outcast, slightly scruffy world of football was in fact a potential goldmine. In 1983, with Thatcherite dreams of share option windfalls in the air, Scholar floated Spurs on the Stock Exchange. To do this he sidestepped the FA's long-standing Rule 34 (limiting the size of return on dividends payable to shareholders) by setting up a company, Tottenham Hotspur PLC, and including the football club as a subsidiary. Others were quick to follow Spurs' lead, most notably Manchester United. Operating as companies, the structure of football clubs changed irrevocably.

Now listed on the Stock Exchange (like all floated clubs, under Leisure, Entertainment and Hotels), Manchester United appointed Martin Edwards as chief executive, a new breed in the upper eche-lons of the modern game. Whereas the old-fashioned chairmen were lords of all they surveyed, chief executives had to balance the demands of various inves-tors, duty-bound to act in the interests of shareholders.

Investors in football clubs are either looking for an 'emotional' return – the chance to be involved in their team – or a financial one, hoping for a profit from television rights, merchandising and various sponsorships. It's the latter group the chief executive works for, often to the total exclusion of the former (protests against the failed BSkyB takeover at Old Trafford saw shareholding United fans evicted from the club offices; turfed out of the company they partially owned).

Who actually regulates these money men is a moot point. Market forces perhaps, but what market? Terrace chants of 'Sack the Board' lose their potency if that Far East pre-season tour has opened lucrative new sponsorship deals. Football clubs didn't start to make substantial amounts of money until the 1990s, with the arrival of the Premier League, but even now it's only Manchester United who have any real clout in the City, and even they, compared with (for instance) a hotel group, are relatively small fry.

Lower-league clubs are increasingly having to consider ways of restructuring (the unlovely Edwards believed in natural wastage, declaring smaller clubs were 'bleeding the game dry . . . they should be put to sleep'; a sentiment echoed by his replacement Peter Kenyon, now at Chelsea, who wants to see such clubs go part-time). Supporter representation on the board is more viable on the lower rungs of the League ladder, as clubs revert to positioning themselves as localized cultural assets, their fans able to vent their frustration and exercise their

rights as consumers with some sort of effect. In 2005, Manchester United fans formed a non-League team, FC United of Manchester, in response to the contro-versial takeover of their club by American billionaire Malcolm Glazer. Small, it seems, can still be beautiful.

substitutes

For nearly a century of organized football the use of substitutes was considered to be somewhat against the spirit of the game – when a player went off through injury, it was simply a test of his team's character to continue with ten men. That led to any number of heroic perform-ances, but also a lot of unnecessarily one-sided games. With the advent of tele-vision and the increasing frequency of international club and country matches, views began to change.

FIFA first sanctioned substitutes for youth competitions in 1956, for a goal-keeper and one other player, provided they were injured. Two years later, national associations were free to adopt the rule for all competitions, though many were slow to do so. In England, the push for substitutes was given momentum by a freak series of injuries in the FA Cup Finals of the 1950s, which ruined many of the contests – among them Wally Barnes (split cartilage, 1952), Jimmy Meadows (broken leg, 1955), Bert Trautmann (broken neck, 1956), Ray Wood (broken jaw, 1957), Roy Dwight (broken leg, 1959). Finally, the League permitted the use of one sub, initially for injured players only, for the start of the 1965–66 season. Charlton's Keith Peacock replaced the injured goalkeeper Mike Rose after 11 minutes of their game at Bolton on 21 August 1965, to become the first sub used in League football (Bolton won 4–2).

It wasn't until the 1970 World Cup finals that FIFA themselves gave way, though two subs were permitted from the start – Anatoly Puzach of the Soviet Union was the first used, in the 0–0 draw against Mexico. Alf **Ramsey**, often unfairly criticized as a manager who never quite got the hang of substitutions, set an unfortunate precedent by taking off Bobby **Charlton** with England 2–1 up against West Germany in the quarter-final, an act that effectively ended Charlton's international career. Twenty-two years later, Graham **Taylor** provided a neat parallel by substituting Gary **Lineker** in his last match for England, the 2–1 defeat by Sweden at Euro 92, when he was one goal short of Charlton's record total for England.

The 1970s and 1980s were the golden age for substitutes. A few players, Liverpool's David Fairclough above all, made frustrating reputations as 'supersubs'. Some had their finest moments as subs, such as Arsenal's Eddie Kelly, the first man to score as a sub in the Cup Final (2–1 v Liverpool in 1971) and Aston Villa's Nigel Spink, who came off the bench after ten minutes of the 1982 European Cup Final against Bayern Munich, for only his second appearance for the club.

The one-sub era also allowed a brief heyday for outfield players who could go in goal if necessary – Chelsea's David Webb being the best-known. That all came to an end in the 1990s, as first two, then three substitutions were permitted, to be chosen from a bench of five (or the entire squad at international tournaments): luxury for coaches, misery for so many goalkeepers forced to sit and watch week after week. The proliferation of substitutes has given coaches the chance to waste more time, give retiring players a chance to salute the crowd by bringing them off just before the end and even to indulge in quirky history-making, as when 16-year-old Eidur Gudjohnsen was sent on as a sub for his father Arnor,

in Iceland's match against Estonia in 1996.

At international level, the situation reached farcical levels when unlimited substitutions were allowed in friendly matches, leading to games such as Malta v England in 2000 and England v Australia in 2003, in which one side changed its entire team during the match.

While FIFA belatedly curbed such extravaganzas, the pressure is on from coaches such as Arsène **Wenger** to allow even more flexibility with substitutes. If recent radical changes are anything to go by, football may end up not with a substitutes bench, but an interchange bench along the lines of rugby league or American football.

Sunderland

Sunderland were once known as 'The Team of All Talents' and later as 'The Bank of England Club'. Today, they are 'The Black Cats'. Gone is the aura of on-field ability and off-field wealth. Superstition and a connotation of bad luck now hold sway on Wearside, though the club have had recent cause for celebration, winning the Championship, and so promotion to the Premier League, in 2005.

Formed in 1879 by Scottish schoolteacher James Allan, the club arrived in the Football League in 1890, underpinned by money from shipbuilding and coal. Drawing on a stream of talented Scottish players, the club swiftly made their mark, winning the title in 1892, 1893 and 1895. A move to Roker Park in 1898 and a further title in 1902 established the club's reputation and made stars of the like of flat-cap-wearing keeper Ned Doig, notoriously touchy about his baldness and virtually ever-present for 14 seasons.

Success temporarily dried up amid a

bribery scandal in 1903–04. It resulted in the suspension of six directors and was the first example of an endemic boardroom incompetence that has blighted the club to the present day. Under the guidance of Robert Kyle the club rebuilt, winning the title in 1913 and narrowly losing to Aston Villa in the FA Cup Final the same year, in front of 120,000 at the Crystal Palace Stadium. The First World War brought the revival to a halt.

The post-war decade was dominated by three sensational goal-scorers: Charlie Buchan (413 games, 224 goals), Bobby Gurney (388 games, 228 goals) and Dave Halliday (whose 162 goals included 43 in one League season, 1928–29). Gurney was one of the key players in the 1930s, the club's last sustained period of success. He and Raich **Carter** propelled the team to a fifth and final League title in 1936 and a first FA Cup crown the following year. But with the club set for a new spell of dominance, world war intervened once more and broke up a team of enormous ability. Post-war euphoria saw massive crowds at Roker Park, the rich on-field talents of Len **Shackleton** and Stan Anderson (one of the few to have played for the three big north-east clubs), and a bewildering revolving-doors transfer policy. Though the club continued to challenge for honours, momentum had faltered. Another illegal-payments scandal in 1957 was followed by relegation in 1958, ending 68 years of continuous top-flight football.

Although fine players, striker Brian **Clough** and Irish centre-back Charlie Hurley among them, ensured the fans still had their heroes, success was now fleeting. Despite promotion in 1964, survival was a struggle. Relegation in 1970 began a dispiriting and on-going cycle of promotion and relegation, including a humiliating, though short-lived, drop to the third flight in 1987.

The one moment of enduring delight over the past three decades was the 1973 FA Cup Final win over Leeds. The day provided two iconic moments: Jim Montgomery's double-jointed double save and manager Bob Stokoe's full-time dash across the Wembley turf in his trilby, brown mac and red tracksuit. However, the fact that a club of Sunderland's pedigree were now 'giant-killers' simply highlighted how far the club had fallen. It was a decline that went hand in hand with a decline in the traditional heavy industries of the north-east. By the 1990s, crowds, originally drawn from a wide geographical area, including Wearside, large swathes of County Durham and parts of what is now Teesside, had dwindled.

A move away from the much-loved but dilapidated Roker Park in 1997 to the glitzy, if pompously named, Stadium of Light coincided with Peter Reid's brief resurrection of the club. The form of strikers Kevin Phillips and Niall Quinn suggested the good times might return. But relegation in 2003 with a dismal 19 points ended any such hopes, with mismanagement off the pitch plunging the club into alarming debt prior to their revival under the managership of Mick McCarthy. However, a disastrous season in the Premiership in 2005–06 saw McCarthy depart without having won a home match.

superstitions

Football is an inherently ritualistic occupation. The earliest recorded organized games took place on holy days, such as the Ashbourne Shrovetide Football Game, which dates back beyond the 12th century, and the professional changing room has long been a repository of rituals, rune-reading, hoodoos, jinxes and all manner of occult practices.

Footballing superstitions tend to take

on certain prescribed forms: the Gypsy Curse; the Changing Room Routine and Match Day Quirk; and the more general Jinxes and Bad Luck. The Gypsy Curse is traditionally invoked as a punishment by disgruntled Romanies displaced by the building of a club's home ground. Derby County boast the oldest recorded curse, laid down by local gypsies made homeless by the building of the Baseball Ground in 1895. The curse was famously 'lifted' by club captain Jack Nicholas, who paid a conciliatory visit to a local soothsayer before the 1946 FA Cup Final. Derby duly beat Charlton 4–1 to claim their first major trophy.

More recently Birminhgam City manager Barry Fry was encouraged to urinate in all four corners of the St Andrews pitch in an attempt to lift an ancient curse attached to the Blues' home ground, which had prompted the club to paint crosses on dressing room doors and players' boots during the 1980s. Similarly, Maine Road was rumoured to have been given the evil eye by gypsies evicted from the stadium site in 1921, although the curse appears to have been rather ineffectual, falling to prevent City from winning the FA Cup 13 years later and the League title shortly afterwards.

The recent surge in stadium building has provided the gypsy curse with a new lease of life: in 2001 Oxford United called in the Bishop of Oxford to say a prayer of exorcism in the centre circle at the new Kassam Stadium, in a bid to ward off any possibility of contagion from the curse that had previously dogged the Manor Ground. Similarly, a tip-off from a local witch that their new St Mary's Stadium was built on the site of a Saxon burial ground prompted Southampton to enlist a pagan priestess to do a job for them out on the pitch after they failed to win any of their first five games at their new stadium; the Saints, of course, won their next three home games without conceding a goal.

The famous 'Wembley Hoodoo' – the curse of England's national stadium – expressed itself though a series of injuries in FA Cup Finals and international matches during the 1950s, supposedly ushered in by a broken cheekbone suffered by Wilf **Mannion** in the 13th minute of England's 3–2 defeat by Scotland in April 1951. Further match-shaping breaks, strains and blows would mar Cup Finals for the rest of the decade, among them Eric Bell – Stanley **Matthews**'s opposite number – spending almost all of the 1953 Cup Final limping around trying to stay out of the way on the right wing, Manchester City's ex-POW goalkeeper Bert Trautmann breaking his neck in the cause in the 1956 Final after clashing with Birmingham City's Peter Murphy, and Elton John's uncle, Roy Dwight, breaking his leg playing for Nottingham Forest against Luton Town. The jinx of Wembley Finals affected by serious injuries to players was eventually 'exorcised' by the introduction of substitutes in July 1965.

A similar hoodoo seemed to be attaching itself to the south changing room at the Millennium Stadium in Cardiff prior to Stoke City's victory in the Division 2 play-off final in May 2002. The preceding 12 major cup and play-off finals had been won by the team changing – into their lucky shorts, right sock on first, last one out the door – in the dressing rooms at the north end of the ground; this despite the stadium manager enlisting a feng shui expert to carry out a blessing, and employing a Welsh artist to paint a mural designed to defeat any resident evil spirits – evidence more of an innate footballing fear of the jinx than any lurking supernatural activity.

Players' superstitions tend to revolve around a traditional match day ritual, usually bound up with the order in which vital pieces of clothing are either removed or put on, what order to emerge from the dressing room, or a refined combination of turf-stroking, badge-touching or limb-stretching when they finally make it on to the pitch. Many a beard has thrived during an unexected Cup run, or a lucky suit been wheeled out to keep a hot streak going.

While every players' questionnaire ever devised contains a space for professional footballers to list their arcane, futile pre-match rituals, it is among supporters, for whom the gulf between the desire for success and the possibilty of influencing events on the field of play is greatest, that superstition and ritual are most commonplace. Lucky routes to a ground, lucky seats, lucky pre-match meals, lucky friends are all widespread and often fleeting afflictions of the anxious supporter.

supporters' organizations

The relationship between those who run football and those who watch it has been transformed over the last 20 years. This has been almost entirely through the efforts of supporters and their organiza-tions. In the mid-1980s new kinds of inde-pendent fans' associations emerged alongside fanzines to change the way supporters are seen in the eyes of the media, the public and, to a limited extent, the football authorities. Twenty years ago, fans' views on issues affecting the game were virtually never heard; now, hardly an incident goes by without supporters being asked for their opinions.

Not that these were the first supporters' organizations; there have been supporters' clubs for almost as long as there have been clubs to support. In his book *Football and Its Fans* Rogan

Taylor reveals that the earliest supporters' organizations were called 'brake clubs'. Established in the 1880s, they existed primarily to organize travel to and from matches. The first 'tradi-tional' supporters' clubs emerged slightly later, around 1900. According to Taylor they tended to be 'model organizations of respectability, manned, and very occasionally womanned, by a selection of local worthies', such as councillors, aldermen and mayors – not unlike the club boards themselves.

Many such clubs were formed at the instigation of the directors and were often little more than fund-raising vehicles, called on to pull in extra money in times of financial crisis or when a new player was needed. Supporters who tried to organize independently, or protest about their treatment, were given short shrift. The relationship between these 'official' supporters' organizations and their clubs was best summed up by the motto of the National Federation of Foot-ball Supporters' Clubs (Nat Fed), set up in 1927: 'To help, not hinder'.

By the 1950s the Nat Fed had half a million members, but while the individual supporters' clubs busied themselves raising funds, its role in campaigning on supporters' behalf remained distinctly low-key. Perhaps this explains its decline, for by 1988 only 40 clubs were represented at its AGM. By then, though, a new kind of organization had emerged.

The Football Supporters' Association was set up (by Rogan Taylor among others) in 1985, the year of the **Heysel disaster** and the **Bradford fire**. Attendances were falling, the image of the game was at an all-time low, and most fans were seen by the media and the government as little more than hooli-gans. The FSA was created to represent the views of supporters at a national level. From the start it was independent of club affiliation, political in tone and intention, with a campaigning stance. Along with the newly emerging fanzines, it started to give fans a presence in the media and a say with the authorities. By the 1988–89 season it had 5,000 members. More importantly, perhaps, it began to be seen as the authentic voice of supporters.

Its first success was a significant one – helping to stop the Thatcher government's plans for an ID card scheme with a 250,000-signature petition. It also campaigned for refunds for abandoned matches; for 70 per cent of Cup Final tickets to go to supporters of the teams involved; and for 10 per cent of ground capacity to be reserved for away supporters. It conducted a high-profile campaign against racism and played a significant part in establishing the national Kick It Out campaign. From the 1990 World Cup onwards, it has organized fans' embassies at all the major international tournaments, providing travelling fans with much-needed advice, helping to counter some of the worst media coverage of England supporters, and fostering relations with fans from other countries.

The FSA's campaigning voice provided a model for a number of club-based initiatives started by fans fed up with the compliance of traditional supporters' clubs. Independent supporters' associations, which first sprang up in the late 1980s and early 1990s, aim to make football clubs more accountable. Tottenham Independent Supporters' Association (TISA) was set up in 1991, when the club faced bank-ruptcy; Hammers ISA defeated West Ham's attempt to impose a bond scheme in 1993 (a success repeated by Arsenal fans); and the Independent Manchester United Supporters' Association (IMUSA) was instrumental in seeing off the

takeover threat from Rupert Murdoch's BSkyB in 1999 and was central to the fight against Malcolm Glazer's takeover. It says something for the power of these organizations that every Premier League club now has a supporters' panel.

After years of not quite seeing eye-to-eye, the FSA joined forces with the Nat Fed in 2002 to give fans a unified voice, forming the Football Supporters' Federation (FSF), which currently represents over 130,000 football fans throughout the UK. Almost all clubs now have an ISA and many of them also have a **supporters' trust**, organizations seeking to acquire some degree of owner-ship and a decision-making role in their clubs.

The achievements of all these organiza-tions shouldn't be underestimated as they have given fans a say at many levels of the game and influence with other significant bodies such as the Football Task Force and Parliament's All-Party Football Committee. However, there is still no fan representation at the Football Association (while the armed services and public schools continue to be repre-sented); there are no fans on the boards of Premier League clubs; and the decisions made by those who control football are still dictated more by commercial considerations than the interests of fans. Over the last 20 years, supporters' organiz-ations have given fans an independent, influential and active voice. The next step is to gain some control.

supporters' trusts

Over the last six years supporters' trusts have become an influential force at a number of football clubs around Britain, for the first time giving fans a collective stake in the ownership and control of the clubs they support. Essentially they are set up not just to campaign for a better deal for supporters, or to protest against the activities of a chairman or board, but to do the job for them by holding shares in the club and voting collectively on behalf of all fans.

The first supporters' trust in the country was set up by fans of Northampton Town in 1992 when the club fell into debt and was under threat of extinction. The money raised by the trust, and its relationship with the local council, helped to save the club, build a new ground, and gave the trust two seats on the club's new board – the first supporters' directors on the board of an English League club. Brian Lomax, one of those fan-directors, explained that the trust 'marked itself out as being distinct from normal supporters' clubs in that, from its inception, it has had an inescapably political dimension'.

The success of the Northampton Town supporters' trust led to many similar organizations at other clubs, winning varying degrees of ownership, control and influence for fans. Often these are most successful at relatively small clubs that fall into similar financial crises – trusts have been particularly successful at clubs like Bournemouth, Exeter and York City, for example. Occasionally, however, as with Shareholders United at Old Trafford, they are active at clubs whose huge assets have made them attractive takeover propositions for commercial interests. Shareholders United owned 2 per cent of Manchester United's shares but it was able to work with other fans' groups to prevent the club being taken over by Rupert Murdoch's BSkyB, though it could not prevent American businessman Malcolm Glazer seizing control in 2005.

Whatever the reasons, there's no doubt the trust movement has mushroomed in recent years. By January 2005 there were 122 supporters' trusts in England, Wales and Scotland, 59 of which held equity. Trusts at 39 clubs were represented on the board of their clubs, and at eight (two in the Football League, Brentford and Chesterfield, and six non-League) they have control. Supporters Direct, the government-funded umbrella body for trusts, estimates that trusts have helped to save at least 19 clubs from extinction and brought some £10m into the game, involving more than 85,000 fans.

Supporters Direct was established by the government in 2001, when only a handful of trusts existed, and few had any real influence at their club. It emerged out of the Football Task Force, a public enquiry into football set up by the new Labour government in 1997 and led by former Tory MP and 'celebrity' Chelsea fan David Mellor. It was the first time taxpayers' money had gone into a football fans' organization and marked, according to Dave Boyle, Supporters Direct's assistant director, 'a fundamental shift in how fans are perceived, both by clubs and football authorities'.

Funded by the Football Foundation, Supporters Direct acts as an umbrella and advice body for trusts, helping fans set them up and encouraging them to become mutual organizations – Industrial and Provident Societies to use the legal jargon – which push for representation on club boards and seek ownership by pooling fans' shares. Boyle comments that 'through trusts we've proved that the sky doesn't turn black if supporters are on the board'.

It could take years for trusts at large clubs like Arsenal or Manchester United to gain any decision-making power, and decades for clubs to become genuine fan-owned democracies, but Supporters Direct is at least confident that it will soon have a voice among the decision-makers at the Football Association.

Swansea City

Swansea City were called Swansea Town until 1970. Despite this their ground, nickname and – with minor variations – colours have remained the same since they were founded in 1912 and immediately elected to the Southern League.

All-white colours and their name led logically to the 'Swans' nickname. The Vetch Field, close to both seafront and town centre on a site whose tightness makes it noisily atmospheric, was constructed during the summer of 1912. The club was immediately successful. It won the Welsh Cup in 1913, knocked League champions Blackburn out of the FA Cup in 1915 and – elected to the Football League in 1920 – won promotion to Division 2 within five years.

Subsequent history divides neatly into two eras. The years 1925 to 1965 were spent almost entirely in Division 2, the last 40 mostly in the lower leagues. Fifth place, plus an FA Cup semi-final, in 1925–26 proved a high point but Division 2 survival through the inter-war years represented achievement while Aberdare, Merthyr and (briefly) Newport were losing League status. Continuity was supplied by full-back Wilfred Milne, whose club record 585 League appearances included a 15-year wait for his first goal.

Having been lost immediately after the war, Division 2 status was regained in 1949 with manager Bill McCandless's third promotion in four seasons with different Welsh clubs. The following decade saw a remarkable flowering of local, mostly attacking, talent. Ivor **Allchurch** – described by Real Madrid president Santiago Bernabéu in 1958 as 'the finest inside-forward in the world' – was followed by Cliff Jones, Terry Medwin and Mel Charles. Failure to replace injured centre-half Tom Kiley in November 1955 when the Swans led Division 2 remains in folk memory as exemplifying a decade of missed opportunity. Subsequent decline, briefly masked by an FA Cup semi-final in 1964 – a still bitterly remembered defeat by Preston – led to relegation in 1965.

Expected to return rapidly, they instead went down again in 1967 and had to apply for re-election in 1975. The recovery initiated by Harry Griffiths and brought to fruition by John Toshack has no parallel. Between 1978 and 1981 the Swans were promoted three times and, after leading at Easter, finished sixth in the old Division 1. Widely ascribed to Toshack's Liverpool links, the success owed more to an inheritance of youthful local talent, including Alan Curtis, Robbie James and Jeremy Charles, adventurous signings like Yugoslavs Ante Rajkovic and Dzemal Habziabdic and an innovative formation – refined into the *sistema Toshack* when he subsequently managed Real Madrid – using wing-backs and a sweeper.

The return journey, though, was just as rapid. Surviving a near-death experience at Christmas 1984 – as the club almost went bankrupt – the Swans were back in Division 4 by 1986 and have since divided time between the two variously named and numbered lower divisions. The last of seven European campaigns as Welsh Cup-winners, spread over 30 years and invariably generating more memories than victories, ended in 1991. Winning the Autoglass Trophy in 1994 was no compensation for losing in the Division 2 play-offs a year earlier. The Division 3 championship winners of 2000 were exceptional for scoring fewer goals than any champions in League history, and their fans for reversing normal football patterns by believing them not as good as their results – belief confirmed by relegation 12 months later. League status was retained only in the final 45 minutes of the 2002–03 season.

Toshack has been followed by 17 managers in 20 years, none lasting more than three years, two little over a week apiece. Continuity was instead represented by the much-loved but decaying Vetch and outstanding goal-keeper Roger Freestone, who made 566 League appearances in 14 seasons. Free-stone's departure in 2004, the move to the new all-seater White Rock stadium – shared with Neath–Swansea Ospreys rugby club – and unprecedented fan involvement at board level created an air of renewal at the club, boosted further by promotion in 2005. The following season they lost on penalties to Barnsley in the League One play-off final.

Swindon Town

Swindon Town was formed in 1881 by a local clergyman who convinced two sports clubs from the fractious farming and railway communities of Old and New Swindon to resolve their differences through the medium of football. By 1900 the club had moved from its first ground by the side of a quarry after a spectator fell to his death, settled on red shirts after giving up on finding a suitable green dye for their old white kit, and were nick-named 'The Robins'. 'The Railwaymen' nickname had faded from the memory by the time the GWR works closed down in the mid-1980s.

Before the Great War Harold Flemming, an enigmatic winger who played with his cuffs flapping by his sides, inspired the club to the Southern League champion-ship, two FA Cup semi-finals, the Dubonnet Cup (an FA Cup third-place play-off) and a Charity Shield match which Manchester United won 8–4. Flemming is commemorated in the

naming of a road that radiates from the contemporary Magic Roundabout outside the County Ground. It wasn't until the 1960s that the club's fortunes took off again. Bert Head produced a crop of talented young players and laid the foundations for a decade of relative success. Amongst the most famous of Bert's Babes were Mike Summerbee and Ernie Hunt, who lodged together in a terraced house and organized kickabouts with local youngsters.

The club's finest moment remains the 1969 League Cup victory over Arsenal on a heavy Wembley pitch. The photo-graph of Don Rogers scoring his second extra-time goal in a spotless white shirt is an iconic image in Swindon – 'A proud ocean liner sailing on a sea of mud', according to a poem in a local news-paper's coverage of the game. Inter-national silverware followed in the shape of the hastily arranged Anglo-Italian League Cup Winners' Cup in 1969. By the mid-1970s the club were back in what many still believe is their natural level, the old Division 3. Neverthe-less a series of good FA Cup runs, and a League Cup semi-final appearance brought record attendances.

The late 1980s marked a renaissance as Swindon rose through the divisions again under the inspired leadership of first-time managers Macari, Ardiles and **Hoddle**. Ossie Ardiles assembled the most technically gifted side in the club's history and won promotion to the old Division 1 via the play-offs in 1990. Ten days later the club was de-moted because of financial irregularities. 'Swindle Town' is still sung by some away supporters.

Three years later a memorable 4–3 play-off win against Leicester saw Swindon promoted to the Premiership. Two successive relegations followed, before promotion, relegation and a spell in administration. The club survived a second spell in adminstration after 'Razorgate' (paying off an unfit Neil Ruddock's weighty contract) and donations of office equipment from supporters. Despite such recent excitement Swindon Town remain the epitome of an unfashionable provincial club, short on cash and high on hopes. They were relegated to League Two in 2005–06.

tackling

Of all the basic footballing arts, the tackle is undoubtedly the darkest. Tackling defines the outer limits of what is and isn't football. The *Oxford English Dictionary* may describe it as simply 'intercepting a player in an effort to get the ball away from him', but the thin line between the tackle and the foul has increasingly preoccupied those who dictate the way the game is played.

According to English footballing lore, Bobby **Moore**'s challenge on Jairzinho during the 1970 World Cup between England and Brazil represents the Platonic ideal of the perfectly timed tackle. In a match tinged with nostalgic hyperbole – also said to have contained the Greatest Save (see Gordon **Banks**) – Moore's tackle still stands out as an example of perfect timing and balance, the England captain removing the ball from his opponent's foot so cleanly that neither player even breaks his stride.

Football's lawmakers have always tended to define tackling by what it isn't. Any challenge that doesn't fall foul of Law 12 of FIFA's much-tinkered-with laws of the game can be called a tackle. In fact, the ability to tackle without infringing Law 12 is a skill that many feel is being lost, partly owing to changes in the way the game is refereed. The most significant of the rule changes affecting tackling was implemented before the France 98 World Cup, 'Decision 5' of Law 12 decreeing that a mistimed challenge from behind should be punishable by a straight red card, dramatically increasing the risks for players still willing to attempt an old-style tackle.

As a result, tackling has become less a test of physical strength and more an exercise in subterfuge. For a while shirt-pulling became the dark practice of choice for the defender looking for an edge – although FIFA have since addressed this tactic by instructing referees before the 2002 World Cup to treat the tugging of shirts as a cautionable offence.

A variety of factors have combined to lessen the importance of the traditional bone-crunching tackle. The rules may have changed, but so have pitches: the ploughed fields and swamps of the 1970s and early 1980s are a thing of the past. Similarly, tactics have evolved. Fewer players travel with the ball at their feet. Wizards of Dribble no longer hug the touchline.

But while traditionalists may mourn the demise of the sliding lunge on a bog-soaked swamp of a pitch – which takes ball, player and three wheelbarrows of turf slithering into the stands – it will surely only be a matter of time before tackling is back again, albeit in modified form. After all, the game can hardly be expected to do without nicknames, the best of which have always tended to relate to tackling. Norman 'pulls your shirt' Hunter doesn't quite have the same ring.

Graham Taylor

Former Lincoln, Watford, Aston Villa, Wolves and England manager Graham Taylor represents much of what is best about English football. This is despite the fact that, tactically, his coaching embodies aspects of the English game at its worst. Taylor emerged from the lower divisions to reach the highest level of English management, where he endured a traumatic four years in charge of the national team.

Born in Worksop in 1944, Taylor played for Grimsby Town in Division 3 and then made over 150 appearances for Lincoln before being forced into early retirement by a hip injury. Appointed manager of Lincoln at the age of 28, he took the club to the Division 4 championship in 1976, in the process catching the eye of newly appointed Watford director Elton John. Elton himself approached Taylor over a move to Vicarage Road, although his initial impressions were sceptical. 'I thought it was the last thing I wanted,' Taylor admitted later. 'To go back into the fourth division with an outrageous pop star messing around as chairman.' Elton's patience eventually won Taylor round, and in 1977 he accepted the job that would transform his career.

Within five years Watford were in Division 1 for the first time in their history. In 1983 they finished second in the League behind Liverpool, and in 1984 they reached a first-ever FA Cup Final, losing 2–0 to Everton as Elton wept in the stands. Taylor nurtured a generation of young players, among them Luther Blissett and John Barnes, both of whom would go on to higher things with England, and respectively Milan and Liverpool.

Their success reflected Taylor's other great innovation, his bridge-building with the local community. Under his guidance, Watford players were contractually obliged to do several hours of community work every week. Local links were sought out and cultivated. Families were encouraged to attend games and talent was sourced and developed. At the same time Taylor's unusual relationship with his chairman had reached a particular level of intimacy. 'For a while, I was his reality,' Taylor later admitted. At one point Elton even credited his manager with helping to ward off his burgeoning alcoholism.

Inevitably Taylor was poached by a larger club. His move to Aston Villa led to further success on the field, a second-place finish in 1990. Taylor was by now the hottest young English managerial property. He seemed an automatic choice when Bobby **Robson** left his post as England manager after the World Cup finals in Italy. However, this was where the other side to Taylor's career emerged: his methods were never those of the footballing purist. An acolyte of the FA Coaching Director Charles Hughes, who favoured the direct football of the long-ball game, Taylor took his Watford methods with him on to the international stage. This was his undoing. The enduring images of Taylor's reign as England manager are all of gripping failure.

Euro 92 saw an England squad containing Carlton Palmer, Keith Curle and Tony Daley crash out to Sweden in gormless circumstances; Gary **Lineker** was substituted on his last international appearance in favour of the taller and more target-like Alan Smith. Then came World Cup qualifying failure: witless defeat to Norway in Oslo, with Taylor's wonky backline hopelessly bemused by the towering Jostein Flo. There followed elimination from the World Cup at the hands of Holland in Rotterdam, Taylor twitching hopelessly and unluckily on the touchline; and finally the goal conceded inside seven seconds to San Marino. Taylor's England even found time to lose to the US. Eventually his head was morphed cruelly into a turnip on the back page of the *Sun* and his every mannerism distended into a ludicrous cartoon by the prying cameras of a *Cutting Edge* documentary team (instant catch phrases: 'Can we not knock it?' 'Do I not like that?', 'Carlton! Carlton!'). Taylor eventually resigned in November 1993.

After a spell with Wolves, he returned to Watford a few years later, winning successive promotions from Division 2 in 1998 and into the Premiership in 1999.

Having announced his retirement he then surprised many observers by returning to Aston Villa in 2002 for a fruitless season and a half back in the top flight. Taylor remains a very nice man, apparently unscarred by his travails as England manager.

Taylor Report

The inquiry into the **Hillsborough disaster** was led by Lord Justice Taylor, a High Court Judge, whose brief was: 'To inquire into the events at Sheffield Wednesday Football ground on 15th April and to make recommendations about the needs of crowd control and safety at sports events.' It was the ninth official inquiry commissioned into ground safety and crowd control at football matches in Britain. Indeed, the list of football stadium tragedies stretches back to 1902 when a terrace collapsed at Ibrox, killing 26 and injuring over 500. Since 1900 at least 306 fans have died supporting football in 27 separate incidents; a further 3,500 fans have been injured. Since the Second World War around 186 people have been killed in accidents at League matches.

The Taylor Report came in two parts. An interim report in 1989 made 43 recommendations to be implemented immediately, including calls to restrict the capacity of grounds by 15 per cent, open perimeter fences, and review all ground safety certificates. The final report in January 1990 criticized virtually everyone in football and many aspects of the game: the football authorities and their leaders; football grounds and facilities; players for poor behaviour; clubs for selling alcohol and not consulting fans; the media for its attitude; and some fans for hooliganism and segregation. Its 76 recommendations included demands for terraces to be replaced by seating; for a

Football Stadium Advisory Design Council to advise on ground safety and construction; for perimeter fencing to be restricted and spikes removed; for new laws to outlaw ticket touting, racist chanting and missile throwing; and for better relations between fans and police.

It was probably the most comprehensive and significant review ever of the condition of British football and 15 years later its effects are still evident – all-seater stadiums, many of them brand new, are now the norm; perimeter fences no longer exist; the nature of crowd **policing** has been transformed; the views of fans are courted persistently by the media; and football **grounds** are no longer seen as sites of social disorder but an economic boon to local areas.

It's not all good though. Racist chanting is still heard, sometimes, and very rarely dealt with effectively, though the law's been toughened up still further. Ticket touting carries on with little apparent restriction. And fans still struggle to have any real influence over their clubs' or the football authorities' decisions and policies.

Most significantly, Taylor envisaged safe and accessible grounds available to all at reasonable prices, but the reality has been quite different as clubs have used 'safety' to cleanse and market the sport to a new kind of consumer. Some fans complain that grounds have become sanitized entertainment venues in which the atmosphere of a crowd has been replaced by the passive engagement of a high-paying audience. Some, especially in the Premier League, have been priced out of the game as clubs have put up admission fees in order to pay for their new stadiums. And some, keen to participate not just spectate, continue to campaign for grounds to have some area where fans who want to will be allowed to stand in safety.

television

If football and television are a married couple then their relationship is currently rekindling early passions following a near-terminal break-up in the 1980s.

Regular television coverage of the game began in the late 1950s, although the most famous and long-running TV football programme (BBC's Saturday night *Match of the Day*) did not begin until 1964. Most ITV regions were already broadcasting a variety of local football programmes at this stage but the reallocation of ITV franchises in 1968 created a pattern of coverage that would endure for the next 15 years. Seven regions elected to screen local football programmes on a Sunday afternoon, with each taking a match featuring a local team plus highlights of a couple of other games.

The weekend highlights programmes were supplemented by Saturday lunchtime previews (*Football Focus* on BBC, *On the Ball* on ITV) and alternating midweek coverage of European games, League Cup ties and FA Cup replays. The BBC's midweek games were broadcast in their *Sportsnight* programme and ITV aired them under the banner of *The Midweek Match*. All matches were shown in highlights format and live games were an infrequent treat. Only about four or five live fixtures were screened every season, comprising the FA Cup Final, the annual England v Scotland clash, occasional major internationals and selected European finals (especially if a British club was involved).

By the late 1970s, football on television seemed to have settled into a cosy pattern. Coverage was thorough but hardly incisive. Broadcasters appeared reluctant to delve into the problems of the game, such as hooliganism, dull play or the financial problems facing many clubs. There was criticism of cliché-ridden commentaries and excruciating post-match interviews with uncomfortable kipper-tied footballers.

There was a brief attempt to shake up the system in 1978, when ITV (led by LWT chief Michael Grade) signed a new deal giving them exclusive rights to League football – a move which the press inevitably billed as 'Snatch of the Day'. Their audacious bid was rebuffed after the intervention of the Office of Fair Trading, but the new four-year deal signed by both channels for the first time allowed ITV to screen matches on a Saturday night (alternating season by season with the BBC). This incident apart, ITV and BBC always made joint bids to cover football, effectively creating a duopoly (at least until the arrival of satellite television).

By this stage, audience figures for televised football were dropping almost as fast as attendances at live matches. Each side blamed the other for their difficulties. Some football figures (including Brian Clough) felt that too much football on television put off spectators from attending their local ground. TV chiefs meanwhile, such as ITV's Head of Sport, John Bromley, chafed at boring matches and the contractual requirement to cover a fixed number of lower-division games each season. Bromley's anger boiled over in a newspaper interview: 'They have hooligans kicking each other on the terraces, lousy facilities and boring players and they say it's television's fault nobody goes to the game any more!'

At the end of the 1982–83 season, a TV blackout was threatened and there was even a bizarre proposal by a firm called Telejector to broadcast games every Monday night on large video screens in pubs and clubs, replacing conventional television coverage. A two-year deal was finally cobbled together for a limited number of live games, five per channel each year, but like the rumblings that precede a major earthquake, the arguments were a sign that worse was to follow.

With the new deal due to expire at the end of the 1984–85 season, the two sides became even more divided. Oxford United chairman Robert Maxwell was amongst the most vocal critics of the TV companies. He labelled their new offer 'mad, bad and sad' and found strong support from Ken Bates and Tottenham's Irving Scholar. The TV companies were offering £19m per season for a beefed-up programme of live games but many chairmen had convinced themselves that television had long enjoyed football on the cheap and figures of £90m per season were being bandied about.

But football's bargaining position was weak. BBC and ITV refused to negotiate separately and satellite or cable competition was some years off. Moreover, end-of-season tragedies (supporter deaths at Middlesbrough and Birmingham, plus the **Bradford fire** and **Heysel disaster**) made the game appear ugly, badly run and violent. Robert Maxwell quit the negotiating committee in a fit of pique and the TV companies left football to twist in the wind for the first half of the 1985–86 season. Barring midweek internationals and Saturday lunchtime preview programmes, the game was off the screen and hopes that this might result in spectators returning to the terraces were short-lived; attendances actually dropped.

The by now desperate chairmen were forced to accept much less money than they had first been offered and, over the next few years, the TV companies turned the screw by downgrading coverage of the game. They claimed (falsely) that snooker was more popular than football and that viewers were no longer interested in recorded games, even though ratings for the few weekend highlights that were broadcast still remained good. At one stage, the BBC even showed highlights of American basketball in the Saturday night *Match of the Day* slot.

The mid-1980s were a low point for football on television. By the end of the decade, the game was regaining its popularity and appeal, both to spectators and to TV viewers. The 1990 World Cup and England's erratic but exciting progress to the semi-finals attracted huge audiences. Suddenly football was fashionable again. Newspapers that had once branded football 'A slum game, played in slum stadiums, watched by slum fans' (the *Sunday Times*) now filled their *Style* supplements with articles about it.

Famine had turned to feast and feast turned to gluttony in the 1990s with a deluge of matches, both live and recorded, on all stations. The first real step in breaking up the BBC–ITV duopoly had come in 1988, when the League signed an exclusive deal with ITV for live football, a move masterminded by future BBC Director-General Greg Dyke. Fortunately Dyke's attempt to create a ten-club 'ITV Super League' as part of the deal fell through, although fans were left to suffer *The Match* presented by the vacuous Elton Welsby for the next four years. Recorded football was meanwhile banished to ever more remote corners of the schedule (9.25 on a Sunday morning in the case of LWT) and unfashionable clubs like Norwich were ignored even when they were performing better than the so-called 'Big Five' (Everton, Liverpool, Arsenal, Tottenham and Man Utd).

With the advent of Sky, technical standards have improved massively. Probably more important to football chiefs, so has the money on offer. Sky's first deal, concluded in 1992, was worth £304m to the Premier League over five years. Wisely learning a lesson from the 1980s, football chiefs also dictated that the action be spread around. Even Premiership strugglers now receive regular live coverage whilst a separate deal with the Football League has brought us live broadcasts from some unlikely venues – who would have predicted back in the 1970s that Halifax v Hartlepool would one day be beamed live?

Highlights have come back into favour with the two main networks, since neither can compete with Sky's millions where live games are concerned. *Match of the Day* returned in 1992, lost the contract to ITV in 2001, and regained it in 2004, just in time for the programme's 40th anniversary celebrations. *The Premiership* had earlier tried to shake up the highlights format a little, but their innovations (such as Andy Townsend's 'Tactics Truck') didn't work; the new early-evening viewing slot may have been welcomed by Des Lynam ('better for you, better for us') but was a ratings flop.

Much of the analysis and presentation remains bland and vacuous, reaching a nadir in comments such as Peter Reid's sage analysis of the Scarborough–Chelsea FA Cup tie ('Well, it's a massive game for Scarborough'). Against that, fans' views feature a little more frequently, especially in the ubiquitous post-match phone-ins, and fanzine culture seems to have encouraged the broadcasters to loosen up a little, with a 'Cult Heroes' slot on *Football Focus* and the blokey banter, enjoyed by some, on Sky's *Soccer AM*.

Sky have also influenced the terrestrial broadcasters – the now ubiquitous on-screen captions giving the latest score were first introduced by them and the BBC's *Football Focus* is now copying the *Soccer Saturday* approach with ex-players watching games on mini-screens. But whatever stylistic innovations we see, one thing seems reasonably certain – we won't have another TV blackout. Both sides need each other too much for that.

terraces

Standing up has been the accepted way to watch a football match for most spectators throughout its history. Only since the 1990s has it seemed normal to sit down. The concept of the terrace came naturally (it was at least as ancient as the amphitheatre, after all) in the late 1880s, when football's crowds had grown too large to be held behind a rope, or to see anything without elevation. Less certain were the right materials and design to accommodate the unprecedented masses in safety, still less in comfort, which was barely a consideration for a century. The first lesson was learnt early, when the timber framework supporting terracing at Ibrox Park collapsed in 1902, killing 26 people. After that, large terraces were built only on solid embankments.

However, that did nothing to tame the pressures caused by the flow of huge numbers of people on an often steep slope. Photographs of ramshackle wooden crush barriers placed seemingly at random on the terraces show how little science was involved in early crowd control. What is astonishing is how long it took to make any serious advances on those haphazard methods, and how few spectators lost their lives in the intervening period. The terraces in their heyday were both magnificent and terrifying to a modern eye. In 1937, when Hampden Park recorded the largest crowd for any match in Britain (149,415 for Scotland v England), fewer than 15,000 of the spectators were seated.

But it was the classic square-on ends that gave terracing its later reputation

(for better and worse), rather than gargantuan bowls such as Hampden, Wembley or Stamford Bridge. The rise of a distinctive terrace culture in the 1960s, popularly associated initially with Liverpool, ran parallel with the emergence of the teenager as a social phenomenon, with its own fashions, **music** and attitudes. The terraces meant freedom: freedom simply to move around the ground at will, to lose yourself in a crowd away from any supervision, or to behave in ways that would not be tolerated in any other public place.

That gave rise to the distinctive atmosphere of grounds all around Europe, but led by Britain, in which rituals of singing, chanting, clapping, gestures and displays of colour gave football its recognizable background for the best part of 30 years. In some countries, such as Italy and Spain, terrace behaviour evolved into highly organized displays of **banners** and messages, led by groups often on the fringes of the hooligan scene. There was another side to the terraces, particularly in the lower leagues, where crowds were smaller, rituals more homely (the cup of tea and pie at half-time, for example) and atmosphere, by reputation at least, friendlier. Either way, they seemed resistant to change, despite the pioneering all-seater efforts at clubs such as Coventry and Aberdeen.

By the 1980s, however, the terraces had become inextricably linked with violence and racism. After the **Hillsborough disaster** in 1989, few had the heart to argue for the positive aspects of terrace culture and within a few years all-seaters had been imposed throughout the top two divisions in England. As the Premiership took off, terraces were associated only with the bad old days of hooliganism, shrinking crowds and disasters. The last to survive in the Premiership was at Craven Cottage, where exemptions to the all-seater rule kept standing alive until 2002.

However, other countries found compromises to keep big terraces despite the preference of FIFA, UEFA and many national associations for seats. Germany, above all, experimented successfully with terraces that could be converted to seating and as late as 1996 Borussia Dortmund built a 26,000-capacity terrace at one end of their Westfalenstadion. Campaigns to introduce similar concepts in Britain, for example at the City of Manchester Stadium, have so far fallen on deaf ears. And with the glow that surrounds almost any phenomenon that is getting on for 20 years old, the old days of packed terracing have become sentimentalized, as well as demonized, for the supposedly razor-sharp wit and banter of the fans, and an atmosphere that no all-seated stadium can match. Few of the nostalgics, however, are women, pensioners or anyone under about 5 ft 7 in.

testimonial games

At his own testimonial game in 2004 Arsenal defender Martin Keown ended the evening by standing in the centre circle at Highbury and serenading the crowd over the public address system. 'Ke-own. There's only one Ke-own. There's only one Keown. Ke-e-own . . .' the retired defensive linchpin sang – strangely given that he was surrounded by his children at the time, all wearing Arsenal shirts with the name 'Keown' on the back.

Traditionally testimonial games have been staged as a reward for ten years' service at a single club. The player being honoured will captain his own team against a select XI in a friendly exhibition match with all receipts from tickets sold going to his benefit fund. The testimonial is intended as a financial reward for a

player who may be on the verge of retirement and who has during his career refused the financial rewards of a transfer in favour of loyalty to a club, a place and a set of fans.

In the leagues below the Premiership this ideal may still hold true. Most footballers, even long-serving ones, won't make enough money out of the game to retire comfortably. Some players have been given testimonials long after their playing days ended simply as a way of helping them out of financial difficulties – Everton staged one such game for their pre-War player Tommy **Lawton** in 1972.

Testimonials provide a tax-free lump sum, a nest egg for a faithful footballer, and a fitting farewell from those supporters interested enough to buy a ticket for the game. At the top end of the scale, however, the testimonial has begun to seem slightly ridiculous. Hyper-inflation in both players' wages and ticket prices has made the principles behind them seem redundant.

This was reflected in Sunderland striker Niall Quinn's decision to give all proceeds from his 2003 testimonial to charity. At the time Quinn, slightly sanctimoniously, called on all Premiership players to follow his lead in future. It hasn't happened yet.

Texaco Cup

When Newcastle United went to Washington DC in 2001 for a pre-season friendly against Major League Soccer's DC United, they were greeted with the warm banner, 'Welcome to Newcastle United FC – Texaco Cup Winners 1975'. For those who weren't baffled by the reference, it was a knowingly backhanded compliment, the Texaco being the last senior trophy won by the Geordies.

What was the Texaco? It began life in

1969–70 as a knock-out cup for the leading teams who had not qualified for Europe in Scotland, England, the Republic of Ireland and Northern Ireland (Welsh teams being excluded because they did not have a league of their own). Irish clubs withdrew after two years owing to the political situation and competed in their own Texaco Irish Cup for two further seasons. The mainland version lasted only five years and folded when Texaco withdrew its backing, after which it morphed into the even less prestigious Anglo-Scottish Cup. Newcastle remain the tournament's giants, having won the competition during its final two seasons in 1974 and 1975.

During the Texaco's short history only two Scottish teams reached the final, Hearts falling 4–1 to Wolves over the two-game final in 1970, Airdrie losing 2–1 to Derby a year later. The other finals were all-Anglo affairs, including an East Anglian derby in 1973, when Ipswich came out tops over Norwich, 4–2. The Magpies' hour of glory finally came with a 2–1 win over Burnley in a single game, and then a two-legged, 3–1 despatch of Southampton in the tournament's death-knell era.

Bobby **Robson**'s programme notes for Ipswich's first-round, first-leg tie with St Johnstone on a Tuesday night in 1972 perhaps best reflect the pitfalls of organizing yet another gratuitous club tournament. 'A warm welcome is extended to St Johnstone,' he wrote, adding as an afterthought, 'and any of their supporters who may have followed them down from Perth.'

The Anglo-Scottish Cup lasted only six years, and was scrapped in 1981 when clubs in Scotland withdrew owing to lack of public interest and the increasingly low stature of the English entrants, reflected by the 1981 Chesterfield v Notts County final (which the Spireites,

having knocked out Rangers on the way, won 2–1 on aggregate). St Mirren were the most successful Scots, reaching the final twice, and taking the title in 1980 after overcoming Bristol City and avenging defeat at the hands of the same opponents two years earlier.

throw-ins

Evolved out of necessity as the only sensible answer to the question of what to do when the ball goes out of play, a throw-in is also the only occasion on which an outfield player is required to handle the ball, and the only physical movement on a football field governed by distinct rules of choreography.

The laws of the game dictate that a throw-in is awarded to the opponents of the player who last touched the ball ('if there is the slightest doubt, players will appeal', the Referees' Association notes darkly in its training guidance) when the whole of the ball passes over the touchline, either on the ground or in the air, and that the throw shall be taken from the point where the ball first crossed the line. A throw-in is correctly taken while standing on or outside the touchline, releasing the ball two-handed from a point above or behind the head. Failure to observe any of these strictures – referees are warned to be particularly censorious of the practice of 'dropping' the ball in front of a team-mate – will result in a 'foul throw', with the throw-in awarded to the opposition.

Long throw-ins have increasingly been used as an attacking weapon, particularly as match balls have become lighter and throwing techniques more refined. The attacking long throw tends to be released from well behind a player's head with thumbs and fingers spread, combined with a flexing of the knees to deliver a fast, flat trajectory. Periodically the long throw-in-coupled-with-somersaulting-approach-to-the-touchline has surfaced in various parts of the world, prompting a ruling from FIFA that such a throw is not necessarily illegal; just, as it turned out, likely to be wildly inaccurate.

Notable exponents of the attacking long throw include Dave Challinor who, during his time at Tranmere Rovers, became notorious for his ability to propel the ball accurately across distances of up to 40 metres. Challinor's use of towels to dry the ball before hurling it into play caused a certain amount of controversy during Tranmere's run to the Final of the Worthington Cup in the 1999–2000 season, notably when Bolton Wanderers tried to persuade match officials to ban Challinor's towels from the sidelines for their semi-final meeting. During a League game at Barnsley the home team confiscated the offending materials, moved the perimeter hoardings closer to the pitch and instructed substitutes to warm up in areas that would restrict the Tranmere man's run-up.

Outside Challinor's *reductio ad absurdum*, the long throw-in remains an important attacking ploy in English football. Vinnie Jones's long throws were a notable source of attacking success for Dave Bassett's Wimbledon during the 1980s, while the fastest goal in England's World Cup history was scored by Bryan **Robson** (27 seconds into England's opening game against France at Spain 82) from a long throw headed into his path, a move perfected on the training pitch by Don **Howe**. A throw-in by Chelsea's Ian Hutchinson, the most revered long-thrower of his era, created the winning goal in the 1970 FA Cup Final replay between Chelsea and Leeds United, Hutchinson spearing the ball into the Leeds United six-yard box from the left-hand touchline, where it was headed home by David Webb.

Periodic attempts are made to tinker with the throw-in. As early as 1951 US college soccer leagues introduced the 'kick-in', whereby a free kick was awarded every time the ball went out of play. Rather than consigning this experiment to the same dustbin as other US innovations such as dividing the game into quarters, wearing protective headgear and structuring a World Cup opening ceremony around Diana Ross taking a penalty, FIFA recently toyed with the idea of introducing the kick-in, before the idea was ultimately rejected by the International Football Association Board. This didn't stop the kick-in receiving high-profile support at a FIFA conference held before the 2002 World Cup from (for some reason) Pelé. But then, he also took the opportunity to call for the outlawing of the defensive wall on the grounds that 'it's not fair'.

Torquay United

Were Torquay United to have a motto, 'By the skin of its teeth' would be most apposite. For 80 years the club has survived through a detailed history of scrapes and near-misses, the first being the very act of entering the League in 1927. After a tied first ballot Torquay prevailed at the expense of Aberdare with the help of a sympathetic scrutineer. The season 1927–28 proved a difficult initiation as Torquay finished bottom of the League (an achievement unmatched until 1985). Thereafter League life was uneventful until the mid-1950s, when, fortified by club greats Don Mills and Sammy Collins, Torquay nearly won Division 3 (South) only to lose on goal average to Alf **Ramsey**'s Ipswich Town. A few more Torquay goals and the World Cup may have never been won.

Decline followed with Torquay generously supporting the new fourth division as founder members. With one or two breaks the club has continued to support this particular institution for most of the last 45 years. (Torquay fans have rarely had the welcome distraction of a Cup run either – the club has never got past the fourth round of the FA Cup or the third round of the League Cup.)

The biggest break from the basement came in the late 1960s, the glitziest period in the club's history. With Frank O'Farrell at the helm, and Robin Stubbs as cult hero, Torquay nearly made it to Division 2. A fondly remembered era of regular 9,000 crowds, and appearances on *Match of the Day*, it was also when Torquay became 'The Gulls'.

Notwithstanding the seabird's place as foremost local public enemy the nickname persists (leading to cries of 'chip eaters' in rival circles). Torquay slumbered through the 1970s, a decade of Saturday evening kick-offs featuring the world's fastest-ever own goal (six seconds against Cambridge in 1977), only to be rudely awakened by the arrival of owner-manager-player Dave Webb in 1984. The promised revolution materialized into successive 92nd places in 1985 and 1986 (as average crowds dwindled to 1,240).

Rejuvenation came by dint of rule change. In 1987 Torquay were nearly the first team to be relegated to the Conference. Only a late goal saved the day, scored in injury time added on after midfielder Jim McNichol was attacked by a hungry police dog. Spirits lifted, the next four years saw a failed play-off attempt, a Wembley visit for the Sherpa Van, and, in 1991, promotion by play-off. This was achieved on penalties (with the goalkeeper scoring the winner) in a year that, uniquely, saw five teams promoted.

Life in a faster lane lasted one season as Torquay were relegated from Division 3 (to . . . Division 3). Unsuccessful

play-off attempts in 1994 and 1998 were punctuated by a rock-bottom performance in 1996, when only Stevenage's sub-standard ground prevented relegation. Yet some of the greatest drama has been reserved for the new century. Victory in a last day them-or-us dogfight against Barnet in 2001 saw League status maintained again. Three years later another final day victory meant Torquay's first automatic promotion for 38 years – from Division 3 to League One.

By this time, under Mike Bateson (chairman and sole owner since 1990), the club resembled a no-frills, low-cost airline that occasionally gives the public what it wants whilst sometimes leaving them grounded. Some customers complain about lack of ambition in failing to expand operations; others appreciate measured pragmatism. For a club that, ordinarily, remains one of the smallest in the lowest division it's clear that, when promotion comes, it isn't easy to add new routes. Torquay returned to the basement division in 2005.

Tottenham Hotspur

In true north London suburbanite fashion, Tottenham Hotspur have spent much of the last 20 years tantalized by aspirations towards something greater. The game is about glory, Danny **Blanchflower** told them. It's about playing 'the Spurs Way', about footballers with the flair of **Greaves**, Ardiles and **Hoddle**. Unfortunately, it's also about finishing 9th in the Premier League, about Alan Sugar (irascible vendor of satellite boxes), George **Graham** (even among dour Scots, a dour Scot) and Sergei Rebrov (£11m record signing; scorer of ten League goals in three seasons).

A financially secure club accustomed to the odd lightning strike of success, Spurs find themselves in an uncomfortable historical position, deprived of their occasional fix of glory by the increasing tendency for an elite of the four or five wealthiest clubs to dominate the domestic game. At the same time Spurs have never suffered any real period of footballing failure, having existed outside the top flight for just two post-war seasons. The result is an uneasy mix: a hankering after glory that may never come again; a perception of being a leading club that endures, albeit in fading fashion, only within Spurs' support.

Tottenham Hotspur has its roots in the Hotspur football club founded in 1882 by a group of cricketers from local schools. The name is derived from Harry 'Hotspur' Percy, a legendary medieval soldier, whose powerful Northumberland family also owned large amounts of land around what is now north London. In 1898 Spurs moved to their first and current home ground, White Hart Lane, designed by stadium architect Archibald Leitch and named after the White Hart Inn formerly on the site. Three years later they became the last non-League club to win the FA Cup, defeating four Division 1 teams in the process, and paving the way for League membership in 1908.

Spurs won the FA Cup for a second time in 1921, and went on to spend the next 30 years oscillating between Divisions 1 and 2. After winning a second League title in 1950–51 Spurs embarked on the most successful period in their history: a 27-year spell in Division 1, including the club's greatest-ever season, 1960–61, when Bill **Nicholson**'s team won the first League and Cup Double of the 20th century. Tottenham also won the FA Cup in 1962 and 1967, the European Cup Winners' Cup in 1963 – becoming in the process the first British team to win a European trophy – the League Cup in 1971 and 1973 and the UEFA Cup in 1972, a period of success characterized by the flowing style of football developed by managers Arthur Rowe and then Nicholson. They enjoyed a second purple patch under Keith Burkinshaw in the early 1980s, winning the FA Cup in 1981 and 1982, and the UEFA Cup in 1984; since when – an FA Cup win in 1991 and a League Cup in 1999 apart – events off the field at White Hart Lane have made more headlines than any success on the pitch.

Financial near-collapse after flotation on the stock market in 1983 (an exasperated Burkinshaw departed a year later famously saying, 'There used to be a football club over there') was followed a decade later by the protracted dismissal of manager Terry **Venables**, with attendant court case and allegations of shady dealing all round. Under the uneasy stewardship of chairman Alan Sugar, short-term managerial eccentrics Ossie Ardiles and Christian Gross came and went before Sugar eventually sold his controlling stake in the club to leisure company ENIC, precipitating another acrimonious managerial departure as George Graham was sacked after making comments about a lack of transfer funds during a television interview.

The return of Glenn Hoddle to White Hart Lane as manager may have failed to inspire a return to trophy-winning form, but Hoddle's spell in charge, which ended in 2003, did serve to emphasize the reverence in which the club's many distinguished former players are held. Tottenham have a long tradition of celebrated star players. Weaned on the Double-winning team of Blanchflower, Cliff Jones and Bobby Smith, through to Ardiles, Hoddle and Waddle during the 1980s, and the more recent exploits of **Gascoigne**, **Lineker** and Ginola, Spurs supporters have tended to delight in skilful attacking footballers, and their teams have always boasted a dispro-portionately large number of inter-national players – another reason, perhaps, for the mild sense of unfulfilled ambition that is currently the club's defining feature. In January 1975 an inter-view in *Shoot!* magazine with future club captain and holder of the club record for appearances, Steve Perryman, ended with the lament, 'Spurs are one of the greatest clubs in soccer and it's high time we proved it by finally winning the title.' Two seasons later they were relegated.

Tranmere Rovers

Contrary to what some think, Tranmere are not Liverpool's 'third club'. Formed in 1884, and League members since 1921, they are based in Birkenhead on the Wirral peninsula, an area with a distinct identity separate from that of the city on the opposite side of the Mersey. But while so many of the Wirral's football fans continue to support Liverpool or Everton, Rovers will always be the poor relations.

Two locally born goalscorers were the stars of the club's early League history. Dixie **Dean** began his career at Tran-mere aged 16 in 1923, while Robert 'Bunny' Bell's 104 goals in 114 League appearances included nine in the team's League record 13–4 win over Oldham Athletic in 1935. Bell followed Dean to Everton but with little success.

Aside from one season in Division 2 in 1938–39, Tranmere were confined to the bottom division until the League's reorganization in 1958, after which they spent three years at the third level. By the time they were promoted again in 1966–67, the club's gates, which had been a healthy five figures in mid-decade, had started to wane. Rovers remained in Division 3 for all but one of the next 12 seasons and had the occasional triumph

– a team containing future FA chief executive Mark Palios won at Arsenal in the League Cup in 1973–74; two years earlier a record gate of 24,424 had seen a 2–2 draw with Stoke City in the FA Cup fourth round. But the early 1970s also saw the rise of Liverpool as one of the best teams in Europe. Despite playing on Friday nights to avoid clashing with the two big neighbours, Rovers' support began to melt away.

Tranmere's decline reached its lowest point during 1982–83 with the club in the re-election zone in Division 4, and weeks away from closure. A £200,000 loan from Wirral Council, and fund-raising matches against Liverpool and others, kept Rovers afloat. For the next few years they limped along, with games attracting between 1,500 and 2,000 – barely enough to keep the club alive – despite finishing tenth in 1984 and sixth the following year. In 1986–87, bankrupcy was averted by the intervention of Wirral businessman and Liverpool season ticket holder Peter Johnson, who brought back former manager John King for his second spell with the club.

Going into the last game without a win in nine, the team looked destined for relegation to the Conference, but King's collection of non-League free transfers, old pros and youngsters (including long-term fans' favourite, winger John Morrissey) got the victory they needed against Exeter. The victory triggered a pitch invasion by most of the 7,000 fans in the ground.

Revitalized by Johnson's cash, the club entered the best period in their history, being promoted twice then reaching the Division 1 play-offs three years running. In 1999–2000 John Aldridge's team lost to Leicester City in the League Cup Final and got to the last eight of the FA Cup. The latter feat was repeated the following year (Rovers beating Everton

3–0 away in the fourth round and coming back from three down to defeat Southampton 4–3 before losing to Liverpool), but they lost almost all of the backlog of matches built up during their cup runs and were relegated. Peter Johnson had left to take over Everton in 1994, but four years after he had supposedly sold Tranmere to chairman Frank Corfe, it transpired that, contrary to League rules, he still owned the club. Johnson finally sold his stake in Everton, where he had been hugely unpopular, in 1999, and he has been largely an absentee owner since, having previously appointed his one-time partner Lorraine Rogers as the club's chief executive.

In 2002 Chester owner Stephen Vaughan announced plans to merge his club with Tranmere. It was reported that Rovers would be forced to sell Prenton Park, their home since 1912, to pay the £5.3 million owed to owner Peter Johnson but that Vaughan would build a new stadium in Birkenhead on the site of the Cammell Laird shipyard, once the town's main employer. Vaughan backed down after supporter opposition and the club remains in Johnson's control. After several moderate seasons at the third level, the team has recently been revived by manager Brian Little.

travel

By the 1980s the expanding train network enabled fans to travel relatively cheaply to distant matches. As cities once grew up around rivers, so clubs started to develop near train stations. Spurs, Aston Villa, QPR and Arsenal were among teams who, in part, owe their sturdy development to a good strategic positioning in railway terms. Despite the cheapness and availability of the train services, though, there was still no nationwide away support of any

significant and sustained numbers because for many it would have meant forfeiting half-day wages on Saturday morning.

Big matches such as the first Wembley FA Cup Final and England v Scotland games saw fans brought in on large-scale, highly organized railway operations, including special service trains; by the end of the 1930s, supporters were travelling further to see their team and in larger numbers. For the FA Cup semi-final of 1979 between Man Utd and Liverpool, six football special trains, or Footexes – a total of nigh on 150 coaches – were made available to each set of supporters. Not all hard-core fans travelled on the Footex. Infamous outfits such as the Inter-City Firm (West Ham), Service Crew (Leeds) and 6.57 Crew (Portsmouth) derived their names from the trains they took to avoid the police escort on the specials. A large host of away fans swarming through an alien town centre, terrorizing shoppers outside Timothy White's, was a familiar spectacle throughout the 1970s. Train travel was also responsible for the tradition, now largely lost, of toilet rolls pinched from Footex WCs being hurled on to the pitch from behind the goal.

The railways' association with hooliganism continues as, with increased security inside the grounds, much of today's football-related violence now occurs on the railway platforms of Britain, where opposing fans ambush each other or, more convivially, arrange beforehand to turn up and fight.

By the 1960s, increased car ownership, improved coach travel and station closures began the football special's decline, which was accelerated by the railways' redeployment of rolling stock and their reaction to hooliganism on the trains in the 1970s. Nowadays the preferred way to get to the game is by car or air-conditioned coach and the clubs, like the big out-of-town supermarkets, are gradually moving away from the residential areas to the outskirts, where there is plenty of room to lay out the 21st century hyper-car-park.

Away games are still a big commitment, however. Newcastle United fans making their way to every away game in a season can expect to pay around £1,000 in petrol over a total distance of 8,500 miles.

trophies

Football has given out silver cups to its winning teams since the very earliest days, following in the established tradition of sports such as horse-racing. The first cup in football history – the FA Cup – is still its most famous, although the current shape of the trophy dates only from 1911. The original cup (known as the 'little tin idol') was bought for £20 in 1872 by the FA's visionary secretary, Charles Alcock. It was stolen from a Birmingham shop window after Aston Villa's victory in 1895 – one of the thieves confessed, but not until 1958, when he was 83. The second was withdrawn after it was discovered pirate copies had been made. The cup has survived ill-treatment at the hands of many a holder (Wimbledon left it locked in a car boot overnight after their 1988 victory), not to mention the ritual 'lid-on-head' routine of the class clown in each winning side as it is paraded after the Final.

The World Cup itself has never been a cup, although the original art deco Jules Rimet trophy (a rare football prize made of gold, rather than silver) portrayed an allegorical figure of 'winged victory' holding up an eight-sided chalice. The Jules Rimet survived the Second World War hidden in a shoebox under the bed of FIFA's vice-president, Ottorino Barassi. It was saved again by the most famous dog in football history, Pickles, after being stolen from a London exhibition before the 1966 tournament. But thieves finally got their hands on it for good after it was given to Brazil in recognition of their third World Cup triumph in 1970.

Of the other significant international trophies, the European Cup ('the cup with the big ears') is undoubtedly the largest, although the hefty Copa America is even harder to lift, having no handles. The number of pots available to British teams has steadily increased since the introduction of the (cutely three-handled) League Cup in 1961, although even the most devoted fan would have trouble identifying the defunct Watney Cup, Texaco Cup, Full Members' Cup (the latter was appropriately modest in size), or even the trophy that is incongruously handed to winners of the play-offs. The Community Shield (formerly Charity Shield) and FA Vase still fly the flag for non-cup-shaped awards.

Most shabbily treated of the old cups has been the ornate monster that used to accompany the League championship. First usurped by modernist atrocities when the League was sponsored in the 1980s (the black phallic affair awarded to the winners of the Canon League stood out), it was downgraded altogether by the advent of the Premiership in 1992, which spawned yet another new trophy, complete with a slightly child-like crown effect. The prize for the most ludicrous trophy on offer must surely go to the Intertoto Cup, however, for its size (tiny), design (a tennis ball on a stick) and quantity, with three given out each year to the 'winners', who qualify for the UEFA Cup.

UEFA

The Union des Associations Européennes de Football – UEFA – was founded in the Swiss city of Basle on 15 June 1954. The organization was the brainchild of Frenchman Henri Delaunay (who was appointed the first general secretary), and set up with the help of Ottorino Barassi, the Italian vice-president of FIFA and the Belgian José Crahay.

The trio wanted to create an umbrella organization to preside over European football, working as a confederation of FIFA and promoting and developing the game within the continent. Delaunay had been keen on the idea for some years; he had been pushing for a cup competition for European clubs as far back as the late 1920s (he also had plans for a European nations' tournament).

FIFA had been in existence exactly 50 years before the Europeans finally got together (the South Americans had formed the Confederación Sudamericana de Fútbol in 1916). Things moved quickly: within a year the first European Champion Clubs' Cup and Inter-Cities Fairs Cup, the forerunners of the Champions' League and UEFA Cup, were up and running. Sadly, Delaunay wasn't around to see his long-cherished vision take shape. The Frenchman died within a year of the opening of UEFA's original offices. Delaunay's son Pierre took over, retiring at the end of the decade.

Delaunay junior, combining his new role with that of general secretary of the French FA, had teamed up with Gabriel Hanot, editor of sports paper *L'Équipe*, to sell the idea of club competitions among the 25 national associations then under UEFA's wing. The number has since increased to 52. Most were enthusiastic about the idea – some, however, were not.

The English FA in particular reacted to the French with haughty disdain, unhappy at the thought that their standing as founders of the modern game stood to be undermined (FIFA received similar short shrift in its formative years). The 1955 League champions Chelsea were advised not to take part in the inaugural tournament; Matt **Busby**'s Manchester United, similarly expected to refuse UEFA's invitation the following year, famously went against the FA's wishes, becoming the first English club to enter the competition.

In 1958 qualification rounds for the first European Nations' Cup got underway. The finals would be held in France in 1960 (and the trophy itself named after Henri Delaunay). Just 17 teams took part but the tournament grew in stature – and size – as the decade wore on. The club competitions caught the imagination from the off; the European Cup, as it was now known, enjoying something of a golden age in the 1960s and 1970s, with the successes of Celtic and Manchester United cementing its appeal in the once sceptical Home Nations, and making the FA's previous reluctance to get involved look ever more blinkered.

Clubs like Ajax, Barcelona, Real Madrid, Juventus and Milan became household names. European nights were glamorous, exciting and different. UEFA went through the 1980s and into the 1990s with high hopes, presided over by the Arsenal-supporting Swedish president Lennart Johansson, who fought his corner in a series of disputes with FIFA president Sepp Blatter (Johansson is also a vice-president of the international federation).

But UEFA now enjoys an uneasy relationship with the larger European clubs, torn as it is between the need to promote the best of the continent, and a duty to protect the wishes of other members. Things were thrown into sharp relief in the early 1990s with the forma-

tion of G14, a lobby group representing clubs keen to maximize revenue from broadcasting rights, and instrumental in the formation of the Champions' League (having grown impatient at UEFA's heel-dragging over the mini-league format).

At the same time, UEFA found itself caught up in a succession of court cases, as Belgian footballer Jean-Marc **Bosman** sought to use European Union employment legislation to become a free agent, allowing him to move to a club once his contract was up without the need for a transfer fee. Bosman won, catching a complacent UEFA on the hop and adding another serious dent in the organization's credibility.

Recent proposals, like the mandatory inclusion of four home-grown players in every squad, have rattled G14 further, and look set to incur the disapproval of the EU law lords once again. If anything, UEFA has become something of a victim of its own success; the wealth and power of European clubs has grown to such an extent that they now pose a very real threat to the organization's authority. Having come so far in such a relatively short space of time, the next few years could prove crucial to the UEFA; in danger of looking increasingly toothless, it has to keep in check the more excessive tendencies of the G14 members if it is to continue to govern the European game.

UEFA Cup

The UEFA Cup began life as the Fairs Cup, a competition for cities that hosted trade fairs, a criterion described by French film director Louis Malle as like having 'a tournament for cities with brothels'. If only UEFA had ideas that good.

Starting life in 1955 as the tortuously named International Inter-City Industrial

Fairs Cup, the first tournament was equally drawn out as it took the ten entrants, including a London select side, three years to drag the tournament to a two-legged final, Barcelona beating the English capital 8–2 on aggregate.

The next competition, which abolished the group stage of its predecessor and became a straight knockout over two legs, was finished in just two years, Barcelona again trumping English opponents in the form of Birmingham City. From then on, however, the Cup was annual and drew increasing numbers of entrants. By the end of the 1960s qualification was based on domestic league position rather than fortuitous fairs, with the more competitive leagues allowed to enter a greater number of teams. A one club–one city rule, which was dropped in the 1970s, allowed the 1968–69 winners, Newcastle, to qualify for the competition despite having finished only 10th in the league, below both Liverpool clubs and three from London.

Spanish sides dominated the early to mid-1960s, Valencia winning twice and Barcelona and Zaragoza once apiece, until Leeds (in both 1968 and 1971), Newcastle, Arsenal, Spurs (in an all-English 1972 final versus Wolves) and Liverpool (3–2 over two games against the fine Borussia Mönchengladbach team that included Gunther Netzer) took the trophy off the mainland for six successive years. By this time the cup had become the UEFA Cup, Barcelona and Leeds having played off to decide who kept the Fairs Cup in a one-off game in the Catalan capital that the home side won 2–1.

Mönchengladbach finally laid hands on the trophy in 1975, beating Twente Enschede 5–1 in the away leg, with a hat-trick for Jupp Heynckes, after they had only drawn 0–0 at home. Between that and the German side's second triumph, over Red Star Belgrade in 1979, Liverpool were winners again, to be followed by Ipswich in 1981 and Tottenham for the second time in 1984, beating Anderlecht on penalties, although that was the end of English success for almost two decades.

In the 1980s and early 1990s the competition began to become a victim of its own success. Compared with the European Champions' Cup and Cup Winners' Cup, the winners had to negotiate an extra round and generally much stronger teams in the later stages, and it was viewed as the toughest of the three competitions. The absorbing Juventus–Dortmund final of 1993, when the Turin side came back from a first leg 3–1 reverse to take the tie 4–3, was probably the last time the cup will be fought for by two such high-ranking opponents.

Meanwhile Bayern Munich whined, upon being knocked out in the first round of the 1996–97 competition by Valencia, that it was financially not worth their while to take part. The Champions' League was to be expanded so that clubs like Bayern were virtually guaranteed qualification and a certain number of income-generating European fixtures. The UEFA Cup took in domestic cup-winners after the demise of the Cup Winners' Cup, and changed to a single-game final at a neutral venue in 1998. Even a see-saw 5–4 thriller in Dortmund between Liverpool and Alaves of Spain in the 2001 final could not disguise the fact that UEFA now regarded their own creation as something of an inconvenience. For the 2004–05 model they introduced an unwieldy group stage between round one and the last 16, thus completing the financially driven homogenization of their three once unique knock-out contests.

Terry Venables

Terry Venables was the first English player to represent his country at every possible level, from schoolboy and amateur through to full international. He won the Spanish title in his first season at Barcelona and led the England team to its best-ever performance at a European Championships; and his tactical prowess, particularly in organizing a defence, is generally regarded as being of the highest class.

Unfortunately, Venables is also the only England manager ever to resign from his post because of the muddy personal details set to be showcased in a high-profile trial related to financial irregularities. He is also the only disqualified company director ever to be indirectly accused of accepting bribes to sign players while also being involved in a courtroom battle with Tottenham Hotspur. A tangle of complex accusations and counter-accusations seems to have followed Venables wherever he has managed in recent times, much of it painstakingly detailed in the biography, *False Messiah*, by Mihir Bose, the title of which says more about the state of English football over the last 20 years than about the man himself. But, everybody loves a showman and Venables has certainly been one of those.

Born in Dagenham in 1943, Venables began his playing career as a right-half at Chelsea, making his debut as a 16-year-old, captaining the team a year later and playing 202 League games in total. He made his England debut in 1964, winning two caps as a 21-year-old and never playing for the national team again, before moving to Tottenham in 1966. Moves to Queens Park Rangers and Crystal Palace followed; he became the latter's first-team coach in 1976, in succession to his early managerial mentor, Malcolm **Allison**.

Venables went on to win promotion to Division 1 with the Palace team that was briefly but famously hailed as the 'Team of the '80s' (in a newspaper article by a friend of the manager, Jeff Powell of the *Daily Mail*). He moved to Queens Park Rangers, taking the club to the 1982 FA Cup Final as a Division 2 club, then to fifth place in the top division. This was followed by the mind-boggling step up from Loftus Road to the Nou Camp in May 1984. A year later, 'El Tel' took Barcelona to their first Spanish League title in 11 years, and the season after to the final of the European Cup, where they would lose on penalties to Steaua Bucharest. Following a second-place League finish, Venables was sacked in September 1987 and appointed manager of Tottenham Hotspur a month later.

Despite an FA Cup win in 1991, and despite bringing players such as Paul **Gascoigne** and Gary **Lineker** to White Hart Lane, Venables's purchase of the club in partnership with Alan Sugar would prove disastrous. Within three years the two had fallen out, leading to lengthy, acrimonious and very tedious court cases, and subsequent investigations into Venables's financial dealings. What went wrong? At the age of 17 Venables had made himself a limited company, one whose stated aim was 'to exploit the talents of Terence Venables'. But what are those talents exactly? Over the years Venables has dissipated his energies into countless business ventures. A glance at the index of his biography gives a résumé under 'Venables, Terry': 'business ventures . . . marriages . . . music performance . . . writing . . . plans to take over Tottenham Hotspur . . . breakdown of partnership . . . ousted from Tottenham Hotspur . . . court cases . . . financial investigation . . . becomes England manager'.

Venables has been a coach, a big-band crooner, a novelist, a board game inventor (he helped to create a game called *Manager*), a successful businessman, a failed businessman, a nightclub owner, a bankrupt businessman, a TV pundit and manager of the England football team. He remained in the England job for two years, playing a lot of friendlies and taking a talented team to the semi-finals of Euro 96, where they lost to Germany on penalties. Venables then resigned in order to fight more murky and tedious court cases, effectively signalling the end of his credible coaching career.

Spells at Crystal Palace (disastrous), Middlesbrough (saved Bryan **Robson**'s men from relegation) and at the moribund Leeds United ('Ell Tel') proved staging posts on the path to semi-retired TV punditry. Venables may have been a great coach. But thanks mainly to his own litany of self-generated distractions, no-one will ever know quite how good he could have been.

Wales

The history of the Welsh national football team is one of consistent failure to over-achieve. Wales is one of the smaller nations in FIFA. It has no professional national league and, for most of the last hundred years, rugby union has been promoted within Wales as its national sport (although football has always been more popular). Wales won six Home International Championships during the inter-war period but they have failed to reach the finals of a major tourna-ment since 1958 despite consistently producing excellent players. Among those never to have competed at an inter-national finals, the principality can boast Ryan **Giggs**, Ian **Rush**, Mark Hughes and Neville Southall.

Wales have qualified for the finals of the World Cup just once. At the 1958 tournament in Sweden a fine Welsh side containing the prodigious John **Charles** at centre-back and Ivor **Allchurch** at inside-left, reached the quarter-finals of the competition. Wales had come from behind to beat a great Hungary team 2–1 in a group stage qualifying play-off, and at that stage had a fair chance of winning the trophy. However, they lost 1–0 to Brazil in Malmö in the knockout stages, the 17-year-old Pelé scoring the winner.

A Wales team featuring John Toshack, Terry Yorath and Leighton James reached the last eight of the 1976 Euro-pean Championship after topping their qualifying group, but were then beaten 3–1 over two legs by Yugoslavia. Since then, there have been several near misses. The mid-1980s side included Neville Southall, Kevin Ratcliffe and Pat Van Den Hauwe of the championship-winning Everton team, as well as the attacking partnership of all-time leading scorer Ian Rush (28 goals) and Mark Hughes.

As ever, there were problems with depth in the squad and with consistent quality in every position. The team beat Spain 3–0 in a World Cup qualifier in 1985, but then failed to get the win they needed against Scotland after conceding a late penalty. In November 1993 Wales had to defeat Romania in their final qualifying game at home to reach the World Cup finals in the USA. Paul Bodin had the chance to put them ahead just after the hour but hit the bar from the penalty spot. Wales lost 2–1.

A period of decline saw the likes of Vinnie Jones play for Wales – complete with newly acquired dragon tattoo – and a consistent plummeting in the FIFA world rankings, aided by thrashings in Holland (7–1) and Georgia (5–0). A mini-renaissance under the management of Mark Hughes was suggested by a short run of excellent results in 2002–03, including a home victory over Italy. But the fact remains that Wales are punching their weight in international football and no more. A presence at a major finals looks no nearer and under the current seeding rules a dramatic improvement will be required if Wales are to qualify from groups.

Walsall

Founder members of the Football League Division 2 in 1892, Walsall Town Swifts changed their name to plain Walsall three years later. 'The Saddlers' – leather had been the town's main industry – have spent their entire League history in the shadow of Aston Villa and Birmingham City to the south and West Bromwich Albion and Wolverhampton Wanderers to the west.

Given that Walsall have spent just nine of those 117 years outside football's lower leagues it is perhaps not surprising that most of the town's residents have opted to support its more successful neighbours. A few thousand loyal supporters have enjoyed a handful of promotions and the odd cup run and just one championship (Division 4 in 1959–60). Some may yet be scarred by the club's awful run of 15 successive defeats during the 1988–89 season in the old Division 2, which culminated in a 7–0 home loss to Chelsea. Four years earlier the club had reached the semi-finals of the League Cup, losing 4–2 on aggregate to Liverpool having knocked out Arsenal.

Another victory over Arsenal is still regarded as the the club's finest hour. It came in 1933, when Walsall beat the reigning champions 2–0 in the third round of the FA Cup. This remains one of the greatest shocks in the history of the competition. 'Is it not really a dream that I shall awake and smile at?' asked the correspondent from the *South Staffordshire Advertiser*. Replica match programmes are still on sale in the club shop and one of the Walsall goalscorers on that day, Gilbert Alsop, has lent his name to the ground's main stand. When a recent sponsorship deal resulted in a name change for the stand there was uproar amongst the supporters, even though very few would have ever seen Alsop play.

It is possible that every person in the country has seen the stand that created this ill-feeling. Walsall's Bescot Stadium is located literally next to the M6 motorway at the point where it becomes one of the busiest roads in Western Europe. The ground itself was built in 1990 after Walsall relocated from the dilapidated Fellows Park. At the time this was quite a novel move for a football club, and possibly premature when other clubs of a similar size have built bigger and better grounds in subsequent years (identically designed stands on each side give the Bescot the appearance of a pool table when viewed from the air).

The move was a great commercial success, however: the facilities have since generated a stable cash flow and Walsall have bucked the trend for smaller clubs in consistently recording healthy profits. This has translated to success on the field with promotions to Division 1 in 1999 and 2001, both under manager Ray Graydon, who was harshly sacked during the 2001–02 season. Colin Lee and Paul Merson have since taken charge of a team that quickly slipped back to mid-table in the third level, before being relegated to League Two in 2005–06.

Finally it should be noted that Walsall have led the way in introducing one important aspect of the match day experience to the football community. In 1997 the Balti pie was launched at Bescot and has gone on to be sold at many grounds across the country. At a time when one in five adults across the UK is classed as clinically obese perhaps this is not something to be proud of.

Watford

There may be some confusion over the precise birth-date of Watford FC, but there is complete clarity – symmetry almost – over the 80-odd years the club has subsequently spent in the Football League. Effectively 40 years bouncing around doing nothing much, followed by 40 years making up for it.

That first period was spent in Division 3 (South) and save for the odd near miss, neither promotion, nor failure to achieve re-election, were ever seriously threatened. But having stayed put for almost 40 years, the club has subsequently experienced either promotion or relegation on no fewer than 12 occasions.

Following a successful spell in the Southern League, Watford joined

Division 3 in 1920 and moved to their current home at Vicarage Road a year later. Proof of this remains – just about – in the creaking form of the original main stand. Partly condemned by Health and Safety, and unable any longer to seriously contribute towards the ground's reduced capacity, it nevertheless serves as a useful reminder of the club's predominantly lower-division heritage.

Watford have racked up some outstanding achievements in the last 30 years, but one record will simply never be beaten. On Saturday 30 August 1975, they lost 1–0 at Darlington and fell to the bottom of Division 4. Just seven years later, on 11 September 1982, West Brom were beaten 3–0 in front of a disbelieving Vicarage Road crowd, to take the club to the top of Division 1. That extraordinary season ended with Watford finishing runners-up to Liverpool, having edged in front of Manchester United by beating the champions on the final day.

The chairman/manager combination of Elton John and Graham **Taylor** had come together to make all things possible at the old ground on a gravel pit which has, incidentally, opened up on occasions, to reveal the original earth-workings below: once, during the 1930s, it is said, to a depth such that it could have comfortably accommodated a horse and cart.

Taylor joined from Lincoln in 1977 and, the team, based largely around the free-scoring exploits of Luther Blissett and Ross Jenkins, immediately claimed successive promotions. Three more years saw top-division status being achieved and then comfortably maintained for the five years that he remained at Watford. The FA Cup Final was reached and unconsidered victories won – Sunderland thrashed 8–0 in the League, Southampton beaten 7–1 to overturn a 4–0 first-leg deficit in the League Cup,

Manchester United swamped 5–1 at Vicarage Road, Kaiserslautern swept aside 3–0 to progress in the UEFA Cup – and so it went on until Taylor cried enough.

The following year, 1987–88, relegation was suffered and the fun was effectively over – at least until Taylor returned in 1997. Once again he achieved successive promotions, this time delivering a workmanlike Watford side into the Premiership via a Wembley play-off victory over Bolton. Fine wins over Chelsea and at Liverpool failed to paper over the yawning cracks and they swiftly returned whence they came. Taylor departed once again – this time for good – at which point the wheels came off completely.

The club, suffering from acute board-room delusions of grandeur, appointed Gianluca Vialli as manager, in a futile attempt to regain Premiership status. An arrogant managerial style was entirely inappropriate for the homely Hertford-shire outfit and his overpaid squad simply went through the motions. After just one dreadful season, Vialli left the club in tatters. The ground was sold and immediately leased back, in a desperate attempt to remain nominally solvent, while the better-paid players mostly drifted away. The club was saved by the emergence of chairman and long-term fan Graham Simpson. Under manager Adrian Boothroyd, the team were promoted to the Premier League in 2006, after beating Leeds in the Championship play-off final.

The foundations are now firmly in place for a thoroughly decent, community-based club to emerge from the ruins. But whether Watford will ever repeat 1982–83, discover another John Barnes on the doorstep and finish ahead of modern football's Big Three remains to be seen.

Welsh Cup

If two creations of 1876, the national team and the Football Association of Wales, have given Welsh football its insti-tutional continuity, the competitive thread was supplied a year later with the creation of the Welsh Cup. Wrexham beat Druids 1–0 in the first final and these two clubs dominated the early decades before football spread to the industrial south, Wrexham winning nine times and Druids (based at Ruabon, five miles outside Wrexham) eight before Cardiff City became the first southern winners in 1912. While Druids' last final was in 1904, Wrexham remained the most consistent competitors, appearing in a record 44 finals and winning 22, the same number of victories as Cardiff City.

The competition lost something of its standing in the inter-war years as the strongest clubs progressed in the English system, Cardiff winning the FA Cup in 1927, a year after Swansea had reached the semi-final. Open from its foundation to clubs from just across the border, the Cup was held by English clubs from 1933 to 1947, and has left Wales 19 times in all. It was given a fresh dimension, encouraging the Welsh Football League clubs to treat it more seriously, when the winners were admitted to the European Cup Winners' Cup from 1961 onwards. Cardiff City enjoyed an unprecedented period of dominance with ten victories in 13 seasons from 1964 and earned a considerable European reputation for Cup Winners' Cup performances which peaked in a semi-final in 1968. Swansea's total of ten wins includes a hat-trick (1981–83) during its purple patch under John Toshack.

There was, though, a corresponding loss of status when clubs who play in the English system were excluded after 1995, although winners continue to qualify for

Europe – going into the UEFA Cup once the Cup Winners' Cup was abolished in 1999. Since 1997 it has faced competition from the made-for-television FAW Premier Cup, which includes the Football League clubs and was won five times in its first seven seasons by Wrexham.

Welsh Premier League

The Welsh Premier League, known from its formation in 1992 until 2004 as the League of Wales, epitomizes a national talent for turning unifying projects into sources of divisiveness. A national league, ending a north–south division as old as football in Wales by merging the best of the (southern) Welsh League and (northern) Cymru Alliance, was undoubtedly overdue. The problem was the Football Association of Wales's accompanying attempt to dragoon members of the English non-League pyramid into the new league, forcing clubs like Newport into exile and immediately alienating supporters of those clubs and the three Football League teams.

The League has enabled Welsh representation in Europe to be extended from one Cup Winners' Cup entrant to four in all competitions, but with limited playing success – three victories, all by Barry Town, in 56 ties. Barry, who also beat Cardiff City to take the Welsh Cup in 1994 and Wrexham to win the 1999 FAW Premier Cup, have been the outstanding team. They won seven titles between 1996 and 2003 before a spectacular implosion and relegation to the Welsh League – with the Cymru Alliance a feeder league – in 2004. Founder champions Cwmbran, Bangor City (twice), Total Network Solutions (formerly Llansantffraid) and, in 2003–04, Rhyl, have won the other titles. If most championships have gone south, north and mid-Wales predominate numerically,

providing 12 of 18 teams in 2004–05. Facilities have undoubtedly improved, but crowds remain small, rarely reaching four figures.

Wales defender Mark Delaney, who started at Carmarthen, is the most significant player to emerge from the competition, along with two notable lower-division strikers, Eifion Williams – who scored 131 goals in 135 games for Caernarfon before joining Torquay then Hartlepool – and Lee Trundle, whose exotic ball-skills were displayed at Rhyl before Wrexham and Swansea. In January 2005 Marc Lloyd Williams (of TNS) became the first player to score 200 goals, the majority for Bangor.

Wembley

The idea of a national stadium for English football existed long before Wembley, but the two became synonymous in the second half of the 20th century. Some may feel the concept should have been put to rest before so much time, money and anguish were spent on rebuilding the famous old stadium at the start of the 21st.

England's devotion to a national stadium, not shared by most other European countries, stemmed from the special place of the FA Cup in its history and the decision from the start to play the final at a neutral venue. After the Oval, the Crystal Palace Stadium was the first long-term venue, though several other stadiums were planned (and, like Stamford Bridge, even built) with the intention of usurping its role. Nevertheless, the Palace was never envisaged as the permanent home of the national team, and nor was Wembley in its early years – between its construction in 1923 and the Second World War, only seven England games were played there, all against Scotland. Even in the 1950s and 1960s England appeared sporadically at other venues, such as Hillsborough, Highbury and even Molineux. As late as 1966 they played Poland at Goodison Park (as a warm-up for a possible World Cup semi-final there), the last England home match away from Wembley until they met Sweden at Elland Road in 1995.

Although often mooted as a possible club ground (Arsenal even played their home European games there in the late 1990s, with unsatisfying results), Wembley has never attracted a regular tenant. In the days before the League Cup, play-offs and European finals, therefore, football at Wembley was a very occasional event. Built as the centrepiece of the British Empire Exhibition (hence the official name of the Empire Stadium), it seemed likely to live on as a vast white elephant after the exhibition closed in 1925.

The stadium was saved not by football but by the fortuitous arrival of greyhound racing, which was an instant success when it began in Britain in 1927. As well as the mainstay of the dogs, the private company that owned Wembley has always relied on other events for survival: the rugby league Challenge Cup final, speedway, horse shows (which ruined the pitch for the 1970 FA Cup Final) and rock concerts. It also took centre stage as London hosted the Olympics, memorably but austerely, in 1948.

But while dog racing paid the bills, it was only thanks to football that Wembley came to mean something quite different from, say, Neasden. The place had an indefinable aura, bequeathed in part by the drama of the first Cup Final (though that might just as easily have ended in tragedy) and of the great events linked with it since: Scotland's Wembley Wizards of 1928, the Matthews final of

1953, the Hungarian triumph in the same year, European wins for West Ham (1965), Manchester United (1968) and Liverpool (1978) and, of course, England's 1966 World Cup win.

Yet its past was never quite as grand as the legend suggested. Foreign vistors genuinely loved it and feared it; English fans who visited more often loved it, too, but also hated it for its grossly inadequate sightlines and facilities. Nor did it have the one great redeeming feature of the old Crystal Palace, a dramatic setting. Fans were pictured on TV each year arriving excitely for the Cup Final, but never leaving it for the deflating walk through the dismal surrounding landscape of light industry and suburban shops, or even (in earlier days) staying on for the evening greyhound races. Like its cheap construction of concrete made to look like masonry, the old Wembley was tackier than the ceremonial surrounding its grand occasions suggested.

In the 1990s the stadium's vital link with the Cup Final lost much of its appeal. The replacement of the terracing with seats after the **Taylor Report** reduced its traditional capacity of 100,000 by a fifth. The vast increase in the number of televised matches diminished the final's special status, as did the decision to play semi-finals at Wembley, beginning with Tottenham v Arsenal in 1991. Some of the pomposity went out of Cup Final day, but it was replaced mostly by cheap and irritating gimmicks such as fireworks and noisy DJs. A new low was reached when Cliff Richard massacred *Abide With Me* before the 1997 final.

The dismal circumstances of Wembley's last international, England's miserable, rain-soaked 1–0 defeat by Germany in Kevin **Keegan**'s last match in charge in October 2000, summed up the condition to which it had sunk in the eyes of many fans. Even the media's frenetic (and unsuccessful) campaign to save Wembley's landmark Twin Towers in its reconstruction never generated much popular enthusiasm.

Wembley was at its best when a spark of genius or unexpected informality pierced its stiff ways: Stanley **Matthews** and Puskás, George **Best** and Geoff **Hurst**, of course. But other less revered names are also indelibly linked with the stadium: Poland's goalkeeper Jan Tomaszewski, whose saves eliminated England in their 1973 World Cup qualifier; unheralded FA Cup heroes such as Roger Osborne, Keith Houchen and Jim Montgomery; rugby league's inconsolable Don Fox after missing what would have been the winning kick in the 1968 Challenge Cup final; even Eddie Cavanagh.

Wembley as a place may have looked much better on TV than in real life. But as an ideal it had a magic unsurpassed by any other stadium. For Scotland fans it represented a citadel to be stormed every two years (an idea taken rather too literally when the goalposts were abruptly dismantled and the turf dug up after their 2–1 win in 1977) until the end of that regular date in 1989. For English club fans it was the end of the Cup rainbow, a journey celebrated or earnestly wished for in countless songs, with rhyming possibilities that Cardiff can never match. And for all England fans it was Nobby Stiles and Alf **Ramsey**, Geoff Hurst and Bobby **Moore**, Tofik Bakhramov and Kenneth Wolstenholme, one sunny afternoon.

For all its diverse appeal, Wembley missed its best chance to become a national sports stadium, capable of staging international events in all sports. That came in the 1990s, when its dilapidated condition, advances in stadium technology and Britain's lack of a remotely suitable venue even for the

athletics world championships, let alone the Olympics, offered the chance of public funds being used to reinvent what had always been a privately owned concern.

The saga of choosing a city for the national stadium in the mid-1990s – Manchester, Birmingham, Sheffield and Bradford also offered themselves – and the appalling mess of the plans to rebuild Wembley once it had been selected, will no doubt be told at suitable length when it is over (a West End musical may prove to be the most appropriate format). Suffice to say here that it led to the closure of Wembley for at least six years, the tarnishing of reputations in the Labour government and in football's administration – the former FA chief Adam Crozier and Ken Bates among them – and the building of a stadium that may prove as frustratingly imperfect as its predecessor.

In the 1995 edition of his definitive *The Football Grounds of Britain* (published when Wembley was fighting it out with Manchester for national stadium rights), Simon Inglis offered three compelling reasons why Wembley should survive as the venue for cup finals and internationals, even after the chance to incorporate athletics facilities had been butchered: first, it could offer a capacity far in excess of even the biggest club ground; second, the FA Cup was such a distinctive English tradition that it must have a neutral venue; and third, Wembley was in the area best placed to handle huge crowds, especially by public transport.

But in the years that Wembley has been a building site, circumstances have changed. Several club grounds have been dramatically enlarged and new ones built or planned (in 1995, Old Trafford was the second-biggest football ground in England and Wales, with a capacity of only 55,000). The Cup has shrunk tragically in stature, thanks largely to the flippant attitude towards it of the biggest clubs and even, pathetically, the FA itself. Taking England internationals around the country again has proved extraordinarily popular. And, above all, Cardiff's Millennium Stadium has shown that another city and another stadium are perfectly capable of handling the big events.

England will again have a national stadium, but whether it needs one is not much clearer than it was in 1923. As a result Wembley faces a struggle to regain that old aura, no matter how stunning the construction of the new stadium proves.

Arsène Wenger

Arsène Wenger is the latest in a select line of great Arsenal managers. Appointed in September 1996, Wenger has transformed not only the fortunes and the structure of the club, but basic English notions of how teams can be run and players managed. Wenger's reign at Arsenal has proved to be the most significant single part of the opening up of English football's borders. Forcibly assimilated into an insular League by the sheer weight of his domestic success, he was the first to provide a definitive template for the progressive domestic coach. This is a state of affairs that would have seemed highly unlikely while he was leading Nagoya Grampus Eight to second place in the Japanese League in the season prior to his arrival at Highbury.

Wenger was recommended to Arsenal vice-chairman David Dein by Glenn **Hoddle**, who played under him when Monaco won the French title in 1987; Wenger also took the club to a Champions' League semi-final during eight largely successful seasons. Born in Strasbourg, Wenger had begun playing as an amateur with Mutzig in the French third division, before graduating in 1974 with a degree in economics from Strasbourg University. A central defender, he turned professional with Strasbourg in 1978 before becoming youth team coach in 1981.

After a brief spell as assistant coach with Cannes, he was appointed coach of Nancy before getting his big break with Monaco in 1987, although his time there ended in bizarre circumstances as he was sacked just weeks after committing his future to the club and rebuffing the advances of both Bayern Munich and the French national team.

At Arsenal, Wenger inherited an ageing team whose recent League and European triumphs had been built around a veteran back four and a rigidly English style of play. One of his first acts as manager was to sign unknown French teenager Patrick Vieira from AC Milan's reserve team. Marc Overmars, Nicolas Anelka and Emmanuel Petit followed, and in Wenger's second season Arsenal won a League and Cup Double for the second time in the club's history. After a gradual renewing of the major components of his team, Wenger's Arsenal won another League and FA Cup Double in 2002, another League title in 2004 and an FA Cup the following season.

It is in his signings and his ability to improve the players in his charge that Wenger has excelled. Thierry **Henry** was a wayward left-winger signed for £10m following a troubled time at Juventus. Under Wenger he has been transformed into perhaps the finest centre-forward in the world. At the lower end of the scale, Ray Parlour progressed from a one-paced but fast-living under-achiever to an important part of Wenger's success, a convert to the dietary guidance and physical conditioning that have prolonged his top-level career.

Arsenal have an occasionally peerless

attacking team, a revitalized youth team structure and a new stadium, which opened for 2006–07. Wenger's nine years in charge of the club have proved as much of a definitively modernizing influence as Herbert **Chapman**'s tactical and commercial innovations and George **Graham**'s ruthlessly direct successes of the late 1980s and early 1990s.

West Bromwich Albion

As anyone who has shivered through a winter match at the Hawthorns will know, West Bromwich play at the most elevated League ground in the country, at 551ft above sea level. The club lived a nomadic existence before the stadium was opened in 1900, and had used the Plough and Harrow pub as an unofficial HQ. The landlady there kept a pet thrush, or 'throstle', which was adopted as a mascot and features on the club badge. Many reference books claim 'The Throstles' as the club nickname but the fans always preferred 'The Baggies' in light of the voluminous shorts worn by the team in their early days.

In 1878 employees of the George Salter Spring Works in West Bromwich decided to form a football club. One amongst them was dispatched, on foot, to nearby Wednesbury to buy a ball and West Bromwich Strollers were born. Three successive FA Cup Final appearances from 1886 to 1888 – the last of which was won, 2–1 against Preston North End – helped to secure entry to the Football League, with the suffix Albion now added to the club name. Soon after, the club adopted their familiar blue and white stripes, having played in a variety of colours previously, including yellow and white quarters. A second Cup win was recorded before the First World War and a first, and so far

only, League title was secured immediately upon resumption of competitions in 1919–20. And in some style: with 104 goals being scored by a team amassing a then record 60 points.

The next 30 years were shared equally between the first and second divisions – a runners-up spot in 1925 and a still-unmatched double of promotion and FA Cup win in 1931 the highlights of the period – before an unbroken run of top-flight football commenced in 1949, lasting 24 seasons. The 1950s side managed by Vic Buckingham, who later had a hand in the development of the great Ajax team, was probably Albion's best. Fusing the 'push-and-run' style pioneered by Spurs with ideas taken from the great Hungarian team, the side reach its peak in 1953–54, coming within a whisker of winning the first League and Cup Double of the 20th century. While leading the League in April, forwards Ronnie Allen and Johnny Nicholls received rare call-ups to an England squad to face Scotland, missing a derby match against second-placed Wolves. Albion lost the game and then their sparkle, winning just one of their final six games, and, hampered by injuries, surrendered the title to their neighbours. A 3–2 success in the FA Cup Final was scant consolation for the loss.

The following decade saw the rise of two of the club's greatest goalscorers: Tony Brown and Jeff Astle, who starred in teams that reached four cup finals in five seasons. Albion beat West Ham in the last of the two-legged League Cup Finals in 1966, then lost two more in 1967, after holding a two-goal lead against QPR, and 1970. They also won their fifth FA Cup in 1968, defeating Everton with a blistering strike from Astle, who scored in every round of the competition that year.

Tony 'Bomber' Brown, meanwhile, still

holds the record for appearances and goals scored for the club – 720 and 279 respectively in a career that spanned two decades. Brown and veteran goalkeeper John Osborne were the only members of the 1960s team still at Albion when their last great side developed. Johnny **Giles** began the process after taking the club to promotion in 1975, and it was brought to fruition by Ron Atkinson, who took over in 1978. Albion were to finish third in 1978–79, also reaching the quarter-finals of the UEFA Cup, and fourth two years later. Atkinson's team were the first in England to regularly feature three black players, full-back Brendan Batson, striker Cyrille Regis and winger Laurie Cunningham, whose displays in the UEFA Cup run led to a transfer to Real Madrid.

A long decline began in 1981, when Atkinson moved to Manchester United, taking the influential midfielders Bryan **Robson** and Remi Moses with him. Albion suffered a calamitous relegation from the top level in 1985–86 – they were bottom throughout the season and won only four matches – and fell to the third tier for the first time at the end of 1990–91. Recovery was swift via the play-offs but then the club stagnated in the second level for a decade. Under Gary Megson, Albion lost in the 2001 play-off final to Bolton, but went up the following year, pipping bitter rivals Wolves at the death after winning seven of their last eight games. Latterly they struggled in the Premiership but managed to stay up, after a win on the last day, in 2005. Bryan Robson's team went down the following season.

West Ham United

West Ham United were formed as Thames Ironworks Football Club in 1895, a team made up of east London shipyard workers and run by the Ironworks company. Known as 'The Irons', the club was initially funded by an enthusiastic managing director called Arnold Hills, who arranged the club's early fixtures, including a debut season appearance in the FA Cup and a series of friendlies under innovative artificial lights supplied by the dockyard engineers.

In 1900 the club was officially divorced from the shipbuilding company that spawned it, and relaunched with an issue of 20,000 ten-shilling shares (under the name West Ham United). Four years later the club moved to its current home, the Boleyn Ground at Upton Park. Early players included Charlie Satterthwaite, reputedly one of the hardest strikers of a ball in the country, who in 1906 took part in the first of many explosive derby games with Millwall. The *East Ham Echo* report describes a game in which 'all attempts at football were ignored', climaxing in West Ham's Jarvis smashing the head of Millwall's Deans against a metal advertising board, seriously injuring his opponent, for which he received only a caution.

Twenty years of modest success in the Southern League followed, buoyed by an FA Cup run in 1911 that brought the club to national attention for the first time. The Hammers beat three previous trophy-winners in reaching the fourth round, including a first-round victory over Nottingham Forest played in such thick fog that newspaper reports described the game as a 'pure farce'. Hammers forward Frank Carruthers later admitted punching both West Ham goals into the Forest net in full view of several opponents.

West Ham joined the Football League

in 1919, losing their second game of their first season 7–0 to Barnsley at Oakwell, still the club's equal record defeat. Four years later they reached the final of the FA Cup, the famous **White Horse Final** against Bolton Wanderers. The same year they earned promotion to Division 1 on the final day of the League season. West Ham were relegated in 1932 and only returned to the first division 26 years later. That year the Hammers scored 101 goals in winning the second-division championship under Ted Fenton's management, the club's first major honour. Fenton was only the club's third manager and as recently as John Lyall's departure in 1989 West Ham had only ever had five managers, the others being Syd King, Charlie Paynter and Ron **Greenwood**.

The Hammers would stay in the top flight for 20 years, during which time an illustrious generation of home-produced players emerged, including the World Cup-winning trio Bobby **Moore**, Geoff **Hurst** and Martin Peters, who won 224 caps between them and played together for England on 37 occasions. During this period Billy Bonds made a record 663 appearances for the club, finally retiring in 1988. Under Greenwood, West Ham developed a reputation for playing attractive attacking football and for fielding locally sourced players, prompting the notion of the West Ham 'academy'. This was the club's most successful period to date, during which they won the FA Cup in 1964, 1975 and 1980 and the Cup Winners' Cup in 1965, finishing runners-up in the competition in 1976, and losing a League Cup final in 1966. The club's League form was always erratic, though: the team featuring the World Cup-winning trio never finished higher than eighth.

The FA Cup win of 1980 was as a Division 2 club, Trevor **Brooking**

scoring the winning goal and the 17-year-old Paul Allen becoming the youngest player ever to take part in an FA Cup Final. The Hammers were promoted the following season and spent nine years in the top flight, finishing third in 1986, their highest-ever League placing, with a team containing the likes of goalscoring darling of the tabloids Frank McAvennie and the home-grown Tony Cottee, who scored well over a hundred League goals in two spells at the club.

During the mid-1990s West Ham produced a new generation of young players, many of whom were sold to finance the club's escalating wage bill and a catastrophically timed relegation in 2003. Rio Ferdinand, Frank Lampard, Joe Cole and Glen Johnson, all home-produced England internationals, were sold for a combined fee of £42m, mainly to finance the drop to Division 1 under the guidance of manager Glenn Roeder. Roeder had replaced Harry Redknapp, who was sacked after eight years in the job following a seventh-placed finish in the Premiership. Current boss Alan Pardew, brought from Reading in 2003, achieved promotion through the play-offs in 2005. The Hammers were a minute away from winning the FA Cup in 2006, finally losing on penalties to Liverpool after a 3–3 draw.

White City

The huge White City stadium in west London flitted in and out of football history without ever finding a satisfactory role. Originally conceived as part of an Empire exhibition site (like Wembley), the stadium was completed in time to stage the 1908 Olympics, where Britain's amateurs beat Denmark 2–0 in the final.

Plans for an all-seated 'London Colosseum' holding 367,000 had thankfully been scaled back, but White City always suffered from grandiose expectations. It was a vast elongated bowl with a final capacity of 130,000. Spectators were separated from the pitch by a 525-yard running track and huge infield, including a swimming pool. It should have been an obvious candidate to stage the FA Cup Final once the old Crystal Palace Stadium became manifestly inadequate, but by 1914 White City had fallen into disrepair. It did not revive until the new sport of greyhound racing came on the scene in 1927, when the stadium came under the control of one of the forgotten giants of British sport, the visionary and dictatorial Brigadier-General Alfred Critchley.

In the 1930s he planned to wrest control of the FA Cup Final from his rivals at Wembley by expanding White City's capacity to 163,000, floated the idea of a world club championship at the stadium and experimented with floodlit games (despite the FA's ban). But typically for White City, none of the schemes ever quite came off. The stadium was also used periodically by QPR, notably in 1912, 1931–32 and 1962–63, but even their biggest crowds (41,097 against Leeds in 1932 is a club record) were dwarfed by their surroundings.

In 1966, White City staged the World Cup group game between France and Uruguay, watched by 45,662 – Wembley being unavailable because of its regular greyhound night. The stadium was demolished in 1985 after the Greyhound Racing Association fell into financial crisis.

White Horse Final

The first FA Cup Final at Wembley in 1923 became one of the most celebrated popular moments in football's early history as a mass spectator sport. The Empire Stadium was built partly with the 1924 British Empire Exhibition in mind, and partly as a response to the growing popularity of the game. Thousands of those attending the 1913 final at the Crystal Palace Stadium had complained of being unable to see anything of the pitch. At a cost of £750,000, the twin-towered colossus was erected in the quiet commuter belt of Wembley and finished just four days before the Cup Final was played on 28 April.

The FA threw open the doors of the Empire Stadium for its first competitive game, and a quarter of a million people gathered at Wembley to fill a ground with a capacity of 127,000. By one o'clock the terraces were already full. Those already in the stadium were forced on to the pitch by people flooding in behind them. In the chaos, up to 1,000 spectators were injured and, at a conservative estimate, many dozens of cloth caps and derbies were mislaid.

The confusion was temporarily halted when King George V arrived at 2.45pm to behold a writhing mass of his subjects covering every available vantage point and blade of grass. Remarkably, everybody managed to collect themselves in time to stand still for the national anthem. With some order restored, a small band of mounted police, aided by several of the Bolton and West Ham players, were able to edge the crowd slowly back to the touchline by herding them in ever increasing circles from the centre of the pitch.

Just as on the *Titanic*, 11 years earlier, the band played on from somewhere in the middle of the throng. On the monochrome film of the time, Billy, the only white horse present, ridden by PC George Scorey, appeared as a brilliant beacon of crowd control and, despite the near disaster that occurred, the day was remembered as a miraculous display of British reserve.

The game itself, 45 minutes late in starting, was little short of a farce. Bolton scored in the first two minutes. With crowds hugging the touchline, a West Ham player was swallowed by the mob as he attempted to reclaim the ball and, while he was still excuse-me-ing his way back on to the pitch, David Jack nodded Bolton 1–0 up. The players had been forced to stay on the pitch during the interval as any journey to the dressing rooms would have required an effort of Himalayan proportions and it was all over ten minutes into the second half when John Smith blasted Bolton into a 2–0 lead, the ball rebounding straight back into play off the spectators crammed against the goal net. There is also strong eye-witness testimony to the effect that a civilian foot kept the ball in play for the cross to be made into Smith's path.

Wigan Athletic

Wigan Athletic are a modern phenomenon, and a club on the rise. For nearly half a century the club was merely a footnote in Lancashire football – overshadowed not just by big-city rivals in Manchester and Liverpool, but by the town's historical strength in rugby league. Election to Division 4 in 1978 proved the first step in a steady rise to footballing prominence. In 2005, the club were promoted to the Premier League, where they enjoyed an impressive first season in the top flight. Before this Wigan had been relegated only once in their 27-year League existence. During that time there have been four promotions, Divisions 2 and 3 championships in 1997 and 2003 and five further appearances in the play-offs.

The home support at the 25,000 capacity JJB Stadium is still small, the team attracting an average gate of 11,563 in their 2004–05 promotion season. However, the financial backing of local sportswear magnate and club chairman

Dave Whelan has been both consistent and sensibly applied. During the financial chaos of the last few seasons Wigan have been an island of stability and ambition, a template for a new type of footballing success, the kind of localized corporate sponsorship more familiar in American sport than in the UK.

Formed out of the ashes of the defunct Wigan Borough, Wigan Athletic were founded at a public meeting at the Queen's Hall in May 1932. Borough had been a League club prior to their resignation, and the intention was that the new club, based at Springfield Park, which the directors bought for £2,250, would rise to take its place. However, it would take 46 years for the plan to come to fruition.

During their years as a semiprofessional club Wigan competed in the Cheshire League, winning the championship as early as 1935, the same year the club made it to the third round proper of the FA Cup for the first time, scoring 27 goals in seven ties. In 1953 a crowd of 27,500 gathered at Springfield Park to witness a 4–1 FA Cup second-round victory over Hereford United, the highest ever for a meeting of two non-League clubs outside a Wembley final.

Election to the League in 1978 was followed by promotion from Division 4 in 1982 and the Freight Rover trophy in 1985. A period of steady consolidation, undermined by dwindling crowds, gained impetus with the purchase of the club in 1995 by Whelan, former Blackburn player turned successful local businessman. From the prospect of extinction – the crowd at Springfield Park for Whelan's first game as owner was 1,452 – the club began to invest in players, signing a trio of Spaniards to play in Division 3, one of whom, Roberto Martinez, went on to make nearly 200 appearances for the club.

August 1999 saw the club move from

Springfield Park to the new all-seater JJB Stadium at Robin Park, a venue that has also hosted rugby league internationals and Wigan Warriors fixtures. The appointment of former Wigan player Paul Jewell as manager in 2001 was followed by the Division 2 title in his second season in charge, the club signalling its intentions by spending over £3m on players (including a club record £1.2m on Nathan Ellington) at a time when many of its competitors were facing financial collapse. Jewell's team finished tenth in their first season in the Premier League and reached the League Cup Final where they were beaten by Manchester United.

In 1987 the *Daily Express* reported that former Soviet premier and architect of *glasnost* Mikhail Gorbachev is a Wigan supporter, having visited the town for a friendly match in 1970 while he was secretary of Ukrainian team Metalist Kharkov. Characteristically miserly with privileged information, Gorbachev's spokesman refused to confirm or deny the reports.

Wimbledon

On the face of it, the combined history of Wimbledon FC and AFC Wimbledon is a perfect circle – a team formed on Wimbledon Common rises to the highest echelons of the English game, falls dramatically from grace in controversial circumstances, regroups on that self-same common and starts another triumphant against-the-odds ascendancy.

The perfect circle has some jagged edges, however. This is a club deemed 'not in the wider interests of football' by the FA. A club which should by rights never have existed. Wimbledon FC began life as Wimbledon Old Centrals, on the Common, in 1889, simplifying their moniker in 1905 and joining the Isthmian League in 1921 at their new Plough Lane

home. They would win the title eight times in the next 50-odd years, though the finest hour of their initial existence came courtesy of four Eddie Reynolds headers at Wembley in 1963, which secured the FA Amateur Cup at the third time of asking. A year later they joined the semi-professional Southern League.

It could be argued that had Wimbledon remained at this level, all would have been well. Ron Noades, however, spotted the potential for greater things and, as chairman, oversaw elevation to the Football League in 1977. With Sam Hammam in the boardroom and Dave Bassett as manager, a collection of rejects and has-beens took the Dons, inexplicably, to Division 1 by 1986. The strong-arm tactics of John Fashanu and, later, Vinnie Jones, the unsung heroics of Lawrie Sanchez, Alan Cork and Dave Beasant, and Bassett's dogged rewriting of the rulebook via relentless hoofing of the ball downfield upset numerous apple carts. Most notably, it made monkeys of the free-flowing Liverpool team in the 1988 Cup Final, Sanchez's looping header securing the unlikeliest Wembley victory of all time.

The Dons stayed there, too, consistently securing top-half Premiership finishes well into the latter part of the 1990s, though a European place consistently evaded them. Behind the scenes, however, life looked less rosy. Plough Lane was redundant after the **Taylor Report** and Hammam sold it to Safeway (conveniently ignoring a covenant promising it would be kept for the football club) and after ten years of sharing Selhurst Park and searching fruitlessly – some would say half-heartedly – for a ground in the club's home borough of Merton, stories began to surface of outlandish moves to Dublin, Manchester, Cardiff and, most chillingly of all, Milton Keynes. Concerted campaigning by

WISA (Wimbledon Independent Supporters' Association) and widespread condemnation in the media saw Hammam's Irish dreams turn to dust, and he duly offloaded the club for a tidy profit to Norweigan multi-millionaires Kjell Inge Røkke and Bjorn Rune Gjelsten.

Their unique brand of parsimony, and the sterling efforts of hapless former Norway boss Egil Olsen, guaranteed relegation to Division 1 and gave new puppet chairman Charles Koppel the perfect platform to plead the case for a move to Buckinghamshire. The FA cravenly agreed in May 2002 (via a three-man commission), and crowds dwindled to three figures.

What followed was remarkable. At a packed meeting in the Fox and Grapes pub in Wimbledon Village, supporters voted overwhelmingly to set up and back a new team, AFC Wimbledon. Their first game, against Sutton in July 2002, was watched by over 4,500 and the new team began 2002–03 in the Combined Counties League.

By the summer of 2005, promotion to the Ryman Premier League had been achieved. With crowds regularly topping 3,000 at Kingsmeadow, the stadium they now own and share with Kingstonian a couple of miles outside Merton, the club is edging nearer the ultimate aim of a return to the professional ranks.

Windsor Park

The home of Linfield and Northern Ireland for most of the past century, south Belfast's Windsor Park has had a turbulent history and, at the time of writing, appears to have a doubtful future. After Linfield had wandered through several grounds in the early years of the 20th century they finally secured a piece of land to call home and

Windsor Park (built on a site originally known as the 'bog meadows') was opened on 2 September 1905 with a game against Glentoran. The official history of the IFA called it 'a magnificent arena, the ultimate and obvious venue for international football', yet it was not until 1910 that it hosted its first British championship match, a 1–0 win over Scotland. A 1–1 draw with the same opponents in front of 31,000 at Windsor Park in 1914 took Ireland to their first outright British championship triumph (and their last until 1980), but until the First World War Cliftonville's Solitude and Dublin's Dalymount Park were also frequently used for internationals.

After the war and the political division of Ireland in 1921, Windsor Park became the almost exclusive venue. However, its 'obviousness' as the home of the IFA helped to align the association more tightly with Protestant Linfield, at a time when Belfast Celtic's vast open arena might have served as more than just an occasional international venue. Celtic Park did at least have the satisfaction of hosting (Northern) Ireland's record win, a 7–0 thumping of Wales in 1930. A crowd of 57,000 welcomed England back to Windsor Park for the first Home International after the Second World War (England won 7–2) and a few hundred more squeezed in for the stadium's record attendance, on 13 August 1955, in a match to mark the 75th anniversary of the IFA. 'Britain's already dwindling soccer prestige has faded away to a faint shadow,' wrote one local paper after the United Kingdom team had gone down 4–1 to Europe (the first time a team had been assembled under the auspices of the newly formed UEFA).

Much less happily, Windsor Park was also the site of the vicious attack by Linfield fans on Belfast Celtic's Jimmy Jones in 1948, which left the Celtic striker with permanent leg injuries and led to the club's withdrawal from the Irish League. The onset of political violence in Northern Ireland in the late 1960s brought more tensions to football and no international teams visited Windsor Park (or anywhere else in the North) between the European Championship qualifiers against the Soviet Union in October 1971 and Yugoslavia in March 1975 – Scotland refused to return until 1980.

While things improved on the pitch, with Northern Ireland qualifying for the 1982 and 1986 World Cups, Windsor Park had become a hazardous place to visit for Catholic fans. The area around the stadium, adjacent to the Loyalist Village area of the city, was often used by paramilitaries to dump the bodies of their victims and by the mid-1980s matches at Windsor Park were played against a backdrop of increasingly overt Loyalist identification on the terraces. It hardly helped that Republican groups set off bombs near the stadium after the matches against England in 1985 and 1987, in an attempt to deter foreign teams from coming to Belfast.

In the midst of such trauma João Havelange was on hand to open the new 6,800-capacity North Stand in 1984. That came too late to witness the last British championship match at Windsor Park, a 2–0 win over Scotland the previous December, in front of 10,000 people and a building site, which ultimately gave Northern Ireland a bitter-sweet championship triumph and the right to keep the trophy they had won only three times in its 100-year history. More improvements came in the late 1990s, with the 4,000-seat Kop Stand leaving the capacity at just over 20,000, but Northern Ireland's woeful form and the persistently poisonous atmosphere at Windsor Park made it a glum era as the stadium

reached its centenary. Indeed, the peace process may spell the end for international football at the stadium, whose location and connection with Linfield make it an unacceptable venue for many Catholics.

In 2004 the Gaelic Athletic Association remarkably agreed to support a proposal for a new 30,000-seater stadium that would host big GAA, football and rugby matches in the province – the government had insisted it would only get funding if backed by all three sports. In early 2005 three locations were shortlisted, with the site of the notorious Maze Prison in Lisburn the favourite.

Sir Walter Winterbottom

Walter Winterbottom spent 16 years as England's first national team coach, a major achievement bearing in mind his reign coincided with the side's humiliating 1–0 defeat to the USA in the 1950 World Cup, then the 6–3 hammering from Hungary at Wembley three years later. Winterbottom once admitted that the other job he held at the same time, as FA director of coaching, was more important to him, and it was just as well.

He was born in Oldham in January 1913, and played 27 games as centreback for Manchester United before a back injury forced him to quit aged 26. By then he was already moonlighting as a PE teacher and lecturer, and in 1946, after spending the Second World War as an RAF Wing Commander, he was appointed by the FA as director of coaching and was responsible for managing England's senior, amateur and youth sides.

He faced immediate suspicion as he had never coached a professional team before, and that grew after he recommended the need for better-qualified English coaches to focus on the development of technique and skill, rather than just fitness. He also demanded floodlit training pitches for evening practice sessions. He eventually found support for his new methods and his disciples included future England coaches Ron **Greenwood** and Bobby **Robson** and successful Spurs boss Bill **Nicholson**.

The England team itself was always picked by a selection committee of club directors (or, in the case of the USA game, just one selector) and Winterbottom just had to coach them. The problem was, Winterbottom was better at getting results out of coaches than players: he was not a great communicator – a young Bobby **Charlton** once admitted, 'He gave us a lovely talk but I don't know what he meant' – while tactics were not his forte, as six months after the Hungary defeat Winterbottom took his side to Budapest for a return match and lost 7–1.

But he did achieve some success with an England side that qualified for four straight World Cups between 1950 and 1962, though they never went further than the quarter-finals. That Winterbottom stayed in the job so long was down to his mentor, the FA's powerful secretary Stanley **Rous**. When Rous became FIFA president in 1962, Winterbottom was expected to succeed him, but he was thwarted by Rous's nemesis, FA vice-president Sir Harold Thompson, who ensured Winterbottom was overlooked.

Instead, Winterbottom was appointed secretary of the Central Council for Physical Recreation and in 1965 became the first director-general of the Sports Council, establishing coaching structures for his successors. He was awarded an OBE in 1963, a CBE in 1972 and a knighthood in 1978. By the time Winterbottom died aged 88 in February 2002,

Sven-Göran **Eriksson** was England's first foreign coach. Many still believe that would never have happened had Winterbottom replaced Rous as FA secretary and continued his education of English coaches. Although fondly remembered as England coach, he might have achieved more for the game from a position of power within the FA.

Wolverhampton Wanderers

It is no exaggeration to suggest Wolves were one of the pre-eminent forces in European football during the 1950s. Manager Stan **Cullis** fashioned a combative side captained by Billy **Wright**, who formed a formidable half-back trio with Eddie Clamp and Bill Slater (the latter voted Footballer of the Year in 1960), also featuring among others hard-working inside-forward Peter Broadbent and winger Jimmy Mullen. The League title was claimed three times, in 1953–54, 1957–58 – with a century of goals recorded – and a year later. In 1959–60 a single point denied them a hat-trick of championships and the first League and Cup Double since the turn of the century.

In the days before international club tournaments, Wolves beat a series of top European teams – Real Madrid, Moscow Dynamo, Moscow Spartak and the formidable Honvéd of Hungary – in floodlit friendlies at their stadium, Molineux. That success, however, could not be carried into European competition proper; Cullis's team tumbled at the first hurdle of the European Cup in 1958 to German side Schalke 04 and were heavily beaten by Barcelona a year later.

Wolves' roots can be traced back to school side St Lukes FC, founded in 1877 as a reward for the students after an exceptional year's academic achievement. Two years later the team merged with a local cricket-and-football club known as the Wanderers to become Wolverhampton Wanderers. Founder members of the Football League in 1888, the team first excelled in the FA Cup. They made three final appearances in eight years but won only one, beating Everton 1–0 in 1893, by which time they had ditched their original red-and-white-striped shirts for 'old gold'. By the early part of the 20th century, however, Wolves were languishing in Division 2; the struggle to restore top-flight status continued either side of the First World War. Succour was gleaned from a shock 1908 FA Cup Final win over odds-on favourites Newcastle.

The side fell further down the scale before, under the stewardship of Major Frank Buckley, they were restored to the top level with Stan Cullis a regular at centre-half. There were two second-place finishes before war broke out again, coupled with another FA Cup Final defeat in 1939. In 1964, Wanderers controversially ended their association with Cullis, who was sacked after a disappointing start to the season. The club were relegated and oscillated between the top two divisions for a decade before a fourth-place finish in 1971 returned them to Europe. Juventus were among the teams dispatched en route to the first all-English UEFA Cup Final, which ended with a 3–2 aggregate defeat by Spurs, Northern Ireland centre-forward Derek Dougan scoring nine in the competition.

Dougan and his strike partner John Richards were key figures in the team that took the League Cup in 1974; the trophy was won again with a goal from Andy Gray in 1980. By the early 80s, however, Wolves were in near-terminal decline having gone badly into debt over the construction of a huge new stand named after then chairman John Ireland. Three consecutive relegations found Wolves playing in the bottom division in 1986, attendances having fallen almost as dramatically as the team's standing. With two sides of Molineux closed down in the wake of the **Bradford fire**, the club might have folded but for an 11th-hour intervention from the council and builders Gallaghers, who paid off the club's debts in exchange for building a supermarket behind one end.

One player almost single-handedly revived Wolves' fortunes. Steve Bull scored over 50 goals in consecutive seasons as Division 4 and then Division 3 were won. England recognition followed and he went on to become the club's record scorer with 306 goals in a career spent entirely outside the top flight; Bull, like Wright before him, remained loyal despite interest from more elevated clubs.

Sir Jack Hayward, a multi-millionaire and keen fan, bought the club for £2.1m in 1990 and ploughed a large part of his fortune ('I'm the Golden Tit' he later claimed) into attempting to restore the club to its 'rightful' position. Molineux was transformed into one of the most modern grounds in the League, but improving the playing side proved a harder task. Graham **Taylor**, Mark McGhee and Colin Lee all proved inept at spending Hayward's money. Millions were squandered with only three play-off semi-final defeats to show for it.

Finally, in 2003, 19 years after leaving the top flight, Dave Jones's team snatched promotion in an emphatic play-off win over Sheffield United and Sir Jack Hayward handed over the club to his son. An immediate relegation followed by a season of turmoil led to Jones's sacking. Former England boss Glenn **Hoddle** is now challenged with the task of matching Molineux's 'big club' aspirations. Another long spell in England's second tier is a real possibility.

women's football

The Scottish town of Inveresk was the location for regular football contests between two teams of women, married and unmarried, towards the end of the 17th century, but the first official women's football match took place in England on 23 March 1895. Organized by Lettie Honeyball, the secretary of the British Ladies' Football Club, the game drew a crowd of 10,000 to Crouch End to witness a team of upper-class northern schoolgirls defeat their southern counterparts 7–1.

The women's game then grew steadily in popularity up until the First World War and beyond. At its height, crowds in excess of 50,000 attended women's matches featuring the legendary Dick Kerr Ladies of Preston, a roving team that played to raise money for charity – up to a peak of 67 times in one year. The Dick Kerr Ladies toured France, playing against representatives of the nine French women's teams then in existence, and later played teams in Belgium and Holland, and men's soccer teams in the USA. The side supplied nine of the England XI that beat Scotland 22–0 in, unofficially, the first women's international in 1920.

Despite plenty of adverse reaction, great strides were made during the First World War. With huge numbers of girls and women placed in strange working environments, the government feared social problems and so encouraged contemporary organizations such as the YWCA, the church and the working women's union to create football teams. Women's football began to develop all over Britain, particularly in the north-east

of England where, in a time of post-war hardship and political disquiet, its fund-raising capabilities associated it briefly but distinctly with the labour movement.

During the 1921 miners' lock-out, miners' wives and other local women played matches to raise money for food. Coincidentally perhaps, it was in 1921 that the FA banned women from playing on League grounds, pronouncing football 'unsuitable for females'. Women's matches continued but were forced to decamp to rugby pitches, and with the sense of structure and cohesion diminished, the game inevitably floundered. It was only half a century later, in 1971, that the FA lifted the ban.

After England won the World Cup in 1966, a general resurgence of interest in football led to the formation of the Women's Football Association, which developed a successful national team, league and FA Cup competition. The first fully sanctioned English women's international finally took place in 1971 and England were beaten finalists in the inaugural European Championship of 1984, losing to Sweden. The first World Cup took place in China in 1991, won by the USA. Despite this, the women's game in the UK was struggling to build a chain of progression from schools to youth to adult league.

The FA finally offered its support in 1993, a crucial intervention which transformed the 80 girls' teams of 1993 into over 3,000 in schools and clubs – with approximately 2 million girls playing football in schools – by the turn of the century. With the FA giving their full encouragement, Fulham became the first professional women's team in 2000. Perhaps more significantly, the number of female coaches and women in key positions at committee level was beginning to rise steeply by this time. Having overcome open hostility and legal restrictions, the chief obstacle for the women's game today seems to be an alternating attitude of indifference and facetiousness from the British media, although BBC television did at least give wide coverage to England's hosting of the 2005 women's European Championships.

The FA Women's Premier League currently has ten teams in a National Division and 12 each in the North and South divisions. Sides such as Arsenal, Croydon, Millwall and Fulham have given a southern dominance to the League and Cup but Doncaster Belles, winners of the 93–94 championship, have challenged this supremacy while earning themselves a prominent public reputation on a par with the pioneering Dick Kerr Ladies.

World Club Championship

A club competition between the winners of the European Cup and the South American Copa de los Libertadores sounds a simple enough idea, but ever since its inception in 1960 the contest has been beset with problems.

First was the format. Initially there were two games, home and away, but until 1968 the championship was decided on games won. This meant that if each side won a game, a decider was played on the continent of the home team in the second leg, clearly giving an unfair advantage to the team who played an extra home match.

From 1969 the winner was decided on the aggregate score over two legs, then between 1980 and 2004 the championship was decided in a single game played in Tokyo, meaning that few fans of either side were there, and whoever wanted to watch it at home had to get up in the middle of the night.

To add to the confusion (and, for many, the pointlessness), in January 2000 FIFA added an eight-team Club World Championship tournament in Brazil, won by Corinthians, to the already crowded global football schedule. This tournament became most famous for being entered by Manchester United because the English FA thought it would enhance England's 2006 World Cup bid. United sacrificed their place in that season's FA Cup, flopped in Brazil and Germany were awarded the World Cup.

The second problem, particularly in the early years, was on-field violence, which had become so bad that by 1971 European Cup winners Ajax refused to travel to Nacional of Uruguay, being replaced by runners-up Panathinaikos. Later in the decade Ajax (again), Bayern Munich, Liverpool and Nottingham Forest also declined, while in 1975 and 1978 no competition took place at all. The most notorious tie was between Celtic and Racing Club of Argentina in 1967. Celtic won the first game in Glasgow. In the return leg their goalie, Ronnie Simpson, had to be replaced after being hit by a stone before the game had even started. The Argentines fouled their way to victory, as they did in the ensuing play-off that saw six players sent off – two from Racing and four from Celtic. Over the next three years Manchester United, AC Milan and Feyenoord all suffered violent conduct at the hands and feet of the same Argentine team – Estudiantes de la Plata.

It wasn't all bad. The Santos side of Pelé and Zito triumphed in 1962 and 1963, topping Benfica 8–4 overall in their first victory, while the much-maligned Internazionale side of Facchetti and Mazzola took the trophy in 1964 and 1965, largely by fair means. English sides have little reason to remember the competition, despite several European

Cup successes – only Manchester United have won it, scraping a 1–0 victory over Palmeiras in 1999 a few months before their ill-fated trip to Brazil (see above).

FIFA President Sepp Blatter has an almost evangelical zeal about making a multi-team Club World Championship a regular event, despite opposition from Europe's group of wealthy G14 clubs (a body Blatter refuses to recognize). The 2001 tournament in Spain was scrapped after FIFA's marketing arm collapsed, leaving it without a sponsor. Despite this Blatter doggedly scheduled another six-team event (with one from each Confederation) to take place in Tokyo in late 2005 – where Sao Paulo beat Liverpool in the final – to be played annually and to replace permanently the single-game event. What might have been a show-piece event to crown the best club side in the world has somehow become a burdensome and deeply unwatchable political football.

World Cup 1966

The 1966 World Cup has become not only English football's most celebrated occasion but also an object of fetishist nostalgia in the tabloid press and a constant source of negative comparison with successive generations of the national team. In the build-up to the 1986 World Cup in Mexico Bryan **Robson** confessed to an interviewer that he 'hated' the famous picture of Bobby **Moore** on the shoulders of his team-mates holding the Jules Rimet trophy. At this time the notion of '30 years of hurt', as celebrated in the Skinner and Baddiel Euro 96 anthem 'Three Lions', was yet to emerge in earnest. The England World Cup-winning team of 1966 were yet to band together into a nostalgia-fuelled money-making operation and nobody outside *Match of*

the Day watchers knew who Kenneth Wolstenholme was.

The 1966 World Cup in England was notable for two things. Firstly, it was the best-organized and best-attended tournament in the competition's history. The games took place in large, modern stadiums spread across the length and breadth of the country and there were few of the organizational hitches that had blighted previous World Cups. Despite this, and secondly, the standard of football was poor compared to previous competitions. A thrilling Wembley final only partially compensated for the lack of excitement that had preceded it. England were competent hosts and emerged as the strongest of a largely uninspiring pack, making use of home advantage and a well-organized team in much the same way as France in 1998.

The months leading up to the tournament provided their own excitement. The Jules Rimet trophy was recovered from some bushes in South London by Pickles the dog after it had been stolen from an exhibition in March of 1966. Pickles received a reward and achieved a lasting celebrity, although he would die tragically some years later after strangling himself on his own lead.

England started slowly but qualified from their group as winners, drawing 0–0 against Uruguay and winning 2–0 against both Mexico and France. It was during the Mexico game that the phenomenon of chanting from the stands was noted at an England game for the first time by many sections of the media. 'We want goals,' sang the crowd, and against Mexico they got one, a beauty scored by Bobby **Charlton**.

As he had been four years earlier in Chile, Pelé was effectively kicked out of the tournament by the thuggish marking tactics of his first-round opponents. Injured against Bulgaria, he missed the defeat against Hungary before being carried off again against Portugal. North Korea were the surprise team of the tournament. They beat Italy 1–0 at Ayresome Park to provide one of the World Cup's greatest-ever shocks and then went on to lose 5–3 in the quarter-finals to a Eusébio-inspired Portugal, the Koreans having led 3–0 after 20 minutes.

Meanwhile England reached the last four by beating Argentina 1–0 in a foul-tempered match. Argentina captain Rattin was sent off and at the final whistle Alf **Ramsey** refused to allow his players to shake hands with opponents whom he later described as 'animals'. In the semi-finals England played extremely well to knock out the Portuguese, Bobby Charlton rising to the occasion and scoring twice to send the hosts through to the final.

After a low-key tournament, the eighth World Cup provided perhaps the most dramatic final of all. It had been billed as a contest between Franz Beckenbauer and Bobby Charlton, but neither player shone in the final. Germany started well, taking the lead through Haller, only for England to equalize through Geoff **Hurst**'s header from a cross by West Ham team-mate Bobby **Moore**. England took the lead in the 78th minute through another Hammer, Martin Peters, and held on until seconds from the end when Weber converted from close range after a fortunate ricochet to take the game into extra time.

Midway through the first period of extra time Alan Ball crossed for Hurst to turn and hit a shot that cannoned down and just over the line – according to the Azerbaijani linesman who was ideally positioned. To this day many still claim that the ball did not actually cross the goal-line. England completed their 4–2 victory in the final seconds, Hurst scoring from the edge of the area with a left-footed shot. This prompted a famous

piece of commentary by the BBC's Kenneth Wolstenholme, who had spotted some fans racing on prematurely: 'Some people are on the pitch, they think it's all over . . . it is now.' Hurst later admitted he hadn't really expected to score, but had wanted to send the ball as far as possible into the crowd in order to waste some time. Hurst was the first and only player to score a hat-trick in a World Cup Final, and for the third time the host nation had won the World Cup.

Bobby Moore received the trophy from Queen Elizabeth; Nobby Stiles, terrify-ingly toothless, pranced across the Wembley turf; and somebody stole the ball. The Germans would be back. But for England, this remains their finest hour.

World Wars

After consultation with the War Office, the FA and Football League decided to continue playing despite war breaking out at the very start of the 1914–15 season. But soon after, all competitive football was banned by the FA. For the following three seasons, emergency com-petitions were held via three regional leagues: Lancashire Section, Midland Section and London Combination. With the majority of young and fit footballers ideal recruits for the armed forces, many joined up and were posted overseas. Consequently, guest players were common-place and players were no longer allowed to be paid: Leeds City were found to have paid wages and were disbanded after a sensational inquiry. Dozens of pro-fessional players died on the front lines.

The League closed down immediately and the threat of air strikes led to crowds being discouraged when the Second World War broke out three weeks into the 1939–40 season. No games were played at first, then only friendlies in specified 'safe' areas. Eventually, in

October 1939, ten regional leagues began and the season was extended to 8 June.

All but 20 of the League's 88 clubs were back in action for 1940–41 but air strike threats caused two games at Southampton to be delayed. The problem of getting teams together when players were heading off to serve all over Europe, Africa and Asia was exemplified by Brighton, who turned up at Norwich with only five players. They borrowed various local soldiers and Norwich reserves but still lost 18–0. Most clubs managed to fulfil their fixtures.

A League Cup competition was played for the first three seasons of wartime, with West Ham, Preston and Wolves triumphing. Preston drew their 1941 final with Arsenal at Wembley before winning the replay at Blackburn. In 1942–43, League Cup North and South tournaments were introduced and two systems that are now commonplace were tried: the North played home and away two-legged ties while in 1945 and 1946 cup ties had to be played to a finish with extra time and a sudden-death golden goal. In March 1946, Stockport and Doncaster set a record when they played for 3 hours and 23 minutes in the Division 3 (North) Cup before darkness fell with the score locked at 4–4 and a replay was forced. The League Cup North winners were Blackpool, Aston Villa and Bolton; the South's were Arsenal, Charlton and Chelsea. However, none of the honours are official. The FA Cup proper resumed in 1945–46 and the Football League in 1946–47.

Unlike in 1914–18, England continued to play internationals during the Second World War, with Scotland usually the opposition in front of huge crowds raising funds for the war effort. Of more interest were the touring sides, such as the Wanderers, in which star players such as Tom **Finney** entertained fellow troops overseas by playing exhibition matches.

Wrexham

Wrexham's club badge stubbornly features 1873 as the date of its creation despite the fact that it was founded a year earlier. Although not a member of an organized league until joining the Combination League in 1890, they had won the inaugural Welsh Cup, the first of 22 victories to date, in 1878. There was no presentation ceremony, however, as the Welsh FA couldn't afford to buy a trophy or medals.

Based at the Racecourse Ground – originally a cricket venue as well as a racecourse – for all but four years since their foundation, Wrexham became members of Division 3 (North) in 1921. Arguably the high point of their first 90 years was a 5–0 thrashing of Manchester United in a January 1957 FA Cup tie watched by a record home crowd of 36,000. That wasn't the only big attendance that month: 18,000 queued to get into a reserve match against Winsford, although once they had vouchers for the Manchester United tie, few stayed for the game.

Wrexham got their first promotion by finishing 12th. In the reorganization of the League in 1958 they squeezed into the top half of the table on the last day of the season, but were soon relegated and in 1966 finished bottom of Division 4. However, unprecedented good times were just around the corner.

Under the shrewd management of John Neal success finally arrived in the 1970s. Promotion to Division 3 and a run to the quarter-finals of the FA Cup were followed in 1976 by an appearance in the last eight of the European Cup Winners' Cup, losing 2–1 on aggregate to Anderlecht. Neal left in 1977 after missing out on promotion to Division 2 on the last day of the season. The club appointed popular former player Arfon Griffiths as manager, and immediately enjoyed the greatest season in its history. Playing dashing football, a team containing six players capped by Wales swept to the Division 3 championship, won the Welsh Cup and reached the quarter-finals of both the FA and League Cups.

Four years in Division 2 were followed by a dramatic plummet. The nadir of a dismal decade in the bottom division was reached when 45-year-old manager Bobby Roberts, an outfield player in his career, had to play as goalkeeper in a Welsh Cup tie. Yet amidst the dross Wrexham pulled off some remarkable victories; in 1985 in the middle of a run of four League defeats they knocked Porto out of the European Cup Winners' Cup. In the next round, Sven-Göran **Eriksson**'s Roma squeaked through by virtue of two goals which TV replays showed should have been disallowed.

With Wrexham apparently heading for the Conference, manager Dixie McNeil resigned after the club's poverty forced the players to travel to Maidstone by public transport, lugging the kit lockers across London by tube. Brian Flynn took over in 1989, avoided relegation and fashioned another astonishing upset in 1991–92. With seven minutes left in an FA Cup tie, champions Arsenal led 1–0, but two goals in three minutes by Mickey Thomas and Steve Watkin secured a stunning win.

The following season the club began a lengthy spell at the third level, often flirting with a play-off place. There was cup success to savour too, most notably a run to the FA Cup quarter-finals in 1997, ended by a 1–0 defeat at Chester-field. When Flynn departed, new manager Denis Smith was unable to prevent relegation but, aided by the country's top scorer, Andy Morrell, the

team immediately won promotion. Smith did sterling work to consolidate the club's status, but found himself battling against prohibitive odds after its purchase by a property developer keen to profit from the Racecourse Ground's location. In 2004 Wrexham became the first to suffer a ten-point penalty for going into administration and were subsequently relegated.

Billy Wright

Alongside the likes of Tom **Finney** and Sir Stanley **Matthews**, Billy Wright ranks among the giants of the English game in the immediate post-war era. An accomplished half-back and central defender for Wolverhampton Wanderers, he was the first player to win 100 caps for England and skippered the side over 90 times.

Oft cited as one of the first modern footballers, chiefly for his 'showbiz' marriage to Joy, one of the Beverly Sisters, Wright was nonetheless cast in the classic mould of the respectable and dutiful sportsman emblematic of the age: he played for only one club (except for a brief wartime guest period for Leicester City) and had the distinction of never being booked, let alone dismissed, throughout his career.

Dubbed the 'Ironbridge Rocket', Wright made his debut for Wolves B at just 14, but struggled to impress the club's legendary manager, Major Frank Buckley. After he was eventually awarded a contract at 17, his early career was interrupted by the war, but under the managerial guidance of Stan **Cullis**, Wright became the fulcrum of Wolves' most successful side ever. He won three League championships, in 1954, 1958 and 1959, and an FA Cup winners' medal in 1949. The Football Writers' Association voted him Footballer of the Year in 1952, and in 1957 he finished second to Alfredo Di Stefano in the vote for European Footballer of the Year. Wright also played a starring role in the famous floodlit friendlies at Molineux, in which Wolves played host to some of the continent's most famous sides, including Honved and Moscow Dynamo, experiments that did much to usher British sides into European competition.

Internationally, Wright was arguably England's most consistent performer. In 13 years he missed only three games, winning 105 caps. Wright played a starring, if unwanted, role in the 6–3 mauling handed out to England by the fluent Hungary side of 1953. In the first-ever defeat to continental opposition on home soil, England's rigid formation and tactics were ruthlessly exposed by the 'magical Magyars', with Wright a flummoxed victim of one particularly famous drag-back by Puskás. Wright admitted afterwards: 'When we walked out at Wembley, I noticed that the Hungarians had on these strange, lightweight boots, cut away like slippers under the ankle bone. I turned to Stan Mortensen and said, "We should be alright here, Stan, they haven't got the proper kit."'

After being awarded a CBE, Wright enjoyed a mixed post-playing career. Following an unsuccessful spell as manager of his boyhood favourites, Arsenal, the pressure of working as a television executive contributed to problems with alcohol. Overcoming this, he later returned to Wolves as a director and died in 1994 aged 70; as a measure of his immense popularity, his statue today takes pride of place outside Molineux.

Ian Wright

Ian Wright was already 26 and an England B international when he scored two late goals as a Crystal Palace substitute in the 1990 FA Cup Final against Manchester United. Wright had rejected interest from Spurs and Liverpool the season before but within a year of those goals he joined Arsenal for a club record £2.5m and went on to break Cliff **Bastin**'s record for most goals scored in a Gunners shirt.

Wright was born in 1963 in south London, the third son of Jamaican immigrants. His father Herbert left home when he was four and he was brought up by his mother Nesta. He trained as a bricklayer and plasterer when he left school at 16, and spent a week in Chelmsford Prison for not paying motoring fines. It scared him on to the straight and narrow, and he focused his energy on playing for local side Ten Em Bee. He was rejected by Millwall and Brighton before Palace manager Steve Coppell signed him from non-league Greenwich Borough when he was 22 on a £100-a-week contract. When Mark Bright joined him two years later, the partnership clicked and Wright blossomed.

Wright and Palace's other young black players, Andy Gray and Tony Finnegan, had been racially abused on the training-ground by their team-mates, perhaps unsurprising given chairman Ron Noades's remarks. Wright reported Noades to the Commission of Racial Equality. Abused on his England B debut at Millwall and fined for spitting at racist fans at Oldham and QPR, Wright became an effective spokesman against racial prejudice in football.

He was capped by Graham **Taylor** before he moved to Arsenal, where he became as well known for his spats – with David Howells, Steve Walsh, Alex Rae and famously Peter Schmeichel, and numerous referees – as for his goals record, which started with a debut hat-trick against Southampton. Wright played on the threshold of his emotions, sulking one minute, celebrating the next, and liable to explode at any time. Under George **Graham**, Wright helped Arsenal win the FA Cup and the League Cup in 1993 and the European Cup Winners' Cup in 1994, though he was suspended for the final. Arsenal relied on Wright for goals, but with a midfield woefully short on creativity they had little choice. The '1–0 to the Arsenal' chant was as much down to his ability to fashion a goal from nothing as it was to Graham's defence. The European trophy, if anything, was an over-achievement for a club that also finished 10th and 12th in the midst of three top-five finishes.

When Arsène **Wenger** arrived and won the League in 1998, Wright missed 22 games of the season and only scored 11 goals. His high point of that season was against Bolton, when he scored his record-breaking 179th goal for Arsenal. Highbury had not seen jubilation like it. He left in 1998, the year when a hamstring injury cost him an assured place in Glenn **Hoddle**'s World Cup squad – his best performance for England had come in a 0–0 draw away to Italy in a qualifier when he held the ball up as the sole striker. After Arsenal, Wright had brief spells with West Ham, Nottingham Forest, Celtic and Burnley before retiring in 2000.

His iconic appeal persuaded ITV to give him a chance as a chat-show host on *Friday Night's All Wright*. The show was a hit – even though he sang a duet with Lionel Ritchie on his debut – and he was soon poached by the BBC to become their face of Saturday evening TV.

Wycombe Wanderers

With a Football League history dating back to only 1993, most football followers will recognize Wycombe Wanderers as the team that play in light- and dark-blue quarters at the end of an industrial estate on the edge of the Buckinghamshire countryside. The ground, Adams Park, was opened in 1990, Wycombe being one of the first clubs to move from a town centre location to a remote site. With the move Wanderers left behind more than 100 years of history of playing in or around the centre of High Wycombe, a market town 30 miles west of London.

The club was formed around 1887 when High Wycombe was famous for its chairmaking. 'The Chairboys' quickly became a nickname for those early teams but was soon replaced by the bland 'Blues'. The original nickname was resurrected by the fanzine *Chairboys Gas* in the 1980s, the suffix coming from the 'Gasworks End' terrace at Loakes Park, Wanderers' ground between 1895 and 1990.

A highlight of those amateur days was winning the 1931 FA Amateur Cup in a final played at Highbury. Wycombe reached the final of the competition again in 1957, losing to Bishop Auckland in front of 90,000. It was during this time that Frank Adams, former captain and later secretary, secured the freehold of Loakes Park and donated it to the club. When the old ground was sold to developers in the late 1980s its replacement was named after him.

There was a chairmaking industry connection to one of Wanderers' most famous players, Tony Horseman, who scored over 400 goals between 1961 and 1978. His profession in the furniture trade led him to be known as 'Bodger' – a local term for a chairmaker. During Horseman's heyday, Wanderers took four Isthmian League titles in five seasons and held Jackie Charlton's Middlesbrough to a 0–0 draw in front of 12,000 at Loakes Park in a 1975 FA Cup third-round tie, before narrowly losing the replay.

After a relatively fallow period, barring

an Isthmian League title in 1987, Wanderers were galvanized by the arrival of Martin O'Neill as manager in 1990 and the subsequent move to Adams Park. By the time the Irishman left five years later, the club had been to Wembley three more times, won the non-League version of the 'Double', gained promotion to the Football League and within another 12 months moved up again to what was Division 2. Only the restructuring of the leagues in preparation for the Premier League in 1994 prevented Wycombe from having a chance of a third consecutive promotion via the play-offs. After ten years at the third level, the club were relegated to League Two in 2004.

Crowds, averaging under 500 in the mid-1980s, had risen tenfold by the time Wanderers had gained entry into the Football League. In the midst of a decade of steady performances in the third tier of English football was the remarkable FA Cup run of 2001, when manager Lawrie Sanchez led Wycombe to the semi-final before losing 1–0 to Liverpool at Villa Park. That feat could well come to be seen as the greatest achievement in the history of a club who seem set to continue in the lower half of English professional football.

Yeovil Town

Yeovil Town first came to national attention during their FA Cup run of 1949,
when the Somerset club, members of the
Southern League since 1922, knocked
out Sunderland's expensively assembled
team 2–1 in the fourth round. In the
build-up to the match much had been
made of the ten-foot slope at their
ground, the Huish – it ran from the side
of the pitch under the main stand over
to the far touchline – with the vistors
refused permission to train on it.

Player-manager Alec Stock, said to
have prepared his team on a special diet
including glucose tablets and sherry, put
Yeovil ahead in the first half. Sunderland
equalized with half an hour to go, after
which goalkeeper Dickie Dyke, playing
only his second match, kept them at bay
until striker Eric Bryant scored the
winning goal in extra time, seizing on a
mistake by Len **Shackleton**. In the next
round over 81,000 saw Yeovil lose 8–0
to Manchester United at Maine Road, the
biggest FA Cup attendance ever outside
the final.

Nicknamed 'The Glovers' after one of
the main local industries (members of the
1949 Cup team were glove cutters), the
club had begun as Yeovil Casuals in
1895, becoming Yeovil & Petters United
through a merger during the First World
War, then taking the name 'Town' in
1946. The club were runners-up in the
Southern League in their second season
and made the first of several unsuccessful applications for Football League
membership in 1927.

They were to win the Southern League
three times after the Second World War
but the FA Cup became Yeovil's speci-
ality. Beginning with a match against
Plymouth in 1928–29, they reached the
first round of the Cup on over 40
occasions and knocked out League teams

a record 20 times. Yeovil's Cup exploits led to their being the first non-League club to have a Subbuteo team made in their honour.

Yeovil were invited to be founder members of the inaugural Alliance Premier League in 1979, but despite being the best-supported club, they finished in the bottom half each year until going down for the first time in their history in 1984–85. Local resident Ian Botham boosted gates home and away when turning out in their relegation season, but Alec Stock, back at the Huish as a spectator, was unimpressed: 'As a footballer, he's an exceptional cricketer.'

Yeovil were relegated from the Conference again in 1995 but could still count on massive support – their Isthmian League promotion decider against Enfield two years later attracted a crowd of 8,000 to Huish Park, their ground from 1990 (the sloping pitch was sold to Tesco). The club began to challenge for promotion to the Football League after going full-time in 2000–01, finally achieving their goal under manager Gary Johnson two seasons later. In 2005, they moved up to League One.

youth football

When the 16-year-old Wayne **Rooney** crashed in two spectacular goals to take Everton into the FA Youth Cup Final in 2001–02 he not only lived out many a schoolboy's dream but also embodied the fantasies of many a club – the notion that one day they will unearth their own teenage footballing phenomenon.

Football clubs are always full of talk of some young talent who's going to be better than **Best**, **Beckham** and **Owen** all rolled into one. And they've always spent a considerable amount of time and effort scouring the country in hope of finding such a player. Rooney came

through the academy system – a structure now in place at every Premiership and many Football League and non-League clubs for recruiting and training every potential young talent from nine to 16 in the local area.

The development of young footballers has not always been so organized, however. In the earliest days of the professional game clubs merely advertised for players in local newspapers and the sporting press, while from 1904 the English Schools' Football Association administered the transition of suitably skilled schoolboys to professional status. But as the cultural and financial importance of the game grew, clubs developed their own scouting structures, relying on personal recommendations, word-of-mouth 'tip-offs' and the championing of individual players by friends and family.

By the 1930s, a semi-formalized apprenticeship system had developed. At the time it was illegal to employ under-17s as professional players, so clubs would take a small number of boys on to their ground staff. The young men's days were spent tending the pitch, washing the dressing rooms and picking up litter. Many a future first-team player spent his 'apprenticeship' cleaning the boots of the current stars. Such menial tasks were part of a young player's induction into the hierarchical world of professional football, sometimes to the exclusion of playing football. Liverpool defender Tommy Smith wrote about being an apprentice in the late 1950s: 'The only time I got to see a football was on Friday mornings when we'd play against the bin-men in the car park.'

In 1960 the FA and Football League introduced an official Apprenticeship Scheme, and recognized youth footballers as a category of player. Although their day-to-day tasks changed very little, the numbers of apprentice players increased from 220 in 1960–61 to 592 in 1966–67. As the economic problems of the 1970s bit into football finances, however, clubs recruited fewer youngsters and began to look to the state for financial help.

The government-funded Youth Training Scheme (YTS) into professional football started in June 1983, and by the early 1990s the number of registered apprentices had soared from 200 to 600. Not that any more young players became full professionals, however, as the proportion released at the end of their two-year apprenticeships also grew. In fact, the YTS scheme was heavily criticized for providing employers with cheap labour – apprentices cost clubs very little and gained little in the way of training for an alternative career once they were released.

Meanwhile, in 1984, amid growing concern about the decline of basic skills in the English game, the FA set up 150 Centres of Excellence to coach 5,000 schoolboys a week, plus a National FA School at Lilleshall Hall in Shropshire which trained and (in conjunction with a local comprehensive school) educated 16 teenage boys a year. Criticized by some as an elitist experiment, the school did help to produce a number of future professionals and nearly 50 per cent of graduates went on to play for League clubs.

Eventually schools of excellence were replaced by football academies. Introduced in 1998 by the FA's then director of coaching, Howard Wilkinson, the academies were at the centre of the FA's Charter for Quality programme – a kind of vision for the development of young players and a belated response to the long-established and highly successful youth-coaching programmes run in countries such as the Netherlands and France.

Every Premier League club now has to have an academy, and many in lower divisions do too. Young players are recruited to academies from the age of nine to 16, and train three to five times a week, although no 11-a-side football is allowed until they are 12 and even then they are limited to a maximum of 30 games a season. FA regulations decree that 13- to 16-year-olds must live within a one and half hour's travelling time of the ground; and under-12s within one hour. Each year an academy awards three-year Football Scholarships to the best players, those few who have demonstrated the potential to 'make it'. Only the best of these go on to get full professional contracts but all are guaranteed three years of vocational and/or academic education.

All academies are monitored by the Premier and Football Leagues, and must not only provide top-quality coaching, but education and medical care too. Whereas under the old system, a top club might have employed three or four full-time youth coaches, they now have at least ten full-time and even more part-time staff, including at least one education and welfare officer who liaises closely with the young player's school and parents.

However, while the whole system is far more structured than the old, ad hoc and often ruthless apprenticeships, it's not been without its critics. There are still rumours of promising young players being 'poached' by richer clubs as soon as they reach the scholarship stage; and the proportion of local lads who become professional players is still pitifully low at about 15 per cent. The academy model has been successful, however: some of the richer clubs even have 'satellite' academies based abroad to nurture young players from overseas; some lower and non-League teams run their own schemes by linking with local further education colleges which enable young players to train almost full-time while taking courses. When even Chester-le-Street Town can field a 'giant killing' team in the FA Youth Cup (they won at Derby County in 2003–04), it's clear the development of youth football has come a long way.

Index

Figures in bold type indicate main references.

Index

457

Index

Index

469

Index

471